Community Reinvestment Performance

Making CRA Work for Banks, Communities and Regulators

Kenneth H. Thomas, Ph.D.

PROBUS PUBLISHING COMPANY
Chicago, Illinois
Cambridge, England

ISBN 1-55738-379-0

Printed in the United States of America

BB

1 2 3 4 5 6 7 8 9 0

HG 1642
.U5747
1994 α

This book is dedicated to those in Congress who believe in the
"Positive Power of Public Disclosure."

TABLE OF CONTENTS

Preface

INTRODUCTION

This book is a reference tool for banks, community groups, regulators, and others interested in the whos, hows, wheres, and whys of the highest and lowest bank ratings under the Community Reinvestment Act (CRA). These ratings refer to a bank's assessed performance in complying with CRA and have nothing to do with safety and soundness ratings, which are not public.

This book represents the first comprehensive examination of CRA ratings under the new examination procedures and public disclosure requirements that have been in effect since July 1, 1990. It contains the results of our detailed analysis of the 6,706 CRA public evaluations made as of December 31, 1991. This represents one-and-one-half year's worth of ratings under the new system. Updated data recently made available on approximately 5,400 more CRA ratings through December 31, 1992, are also included here. Thus, a total of 12,115 CRA ratings are analyzed here.

The publicly available ratings that were reported by the federal bank regulators through December 31, 1991, represented about one-half of all banks and thrifts in the country. Therefore, roughly one out of every two banks and thrifts in the nation had yet to be rated under the new publicly disclosed system as of year-end 1991. The updated data on approximately 12,100 ratings as of December 31, 1992, reflect about three out of four banks. Information on the other unrated banks will not be available for some time. In fact, it will probably be well into 1993 before all the banks and thrifts in the nation, with the exception of some smaller national banks, have been evaluated at least once under the new rating system.

WHICH RATINGS ARE INCLUDED AND WHICH ARE NOT

Data on the highest and lowest bank and thrift CRA ratings as defined above that were available as of December 31, 1992, are included here. We obtained and reviewed several thousand of the bank and thrift evaluations that were publicly released as of December 31, 1991. Additional updated data on ratings made in 1992 are included here, but lack of availability precluded those evaluations being reviewed and analyzed in the same way.

Nationwide only 8.7% of all banks and thrifts evaluated as of December 31, 1991 received the highest "outstanding" rating. A full 11% received one of the two lowest ratings which include "needs improvement" (10.1%) and "substantial noncompliance" (0.9%). There were only 59 of the latter lowest possible ratings.

The remaining 80.3% of all banks and thrifts received a "satisfactory" rating. Except for a few cases of multiple ratings, detailed data and actual evaluations for these banks are not included here. Rather, the emphasis is on the roughly 20% in the one highest and two lowest categories. This rating distribution was quite similar through year-end 1992, with the proportion of outstanding ratings increasing to 10.3% and below average ratings decreasing to 10.5%.

A stratified sample of approximately 250 CRA public performance evaluations with high and low ratings made as of December 31, 1991, is analyzed in detail in this book. This sample includes nearly 20 percent of all outstanding and needs improvement and 100 percent of all substantial noncompliance evaluations that were publicly available as of year-end 1991.

These evaluations also represent a mix by regulators and length. About 80 percent of the sample evaluations were retyped in a standardized format. These evaluations averaged five retyped pages each, with a range from a low of just two pages in a few cases for the FDIC and OTS to a high of 22 pages for the FED. The FDIC had the shortest evaluations, averaging only 3.8 pages, and this was followed by the OTS at 4.2 pages. The OCC was about average at 5.2 pages, and the FED was the longest at an average 7.0 pages.

Any of the public evaluations that are listed or referenced here are available from the subject bank or thrift, or the federal regulator as a last resort. These banks or thrifts will also make available upon request (a telephone call is sufficient) a copy of their CRA statement and any rebuttal or further explanation of their evaluation (which is often available with the lower-rated banks). Of course, the nonpublic portions of the CRA examination or the overall compliance rating are not released with these public evaluations. A bank may charge a nominal fee for mailing these documents, but a fee is the exception rather than the rule; the most we have been charged by a bank is $10.

REPEAT RATINGS—ONLY 2% OF THE TOTAL

Of the approximately 6,700 ratings we analyzed as of year-end 1991, only 142 of them (2% of the total) were multiple ratings, almost all double ratings with a few triple ratings. Most of the second evaluations represented either the same ratings or upgrades. There were only four downgrades. The differences between the two evaluations for those institutions with improved ratings (42% of the total) indicate the affirmative changes they made in their CRA program during a relatively short period. The reverse is true for those four with downgraded ratings. Approximately 15% of the 12,115 ratings made as of year-end 1992 were multiple ratings.

Because federal regulations do not require an institution to place more than the most recent evaluation in its public file, interested parties may not be able to make such a comparison at a particular bank. While it can be argued that the present set of circumstances and examination is all that is relevant at a bank, we find it informative to compare previous evaluations when they are available to examine changes in CRA activities. Also, the first public evaluation is in many respects the most informative as it reflects CRA activities that have existed over a long period. Therefore, the companion volume contains multiple evaluations for many of the banks receiving repeat ratings.

HOW THIS BOOK CAN HELP BANKS

A primary purpose of this book is to help banks and thrift institutions improve their CRA performance. This should in turn result in an improved rating for a bank. The term *bank* is used generically in this book to refer to both commercial banks and thrift institutions which include savings banks and savings and loan associations. Credit unions and other financial institutions are not affected by CRA.

Many bankers oppose the idea of any disclosure of examination ratings and, of course, further publication and visibility of them. We believe that a key to improving a bank's CRA performance and rating is through learning from the good *and* bad experiences of other banks around the country.

A community bank in New York can learn from the successes and failures of a big thrift in California. Likewise, a small thrift in Florida can benefit from the experiences of a big bank in Chicago. Of course, peer comparisons by size, geographic region, business specialization, and regulator are most useful.

Should bankers require more detailed information on any individual program from another bank they believe is an appropriate peer, they will be able to contact that bank since its name and location are indicated in this book. Our purpose is not to embarrass or make examples of any banks but merely to learn from their experiences. This requires that the reader know the name, location, and background of each bank.

Chapters 4, 6, and 8 containing profiles from banks receiving "outstanding," "needs improvement," and "substantial noncompliance" will be of particular interest to banks desiring information on what to do and not do in their CRA programs. Specific tips with particular reference to individual banks are included in these chapters.

Many bankers have already reviewed CRA performance evaluations of competing banks. Some banks receiving needs improvement ratings have complained that they should have received at least a satisfactory rating after they reviewed ratings received by peer banks.

Because ratings are subjective and may be based upon information not reflected in the public evaluation, the regulator may always be able to defend a specific rating. Nonetheless, a banker desirous of improving a bank's CRA rating may decide to use examples and other information cited in this book as a basis for attempting to justify an upgraded rating.

Bankers may also choose to use the information in this book to improve their communications with local community groups. For example, bankers may be able to place their evaluation in better perspective relative to appropriate peers around the country. A very large bank being criticized by a community group for a needs improvement rating may find it useful to compare its performance by assessment factor to another large bank with an outstanding rating to highlight the positives in its own CRA performance. Although all comparisons have limitations, this approach can encourage an informed dialogue between bankers and community groups.

In some cases the CRA program of a bank receiving a satisfactory evaluation may appear to be as good as one at another bank with an outstanding rating. Also, some banks receiving needs improvement ratings may have been categorized that way as a result of one "mistake" (e.g., a technical violation of a consumer compliance requirement).

It would clearly be in a bank's interest to explain any relevant background and comparative information to any community group that is challenging or is very interested in a bank's CRA record. Remember, Congress mandated the disclosure of not just the rating but also the public evaluation supporting it.

One of the case studies on outstanding banks in Chapter 5 involves a CRA "turnaround" for a bank that went from a likely failure to an outstanding rating in roughly one year. The eight-step program identified there should be useful for bankers looking for a "how-to" approach to improving their CRA performance and rating.

HOW THIS BOOK CAN HELP COMMUNITY GROUPS

This book will enable community groups to review and compare the highest and lowest bank CRA ratings available to date. We have found that many community groups are not fully aware of the broad range of CRA compliance efforts that exist at many banks.

The banks themselves are partly to blame for this because most use "no frills" CRA statements as compared to the expanded ones recommended by regulators. The latter statements provide considerably more detail on how banks ascertain and meet local credit needs. While an expanded CRA statement is a substantial improvement over a no frills one, there is no comparison to the adequacy and objectivity of information that should be found in public evaluations.

Community groups should become familiar not

just with CRA programs in their local markets but also with those of relevant peer banks throughout the country. Small and large banks in other parts of the country have developed unique and innovative CRA programs, many of these in concert with local community groups. Therefore, a community group in one area may find an outstanding idea in this book that is being used by a bank in conjunction with a community group in another area.

This may be used as a basis for a dialogue with a local bank on a suggested improvement to an existing program or perhaps an altogether new one. True and tested CRA ideas from other banks throughout the country can hardly be dismissed by another banker regardless of location, especially if the CRA ideas have contributed to an outstanding CRA rating. Viewed in this way, a community group can actually benefit the local bank and the community by suggesting new ideas.

Community groups must be aware that the evaluations and ratings in this book are as of the cited date. Many of those banks receiving needs improvement and substantial noncompliance ratings have improved their programs in response to these public evaluations since that date. Any such upgrades reported by the regulators after December 31, 1991, are not included in this analysis.

Community groups can therefore use the evaluations in this book to gauge the extent of improvement at an individual bank. That is, a bank should be viewed not only in terms of its current or past public evaluation but also on the basis of improvements it has made since the last one. It is quite likely that many of the substantial noncompliance and needs improvement ratings may be upgraded the next time around.

Because only one out of two banks have been evaluated as of December 31, 1991, and three out of four as of December 31, 1992, many community groups may be frustrated with the lack of public evaluations. Unfortunately, because some CRA exam cycles may be as long as three or more years, it is likely we will not have evaluations for all banks, with the exception of some smaller national banks, until at least the end of 1993.

Banks with low ratings generally receive their reevaluations more quickly. Obviously, a bank that receives the same low rating the second time around

will attract the most attention in this regard. The worst case scenario is a needs improvement bank dropping to substantial noncompliance or a bank in the latter category failing to get out of it. We provide examples of banks under both of these scenarios.

The information in this book will be useful to those community groups that attempt to create their own evaluation of a bank. Just as a bank is recommended to make an *internal* self assessment and come up with its own CRA rating, community groups may find it beneficial to make an *external* assessment. Community groups can develop their own "shadow" assessment factor, performance category, and overall CRA ratings for banks that have yet to be evaluated and then compare those to the actual ratings. This can also be done for repeat exams.

If done on an objective and analytical basis, this may be an interesting and informative exercise. Also, it will likely serve to increase the dialogue between bankers and community groups in understanding the full range of a bank's CRA compliance efforts. Moreover, a truly objective and analytical internal or external self-assessment can be used to document any alleged cases of CRA grade inflation or deflation.

Of course, community groups and outsiders have limited access to much of the information that regulators consider. The availability of CRA statements, especially expanded ones, as well as other information in the CRA public file, plus readily available and expanded data under the Home Mortgage Disclosure Act (HMDA) can be quite useful for this purpose.

Bank customers and other members of the community who may not be affiliated with a community group will also find this book helpful in better understanding the CRA evaluation procedure and how they can access this information. Information in the public evaluations on available credit services and special programs, including those for low- and moderate-income individuals, may be especially useful.

Also, governmental bodies involved in community affairs and outreach programs will likewise find this information helpful. Many CRA "interested" parties have little knowledge as to the breadth or depth of many bank CRA programs, and this is one way to find out.

A "must" supplemental reference for community groups, consumers, and other interested parties is *A*

Citizen's Guide To CRA, revised in June 1992 by the Federal Financial Institutions Examination Council (FFIEC). This CRA publication is reproduced as Appendix 1. Two 1990 publications of great interest published by the FFIEC include *Community Reinvestment Act Performance Evaluations* and *HMDA Reporting, Getting It Right!*

Another pamphlet entitled *Is My Bank Meeting Its Community Reinvestment Obligations?,* by the Federal Reserve Bank of Atlanta, is quite useful. Eight other Federal Reserve Banks and some Federal Home Loan Banks such as those in Atlanta and San Francisco produce a no-charge monthly or quarterly publication on CRA and related housing issues.

HOW THIS BOOK CAN HELP REGULATORS

Each of the four federal regulators involved in CRA exams take somewhat different approaches to performance evaluations. However, the differences are more in degree than kind.

The individual agencies provide substantial training and information for its compliance examiners to attempt to ensure consistency throughout all regions. Likewise, the FFIEC is a joint training and information resource to attempt to develop consistency among compliance examiners across the four regulators. Unfortunately, not all evaluations are consistent by regulator or even by region for a given regulator. Also, we have noted examiner subjectivity in many cases that has resulted in both grade inflation and even deflation.

Prior to the disclosure of CRA ratings and evaluations, there was little information available as to the degree of consistency or inconsistency among regulators or among districts for a specific regulator. The results to date indicate that there are indeed substantial differences in the format and content of examinations.

Regulators can use this information to examine similarities and differences in both form and content for a given regulator by district and for the different regulators. Likewise, those handful of state regulators charged with CRA examination responsibilities will find this material quite useful.

For example, we have found certain examiners to be much more analytical than others in terms of their evaluation of loan distribution data, which may or may not be in conjunction with HMDA data. There is a substantial difference in the length of evaluations, although we have noticed no correlation between the length of a public evaluation and the resultant rating.

The CRA rating applies to an entire bank. As such, it is a composite rating of all 12 CRA assessment factors grouped under five performance categories. Some examiners at the FED and the West Region of the OTS initially provided individual ratings of a bank's performance under each of the assessment factors. This further disclosure raises, of course, the question as to the appropriate weighting of the assessment factors vis-à-vis the overall bank rating.

The review of the cross-section of evaluations in this book by district for each individual regulator and across all regulators should therefore prove most informative to the regulators themselves as they strive for further consistency in this regard. Ideally, an informed OTS examiner from the West Region should provide the same CRA rating to a bank in Florida that would be given by one of the three federal banking regulators there.

Individual examiners can review the evaluations discussed in this book to determine whether or not they would have agreed with those evaluations based upon the data presented here. Of course, there will always be additional information not available in the public evaluation that may have influenced the examiners, especially in cases where they were on the fence between two ratings.

The representative sample of public evaluations analyzed here was designed so that there was at least one evaluation for each region of each regulator. Multiple evaluations within a given district for a given regulator may or may not have been completed by the same examiner, although a particular examiner's writing and analytical style becomes apparent over time.

Chapters 4, 6, and 8 in this book contain rating profiles which will be useful to examiners in obtaining a sense of uniformity across regions and regulators. In fact, examiners who are truly interested in the encouragement of affirmative CRA performance may identify potentially good ideas that they can mention to banks and thrifts as appropriate to enhance their CRA program.

The best ideas from the top-rated programs are found in Chapter 4 on outstanding CRA ratings. Likewise, an examiner may become more adept at spotting potential pitfalls or trouble spots with low-rated CRA programs by examining the needs improvement (Chapter 6) and substantial noncompliance (Chapter 8) profiles.

There is yet another reason why this book will be helpful to CRA examiners. Because of the increasing availability of CRA public evaluations, bankers undergoing CRA exams will be asking their examiners some hard questions. For example, "Why didn't we get an outstanding or satisfactory rating if we did all that another bank did that got that rating?"

Bankers undergoing a second exam that received a needs improvement or even substantial noncompliance the first time around will likely be prepared with examples of peer and nonpeer bank evaluations to justify an improvement in their own rating. Again, a banker may state, "We are at least entitled to a satisfactory rating if this other peer bank that didn't do as much as we did got an outstanding rating."

Examiners may be placed in the uncomfortable and arguably unfair position of trying to justify another examiner's rating without full knowledge of that situation. Even though it may be irrelevant to the exam at hand, examiners who have familiarized themselves with the work of other examiners around the country may be better prepared to handle these situations.

OUTLINE OF BOOK

Chapter 1 explains what the CRA rating is and what it is not. The four ratings are explained here in the context of the five performance categories and 12 assessment factors.

Chapter 2 provides a detailed accounting in their own words of what each of the elements of the "CRA triangle" really think about CRA. Specifically, we have excerpted passages from public comment letters by bankers, community groups, and regulators as to how they really feel about CRA evaluations and their public disclosure.

Chapter 3, "CRA Watch," begins with an historic comparison of CRA ratings going back to 1982 by region. All of the new CRA ratings that are available between July 1, 1990, and December 31, 1991, are then analyzed. These data are based upon one-and-one-half year's worth of ratings under the new system for 6,706 banks and thrifts, roughly half of them throughout the nation. Additionally, 5,400 updated ratings through December 31, 1992, are summarized in that chapter.

Chapter 4 presents a composite profile of the banks and thrifts that have received the highest, "outstanding" CRA ratings to date, and Chapter 5 contains case histories on selected outstanding banks. Comparable profiles and case histories for banks with needs improvement ratings are found in Chapters 6 and 7, respectively. Chapters 8 and 9 contain profiles and case studies for banks with substantial noncompliance ratings, respectively.

Specific examples, using the names of individual banks and thrifts, are cited in each of the profile chapters. The profiles are organized by the five performance categories and component assessment factors. The case studies represent a detailed analysis of several specific situations of interest.

Chapter 10, which represents our conclusions and recommendations, presents a summary of what we have learned from two and one-half year's worth of publicly disclosed ratings under the new CRA procedures. The emphasis is on public policy issues that affect banks, community groups, and regulators. Various recommendations to improve CRA are described in this chapter.

The Appendix to this book contains various CRA rating summaries and charts. Several maps and telephone and address lists identify key CRA regulatory contacts around the country. A glossary of CRA-related acronyms is also included.

ACKNOWLEDGMENTS

My first debt of gratitude goes to Professor Jack M. Guttentag of The Wharton School, with whom I have worked since 1970—first as a doctoral student and later as co-researcher. Professor Guttentag, a pioneer in public policy research in banking and housing finance, is one of the few academicians who successfully bridged the gap between the classroom and the real world.

I am also grateful to the countless banks providing requested CRA statements, public performance evaluations, and related material to me for this research. And, to the four federal regulatory agencies who forwarded CRA evaluations in the handful of cases where the banks refused my verbal and written requests for them.

A special thanks to Editorial Director Jim McNeil and his associates at Probus Publishing who accepted my complete manuscript without requiring me to delete references to individual banks. Freedom of the press is alive and well at Probus! Also on the production side, my thanks to Wanda Janke for her word processing expertise.

My greatest gratitude goes to my family, and especially my parents, for their nonstop and never-ending support.

A final "thanks" to Hurricane Andrew for trashing most (but not all) of our home in the early morning of August 24, 1992. Those four hours in Andrew's northern eye, which I spent running from room to room with my family and the manuscript of this book, will never be forgotten.

1. SHEDDING LIGHT ON BANKING'S LEAST-LIKED LAW

INTRODUCTION

The "CRA triangle" represents the three most prominent players in CRA: community groups, regulators, and, of course, the banks. This chapter will summarize the interrelationships among these three groups and emphasize their similarities and differences regarding CRA.

We will first review the relevant background of CRA and how its development was in part based upon conflicting views by bankers and community groups. We then enter the regulatory element to complete the CRA triangle.

We trace the evolution of CRA through the 1989 Congressional requirement to disclose the previously confidential CRA ratings and evaluations. We discuss what the CRA rating is and what it is not.

We include a detailed description of the five performance categories (which are subdivided into 12 assessment factors) upon which banks are evaluated. We then define the four CRA ratings: outstanding, satisfactory, needs improvement, and substantial noncompliance.

These ratings are further described relative to the five performance categories and 12 assessment factors. We use many of the same descriptive exhibits that the regulators use to train their CRA examiners about the evaluation process.

THE CRA TRIANGLE

Figure 1-1, The CRA Triangle, summarizes the relationships among the three most prominent players in CRA:

1. "C" is for Community groups, which are the most visible representatives of consumer interests;

2. "R" is for Regulators, who usually work closely with Congress to implement and enforce relevant consumer legislation; and

3. "A" is for America's banks and thrifts, which exclude credit unions that are not subject to CRA.

This CRA triangle will be referred to throughout this book. We find it most useful as a model to help explain and understand the interaction, including both conflict and cooperation, among these three CRA players. Of course, there are other interested parties, but these are the primary ones.

CRA—BANKING'S LEAST-LIKED LAW

The banking and thrift industries in the United States taken collectively are probably the most heavily regulated businesses anywhere in the country. It can be argued that all banking laws and regulations, except those that reduce or inhibit competition or otherwise improve profitability, are unpopular with banks. Of the myriad of laws and regulations affecting banks,

Figure 1-1   The CRA Triangle©

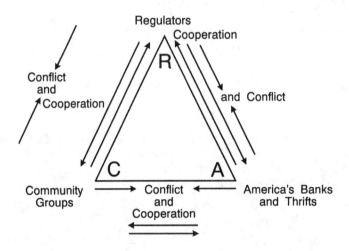

one stands out, however, as being the most disliked by bankers in our opinion.

This is the Community Reinvestment Act of 1977, which was introduced by Senator William Proxmire of Wisconsin, and signed into law by President Jimmy Carter. CRA was one of many pro-consumer pieces of banking legislation enacted in the 70s in response to the new consumer movement in banking. CRA was immediately hailed by consumer groups as a new type of antidiscrimination legislation that would prevent banks from "redlining." Redlining refers to the practice of geographic (not racial) discrimination in the granting of credit to qualified applicants in certain "redlined" or targeted neighborhoods. These neighborhoods presumably were circumscribed by a red "magic marker" on a city map in a bank's board room.

An extreme community activists' view would argue that most of our nation's dilapidated ghettos and

inner-city areas are mainly the result of a systematic and continued process of redlining. It would further be argued that banks have a social responsibility to act in an affirmative manner because they have been the recipients of (underpriced) deposit insurance and other federal benefits such as access to the Federal Reserve discount window and barriers to entry.

An extreme view by the banking community would consider CRA an unprecedented form of "credit allocation" where the government assumes an unnecessary role in a bank's lending decision. After all, the major function of a bank is to lend money, and the market, not the government, in our capitalistic system should tell a bank where and where not to lend. The extreme bankers' view further would argue that the alleged practice of redlining never existed; our nation's most dilapidated ghettos and inner-city areas are the result of social and other changes beyond the banks' control.

Obviously, the truth is somewhere in the middle between these two extremes. Nonetheless, there are still many bankers and community activists who would be viewed as extremists in their respective camps. Bankers themselves are not a homogeneous group since big and small banks, for example, often have different objectives and problems. In one unusual case the trade group for small banks, the Independent Bankers Association of America, filed a May 1991 request with the OCC and FED to investigate the CRA record of NCNB Texas National Bank. Thus, a major banking association attempted to use the CRA to benefit its members, much like a community group would do on behalf of its members.

As would be expected with banking's least-liked law there have been numerous efforts by the banking lobby to significantly reduce (or "gut," in the words of many community group leaders) CRA enforcement. Serious and well-organized efforts by the banking lobby in 1991 were nearly successful. The salvo of attacks on CRA in 1992 with the former Bush Administration's full backing have been in the name of a reduction in the bank regulatory burden. While the Bush Administration took a generally anti-CRA position, the Clinton Administration is expected to take a pro-CRA position in accordance with the national platform of the Democratic party.

The conflicting positions between bankers and community groups is often overemphasized in discussions of CRA. This is an overly simplistic view that has the trappings of a classic rich-versus-poor or even capitalism-versus-socialism confrontation.

Viewing CRA solely as a struggle between bankers and community groups is incorrect. First, it ignores the key role of the regulators. And, second, banks need the support of their community to succeed as much as the community needs their bank. Most of our nation's banks are small ones in rural areas where they maintain good community relations. The more vocal consumer groups are in our major metropolitan areas, although this has changed in recent years. The most well-known and visible consumer groups that have taken a strong and affirmative role in defending CRA against the above-mentioned attacks include the Association of Community Organizations for Reform

Now (ACORN), the Center for Community Change, and the Consumer Federation of America.

Community groups, like banks, represent a heterogeneous group. It is, therefore, a mistake to consider all community groups as "trouble-making activists" looking for a highly visible confrontation. This would be equivalent to viewing all our nation's banks and thrifts as troubled because of the condition of only some of them.

Misconceptions regarding CRA are not limited to bankers or community group representatives. Members of the press themselves sometimes get caught up in the debate and put an unusual spin on CRA. In an article titled "All Tied Up" in the August 10, 1992 issue (page 15) of the *South Florida Business Journal,* CRA was not portrayed as benefiting the 40% of American households that are low- and moderate-income but as something much different. This article went beyond the most common interpretation that CRA is for the "poor and/or minorities." For the first time, to the best of our knowledge, this article identified an additional "risk" bankers must be concerned about in CRA lending—making sure the loans aren't going to "potential criminals":

> The Community Reinvestment Act (CRA) insists they [the bankers] become philanthropists, lending a significant amount of money to folks in the neighborhood who are poor and/or minorities, yet at the same time making sure they are neither bad credit risks nor potential criminals. Under the provision of the federal civil and criminal forfeiture act, financial institutions which lend money to businessmen who are later proven to be criminals, especially drug dealers, run the risk of losing their collateral. They are considered guilty of knowing that their client was a criminal, unless they can prove they made an effort to find out he wasn't a criminal, or unless they show that there was no way they could know. Otherwise they lose their investment.

THE REGULATORS COMPLETE THE TRIANGLE

The first two components of the CRA triangle, namely banks and community groups, developed naturally with the creation of CRA. The third element, which brings the CRA triangle together, is the regulators, namely federal ones but also an increasing number of state ones.

The regulatory link is critical to balance what might otherwise be an adversarial and emotionally charged relationship between bankers and community groups. For example, the July 1980 opinion of the New York State Banking Department denying the branch application of the Jamaica Savings Bank of Queens on CRA grounds cited such a relationship. The bank's president testified then that a community group's written request for a meeting was thrown away because it did not have a letterhead, the return address was a post office box, and the letter was otherwise "unimpressive." That bank allegedly refused to meet with community group representatives unless they had a minimum $1,000 deposit at the bank for at least one year. As pointed out in Figure 1-1, regulators usually work closely with community groups, ideally in furtherance of congressional and governmental consumer objectives. Conflicts will, however, develop between regulators and community groups if they believe the regulators are too lax in their CRA enforcement, a major item of concern in the last few years. Members of Congress themselves are often critical of regulators for this same reason. Banks also work closely with regulators, sometimes too much so, but both end up on the opposite side of the fence in some instances. Therefore, the regulators represent not only a buffer between banks and community groups but also a facilitator to encourage better relationships between them. As seen in Figure 1-1, conflicts can develop with regulators because community groups may believe the regulators aren't doing their CRA enforcement job or because bankers may believe the regulators are doing far too much of their job.

Our federal regulatory structure consists of three agencies regulating commercial banks and one for thrift institutions. The federal bank regulators are the Board of Governors of the Federal Reserve System and its 12 Federal Reserve Banks (FED), the Federal Deposit Insurance Corporation (FDIC), and the Office of the Comptroller of the Currency (OCC). The Office of Thrift Supervision (OTS), which was formerly known as the Federal Home Loan Bank Board (FHLBB), regulates thrift institutions. The latter agency, like the Office of the Comptroller of the Currency, is part of the administration's Treasury Department.

The Federal Financial Institutions Examination Council (FFIEC) is the closest thing to a "super regulator" of financial institutions in our nation. In addition to the four bank and thrift federal regulators, it includes a representative of the National Credit Union Administration (although credit unions are not affected by CRA).

CRA requires that the four federal regulatory agencies not only encourage institutions to ascertain and help meet the credit needs of their local communities, but also assess their performance through special compliance examinations. Because an institution's CRA record is considered in a branch, merger, or other applications, the regulators represent the enforcement side of CRA.

CRA'S WATERSHED YEAR—1989

Some will argue that CRA sat around since 1977 as one of many pro-consumer regulations on the regulators' and compliance officers' shelf. Actually, there was some CRA enforcement going back to early 1979 when the FDIC denied the first application on CRA grounds. This was the April 23, 1979 denial of a branch application for New York's affluent Upper East Side by the Greater New York Savings Bank. Later that year the OCC denied the first merger on CRA grounds involving the Bank of Indiana, N.A. of Gary, Indiana. CRA was still, however, not a major issue for most of the deregulation-minded 80s.

That was until 1989. The regulators finally flexed their CRA muscles in four ways that year. First was the landmark case involving the FED's denial on CRA grounds of the application of Chicago's Continental Illinois to acquire the Grand Canyon State Bank of Scottsdale, Arizona, in February 1989. The fact that Continental Bank was partly owned by the government as a result of a previous bailout may have had a bearing on the denial. Nonetheless, it was the FED's first CRA denial ever, and Continental was the biggest bank ever to be affected by a CRA denial.

The second CRA development in 1989 was increased enforcement by other regulators resulting in the most CRA denials (four) ever in one year. In July 1989 the FHLBB denied a branch application, the agency's second CRA denial ever, for Leader Federal Savings and Loan Association of Memphis on the basis of poor CRA compliance and documentation. Additionally, the OCC denied two applications on CRA grounds in 1989. Other CRA protested applications were approved that year but with various CRA conditions.

The third major CRA event that year was the March 21, 1989, interagency joint public CRA statement by the FFIEC, which outlined more specific methods of compliance and CRA enforcement. This document was partly in response to the March 1988 Senate Banking Committee hearings which were critical of CRA enforcement.

The fourth way in which 1989 was a watershed year for CRA enforcement was the most important: the thrift bailout law, formally known as the Financial Institutions Reform, Recovery, and Enforcement Act of 1989 (FIRREA), mandated the disclosure of a new CRA rating and public evaluation. For the first time in the history of American banking, previously confidential examination reports were to be released to the public in this one area.

In addition to the four federal financial institution regulators, a handful of state banking departments have their own CRA regulations. The forerunners among these were New York and Massachusetts, with New York being the leader in state CRA legislation in most respects. In fact, bank regulators in each of these states denied an application on CRA grounds during the 1979-1980 period. These and a few other states have their own CRA exams and rating systems which in some cases include other financial institutions such as credit unions, which are not covered by the federal law.

THE BATTLE OVER CRA DISCLOSURE

The degree of conflict and cooperation among the three elements of the CRA triangle was never more evident than in the 1989 debate involving the disclosure of CRA ratings and evaluations. Chapter 2 contains the first detailed published account of some of the actual comments of each of these three elements to show what they really think about CRA.

Banks were adamantly opposed to any increased enforcement of the least-liked law in banking, much less the public disclosure of previously confidential ratings and evaluations. Community groups across the nation were enjoying an upsurge in popularity and power in banking matters in 1988 and 1989, much of it the result of the increasingly huge S&L bailout. Congress was unhappy with the S&L bailout and clearly receptive to the new wave of consumerism in banking. The consumerists ultimately prevailed on the issue of CRA disclosure.

FIRREA amended the CRA in several important ways. First, it replaced the previously used five-tier numerical rating system for CRA evaluations with a four-tier descriptive rating system. Second, all ratings made on July 1, 1990, and later would be publicly disclosed. Third, the actual performance evaluation with the examiner's conclusion on each of the different CRA regulatory assessment factors would also be disclosed.

OVERVIEW OF THE CRA RATING PROCEDURES

The FFIEC's publication *A Citizen's Guide to the CRA* prepared in June 1992 is reproduced in Appendix 1. This booklet provides an overview of CRA as well as maps, addresses, and phone numbers for each of the four regulatory agencies.

While the FFIEC brochure was designed primarily for members of the public interested in CRA evaluations, more technical information is required for bankers, community groups, and the regulators. For this reason, exhibits are reproduced in the Appendix from the FDIC publication *Uniform Interagency Guidelines for Disclosure of CRA Evaluations and Revisions to Ratings* dated June 27, 1990, as well as updates to that publication.

These are actual examination procedures used by CRA examiners to form the basis for their public ratings and evaluations. An understanding of these procedures is therefore critical for bankers undergoing examinations and helpful to community groups' better understanding of them.

Appendix 2 is a June 17, 1992, document containing an updated statement on CRA requirements as well as revised CRA examination procedures and a checklist. These examination procedures explain some of the concerns of both bankers and community groups and why CRA examiners must try to be objective and comprehensive.

Minimum CRA requirements are spelled out in that document as well as recommended requirements such as an expanded CRA statement. We have found that the marginal effort required to produce such an expanded CRA statement more than pays off in terms of benefits not only to the community but also to the bank in its performance evaluation.

Regulators are well aware of the subjectivities involved in the examination process and the pressures upon them to be both fair and balanced. The unique and complex set of factors relevant to each bank must be considered on a case-by-case basis in the evaluation process. Different banks' CRA performances are not supposed to be compared to each other by the examiner during this process. We disagree with this position and believe that the increasing number and availability of such evaluations will likely encourage such comparisons by all involved parties.

In addition to making various assessments and determinations of an institution's CRA performance, the examiner is also charged with encouraging an institution to help meet local credit needs consistent with safe and sound operations. This, of course, places an additional burden on examiners. Such encouragement will not only result in a better CRA program at a bank but also in a more informed and involved examiner.

The examination procedures relating to the 12 specific assessment factors grouped according to the five performance categories are particularly noteworthy. The wording in these procedures is identical to that found in many public evaluations.

The 32-point examination checklist at the end of these procedures should be fairly familiar to every CRA compliance officer. It is bad enough to perform poorly on any examination, but it is worse when the actual examination questions and procedures to be used are known in advance!

The argument can be made that with the availability of these examination procedures and checklist any bank receiving a below-average rating (i.e., needs improvement or substantial noncompliance) should have probably known about it well in advance of the examination by doing a self-assessment using these procedures and checklist. More than a few "No's" on that checklist will probably knock a bank out of the outstanding range and a large number of "No's," especially in certain categories, will likely drop a bank to a below-average rating.

Most banks are informed of their likely rating upon the exit interview, but there are sometimes surprises. We have learned of at least one instance where a bank was told that it would get an outstanding rating upon the exit interview and was later shocked to see that the decision was overturned back at the regulator's office, where a satisfactory rating was given.

Some of an examiner's biggest dilemmas occur when they are on the fence between a satisfactory and the higher or lower rating. Bankers who thoroughly prepare for an examination through reviewing these procedures and performing a self-assessment are more likely to receive the higher rating.

As pointed out in a few case studies in this book, the examiner's perception of a bank's "CRA spirit" or attitude often makes a difference in fence-sitting decisions. That is, banks that truly demonstrate an "I really care about CRA and am doing my best to improve my performance" attitude will usually get the benefit of the doubt. Conversely, the bank displaying the "unnecessary paperwork burden," "credit allocation" or "give me a break" attitude may likely see the reverse result.

There are two additional publications besides the June 27, 1990, *Uniform Interagency Guidelines* and the June 17, 1992, revised procedures which should be in the hands of all individuals serious about CRA.

The first of these is the February 16, 1993, revised version of *Interagency Questions and Answers Regarding CRA* by the FFIEC. The 31 questions and answers in this document are reproduced as Appendix 3. Of particular interest are the questions which provide CRA guidelines to specialized lenders such as wholesale or credit card banks.

The second important publication, which is reproduced as Appendix 4, is the December 17, 1991, FFIEC *CRA Policy Statement on Analyses of Geographic Distribution of Lending.* This statement directly impacts two CRA assessment factors (C and E).

CRA EVALUATION FORMAT

CRA public evaluations follow a rigid format based around five performance categories subdivided into 12 assessment factors.

In reality there are 13 assessment factors. The 13th, or "non-letter," assessment factor relates to the reasonableness of the delineated community, which is the first item covered under performance category III.

The assessment factors, which are alphabetized, were apparently developed as a CRA "laundry list" but later forced into five performance categories. The result is that assessment factors A and C are in performance category I while assessment factors B and D are in performance categories II and IV, respectively. This is confusing to many readers of these evaluations. Furthermore, the 13th, or missing, assessment factor pertaining to the community delineation is at the beginning of performance category III.

Appendix 5 contains the actual CRA evaluation format as taken from the above-referenced FDIC guidelines publication. Sometimes, the date of evaluation on the cover page will differ from that on the first page under the section titled "General Information." This is because the latter date may represent when the overall compliance, but not the specific CRA portion of the exam, began or ended versus the official date of record for the CRA evaluation which is on the cover page.

Various regulators and even certain districts for certain regulators may have a unique format. Some evaluations have detailed "other information" summaries at the end, and others have special background bank and community profiles at the beginning.

The institution's final CRA rating is most often included on the first page of the Discussion section. Sometimes it is located at the bottom of the Assignment of Rating page. The West Region of the OTS and some FED examiners used to be unique in that they sometimes provided individual ratings for each of the assessment factors in addition to the overall rating for the entire bank. However, some of their evaluations indicated certain factors were "not rated" for one reason or another.

Actually, Congress may have intended that public evaluations be made with individual assessment and/or performance category ratings. We are an advocate of this approach, as we believe that this additional disclosure provides banks, community groups, and other interested parties with greater feedback and insight as to a bank's actual performance.

One of the criticisms of the current procedure is the lack of a weighting scheme relative to the assessment factors and performance categories that result in the final rating. The CRA rating guidelines are, however, specific in noting that no relative weights are assigned to assessment factors or performance categories purposefully, to allow the necessary flexibility for examiners in their case-by-case evaluations. This "flexibility" unfortunately can also be the basis for undue subjectivity by examiners.

When we are provided with individual ratings for the assessment factors and a final rating for the entire bank, we have a better idea as to the implicit weighting procedure being utilized by the examiners. Unfortunately, all regulators have moved away from such a system. Ironically, we have less of this type of information now than we had when these ratings and evaluations first became public.

CRA RATING PROFILES

One of the major differences between the old and new CRA rating systems is the FIRREA-mandated change from the five-tier numerical to a four-tier descriptive or narrative rating.

The old system is similar to the regulatory safety and soundness examination system, which ranges from the highest rating of 1 to the lowest rating of 5. There were some differences among the definitions of these ratings between the three federal banking agencies and that of savings and loans (i.e., the

FHLBB, the OTS predecessor). Under the old rating system the bank regulators considered a rating of 2 and above to be satisfactory or better, but the FHLBB considered a rating of 3 or above to be satisfactory or better.

The present CRA rating system, which is consistent for all four federal regulators, uses one of four descriptive categories: outstanding, satisfactory, needs improvement, or substantial noncompliance. Chapter 3 on CRA Watch provides the most comprehensive summary of both past and present CRA ratings.

The logic behind the change in the CRA ratings system was the fear, mainly by bankers and regulators, that the public might somehow confuse a bank's CRA rating with that of its safety and soundness. The real concern was not whether a financially weak bank might be misinterpreted as a strong bank to its own advantage with a good CRA rating, but the opposite case. Specifically, the greatest fear was that a strong bank with a below-average CRA rating might somehow be perceived by the public as being in an unsafe or unsound condition.

We believe that most of these fears were unwarranted to begin with. First of all, the public is more knowledgeable about bank and thrift matters than ever before with all of the press devoted to this area in the last few years. We believe most people are able to discern the difference between the two rating systems, especially considering the increasing number of private bank-rating services that are widely available and well publicized. Also, the past experience of the State of New York, which has disclosed its numerical CRA ratings for the institutions it regulates since 1984, has never had this potential confusion problem develop as a major concern.

One advantage of the new rating system, with an even rather than odd number of categories, is that a bank is either rated average (satisfactory), above average (outstanding), or below average (needs improvement or substantial noncompliance). However, because roughly 80% of all banks are receiving a satisfactory rating, we believe we are losing much of the richness of the data which would allow us to distinguish between those banks that are more satisfactory than others.

Appendix 6, which is an excerpt from the FDIC guidelines publication, contains a summary of the CRA profiles. The first three pages of these profiles explain the differences among the four categories in terms of their overall ratings. The remainder of that appendix explains the differences among the four ratings in terms of each of the assessment factors.

Appendix 7 is a very useful condensed summary of that same rating system. This grid was developed by the Individual Banking Regulatory Compliance Division of Chase Manhattan Bank, N.A. and is reproduced with their permission.

THE CRA RATING — WHAT IT IS AND WHAT IT ISN'T

A bank's CRA rating is a subjective evaluation of the bank's overall performance based upon an unknown and again subjective weighting system relative to the different performance categories and assessment factors as perceived by the examiners.

Yes, these ratings are subjective. Yes, they are based upon perceptions of performance. And, yes, they are based upon a subjective and unknown weighting scheme where the 12 plus one assessment factors and five performance categories are assigned implicit values relative to each other to reach the overall rating.

Can these CRA ratings be wrong? Any subjective rating based upon perceptions and a subjective weighting scheme certainly can be wrong as there is no absolute standard for comparison. As noted above, examiners are not supposed to compare a bank's CRA performance with that of its peers during the evaluation process.

We are at the beginning of a new type of rating system that has been made public for the first time ever, and the natural self-correcting mechanisms which occur over time should help improve this system.

The most common rating errors are probably between the satisfactory and higher or lower ratings. When in doubt the answer seems to be a satisfactory rating—where four out of five banks end up. The greatest source of criticism we have seen to date is by those banks that have received what they believe to be an unwarranted needs improvement rating.

Those banks that receive satisfactory ratings and thought they deserved the higher one are not as disappointed because they are in the "category of the masses" representing 80% of all banks. Those banks, however, that are rated as needing improvement are in the lowest decile of all rated banks, a matter of obviously greater concern.

Our review of the roughly 1% of banks receiving the lowest possible substantial noncompliance rating indicates they deserve it for the most part. These were typically banks that had substantially deficient CRA programs almost across the board. While some will bootstrap themselves out of that category, others are likely to remain there because of the wrong CRA spirit or other reasons. We could only document what we believe to be one example of grade deflation involving a bank rated as being in substantial noncompliance.

We believe that many of the banks that have received needs improvement ratings will upgrade themselves with a new examination. Unfortunately, most banks don't have the luxury of a quick reexamination because of the current backlog in compliance examinations. The FED is moving the most quickly within an approximately 6- to 24-month reexamination schedule depending upon the past rating as follows: substantial noncompliance – 6 months, needs improvement – 12 months, satisfactory – 18 months, and outstanding – 24 months. It can be much longer with some other agencies (especially the OCC) that do not enjoy the FED's high ratio of examiners to regulated banks. The FDIC sets the following maximum exam intervals: 24 months for outstanding and satisfactory and 12 months for either below-average rating. The OTS has a similar schedule but may rate on a 6-month interval depending upon the severity of the deficiencies. The OCC rates regional and multinational banks on a 24-month interval. The OCC, however, reportedly can go as long as seven years between compliance exams at some of its community banks, and it therefore may be 1996 before they provide CRA ratings for all national banks.

For this reason CRA ratings, as noted in the general information section of the evaluation, are really only appropriate for the date cited thereon. The bank's CRA performance may have gotten better or worse since the date of that examination. The likelihood is that it has improved because of the disclosure of the ratings and increased public awareness of them.

Many banks receiving one of the two below-average ratings have produced detailed responses or rebuttals to their current CRA evaluations, which they often disagree with as being harsh, unfair, or outright wrong. Some bankers in their responses have admitted to problems with their program but report they have quickly remedied them. Those banks taking such affirmative action may likely receive an improved rating, assuming everything else is as least as good as it was before. These responses are placed in a bank's public file.

The most important thing CRA ratings are *not* is an evaluation of a bank's safety and soundness. These disclosures are most visible on all public evaluations, including those reprinted in this book.

A CRA evaluation is not relevant for a bank holding company but for its individual bank affiliates. We have noted significant differences in ratings among banks within a given bank holding company. Several very large interstate and intrastate multibank holding companies have received a mix of ratings, including one case where affiliates of one of our largest bank holding companies received at least one of all four CRA ratings.

These findings seem to question the belief by some that size alone is a determinant of a bank's CRA rating. Since each affiliate bank has access to the CRA compliance resources of the holding company, it would be reasonable to assume that all banks in a large holding company would receive above-average ratings because the documentation ability is there. Because we are finding a number of needs improvement ratings at banks within large interstate and intrastate bank holding companies, it appears that size is not the sole predictor of CRA ratings.

A CRA rating is specific to a bank and not the individual market which it serves. For this reason, CRA ratings for large banks serving many markets within a state and especially many different states will not be as revealing as the rating of a small bank serving its local community.

We use the terminology "above average" to refer to the top rating and "below average" to refer to the bottom two ratings. The satisfactory rating may be a combination of both average and above-average ones, but we have no way to prove this hypothesis. That is, if we were to force the current system into the typical academic grading scale, it would be as follows:

CRA Rating	Grade Equivalent	Our Terminology
Outstanding	A	Above Average
Satisfactory	B or C	Average

CRA Rating	Grade Equivalent	Our Terminology
Needs Improvement	D	Below Average
Substantial Noncompliance	F	Below Average

Our above interpretation of the current system means that banks receiving a satisfactory rating may in reality be a combination of those with B+ and C– grades as well as others in between these two. This is important because four out of five banks receive a satisfactory rating.

2. WHAT BANKERS, COMMUNITY GROUPS, AND REGULATORS *REALLY* THINK ABOUT CRA

INTRODUCTION

Very few bankers will go on record as to their true feelings on CRA. Community group representatives are usually more outspoken with their opinions on this subject, especially as they pertain to banks. And the views of the regulators themselves on CRA, when they are made public, are usually in the form of carefully drafted statements.

Our object was to find out what representatives of the three elements of the CRA triangle *really* think about CRA. We decided to examine actual written comments placed into the public record by representatives of each of these three groups. These comments, which were on proposed regulations regarding the content and disclosure of CRA performance evaluations, will form the body of this chapter. They will provide the reader with an inside view of how bankers, community groups, and regulators really feel about CRA.

A FOIA FOR FIRREA

FIRREA amended the CRA by requiring the public disclosure of a new four-tier bank rating along with an evaluation for the first time. The FFIEC, the super regulator of the banking industry, published proposals to implement the CRA amendments for public comment in the *Federal Register* on December 22, 1989.

A total of 129 comments were received from banks, community groups, regulators, and other interested parties. Under the Freedom of Information Act (FOIA), we obtained a copy of each of these comment letters, which totaled over 500 pages, to ascertain how banks, community groups, and regulators really felt about CRA.

Some of these comment letters were handwritten, and others were likely the result of several drafts. Most were on official letterhead, but some were not. The best part about this sample is that any person, company, or organization in the country could comment and put their true CRA views on record. The sample was not limited to those individuals who might be quoted in the media, asked to testify before Congress, or speak before a banking or community group.

GOING ON THE RECORD

Each of the commentors recognized that their letters would be part of the public file. Almost all of the 129 comments were from the CRA triangle, namely banks, community groups, and regulators.

We extracted relevant sentences and paragraphs from letters in each of these categories. The only corrections were for punctuation or spelling. As much of a passage is included as possible to reflect the writer's view on a particular subject.

Obviously, there is not enough space here to reproduce each letter. These are available through a

FOIA request with the FFIEC. We realize that we will be subject to the "taking out of context" criticism for utilizing only a portion of certain comments, but we attempted to be as fair as possible in our selection of various passages. We indicated where phrases, sentences, or paragraphs were omitted through the use of . . . or *****.

The printing of these excerpts from this public record is meant to be informative and descriptive of views on CRA. There is no intent here to embarrass or discredit any of the authors or their banks, organizations, or agencies. They felt strongly enough about CRA to take the time to write a letter to have their voice heard, and these commentors should be praised for this initiative. We did not include the name of the individual writing each letter but included the name of the bank, organization, or agency as was appropriate.

We attempted to provide a distribution of different commentors that was representative of all 129 letters. Bankers and/or representatives of associations or groups representing bankers accounted for 70% of all comments. Community groups and agencies including research organizations who consult with such groups were the second most prolific commentors, representing 17% of the total. The third largest group included the regulators, with 7% of the total. All three of these elements of the CRA triangle represented 94% of all 129 submitted comments. The remainder were submitted by government agencies, congressional representatives, unaffiliated individuals, and others.

WHAT COMMUNITY GROUPS REALLY THINK ABOUT CRA

Community groups and consumer agencies and centers represented 17% of all comment letters to the FFIEC. Excerpts from 14 of the 22 letters are contained in this section.

Community group commentors generally pushed for tougher CRA enforcement rules and sanctions for violators. These groups were very concerned about convenient access to public evaluations and in fact were granted some relief in the final rules. The only area where community groups agreed with both regulators and bankers was concern over the subjectivities in the rating process.

Some community groups felt that the emphasis of CRA evaluations should be by local community rather than for an entire bank operating in many communities. While this emphasis did not change, there have been some proposals before Congress calling for CRA ratings by state and/or metropolitan area for large multistate banking operations.

The excerpts which identify only the name of the community or consumer organizations are as follows:

1. East Harlem Community Coalition for Fair Banking
   New York, New York
   Of particular concern to us has been the devastating and divisive impact of bank policies upon predominantly low and moderate income populations such as exists in East Harlem. . . .

   The Fair Banking Coalition is particularly dismayed with the continued bank practice of grouping different neighborhoods with varying needs, as consolidated "communities." This practice continues to do more social and economic injustice to impoverished populations than any other aspect of the banking industry. It relieves banks from maintaining a high degree of involvement throughout the many neighborhoods of a "community."

2. Action for Boston Community Development Inc.
   Boston, Massachusetts
   Financial institutions should be *required* to establish active CRA Advisory Committees. The purpose of these Committees will be to advise the financial institution on and to actually develop with the financial institution, meaningful and effective CRA Plans that meet the needs of the entire community, including the low income and minority community. The Federal government should mandate that the composition of the CRA Advisory Committee be representative and that at least one-third of the Advisory Committee membership represent minority, low income and anti-poverty concerns.

*****

While I recognize that no institution's Board of Directors will be willing, or should be willing, to abdicate their authority and responsibility for dealing with CRA or other matters, they should be compelled to have a community group which advises them. Financial institutions too often do not have adequate representation or day to day involvement with the low income community. A CRA Community Advisory Committee would provide this input.

3. Ohio State Legal Services Association, State Support Unit Columbus, Ohio

I also hope that these four rating levels shall not become inflated. It would be surprising and disturbing if more than a small percentage of financial institutions achieved the "outstanding" rating. I hope that there will be a bell curve approach to rating the institutions such that there are very few "outstanding" and "substantial noncompliance" ratings for institutions and the bulk of institutions will be in the "satisfactory" and "needs to improve" categories.

4. University of Minnesota, Center for Urban and Regional Affairs Minneapolis, Minnesota

Financial institutions, understandably, have found numerous ways to make their CRA report difficult to obtain. Copying charges are sometimes fixed at discouraging rates, reports are available only through obscure officers who are difficult to contact, or available only through personal application where the potential for subtle intimidation proves irresistible.

5. University of Minnesota, Hubert H. Humphrey Institute of Public Affairs Minneapolis, Minnesota

However, it is abundantly clear that the level of misunderstanding by the public and government would be far less if they knew how these guidelines are to be used and what is behind a specific rating. The Regulators, by their own hand will be responsible for much of the misinterpretation that will result from these evalua-

tions. I do not think this is in the best interest of the public, the banks or the regulators to make public only half of the evaluation.

6. CONSERVE, Inc. New York, New York

There is clearly a compelling need for the kind of positive public intervention in banking activities proposed under FIRREA by the Examination Council to make financial services much more accessible to low-income communities. This is apparent to CONSERVE from the experiences we have had with financing low-income buildings with loans from commercial banks in New York City. Most of the banks we contacted were either not interested in lending, or their policies effectively excluded our customers. Those few banks that were interested in working with us were mainly large commercial banks. One bank appeared to be primarily interested in satisfying its CRA requirements.

7. Oak Park Northwood Neighborhood Association San Antonio, Texas

In addition, we see nothing in the guidelines to address the "minority-front" problem which will be used to obtain questionable loans for inner-city development. Several such companies have cost our city, federal government and lending agencies a great deal of money and have not provided the intended benefits. This play could also be used by the lending institutions to circumvent the guidelines. We would like to see a stiff penalty imposed to discourage this as a means to ignore the guidelines.

8. Fair Housing Center Toledo, Ohio

The regulation should state that whether an institution has had an application protested will be reviewed and that the willingness or unwillingness of the institution to communicate and/or negotiate with the filing community group will be seriously considered. Oftentimes, before a community group protests an institution's application, it has requested meetings with the institution to address community concern.

If an institution does not agree to meet with a community organization to discuss community credit issues, this should be reflected in a rating of substantial noncompliance under factor(s) A and/or L.

9. Citizens Research Education Network
   Hartford, Connecticut
   We find in our city that banks which do CRA related programs in low income neighborhoods often do not actually lend to low and moderate income persons. Instead, they make loans to wealthier individuals, thereby "gentrifying" a neighborhood, or they loan to landlords who take out loans as owner-occupants, but actually do not intend to live in those neighborhoods.

10. Community Redevelopment Center, Inc.
    Fort Worth, Texas
    We suggest that the following criteria be added to the uniform rating system:

    IV. Discrimination and Other Illegal Credit Practices
        Manifests its anti-discrimination policies by engaging qualified minorities in highly responsible and visible positions. This includes the board of directors and senior management.

11. Woodstock Institute
    Chicago, Illinois
    Any institution found to have engaged in illegal or discriminatory practices, regardless of the rest of their evaluation, should not be assigned any rating other than "Substantial Non-Compliance."
    As a case in point, the proposed guidelines call for the assignment of a "Needs-to-Improve" rating to institutions that have been found to have possibly engaged in "isolated prescreening or discouraging of applicants." This is totally unacceptable. Such practices should not be disregarded simply because they are isolated or not fully documented. Where there is evidence of such practices, a serious problem exists that should be thoroughly investigated. In such in-

stances an institution should be considered "Non-Compliant" until it makes a concerted effort to correct such problems and to make fair lending a clearly understood organizational priority from top to bottom. Financial institutions should no more be able to flirt with discriminatory practices than they are with "isolated" fraudulent financial practices.

12. National Training and Information Center
    Chicago, Illinois
    In the past, the regulators claimed that they would seek out local community groups and discuss CRA compliance as part of an examination. This was rarely done. Until Senator Proxmire called CRA hearings in 1988, the National Training and Information Center, the organization that had been involved with the largest number of CRA challenges and agreements and an organization that had asked regulators to contact them about CRA exams, had never been contacted by a single regulator. Then there was a flurry of contact for a short time. Now, the policy statement of April of 1989 seems to suggest that rather than getting out to meet with community groups as promised, the regulators are simply stating that if a group has not placed comments in a lender's file, there will be no community input in the exam.

13. National Business League, Austin Cen-Tex Chapter
    Austin, Texas
    The application of the law appears to give banks, what they were unable to obtain through lobbying efforts "A way around CRA compliance." Regulator enforcement should protect the rights of the minority groups, such as low- to-moderate residents who are unable and often unwilling to participate in an interactive system as CRA.
    Banks have the resources to conduct formal needs assessment studies. They also recognize the importance of business plans and marketing studies. . . . To all of us, it is ludicrous when they

require my clients to present voluminous documents that most often do not produce loans.

14. Center for Community Change
    Washington, D.C.
    Congressional oversight hearings revealed rampant grade inflation which assured that virtually all lending institutions received passing marks, regardless of their actual record in serving community credit needs.

*****

The disclosure of CRA ratings and evaluations represents a major departure from the less than open way in which the regulators conducted their examinations in the past. The agencies have made it clear over the twelve year history of CRA that they much prefer to evaluate the lending institutions they supervise behind closed doors, keeping the public largely uninformed about the CRA records of the institutions they supervise.

WHAT REGULATORS REALLY THINK ABOUT CRA

Only nine federal regulators and one state regulator (the Michigan Financial Institutions Bureau) submitted written comments to the FFIEC. Excerpts from all nine federal regulatory comments are included here.

Most surprising was the fact that eight of the nine federal regulators represented different Federal Reserve Bank districts. The only representatives of the other three federal regulatory agencies submitting comments were two national bank examiners from the Sioux City duty station. For this reason, these regulatory comments are not representative of a cross-section of all four federal regulators.

The most important concern by the regulators who did comment was the need for a more objective and quantifiable system to come up with CRA ratings. Many regulators were in favor of increased availability of CRA ratings and performance evaluations. A number of regulators insisted on maintaining the confidentiality of the name of the actual examiner conducting a given examination.

Selected comments from the regulators, all but one of whom represent Federal Reserve Banks, are as follows:

1. Federal Reserve Bank of Cleveland
   Cleveland, Ohio
   We agree with the value of publicly disclosing the ratings and having all the regulatory agencies working under similar guidelines. However, we find little merit in changing the rating levels from five to four.
   We also do not totally agree with the need for all institutions to be covered by the act. From our experience, we believe that most of the smaller community banks are strongly committed to their community's improvement and work closely with them in this regard. They understand that if the community does not prosper, the bank will not prosper. It is unfortunate that this message was not conveyed effectively during the discussions on this bill so that a minimum cut off would have been included.

*****

We understand the purpose of requiring institutions to publicly state their delineation is to provide customers or others with a basis for determining the community boundaries where the bank markets its lending programs and expects to do the majority of its business. With this thought in mind, during our examination, we evaluate the reasonableness of a delineation by reviewing the loan extensions, the bank's HMDA reports, if required, and its marketing efforts or strategies within that community.

If we find that a delineation is either too large or too small, we generally suggest that the institution adjust its delineation to more accurately reflect one that they are capable of serving and the desire to serve. In most cases, there is a direct correlation between the size of the institution and the size of a reasonable delineation.

2. Federal Reserve Bank of Boston
   Boston, Massachusetts
   A financial institution which is in unsatisfactory financial condition may not be actively en-

gaged in lending because of a necessity to reduce asset size or to improve liquidity. In such situations, we are concerned as to how to rate an institution's performance without commenting publicly on the safety and soundness of the institution. Would a financial institution in distressed condition necessarily receive a rating of "needs to improve" or "substantial noncompliance" because of its inability to actively participate in lending to community development programs, or would efforts to provide technical assistance to these programs be considered evidence of satisfactory performance commensurate with the institution's limited abilities?

3. Federal Reserve Bank of New York
    New York, New York

    We believe that if a bank does analyze the geographic distribution of its loans but ignores evidence that it is excluding low- and moderate-income areas, it should be criticized more severely than the bank that does no analysis but has a presence in such neighborhoods; however, it is not clear that all Agencies would treat this situation the same way.

4. Comptroller of the Currency, Administrator of National Banks
    Sioux City, Iowa

    We suggest that the new rule adopt a numerical system to help determine priorities and substantive issues in regards to CRA. A numerical system assigning weights for each of the twelve assessment factors would alleviate much confusion and help to ensure consistent evaluations between examiners and regulatory agencies.

    For example, is the bank whose Board of Directors does not actively participate in formulating CRA policy (12 CFR 25.7(c)) as negligent as the bank that engages in discriminatory or other illegal credit practices (12 CFR 25.7(f))? Assigning different weights to the assessment factors will help examiners arrive at conclusions when the distinction is less obvious than in the example above.

5. Federal Reserve Bank of Richmond
    Richmond, Virginia

    We suggest clarification that an "informal" CRA program, described under "Assessment Factor C" for a satisfactory rating in ascertaining community credit needs, does not include an "unwritten" program. To receive a satisfactory evaluation in this category, an institution should have at least some general written goals, objectives, and methodology for self-assessment, though they may be "informal."

6. Federal Reserve Bank of Atlanta
    Atlanta, Georgia

    Because of the need to protect the privacy of bank customers and maintain the confidentiality of certain examination findings, some data in the examination report will not be disclosed in the public disclosure. In some cases, this will make it extremely difficult for examiners to support their conclusions. By not including specific statistical and financial data, the public disclosure might appear too generic. We request that additional information be provided to assist examiners in determining the information that can be included in the public disclosure. This additional guidance would not only ensure a more complete public disclosure, but also ensure consistency among the regulatory agencies in their disclosures.

7. Federal Reserve Bank of Minneapolis
    Minneapolis, Minnesota

    . . . the proposed revisions to the CRA rating system state that "the regulators believe it would be especially useful for a financial institution to expand its CRA statement to include a description of the activities the institution has undertaken to meet its responsibilities under CRA." It is our experience that institutions generally will not amend their CRA statements unless they are required to do so. It would be beneficial to the public and helpful for examiners to have this additional information and, accordingly, the FFIEC may wish to consider making such an expansion mandatory.

8. Federal Reserve Bank of Kansas City
   Kansas City, Missouri

   We are concerned that the phrase "other illegal credit practices" in performance Category IV may encourage unjustified lawsuits and recommend it be eliminated. The discussion under Category IV should not encompass all consumer-related laws and regulations, as is the case under existing Council rating guidelines for CRA, but be restricted to discriminatory practices that affect an institution's ability to [meet] or record of meeting community credit needs.

9. Federal Reserve Bank of San Francisco
   San Francisco, California

   In meetings with our compliance examiners on the matter of disclosed evaluations and the institutions' responses to them, we have heard expressions of deep concern over the prospect that an institution, in its response to a disclosed evaluation, may include defamatory or otherwise abusive language in reference to the examiner(s) who conducted the examination. We believe this concern is a valid one and that the Council should deal with it. Each supervisory agency should provide guidance to its institutions cautioning against referring to agency personnel, either by name or innuendo, in the institutions' responses to disclosed evaluations. Institutions should be encouraged to recognize that CRA examinations involve procedures established by the agency and that the examiners' findings are reviewed by the agency; responses by institutions should relate to the findings and methodology of examinations and not to individuals conducting them.

WHAT BANKERS REALLY THINK ABOUT CRA

Banks and thrift institutions and their representatives (trade associations and lawyers) represented 70% of all comments submitted to the FFIEC on the subject proposal. While some bankers were supportive of the new disclosure procedure, most questioned the need for it.

The grounds for opposition to CRA disclosure by bankers included the most common arguments, such as credit allocation; possible confusion with safety and soundness ratings; a perceived conflict between CRA and sound banking principles; unfairness compared to credit unions and other institutions not covered by CRA; the mounting paperwork burden and costs, especially for smaller banks; and, the overall subjectivity and inconsistency, especially in states with their own CRA regulations. Bankers were granted few concessions in the final regulations.

Bankers were particularly concerned about the need for some type of review process before the final rating was made and an appeals process before its public disclosure. Many bankers felt that examiners would be unfamiliar with their local market and might inadvertently make errors which could result in a low rating. Fearing the stigma associated with the low rating, many banks in that situation called for a relatively quick reexamination. As pointed out earlier, only a few banks received two examinations under the new system as of year-end 1991.

Bankers were granted no relief on the issue of reviews, appeals, or reexaminations. The only victory for bankers was a little more time in making the evaluations public (30 *business* days rather than 30 total days after receipt) and the ability to assess mailing fees for public requests of CRA statements. Additional regulations went into effect in July 1991 to clarify some of these technicalities.

Because of the large volume of bank comments to the 1989 FFIEC proposals and because banks are a far from homogeneous group, the comments are divided into three sections. The first section contains selected comments from representatives of 28 small banks. The second section contains selected comments from representatives of 26 larger banks, including a few "wholesale" banks. Finally, selected comments from representatives of eight bank trade associations are included in the third section.

What Bankers at Small Banks Really Think About CRA

1. Anderson National Bank
   Anderson, South Carolina

   There are currently tremendous pressures on small banks emanating from many sources and to propose yet another goal that is in effect unattainable is absurd.

2. The First National Bank of Arcola
   Arcola, Illinois
   . . . the massive resources now being used to enforce and expand the CRA are merely a means of denying the truly poor the funds which they do need. In an attempt to force the issues, your council is spending a great deal more money than necessary and the banks who must comply are also spending money which is not going to the poor. Why doesn't the council resign enmasse provided that these funds be directed to the poverty level individuals who need them?

3. Backus State Bank
   Hackensack, Minnesota
   Lastly, I definitely feel that if our bank or any other bank receives an adverse rating that we have the right to contest the rating prior to it being made public. This to me seems that you're "guilty" before you've had the chance to prove your innocence and the entire community knows you're guilty even if later you prove you're innocent.

4. Bank of Columbia
   Columbia, Alabama
   I am writing in response to the proposed guidelines for disclosure of CRA evaluations and revisions to the assessment rating system. I think this is ridiculous! It is nothing but an entrapment by a minority group or groups when it relates to a small rural bank.

5. Bethalto National Bank
   Bethalto, Illinois
   We here at Bethalto National Bank feel that making any CRA information available to the public other than what's available to them right now is a mistake. The public, as a whole, understands very little of the information coming out of the various regulatory agencies, as a result of laws, rules and regulations passed by Congress.
   I do not think that making any CRA rating or

any other type of rating of any bank available to the public does anything except bring attention to the banks. This would possibly cause more litigation, trouble and more expense which in turn is going to make the banks raise the price of their product just like everybody else does when something like this happens.
. . . This comes at a time when Congress is thinking about legislating all kinds of free and low cost services to all segments of society. I think what we are doing here is asking the public to accept something that they really do not understand or know that much about. At the same time expecting them to pay for it without explaining, they are going to be the ones that will pay.
I respectfully request that no information regarding CRA ratings or any information be made available to the public other than what is already printed in every newspaper in the country from all banks four times a year. I believe this is adequate.

6. Citizens Bank
   Flint, Michigan
   "How much is enough" has frustrated all parties involved in CRA. When community groups come in and say an institution can do better, they immediately attach a dollar amount to that expectation. In some cases, this has been a significant portion of the institution's capital. Unmet demands such as this have been seen as uncooperative and public pressure is applied through the media. Regardless of the institutions other benefits and contributions to the community, the image of the institution is damaged and its safety and soundness is jeopardized.

7. Citizens State Bank of Giddings
   Giddings, Texas
   It would appear that there seems to be a continuing effort to force small banks to close their doors due to all the ongoing requests for more paper work for the regulators.
   Sure, we must see that the low and moderate income persons are not discriminated against but

what about the little old ladies and gentlemen who want to remain independent and come to their small town bank for personal help and attention?

The posting of such public rating will only confuse our customers and lead them to believe that we are a troubled or insolvent institution.

We feel that banks, especially our small independent banks, are being overcome and buried in masses of paper work and log sheets.

8. Farmers Bank of Liberty
Liberty, Illinois

The general public, particularly in a small community such as ours, will never be aware of, or utilize this law.

The only thing it will accomplish is to give a few militant "public-interest" groups a way to fight with urban banks.

It is this type of nonsense that makes it increasingly difficult for a small bank to stay afloat.

We need smarter regulation, not *more* regulation.

9. Farmer's National Bank
Williamsburg, Kentucky

I believe the new proposed CRA guidelines and rating system is a form of socialism and a way to incur extra costs. In my thirty (30) years of banking experience I am not aware of any customer complaints.

10. First Federal Savings and Loan Association of McMinnville
McMinnville, Oregon

. . . past experience with the examiners relative to our CRA performance, would reflect that the CRA rating system does not provide a uniform method for evaluating CRA performances. Why? Because the system does not evaluate each deposit facility in each community on its own CRA merits. Why should it be? Because it's going to be publicly posted in *each* office as if it were individually earned and rated.

What you are doing is misleading a lot of communities that have deposit facilities in their area, and in some cases, not even adequate staff

to make loans back to the community. Yet, they can potentially share in a good overall CRA rating earned by their home office, which in some cases are out of state.

Publicly posting the CRA rating, mailed to them by [the] home office, gives the impression to *their* community that *they* are meeting the CRA requirements locally. Not true!

Prior to the rating being made public it was not a critical issue. Making it public, where competitive community institutions can be compared on the CRA performance ratings locally, is critical and misleading. Some institutions will do more for a local community and technically end up with a lower CRA rating than a competitor because the system allows the overall association rating to be used in *all* offices even if some are mere deposit takers. To be fair *publicly,* each office in each community needs a rating.

11. First National Bank
DeWitt, Arkansas

Small town, rural banks know how and do serve the needs of their town, and the whole county in many cases. We do not have the same problems as our big city, sister banks. Our problems are entirely different, yet we are subjected to the same set of regulation interpretations of the big city banks.

We are not saying that we are not or should not be subject to the CRA. However, we do feel that being subjected to the same criteria of the big city banks places an unfair disadvantage on us.

12. First National Bank
Quanah, Texas

When examiners come to a bank in a small town, there is no way they can judge your bank on how it serves the community. The only way this could be done would be to trace the officers' and employees' activities over a long period of time. I would be opposed to any additional requirements placed on a bank concerning the Community Reinvestment Act.

During the last two weeks our bank has made

two loans to people of minority races who had no money on deposit, to cover the burial of a family member. Our chances of getting this money repaid is very slim. How can services of this type be put into a rating system?

I have always felt like in the 30 years I have been with this bank that our goal was to serve the entire community. Our bank has been run on this basis and I do not feel that any additional regulations are necessary for communities of our size. I feel that if you would go to any bank in a small community you would find the same is true with their institution.

13. The First National Bank
    Strasburg, Virginia

    Where will all of this stop? A small bank cannot continue to comply with all the regulations implemented for banks and still produce expected profits. In order to achieve an "Outstanding" rating under CRA, we would need to have a full-time employee to comply with the criteria as set forth by CRA.

    Please be as liberal as you can on the small banks.

14. First National Bank in Alamogordo
    Alamogordo, New Mexico

    At a time when financial institutions as a general rule need to be strengthened, it would appear that a public notice could generate adverse publicity. This would do nothing but present a whole new host of problems, one of those being a run on the bank's deposits, thereby threatening the institution itself and certainly would not correct the problem. The correction of the problem should be through the regulatory process and not having the institution adjudicated by public sentiment which very well may be a small vocal minority that could adversely affect the bank.

    I hope that cooler heads would prevail and although, I am certainly not objecting to the Community Reinvestment Act concept nor to its rating system, I have serious doubt that the public would best be served by a public notifica-

tion of this action. I believe that the regulatory officials through a process similar to the CAMEL rating can just as effectively serve its purpose.

15. First National Bank in Pampa
    Pampa, Texas

    We are a community bank that has been operating in Pampa for 83 years and feel that we have a handle on the needs of our area. It is disturbing to realize that someone will have the power to imply that we are not meeting the needs of our community with the benefit of only a brief visit. I know, however, that you have been mandated by the FFIEC to accomplish this task.

*****

To be perfectly honest, we believe that the publishing of a CRA rating is a serious mistake and should be postponed until the politicians wake up to the fact that they have again created a monster. It is okay for examiners to access and rate an institution much like they do with the CAMEL rating, but the power to publish that rating is inappropriate in every sense of the word.

16. Grayson National Bank
    Independence, Virginia

    There are many small banks (including ours) that are completely community oriented but are not able to supply, for various reasons, what to examiners is adequate documentation . . . the disclosure [of a low CRA rating] to the public could possibly cause the community to believe the bank substandard when indeed their only crime is in not being able to provide the documentation necessary to show that they are more than adequately meeting the credit needs of the community.

17. Great Southern National Bank
    Meridian, Mississippi

    In addition to the above problem, there will be significant variances among the ratings because they are highly subjective. Be prepared for cases where one regulatory group gives a satisfactory rating while another gives a less than satisfactory rating when the performance is virtually the same. Institutions will tend to copy CRA programs that are rated satisfactory, thus many will have very similar programs.

18. Greene County National Bank in Carrollton
    Carrollton, Illinois
    While I do feel my comments will not have a large effect on what will happen, I see no purpose in disclosing the CRA rating to the public. I could understand this, in cases where a bank has been a habitual violator or will not cooperate with the examiner and take appropriate actions.

    Most likely, with today's "suit-happy" society, you are asking for more trouble for banks. More than likely, we would have to go to court to protect ourselves against a nuisance suit. If the proposed guidelines for disclosure of CRA are passed then they should apply this same rule to all finance companies, credit unions, insurance companies and anyone else who lends money to the public.

19. Horicon State Bank
    Horicon, Wisconsin
    It is difficult to keep up with the regulatory burden placed on banks.

    The Community Reinvestment Act revisions proposed in your letter of December 29, 1989 is another straw for the camel's back.

    Please lighten our load so we can provide better financial services to our customers.

20. Marion State Bank
    Marion, Wisconsin
    First of all, I find it incredible that a Federal agency can walk into our bank, make an evaluation of our institution's CRA performance, rate us, and then require us to make that evaluation public without an opportunity on our part to either appeal or contest the rating prior to its publication to the public.

                    *****

    I feel it would be next to impossible for a community bank like ours ever to be given an outstanding record. It appears to me that the rating would be more in the eye of the examiner

and even that rating could vary from examiner to examiner at the same institution.

    I would hope that the regulatory agencies would get together and actually test the proposal before proceeding with something that appears to be the whim of someone who has never been in the trenches!

21. Midway National Bank
    Saint Paul, Minnesota
    Public misunderstanding, rumor and bad press could affect safety, soundness and continued viability of a financial institution. CRA is not a big issue for a closed bank.

    Finally, we disagree with the rating disclosure because of the subjective nature of the rating process. Assessing CRA performance of an institution is a process that does not rely on absolute standards. Too much discretion is given to the examiner in determining the rating. What happens when there are "personality differences" or "philosophical differences" between the examiner and the bank staff? What recourse does the bank have? Agreed, we can make our response part of our CRA file, but the chances of an inquirer requesting that information at the same time they request the ratings are slim.

22. Page County State Bank
    Clarinda, Iowa
    All we ask for is something we can hang our hat on. . . . It's rather like playing a golf hole with no clearly defined par. You're saying to bankers that after we've played the hole you'll tell us what constitutes par based on a bunch of subjective factors. I don't know about you, but before I play a hole I want to know what the accepted standard of performance is and then try to execute my way towards meeting or beating it. Can you tell me what par is for CRA in terms that my officers and staff can understand and attain?

23. Peoples State Bank
    Rocksprings, Texas
    The CRA report can be very damaging to a Bank if it is not done in a proper and professional manner. In today's environment everyone has

almost perfect knowledge of what his or her rights and remedies for problems consist [of]. There are many free organizations which are readily available to help and assist an individual who feels that they have been wronged.

24. Security National Bank
    Sioux City, Iowa

    Once things that are held close or secret are made public, are they oftentimes misinterpreted or miscommunicated? I feel this very problem could result from the examinations of banks for CRA.

25. State National Bank
    Eufaula, Oklahoma

    Our Board is very concerned that when these evaluations are performed and the ratings given, that the banks will become so caught up in receiving a satisfactory rating that in meeting the credit needs of their Communities that they will make credits that will be detrimental to their financial health.

*****

Being a small Community Bank and having made an honest effort to make credit available to all aspects of the communities we serve, we have also been concerned that what we loan out will be collected.

We can foresee that under the Expanded Act and your proposed guidelines that to achieve at least a satisfactory rating that we may be put in the position that we will be pressed to make credit available that may be difficult or nearly impossible to collect.

Our Board wants to go on record that we feel that the question of making credit available to our communities should pass the test of proper credit standards and only be made with a Bank's safety and soundness in mind.

26. Tri-County Community Bank of Lehigh Acres
    Lehigh Acres, Florida

    There is an old saying "If something isn't broke—don't fix it." Unfortunately, the mental-

ity in Washington is "Keep fixing till you break it!"

This CRA rating system has to be another ride through "Bureaucratic Heaven," for now the folks in Washington have more work to do!

All the things that will be done will certainly cost the taxpayers far more than any good that may someday come to some "poor maligned consumer."

Since the regulatory people did such a poor job in regulating the Savings and Loan Industry now they all want to see how many layers of garbage they can put on the backs of the financial institutions that have always tried to comply with their regulations, and survived to enjoy the efforts of all their great wisdom.

This writer recognizes that his efforts will be of no avail and that common sense departed Washington many years ago!

27. Twin City State Bank
    Kansas City, Kansas

    The idea of putting out the evaluation to the public which will immediately become subject to comment, no matter what it is, and not giving the banks a method of complaining or clarifying or feeling the rating is just not the American way of doing things.

28. Ventura County National Bank
    Oxnard, CA

    Troubled banks are more likely to have frequent examinations than untroubled banks and would be required to make their examiner prepared CRA Evaluations available sooner. The earlier troubled banks make their examiner prepared CRA Evaluations, the more likely protests will develop at these banks and delays in merging the troubled banks with untroubled banks will result.

    I suggest using the same time frame for all banks to provide their most recent CRA Evaluations in the examiner format. Requiring all banks to provide CRA Evaluations at the same time may not concentrate or attract protestors to all of the troubled banks and may allow more efficient merging with untroubled banks.

What Bankers at Big Banks Really Think About CRA

1. Ameritrust
   Cleveland, Ohio
   We believe that an excessive amount of involvement is being expected from the Board of Directors. There must be an allowance for more delegation of responsibility for such matters.

2. AmSouth Bancorporation
   Birmingham, Alabama
   The guidelines should make it clear that absent evidence of an intent to impermissibly discriminate against some protected class of people, the financial institution's judgment about such credit needs is determinative.

*****

The CRA is *not* a credit allocation measure; it requires an institution to *ascertain* the credit needs of its community and to *help meet* those needs. If the needs are great and can be met by an institution, the amount of credit should be commensurately great; if the needs are small, the amount of credit will be small. Thus, the amount of loans in any given area is probative of nothing.

We suppose some would argue that a large percentage of denials in a low- or moderate-income neighborhood[1] would tend to prove that an institution discriminates against the residents of that neighborhood. But, the ratio of denials to applications proves nothing at all. The only relevant statistic is the ratio of denials to *credit-worthy* applications and the Guidelines do not provide for such a comparison.

Compiling such records will do two things. It will give regulatory agencies ammunition to covertly force financial institutions to allocate credit among the various segments of its community (with the probable result either of lowering the institution's credit quality or subjecting it to

punitive action for a perceived imbalance in the allocation). And, it will provide data that can be used by critics to level charges of discrimination against the institution but that proves no such thing. We fear that this will lead to a lot of bickering about a red herring, deflecting attention from the main issue—how to ascertain and help meet the real credit needs of the community.

*****

No one can dispute that conditions of economic deprivation exist that money would cure, at least temporarily. But, loans, no matter how innovative they are or how many special features they have, are not the answer to many of those problems. As we have so clearly seen in the third-world loan problems, forcing ill-conceived lending programs (at the time they were made, those loans could well have been called innovative) into a situation in which they don't fit can result in calamity for the borrower as well as the lender. . . . Financial institutions are not charitable organizations and their stockholders should not see their investment eroded by a well-meaning but ill-fated governmental edict that will pressure financial institutions into making poorly conceived loans.

3. Banc One Corporation
   Columbus, Ohio
   Certain Banc One banks, for example, have been advised that directors are to be personally engaged in making CRA ascertainment calls within the community. This is in contravention of Banc One Corporation's assignment of duties to affiliate bank directors who are charged with directing, not managing or conducting, bank business. Banc One holds the opinion that the proposed CRA guidelines, as written, blur the legitimate distinctions between the appropriate role of the director and the appropriate role of senior management.

---

1 One would naturally expect that lower-income neighborhoods could have a higher rate of loan denials than higher-income neighborhoods, simply because income is such an important factor in judging creditworthiness.

4. Bankers Trust Company
   New York, New York

   The Bank is concerned that the Rating System and Disclosure Guidelines do not take into account the special nature and limitations of wholesale banks with the likely result that such institutions will receive ratings that are disproportionately and unfairly low relative to the ratings achievable by retail oriented institutions in the ordinary course of business. Wholesale institutions should not be expected to develop retail products to comply with CRA and they should not be penalized for dealing with intermediary community groups, as would clearly be the case if wholesale banks were compared to retail banks head to head.

   *****

   . . . it would seem impossible for a wholesale bank, by its very nature, to receive a rating of "outstanding" and difficult for it even to receive a rating of "satisfactory."

5. BayBanks, Inc.
   Boston, Massachusetts

   BayBanks opposes any proposal that would make the confidential CRA examination report publicly available. BayBanks also recommends that a mechanism be developed to permit banks to participate with the agencies in identifying information that is confidential and that should not be disclosed in the stand-alone document which would be available to the public.

   *****

   . . . safety and soundness considerations, in particular, as they relate to lending activities, need to be taken into account more specifically and more frequently throughout the description of the assessment factors.

6. Continental Bank
   Chicago, Illinois

   A wholesale bank that makes loans to individuals to enhance a business relationship will not surprisingly evidence a geographical imbalance in its loan distribution. A wholesale bank should, however, be able to demonstrate the number of loans or calls made by its banking officers in low- to moderate-income areas. However, since most commercial borrowers choose to locate outside low- to moderate-income areas for reasons unrelated to availability of financing, wholesale banks will, of necessity, show some geographical imbalance in their loan distribution.

7. Cullen/Frost Bankers
   San Antonio, Texas

   It is our experience and that of other banks that there can be a considerable difference between what examiners say in oral examination closings and what appears in written reports. Also, it is probable that a bank's "response" to a criticism will not carry the weight with activist groups nor get as much prominence in newspaper reports as negative examination remarks.

8. First City Bancorporation of Texas
   Houston, Texas

   This section provides for disclosure of any evidence of prohibited discrimination or other illegal credit practices. Public identification of any violations in this section could be a confession of judgment or self-incrimination of the bank unless an investigation has been made and a violation of law clearly documented. The examination process should continue to include such an evaluation; however, the results should not be part of the written report which is made public since it may compromise the bank's ability to provide a defense against discrimination under Regulation B or other litigation brought to court.

9. First Tennessee Bank, N.A.
   Memphis, Tennessee

   Even though examination personnel and bank personnel generally cooperate closely during the examination process, we have found that miscommunication or misunderstandings do arise from time to time, sometimes resulting in outright errors in the examination report. Heretofore, those errors could be pointed out to the regulatory agency afterwards and would have no adverse impact. However, under the new guidelines, it is important that any errors be identified and corrected before the institution is harmed by public disclosure.

10. Glendale Federal Bank, FSB
     Glendale, California
     It is unreasonable, unfair and wholly ineffectual for an institution to be able to respond, if necessary, only after the rating is public.

11. IBJ Schroder Bank & Trust Company and Morgan Guaranty Trust Company of New York
     New York, New York
     Finally, two problems which have already arisen in the CRA examinations of some wholesale banks should also be mentioned. The first is the tendency of examiners to give CRA credit for the first couple of years of a loan or investment and to thereafter discount it. The unintentional effect of such an approach is to discourage institutions from making long-term commitments because they know they will not receive multiple-year CRA credit for them. Since community groups prefer the certainty and stability of a long-term commitment, this policy undermines the very goals that the CRA is intended to further. The second problem is the reluctance which some CRA examiners have shown to giving an institution full credit for a loan commitment which is only partially used. If an institution makes a commitment to lend a certain amount of money, it has a legal obligation to honor that commitment if it is requested to do so and the ready availability of such funds is of continuing benefit to the borrower. Whether the recipient of that commitment decides to borrow all or part of the amount of the commitment is beyond the control of the financial institution. The CRA examiner should not discount the institution's commitment because it has not been fully utilized.

12. International Bancshares Corporation
     Laredo, Texas
     I wish to go on record as being adamantly

opposed to the disclosure of CRA Ratings or any other ratings to the public. It has been my experience, especially over the last 3 or 4 years, that the examiners make a lot of errors in their judgment and decisions. The one thing examiners never admit is that they make mistakes. Once a bank has been "labeled" by an examiner, the regulators will not change that determination until another complete examination takes place.

*****

I'm very concerned with the whole process of labeling that is going on in the regulatory network. Once you are on a bad list, you tend to get marked by the whole system, i.e., the Federal Reserve, the FDIC, the OCC, the State Banking Department, etc. You are a black sheep, and there is no recovery from that verdict.

I'm totally opposed to any disclosure of CRA Ratings or any other rating, unless there is some sort of appeal process that removes the ultimate decision from the regulator. They never admit that they make mistakes. No business can survive with that attitude. It seems that only government can take that position.

13. Manufacturers National Bank
     Detroit, Michigan
     This language constitutes a form of credit allocation, dictating the types of loans that count toward successful achievement of high CRA rating goals and leading to a "numbers game" in dealing with the regulators and community groups. We believe that this method of evaluating for Factor I is inconsistent with the statement that an institution is not required to adopt specific activities or to offer specific types or amounts of credit. It also removes from the institution its flexibility in determining how it best can help meet the credit needs of its entire community and may lead an institution into unsafe and unsound activities in order to meet CRA goals. The directors and management of a bank have fiduciary duties to their shareholders that may at times conflict with the achievement

of high CRA ratings if the criteria remain as stated in Assessment Factor I.

14. Mellon Bank
    Pittsburgh, Pennsylvania
    We are also concerned about the potential for adverse consequences from the public notification of Section IV *(Discrimination and Other Illegal Credit Practices)*. . . . Such disclosures could encourage litigation, individual and class action, against the institution irrespective of the basis for the criticism in the examination. We further question if such disclosure would be contrary to the provisions of the Freedom of Information Act.

15. Meridian Bancorp, Inc.
    Reading, PA
    Disclosures on a bank-by-bank basis could cause confusion and misinterpretation about the bank holding company's overall CRA compliance record, potentially provoking inappropriate and unwarranted consumer activism. (For example, one bank out of eight may have a poor CRA rating. If the other "good" banks are not also examined at the same time, one bank's "poor" CRA review affects the entire BHC evaluation.)

16. National Bank of Commerce of Mississippi
    Starkville, Mississippi
    No other enterprises or even governmentally regulated businesses are hampered by the restriction to demonstrate and prove that marketing efforts and contacts are made to every person and business within its client base. The cost and effort to accommodate such a requirement would be incomprehensible.

17. National City Corporation
    Cleveland, Ohio
    With all due respect to the concerns and efforts of the Council, I am extremely sensitive to the impact public disclosure of the results of a CRA examination can have. The ability of the examiners to make judgments based on what could be limited knowledge of the needs of communities, federal, state and city financing

programs including the operation cost and problems associated with them could have a negative impact upon the bank.

18. Norwest Corporation
    Minneapolis, Minnesota
    We are deeply concerned about a public rating system that is not uniformly applied or fairly administered. We have experienced over zealous examiners in the past who have not been objective evaluators. Accordingly, we strongly urge the Council and its member federal banking supervisory agencies to prepare their examiners for this major change in the CRA process. The banking industry did not seek nor did the banking supervisory agencies support the concept of public ratings.

                             *****

    To ignore the activities of affiliated companies would result in unfair evaluations of banks with affiliates that are actively involved in addressing needs in local communities. In our case affiliates provide mortgage banking and municipal securities underwriting products and services and have made community development investments.

19. Signet Banking Corporation
    Richmond, Virginia
    The rating term "substantial noncompliance" does not appear to be in keeping with the spirit of the CRA. While a poor performance assessment rating may result from violations of other antidiscrimination laws, neglect of community credit needs does not constitute a violation of the CRA. Perhaps a better rating term would be "substantially deficient record of helping to meet community credit needs."

20. South Carolina National Corporation
    Columbia, South Carolina
    We submit that this wording is so non-definitive as to be confusing to all concerned, be it institutional management, regulatory agency examining personnel or community interest groups.

The definitions of:
    proactive
    high degree
    satisfactorily
    limited
    rarely
are entirely discretionary with any and each individual.

* * * * *

Although we have no suggestions as to how the description of these levels of performance could or should be defined in order to clearly communicate, surely (hopefully) some wording can be developed that will provide meaningful guidance to the industry and the examining authorities within the regulatory agencies.

21. SunTrust Banks, Inc.
    Atlanta, Georgia
    Unless one believes that discrimination is the only possible cause for disparities in lending among segments of the community, there are numerous factors involving both economics and personal behavior which may result in these disparities. A bank can offer below market interest rates and reduced or zero closing costs and it can reduce or even eliminate its credit standards (the factors within its control) to try to reduce disparities, but these are only band-aids which do not address the underlying factors causing disparities.

    Encouragement through CRA for institutions to reduce credit standards and to offer below-market, fixed rate term loans such as for home mortgages is also directly in conflict with recent efforts by the regulators to emphasize safety and soundness by promoting stronger credit underwriting and better asset/liability management practices.

* * * * *

Despite all the highly publicized allegations of discriminatory practices by institutions, and recognizing the huge financial awards possible for any persons receiving discriminatory treat-
ment and lawyers who represent them, there are virtually no individual allegations of discriminatory treatment. It may very well be that disparate patterns are justified and reasonable based on the individual decisions which resulted in that pattern. Unfortunately, the standards in this proposal focus on the pattern and not the reasonableness of the decisions resulting in the pattern. Credit decisions should be made using fair standards which are fairly applied, and that includes neither discrimination nor preference based on irrelevant factors such as sex, race and geographic location.

22. TCF Bank
    Minneapolis, Minnesota
    We are aware of studies which indicate higher rejection rates for residents of minority census tracts and the belief by some that this is indicative of redlining. Although we deplore redlining, we believe that there is, at best, an open question as to whether the existence of redlining can be established solely on the basis of rejection rates. We believe that a CRA evaluation should not, on the basis of rejection rates alone, necessarily conclude that an institution engages in redlining.

23. Trust Company Bank
    Atlanta, Georgia
    . . . we believe that the present language and content of these proposed standards will make the achievement of an outstanding rating virtually impossible (or, if possible, extremely time consuming and expensive) for a bank. We believe that the cost in administering such a program, particularly for larger institutions, will be very great. And, at least in the context of dealing with CRA protests, there really is no benefit in achieving such a rating.

* * * * *

. . . However, those institutions with good examination ratings which have submitted applications, and have subsequently found those applications protested, have found little consolation from their good ratings. In fact, an institution with an outstanding rating is just as vulnerable to a lengthy and complicated application delay as one with a satisfactory rating.

* * * * *

I know of a specific circumstance where an institution decided not to offer government-guaranteed loans because they did not believe these types of loans were going to meet a credit need. Instead, they decided to make the loans direct, i.e., with no guarantee other than the applicant's. They were truly meeting the spirit of this CRA factor, yet they were downgraded for not offering government-guaranteed loans, i.e., if it wasn't on the checklist it didn't count.

24. UJB Financial Corp
    Princeton, New Jersey
    To recapitulate, I would strongly recommend that "product/results" outweigh "process" in the evaluation of institutions. Secondly, evaluation should stick with the spirit of CRA in "Criteria IV," not be based on technicalities of whether or not a form was filled out properly by a clerk.

    In the final analysis, I believe we will all be judged on results or the lack thereof, not on our form or process.

25. United American Bank
    Memphis, Tennessee
    We firmly believe that our bank should be involved in the community and should put something back into the community. However, we feel that the method proposed by the Federal Financial Institutions Council is a means to blackmail organizations into compliance by stating that if they don't do this or that for a particular organization, they will do something to cause the regulators to lower the bank's grade.

* * * * *

There are groups holding courses in minority neighborhoods throughout the country to teach people how to make banks do what they want done. In effect, preferential treatment is demand-

ed of banks, or they will complain in mass to regulatory authorities. This is wrong and your proposed revision plays into their hands.

I can't see why the existing system of regulatory grading as it exists now would not continue to work without making this matter a matter of public record.

26. Wilmington Trust
    Wilmington, Delaware
    Secondly, your proposed regulations do not reflect the real world. Boards of Directors do not get involved in the planning process nor the day to day operations of an institution. Rather, Boards react to proposals by management rather than generating plans or proposals themselves. Except in the smallest of institutions, Board members will not get involved in any facet of running a bank, including CRA programs as your descriptions would seem to expect. The planning and the details of the day to day running of the bank, including the setting of goals (including the CRA) is done by its management and reacted to by its Board.

What Bankers Associations Really Think About CRA

1. American Bankers Association
   Washington, D.C.
   The proposal does not give adequate consideration to the overriding importance of safety and soundness, which underlies the operation of every bank and should be an integral part of any CRA evaluation. Also, the proposal in its reference to the geographic spread of specific types of credit as important assessment factors fosters credit allocation and therefore denies a bank the flexibility it should have in meeting its community's credit needs.

* * * * *

At the time CRA was enacted in 1977 commercial banks held about thirty-seven (37) percent of the total financial assets of all financial institutions. Currently banks hold only thirty

(30) percent of total financial assets. . . . The decline in bank market share indicates that the available resources within any particular community are shifting to other financial intermediaries such as money market funds, insurance companies and market securities which are not subject to CRA. The continued imposition of CRA on commercial banks and the expansion of the burden associated with CRA under the pending proposal greatly accelerates the competitive problems facing banks in today's marketplace.

2. Association of Reserve City Bankers
   Washington, D.C.

   The information to be publicly disclosed under the new requirements could be quite substantial. A particularly troubling aspect is that misunderstanding of CRA ratings could have severe consequences for the image and customer relations of ARCB-member institutions. Equally important, care will need to be taken to assure that CRA disclosure requirements do not provoke frivolous consumer advocacy actions. There is also a potential for public disclosure of confidential information, since the new legislation allows the bank regulatory agencies to disclose such information if it determines that it would "promote the objectives of this Act."

3. Consumer Bankers Association
   Arlington, Virginia

   An inordinate level of "hands-on" involvement is expected of an institution's Board of Directors.

   *****

   Boards of Directors should be kept informed by management of the effectiveness and degree of success in carrying out the Board's policies but should not be required to create or manage programs, or serve as CRA loan committees.

   *****

   CBA, with all due respect to the energies and efforts of agency exam personnel, question whether this level of expertise could ever be realized by more than a few staffers. In its absence, examiners would be expected to make subjective assessments of CRA programs with little working knowledge of the day to day realities of providing "loans that significantly benefit the community."

4. Independent Bankers Association of America
   Washington, D.C.

   We believe that in many of the smaller towns, especially those in rural America, a public CRA rating is not relevant nor is it useful to the consumers or the institution itself. In fact, it would only add to the paperwork burden with which banks must comply. Hometown banks are already drowning in a sea of paperwork in their attempts to cope with the enormous regulatory burdens imposed by recent laws.

5. Maine Bankers Association
   Augusta, Maine

   Banks with needs improvement or worse CRA ratings may be taken to task by the media or special interest groups for an extended period of time even though the correction was made relatively quickly. Negative publicity of this sort can be extremely difficult to overcome. Any negative publicity can affect public perception of the entire banking industry.

   *****

   Economic conditions have made it necessary for some banks to close branches. . . . don't we have the potential for conflict between CRA standards and "safety and soundness" decisions?

6. Massachusetts Bankers Association
   Boston, Massachusetts

   Since many banks are now faced with the challenge of both state and federal compliance, we would ask that all efforts be made to mitigate any regulatory overlap at the federal level.

   *****

   Discrimination and Other Illegal Practices: While the purpose of the CRA exam is to review the credit practices of banks, the requirements of this section will force examiners to make legal judgments and disclosures regarding existing anti-discrimination laws. We believe this section is inappropriate and should be eliminated from the evaluation. We would urge that any lender found guilty of discriminatory practices should be prosecuted to the full extent of the law. Examiners, however, should not be judge and jury for alleged violations.

7. Oregon Bankers Association
   Salem, Oregon

   We believe that this section in particular should be in plain language. . . . instead of saying "consistent with the safe and sound operations of the institution" which may or may not be understood by all of the "general public," we urge a plain language statement such as "an institution is not expected to make a bad loan."

8. United States League of Savings Institutions
   Washington, D.C.

   We remain concerned by the problem of integrating into a consistent rating scheme the dramatic differences in credit needs, community development resources, social values, etc., that exist among communities. . . . The institution may have had its fingers on the pulse of that community for many years, while the examiner knows it for only a few weeks. If the examiner points to what some community group may say it wants, that does not necessarily describe what a community truly needs.

3. CRA Watch

INTRODUCTION

The purpose of this chapter is to provide an important historic perspective of CRA ratings and then to tie this perspective into the most recently available ratings. The historic data on CRA ratings presented here represents the first such published analysis. The focus again will be on the highest and lowest CRA bank ratings.

IMPORTANT PUBLIC POLICY QUESTIONS

An analysis of CRA ratings can provide input for answering several important questions relating to public policy. The first and probably most important question is What are the costs and benefits of the public disclosure of CRA ratings and evaluations? We will address this question mainly in terms of public policy benefits, but much more research will be needed in the future.

The second question is What is the actual and ideal distribution of CRA ratings among banks? Has this distribution changed over time, particularly with the disclosure of ratings and the use of specialized compliance examiners? The question of the appropriate distribution of CRA ratings has a bearing on the alleged "grade inflation" claimed by many community groups. That is, have CRA grades been inflated, especially before they were made public?

The third question involves the appropriate form of the ratings themselves. Is a numerical or descriptive rating preferred? Also, is the current four-tiered rating system better than the previous five-tiered ones?

The fourth question pertains to rating differences among the four federal bank regulators. Can we say that one of the four is the "toughest" or "easiest" grader? Do low ratings from an agency reflect on an agency's unique rating policies or on the institutions being rated? Related to the difference in ratings by regulator, is there a difference by industry? Specifically, since the Office of Thrift Supervision is the primary regulator of thrifts (the FDIC also regulates state savings banks), differences in ratings between the OTS and the other three bank regulators combined will reflect variations between the thrift and bank industries.

The fifth question, which has become especially important during the recent debate over a proposed CRA exemption for small banks, concerns the size distribution of ratings. Particularly, how are CRA ratings related to bank asset size? What would be the impact of exempting small banks from CRA compliance?

The sixth question requiring research is how the distribution of CRA ratings differs on a geographic basis. For example, how are CRA ratings distributed on a state-by-state basis? We present data only for the highest and lowest rated banks in this regard. Another important question not answered here relates to the distribution of CRA ratings among the major metropolitan areas. Moreover, within a given market, how are the ratings distributed among banks in different neighborhoods or economic submarkets?

The seventh question asked here is What do multiple CRA ratings reveal about bank CRA performance under disclosure? That is, how have the same banks performed that have been rated more than once under the new system? Do we see more upgrading or downgrading, or perhaps no change?

The eighth question of importance is How have our nation's largest banks and thrifts performed on CRA exams? We focus on the 100 largest banks and 50 largest thrifts. Actual ratings for each bank and thrift in these categories are presented here. This analysis allows us to directly address the claim that big institutions get the best ratings because they have the most resources to document their CRA efforts.

The CRA ratings and analysis summarized in this section will address the above and related questions. There are, however, other important issues not addressed here in detail which relate to CRA ratings. For example, what is the relationship between CRA ratings and bank financial strength? Do the strongest banks get the best CRA ratings or is the reverse true? A limited analysis of this relationship for the substantial noncompliant banks is found in Chapter 8.

CRA RATINGS DATA LIMITATIONS

The establishment of a single relationship between a CRA rating and another variable doesn't necessarily prove a cause and effect pattern. Also, there are various limitations in using CRA ratings data of which the reader should be aware.

For example, CRA ratings pertain to an entire bank which may have offices in a multi-state area. Also, banks in multi-state metropolitan areas grant credit across state lines, even though they may have no offices on the other side of the river in the adjacent state. Although they may be important participants in the metropolitan credit market, their CRA ratings will be recorded in their home-office state. This may limit the ability to conduct an interstate or intrastate geographic analysis of CRA ratings. More importantly the significant differences which may exist in CRA performance by state or region may limit generalizations that can be made about a given bank's overall performance.

Multi-bank holding companies with a large number of banks receive ratings for each of these banks but not for the holding company in its entirety. A comparably sized branch bank would receive one rating, even though there would likely be important differences by branch. This impacts the question as to what effect size of bank has on CRA ratings.

For example, a very large bank with a low CRA rating would present a greater potential public policy concern than a very small bank with the same rating because of the amount of assets under their respective control. Moreover, a low rated very large bank with the dominant position in a concentrated local banking market would have a more adverse public policy impact than the same bank with a relatively small market share in an unconcentrated market. Furthermore, given two markets of equal population size, there would be relatively greater CRA public policy concern for the market with more low- and moderate-income individuals.

A simple analysis of CRA ratings without any weighting by size would treat a low rating for a $10 million dollar bank in the same way as a low rating for a $1 billion dollar bank. We did not attempt any type of rating weightings by size or market variables to reflect this difference. Any attempt to aggregate weightings or to calculate central tendency summary statistics (e.g., the "average" CRA rating in a state) would have to account for important size and related differences.

Likewise, our analysis categorizes both substantial noncompliance and needs improvement ratings as "low" ones (compared to "high" outstanding ones) without weighting the former ratings more. Would we weight substantial noncompliance ratings twice as bad as needs improvement ratings, or ten times as bad to reflect their relative frequency? This is another data limitation in this type of analysis.

There are other technical data problems. For example, two CRA ratings don't always mean two banks, because of the increasing incidence of multiple ratings of the same bank. Also, the number of CRA ratings reported through a certain date (e.g., December 31, 1992) generally increases as time goes on because CRA ratings made before that date may not be publicly available when the ratings are reported. Thus, the "call report" mentality in banking of assuming that year-end totals are complete is inappropriate in CRA research, because of the continual flow of previous CRA ratings that become public daily.

CRA DATA AVAILABILITY

There have been at least four distinct phases of CRA data availability. These phases are as follows:

Phase I: 1977 to 1981—Little to No CRA Data.

CRA was signed into law on October 12, 1977. Regulations implementing the CRA became effective on November 22, 1978. Importantly, there is little available data on CRA ratings that may have been made in late 1978 or during the years of 1979 – 1981. These early years of CRA ratings represent the only void of CRA data. We made multiple verbal and written FOIA requests at all four federal banking agencies for such CRA data, but we were not successful in obtaining *any* CRA ratings, even on an aggregated basis for this early period. Some annual reports for some of these agencies for these years reference CRA exams but do not contain any CRA ratings distributions. For example, the FHLBB reported 1,121 CRA performance assessments between November 1978 and June 1979 and 3,177 assessments in 1981 (of which 2.5% received less-than-satisfactory ratings). Also, a November 1981 *Federal Reserve Bulletin* article reported there were 894 CRA exams at the FED in 1980, with 3.5 % rated outstanding, 36.7% good, 56.7% satisfactory, 2.9% needs improvement, and 0.2% unsatisfactory. This may have been one of the most "inflated" ratings distributions ever, with four out of ten member banks receiving an above-average CRA rating.

Phase II: 1982 to 1988—Good Aggregated CRA Data.

The FFIEC was established on March 10, 1979, primarily as a formal interagency body of the federal financial institution regulators. In an effort to maintain communications and consistency among the different bank regulators, the FFIEC collected and disseminated data from the different agencies. We were successful in obtaining CRA data from this source beginning with calendar year 1982. They informed us that they did not collect such data for previous years. The data for the 1982—1988 period were aggregated for the three federal bank agencies and separately for the thrift agency, since the latter one had a distinct CRA rating mechanism. As a result, the 1982—1988 period was one of relatively good aggregated CRA data, not only on the basis of the bank versus thrift industries, but also by geographic region and by size of institution.

Phase III: January 1989 to June 1990—Inconsistent Aggregated CRA Data

This period represented a data problem since the FFIEC discontinued collecting aggregate data as it had previously done. This was because FIRREA was being debated and the entire CRA ratings and examination procedure was being revamped by Congress. As a result, what CRA ratings data that are available during this period are spotty and inconsistent. This is because they come from different regulators in their own format rather than being filtered through the FFIEC. The data in this phase are not consistent with previous years, either by size or by geographic region. Also, during this period the FHLBB (which became the OTS) changed its rating scheme, which further complicated matters. CRA ratings data during this period, like the two previous ones, were only available on an aggregate basis by regulator or by industry, but not for individual institutions.

Phase IV: July 1990 to Present—Complete Individual Bank CRA Data

As a result of FIRREA, CRA ratings and evaluations made on July 1, 1990, or later were made public. For the first time, individual CRA ratings data would now be available rather than being aggregated by industry or regulator, as in the past. As of December 31, 1991, roughly half of all banks and thrifts in the United States have been rated under the new CRA procedures since July 1, 1990. Detailed data to be presented here will reflect the results of approximately 6,700 such evaluations throughout the nation. Updated data on the 5,400 evaluations made during 1992 will also be included here.

DIFFERENT CRA RATING SYSTEMS

CRA rating systems differ in terms of whether they are numerical or descriptive ratings, and also in terms of the number of rating levels. Although there is consistency among regulators today in this respect, this was not always the case.

Table 3-1 compares the current and two former CRA rating systems on the basis of three simple categories: above-average, average, and below-average.

The former commercial bank system consisted of five ratings with both numerical and descriptive identifiers (see Table 3-2). As noted in Table 3-1, this translated into one above-average rating, one average rating, and three below-average ratings. This was clearly a skewed rating system with three low ratings but only one high one.

The former thrift CRA rating system (Table 3-3) likewise had five numerical ratings, but they differed in terms of their description. In the case of this system, the FHLBB used a "normal" distribution where the first two ratings were above average, the middle one was average, and the last two were below average. The FED actually used such a system in 1980, but it was revised by 1982. Because none of the four federal regulators were able to provide us with any information on CRA ratings over the 1977–1981 period, we have no idea so to the type of CRA rating systems used then.

This unique system provided the FHLBB and only them an opportunity to make a distinction between above-average banks as being either "outstanding" or "good," unlike the system previously or currently used by the commercial bank regulators. Conversely, the FHLBB still had an opportunity to distinguish between below-average banks with two rather than three different ratings.

Another reason why the former thrift rating system (Table 3-3) is different than that formerly used by the bank regulators (Table 3-2) is that the former thrift system is much more specific with less room for examiner interpretation and, therefore, subjectivity. Especially noteworthy is the FHLBB's explanation for the lowest rating of unsatisfactory as normally being given for either one of two conditions, the first one

Table 3-1   Comparison of CRA Ratings under the Current vs. Former Systems

Category	Current System for Banks and Thrifts[a]		Former Commercial Bank System[b]		Former Thrift System[c]	
	Rating	Description	Rating	Description	Rating	Description
Above Average	N/A	Outstanding	1	Strong	1	Outstanding
					2	Good
Average	N/A	Satisfactory	2	Satisfactory	3	Satisfactory
			3	Less than Satisfactory		
Below Average	N/A	Needs Improvement	4	Unsatisfactory	4	Needs Improvement
	N/A	Substantial Noncompliance	5	Substantially Inadequate	5	Unsatisfactory

a/ Effective July 1, 1990, for all federal bank and thrift regulators.
b/ Utilized by the FDIC, FED, and OCC from 1982 until June 30, 1990, and by the FHLBB from July 1, 1989, to June 30, 1990.
c/ Utilized by the FHLBB until June 30, 1989.
N/A Numerical ratings not applicable under current system.

Source: FFIEC
                 K.H. Thomas Associates

Table 3-2   Description Of Former Bank CRA Rating System

The performance categories are individually assigned a numeric rating. In assigning the overall composite CRA rating, the performance categories will be weighed and evaluated according to how well the institution meets the descriptive characteristics listed below.

Rating 1 (Strong)

The institutions in this group have a strong record of meeting community credit needs. Both the Board of Directors and management take an active part in the process and demonstrate an affirmative commitment to the community. Institutions receiving this rating normally rank high in all performance categories. Such institutions have a commendable record and need no further encouragement.

Rating 2 (Satisfactory)

Institutions in this group have a satisfactory record of helping to meet community credit needs. Institutions receiving this rating normally are ranked in the satisfactory levels of the performance categories. Institutions in this category may require some encouragement to help meet community credit needs.

Rating 3 (Less than Satisfactory)

Institutions in this group have a less than satisfactory record of helping to meet community credit needs. The Board of Directors and management have not placed strong emphasis on the credit needs of the community. Institutions receiving this rating have mixed rankings surrounding the mid-range levels of the performance categories. Such institutions require encouragement to help meet the community credit needs.

Rating 4 (Unsatisfactory)

Institutions in this group have an unsatisfactory record of helping to meet community credit needs. The Board of Directors and management give inadequate consideration to the credit needs of the institution's community. Institutions receiving this rating generally rank below satisfactory in the majority of the performance categories. Such institutions require strong encouragement to help meet community credit needs.

Rating 5 (Substantially Inadequate)

Institutions in this group have a substantially inadequate record of helping to meet community credit needs. The Board of Directors and management appear to give little consideration to the credit needs of the institution's community. Institutions receiving this rating generally rank in the lowest levels of the performance categories. Such institutions require the strongest encouragement to be responsive to community credit needs.

Note: Utilized by the FDIC, FED, and OCC from 1982 until June 30, 1990, and by the FHLBB from July 1, 1989 to June 30, 1990.

Source: FFIEC
K.H. Thomas Associates

---

being material, unresolved, or numerous repetitive compliance regulation violations (Table 3-3).

The FHLBB system, which is described in Table 3-3, was utilized until June 30, 1989, when they adopted the former commercial bank system for one year. The FHLBB was in the pre-FIRREA process of being phased out then, and the agency ultimately became the OTS under the Treasury Department.

Therefore, prior to the current system, the four federal bank regulators had the same CRA rating system in effect for only one year, between June 30, 1989, and June 30, 1990. Still, though, data were aggregated with no disclosure for individual banks.

The current system for both banks and thrifts adopted by FIRREA differed in two salient respects. First, there was to be no numerical rating for fear that

Table 3-3   Description of Former Thrift CRA Rating System

Rating 1 (Outstanding)

The association has assumed an active leadership role in furthering the objectives of CRA. This will be usually evidenced by its aggressive efforts acting in concert with various governmental and community groups to identify the special credit needs of its community, particularly in the low/moderate income neighborhoods, and by its efforts in helping to meet such credit needs through a variety of effective, and often innovative, marketing, lending and redevelopment programs. The association normally will have devised prudent programs to help meet the credit needs of its community even in the face of legal or economic impediments and will have committed substantial managerial resources to its efforts.

Rating 2 (Good)

The association is meeting its obligations under CRA in a positive and aggressive manner. This usually will be evidenced by numerous contacts with community groups and the extent of its affirmative marketing and lending programs. The association for its size and financial condition must have a good record of serving the credit needs of its entire community, particularly in low/moderate income neighborhoods, or it must actively be working to remove roadblocks to such full community involvement.

Rating 3 (Satisfactory)

The association's community delineation appears reasonable and it has taken steps to identify and help meet the credit needs of its entire community. The association's lending record in its community appears adequate when legal, economic, or business grounds are taken into consideration. The association's loan policies and practices must comply with the Bank Board's nondiscrimination regulations. Complaints alleging discrimination or unacceptable CRA performance must have been resolved in the associ-

ation's favor, or the institution must have taken appropriate corrective action.

Rating 4 (Needs Improvement)

The association's community delineation does not appear consistent with the spirit and intent of CRA, and/or the association has taken few, if any, productive steps to identify and help meet the credit needs of its community, or the association's efforts are so recent that their probable impact cannot be adequately assessed. The examination report does not disclose any material violation of the Bank Board's nondiscrimination regulation or numerous, repetitive violations of the technical/procedural requirement of the nondiscrimination or CRA regulation. Although the institution cannot fully justify the lack of lending in its community, particularly in low/moderate income neighborhoods, there are clear indications that the institution is becoming increasingly aware of its community responsibilities and that improvements in its CRA performance can be reasonably anticipated.

Rating 5 (Unsatisfactory)

An association should normally be rated "Unsatisfactory" because of either of the following reasons:

A. The examination report discloses material, unresolved violations of the Bank Board's nondiscrimination regulations, or numerous repetitive violations of the technical/procedural requirements of the nondiscrimination or CRA regulations, or

B. The association cannot provide any reasonable justification for its community delineation or its lack of lending in its community, particularly in low/moderate income areas, and material improvements in its CRA performance cannot be reasonably anticipated in light of management's attitude.

Note: Utilized by the FHLBB until June 30, 1989.

Source: FFIEC
          K.H. Thomas Associates

a disclosed number could somehow be misinterpreted as a safety and soundness CAMEL or MACRO rating. Rather, there would only be descriptive ratings using various adjectives of differing degrees.

The second major change was that the previous five-tiered system was to be compressed into a four-tiered system. The logic was likewise based on the same (what we have shown now to be unfounded) fear of the public's possible confusion of CRA with safety and soundness ratings.

The new system under FIRREA would have only one above-average category like the former commercial bank system, but two rather than three below-average categories. With an even rather than odd number of categories, the examiner would now be forced to place a bank in either the top two or the bottom two categories, with no choice of a middle category. Reportedly, there was some effort by the bank lobby to push for a simple two-tiered "pass-fail" system, but that was never adopted.

1982 – 1988 CRA RATINGS TRENDS

Little to no CRA ratings data are available for the earliest phase of 1977–1981. Tables 3-4 through 3-17 display all of the available FFIEC aggregated CRA ratings data that exist for the second phase of CRA data availability, namely 1982 – 1988. There are two tables for each year over this period. Data for the three commercial bank regulators are aggregated into one table by FDIC region and by asset size. Therefore, it is not possible to compare CRA ratings for the three bank regulators over this period.

Data for the FHLBB are in two tables for each year, one by FHLBB region and the other by asset size. Only in 1988 did the FHLBB complete one table showing CRA ratings by both region and asset size.

Figures 3-1 and 3-2 describe the boundaries of the FDIC and FHLBB regions, respectively, that existed over most of this period. The FDIC regions shown in Figure 3-1 were consolidated into 9 regions in 1985 (see note in Tables 3-10 and 3-12) and 8 regions in 1987, which represent the current FDIC regional boundaries (see map in Appendix 1). Although these regions experienced some changes, these data do reflect some important differences by region.

JANUARY 1989—JUNE 1990 CRA RATINGS TRENDS

The third phase of CRA data availability covers the January 1989 – June 1990 period. Tables 3-18 through 3-26 present CRA ratings data that are available by both size and region over this period. The maps in the back of Appendix 1 show the relevant regional boundaries. Because the FFIEC no longer collected data over this period, there was a lack of consistent CRA information.

Both the FDIC and the FED were able to provide consistent size distribution data for 1989 and the first half of 1990. Neither of these agencies was able to provide a geographic distribution of ratings similar to the ones previously prepared for the FFIEC.

Tables 3-18 and 3-19 present CRA ratings by the FDIC by size for 1989 and the first part of 1990, respectively. Tables 3-20 and 3-21 present the same respective data for the FED.

CRA records at the OCC were even worse. The OCC did not make available CRA ratings by region or by a similar size breakdown for this period. They could only provide CRA ratings by a different size breakdown. These data are shown for 1989 and the first half of 1990 in Tables 3-22 and 3-23, respectively. Because their smallest asset size breakdown is under $100 million, we were not able to reach any conclusions regarding their ratings of very small banks over this period.

Data from the FHLBB, and its successor the OTS, definitely were the most difficult to obtain for this period. They had no data available by thrift size whatsoever. The only data that were available were by region, and these data were not even available for the first quarter of 1989. Obviously, 1989 was not a good year for the thrift industry or its regulator. Table 3-24 shows CRA ratings by region for the second quarter of 1989. Comparable aggregated data for the first quarter are shown in the footnote to that table, but those data are not available by region or by size. Table 3-25 shows thrift CRA ratings by region for the second half of 1989. These data are based upon a different rating system than was used by that regulator during the first part of 1989 (Table 3-24). Table 3-26 provides comparable data for the first half of 1990. Table 3-1 summarizes the different rating sys-

Figure 3-1   Former FDIC Regions

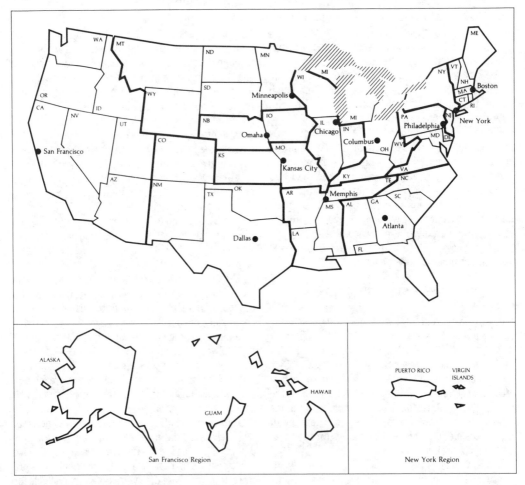

Source: *A Citizens Guide to CRA*, FFIEC, 1985.

tems that existed for this thrift regulator over this period.

THE EFFECT OF A SPECIALIZED COMPLIANCE PROGRAM

The FHLBB did not institute a specialized compliance program until April 1, 1989. This meant that there was only one examination team for both safety and soundness and compliance prior to the inception of that program. In many cases this meant "stale" ratings, a carrying over of the previous compliance ratings, since the examiners were not specialized in that area. Of course, the emphasis during these critical years of the thrift crisis was on safety and soundness.

Figure 3-2   Former FHLBB Regions

Source: *A Citizens Guide to CRA,* FFIEC, 1985.

Since 1977, the FED has had specialized compliance examiners, and the FDIC only began such a program in 1991. The OCC is the only one of the four federal regulators without specialized compliance examiners, although the OCC has had a "Compliance Program" since 1987. We expect that the OCC will soon switch to a specialized compliance examination force.

In addition to developing the specialized compliance program on April 1, 1989, the FHLBB adopted the bank CRA rating system on July 1, 1989, for purposes of consistency. Again, this was during the pre-FIRREA period when the FHLBB was on the eve of being dismantled and changed into the OTS under the Treasury Department.

Table 3-4 Commercial Bank CRA Ratings by Region and Size, 1982

ASSET SIZE (MILLIONS)

FDIC REGION*	<$25 RATING					$26 – $99 Rating					$100 – $499 RATING					>$500 RATING					TOTAL RATING				
	1	2	3	4	5	1	2	3	4	5	1	2	3	4	5	1	2	3	4	5	1	2	3	4	5
Boston	3	46	2	0	0	6	130	8	0	0	11	73	4	0	0	7	16	2	0	0	27	265	16	0	0
New York	7	36	1	0	0	6	108	7	0	0	12	70	5	0	0	14	52	4	0	0	39	266	17	0	0
Philadelphia	12	115	4	1	0	27	217	0	1	0	15	61	0	0	0	20	30	0	0	0	74	423	4	2	0
Atlanta	49	328	4	0	0	50	326	2	0	0	18	63	0	0	0	8	16	1	0	0	125	733	7	0	0
Columbus	29	255	17	1	0	50	349	11	1	0	29	113	2	0	0	17	12	1	0	0	125	729	31	2	0
Chicago	57	520	28	3	2	129	464	20	3	0	46	94	3	0	0	11	5	0	0	0	243	1083	51	6	2
Memphis	1	188	1	0	0	15	272	4	0	0	11	55	1	0	0	8	12	2	0	0	35	527	8	0	0
Dallas	58	529	19	1	1	72	499	9	0	0	27	96	2	0	0	11	22	1	0	0	168	1146	31	1	1
Kansas City	99	371	11	2	0	69	210	3	0	0	12	26	0	0	0	5	3	0	0	0	185	610	14	2	0
Omaha	52	383	6	0	0	39	170	1	0	0	9	21	0	0	0	3	4	0	0	0	103	578	7	0	0
Minneapolis	91	318	7	2	0	100	151	1	0	0	20	12	0	0	0	5	1	0	0	0	216	482	8	2	0
San Francisco	11	172	8	0	0	12	143	6	0	0	9	57	3	0	0	17	13	3	0	0	49	385	20	0	0
TOTAL	469	3,261	108	10	3	575	3,039	72	5	0	219	741	20	0	0	126	186	14	0	0	1,389	7,227	214	15	3

* See Figure 3-1 for map of former FDIC regions.

Source: FFIEC
K.H. Thomas Associates

Table 3-5   Thrift CRA Ratings by Region and Size, 1982

FHLBB REGION*	RATING					TOTAL
	1	2	3	4	5	
1–Boston	1	9	81	0	0	91
2–New York	0	7	238	1	0	246
3–Pittsburgh	0	7	210	0	0	217
4–Atlanta	1	26	419	8	0	454
5–Cincinnati	0	22	309	4	0	335
6–Indianapolis	1	7	134	4	1	147
7–Chicago	0	9	384	0	0	393
8–Des Moines	0	7	205	2	0	214
9–Dallas	0	10	352	16	1	379
10–Topeka	0	5	157	4	0	166
11–San Francisco	2	11	144	8	0	165
12–Seattle	0	23	85	0	0	108
TOTAL	5	143	2,718	47	2	2,915

ASSET SIZE (MILLIONS)	RATING					TOTAL
	1	2	3	4	5	
< $25	0	16	622	21	1	660
$26 – $99	0	31	1,182	15	1	1,229
$100 – $499	2	63	754	8	0	827
> $500	3	33	160	3	0	199
TOTAL	5	143	2,718	47	2	2,915

*See Figure 3-2 for map of former FHLBB regions.

Source: FFIEC
             K.H. Thomas Associates

Table 3-6 Commercial Bank CRA Ratings by Region and Size, 1983

ASSET SIZE (MILLIONS)

FDIC REGION*	< $25 RATING					$26 – $99 RATING					$100 – $499 RATING					> $500 RATING					TOTAL RATING				
	1	2	3	4	5	1	2	3	4	5	1	2	3	4	5	1	2	3	4	5	1	2	3	4	5
Boston	1	12	1	0	0	5	35	0	0	0	9	18	1	0	0	4	8	0	0	0	19	73	2	0	0
New York	2	10	0	0	0	5	60	5	0	0	7	39	4	0	0	11	45	0	0	0	25	154	9	0	0
Philadelphia	4	70	3	0	0	23	127	3	0	0	15	40	2	0	0	18	21	0	0	0	60	258	8	0	0
Atlanta	50	165	2	0	0	58	208	5	0	0	16	60	0	0	0	12	17	0	0	0	136	450	7	0	0
Columbus	20	127	9	0	0	46	196	5	0	0	19	48	0	1	0	5	11	0	0	0	90	382	14	1	0
Chicago	34	302	36	3	0	79	305	20	2	1	34	61	3	2	0	6	8	0	0	0	153	676	59	7	1
Memphis	1	51	0	0	0	7	104	1	0	0	8	28	0	0	0	8	5	0	0	0	24	188	1	0	0
Dallas	63	296	7	0	0	87	273	11	0	0	18	63	2	0	0	13	15	0	0	0	181	647	20	0	0
Kansas City	56	243	19	0	1	68	160	6	0	0	10	29	0	0	0	4	2	0	0	0	138	434	25	0	1
Omaha	21	201	9	1	0	40	113	3	0	0	2	18	0	0	0	5	0	0	0	0	68	332	12	1	0
Minneapolis	87	311	8	1	0	72	112	1	0	0	25	13	0	0	0	4	2	0	0	0	188	438	9	1	0
San Francisco	4	63	2	0	0	1	30	4	0	–	3	9	0	0	–	9	11	1	0	–	17	113	7	0	0
TOTAL	343	1,851	96	5	1	491	1,723	64	2	1	166	426	12	3	0	99	145	1	0	0	1,099	4,145	173	10	2

* See Figure 3-1 for map of former FDIC regions.

Source: FFIEC
K.H. Thomas Associates

Table 3-7   Thrift CRA Ratings by Region and Size, 1983

FHLBB REGION*	RATING					TOTAL
	1	2	3	4	5	
1–Boston	0	5	78	1	0	84
2–New York	0	5	189	0	0	194
3–Pittsburgh	0	2	161	0	0	163
4–Atlanta	1	16	328	1	0	346
5–Cincinnati	0	12	220	0	0	232
6–Indianapolis	0	4	104	0	0	108
7–Chicago	0	5	284	0	1	290
8–Des Moines	0	6	186	1	0	193
9–Dallas	0	3	218	1	0	222
10–Topeka	0	8	87	2	0	97
11–San Francisco	2	6	118	6	0	132
12–Seattle	0	16	77	1	0	94
TOTAL	3	88	2,050	13	1	2,155

ASSET SIZE (MILLIONS)	RATING					TOTAL
	1	2	3	4	5	
< $25	0	18	405	7	0	430
$26 – $99	0	21	854	4	0	879
$100 – $499	1	32	628	1	1	663
> $500	2	17	163	1	0	183
TOTAL	3	88	2,050	13	1	2,155

*See Figure 3-2 for map of former FHLBB regions.

Source: FFIEC
K.H. Thomas Associates

Table 3-8 Commercial Bank CRA Ratings by Region and Size, 1984

ASSET SIZE (MILLIONS)

FDIC REGION*	< $25 RATING					$26 – $99 RATING					$100 – $499 RATING					> $500 RATING					TOTAL RATING				
	1	2	3	4	5	1	2	3	4	5	1	2	3	4	5	1	2	3	4	5	1	2	3	4	5
Boston	1	14	2	0	0	6	56	0	0	0	5	43	0	0	0	6	7	0	0	0	18	120	2	0	0
New York	0	4	0	0	0	2	29	1	0	0	3	27	2	0	0	5	32	0	0	0	10	92	3	0	0
Philadelphia	2	60	0	0	0	15	98	0	0	0	16	33	0	0	0	17	14	1	1	0	50	205	1	0	0
Atlanta	12	130	4	0	0	18	162	2	0	0	11	42	1	0	0	13	14	0	0	0	54	348	7	0	0
Columbus	8	101	3	0	0	28	169	3	1	0	12	55	2	0	0	6	13	0	0	0	54	338	8	1	0
Chicago	10	220	9	2	1	44	252	3	3	0	32	64	4	2	0	7	4	1	0	0	93	540	17	7	1
Memphis	1	44	3	0	0	12	61	1	0	0	9	23	0	0	0	7	8	0	0	0	29	136	4	0	0
Dallas	48	396	5	0	0	69	374	8	0	0	14	95	0	0	0	9	10	0	0	0	140	875	13	0	0
Kansas City	22	149	1	0	0	22	110	0	0	0	3	26	0	0	0	2	3	0	0	0	49	288	1	0	0
Omaha	4	76	0	0	0	7	49	0	0	0	3	11	0	0	0	1	3	0	0	0	15	139	0	0	0
Minneapolis	58	181	1	0	0	64	101	1	1	0	20	13	0	0	0	3	0	0	0	0	145	295	2	0	0
San Francisco	2	122	4	1	0	7	93	3	0	0	4	32	0	0	0	6	12	2	0	0	19	259	7	1	0
TOTAL	168	1,497	32	3	1	294	1,554	22	4	0	132	464	9	2	0	82	120	2	0	0	676	3,635	65	9	1

* See Figure 3-1 for map of former FDIC regions.

Source: FFIEC
K.H. Thomas Associates

Table 3-9   Thrift CRA Ratings by Region and Size, 1984

FHLBB REGION*	RATING					TOTAL
	1	2	3	4	5	
1–Boston	0	4	28	1	0	33
2–New York	0	3	78	0	0	81
3–Pittsburgh	0	1	89	0	0	90
4–Atlanta	0	11	143	2	0	156
5–Cincinnati	0	9	150	1	0	160
6–Indianapolis	0	3	42	1	0	46
7–Chicago	0	6	149	0	1	156
8–Des Moines	0	0	22	0	0	22
9–Dallas	0	2	157	1	0	160
10–Topeka	0	6	67	1	0	74
11–San Francisco	0	5	77	4	0	86
12–Seattle	0	14	49	1	0	64
TOTAL	0	64	1,051	12	1	1,128

ASSET SIZE (MILLIONS)	RATING					TOTAL
	1	2	3	4	5	
< $25	0	13	191	2	0	206
$26 – $99	0	12	425	3	0	440
$100 – $499	0	26	333	6	1	366
> $500	0	13	102	1	0	116
TOTAL	0	64	1,051	12	1	1,128

*See Figure 3-2 for map of former FHLBB regions.

Source: FFIEC
          K.H. Thomas Associates

Table 3-10   Commercial Bank CRA Ratings by Region and Size, 1985

ASSET SIZE (MILLIONS)

FDIC REGION*	< $25 RATING					$26 – $99 RATING					$100 – $499 RATING					> $500 RATING					TOTAL RATING				
	1	2	3	4	5	1	2	3	4	5	1	2	3	4	5	1	2	3	4	5	1	2	3	4	5
Boston	3	4	0	0	0	4	27	0	0	0	5	11	0	0	0	7	5	0	0	0	19	47	0	0	0
New York	3	20	1	0	0	12	54	3	0	0	13	46	0	0	0	23	35	2	0	0	51	155	6	0	0
Atlanta	12	138	1	1	0	22	153	2	0	0	14	27	0	0	0	14	13	0	0	0	62	331	3	1	0
Columbus	10	67	0	0	0	34	179	1	0	0	22	76	1	0	0	16	21	0	0	0	82	343	2	0	0
Chicago	11	176	4	0	0	30	271	6	3	0	23	60	2	0	0	7	7	0	0	0	71	514	12	3	0
Memphis	1	40	0	1	0	8	74	1	0	0	6	25	1	0	0	9	7	0	0	0	24	146	2	1	0
Dallas	24	310	3	1	0	30	244	5	1	0	6	55	1	0	0	4	12	0	0	0	64	621	9	2	0
Kansas City	25	211	5	2	0	36	196	0	0	0	22	35	0	0	0	10	9	0	0	0	93	451	5	2	0
San Francisco	6	134	5	1	0	6	130	2	0	0	2	45	1	1	0	10	18	2	0	0	24	327	8	1	0
TOTAL	95	1,100	19	6	0	182	1,328	20	4	0	113	380	6	0	0	100	127	2	0	0	490	2,936	47	10	0

*   See Figure 3-1 for map of former FDIC regions. In 1985 the following three former FDIC regions were sonsolidated as follows: Most of the former Philadelphia Region merged into the New York Region except for VA, which merged into the Atlanta Region; all of the former Omaha Regiion plus a portion (MN, ND, and SD) of the former Minneapolis Region merged into the Kansas City Region; and the remaining portion (MT and WY) of the former Minneapolis Region merged into the San Francisco Region.

Source: FFIEC
          K.H. Thomas Associates

Table 3-11   Thrift CRA Ratings by Region and Size, 1985

FHLBB REGION*	RATING					TOTAL
	1	2	3	4	5	
1–Boston	0	11	37	1	0	49
2–New York	0	8	142	0	0	150
3–Pittsburgh	0	3	112	0	0	115
4–Atlanta	0	22	253	1	2	278
5–Cincinnati	1	10	170	0	0	181
6–Indianapolis	2	0	16	1	0	19
7–Chicago	1	11	174	1	3	190
8–Des Moines	0	1	165	2	1	169
9–Dallas	0	4	110	1	0	115
10–Topeka	0	13	93	4	0	110
11–San Francisco	2	5	75	6	2	90
12–Seattle	0	7	42	0	0	49
TOTAL	6	95	1,389	17	8	1,515

ASSET SIZE (MILLIONS)	RATING					TOTAL
	1	2	3	4	5	
< $25	1	14	195	4	0	214
$26 – $99	1	33	541	6	4	585
$100 – $499	1	34	477	5	2	519
> $500	3	14	176	2	2	197
TOTAL	6	95	1,389	17	8	1,515

*See Figure 3-2 for map of former FHLBB regions.

Source: FFIEC
           K.H. Thomas Associates

Table 3-12 Commercial Bank CRA Ratings by Region and Size, 1986

ASSET SIZE (MILLIONS)

FDIC REGION*	< $25 RATING					$26 – $99 RATING					$100 – $499 RATING					> $500 RATING					TOTAL RATING				
	1	2	3	4	5	1	2	3	4	5	1	2	3	4	5	1	2	3	4	5	1	2	3	4	5
Boston	3	30	1	0	0	3	31	0	0	0	3	32	1	0	0	6	14	1	0	0	15	107	3	0	0
New York	17	86	2	0	0	9	91	2	0	0	13	87	0	0	0	18	58	2	0	0	57	322	6	0	0
Atlanta	13	164	1	0	0	19	165	2	0	0	10	59	1	0	0	14	27	0	0	0	56	415	4	0	0
Columbus	15	99	3	0	0	38	199	1	1	0	23	86	1	0	0	12	26	0	0	0	88	410	5	1	0
Chicago	34	213	4	0	0	47	267	1	0	0	41	83	1	0	0	6	20	3	0	0	128	583	9	0	0
Memphis	12	81	2	0	0	16	132	0	0	0	6	46	1	0	0	6	13	2	0	0	40	272	5	0	0
Dallas	38	550	10	0	0	38	330	2	1	0	12	76	0	0	0	5	19	1	0	0	93	975	13	1	0
Kansas City	53	388	4	0	1	57	297	5	0	0	17	61	0	0	0	8	12	0	0	0	135	758	9	0	1
San Francisco	18	184	3	1	0	5	174	6	0	0	4	41	1	0	0	9	30	1	0	0	36	429	11	1	0
TOTAL	203	1,795	30	1	1	232	1,686	19	2	0	129	571	6	0	0	84	219	10	0	0	648	4,271	65	3	1

* See Figure 3-1 for map of former FDIC regions. In 1985 the following three former FDIC regions were sonsolidated as follows: Most of the former Philadelphia Region merged into the New York Region except for VA, which merged into the Atlanta Region; all of the former Omaha Regiion plus a portion (MN, ND, and SD) of the former Minneapolis Region merged into the Kansas City Region; and the remaining portion (MT and WY) of the former Minneapolis Region merged into the San Francisco Region.

Source: FFIEC
          K.H. Thomas Associates

Table 3-13   Thrift CRA Ratings by Region and Size, 1986

FHLBB REGION*	RATING					TOTAL
	1	2	3	4	5	
1–Boston	0	3	28	1	0	32
2–New York	0	3	128	1	0	132
3–Pittsburgh	0	1	80	0	0	81
4–Atlanta	0	13	230	4	0	247
5–Cincinnati	0	2	142	4	1	149
6–Indianapolis	0	0	54	1	0	55
7–Chicago	0	4	209	1	0	214
8–Des Moines	0	0	117	2	1	120
9–Dallas	1	8	256	6	7	278
10–Topeka	0	7	96	0	0	103
11–San Francisco	0	6	99	11	0	116
12–Seattle	0	12	75	1	0	88
TOTAL	1	59	1,514	32	9	1,615

ASSET SIZE (MILLIONS)	RATING					TOTAL
	1	2	3	4	5	
< $25	0	8	200	4	2	214
$26 – $99	0	23	615	13	2	653
$100 – $499	0	20	544	13	4	581
> $500	1	8	155	2	1	167
TOTAL	1	59	1,514	32	9	1,615

*See Figure 3-2 for map of former FHLBB regions.

Source: FFIEC
          K.H. Thomas Associates

Table 3-14 Commercial Bank CRA Ratings by Region and Size, 1987

ASSET SIZE (MILLIONS)

FDIC REGION*	< $25 RATING					$26 – $99 RATING					$100 – $499 RATING					> $500 RATING					TOTAL RATING				
	1	2	3	4	5	1	2	3	4	5	1	2	3	4	5	1	2	3	4	5	1	2	3	4	5
Boston	1	14	1	0	0	2	27	2	0	0	2	37	2	0	0	0	15	1	0	0	5	93	6	0	0
New York	5	57	2	0	0	6	75	0	0	0	14	73	2	0	0	12	49	4	0	0	37	254	8	0	0
Atlanta	17	218	8	0	0	43	286	6	1	0	16	73	1	0	0	10	19	2	0	0	86	596	17	1	0
Chicago	39	366	11	1	0	96	523	12	2	0	59	228	5	2	0	9	44	4	0	0	203	1,161	32	5	0
Memphis	12	127	2	0	0	27	218	1	0	0	4	59	3	0	0	3	11	1	0	0	46	415	7	0	0
Dallas	17	240	6	0	0	16	225	13	1	0	3	42	1	0	0	3	12	1	0	0	39	519	21	1	0
Kansas City	47	591	6	2	1	44	326	6	0	0	13	56	1	0	0	4	13	0	0	0	108	986	13	2	1
San Francisco	2	113	2	1	0	9	158	2	0	0	6	54	1	4	0	5	24	1	0	0	22	349	6	5	0
TOTAL	140	1,726	38	4	1	243	1,838	42	4	0	117	622	16	6	0	46	187	14	0	0	546	4,373	110	14	1

* See map of currentr FDIC Regions in Appendix 1.

Source: FFIEC
K.H. Thomas Associates

Table 3-15   Thrift CRA Ratings by Region and Size, 1987

FHLBB REGION*	RATING 1	2	3	4	5	TOTAL
1–Boston	0	16	57	0	0	73
2–New York	0	9	125	1	0	135
3–Pittsburgh	0	5	127	0	0	132
4–Atlanta	0	16	399	6	2	423
5–Cincinnati	0	14	274	2	0	290
6–Indianapolis	2	6	137	3	1	149
7–Chicago	1	6	223	1	2	233
8–Des Moines	0	1	148	3	1	153
9–Dallas	3	27	233	7	3	273
10–Topeka	0	17	98	1	0	116
11–San Francisco	0	13	77	6	2	98
12–Seattle	0	10	84	0	0	94
TOTAL	6	140	1,982	30	11	2,169

ASSET SIZE (MILLIONS)	RATING 1	2	3	4	5	TOTAL
< $25	0	9	238	5	0	252
$26 – $99	2	62	810	9	5	888
$100 – $499	3	44	711	11	4	773
> $500	1	25	223	5	2	256
TOTAL	6	140	1,982	30	11	2,169

*See Figure 3-2 for map of former FHLBB regions

Source: FFIEC
           K.H. Thomas Associates

Table 3-16　Commercial Bank CRA Ratings by Region and Size, 1988

ASSET SIZE (MILLIONS)

FDIC REGION*	< $25 RATING					$26 – $99 RATING					$100 – $499 RATING					> $500 RATING					TOTAL RATING				
	1	2	3	4	5	1	2	3	4	5	1	2	3	4	5	1	2	3	4	5	1	2	3	4	5
Boston	0	12	1	2	0	2	36	4	0	0	4	39	5	0	0	1	12	0	0	0	7	99	10	2	0
New York	3	33	4	0	0	9	71	3	1	0	13	83	5	0	0	13	64	5	0	0	38	251	17	1	0
Atlanta	15	204	10	0	0	50	350	17	3	0	18	93	6	1	0	10	26	3	0	0	93	673	36	4	0
Chicago	27	356	12	2	0	86	519	10	4	0	49	210	8	2	0	7	59	4	1	0	169	1,144	34	9	0
Memphis	7	116	1	1	0	11	256	7	0	0	8	67	4	1	0	2	13	2	0	0	28	452	14	2	0
Dallas	3	129	17	2	0	9	164	16	1	0	5	43	3	0	0	0	18	2	0	0	17	354	39	3	0
Kansas City	37	616	8	2	1	55	415	8	0	0	13	69	3	0	0	2	21	2	0	0	107	1,121	21	2	1
San Francisco	4	128	8	1	1	8	169	3	0	0	6	73	6	4	0	8	29	2	1	0	26	399	19	1	1
TOTAL	96	1,594	61	10	2	230	1,980	68	9	0	116	677	41	4	0	43	242	20	1	0	485	4,493	190	24	2

* See map of current FDIC regions in Appendix 1.

Source:　FFIEC
　　　　　K.H. Thomas Associates

Table 3-17 Thrift CRA Ratings by Region and Size, 1988

ASSET SIZE (MILLIONS)

FHLBB REGION*	< $25 RATING					$26 – $99 RATING					$100 – $499 RATING					> $500 RATING					TOTAL RATING				
	1	2	3	4	5	1	2	3	4	5	1	2	3	4	5	1	2	3	4	5	1	2	3	4	5
Boston	0	0	3	0	0	0	7	18	1	0	0	3	18	0	0	0	4	2	0	0	0	14	41	1	0
New York	0	0	12	0	0	0	4	42	0	0	0	1	63	1	0	0	1	28	1	0	0	6	145	2	0
Pittsburgh	0	1	12	0	0	0	0	41	0	0	0	2	37	0	0	0	2	9	0	0	0	5	99	0	0
Atlanta	0	2	48	2	0	0	3	137	3	0	0	6	124	0	0	0	5	43	3	0	0	16	352	8	0
Cincinnati	0	2	26	0	0	0	2	72	1	0	0	2	51	0	0	0	0	18	0	0	0	6	167	1	0
Indianapolis	0	0	7	0	0	0	2	55	0	0	0	1	38	0	0	0	0	12	0	0	0	3	112	0	0
Chicago	0	0	36	1	0	0	1	95	6	1	0	0	81	0	1	0	0	22	1	0	0	1	234	8	2
Des Moines	0	0	16	1	0	0	0	68	0	1	0	0	56	0	0	0	0	13	0	0	0	0	153	1	1
Dallas	1	4	34	1	1	0	12	109	4	1	2	9	96	6	0	0	2	31	1	0	3	27	270	12	2
Topeka	0	2	5	0	0	0	4	42	0	0	0	10	24	0	0	0	3	10	0	0	0	19	81	0	0
San Francisco	0	0	3	0	0	0	11	35	5	1	0	4	39	5	4	0	8	22	0	2	0	23	99	10	7
Seattle	0	1	3	2	0	0	3	14	0	0	0	3	30	0	0	0	0	9	0	0	0	7	56	2	0
TOTAL	1	12	205	7	1	0	49	728	20	4	2	41	657	12	5	0	25	219	6	2	3	127	1,809	45	12

* See Figure 3-2 for map of former FHLBB regions.

Source: FFIEC
          K.H. Thomas Associates

Table 3-18   FDIC CRA Ratings by Size, 1989

RATING	ASSET SIZE (MILLIONS)				TOTAL
	< $25	$26 – $99	$100 – $499	> $500	
1	70	138	103	24	335
2	1,009	1,195	346	87	2,637
3	22	25	8	11	66
4	1	3	0	0	4
5	1	0	0	1	2
TOTAL	1,103	1,361	457	123	3,044

Source: FDIC
            K.H. Thomas Associates

Table 3-19   FDIC CRA Ratings by Size, 1/1/90 – 6/30/90

RATING	ASSET SIZE (MILLIONS)				TOTAL
	< $25	$26 – $99	$100 – $499	> $500	
1	47	140	61	10	258
2	581	691	204	35	1,511
3	38	33	19	6	96
4	1	2	1	0	4
5	0	0	0	1	1
TOTAL	667	866	285	52	1,870

Source: FDIC
            K.H. Thomas Associates

The effect of implementing a specialized compliance program at the FHLBB was dramatic in terms of CRA ratings. Table 3-27 documents the three different CRA rating categories for a 15 month period both before and after the inception of the specialized compliance program.

The most dramatic difference in instituting that program is the roughly six-fold increase in the percentage of below-average ratings. As shown in Table 3-27, the percentage of below-average ratings went from just 3.7% before the program to 22.5% after it. As pointed in the footnote to that table, excluding the first "transition" quarter under the new system would have resulted in an even greater difference due to the large drop in the percentage of above-average ratings during that first quarter. Table 3-27 also indicates a slight drop in the percentage of above-average ratings, which likewise would have been more dramatic excluding that first quarter.

This evidence, although only for one federal regulator, suggests that the use of specialized compliance examiners results in much stricter enforcement of CRA defined in terms of a greater percentage of below-average ratings and a lesser percentage of

Table 3-20   FED CRA Ratings by Size, 1989

| | ASSET SIZE (MILLIONS) | | | | |
RATING	< $25	$26 – $99	$100 – $499	> $500	TOTAL
1	8	19	12	6	45
2	162	251	89	24	526
3	15	16	9	5	45
4	1	0	0	4	5
5	1	0	0	0	1
TOTAL	187	286	110	39	622

Source: FED
          K. H. Thomas Associates

Table 3-21   FED CRA Ratings by Size, 1/1/90 – 6/30/90

| | ASSET SIZE (MILLIONS) | | | | |
RATING	< $25	$26 – $99	$100 – $499	> $500	TOTAL
1	4	10	4	2	20
2	74	111	53	24	262
3	9	11	5	3	28
4	0	0	0	1	1
5	1	0	0	0	1
TOTAL	88	132	62	30	312

Source: FED
          K. H. Thomas Associates

above-average ratings. One might argue that the lower ratings may have been a result of the examiners in that new program attempting to justify their new position by being "tougher" than before, but it would be very difficult to prove or disprove this hypothesis. Then again, many of the previous CRA ratings that were downgraded by the specialized examiners may have been inflated by previous safety and soundness examiners.

The significant increase in the percentage of below-average ratings by the FHLBB after the implementation of the specialized compliance program may also reflect the environment in most of 1989. During that period FIRREA was being debated, and as the real magnitude of the S&L crisis became apparent, many in the S&L industry felt that there was a prevalent "get S&Ls" or "get S&L regulators" attitude.

There also was a strong reregulation, as compared to a deregulation environment, in early 1989. Moreover, as previously described, 1989 was a watershed year for CRA with a new emphasis on enforcement. All of these factors in an anti-S&L, proconsumer, reregulation environment may have had an impact on newly specialized CRA examiners at the FHLBB,

Table 3-22   OCC CRA Ratings by Size, 1989

RATING	ASSET SIZE (MILLIONS)			TOTAL
	< $100	$100 – $250	> $250	
1	35	19	22	76
2	442	191	199	832
3	66	22	27	115
4	6	1	2	9
5	0	0	0	0
TOTAL	549	233	250	1,032

Source: OCC
          K.H. Thomas Associates

Table 3-23   OCC CRA Ratings by Size, 1/1/90 – 6/30/90

RATING	ASSET SIZE (MILLIONS)			TOTAL
	< $100	$100 – $250	> $250	
1	16	8	11	35
2	275	80	84	439
3	50	11	9	70
4	3	2	1	6
5	0	0	0	0
TOTAL	344	101	105	550

Source: OCC
          K.H. Thomas Associates

resulting in a very high proportion of below-average ratings.

Nonetheless, based on current thrift CRA rating distributions with below-average ratings in the 20% range, the percentage of below-average ratings of only 3.7% before their specialized compliance program appears to have been much too low.

CRA RATINGS UNDER THE NEW SYSTEM

CRA ratings and public evaluations for individual institutions first became available on July 1, 1990. We have been closely tracking these ratings since that time, and there have been various published accounts of our research in this respect.

The first major comprehensive analysis of newly available CRA data was on March 26, 1991, when we released our study of the ratings of 1,659 financial institutions made through February and March 1991. According to that study, 8.0% of all banks and thrifts received outstanding ratings, 80.7% received satisfactory ratings, 10.8% received needs improvement ratings, and 0.5% received substantial noncompliance ratings.

Table 3-24   Thrift CRA Ratings by Region, 4/1/89 – 6/30/89

| RATING | REGION | | | | | TOTAL |
	Northeast	Southeast	Central	Midwest	West	
1	0	0	0	1	0	1
2	9	16	13	33	10	81
3	9	3	46	29	9	96
4	11	0	4	5	2	22
5	0	0	0	0	0	0
TOTAL	29	19	63	68	21	200

Note: Comparable data for the first quarter of 1989 not available, although aggregate ratings are as follows for that period:

Rating	Number
1	7
2	179
3	578
4	41
5	7
Total	812

Source: FHLBB
OTS
K.H. Thomas Associates

Table 3-25   Thrift CRA Ratings by Region, 7/1/89 – 12/31/89

| RATING | REGION | | | | | TOTAL |
	Northeast	Southeast	Central	Midwest	West	
1	1	1	2	1	1	6
2	58	60	114	68	23	323
3	30	14	25	13	3	85
4	3	4	7	7	2	23
5	0	0	0	0	0	0
TOTAL	92	79	148	89	29	437

Source: FHLBB
OTS
K.H. Thomas Associates

Table 3-26   Thrift CRA Ratings by Region, 1/1/90 – 6/30/90

	REGION					
RATING	Northeast	Southeast	Central	Midwest	West	TOTAL
1	4	1	5	6	1	17
2	67	36	117	111	15	346
3	27	16	24	25	10	102
4	4	6	5	3	3	21
5	0	0	0	0	0	0
TOTAL	102	59	151	145	29	486

Source: FHLBB
          OTS
          K.H. Thomas Associates

**Table 3-27   Thrift CRA Rating Categories before and after Specialized
               Compliance Program, January 1988 – June 1990**

	BEFORE 1/1/88 – 3/31/89		AFTER 4/1/89 – 6/30/90	
RATING CATEGORY	NUMBER	PERCENT	NUMBER	PERCENT
Above Average	316	11.3%	105	9.4%
Average	2,387	85.0%	765	68.1%
Below Average	105	3.7%	253	22.5%
TOTAL	2,808	100.0%	1,123	100.0%

Note: FHLBB began specialized compliance program on 4/1/89. Excluding the initial "transition" quarter under the
        new system, the rating distribution between 7/1/89 and 6/30/90 was 2.5%, 72.5%, and 25.0% for the above-
        average, average, and below-average categories, respectively.

Source: FHLBB
          OTS
          K.H. Thomas Associates

Our second comprehensive analysis of CRA ratings was published on September 17, 1991, showing the results of ratings of 4,352 banks and thrifts through mid-year 1991. According to that analysis, 7.5% received outstanding ratings, 81.0% received satisfactory ratings, 10.7% received needs improvement ratings, and 0.8% received substantial noncompliance ratings.

Our third comprehensive analysis of CRA ratings, reflecting 15 months of data through September 30, 1991, was published by us on December 11, 1991. These data for 5,843 banks and thrifts showed 8.5% of them receiving outstanding ratings, 80.2% with satisfactory ratings, 10.4% with needs improvement ratings, and 0.9% with substantial noncompliance ratings.

Our fourth comprehensive analysis of CRA ratings published on April 13, 1992, reflected one and one-half years of experience for approximately 6,700 banks and thrifts under the new system over the July 1, 1990 – December 31, 1991, period. Various tables summarizing these data are presented in this section.

Table 3-28 shows CRA ratings by both size and regulator for the July 1, 1990 – December 31, 1991, period, reflecting 18 months of data under the new CRA rating system. These ratings of 6,706 banks and thrifts accounted for nearly half of the roughly 14,600 banks and thrifts in the United States at that time. Thus, as of year-end 1991, just over half of all banks and thrifts had yet to have had a public evaluation reported. As noted in that table, approximately 2% of the ratings in Table 3-28 are multiple ratings of the same bank.

Our fifth analysis of CRA ratings was published in August 1992. This contained the results of 8,722 published ratings as of June 30, 1992. Even though an increasing number of banks received multiple evaluations in 1992, these updated data as of mid-year 1992 reflected about six out of ten banks.

Table 3-29 represents our most comprehensive analysis to date of 12,115 CRA evaluations by both size and regulator over the July 1, 1990 – December 31, 1992, period. We estimate that approximately 15% of those ratings are multiple ratings of the same bank.

CRA RATINGS BY BANK SIZE

Table 3-30 presents a distribution of CRA ratings for each bank size, and Table 3-31 presents a distribution of bank size for each of the four CRA ratings. These are the same tables showing data over the July 1, 1990 – December 31, 1991 period with the percentages calculated horizontally in Table 3-30 and vertically in Table 3-31. Tables 3-32 and 3-33 display comparable data over the broader July 1, 1990 – December 31, 1992, period.

Compared to the 8.7% of all banks receiving an outstanding rating as of year-end 1991, small banks under $100 million fell short, with only 6.2% in this category (see Table 3-30). By year-end 1992 these ratios increased to 10.3% and 7.7%, respectively (see Table 3-32). Larger banks received higher relative amounts of outstanding ratings, with the percentage increasing positively with size to the 39 – 46% range for the very large banks for both year-end 1991 and 1992.

The size category consistently receiving a higher percentage of the two low ratings than the national average was the $250-500 million range. Whereas the national average for all banks as of December 31, 1991, was 11.0% (10.1% for needs improvement and 0.9% for substantial noncompliance), banks in the $250-500 million range had 13.6% in the lowest categories. This latter ratio dropped to 13.4% as of December 31, 1992, compared to the 10.5% national average then for all banks. The $1 – 10 billion range was second in this respect with a percentage of below-average ratings just at or above the national average.

Small banks under $100 million, which numerically account for most banks, reported 10.8% of ratings in the two lowest categories, almost equal to the national average as of December 31, 1991. The comparable ratio of 10.3% as of December 31, 1992, was again almost identical to the 10.5% national average then for all banks.

The analysis of bank size by CRA ratings (Table 3-31) shows that small banks received 72.0% and 76.2% of needs improvement and substantial noncompliance ratings as of December 31, 1991, respectively). These ratios were 72.1% and 77.4% respectively, as of December 31, 1992 (see Table 3-33). The combined average for both categories was 72.3% and 72.6% for these two dates, respectively.

Care must be taken in drawing conclusions from these data because most banks are small banks. As shown in Table 3-33, 73.3% of all of the banks publicly rated as of December 31, 1992, are small banks of under $100 million. Thus, the fact that 72.6% of the two lowest categories of ratings were given to small banks as of that date is consistent with the fact that most banks are small banks.

Since this is the case, the proposed exemption of small banks from CRA would immediately eliminate roughly three-fourths of all banks in the United States from any CRA obligation, thus, the claim that such an exemption would effectively "gut" CRA.

The last column in Table 3-31 showing the size distribution of all CRA ratings indicates the "ex-

Table 3-28 CRA Ratings by Size and Regulator, 7/1/90 – 12/31/91

ASSET SIZE	FDIC				SUBTOTAL	FED				SUBTOTAL	OCC				SUBTOTAL	OTS				SUBTOTAL	ALL REGULATORS				GRAND TOTAL
	O	S	NI	SN		O	S	NI	SN		O	S	NI	SN		O	S	NI	SN		O	S	NI	SN	
< $100 MILLION	191	2,688	262	17	3,158	70	608	63	7	748	20	382	77	8	487	23	382	84	13	502	304	4,060	486	45	4,895
$100 – $250 MILLION	62	330	34	0	426	19	108	11	0	138	28	127	22	0	177	22	193	37	3	255	131	758	104	3	996
$250 – $500 MILLION	20	82	12	1	115	6	27	0	0	33	14	43	6	0	63	5	82	22	3	112	45	234	40	4	323
$500 MILLION – $1 BILLION	12	33	1	0	46	3	14	3	1	21	10	27	2	0	39	8	50	10	1	69	33	124	16	2	175
$1 – $10 BILLION	16	34	1	1	52	8	25	3	1	37	20	79	9	0	108	13	54	13	3	83	57	192	26	5	280
> $10 BILLION	0	0	0	0	0	4	3	1	0	8	5	13	0	0	18	8	1	2	0	11	17	17	3	0	37
TOTAL	301	3,167	310	19	3,797	110	785	81	9	985	97	671	116	8	892	79	762	168	23	1,032	587	5,385	675	59	6,706

O   =   Outstanding
S   =   Satisfactory
NI =   Needs Improvement
SN =   Substantial Noncompliance

Note: Approximately 2% of ratings are multiple ratings of the same bank.

Source: Individual Regulators
              FFIEC
              K. H. Thomas Associates

Table 3-29   CRA Ratings by Size and Regulator, 7/1/90 – 12/31/92

ASSET SIZE	FDIC					FED					OCC					OTS					ALL REGULATORS				
	O	S	NI	SN	SUBTOTAL	O	S	NI	SN	SUBTOTAL	O	S	NI	SN	SUBTOTAL	O	S	NI	SN	SUBTOTAL	O	S	NI	SN	GRAND TOTAL
< $100 MILLION	481	4,873	413	42	5,889	112	944	100	12	1,168	49	722	151	11	933	44	737	172	17	970	686	7,276	836	82	8,880
$100 – $250 MILLION	142	571	46	2	761	39	173	15	0	227	53	237	40	0	330	53	343	79	5	480	287	1,324	180	7	1,798
$250 – $500 MILLION	49	141	25	3	218	10	44	2	0	56	20	76	8	1	105	19	158	38	3	218	98	419	73	7	597
$500 MILLION – $1 BILLION	28	63	3	1	95	6	25	5	1	37	16	52	3	2	73	18	84	14	1	117	68	224	25	5	322
$1 – $10 BILLION	27	56	5	1	89	13	40	4	1	58	28	135	13	0	176	18	91	21	3	133	86	322	43	5	456
> $10 BILLION	0	0	0	0	0	4	11	1	0	16	13	22	0	0	35	7	3	1	0	11	24	36	2	0	62
TOTAL	727	5,704	492	49	6,972	184	1,237	127	14	1,562	179	1,244	215	14	1,652	159	1,416	325	29	1,929	1,249	9,601	1,159	106	12,115

O = Outstanding
S = Satisfactory
NI = Needs Improvement
SN = Substantial Noncompliance

Note: Approximately 15% of ratings are multiple ratings of the same bank.

Source: Individual Regulators
FFIEC
K. H. Thomas Associates

Table 3-30   CRA Ratings by Size, 7/1/90 – 12/31/91

	RATING								
	OUTSTANDING		SATISFACTORY		NEEDS IMPROVEMENT		SUBSTANTIAL NON-COMPLIANCE		TOTAL	
ASSET SIZE	NO.	%	NO.	%	NO.	%	NO.	%	NO.	%
< $100 MILLION	304	6.2%	4,060	83.0%	486	9.9%	45	0.9%	4,895	100.0%
$100 – $250 MILLION	131	13.2%	758	76.1%	104	10.4%	3	0.3%	996	100.0%
$250 – $500 MILLION	45	13.9%	234	72.5%	40	12.4%	4	1.2%	323	100.0%
$500 MILLION – $1 BILLION	33	18.9%	124	70.9%	16	9.1%	2	1.1%	175	100.0%
$1 – $10 BILLION	57	20.3%	192	68.6%	26	9.3%	5	1.8%	280	100.0%
> $10 BILLION	17	45.9%	17	45.9%	3	8.2%	0	0%	37	100.0%
TOTAL	587	8.7%	5,385	80.3%	675	10.1%	59	0.9%	6,706	100.0%

Note: Approximately 2% of ratings are multiple ratings of the same bank.

Source: Individual Regulators
          FFIEC
          K.H. Thomas Associates

pected" frequency of a given rating based solely on the percentage of ratings made through year-end 1991. Table 3-31 indicates that only 51.8% of the outstanding ratings were given to small banks, a number considerably lower than the 73.0% of all ratings these small banks represented as of year-end 1991. The former percentage increased somewhat to 54.9% by year-end 1992, still well below the latter total of 73.3% at that time (see Table 3-33).

By contrast, most size categories of larger banks with assets over $100 million received a greater than expected share of outstanding ratings through year-end 1992. This was especially true as bank size increased to $500 million and even more beyond $1 billion and $10 billion.

Larger banks, however, fell short in a few size categories with a greater than expected proportion of low ratings. Banks in the $250—500 million range

had a disproportionately higher percentage in the two lowest ratings categories. This percentage, although not calculated in Table 3-31, was 6.0% as of year-end 1991 compared to an expected rate of 4.8%. The comparable level of 6.3% as of year-end 1992, although not calculated in Table 3-33, was also above the 4.9% expected rate.

In summary, small banks are getting less than their expected share of outstanding ratings but generally are receiving their expected share of low ratings. Large banks, by contrast, are receiving more than their expected share of outstanding ratings. The only exception are banks in the $250 – 500 million size category which are receiving disproportionately more than their expected share of below-average ratings. We should point out, however, that over half of the below-average ratings in that asset size category were given to thrifts by the OTS.

Table 3-31   Bank Size by CRA Ratings, 7/1/90 – 12/31/91

	RATING									
ASSET SIZE	OUTSTANDING		SATISFACTORY		NEEDS IMPROVEMENT		SUBSTANTIAL NON-COMPLIANCE		TOTAL	
	NO.	%	NO.	%	NO.	%	NO.	%	NO.	%
< $100 MILLION	304	51.8%	4,060	75.4%	486	72.0%	45	76.2%	4.895	73.0%
$100 – $250 MILLION	131	22.3%	758	14.1%	104	15.4%	3	5.1%	996	14.9%
$250 – $500 MILLION	45	7.7%	234	4.3%	40	5.9%	4	6.8%	323	4.8%
$500 MILLION – $1 BILLION	33	5.6%	124	2.3%	16	2.4%	2	3.4%	175	2.6%
$1 – $10 BILLION	57	9.7%	192	3.6%	26	3.9%	5	8.5%	280	4.2%
> $10 BILLION	17	2.9%	17	0.3%	3	0.4%	0	0%	37	0.5%
TOTAL	587	100%	5,385	100%	675	100%	59	100%	6,706	100%

Note: Approximately 2% of ratings are multiple ratings of the same bank.

Source: Individual Regulators
FFIEC
K H. Thomas Associates

CRA RATINGS BY REGULATOR

Table 3-34 shows CRA ratings as of December 31, 1991, by regulator for the 6,706 ratings made under the new system since July 1, 1990. The comparable data for the 12,115 ratings made through December 31, 1992, are shown in Table 3-35. The majority (57.5%) of all CRA ratings under the new system have been made by the FDIC; this is because just over half of all banks and thrifts are regulated by that agency.

The twelve Federal Reserve Banks of the FED have made the greatest progress in CRA ratings, simply because it has the smallest number of regulated banks (less than 1,000) and also because it has the largest examination staff relative to them. Nearly all FED member banks were rated under the new system by December 31, 1991, with many having received a second evaluation by then. All FED member banks were rated at least once by mid-year 1992. By December 31, 1992, the FED had completed 1.63 CRA exams per regulated bank, meaning that all banks were rated at least once and as many as one-half of its banks may have been evaluated twice.

This proportion is much lower for the other regulators. For example, the FDIC had examined one-half of all of its regulated banks as of year-end 1991 and 67% by mid-year 1992. By year-end 1992 the FDIC had conducted 6,972 CRA exams, but about 12% of them were multiple ratings of the same bank. Excluding those ratings, the FDIC had evaluated about 80% of all of its regulated banks at least once by year-end 1992. Its ratio of CRA ratings to regulated banks of .94 at that time was higher than .80 because of multiple ratings.

Table 3-32   CRA Ratings by Size, 7/1/90 – 12/31/92

	RATING									
	OUTSTANDING		SATISFACTORY		NEEDS IMPROVEMENT		SUBSTANTIAL NON-COMPLIANCE		TOTAL	
ASSET SIZE	NO.	%	NO.	%	NO.	%	NO.	%	NO.	%
< $100 MILLION	686	7.7%	7,276	82.0%	836	9.4%	82	0.9%	8,880	100.0%
$100 – $250 MILLION	287	16.0%	1,324	73.6%	180	10.0%	7	0.4%	1,798	100.0%
$250 – $500 MILLION	98	16.4%	419	70.2%	73	12.2%	7	1.2%	597	100.0%
$500 MILLION – $1 BILLION	68	21.1%	224	69.6%	25	7.8%	5	1.5%	322	100.0%
$1 – $10 BILLION	86	18.9%	322	70.6%	43	9.4%	5	1.1%	456	100.0%
> $10 BILLION	24	38.7%	36	58.1%	2	3.2%	0	0.0%	62	100.0%
TOTAL	1,249	10.3%	9,601	79.2%	1,159	9.6%	106	0.9%	12,115	100.0%

Note: Approximately 15% of ratings are multiple ratings of the same bank.

Source: Individual Regulators
          FFIEC
          K.H. Thomas Associates

The OTS, like the FDIC, had conducted CRA exams for about half of all of its regulated thrifts as of year-end 1991 and 75% by mid-year 1992. The OTS examined nearly all of its thrifts as of year-end 1992, even after counting multiple ratings. Its ratio of CRA ratings to regulated thrifts was .98 at that time. Multiple ratings at the OTS are not as common as they are at the FED or FDIC.

By comparison, the OCC had examined less than one-fourth of its regulated banks by year-end 1991, only 35% by mid-year 1992, and less than one-half by year-end 1992. Counting all ratings the OCC's ratio of CRA ratings to regulated banks was only .46 as of year-end 1992, roughly one-fourth the comparable FED ratio. The OCC is clearly the laggard of the regulators when it comes to frequency of CRA exams, and the FED is at the other extreme.

The most important conclusion resulting from an examination of Tables 3-34 and 3-35 is that thrifts are twice as likely as banks to receive below-average ratings. Of the four federal bank and thrift regulators, the OTS had given out the lowest percentage of outstanding ratings (7.7%) *and* the highest percentage of below-average ratings (18.5%) as of year-end 1991. The latter number is nearly twice the comparable percentage given by all three other regulators combined. These conclusions held true as of December 31, 1992, with the comparable OTS above-average and below-average ratings standing at 8.2% and 18.4%, respectively. In fact, 29 of 106 or 27% of all substantial noncompliance ratings were given by the OTS as of December 31, 1992. This is nearly two times the percentage of all banks and thrifts (14%) that are regulated by the OTS.

Table 3-33   Bank Size by CRA Ratings, 7/1/90 – 12/31/92

	RATING									
ASSET SIZE	OUTSTANDING		SATISFACTORY		NEEDS IMPROVEMENT		SUBSTANTIAL NON-COMPLIANCE		TOTAL	
	NO.	%	NO.	%	NO.	%	NO.	%	NO.	%
< $100 MILLION	686	54.9%	7,276	75.8%	836	72.1%	82	77.4%	8,880	73.3%
$100 – $250 MILLION	287	23.0%	1,324	13.8%	180	15.5%	7	6.6%	1,798	14.8%
$250 – $500 MILLION	98	7.9%	419	4.4%	73	6.3%	7	6.6%	597	4.9%
$500 MILLION – $1 BILLION	68	5.4%	224	2.3%	25	2.2%	5	4.7%	322	2.7%
$1 – $10 BILLION	86	6.9%	322	3.3%	43	3.7%	5	4.7%	456	3.8%
> $10 BILLION	24	1.9%	36	0.4%	2	0.2%	0	0%	62	0.5%
TOTAL	1,249	100%	9,601	100%	1,159	100%	106	100%	12,115	100%

Note: Approximately 15% of ratings are multiple ratings of the same bank.

Source: Individual Regulators
FFIEC
K.H. Thomas Associates

The FED reported the highest percentage of outstanding ratings at 11.2%, as of year-end 1991, and the OCC followed closely at 10.9%. By year-end 1992 the FED widened its lead to 11.8% compared to the 10.8% at the OCC. The FDIC had the lowest percentage of below-average ratings as of year-end 1991 (8.7%) and year-end 1992 (7.8%), and the FED had the second lowest percentage at 9.1% and 9.0%, respectively. One way to interpret these data is that the FED is the "easiest" CRA grader based on the highest percentage of above-average ratings and the second lowest percentage of below-average ratings as of year-end 1992. Two 1992 merger approvals by the FED that just as easily and arguably should have been denials on CRA grounds provide further support to the argument that the FED is the "easiest" CRA grader. In fact, these decisions, but especially the

second one, cause us to question the FED's commitment to CRA enforcement (see case study at end of Chapter 9).

Substantial ratings variations among the regulators may reflect differences among the banks' CRA performance and/or the regulators themselves. If the latter factor is important, than the OTS clearly is the "toughest" CRA grader. Otherwise, the differences may lie in the institutions themselves, meaning that thrifts are nearly twice as likely to be below-average CRA performers than banks.

This would indeed be a difficult conclusion for thrifts to accept considering the severe financial difficulties that industry has gone through in the last several years. Actually, many S&Ls may have concentrated their efforts on safety and soundness problems versus compliance ones. On the other hand, thrifts

Table 3-34   CRA Ratings by Regulator, 7/1/90 – 12/31/91

RATING AGENCY	FDIC		FED		OCC		OTS		ALL REGULATORS	
ALL BANKS IN U.S.*	7,610		976		3,790		2,198		14,574	
TYPE OF BANK	STATE NON-MEMBER AND SSB		STATE MEMBER		NATIONAL		S&L OR FSB			
RATING	NO.	%	NO.	%	NO.	%	NO.	%	NO.	%
OUTSTANDING	301	7.9%	110	11.2%	97	10.9%	79	7.7%	587	8.7%
SATISFACTORY	3,167	83.4%	785	79.7%	671	75.2%	762	73.8%	5,385	80.3%
NEEDS IMPROVEMENT	310	8.2%	81	8.2%	116	13.0%	168	16.3%	675	10.1%
SUBSTANTIAL NONCOMPLIANCE	19	0.5%	9	0.9%	8	0.9%	23	2.2%	59	0.9%
TOTAL	3,797	100%	985	100%	892	100%	1,032	100%	6,706	100%

*As of December 31, 1991

Note: Approximately 2% of ratings are multiple ratings of the same bank.

SSB — State Savings Bank regulated by the FDIC
FSB — Federal Savings Bank regulated by the OTS

Source: Individual Regulators
         FFIEC
         K.H. Thomas Associates

thrifts may argue that an overreaction to the S&L crisis by examiners may partly be responsible for these low CRA ratings.

However, as pointed out previously, the relatively high proportion of below average CRA ratings by the OTS has been the rule rather than the exception since the implementation of the April 1, 1989, specialized compliance program. As indicated before, a number of other factors initially may have influenced these low ratings, but they have been fairly consistent for some time now. This would suggest that the CRA performance of thrifts is as much if not more the reason for these low ratings as their regulators.

Whereas there are many differences between commercial banks and thrifts, we believe commercial banks regulated by the FDIC, FED, and OCC are relatively homogeneous. For this reason, significant CRA ratings differences among these three regulators are probably due more to the regulators themselves than banks' relative CRA performance. For the reason mentioned above plus other reasons discussed in a Chapter 9 case study, we believe the FED is the "easiest" CRA grader and the most lax of all four regulators with respect to CRA enforcement.

Table 3-35   CRA Ratings by Regulator, 7/1/90 – 12/31/92

RATING AGENCY	FDIC		FED		OCC		OTS		ALL REGULATORS	
ALL BANKS IN U.S.*	7,449		957		3,625		1,978		14,009	
TYPE OF BANK	STATE NON-MEMBER AND SSB		STATE MEMBER		NATIONAL		S&L OR FSB			
RATING	NO.	%	NO.	%	NO.	%	NO.	%	NO.	%
OUTSTANDING	727	10.4%	184	11.8%	179	10.8%	159	8.2%	1,249	10.3%
SATISFACTORY	5,704	81.8%	1,237	79.2%	1,244	75.3%	1,416	73.4%	9,601	79.2%
NEEDS IMPROVEMENT	492	7.1%	127	8.1%	215	13.0%	325	16.9%	1,159	9.6%
SUBSTANTIAL NONCOMPLIANCE	49	0.7%	14	0.9%	14	0.9%	29	1.5%	106	0.9%
TOTAL	6,972	100%	1,562	100%	1,652	100%	1,929	100%	12,115	100%

*As of December 31, 1992

Note: Approximately 15% of ratings are multiple ratings of the same bank.

SSB – State Savings Bank regulated by the FDIC
FSB – Federal Savings Bank regulated by the OTS

Source: Individual Regulators
FFIEC
K.H. Thomas Associates

ELEVEN YEARS AFTER—CRA RATINGS FOR THE 1982 – 1992 PERIOD

The four bank regulatory agencies combined have made 72,344 CRA ratings over the last 11 years since information on them has been made available. Table 3-36 summarizes all of these ratings through year-end 1992 in one of the three categories defined in Table 3-1. Several interesting conclusions can be developed from Table 3-36.

First, the 72,344 CRA ratings over 11 years translates into 6,577 ratings per year or one CRA rating per bank or thrift about every two and one-half years

or so. The peak year for CRA ratings was 1982 with nearly 12,000 such ratings. Because there were no data for the more than three full years of CRA ratings previous to that time, there may have been between 25,000 and 35,000 CRA ratings that were made but never publicly reported even on an aggregate basis. Thus, the four federal regulators may have made more than 100,000 CRA ratings, which would average out to roughly five or six exams per institution since CRA was established. This would again average out to roughly one exam per bank or thrift every two and one-half years or so.

A second important conclusion from Table 3-36 is the generally decreasing number of CRA ratings made throughout the 1980s as the deregulation climate grew under the Reagan and Bush Administrations. It is possible that 1980 or 1981 rather than 1982 was the peak year for CRA ratings, but we have no way to prove that from data made available to us by the federal regulators. Now that these data are being disclosed, it would appear that there will be an increase in the number of CRA ratings made on an annual basis.

A third conclusion from the analysis of 11 years of CRA ratings is that the likelihood and actual disclosure of CRA ratings in 1989 and 1990 was associated with a significant increase in the percentage of below-average ratings. This may be suggestive of grade inflation during the pre-disclosure period. The percentage of below-average ratings averaged 4.4% over the 11-year span shown in Table 3-36 and 3.3% for the eight-and-one-half-year pre-disclosure period. The percentage jumped markedly to 6.9% in 1989 when the public disclosure of CRA ratings was being debated, and to over 10% thereafter. The post-disclosure average of 11.0% through year-end 1991 (not shown in Table 3-36) and 10.5% through year-end 1992 was over three times the pre-disclosure average.

A fourth and related conclusion is that CRA disclosure is associated with relatively fewer above-average ratings, and this may also be suggestive of grade inflation during the pre-disclosure period. The percentage of above-average ratings over the 11-year span was 11.6%, and slightly higher at 11.8% over

Table 3-36   CRA Ratings by Category, 1982 – 1992

YEAR	ABOVE AVERAGE NUMBER	%	AVERAGE NUMBER	%	BELOW AVERAGE NUMBER	%	TOTAL NUMBER	%
1982	1,537	13.1%	9,945	84.5%	281	2.4%	11,763	100.0%
1983	1,190	15.7%	6,195	81.7%	199	2.6%	7,584	100.0%
1984	740	13.4%	4,686	85.0%	88	1.6%	5,514	100.0%
1985	591	11.8%	4,324	86.5%	82	1.7%	4,997	100.0%
1986	708	10.7%	5,785	87.6%	110	1.7%	6,603	100.0%
1987	692	9.6%	6,355	88.1%	166	2.3%	7,213	100.0%
1988	615	8.6%	6,302	87.6%	273	3.8%	7,190	100.0%
1989	730	11.9%	4,992	81.2%	425	6.9%	6,147	100.0%
1/1/90 – 6/30/90	330	10.3%	2,558	79.4%	330	10.3%	3,218	100.0%
SUBTOTAL 1/1/82 – 6/30/90*	7,133	11.8%	51,142	84.9%	1,954	3.3%	60,229	100.0%
7/1/90 – 12/31/92**	1,249	10.3%	9,601	79.2%	1,265	10.5%	12,115	100.0%
TOTAL 1982 – 1992	8,382	11.6%	60,743	84.0%	3,219	4.4%	72,344	100.0%

*   Pre-disclosure.

**   Post-disclosure CRA ratings for individual banks and thrifts publicly disclosed for the first time on July 1, 1990.

Source: Individual Regulators
          FFIEC
          K.H. Thomas Associates

the eight-and-one-half-year pre-disclosure period. This ratio went up (peaking at 15.7% in 1983) and down (with an 8.6% trough in 1988) for most of the 80s. This ratio fell from a five-year high of 11.9% in 1989 to 10.3% for the first half of 1990 and to 8.7% for the July 1, 1990 – December 31, 1991, post-disclosure period. With an increased percentage of outstanding ratings in 1992, the average for the entire post-disclosure period was 10.3% (see Table 3-36).

Thus, the public disclosure of CRA ratings between July 1, 1990, and December 31, 1991, was accompanied by the highest percentage of below-average ratings (11.0%) and nearly the lowest percentage of above-average ratings (8.7% vs. 8.6% in 1988) over the period for which CRA ratings data are available. More recent data through year-end 1992, although with a higher percentage of above-average and lower percentage of below-average ratings, suggest similar conclusions.

Since July 1, 1990 (i.e., post-disclosure), the percentage of below-average ratings has been more than triple the eight-and-one-half year pre-disclosure average, and the percentage of above-average ratings has been below the pre-disclosure average. Table 3-36 indicates that grade inflation was probably the greatest during the early predisclosure years. The previously-cited 1980 CRA ratings distribution for the FED, with 40.2% above-average ratings, would support this conclusion. If comparable CRA ratings data for the pre-1982 period were available from the regulators, we would be able to gauge the extent of grade inflation during CRA's formative years.

It would appear that the likelihood and actual public disclosure of CRA ratings and evaluations has had a major impact on the ratings distribution in terms of an increase in the percentage of below-average ratings and a decrease in the percentage of above-average ratings. We therefore refer to this as part of the "positive power of public disclosure."

Distributions of above- and below-average CRA ratings by asset size over the same 11-year period are found in Tables 3-37 and 3-38, respectively. It should be noted that the asset size distributions utilized here are the original ones from the FFIEC and include very small banks of $25 million or less. There are major data gaps for these data beginning in 1989, and these

are pointed out in the footnotes in both of these tables.

The percentage of above-average CRA ratings received by very small banks of $25 million or less has decreased significantly since 1982. By contrast, the percentage of above-average CRA ratings received by most categories of banks larger than $25 million has increased over this time for the most part.

The same data for below-average CRA ratings are shown in Table 3-38. The percentage of such ratings received by very small banks of under $25 million decreased consistently through 1988. Overall, roughly 40% of all below-average CRA ratings were received by very small banks over the 1982—88 period. That same group received just 26% of all above-average ratings over this time span. Comparing Tables 3-37 and 3-38, we conclude that those very small banks were the only size category where the proportion of above-average ratings was below the comparable proportion of below-average ratings.

Counting all banks of $100 million or less in the two smallest size categories results in 67.3% of above-average and 75.9% of below-average CRA ratings having been given out to small banks over the 1982 – 88 period. But, based on the previous finding we know that the very small banks (under $25 million) are primarily responsible for this conclusion. Although more current data are not available for this smallest category, Tables 3-37 and 3-38 suggest that not all banks of $100 million or less in size are homogeneous in their CRA performance.

MORE ON THE POSITIVE POWER OF PUBLIC DISCLOSURE

Table 3-39 compares CRA rating categories by regulator, both before and after the disclosure of CRA ratings. The comparison is based upon the former system of five ratings for the year-and-one-half period before public disclosure, contrasted to the current system of four ratings for the same year-and-one-half period since that time. As noted previously, the likelihood of public disclosure was debated in 1989, although it didn't take effect until July 1, 1990.

This analysis once again shows the positive power of public disclosure in terms of an increase in the percentage of below-average ratings and a decrease in the percentage of above-average ones. While the percentage of average ratings roughly remained the same at 80% over this period, the proportion of above- and below-average ratings literally "flip-flopped" after public disclosure. Of course, the differences would be even more striking by using pre-disclosure data prior to 1989.

This would lend support to the rough rule of thumb that the distribution of "10–80–10" has been consistent for the last several years. A closer evaluation, however, would show that the proportion of high ratings has decreased and the proportion of low ratings has increased since public disclosure. Additional evidence on the positive power of public disclosure is presented in a following analysis of multiple CRA ratings.

HIGHEST AND LOWEST CRA RATINGS BY STATE

This section will address the question of the geographic distribution of CRA ratings. As pointed out previously, we will focus mainly on state-by-state comparisons of high/low ratings, realizing there are various data limitations in such an analysis. Also, we will report complete ratings distributions for selected states and regulators through the first part of 1992 in some cases. The primary data source for this analysis are actual performance evaluations reported for indi-

---

Table 3-37 Above-Average CRA Ratings by Size, 1982 – 1992

ASSET SIZE (MILLIONS)

YEAR	< $25 NO.	%	$25 – $99 NO.	%	$100 – $499 NO.	%	> $500 NO.	%	TOTAL NO.	%
1982	485	31.6%	606	39.4%	284	18.5%	162	10.5%	1,537	100.0%
1983	361	30.4%	512	43.0%	199	16.7%	118	9.9%	1,190	100.0%
1984	181	24.4%	306	41.4%	158	21.4%	95	12.8%	740	100.0%
1985	110	18.6%	216	36.6%	148	25.0%	117	19.8%	591	100.0%
1986	211	29.8%	255	36.0%	149	21.1%	93	13.1%	708	100.0%
1987	149	21.5%	307	44.4%	164	23.7%	72	10.4%	692	100.0%
1988	109	17.7%	279	45.4%	159	25.8%	68	11.1%	615	100.0%
SUBTOTAL 1982 – 1988	1,606	26.4%	2,481	40.9%	1,261	20.8%	725	11.9%	6,073	100.0%
1989[a]	78	20.5%	157	41.3%	115	30.3%	30	7.9%	380	100.0%
1/1/90 – 6/30/90[a]	51	18.3%	150	54.0%	65	23.4%	12	4.3%	278	100.0%
7/1/90 – 12/31/92[b]	N/A	N/A	N/A	N/A	385	30.8%	178	14.3%	1,249	100.0%

a/ Data for FDIC and FED regulated banks only (52% and 84% of all above-average bank and thrift ratings in 1989 and first half of 1990, respectively); OCC and OTS size distribution data not available in this format.

b/ CRA ratings for individual banks and thrifts publicly disclosed for the first time on July 1, 1990. Ratings data for banks and thrifts in two size categories under $100 million not available from federal regulators.

Source: Individual Regulators
FFIEC
K.H. Thomas Associates

Table 3-38   Below-Average CRA Ratings by Size, 1982 – 1992

	ASSET SIZE (MILLIONS)										
	< $25		$25 – $99		$100 – $499		> $500		TOTAL	
YEAR	NO.	%	NO.	%	NO.	%	NO.	%	NO.	%,
1982	143	50.9%	93	33.1%	28	10.0%	17	6.0%	281	100.0%
1983	109	54.8%	71	35.7%	17	8.5%	2	1.0%	199	100.0%
1984	38	43.2%	29	33.0%	18	20.4%	3	3.4%	88	100.0%
1985	29	35.4%	34	41.4%	13	15.9%	6	7.3%	82	100.0%
1986	38	34.6%	36	32.7%	23	20.9%	13	11.8%	110	100.0%
1987	48	28.9%	60	36.1%	37	22.3%	21	12.7%	166	100.0%
1988	81	29.7%	101	37.0%	62	22.7%	29	10.6%	273	100.0%
SUBTOTAL 1982 –1988	486	40.5%	424	35.4%	198	16.5%	91	7.6%	1,199	100.0%
1989[a]	41	33.3%	44	35.8%	17	13.8%	21	17.1%	123	100.0%
1/1/90 – 6/30/90[a]	49	37.4%	46	35.1%	25	19.1%	11	8.4%	131	100.0%
7/1/90 – 12/31/92[b]	N/A	N/A	N/A	N/A	267	21.1%	80	6.3%	1,265	100.0%

a/ Data for FDIC and FED regulated banks only (29% and 40% of all below-average bank and thrift ratings in 1989 and first half of 1990, respectively); OCC and OTS size distribution data not available in this format.

b/ CRA ratings for individual banks and thrifts publicly disclosed for the first time on July 1, 1990. Ratings data for banks and thrifts in two size categories under $100 million not available from federal regulators.

Source: Individual Regulators
FFIEC
KH. Thomas Associates

dividual banks through year-end 1991 rather than aggregate statistics reported by the regulators, the source for the previous tables in this chapter.

Table 3-40 presents a state-by-state listing of the outstanding, needs improvement, and substantial noncompliance ratings that were released over the July 1, 1990, – December 31, 1991 period. This table and the following ones don't reflect the other 80% or so of satisfactory ratings. As noted above, complete distributions with these ratings through the first part of 1992 will be presented narratively in selected cases.

Table 3-40 contains the state-by-state distribution of the 1,120 highest and lowest ratings we reviewed over the July 1, 1990 – December 31, 1991 period.

The 489 outstanding ratings reported there is below the 587 such ratings made as of December 31, 1991, cited in Table 3-28. Thus, roughly 100 more such ratings were given by the regulators as of that date, but they had not been made public at that time. Also, Table 3-40 shows 578 needs improvement ratings, again roughly 100 less than the 675 such ratings noted in Table 3-28. However, the 53 substantial noncompliance ratings in Table 3-40 is quite close to the 59 such ratings cited in Table 3-28.

Of the 1,120 highest and lowest ratings detailed in Table 3-40, 43.7% or less than half were outstanding ones, with the remainder being either needs improvement (51.6%) or substantial noncompliance (4.7%). Texas, with the second largest number of

Table 3-39   CRA Rating Categories by Regulator Comparing Former and Current Rating Systems, 1989 – 1991

RATING CATEGORY	FDIC		FED		OCC		OTS		TOTAL	
	NO.	%	NO.	%	NO.	%	NO.	%	NO.	%
ABOVE AVERAGE										
Former	593	12.1%	65	6.9%	111	7.0%	291	15.0%	1,060	11.3%
Current	301	7.9%	110	11.2%	97	10.9%	79	7.7%	587	8.7%
AVERAGE										
Former	4,148	84.4%	788	84.4%	1,271	80.3%	1,343	69.4%	7,550	80.6%
Current	3,167	83.4%	785	79.7%	671	75.2%	762	73.8%	5,385	80.3%
BELOW AVERAGE										
Former	173	3.5%	81	8.7%	200	12.7%	301	15.6%	755	8.1%
Current	329	8.7%	90	9.1%	124	13.9%	191	18.5%	734	11.0%
TOTAL										
Former	4,914	100%	934	100%	1,582	100%	1,935	100%	9,365	100%
Current	3,797	100%	985	100%	892	100%	1,032	100%	6,706	100%

Note: Former system of five ratings for 1/1/89 to 6/30/90 period vs. current system of four ratings for 7/1/90 to 12/31/91 period.

Source: Individual Regulators
FFIEC
K.H. Thomas Associates

banks and thrifts in the nation, led with 125 high/low ratings or 11.2% of the nationwide total. California, Illinois, and Missouri followed with the greatest number of high/low ratings. These four states alone, which represent four of the five largest in terms of number of banks and thrifts, accounted for nearly one-third of all high/low ratings.

Several states had only a few high/low ratings, and the District of Columbia had none as of December 31, 1991. Our focus was on those states with at least 20 total high/low ratings or at least 10 high or low ratings. With 1,120 high/low ratings nationwide, this averages just over 20 per state. It is difficult to draw conclusions about any state with but a small number of high or low ratings.

The Highest CRA-Rated States

Texas led the nation with the greatest number of outstanding ratings (60) as of December 31, 1991, followed by Wisconsin (39), California (23), and Illinois (23). Wisconsin is the only one of these four states that is not among the nation's five largest in terms of number of banks, and this indicates a disproportionately high representation of outstanding banks.

Of those major states with at least 20 total high/low ratings, Wisconsin led all others by a wide margin with 88.6% of its high/low ratings being outstanding ones. Wisconsin was also the leader in two other calculations in Table 3-40 designed to highlight outstanding ratings, namely the number of highest minus lowest ratings and the ratio of highest to lowest ratings. The higher these high-low and high/low numbers, the better the state, other factors being equal. Our conclusions regarding Wisconsin hold true according to a complete ratings distribution through the first part of 1992. Importantly, all federal bank regulators are consistent in giving the banks in Wisconsin a high percentage of outstanding ratings and a low percentage of below-average ones. Thus, these

Table 3-40 Highest and Lowest CRA Ratings by State, 7/1/90 – 12/31/91

| | HIGHEST | | | | | | TOTAL | | Highest | Ratio of |
| | Outstanding | | Needs Improvement | | Substantial Noncompliance | | HIGHEST AND LOWEST RATINGS | | Minus Lowest | Highest to Lowest |
State	No.	%	No.	%	No.	%	No.	%, ^	Ratings	Ratings
AK	1	100.0%	0	.0%	0	.0%	1	100.0%	1	—
AL	2	18.2%	9	81.8%	0	.0%	11	100.0%	−7	.22
AR	8	80.0%	2	20.0%	0	.0%	10	100.0%	6	4.00
AZ	0	.0%	5	83.3%	1	16.7%	6	100.0%	−6	0
CA	23	28.0%	49	59.8%	10	12.2%	82	100.0%	−36	.39
CO	22	56.4%	16	41.0%	1	2.6%	39	100.0%	5	1.29
CT	2	33.3%	4	66.7%	0	.0%	6	100.0%	−2	.50
DE	2	50.0%	0	.0%	2	50.0%	4	100.0%	0	1.00
FL	3	9.4%	27	84.4%	2	6.2%	32	100.0%	−26	.10
GA	3	16.7%	12	66.6%	3	16.7%	18	100.0%	−12	.20
HI	1	100.0%	0	.0%	0	.0%	1	100.0%	1	—
IA	15	38.4%	23	59.0%	1	2.6%	39	100.0%	−9	.63
ID	2	100.0%	0	.0%	0	.0%	2	100.0%	2	—
IL	23	33.8%	40	58.8%	5	7.4%	68	100.0%	−22	.51
IN	22	66.7%	10	30.3%	1	3.0%	33	100.0%	11	2.00
KS	8	32.0%	17	68.0%	0	.0%	25	100.0%	−9	.47
KY	17	65.4%	9	34.6%	0	.0%	26	100.0%	8	1.89
LA	11	50.0%	11	50.0%	0	.0%	22	100.0%	0	1.00
MA	6	31.6%	13	68.4%	0	.0%	19	100.0%	−7	.46
MD	2	20.0%	5	50.0%	3	30.0%	10	100.0%	−6	.25
ME	3	60.0%	2	40.0%	0	.0%	5	100.0%	1	1.50
MI	13	61.9%	8	38.1%	0	.0%	21	100.0%	5	1.63
MN	14	38.9%	20	55.5%	2	5.6%	36	100.0%	−8	.64
MO	18	26.9%	42	62.7%	7	10.4%	67	100.0%	−31	.37
MS	1	11.1%	5	55.6%	3	33.3%	9	100.0%	−7	.13
MT	8	57.1%	6	42.9%	0	.0%	14	100.0%	2	1.33
NC	0	0.0%	3	100.0%	0	.0%	3	100.0%	−3	0
ND	3	50.0%	3	50.0%	0	.0%	6	100.0%	0	1.00
NE	17	50.0%	17	50.0%	0	.0%	34	100.0%	0	1.00
NH	4	40.0%	6	60.0%	0	.0%	10	100.0%	−2	.67
NJ	6	24.0%	16	64.0%	3	12.0%	25	100.0%	−13	.32
NM	5	71.4%	2	28.6%	0	.0%	7	100.0%	3	2.50
NV	1	50.0%	1	50.0%	0	.0%	2	100.0%	0	1.00
NY	15	51.7%	10	34.5%	4	13.8%	29	100.0%	1	1.07
OH	21	46.7%	23	51.1%	1	2.2%	45	100.0%	−3	.88
OK	22	52.4%	19	45.2%	1	2.4%	42	100.0%	2	1.10
OR	1	11.1%	8	88.9%	0	.0%	9	100.0%	−7	.13

Table continues

Table 3-40   Continued

	HIGHEST		LOWEST				TOTAL		Highest Minus Lowest Ratings	Ratio of Highest to Lowest Ratings
	Outstanding		Needs Improvement		Substantial Noncompliance		HIGHEST AND LOWEST RATINGS			
State	No.	%	No.	%	No.	%	No.	%		
PA	15	46.9%	16	50.0%	1	3.1%	32	100.0%	−2	.88
PR	0	.0%	2	100.0%	0	.0%	2	100.0%	−2	0
RI	3	75.0%	1	25.0%	0	.0%	4	100.0%	2	3.00
SC	3	60.0%	2	40.0%	0	.0%	5	100.0%	1	1.50
SD	4	40.0%	6	60.0%	0	.0%	10	100.0%	−2	.67
TN	7	36.8%	12	63.2%	0	.0%	19	100.0%	−5	.58
TX	60	48.0%	64	51.2%	1	.8%	125	100.0%	−5	.92
UT	2	40.0%	3	60.0%	0	.0%	5	100.0%	−1	.67
VA	5	33.3%	10	66.7%	0	.0%	15	100.0%	−5	.50
VT	3	75.0%	1	25.0%	0	.0%	4	100.0%	2	3.00
WA	13	59.1%	9	40.9%	0	.0%	22	100.0%	4	1.44
WI	39	88.6%	5	11.4%	0	.0%	44	100.0%	34	7.80
WV	6	66.7%	3	33.3%	0	.0%	9	100.0%	3	2.00
WY	4	66.6%	1	16.7%	1	16.7%	6	100.0%	2	2.00
TOTAL	489	43.7%	578	51.6%	53	4.7%	1,120	100.0%	−142	.78

Note: Ratings are most recent ones in cases of multiple ratings of the same bank. Satisfactory ratings were excluded from this tabulation.

Source: K. H. Thomas Associates

ratings are more the result of the banks themselves rather than the regulators.

Wisconsin is clearly the nation's highest CRA-rated state. This is in an historical sense quite fitting, as it was Senator William Proxmire of Wisconsin, the "Father of CRA," who introduced the original CRA legislation in January 1977.

Table 3-41 presents these same two high-low and high/low calculations for each state by regulator. Wisconsin was followed in all of these outstanding categories by Indiana and Kentucky, the second and third highest CRA-rated states, respectively. The states next in these rankings were Michigan and Washington. Other states (for example, Arkansas) ranked favorably in many of these outstanding indi-

cators, but they had fewer than 20 total high/low ratings or 10 of either type as of year-end 1991.

Tables 3-42 and 3-43 contain a distribution of outstanding and needs improvement ratings, respectively, by state and regulator. These data coupled with Table 3-41 help answer the question as to what role one or more of the four federal bank regulators may have had in a state with a very high or low proportion of certain ratings.

If a state is a statistical "outlier," with a very high or low percentage of certain ratings, and all four regulators proportionally made these ratings, then we probably could conclude it is more the banks in the state rather than the regulators responsible for the result. This is generally the case for Wisconsin being the highest CRA-rated state and, to be discussed below, for Florida being the lowest CRA-rated state. Conversely, if a disproportionately high number of the subject ratings were made by one of the four regulators, this would raise the possibility of "selective enforcement." This may have been the case in Tennessee (and Georgia to a lesser extent) regarding below-average ratings made by the OCC's Southeastern District (see below). Still, though, any one regulator singled out for selective enforcement might be totally objective in the CRA evaluation process, and the banks themselves could be responsible for the results.

A given state's outstanding (or needs improvement) rate must be viewed relative to the comparable national rate to ascertain if there is a disproportionately high or low percentage. Also, if the banks evaluated as of December 31, 1991 aren't representative of the distribution of the banks by their four regulators in a given state, this would affect these findings. Because roughly half of all banks and thrifts nationwide had been evaluated as of year-end 1991, these data reflect a broad cross section of banks.

As noted from Table 3-34, the FED's data should be most representative as they had evaluated almost all of their regulated banks as of year-end 1991, although there are significant differences by state. The FDIC and OTS had examined only one-half of their regulated banks as of that time. Since the OCC had examined fewer than one-fourth of its regulated banks at that time, care should be taken in the interpretation of findings pertaining to that agency.

In the case of Wisconsin, the most outstanding state in terms of high CRA ratings, 74.4% of all such ratings were made by the FDIC. This is a much higher percentage than the 51.5% of all outstanding ratings nationwide made by the FDIC (see Table 3-42). We will call these two ratios of 74.4% and 51.5% the state and national FDIC outstanding rates, respectively.

Indiana, the next highest-ranking state behind Wisconsin, followed a similar pattern, since the proportion of outstanding ratings by the FDIC (68.2%) was nearly as high. This was also the case for the third and fourth highest-ranking states, namely, Kentucky with a 70.6% FDIC-outstanding rate and Michigan with a 69.2% FDIC-outstanding rate. Finally, Washington had a similar pattern to Michigan with the same 69.2% FDIC-outstanding rate.

Table 3-41 confirms that the largest high-low rating differences (again, the higher the better) of the major states for the FDIC were for Wisconsin (+27), Indiana (+10), Kentucky (+9), Michigan (+9), and Washington (+7). Importantly, Wisconsin was also the top CRA state in terms of the greatest high/low ratio for the FDIC.

Thus, each of the five most outstanding states as defined here was characterized by a state FDIC-outstanding rate in the 68 – 74% range that exceeded the national FDIC-outstanding rate by 17% to 23%. This suggests that the FDIC's Chicago Region, which covers Wisconsin, Indiana, and Michigan (as well as Ohio and Illinois) has a disproportionately high percentage of outstanding ratings.

A complete ratings distribution through the first part of 1992 comparing all FDIC regions verifies that their Chicago Region had the lowest proportion of below-average ratings to all ratings (including satisfactory ones) of all FDIC regions. Again, we can't say if this is due to factors unique to that region or the banks within them.

Table 3-42 reveals some similar conclusions about the other regulators. The nationwide FED-outstanding rate was 18.0%. The highest FED-outstanding rate for a major state (with at least ten outstanding ratings) was Colorado at 36.4%. Next was Ohio and Minnesota, both with a FED-outstanding rate of 28.6%, and this was followed by Louisiana with a 27.3% FED-outstanding rate. Table 3-41 confirms that Colorado and Ohio had the largest FED high-low ratings differences of all major states, while Colorado had the largest high/low ratio. Data through the first part of 1992 for the Federal Reserve Banks with the most ratings indicated that those in Richmond and Cleveland (which covers Ohio) had the lowest proportion of below-average ratings to all ratings.

In the case of the OCC, the national outstanding rate was 17.8%. Pennsylvania's OCC-outstanding rate was 66.6%, and this was followed by Ohio's 52.4% rate. Table 3-41 shows that Ohio, Pennsylvania, and Wisconsin led all other major states in terms of OCC high-low ratings differences. Ohio, Wisconsin, and Pennsylvania also led with the greatest OCC high/low ratios. Data through the first part of 1992 verifies that the OCC's Midwestern and Central districts reported the lowest proportion of

Table 3-41   Summary of Highest and Lowest CRA Ratings by State and Regulator, 7/1/90 – 12/31/91

STATE	FDIC Hi-Lo	FDIC Hi/Lo	FED Hi-Lo	FED Hi/Lo	OCC Hi-Lo	OCC Hi/Lo	OTS Hi-Lo	OTS Hi/Lo	ALL REGULATORS Hi-Lo	ALL REGULATORS Hi/Lo
AK	1	—	0	—	0	—	0	—	1	—
AL	-1	0.00	1	2.00	-3	0.00	-4	0.00	-7	0.22
AR	4	5.00	0	—	2	3.00	0	—	6	4.00
AZ	-3	0.00	-1	0.00	-1	0.00	-1	0.00	-6	0.00
CA	-14	0.30	2	3.00	-7	0.30	-17	0.39	-36	0.39
CO	-1	0.91	7	8.00	0	1.00	-1	0.50	5	1.29
CT	-3	0.00	0	—	-1	0.00	2	—	-2	0.50
DE	0	1.00	0	—	0	—	0	—	0	1.00
FL	-6	0.00	-3	0.40	-8	0.11	-9	0.00	-26	0.10
GA	1	—	0	1.00	-7	0.13	-6	0.00	-12	0.20
HI	0	—	0	—	0	—	1	—	1	—
IA	-3	0.83	-3	0.00	0	—	-3	0.00	-9	0.63
ID	1	—	1	—	0	—	0	—	2	—
IL	1	1.08	-7	0.13	-1	0.88	-15	0.12	-22	0.51
IN	10	3.00	-3	0.00	4	—	0	1.00	11	2.00
KS	-11	0.27	1	—	2	—	-1	0.50	-9	0.47
KY	9	4.00	-1	0.00	3	4.00	-3	0.25	8	1.89
LA	-2	0.75	3	—	0	—	-1	0.67	0	1.00
MA	-3	0.67	0	—	-1	0.00	-3	0.00	-7	0.46
MD	-4	0.00	2	—	0	—	-4	0.00	-6	0.25
ME	2	—	1	—	0	—	-2	0.00	1	1.50
MI	9	—	-6	0.14	3	—	-1	0.00	5	1.63
MN	-12	0.33	3	4.00	1	1.50	0	1.00	-8	0.64
MO	-31	0.24	-1	0.67	2	—	-1	0.80	-31	0.37
MS	-4	0.00	0	—	-2	0.00	-1	0.50	-7	0.13
MT	-1	0.50	2	1.67	0	—	1	2.00	2	1.33
NC	0	—	0	—	-1	0.00	-2	0.00	-3	0.00
ND	-2	0.33	1	—	1	—	0	—	0	1.00
NE	-7	0.53	3	—	5	6.00	-1	0.00	0	1.00
NH	1	1.33	0	—	-3	0.00	0	—	-2	0.67
NJ	-5	0.17	-1	0.00	1	2.00	-8	0.27	-13	0.32
NM	1	—	1	—	0	1.00	1	2.00	3	2.50
NV	-1	0.00	1	—	0	—	0	—	0	1.00
NY	-2	0.67	1	1.50	-1	0.67	3	2.00	1	1.07
OH	0	1.00	6	—	10	11.00	-19	0.10	-3	0.88
OK	5	1.56	1	1.33	-1	0.75	-3	0.25	2	1.10
OR	-5	0.00	0	1.00	-1	0.00	-1	0.00	-7	0.13
PA	-1	0.75	-4	0.20	7	3.33	-4	0.20	-2	0.88

Table continues

Table 3-41   Continued

STATE	FDIC Hi-Lo	FDIC Hi/Lo	FED Hi-Lo	FED Hi/Lo	OCC Hi-Lo	OCC Hi/Lo	OTS Hi-Lo	OTS Hi/Lo	ALL REGULATORS Hi-Lo	ALL REGULATORS Hi/Lo
PR	−1	0.00	0	—	0	—	−1	0.00	−2	0.00
RI	0	1.00	0	—	1	—	1	—	2	3.00
SC	0	—	1	—	0	—	0	1.00	1	1.50
SD	−2	0.50	2	—	0	—	−2	0.00	−2	0.67
TN	5	3.50	−2	0.00	−7	0.00	−1	0.00	−5	0.58
TX	0	1.00	4	1.57	−9	0.44	0	1.00	−5	0.92
UT	−1	0.50	0	—	0	—	0	1.00	−1	0.67
VA	0	—	4	5.00	−4	0.00	−5	0.00	−5	0.50
VT	2	3.00	0	—	0	—	0	—	2	3.00
WA	7	4.50	0	—	−2	0.00	−1	0.80	4	1.44
WI	27	14.50	1	2.00	6	7.00	0	1.00	34	7.80
WV	−1	0.00	6	—	−1	0.00	−1	0.00	3	2.00
WY	0	1.00	2	3.00	0	—	0	—	2	2.00
TOTAL	−41	0.86	25	1.40	−13	0.87	−113	0.35	−142	0.78

Hi-Lo = Highest minus lowest ratings.
Hi/Lo = Ratio of highest to lowest ratings.

Note: Ratings are most recent ones in cases of multiple ratings of the same bank. Satisfactory ratings were excluded from this tabulation.

Source: Individual Regulators
K.H. Thomas Associates

below-average ratings to all ratings, and the latter district includes Ohio and Wisconsin.

California's OTS-outstanding rate of 47.9% was much higher than the national OTS-outstanding rate of 12.7%. New York's OTS-outstanding rate of 40.0% was likewise much higher, as was Washington's rate of 30.8%. New York was the only one of the three states with a positive OTS high-low ratings difference and a high/low ratio over 1.0.

The Lowest CRA-Rated States

Texas also led the nation with the greatest number of low ratings (65) as of year-end 1991, again because of the large number of banks there. As can be seen in Table 3-40, the states with the next highest number of low-rated banks were California (59), Missouri (49), Illinois (45), and Florida (29). Florida is the only one of those states not in the top five in the nation in terms of overall number of banks and thrifts, and this indicates a disproportionate level of low ratings there.

Of these major states with at least 20 total high/ low ratings, Florida had by a wide margin the highest percentage (90.6%) of its high/low ratings in the low category. Conversely, it had the lowest overall outstanding rate of 9.4%, not for just the major states, but for all states but three (which had no outstanding ratings but a combined total of only low 10 ratings).

A more in-depth analysis of all CRA ratings in Florida, including satisfactory ones, concluded that Florida institutions are twice as likely to receive

Table 3-42   Outstanding CRA Ratings by State and Regulator, 7/1/90 – 12/31/91

STATE	FDIC NO.	FDIC %	FED NO.	FED %	OCC NO.	OCC %	OTS NO.	OTS %	ALL REGULATORS NO.	ALL REGULATORS %
AK	1	100.0%	0	.0%	0	.0%	0	.0%	1	100.0%
AL	0	.0%	2	100.0%	0	.0%	0	.0%	2	100.0%
AR	5	62.5%	0	.0%	3	37.5%	0	.0%	8	100.0%
AZ	0	.0%	0	.0%	0	.0%	0	.0%	0	100.0%
CA	6	26.1%	3	13.0%	3	13.0%	11	47.9%	23	100.0%
CO	10	45.5%	8	36.4%	3	13.6%	1	4.5%	22	100.0%
CT	0	.0%	0	.0%	0	.0%	2	100.0%	2	100.0%
DE	2	100.0%	0	.0%	0	.0%	0	.0%	2	100.0%
FL	0	.0%	2	66.7%	1	33.3%	0	.0%	3	100.0%
GA	1	33.3%	1	33.3%	1	33.4%	0	.0%	3	100.0%
HI	0	.0%	0	.0%	0	.0%	1	100.0%	1	100.0%
IA	15	100.0%	0	.0%	0	.0%	0	.0%	15	100.0%
ID	1	50.0%	1	50.0%	0	.0%	0	.0%	2	100.0%
IL	13	56.5%	1	4.4%	7	30.4%	2	8.7%	23	100.0%
IN	15	68.2%	0	.0%	4	18.2%	3	13.6%	22	100.0%
KS	4	50.0%	1	12.5%	2	25.0%	1	12.5%	8	100.0%
KY	12	70.6%	0	.0%	4	23.5%	1	5.9%	17	100.0%
LA	6	54.5%	3	27.3%	0	.0%	2	18.2%	11	100.0%
MA	6	100.0%	0	.0%	0	.0%	0	.0%	6	100.0%
MD	0	.0%	2	100.0%	0	.0%	0	.0%	2	100.0%
ME	2	66.7%	1	33.3%	0	.0%	0	.0%	3	100.0%
MI	9	69.2%	1	7.7%	3	23.1%	0	.0%	13	100.0%
MN	6	42.9%	4	28.6%	3	21.4%	1	7.1%	14	100.0%
MO	10	55.6%	2	11.1%	2	11.1%	4	22.2%	18	100.0%
MS	0	.0%	0	.0%	0	.0%	1	100.0%	1	100.0%
MT	1	12.5%	5	62.5%	0	.0%	2	25.0%	8	100.0%
NC	0	.0%	0	.0%	0	.0%	0	.0%	0	100.0%
ND	1	33.3%	1	33.3%	1	33.4%	0	.0%	3	100.0%
NE	8	47.1%	3	17.6%	6	35.3%	0	.0%	17	100.0%
NH	4	100.0%	0	.0%	0	.0%	0	.0%	4	100.0%
NJ	1	16.7%	0	.0%	2	33.3%	3	50.0%	6	100.0%
NM	1	20.0%	1	20.0%	1	20.0%	2	40.0%	5	100.0%
NV	0	.0%	1	100.0%	0	.0%	0	.0%	1	100.0%
NY	4	26.7%	3	20.0%	2	13.3%	6	40.0%	15	100.0%
OH	2	9.5%	6	28.6%	11	52.4%	2	9.5%	21	100.0%
OK	14	63.6%	4	18.2%	3	13.6%	1	4.6%	22	100.0%
OR	0	.0%	1	100.0%	0	.0%	0	.0%	1	100.0%
PA	3	20.0%	1	6.7%	10	66.6%	1	6.7%	15	100.0%
PR	0	.0%	0	.0%	0	.0%	0	.0%	0	100.0%
RI	1	33.3%	0	.0%	1	33.3%	1	33.4%	3	100.0%

Table continues

Table 3-42   Continued

	FDIC		FED		OCC		OTS		ALL REGULATORS	
STATE	NO.	%	NO.	%	NO.	%	NO.	%	NO.	%
SC	0	.0%	1	33.3%	0	.0%	2	66.7%	3	100.0%
SD	2	50.0%	2	50.0%	0	.0%	0	.0%	4	100.0%
TN	7	100.0%	0	.0%	0	.0%	0	.0%	7	100.0%
TX	36	60.0%	11	18.3%	7	11.7%	6	10.0%	60	100.0%
UT	1	50.0%	0	.0%	0	.0%	1	50.0%	2	100.0%
VA	0	.0%	5	100.0%	0	.0%	0	.0%	5	100.0%
VT	3	100.0%	0	.0%	0	.0%	0	.0%	3	100.0%
WA	9	69.2%	0	.0%	0	.0%	4	30.8%	13	100.0%
WI	29	74.4%	2	5.1%	7	17.9%	1	2.6%	39	100.0%
WV	0	.0%	6	100.0%	0	.0%	0	.0%	6	100.0%
WY	1	25.0%	3	75.0%	0	.0%	0	.0%	4	100.0%
TOTAL	252	51.5%	88	18.0%	87	17.8%	62	12.7%	489	100.0%

Note: Ratings are most recent ones in cases of multiple ratings of the same bank. Satisfactory ratings were excluded from this tabulation.

Source: Individual Regulators
K.H. Thomas Associates

below-average CRA ratings and only one-fourth as likely to receive above-average ones, compared to the national norm. Although there were only two substantial noncompliance ratings in the state as of year-end 1991, there were only three (2%) outstanding ones out of more than 150 total ratings (representing nearly one-third of all Florida banks and thrifts).

The high minus low ratings column in Table 3-40 indicates that California is the lowest rated state based on this indicator, followed by Missouri, Florida, Illinois, New Jersey, and Georgia. If substantial noncompliance ratings were weighted more than needs improvement, California and Missouri (and Illinois to a lesser extent) would rank even lower.

The ratio of highest to lowest ratings for the major states would definitely place Florida as the lowest CRA-rated state, with a ratio of only .10 compared to the .78 national average. The only states in the nation ranking lower on this ratio are the same three noted

above with a combined total of only 10 low ratings but no high ones.

The next lowest ranking states of the major ones based on this ratio were Georgia, New Jersey, Missouri, and California. Based on this analysis it is apparent that Florida clearly is our nation's lowest CRA-rated state. California and Missouri rank as the second and third lowest CRA-rated states overall, respectively.

Table 3-43 displays needs improvement (but not substantial noncompliance) ratings by state and regulator. In the case of Florida, the lowest CRA-ranked state by most measures, all four federal regulators gave low ratings with no greatly disproportionate imbalance by any one of them. More recent data through the first part of 1992 verifies that all federal banking regulators were consistent in giving out their highest or near-highest proportion of below-average ratings to all ratings in Florida. This suggests that the

Table 3-43   Needs Improvement CRA Ratings by State and Regulator, 7/1/90 – 12/31/91

	FDIC		FED		OCC		OTS		ALL REGULATORS	
STATE	NO.	%	NO.	%	NO.	%	NO.	%	NO.	%
AK	0	.0%	0	.0%	0	.0%	0	.0%	0	100.0%
AL	1	11.1%	1	11.1%	3	33.3%	4	44.5%	9	100.0%
AR	1	50.0%	0	.0%	1	50.0%	0	.0%	2	100.0%
AZ	3	60.0%	0	.0%	1	20.0%	1	20.0%	5	100.0%
CA	18	36.7%	1	2.0%	6	12.3%	24	49.0%	49	100.0%
CO	11	68.8%	1	6.2%	3	18.8%	1	6.2%	16	100.0%
CT	3	75.0%	0	.0%	1	25.0%	0	.0%	4	100.0%
DE	0	.0%	0	.0%	0	.0%	0	.0%	0	100.0%
FL	5	18.5%	5	18.5%	9	33.4%	8	29.6%	27	100.0%
GA	0	.0%	1	8.3%	5	41.7%	6	50.0%	12	100.0%
HI	0	.0%	0	.0%	0	.0%	0	.0%	0	100.0%
IA	17	74.0%	3	13.0%	0	.0%	3	13.0%	23	100.0%
ID	0	.0%	0	.0%	0	.0%	0	.0%	0	100.0%
IL	11	27.5%	7	17.5%	8	20.0%	14	35.0%	40	100.0%
IN	4	40.0%	3	30.0%	0	.0%	3	30.0%	10	100.0%
KS	15	88.2%	0	.0%	0	.0%	2	11.8%	17	100.0%
KY	3	33.3%	1	11.1%	1	11.1%	4	44.5%	9	100.0%
LA	8	72.7%	0	.0%	0	.0%	3	27.3%	11	100.0%
MA	9	69.2%	0	.0%	1	7.7%	3	23.1%	13	100.0%
MD	3	60.0%	0	.0%	0	.0%	2	40.0%	5	100.0%
ME	0	.0%	0	.0%	0	.0%	2	100.0%	2	100.0%
MI	0	.0%	7	87.5%	0	.0%	1	12.5%	8	100.0%
MN	16	80.0%	1	5.0%	2	10.0%	1	5.0%	20	100.0%
MO	35	83.3%	3	7.2%	0	.0%	4	9.5%	42	100.0%
MS	2	40.0%	0	.0%	2	40.0%	1	20.0%	5	100.0%
MT	2	33.3%	3	50.0%	0	.0%	1	16.7%	6	100.0%
NC	0	.0%	0	.0%	1	33.3%	2	66.7%	3	100.0%
ND	3	100.0%	0	.0%	0	.0%	0	.0%	3	100.0%
NE	15	88.2%	0	.0%	1	5.9%	1	5.9%	17	100.0%
NH	3	50.0%	0	.0%	3	50.0%	0	.0%	6	100.0%
NJ	3	18.8%	1	6.2%	1	6.2%	11	68.8%	16	100.0%
NM	0	.0%	0	.0%	1	50.0%	1	50.0%	2	100.0%
NV	1	100.0%	0	.0%	0	.0%	0	.0%	1	100.0%
NY	5	50.0%	0	.0%	3	30.0%	2	20.0%	10	100.0%
OH	2	8.7%	0	.0%	1	4.3%	20	87.0%	23	100.0%
OK	9	47.4%	3	15.8%	4	21.0%	3	15.8%	19	100.0%
OR	5	62.5%	1	12.5%	1	12.5%	1	12.5%	8	100.0%
PA	4	25.0%	5	31.3%	3	18.7%	4	25.0%	16	100.0%
PR	1	50.0%	0	.0%	0	.0%	1	50.0%	2	100.0%
RI	1	100.0%	0	.0%	0	.0%	0	.0%	1	100.0%

Table continues

Table 3-43   Continued

STATE	FDIC		FED		OCC		OTS		ALL REGULATORS	
	NO.	%	NO.	%	NO.	%	NO.	%	NO.	%
SC	0	.0%	0	.0%	0	.0%	2	100.0%	2	100.0%
SD	4	66.7%	0	.0%	0	.0%	2	33.3%	6	100.0%
TN	2	16.7%	2	16.7%	7	58.3%	1	8.3%	12	100.0%
TX	36	56.2%	6	9.4%	16	25.0%	6	9.4%	64	100.0%
UT	2	66.7%	0	.0%	0	.0%	1	33.3%	3	100.0%
VA	0	.0%	1	10.0%	4	40.0%	5	50.0%	10	100.0%
VT	1	100.0%	0	.0%	0	.0%	0	.0%	1	100.0%
WA	2	22.2%	0	.0%	2	22.2%	5	55.6%	9	100.0%
WI	2	40.0%	1	20.0%	1	20.0%	1	20.0%	5	100.0%
WV	1	33.3%	0	.0%	1	33.3%	1	33.4%	3	100.0%
WY	1	100.0%	0	.0%	0	.0%	0	.0%	1	100.0%
TOTAL	270	46.7%	57	9.9%	93	16.1%	158	27.3%	578	100.0%

Note: Ratings are most recent ones in cases of multiple ratings of the same bank. Satisfactory ratings were excluded from this tabulation.

Source: Individual Regulators
K.H. Thomas Associates

banks, not the regulators, are primarily responsible for this result.

California, the next lowest-rated state, was represented by most of the four regulators. The OTS had a disproportionately high needs improvement rate (49.0%) compared to the OTS national rate (27.3%). The Federal Reserve Bank of San Francisco, however, gave out a disproportionately low percentage of below-average ratings relative to all ratings in California compared to the other three regulators, based upon data through the first part of 1992. The analysis of substantial noncompliance ratings in Chapter 9 will show that all regulators were involved in an unusually high concentration of such ratings in the I-405 corridor of L.A.

Missouri, the third lowest-rated CRA state, had the vast majority (83.3%) of its needs improvement ratings given by the FDIC. This is proportionately much higher than the FDIC national rate (46.7%). A further indicator of what may be selective enforcement by the FDIC in Missouri is the fact that all but one of the seven substantial noncompliance ratings there were given by the FDIC. No low CRA ratings were made by the OCC, and only three were made by the FED.

Illinois and Georgia, two other low-rated states, had unique patterns. Illinois had a disproportionately high FED needs improvement ratio of 17.5% compared to the national rate of 9.9%. Also, their OTS needs improvement ratio of 35.0% somewhat exceeded the national average of 27.3%. Not surprisingly, three of the five substantial noncompliance ratings in Illinois were made by the OTS, and the fourth was by the FED.

Georgia had a disproportionately high OCC needs improvement rate of 41.7%, which was more than two-and-one-half times the OCC's national average (16.1%). Moreover, all three of Georgia's substantial noncompliance ratings were given by the OCC. The OTS likewise had a disproportionately high needs improvement rate in Georgia of 50.0% compared to the OTS national average of 27.3%.

There are many other examples of what might be selective enforcement as indicated by disproportionately high below-average ratings and the calculations in Table 3-41. The highest FDIC needs improvement rate for a major state was 88.2% for both Kansas and Nebraska. The comparable national rate was 46.7%. The next highest FDIC needs improvement rate for a major state was in Missouri, as discussed above.

All three of these states with disproportionately high below-average ratings are in the FDIC's Kansas City Region. These results are in stark contrast to the above ones reported for the FDIC's adjacent Chicago Region, where banks it regulates in three states had a disproportionately high level of outstanding ratings. As pointed out above, data through the first part of 1992 verifies that the FDIC's Chicago Region had the lowest proportion of below-average ratings to all ratings of all FDIC regions. Conversely, their New York Region had the highest such proportion.

Missouri led all major states with the smallest FDIC high-low ratings difference, followed by California, Minnesota, and Kansas. Missouri also had the lowest, non-zero, high/low ratio, followed by Kansas, California, and Minnesota.

The national needs improvement rate for the FED was 9.9%. The highest such rate for any major state was Michigan at a very steep 87.5%. A high rate of 31.3% was also the case for Pennsylvania. Illinois and Michigan led all major states with the smallest FED high-low ratings difference and non-zero, high/low ratios. Both Michigan and northern Illinois are regulated by the Federal Reserve Bank of Chicago. Data through the first part of 1992 indicates that of those Federal Reserve Banks with the most ratings, Chicago had the highest proportion of below-average ratings to all ratings.

In the case of the OCC, the national needs improvement rate was 16.1%. The most disproportionately high rate recorded for any state in the country was the 58.3% rate in Tennessee. This was three and one-half times the national rate. The OCC gave out no outstanding ratings there. Texas had the smallest OCC high-low ratings difference of the major states, followed by Florida, California, Georgia, and Tennessee. The smallest, non-zero, high/low ratios

were recorded by Florida, Georgia, and California. The OCC's Southeastern District covers Tennessee, Florida, and Georgia, among other states. Data through the first part of 1992 verifies that this OCC district did in fact have the highest proportion of below-average ratings to all ratings. While the OCC's lowest ratings were in those three states, the FED and FDIC regions covering them gave out a relatively low percentage of below-average ratings to Tennessee and Georgia, but not Florida. Thus, the low CRA ratings appear to be due more to the banks themselves in Florida but possibly more to the regulators in Tennessee and Georgia. The latter two states, especially Tennessee, may be examples of selective enforcement by the OCC.

The nation's highest OTS needs improvement rate for a major state was 87.0% in Ohio. This compares to a 27.3% national rate. The second highest OTS needs improvement rate for a major state was 68.8% in New Jersey. Washington had a 55.6% OTS needs improvement rate. Ohio led all major states with the smallest OTS high-low ratings difference, followed by California, Illinois, and Florida. The smallest, non-zero, high/low ratios in the nation were reported by Ohio and Illinois.

MULTIPLE CRA RATINGS

Approximately 2% of all banks that had public CRA ratings as of year-end 1991 received multiple CRA ratings. We estimate that approximately 15% of all ratings made through year-end 1992 were multiple ratings of the same bank. Because many of the 1992 evaluations were not publicly available, our detailed analysis of multiple ratings is through year-end 1991.

Table 3-44 compares the multiple CRA ratings for the banks that we have been able to determine have received more than one CRA exam between July 1, 1990, and December 31, 1991. Many more banks and thrifts have received multiple ratings since the table's December 31, 1991, cutoff public reporting date. Table 3-45 presents a summary of the data in terms of the number of banks that have been upgraded, downgraded, or remained the same in terms of their CRA ratings.

Of the 142 banks and thrifts listed in Table 3-44, over half (52%) of the multiple evaluations have been

Table 3-44   Multiple CRA Ratings of the Same Bank or Thrift, 7/1/90 – 12/31/91

Name of Bank	City	State	Federal Regulator	First Examination		Second Examination		Change in Rating
				Date	Rating	Date	Rating	
Brundidge Banking Co., Inc.	Brundidge	AL	FED	7/9/90	S	8/19/91	S	Same
Bank of Commerce, N.A.[a]	Auburn	CA	OCC	8/10/90	NI	4/30/91	O	Up
Bay Cities National Bank[a]	Redondo Beach	CA	OCC	7/2/90	NI	12/91[b]	S	Up
Bay View FB, a FSB[a]	San Mateo	CA	OTS	8/13/90	S	5/13/91	NI	Down
California S&LA, a F.A.	San Francisco	CA	OTS	7/16/90	S	2/4/91	S	Same
Citibank, a FSB[a]	Oakland	CA	OTS	7/9/90	S	6/3/91	O	Up
EurekaBank, a FSB[a]	Foster City	CA	OTS	7/25/90	NI	1/28/91	S	Up
Farmers and Merchants Bank of Long Beach[a]	Long Beach	CA	FED	8/6/90	SN	4/22/91	NI	Up
First Nationwide Bank, a FSB[a]	San Francisco	CA	OTS	7/17/90	O	6/17/91	O	Same
Glendale Federal Bank, F.S.B.[a]	Glendale	CA	OTS	7/16/90	S	7/9/91	NI	Down
Great Western Bank, a FSB[a]	Beverly Hills	CA	OTS	7/23/90	S	7/9/91	O	Up
La Jolla Bank, SSB	La Jolla	CA	OTS	9/17/90	S	9/23/91	S	Same
New Horizons S&LA	San Rafael	CA	OTS	7/9/90	S	2/19/91	S	Same
Pacific Valley National Bank[a]	Modesto	CA	OCC	8/15/90	NI	1/31/91	S	Up
San Jose National Bank[a]	San Jose	CA	OCC	7/25/90	NI	1/31/91	S	Up
United Savings Bank, F.S.B.[a]	San Francisco	CA	OTS	7/9/90	NI	3/18/91	S	Up
Bank of Fairplay	Fairplay	CO	FDIC	3/4/91	NI	8/27/91	S	Up
Century Bank of Sterling	Sterling	CO	FED	8/13/90	S	9/23/91	S	Same
Commerce Bank of Aurora	Aurora	CO	FDIC	7/27/90	S	7/19/91	O	Up
First Bank at Arapahoe/Yosemite	Englewood	CO	FED	8/20/90	NI	8/5/91	S	Up
First Community Industrial Bank of Lakewood[a]	Lakewood	CO	FDIC	9/7/90	NI	8/30/91	S	Up
First Community Industrial Bank of Fort Collins	Fort Collins	CO	FDIC	9/11/90	NI	3/15/91	S	Up
Kirk State Bank	Kirk	CO	FDIC	8/7/90	S	7/29/91	S	Same
Valley Bank	Security	CO	FDIC	8/17/90	NI	2/1/91	NI	Same
Vectra Bank of Englewood	Englewood	CO	FED	7/16/90	S	6/3/91	S	Same
Banyan Bank[a]	Boca Raton	FL	FED	7/2/90	NI	7/8/91	S	Up
Commercial State Bank of Orlando	Orlando	FL	FED	7/30/90	S	8/19/91	S	Same
First B&T Co.	Tampa	FL	FED	11/2/90	NI	9/9/91	NI	Same

Table continues

Table 3-44 Continued

| | | | | First Examination | | Second Examination | | Change in |
Name of Bank	City	State	Federal Regulator	Date	Rating	Date	Rating	Rating
First Independence Bank of Florida	Fort Myers	FL	FED	9/21/90	NI	9/3/91	S	Up
Florida First International Bank	Hollywood	FL	FED	7/30/90	S	7/22/91	S	Same
SafraBank II, N.A.[a/]	Pompano Beach	FL	OCC	8/23/90	NI	12/21/90	S	Up
Iowa SB, FSB[a/]	Des Moines	IA	OTS	7/17/90	NI	6/4/91	S	Up
Page County S&LA	Clarinda	IA	OTS	7/31/90	NI	7/29/91	S	Up
Security Savings Bank	Eagle Grove	IA	FDIC	8/24/90	S	8/16/91	S	Same
Friendship State Bank	Friendship	IN	FED	7/16/90	S	8/26/91	S	Same
Scott County State Bank	Scottsburg	IN	FED	7/23/90	S	6/10/91	S	Same
American State Bank	Oswego	KS	FDIC	8/31/90	S	8/16/91	S	Same
Country Hill Bank	Lenexa	KS	FED	11/13/90	S	8/5/91	S	Same
St. Marys State Bank	St. Marys	KS	FED	8/6/90	S	9/30/91	S	Same
Bank of Gueydan	Gueydan	LA	FED	10/9/90	S	9/3/91	S	Same
Commercial Bank[a/]	Bel Air	MD	FED	11/5/90	NI	8/19/91	S	Up
United B&T Co. of MD	Upper Marlboro	MD	FED	10/15/90	S	9/30/91	S	Same
Union Trust Co. of Ellsworth	Ellsworth	ME	FED	10/1/90	S	7/15/91	S	Same
Bank One, Sturgis	Sturgis	MI	FED	8/13/90	S	9/9/91	S	Same
Blaine State Bank	Blaine	MN	FDIC	7/6/90	NI	8/16/91	S	Up
Citizens State Bank of Gaylord	Gaylord	MN	FDIC	10/22/90	S	6/14/91	S	Same
Farmers State Bank of West Concord	West Concord	MN	FED	1/2/91	S	6/21/91[b/]	S	Same
First State Bank of Spring Lake Park	Spring Lake Park	MN	FDIC	7/27/90	NI	8/23/91	S	Up
Frost State Bank	Frost	MN	FDIC	10/1/90	S	6/12/91	S	Same
Kanabec State Bank	Mora	MN	FED	8/13/90	O	8/26/91	O	Same
Marquette Bank Cannon Falls	Cannon Falls	MN	FED	7/2/90	S	7/1/91	S	Same
Marquette Bank Golden Valley[a/]	Golden Valley	MN	FDIC	7/13/90	NI	6/24/91	S	Up
State Bank of Blomkest	Blomkest	MN	FDIC	9/17/90	S	6/7/91	S	Same
State Bank of Springfield[a/]	Springfield	MN	FDIC	7/20/90	S	7/19/91	NI	Down
City B&T Co. of Moberly	Moberly	MO	FED	10/22/90	S	7/15/91	S	Same
First State Bank of Joplin	Joplin	MO	FDIC	7/6/90	S	7/23/91	S	Same

Table continues

Table 3-44   Continued

Name of Bank	City	State	Federal Regulator	First Examination		Second Examination		Change in Rating
				Date	Rating	Date	Rating	
Lindell B&T Co.	St. Louis	MO	FED	8/6/90	S	8/19/91	S	Same
Webster County Bank	Marshfield	MO	FDIC	8/14/90	S	6/21/91	S	Same
Foxworth Bank	Foxworth	MS	FED	11/13/90	S	9/16/91	S	Same
First Bank of Lincoln	Lincoln	MT	FDIC	7/12/90	S	5/6/91	S	Same
Ronan State Bank	Ronan	MT	FED	7/23/90	S	6/17/91	S	Same
First Commercial Bank[a]	Asheville	NC	FDIC	9/17/90	NI	5/13/91	S	Up
Triangle B&T Co.	Raleigh	NC	FDIC	7/9/90	NI	4/1/91	S	Up
Citizens Bank	Bancroft	NE	FED	7/9/90	NI	8/26/91	S	Up
Citizens State Bank	Carleton	NE	FDIC	9/14/90	S	7/19/91	S	Same
First Nebraska Bank	Valley	NE	FED	10/9/90	O	7/29/91	O	Same
Republican Valley Bank	Orleans	NE	FDIC	11/30/90	S	7/19/91	S	Same
Sutton State Bank	Sutton	NE	FDIC	10/12/90	S	7/19/91	S	Same
Thayer County Bank	Hebron	NE	FDIC	9/7/90	S	9/27/91	S	Same
Seacoast Savings Bank	Dover	NH	FDIC	7/30/90	NI	5/30/91	S	Up
El Pueblo State Bank	Espanola	NM	FDIC	10/12/90	NI	8/6/91	S	Up
IBJ Schroder B&T Co.[a]	New York	NY	FED	1/14/91	NI	8/6/91	S	Up
Norstar Bank, N.A.[c]	Buffalo	NY	OCC	10/29/90	NI	5/22/91	S	Up
Custar State Bank Co.	Custar	OH	FED	7/16/90	S	7/15/91	S	Same
Lawrence FS&LA of Ironton	Ironton	OH	OTS	8/20/90	NI	12/91[b]	S	Up
Monroe FS&LA	Tipp City	OH	OTS	7/23/90	NI	9/91[b]	S	Up
Bank of Tulsa	Tulsa	OK	FDIC	7/31/90	S	8/2/91	S	Same
Central Bank of Oklahoma City	Oklahoma City	OK	FED	7/9/90	S	9/9/91	S	Same
Friendly Bank of Oklahoma City	Oklahoma City	OK	FED	7/9/90	S	9/9/91	S	Same
Grand Lake Bank	Grove	OK	FDIC	9/7/90	NI	9/18/91	S	Up
Heritage Bank	Mannford	OK	FDIC	8/17/90	NI	10/18/91	S	Up
Treasure-Land S&LA	Ontario	OR	OTS	9/5/90	NI	9/9/91	NI	Same
Draper State Bank	Presho	SD	FDIC	7/27/90	S	8/16/91	S	Same
Valley Bank	Elk Point	SD	FDIC	12/21/90	NI	7/30/91	S	Up

Table continues

Table 3-44   Continued

Name of Bank	City	State	Federal Regulator	First Examination Date	First Examination Rating	Second Examination Date	Second Examination Rating	Change in Rating
Bank of Nashville	Nashville	TN	FED	9/14/90	S	7/15/91	S	Same
SouthTrust Bank of Middle Tennessee	Nashville	TN	FDIC	12/17/90	NI	5/10/91	S	Up
Alief Alamo Bank[a]	Houston	TX	FED	8/27/90	S	9/23/91	NI	Down
American Bank of Commerce	Grapevine	TX	FDIC	8/23/90	S	9/6/91	S	Same
Bank of Commerce	McLean	TX	FDIC	1/11/91	NI	8/12/91	NI	Same
Bank of San Antonio[a/d]	San Antonio	TX	FDIC	8/17/90	NI	1/28/91	S[d]	Up
						7/12/91	S[d]	Same
Bevans State Bank of Menard	Menard	TX	FDIC	7/20/90	S	7/9/91	S	Same
Carmine State Bank	Carmine	TX	FDIC	10/29/90	S	9/13/91	O	Up
Citizens State Bank	Royse City	TX	FED	9/4/90	S	9/16/91	S	Same
Citizens State Bank	Woodville	TX	FDIC	4/8/91	NI	10/11/91	NI	Same
Commercial State Bank	Garrison	TX	FDIC	5/8/91	S	10/11/91	O	Up
Crockett State Bank	Crockett	TX	FDIC	8/13/90	S	8/21/91	S	Same
Dayton State Bank	Dayton	TX	FDIC	9/17/90	O	9/16/91	O	Same
Donley County State Bank[d]	Clarendon	TX	FDIC	10/26/90	NI	6/10/91	NI	Same
						8/23/91	S[d]	Up
Eagle Bank[d]	Jarrell	TX	FDIC	8/24/90	NI	1/30/91	S	Up
						7/26/91	S[d]	Same
Fidelity Bank of Texas	Waco	TX	FDIC	7/12/90	S	6/7/91	S	Same
First B&T	Cleveland	TX	FDIC	8/24/90	S	10/4/91	S	Same
First B&T	Groves	TX	FDIC	7/26/90	NI	10/9/91	S	Up
First B&T	Springtown	TX	FDIC	8/9/90	NI	9/13/91	S	Up
First B&T Co. of Bartlett	Bartlett	TX	FDIC	7/20/90	S	6/28/91	S	Same
First B&T of Memphis	Memphis	TX	FDIC	8/24/90	S	7/26/91	S	Same
First Bank at Farmersville	Farmersville	TX	FDIC	8/13/90	S	10/28/91	S	Same
First Bank of Deer Park	Deer Park	TX	FDIC	11/9/90	NI	6/10/91	S	Up
First City, Texas – Sour Lake	Sour Lake	TX	FDIC	7/27/90	S	7/10/91	O	Up
First State Bank	Three Rivers	TX	FDIC	8/10/90	S	7/26/91	S	Same

Table continues

Table 3-44   Continued

Name of Bank	City	State	Federal Regulator	First Examination Date	First Examination Rating	Second Examination Date	Second Examination Rating	Change in Rating
First State Bank	Wells	TX	FDIC	8/20/90	NI	8/12/91	S	Up
First State Bank of Shallowater	Shallowater	TX	FDIC	9/28/90	NI	6/11/91	NI	Same
First State Bank of Smithville, TX	Smithville	TX	FDIC	8/17/90	NI	7/17/91	S	Up
Guaranty B&T Co.	Gatesville	TX	FDIC	10/12/90	S	9/16/91	S	Same
Hull State Bank	Hull	TX	FDIC	9/27/90	S	9/10/91	S	Same
Iraan State Bank	Iraan	TX	FDIC	8/20/90	S	9/17/91	S	Same
Johnson City Bank[d]	Johnson City	TX	FDIC	7/13/90	NI	1/25/91	S	Up
						6/7/91	S[d]	Same
Liberty Bank	N. Richland Hills	TX	FDIC	10/5/90	S	10/21/91	S	Same
Marion State Bank	Marion	TX	FDIC	9/24/90	NI	9/3/91	S	Up
Mineola State Bank	Mineola	TX	FDIC	8/31/90	NI	5/28/91	S	Up
North Houston Bank	Houston	TX	FDIC	7/19/90	S	6/25/91	S	Same
Powell State Bank	Powell	TX	FDIC	5/28/91	NI	9/23/91	S	Up
Red Oak State Bank	Red Oak	TX	FDIC	8/10/90	S	9/27/91	O	Up
River Oaks Bank[a]	Houston	TX	FDIC	9/28/90	NI	1/15/91	S	Up
Security State Bank	Farwell	TX	FDIC	7/6/90	NI	1/24/91	NI	Same
Security State Bank	Navasota	TX	FDIC	10/12/90	NI	5/15/91	S	Up
Security State Bank[a][d]	Stockdale	TX	FDIC	9/28/90	NI	2/4/91	S	Up
						9/3/91	O[d]	Up
Spur Security Bank	Spur	TX	FDIC	9/14/90	S	7/26/91	S	Same
Texas Bank	Mont Belvieu	TX	FDIC	8/3/90	S	5/31/91	S	Same
Texas State Bank	McAllen	TX	FED	9/10/90	S	7/22/91	S	Same
Texline State Bank[d]	Texline	TX	FDIC	9/28/90	NI	7/26/91	S	Up
						10/18/91	S[d]	Same
Yorktown Community Bank	Yorktown	TX	FDIC	5/6/91	NI	10/28/91	S	Up
Bank of Suffolk	Suffolk	VA	FED	10/9/90	S	9/23/91	S	Same
Bank of the Commonwealth	Norfolk	VA	FED	1/14/91	S	6/20/91[b]	S	Same
Commonwealth Bank	Richmond	VA	FED	7/30/90	NI	9/3/91	S	Up

Table continues

Table 3-44   Continued

Name of Bank	City	State	Federal Regulator	First Examination		Second Examination		Change in Rating
				Date	Rating	Date	Rating	
Community B&T Co. of Virginia	Sterling	VA	FED	7/16/90	NI	9/3/91	S	Up
F&M Bank/Massanutten, N.A. a/	Harrisonburg	VA	OCC	12/31/90	NI	12/91 b/	S	Up
Peninsula Trust Bank, Inc.	Gloucester	VA	FED	8/13/90	S	9/16/91	S	Same
First FS&LA of Renton	Renton	WA	OTS	8/6/90	NI	8/19/91	NI	Same
Pacific First Bank, a FSB	Seattle	WA	OTS	7/2/90	S	7/8/91	O	Up
Bank of Romney	Romney	WV	FED	7/16/90	O	9/10/91	O	Same
Buffalo FS&LA	Buffalo	WY	OTS	7/23/90	S	9/30/91	S	Same
Uinta County State Bank a/	Mountain View	WY	FED	10/30/90	SN	9/16/91	SN	Same

O   =   Outstanding
S   =   Satisfactory
NI   =   Needs Improvement
SN   =   Substantial Noncompliance

a/ One or more evaluations contained in the sample analyzed in this book.

b/ Date evaluation released to public.

c/ Bank was reevaluated on 5/22/91 based upon additional information submitted to the examiners after original 10/29/90 evaluation.

d/ These banks received a third CRA evaluation.

Source   Individual Regulators
:   K.H. Thomas Associates

Table 3-45   Summary of Multiple CRA Ratings of the Same Bank or Thrift, 7/1/90 – 12/31/91

UPGRADES

RATING CHANGE	FDIC	FED	OCC	OTS	ALL REGULATORS
S to O	5	0	0	3	8
NI to O	0	0	1	0	1
SN to O	0	0	0	0	0
NI to S	30	8	6	6	50
SN to S	0	0	0	0	0
SN to NI	0	1	0	0	1
SUBTOTAL, UPGRADES	35	9	7	9	60

DOWNGRADES

RATING CHANGE	FDIC	FED	OCC	OTS	ALL REGULATORS
O to S	0	0	0	0	0
O to NI	0	0	0	0	0
O to SN	0	0	0	0	0
S to NI	1	1	0	2	4
S to SN	0	0	0	0	0
NI to SN	0	0	0	0	0
SUBTOTAL, DOWNGRADES	1	1	0	2	4

NO CHANGE

RATING	FDIC	FED	OCC	OTS	ALL REGULATORS
O to O	1	3	0	1	5
S to S	31	28	0	4	63
NI to NI	6	1	0	2	9
SN to SN	0	1	0	0	1
SUBTOTAL, NO CHANGE	38	33	0	7	78

SUMMARY

	FDIC	FED	OCC	OTS	ALL REGULATORS
TOTAL, ALL MULTIPLE RATINGS	74	43	7	18	142

O = Outstanding
S = Satisfactory
NI = Needs Improvement
SN= Substantial Noncompliance

Note: In cases of three exams for same bank, only the first two are reflected here.

Source: Individual Regulators
          K.H. Thomas Associates

conducted by the FDIC (mainly in Texas), with the next largest amount (30%) having been done by the FED. The OTS (mainly the West Region) and OCC have been responsible for a relatively small number (13% and 5%, respectively) of multiple evaluations.

Over half (55%) of all multiple ratings maintained the same (usually satisfactory) rating (see Table 3-45). Most importantly, 42% of all the multiple evaluations have resulted in upgraded ratings. This is a very important conclusion since it can be interpreted as part of the positive power of public disclosure on a bank's rated CRA performance.

That is, now that CRA ratings and evaluations are made public, banks with low ratings are making great efforts to improve their CRA performance to upgrade their rating. This analysis assumes consistently objective multiple CRA exams. The OCC was the most lenient grader on reevaluations over this period, with all of the reevaluations being upgrades.

Most of the upgradings were from needs improvement to satisfactory. There have been eight upgrades from satisfactory to outstanding and one from substantial noncompliance to needs improvement by Farmers and Merchants Bank of Long Beach, California.

Of particular interest was a double upgrade in a rating from a needs improvement to an outstanding by the Bank of Commerce, N.A. of Auburn, California. Also, six banks in Texas received triplicate CRA ratings from the FDIC. One of those banks jumped from needs improvement to satisfactory to outstanding (Security State Bank of Stockdale, Texas).

Particularly troubling was the fact that four banks (3%) received downgraded ratings since they have been made public. All of these downgradings have been from satisfactory to needs improvement. These downgradings were received by Bay View Federal Bank, a FSB of San Mateo, California; Glendale Federal Bank, F.S.B. of Glendale, California; State Bank of Springfield, Minnesota; and the Alief Alamo Bank of Houston, Texas.

There were many more multiple ratings in 1992, although complete data are not yet available in a similar format to Table 3-44. We estimate that approximately 15% of the 12,115 CRA ratings made as of year-end 1992 were multiple ratings of the same

bank, most being double ratings with a few triple ratings.

Preliminary data from the FDIC for two and one-half years of public CRA ratings through year-end 1992 indicate approximately 750 double ratings and 32 triple ratings. All but 19 or 2.5% of these multiple ratings were upgrades or the same ratings. Over half of the FDIC downgrades were from satisfactory to needs improvement, with most of the others falling from outstanding to satisfactory. Only two banks were downgraded from needs improvement to substantial noncompliance by the FDIC, and these were the Bank of the Eastern Shore (of Cambridge, Maryland) and the Missouri State Bank and Trust Company (of St. Louis, Missouri).

All but two of the FDIC's 32 triple ratings through year-end 1992 were upgrades or the same ratings. The first exception was Farmers State Bank (of Allen, Oklahoma), first downgraded from satisfactory to needs improvement and then maintained at that rating upon reexamination. The second exception was Walburg State Bank (of Walburg, Texas), likewise downgraded to needs improvement but then upgraded back to satisfactory.

More than two-thirds of all FDIC triple ratings were in Texas, which also had the greatest incidence of FDIC double ratings. Other states in the FDIC's Dallas Region (i.e., Oklahoma, Colorado, and New Mexico) also had significant multiple ratings. This is in stark contrast to the FDIC's Atlanta Region where only a small percentage of banks in Georgia, Florida, Alabama and other states there have received multiple ratings, much less their first one.

According to the FDIC, 564 or 22.9% of the 2,464 unrated banks as of August 24, 1992, are in their Atlanta Region, and this is the highest unrated percentage of all FDIC regions. Their Kansas City (18.2%) and Chicago (16.7%) Regions rank second and third, and these three regions account for 57.8% of all unrated banks in their eight regions. By contrast, the FDIC's Dallas Region reported just 31 banks or 1.3% of the total as unrated, with their San Francisco (5.5%) and Boston (11.9%) Regions in a relatively distant second and third place.

Preliminary data from the FED for 1992 indicate several hundred multiple ratings, but this was expected considering that they completed 1.63 CRA exams per regulated bank by year-end 1992. Although complete data identifying rated banks for 1992 are not yet available, the FED reported several downgrades. At least two of these were into substantial noncompliance, and these were the State Bank of Coloma (Michigan) and the Bank of Garber (Oklahoma). Information on 1992 multiple ratings by the OCC and OTS is not yet available. Preliminary data indicate limited multiple ratings, especially by the OCC, the agency the furthest behind in its CRA ratings.

Most of the multiple ratings at the OTS are by its West Region. Of particular interest were two triple ratings of our nation's largest thrifts, involving both upgradings and downgradings by the West Region, and these are discussed in the following section. Only 17 or 3.4% of the OTS' 503 unrated thrifts as of mid-year 1992 were in the West Region. No other OTS region came close in terms of the proportion of unrated thrifts (Central – 32.8%, Southeast – 25.0%, Northeast – 21.7%, and Midwest – 17.1%). These significant differences are mainly explained by regional variations in compliance examiners. Whereas the OTS averages 20 thrifts per compliance examiner, this ratio ranges from a high of 40 in the Central Region to a low of only 10 in the West Region (the Northwest, Southeast, and Midwest Regions are in the range of 17 – 19 thrifts per compliance examiner).

This analysis of multiple CRA ratings suggests that there may be a misallocation of CRA regulatory resources across regions of a particular regulator and across regulators. The OCC is an example of the latter case where over half of its regulated banks had yet to be evaluated as of year-end 1992 in contrast to the FED where 1.63 CRA ratings per regulated bank were completed. Since the comparable OCC ratio was only .46, the FED's CRA rating process is proceeding nearly four times as fast as that of the OCC.

Another way to view this imbalance is to compare the number of banks per compliance examiner which is only 6 at the FED but 20 at the OTS and 43 at the FDIC. While the OCC doesn't have specialized compliance examiners, we understand from them that the comparable ratio, based on an estimate of approximately 200 examiners in this area, would be about 29 banks per "compliance examiner." These ratios are based on mid-year 1992 data from the regulators indicating 164 compliance examiners at the FED, 98 at the OTS, and 177 at the FDIC. Counting the estimated 200 at the OCC, there would be about 639 compliance examiners nationally responsible for an average of 22 banks each. While the FED had evaluated all of its member banks at least once as of mid-year 1992, the OCC had rated only 35% of its banks compared to 67% at the FDIC and 75% at the OTS.

An example of a misallocation of CRA regulatory resources within a regulator would be the FDIC's Dallas Region or the OTS' West Region. Both of these regions have reported numerous double and even triple ratings of the same bank, while there are banks in other regions of the same regulator that have yet to be evaluated once. This misallocation places uneven regulatory burdens on affected banks. Furthermore, it is a disservice to these communities with unrated banks that are poor CRA performers who have yet to be publicly disclosed and hopefully motivated to improve their community lending record.

CRA RATINGS OF LARGEST BANKS AND THRIFTS

A listing of the CRA ratings of the 100 largest U.S. banks as of December 31, 1992, is shown in Table 3-46. As of December 31, 1991, roughly half, or 51, of the 100 largest banks had been evaluated, with 17 (or 33.3%) of those banks with ratings receiving an outstanding one, 31 (or 60.8%) receiving satisfactory, and just 3 (or 5.9%) receiving needs improvement. The only three big banks receiving needs improvement ratings as of December 31, 1991, were Harris Trust & Savings Bank of Chicago and First Interstate Banks of Arizona and Oregon. None of the largest banks or thrifts have ever received substantial noncompliance ratings.

By year-end 1992, 88 of the 100 largest banks were evaluated once, with 16 having multiple evaluations. Of the 88 most recent CRA ratings, 29 (or 33.0%) were rated outstanding, 58 (or 65.9%) were rated satisfactory, and only one bank (or 1.1%) was rated needs improvement. This distribution was basically unchanged since year-end 1991. The only big bank carrying a needs improvement rating as of year-end 1992 was Chicago's LaSalle National Bank.

Table 3-46   CRA Ratings of the 100 Largest U.S. Banks, 7/1/90 – 12/31/92

Rank	Name of Bank	City	State	Regu-lator	Date of Rating	Rating
1	Citibank, NA	New York	NY	OCC	12/31/90	O
2	Bank of America NT&SA	San Francisco	CA	OCC	9/14/90	O
3	Morgan Guaranty Trust Co.	New York	NY	FED	8/6/90	S
					6/3/92	S
4	Chase Manhattan Bank, NA	New York	NY	OCC	11/8/91	S
5	Manufacturers Hanover Trust Co.	New York	NY	FED	9/24/90	O
6	Security Pacific National Bank	Los Angeles	CA	OCC	4/30/92	S
7	Bankers Trust Co.	New York	NY	FED	5/12/92	O
8	Wells Fargo Bank, NA	San Francisco	CA	OCC	3/15/91	O
9	Chemical Bank	New York	NY	FED	7/22/91	O
10	Bank of New York	New York	NY	FED	3/4/91	S
					7/13/92	S
11	NCNB Texas National Bank	Dallas	TX	OCC	11/15/91	S
12	First National Bank	Chicago	IL	OCC	9/27/91	O
13	Mellon Bank, NA	Pittsburgh	PA	OCC	7/22/91	S
14	First Union National Bank of Florida	Jacksonville	FL	OCC	3/8/91	S
					4/10/92	S
15	First National Bank	Boston	MA	OCC	10/31/90	S
16	Republic National Bank of New York	New York	NY	OCC	8/5/91	S
17	Continental Bank, NA	Chicago	IL	OCC	3/18/92	S
18	NBD Bank, NA	Detroit	MI	OCC	11/8/91	O
19	First Interstate Bank of California	Los Angeles	CA	FED	8/20/90	O
					8/10/92	S
20	Pittsburgh National Bank	Pittsburgh	PA	OCC	9/30/90	O
					12/31/91	O
21	NCNB National Bank of of North Carolina	Charlotte	NC	OCC	11/15/91	S
					5/1/92	S
22	Union Bank	San Francisco	CA	FDIC	N/A	N/A
23	Wachovia Bank of North Carolina, NA	Winston-Salem	NC	OCC	12/11/91	O
24	Marine Midland Bank, NA	Buffalo	NY	OCC	9/7/90	S
					3/31/92	S
25	First Union National Bank of North Carolina	Charlotte	NC	OCC	3/8/91	S
					5/1/92	O
26	State Street B&T Co.	Boston	MA	FED	3/12/91	S
					7/7/92	S
27	CoreStates Bank, NA	Philadelphia	PA	OCC	9/4/91	O
28	National Westminster Bank USA	New York	NY	OCC	1/28/91	O
29	First Fidelity Bank, NA	Newark	NJ	OCC	8/27/90	S
30	Bank One, Texas, NA	Dallas	TX	OCC	3/31/91	S
31	Sovran Bank, NA	Richmond	VA	OCC	10/11/91	S
32	Key Bank of NY, NA	Albany	NY	OCC	9/7/90	S
33	Citizens & Southern National Bank	Atlanta	GA	OCC	10/11/91	S
34	Comerica Bank	Detroit	MI	FED	3/11/91	O

Table continues

Table 3-46   Continued

Rank	Name of Bank	City	State	Regu-lator	Date of Rating	Rating
35	NCNB National Bank of Florida	Tampa	FL	OCC	11/15/91	S
36	Seattle–First National Bank	Seattle	WA	OCC	4/1/91	S
37	Manufacturers Bank, NA	Detroit	MI	OCC	7/2/90	S
38	Maryland National Bank	Baltimore	MD	OCC	N/A	N/A
39	Harris Trust & Savings Bank	Chicago	IL	FED	4/15/91 6/22/92	NI S
40	Shawmut Bank, NA	Boston	MA	OCC	12/31/91	S
41	Norwest Bank Minnesota, NA	Minneapolis	MN	OCC	2/18/92	O
42	Midlantic National Bank	Newark	NJ	OCC	3/28/91	S
43	United States National Bank	Portland	OR	OCC	2/23/92	O
44	Connecticut National Bank	Hartford	CT	OCC	12/31/91	S
45	First Bank, NA	Minneapolis	MN	OCC	1/7/91	S
46	Northern Trust Co.	Chicago	IL	FED	4/6/92	S
47	Crestar Bank	Richmond	VA	FED	N/A	N/A
48	Bank of Hawaii	Honolulu	HI	FDIC	8/13/91	O
49	Chase Manhattan Bank (USA)	Wilmington	DE	FDIC	10/15/91	O
50	Texas Commerce Bank, NA	Houston	TX	OCC	7/9/90 1/21/92	S S
51	Meridian Bank	Reading	PA	FED	N/A	N/A
52	Valley National Bank of Arizona	Phoenix	AZ	OCC	N/A	N/A
53	American Express Centurion Bank	Newark	DE	FDIC	N/A	S
54	Huntington National Bank	Columbus	OH	OCC	7/30/90 3/30/92	S S
55	Fleet National Bank	Providence	RI	OCC	10/29/90	O
56	Boatmen's National Bank of St. Louis	St. Louis	MO	OCC	7/2/90 6/8/92	O O
57	Bank of Tokyo Trust Co.	New York	NY	FDIC	N/A	N/A
58	Michigan National Bank	Farmington Hills	MI	OCC	N/A	N/A
59	Wachovia Bank of Georgia, NA	Atlanta	GA	OCC	12/11/91	S
60	Trust Company Bank	Atlanta	GA	FED	10/28/91	O
61	BayBank Middlesex	Burlington	MA	FDIC	N/A	N/A
62	Boston Safe Deposit & Trust Co.	Boston	MA	FDIC	12/2/91	S
63	Fidelity Bank, NA	Philadelphia	PA	OCC	9/4/90	S
64	Bank of California, NA	San Francisco	CA	OCC	5/15/91	S
65	AmSouth Bank, NA	Birmingham	AL	OCC	9/6/90	S
66	National City Bank	Cleveland	OH	OCC	7/19/91	O
67	Ameritrust Co., NA	Cleveland	OH	OCC	2/25/91	S
68	Society National Bank	Cleveland	OH	OCC	10/1/90	O
69	Fleet National Bank of CT	Hartford	CT	OCC	9/18/92	S
70	Banco Popular de Puerto Rico	San Juan	PR	FED	9/23/91	S
71	Signet Bank/Virginia	Richmond	VA	FED	4/29/91	S
72	Citibank (South Dakota), NA	Sioux Falls	SD	OCC	N/A	N/A

Table continues

Table 3-46   Continued

Rank	Name of Bank	City	State	Regu-lator	Date of Rating	Rating
73	First Tennessee Bank, NA	Memphis	TN	OCC	11/12/91	S
74	Greenwood Trust Co.	New Castle	DE	FDIC	N/A	N/A
75	Provident National Bank	Philadelphia	PA	OCC	9/30/90 1/6/92	S O
76	Sanwa Bank of California	San Francisco	CA	FDIC	1/18/91	S
77	Dominion Bank, NA	Roanoke	VA	OCC	11/8/91	S
78	Fleet Bank of Massachusetts	Boston	MA	OCC	3/9/92	S
79	Manufacturers & Traders Trust Co.	Buffalo	NY	FED	6/24/91	O
80	Security Pacific Bank Washington, NA	Seattle	WA	OCC	1/21/92	S
81	Citizens & Southern National Bank of FL	Fort Lauderdale	FL	OCC	10/11/91	S
82	First National Bank of MD	Baltimore	MD	OCC	3/24/92	S
83	Central Fidelity Bank	Richmond	VA	FED	3/18/91	S
84	Barnett Bank of South Florida, NA	Miami	FL	OCC	11/12/91	S
85	South Carolina National Bank	Columbia	SC	OCC	1/31/91	S
86	First Interstate Bank of Arizona, NA	Phoenix	AZ	OCC	8/31/90 4/30/92	NI S
87	First Alabama Bank	Montgomery	AL	FDIC	6/1/92	S
88	Norstar Bank of Upstate NY	Albany	NY	FED	12/16/91	O
89	First American National Bank	Nashville	TN	OCC	10/10/91	S
90	Citibank (New York State)	Perinton	NY	FDIC	3/12/91	O
91	Security Pacific Bank Arizona	Phoenix	AZ	FDIC	N/A	N/A
92	United Jersey Bank	Hackensack	NJ	FED	N/A	N/A
93	National Westminster Bank NJ	Jersey City	NJ	OCC	1/28/91	S
94	BancOhio National Bank	Columbus	OH	OCC	6/18/91	S
95	Bank One Columbus, NA	Columbus	OH	OCC	5/13/91	O
96	LaSalle NB	Chicago	IL	OCC	12/6/91	NI
97	First Florida Bank, NA	Tampa	FL	OCC	9/16/91	S
98	MBNA America Bank, NA	Newark	DE	OCC	11/1/91	O
99	Team Bank	Fort Worth	TX	FDIC	1/25/91	S
100	First Interstate Bank of Oregon, NA	Portland	OR	OCC	8/13/90 5/6/92	NI S

O = Outstanding
S = Satisfactory
NI = Needs Improvement

N/A —   Not Available as of 12/31/92

Note: 100 largest U.S. banks based on total assets as of 12/31/91

Source: Individual Regulators
          K.H. Thomas Associates

This is because Harris Bank and First Interstate Banks of Arizona and Oregon were upgraded to satisfactory ratings.

LaSalle National Bank has the dubious distinction of being the only big bank with a needs improvement rating at the present time. Their needs improvement status, however, apparently had no affect on the FED, since it approved the acquisition of Talman Home Federal by LaSalle's parent ABN AMRO Bank of the Netherlands on February 27, 1992 (see case study at end of Chapter 9).

Surprisingly, the only big bank downgrade ever reported occurred at First Interstate's lead bank in California, which was lowered by the FED from an outstanding to a satisfactory rating. First Interstate's Arizona, Denver, Oregon, and Washington state affiliates were upgraded from needs improvement to satisfactory ratings. First Interstate Bancard Company, N.A. of Simi Valley, California, was rated needs improvement by the OCC, but we understand that credit card bank is being liquidated and folded into the holding company's lead bank.

Ten of the 16 multiple ratings of big banks were at the same rating, with five upgrades and the one First Interstate downgrade noted above. Three of the five upgrades were from needs improvement to satisfactory (Harris Bank and the First Interstate Banks of Arizona and Oregon). Additionally, the OCC upgraded First Union's lead bank and Provident National Bank from satisfactory to outstanding. Eleven of the 16 multiple ratings were by the OCC. This was because most big banks are regulated by them and also because their ten largest banks are examined through a separate Multinational Banking Division headquartered in Washington, D.C.

The comparable CRA ratings as of December 31, 1992 for the 50 largest thrifts are shown in Table 3-47. As of December 31, 1991, a total of 29 (or 58.0%) of the largest thrifts received CRA ratings. Twelve (or 41.4%) of the 29 thrifts rated as of year-end 1991 received outstanding ratings and 14 (or 48.3%) of them received satisfactory ratings. Only three (or 10.3%) of the largest thrifts rated at that time received needs improvement ratings, and these included Glendale Federal Bank of Glendale, California; HomeFed Bank, FSB of San Diego, California; and Apple Bank for Savings in New York.

The ratings distribution for the largest thrifts as of year-end 1992 was quite similar to that of the year before. Only 37 of the 50 (or 74.0%) of the largest thrifts were rated, since several had failed (including some that were rated). Of the 37 ratings, 17 (or 45.9%) were rated outstanding, 17 (or 45.9%) were rated satisfactory, and 3 (or 8.1%) were rated needs improvement. The only big thrifts with needs improvement ratings as of year-end 1992 were Apple Bank, Hudson City Savings Bank, and the failed HomeFed Bank. Glendale Federal Bank and Coast Federal Bank were previously downgraded from satisfactory to needs improvement, but both were upgraded to their original rating upon their third evaluation.

Counting these two triple ratings and 12 more double ratings, there were 14 multiple ratings, all but one by the OTS' West Region. Eight of the 12 double ratings were repeat ones (four each at satisfactory and outstanding), and four were upgrades (from satisfactory to outstanding). These upgrades were made at Citibank, FSB, Great Western Bank, Pacific First Bank, and Western Federal. Double outstanding ratings were received by Home Savings of America, World Savings, First Nationwide Bank, and American Savings Bank, and these represent four of the seven largest thrifts.

Comparing the 100 largest banks and 50 largest thrifts that have been rated as of year-end 1992, we conclude that the largest thrifts received proportionately more (45.9%) outstanding ratings than the largest banks (33.0%). However, the reverse was true with needs improvement ratings, with 8.1% of the largest thrifts receiving that low rating compared to only 1.1% of the largest banks.

Importantly, this analysis indicates that size alone is not a good indicator of outstanding CRA ratings. This is because only 33.0% of the largest banks analyzed and 45.9% of the largest thrift institutions analyzed obtained such a rating through year-end 1992.

CONCLUSIONS

The first and most important conclusion of this analysis is the documentation we have set forth regarding the positive power of public disclosure. Specifically,

Table 3-47   CRA Ratings of the 50 Largest U.S. Thrifts, 7/1/90 – 12/31/92

Rank	Name of Thrift	City	State	Regu- lator	Date of Rating	Rating
1	Home Savings of America, FA	Los Angeles	CA	OTS	7/10/90 4/6/92	O O
2	Great Western Bank, a FSB	Beverly Hills	CA	OTS	7/23/90 7/9/91	S O
3	World S&LA, a FS&LA	Oakland	CA	OTS	7/12/90 6/29/92	O O
4	Glendale Federal Bank, FSB	Glendale	CA	OTS	7/16/90 7/9/91 5/26/92	S NI S
5	First Nationwide Bank, a FSB	San Francisco	CA	OTS	7/17/90 6/17/91	O O
6	California Federal Bank	Los Angeles	CA	OTS	8/6/90 10/7/91	S S
7	American Savings Bank, FA	Stockton	CA	OTS	7/9/90 8/10/92	O O
8	HomeFed Bank, FSB	San Diego	CA	OTS	7/16/90	NI
9	Citibank, FSB	San Francisco	CA	OTS	7/9/90 6/3/91	S O
10	Dime Savings Bank of NY	Garden City	NY	OTS	12/10/90	O
11	Standard Federal Bank	Troy	MI	OTS	10/15/91	O
12	First Federal of MI	Detroit	MI	OTS	7/15/91	S
13	Coast Federal Bank, FSB	Los Angeles	CA	OTS	7/10/90 11/13/91 8/10/92	S NI S
14	Household Bank, FSB	Newport Beach	CA	OTS	10/10/90 6/3/91	S S
15	Anchor SB, FSB	Northport	NY	OTS	N/A	N/A
16	First Gibraltar Bank, FSB	Dallas	TX	OTS	1/28/91	O
17	Crossland Savings, FSB	Brooklyn	NY	OTS	N/A	N/A
18	Pacific First Bank, a FSB	Seattle	WA	OTS	7/2/90 7/8/91	S O
19	New West FS&LA	Stockton	CA	OTS	N/A	N/A
20	Manhattan SB	New York	NY	FDIC	N/A	N/A
21	Bowery SB	New York	NY	FDIC	2/15/91	O
22	United SA of Texas, FSB	Houston	TX	OTS	N/A	N/A
23	Peoples Bank	Bridgeport	CT	FDIC	8/31/92	O
24	Green Point SB	New York	NY	FDIC	N/A	N/A
25	Washington MSB	Seattle	WA	OTS	11/25/91	O
26	Great American Federal, SA	San Diego	CA	OTS	7/10/90	O
27	First FS&LA of Rochester	Rochester	NY	OTS	N/A	S
28	Sears Savings Bank	Glendale	CA	OTS	N/A	N/A
29	Carteret SB, FA	Morristown	NJ	OTS	12/10/90	O
30	Talman Home FS&LA	Chicago	IL	OTS	N/A	N/A

Table continues

Table 3-47   Continued

Rank	Name of Thrift	City	State	Regu-lator	Date of Rating	Rating
31	Fidelity Federal Bank, a FSB	Glendale	CA	OTS	9/4/90 11/13/91	S S
32	Meritor SB	Philadelphia	PA	FDIC	7/24/90	S
33	Chevy Chase FSB	Chevy Chase	MD	OTS	10/15/90	S
34	Commercial Federal Bank, a FSB	Omaha	NE	OTS	11/30/90	S
35	Metropolitan Federal Bank, FSB	Fargo	ND	OTS	8/19/91	S
36	Georgia Federal Bank, FSB	Atlanta	GA	OTS	8/27/90 8/3/92	S S
37	Franklin SA	Ottawa	KS	OTS	N/A	N/A
38	Western FS&LA	Marina Del Rey	CA	OTS	7/30/90 5/4/92	S O
39	Citizens Federal Bank, a FSB	Miami	FL	OTS	5/28/91	S
40	Apple Bank for Savings	New York	NY	FDIC	7/12/90	NI
41	TCF Bank Savings FSB	Minneapolis	MN	OTS	N/A	N/A
42	Dollar Dry Dock Bank	White Plains	NY	FDIC	N/A	N/A
43	Howard SB	Newark	NJ	FDIC	N/A	N/A
44	TransOhio Savings Bank	Cleveland	OH	OTS	N/A	N/A
45	Hudson City SB	Paramus	NJ	FDIC	2/21/92	NI
46	Guaranty FSB	Dallas	TX	OTS	11/12/91	O
47	Columbia Savings, a FS&LA	Englewood	CO	OTS	3/25/91	S
48	Downey S&LA	Newport Beach	CA	OTS	6/3/91	S
49	Capitol FS&LA	Topeka	KS	OTS	10/18/90	S
50	Northeast Savings, FA	Hartford	CT	OTS	7/30/90	S

O – Outstanding
S – Satisfactory
NI – Needs Improvement
SN– Substantial Noncompliance

N/A, – Not Available as of 12/31/92

Note: 50 largest U.S. thrifts based on total assets as of 12/31/91

Source: Individual Regulators
K.H. Thomas Associates

the *likelihood* of disclosure of CRA ratings in 1989 and the *actual* disclosure beginning on July 1, 1990, have been associated with a significant change in the distribution of CRA ratings.

Specifically, the percentage of below-average CRA ratings has increased significantly, and the percentage of above-average ratings has decreased since public disclosure. This conclusion holds up not only for the approximately year-and-one-half period before and after the actual disclosure, but also for the broader 11-year period for which data are available. The proportion of above-average ratings increased and the proportion of below-average ratings decreased somewhat in 1992, and this may have been due to improved CRA performance under public disclosure.

Further documentation of the positive effect of public disclosure is the significant percentage (42%) of banks and thrifts as of year-end 1991 that have received multiple ratings since July 1, 1990, and improved their ratings. We don't believe such widespread improvement would have occurred had these ratings and evaluations not been made public. This trend continued in 1992 across the board, based on available data.

This important conclusion regarding the positive power of public disclosure would seem to lend credence to the view that serious consideration should be given to making safety and soundness (i.e., CAMEL and MACRO) ratings public. It is quite likely that such public disclosure would have an additional positive impact on financial performance beyond even what the federal regulators are presently able to do with their current arsenal of tools.

This conclusion is by no means meant to be a cost benefit analysis of CRA since we do not have relevant cost data. However, at least from the point of view of public policy benefits defined in terms of improved CRA ratings, they appear to be quite significant based upon this analysis.

Our second conclusion concerns alleged "grade inflation" by regulators. It is difficult to document whether or not grade inflation exists on a widespread basis, because there is no way to determine what the ideal or appropriate distribution of CRA ratings should be as a norm from which to measure. In other words, "inflated" from what? That is, it is difficult to define grade inflation or deflation without a standard or base of comparison.

Significant pre- and post-disclosure ratings differences may, however, be suggestive of grade inflation. We know from 11 years of experience and 72,344 CRA ratings that the percentage of above-average, average, and below-average ratings has been 11.6%, 84.0% and 4.4%, respectively. The eight-and-one-half year predisclosure period from 1982 to mid-year 1990 represented an 11.8%, 84.9%, and 3.3% distribution, respectively.

Since the public disclosure of roughly 6,700 evaluations through year-end 1991, this rating distribution over one and one-half years became 8.7%, 80.3% and

11.0%, respectively. It is possible to interpret the predisclosure distribution as being indicative of grade inflation because of the higher proportion of above-average ratings (11.8% vs. 8.7%) and lower proportion of below-average ones (3.3% vs. 11.0%). More recent data through year-end 1992 suggest similar conclusions but not as strong, since there has been a general improvement in CRA ratings in 1992.

The 10.3%–79.2%–10.5% distribution of 12,196 public ratings as of year-end 1992 is close to a 10–80–10 distribution. It may be viewed by some as appropriate since it is "bell-shaped." But, a 25–50–25 distribution is also "bell-shaped." Thus, the appropriate distribution among these three categories is really a matter of public policy. It appears from the roughly two and one-half years of publicly disclosed data that the federal regulators are comfortable with the 10–80–10 norm.

Our analysis of CRA ratings by state and regulator revealed several instances of disproportionately high or low ratings for a given regulator in a given state. These specific findings could suggest instances of grade inflation or deflation.

We prefer the term "selective enforcement" when there appears to be one regulator in one region with disproportionately high or low ratings. Still, though, it is difficult to generalize in this way because of the various data limitations noted in the analysis. A case study in Chapter 7 will document what we believe to be an example of both grade inflation and deflation. Certain other cases will be identified in this book.

Our third major conclusion is that there is wide distribution of CRA ratings among the states and the four bank regulators, with some regions of some regulators being more consistently liberal and conservative than others. We have identified several states and the appropriate regulator(s) that fit each of these profiles. As noted above, with few exceptions it is quite difficult to draw conclusions as to whether a unique rating pattern is due to the regulators or the banks themselves. We also found a significant difference among regulators (and regions within a given regulator) regarding the frequency of CRA exams, with the FED being the most frequent and the OCC the least frequent CRA grader.

The fourth conclusion from this analysis pertains to the appropriate CRA rating system. Our analysis of both numerical versus descriptive systems and five-versus four-tiered systems has concluded that the preferred system is a five-tiered numerical one similar to the previous FHLBB system. We also prefer that older system because it contained specific conditions for the lowest CRA rating.

The fifth major conclusion we have reached from this analysis is that thrifts are nearly twice as likely to receive below-average ratings as banks. This conclusion may reflect the fact that the OTS is the "toughest" grader or that thrifts themselves are below-average CRA performers. We believe the latter factor is at least as, if not more, important than the former one. Relative to the OTS we have concluded that their adoption of a specialized compliance program resulted in a much stricter enforcement of CRA defined in terms of a greater percentage of below-average ratings and a lower percentage of above-average ones. This finding supports the use of specialized compliance examiners.

On the other side of the grading scale we concluded that the FED is the "easiest" CRA grader based on the highest percentage of above-average ratings and the second-lowest percentage of below-average ones as of year-end 1992. Two merger approvals by the FED in 1992, which are discussed in a case study in Chapter 9, provide further support to this conclusion.

The sixth major conclusion of this analysis is that smaller banks generally receive the greatest percentage of below-average ratings. However, when the proportion of below-average ratings is related to the size distribution of banks, it becomes clear that small banks receive most of the poor ratings because most banks are small banks. Holding constant the size factor, there appears to be evidence to support the view that small banks generally have lower CRA scores than large banks. This is because small banks of $100 million or less in size receive a disproportionately low share of above-average ratings. The analysis over the 1982–88 period suggests that very small banks of under $25 million are primarily responsible for this conclusion.

Our analysis of the 100 largest banks and 50 largest thrifts has concluded that there are significant differences among them in terms of the ratings. Thus, the hypothesis that size alone determines CRA ratings cannot be accepted. This latter view that the resources of a big bank can enable it to document an outstanding CRA rating is not supported by our analysis. In fact, we have identified many banks in the same holding company that have received significantly different ratings, ranging from outstanding to substantial noncompliance in one case (Chemical Banking Corporation of New York). Since all of these banks in the same holding company have access to the same resources, there shouldn't be any difference in their ratings if one subscribed to the view that size alone determines CRA ratings. Otherwise, the 100 largest banks and 50 largest thrifts would all be dominated by outstanding ratings, which is far from the conclusion reached in this analysis.

4. THE HIGHEST CRA RATINGS—PROFILES OF OUTSTANDING BANKS

INTRODUCTION

This chapter summarizes our analysis of the CRA evaluations of the highest rated banks in America—those with outstanding CRA ratings. Chapters 6 and 8 present comparable analyses for those banks receiving needs improvement and substantial noncompliance ratings, respectively.

The highest CRA rated banks must have an outstanding record of, and be a leader in, ascertaining and helping to meet the credit needs of its entire delineated community, including low- and moderate-income neighborhoods, in a manner consistent with its resources and capabilities. As noted in Chapter 3, only 8.7% of all banks with public CRA ratings over the July 1, 1990—December 31, 1991, period received outstanding ratings. This proportion increased to 10.3% by year-end 1992.

This chapter contains the results of our detailed analysis of a stratified sample of outstanding evaluations. A total of 83 outstanding evaluations were selected to represent a cross section of banks and thrifts nationwide. The name and location of the banks in this sample are noted throughout this chapter.

These evaluations represent 17% of the 489 outstanding evaluations that were publicly released by federal bank regulators as of December 31, 1991. As pointed out in Chapter 3, a larger number (587) of outstanding evaluations were made as of that date, but not all were publicly available.

This sample of evaluations was designed to include most of the largest banks and thrifts that were evaluated plus a stratified random sampling of smaller ones. The sample contains banks and thrifts examined by all four federal regulators as well as by each of their different regions where possible. Thus, we believe the sample is representative of the universe of all banks receiving outstanding ratings as of December 31, 1991.

The analysis presented here is in the form of a profile of outstanding banks categorized by each of the performance categories and assessment factors. This same approach is followed in Chapters 6 and 8 on banks with needs improvement and substantial noncompliance ratings, respectively.

There are five performance categories, identified as I–V, in the official CRA evaluation system. Although twelve assessment factors, identified as A–K, are part of this same system, there is a thirteenth assessment factor which pertains to the reasonableness of the delineated CRA local community. This thirteenth, or nonlettered, assessment factor is usually, but not always, covered as a separate item in performance category III, which involves geographic distribution and offices.

Therefore, this profile will be based on all thirteen assessment factors broken down into the five performance categories. This profile lists these five performance categories in order, but the assessment factors within them are not alphabetical. As can be seen from Appendix 5, the CRA evaluation format lists assessment factors A and C under performance category I, but performance category II follows with assessment factors B, I, and J. This seemingly confusing official CRA format is followed in this profile.

The CRA profiles found in Appendix 6 and summarized in Appendix 7 are quite useful as general profiles for each of the individual assessment factors. This analysis will not repeat those general profiles, but focus on specific items and actual examples. The profile that follows should be reviewed in conjunction with the actual performance evaluations whenever possible.

I. ASCERTAINMENT OF COMMUNITY CREDIT NEEDS

Activities to Ascertain Community Credit Needs (Assessment Factor A)

Ascertainment of needs by definition implies some type of research. Outstanding banks for the most part conduct different types of surveys and are involved in multiple and ongoing contacts with community members.

An outstanding rating generally means more than just ascertaining credit needs. It also means developing conclusions about them, recommendations to best meet identified credit needs, and then implementing those recommendations. In other words, the ascertainment of credit needs without any follow-up action is generally not enough for an outstanding bank.

Outstanding banks usually use multiple methods of ascertaining credit needs and then develop new products or modify existing ones to meet these needs. This is not unlike the basic marketing concept which stresses the identification of needs and then the satisfaction of them in a way that meets corporate objectives.

Many Examiners May Prefer In-House Efforts over Outside CRA Vendors

Many outstanding banks conduct all of their ascertainment activities in-house, although an increasing number are relying on outside consultants. It has been our experience that many CRA examiners may prefer in-house efforts where possible. This may be the case because bank personnel can better develop their CRA expertise and at the same time use their background in credit product formation and modification. On the other hand, specialized consultants in this field bring to the table considerable survey research experience and different and innovative methods of credit needs ascertainment.

The First National Bank of Chicago commissioned a national market research firm to conduct an independent study of the credit needs of low- and moderate-income areas in late 1989. Bank Independent in Alabama hired a professional consulting firm to determine whether any unmet credit needs existed in its community. Society National Bank of Cleveland contracted for studies of specific market areas by outside consultants.

Valley Bank of Las Vegas, Nevada, contracted the services of an outside marketing consultant to develop new strategies in ascertaining community credit needs and marketing its products. First Gibraltar Bank of Irving, Texas, entered into an arrangement whereby a consultant contacted housing authorities and nonprofit groups and arranged for meetings with bank representatives.

California Banks Survey Branch Managers and Customers

By far the most common activity of outstanding banks under this assessment factor is the use of surveys to ascertain community credit needs. Many outstanding banks have conducted multiple surveys over different time periods depending upon the particular issues to be addressed.

Surveys can be conducted internal or external to the bank. Internal bank surveys, which are used by a few very large banks, may involve questionnaires directed separately at branch managers, tellers, and other customer contact personnel to determine their perceptions of community credit needs. Because these bank personnel are on the front line dealing with customers daily, the idea is that these employees have a very good understanding of credit needs, especially those that may not be met by the bank. Bank of America of San Francisco, California, surveys its branch managers annually to see how well credit products are meeting identified needs.

Most surveys are external to the bank and can involve multiple groups, such as customers, non-customers, community groups, government leaders, businesses, or representatives of different organizations or groups. Outstanding banks generally conduct broad-based samples representative of the entire community, rather than just a subset, which may not be representative of it. Virtually every marketing research survey technique has been used by outstanding banks in their ascertainment efforts, including surveys by mail, telephone, in-branch questionnaires, focus groups, and so on.

Focus Groups in Spanish and Chinese

Some banks conduct multiple surveys regularly. Great Western Bank conducted three separate ascertainment surveys in 1990, including a written questionnaire to groups or housing organizations; 1,000 telephone interviews with registered voters; and interviews with public and private sector officials.

There are many different examples of alternative credit needs survey assessment techniques employed by outstanding banks. For example, Home Savings of America, the nation's largest thrift, conducted focus group discussions with Hispanic and Chinese customers in their native tongue to better understand their financial needs. Citibank (New York State) of Pittsford, New York, maintains a 24-hour customer telephone line, which is used to gather information for product development and market planning.

No Response from "Piggybacked" Community Lender Survey

Fifth Third Bank of Miami Valley in Ohio uses a postage-paid questionnaire to obtain customer feedback on bank products, employee product knowledge, and convenience factors, among other things. Valley Bank of Nevada includes a questionnaire with its CRA statement, which is available in the brochure display rack at the bank's branches.

Mail-back surveys "piggybacked" onto annual statements or reports usually have lower response rates than stand-alone surveys. Great Western Bank's revised 1991 CRA statement included a community leader survey form, but it had not received any responses as of the date of its CRA examination.

"Tell the President" in Michigan

Many banks provide the opportunity for "point of purchase" immediate feedback by customers. While these efforts do not ascertain credit or other needs of noncustomers, they are useful as a source of relatively inexpensive information. Boatmen's National Bank of St. Louis maintains suggestion boxes at each location to gather data on community needs.

First National Bank of Omaha provides a *First Impressions* survey brochure in all banking offices to allow immediate customer feedback regarding customer service received. First of America Bank in Marquette, Michigan, has a *Tell the President* pamphlet available in all banking lobbies to solicit customer input on the need for additional services. Comerica Bank in Detroit solicits comments from customers through a "Your Opinion Counts" questionnaire form available at all bank facilities.

Magnolia Federal Bank of Hattiesburg, Mississippi, advertises in newspapers of wide circulation throughout the state to solicit comments from the general public concerning credit needs or other subjects relating to CRA. Cattle National Bank of Seward, Nebraska, sent out letters to 21 community groups for help in determining community credit needs. After receiving no response, the bank scheduled follow-up meetings with those groups.

Saving through Shared Surveys

As is clear from the above examples, there are many low-budget and cost-effective ways of ascertaining credit needs. The banks that "outsource" the entire credit needs ascertainment function are the exception rather than the rule. There are, however, alternatives for those banks wishing to economize in using outside survey research and other CRA compliance efforts by sharing these expenses with other banks.

A credit needs ascertainment survey in a given market would have the same general survey objectives for most banks. If an individual bank wants to "piggyback" specific questions about certain products, market share, and the like, then the survey could become more customized. However, a broad-based community credit needs ascertainment survey reflective of the entire community could easily be shared by different banks. In fact, we recommend the sharing of many CRA types of expenses for banks wishing to enhance their performance within certain cost constraints.

CRA Clearinghouse Association in Indiana

City National Bank of Fort Smith, Arkansas, formed a bankers community outreach organization with two other banks in the city and developed a three-page financial needs questionnaire with them. Citizens National Bank of Evansville, Indiana, joined with three other commercial banks in the city to form a clearinghouse association to meet with neighborhood groups. That association sent out a survey to neighborhood groups to ascertain financial services desired by them. Founders Bank and Trust Company of Oklahoma City joined with other local banks in the sharing of information and resources as part of its overall CRA program.

It would appear that the sharing of expenses for broad-based community credit needs ascertainment surveys could also be accomplished through bank trade associations or other groups. If this is not the case, then those banks which are truly outstanding will take a leadership role in using the sharing concept for this purpose. Most marketing research surveys are of a proprietary nature, but this is one exception that makes good sense and provides the basis for communications with other banks on methods of improving CRA performance.

Cleveland Bank Met with One-Half to Two-Thirds of Community Groups

Ongoing, meaningful, and productive contacts with individuals and groups in the community are typical of most outstanding banks. An important starting point is usually the preparation of a list of all relevant community contacts. This is usually done in-house, but as the example from Texas above showed, this activity can also be outsourced.

Citibank, F.S.B. of Oakland, California, has bank affiliates in California, Illinois, and the District of Columbia. The bank in the latter region was primarily responsible for publishing the *Washington Area Bankers Association Resource Guide* designed to inform both local organizations and financial institutions of community investment opportunities.

First American Bank & Trust of Louisiana maintains a community contact list to be used as a reference tool for management. The Bank of Perryville in Missouri maintains a CRA contact list, and five of the seven members of that bank's CRA committee personally contact one person from the list each quarter. Those persons on the contact list not visited during the year receive a mail questionnaire. Sunwest Bank of Roswell in New Mexico maintains and updates annually a list of community contacts.

Outstanding banks maintain ongoing contacts with community groups. For example, Society National Bank of Cleveland has a community relations staff which has met with one-half to two-thirds of the community groups in Cleveland. Some outstanding banks take leadership roles in helping to establish community groups. Some outstanding banks form community development corporations, such as Western State Bank of St. Paul, Minnesota.

"Lunch with the President" in Denver

Outstanding banks may use different methods of reaching out to community leaders. The Illinois division of Citibank, F.S.B. sponsors a bimonthly luncheon to which community leaders are invited and offered the opportunity to share information with senior bank management. Lakeside National Bank of Denver, Colorado, has developed a "Lunch with the President" program where a group of current customers who reside in low- and moderate-income neighborhoods are randomly selected by zip code. This quarterly luncheon meeting is used to help ascertain the credit needs of those residents.

Some outstanding banks carry their relationship with community groups to a higher level by developing formal partnership agreements with them. Delaware Trust Company of Wilmington entered into a five-year partnership agreement with a local community group, whereby the bank provides special programs to residents of 30 economically depressed census tracts. The First National Bank of Chicago formed partnerships with community leaders in two low- and moderate-income neighborhoods. Fleet National Bank of Providence, Rhode Island, maintains written agreements and frequent contacts with two community organizations. Some outstanding banks have had success in working closely with local churches to not only ascertain community credit needs but also as a source of referrals for credit-worthy low- and moderate-income borrowers. Such a borrower personally referred to a bank by a local pastor or priest may feel a greater moral responsibility to keep the loan current so similar borrowers in the congregation or parish can likewise benefit. These banks will usually also make donations to the local church.

Hosting a Seminar in Arkansas Where No One Shows Up Except Bank Employees

Many community groups use seminars as a means of ascertaining community credit needs as well as educating community members on different aspects of credit. Chittenden Trust Company of Burlington, Vermont, hosts community input sessions in each of its designated major trade areas to identify any unmet sound lending opportunities. That bank also provided "seed" money and deposits to a local development credit union which provides services to low- and moderate-income neighborhoods.

Pacific First Bank in Seattle conducts monthly home buyer seminars in Spanish at its offices in Nevada. Firstier Bank of Lincoln, Nebraska, partici-pated in a panel discussion with representatives from neighborhood associations who were invited by let-ters from the bank to attend the meeting on neigh-borhood credit needs.

Even the best laid plans for seminars at outstand-ing banks can go astray if there is little or no attend-ance. City National Bank of Fort Smith, Arkansas, scheduled an educational seminar on basic banking services at a local community center. Despite ad-vertisements in the local newspaper and a local free shoppers guide, poster advertisements at local busi-nesses, and a letter of invitation to all area churches, no one attended the seminar except for bank officers. The seminar was rescheduled.

Deposit-Secured Lending in Denver to Reestablish Credit Histories

Several outstanding banks provide loan counsel-ing services. Although these do not represent credit extensions, these activities are quite important to first-time or infrequent credit users who are un-familiar with the loan process. American Savings Bank in Stockton, California, operates two loan coun-seling centers in low-income communities in Los Angeles. That bank has been able to develop loan products with special features to assist these residents as a result of the centers. Lakeside National Bank of Denver has a loan program in which it counsels individuals with poor credit histories. The bank then extends credit to such individuals at prime interest rates with a certificate of deposit as security to allow them to reestablish their credit histories.

"Street Bankers" in Indianapolis and New York

An important part of many outstanding CRA ef-forts is officer call programs exclusively or primarily for CRA purposes. While most banks conduct some type of officer call program for commercial lending or other purposes, a CRA calling program has specific objectives, such as ascertaining credit needs and meeting them in traditional or nontraditional ways.

Comerica Bank of Detroit has an extensive five-part calling program to help ascertain credit needs. This program involves branch managers, personal bankers, business lenders, real estate contacts, and community relations contacts. The calling program is well documented with various reports. RCB Bank of Claremore, Oklahoma, utilizes an officer call program where officers make at least four calls per month to area individuals in the workplace, and these calls are the subject of a follow-up weekly meeting at the bank.

A form of an officer call activity is a "street banker" program used by at least two outstanding banks. INB National Bank of Indianapolis has employed such a program since 1981 which is in regular communica-tion with over 150 different types of community, government, and business groups. The street banker program at Chemical Bank involves three bankers who ascertain the needs of low- and moderate-in-come areas within specific territories. These street bankers keep local community organizations in-formed about various developments and programs.

Outstanding banks with unique markets adjust their ascertainment efforts accordingly. For example, the Denali State Bank of Fairbanks, Alaska, works closely with the local military in addressing projected housing needs of personnel stationed in that area.

Expensive versus Economical Approaches to Reporting to the Community

Many outstanding banks develop unique methods of regularly communicating with community members. Comerica Bank of Detroit publishes *Comerica Partnerships,* a quarterly publication distributed to community groups, the bank's branches, and employees. That bank also uses an internal publication *Communique* to advise its employees on a monthly basis of relevant CRA information. These efforts certainly can be expensive and are therefore usually only found at larger banks.

A more economical method of informing the community of a bank's CRA activities involves the use of a "report to the community" done on an annual or more frequent basis similar to a shareholder report. These are often prepared as separate documents to include the CRA statement, almost always of an expanded variety, and other relevant CRA information. The most economical approach to a community report is to incorporate it into an expanded and annually updated CRA statement.

Bank One, Appleton in Wisconsin prepares an annual "report to the community" informing the public of its CRA efforts during the past year. First Wisconsin National Bank of Milwaukee prepares an annual *Community Involvement Report* which details specific efforts it makes within low- and moderate-income neighborhoods as well as describing specific credit and deposit products offered within them. Pacific First Bank of Seattle regularly distributes press releases and corporate brochures on the bank's CRA activities to the media and local housing groups.

Examiners Look for Results, Meaning New or Modified Credit Products

Outstanding banks regularly collect and analyze local demographic data, especially those pertaining to lending activities. Census data and considerable information on local communities is generally available at little or no charge. Many banks, however, prefer to purchase these data from outside vendors who have unique data formats to analyze CRA data. Espe-cially valuable are those data which are displayed graphically or on local maps.

The board of directors and senior management at outstanding banks are actively and regularly involved with these and other types of CRA ascertainment efforts. They take a hands-on approach to CRA matters and address them on a systematic and regular basis. Several specifics in this regard will be discussed in the following assessment factor.

The most outstanding banks under this assessment factor are able to document one or more specific new or modified credit products that were a direct result of credit ascertainment activities. An impressive ascertainment effort (e.g., a comprehensive survey) with little or no results is not as desirable as a less sophisticated ascertainment effort resulting in specific new or modified credit programs.

CRA Survival Rule #1: "If It Wasn't Documented, It Wasn't Done"

Many times credit needs of the local community are fairly obvious, but it is important that a bank document its ascertainment efforts and the results of them. Territorial Savings of Honolulu learned from its call program with local housing authorities and community groups that affordable housing was the primary credit need in its delineated area. It proceeded to develop special loan programs responsive to the needs of its community, including low- and moderate-income neighborhoods.

Documentation is important under almost all assessment factors, but perhaps most in the area of ascertainment of credit needs. Outstanding banks generally have comprehensive and systematic documentation procedures that are automatically built into day-to-day operations rather than being disruptive of them in any way. National Westminster Bank of New York City maintains a very extensive, thorough, and centralized CRA document filing system.

Even outstanding banks are criticized if their credit needs assessment efforts aren't translated into conclusions and ultimately implemented (i.e., into new and/or modified credit products). For example, Fleet Bank of Maine was cited for an outstanding record of determining community credit needs, but was criticized for not documenting its conclusions about them. Rather, the examiners themselves briefly reviewed completed surveys and reached their own conclusions regarding the need for certain types of affordable housing financing in certain regions of the state.

Many banks utilize their own documentation systems, while others rely on outside software to help their documentation efforts. Regardless of the approach taken, outstanding banks always keep CRA Survival Rule Number 1 in mind, namely "If it wasn't documented, it wasn't done."

Board of Directors' Participation (Assessment Factor C)

CRA is an integral part of the corporate structure and style of outstanding banks. Board members and senior management are regularly and personally involved in community activities in such banks.

CRA Complexity at Chemical and Comerica

Most large banks have compliance departments and full-time compliance and CRA officers. An increasing number of small banks have full-time compliance people, even those banks that are part of large bank holding companies. For example, Boatmen's National Bank of Belleville, Illinois, hired a full-time Compliance Coordinator who, among other duties, coordinates bank-wide CRA efforts.

Some very large outstanding banks have extensive and seemingly complex CRA organizational structures. For example, Chemical Bank's CRA Coordinating Committee meets quarterly and includes representatives from all the consumer-related departments of the bank as well as the Corporate Social Responsibility Group, Chemical Community Development, Inc., the Community Policy Lending Unit, the Governmental Affairs department, and CRA administration. Chemical also has an Examining Committee responsible for reviewing the regulatory changes affecting CRA, while its Public Policy Committee reviews the bank's ascertainment and community development programs.

Comerica Bank of Detroit adopted a CRA Information Interlock System with five basic levels of communication: Business Units which meet monthly; the CRA Committee which meets monthly and develops the quarterly *CRA Status Report;* the Management Policy Committee which reviews that report quarterly; the Public Responsibility Committee of the board which meets quarterly to discuss CRA; and the board, which receives a quarterly report from that committee regarding the bank's CRA performance. The corporate lines of administration for CRA compliance at that bank begin with the Regional CRA Committee, extend to the Corporate CRA Officer, then to the Executive-in-Charge (the bank's President), through the Public Responsibility Committee, and ultimately to the board of directors.

Pittsburgh National Bank has four community reinvestment committees and boards: advisory boards of directors made up of local businesspeople who meet quarterly in ten business markets; a CRA Policy Committee, which meets semiannually and consists of five bank directors; a CRA Oversight Committee, which meets quarterly and is represented by senior bank managers; and a CDC Committee, which meets quarterly and is involved in community development activities.

Weekly CRA Meetings

Outstanding banks provide many examples of regular reviews of CRA activities and performance by board members and senior management. CRA requires an annual review of certain CRA statement basics, but outstanding banks generally meet quarterly and more often monthly. Some even have committee structures which meet on a weekly basis.

Valley Bank of Nevada has a CRA Committee that meets monthly by itself and also with the bank's Executive Committee. The relatively small Bank of Perryville in Missouri has a CRA Officer and a CRA Committee, which meets quarterly to review the twelve assessment factors and prepare a formal report to the board. Great Western Bank's CRA Committee, officially recognized as an operating committee of the board, meets on a quarterly basis. This is in addition to that bank's Compliance Officers Committee of senior staff members, which meets semiannually. The Northeast Division of Citibank of New York City has an Executive Committee that meets weekly to discuss marketing efforts, special lending programs, and other CRA-related items.

Annual CRA Board Review Not Enough for Outstanding Banks

Surprisingly, some banks with outstanding ratings had a less than outstanding performance in terms of board CRA participation. Board policy oversight and review of CRA activities has been "infrequent" at the Denali State Bank in Alaska. None of the directors of Heartland Federal in Ponca City, Oklahoma, reside there, and participation by the board in ascertaining community credit needs was described as "limited."

Examiners recommended that the board of Eastern Bank in Lynn, Massachusetts increase its efforts in fulfilling its CRA obligations, including methods of self-assessment. Board minutes at the Worcester County Institution for Savings in Worcester, Massachusetts, did not disclose any discussion of CRA other than the required annual approval. Examiners suggested that the bank's CRA Committee, comprised of four bank directors, increase the frequency of its annual meetings to increase its CRA participation.

CRA Manuals at Every Branch at NatWest

The most outstanding CRA banks have formal written CRA programs, which include self-assessment procedures. National Westminster Bank of New York City maintains written policies and plans for meeting stated CRA goals and objectives. Furthermore, that bank provides a CRA manual to each branch to provide uniform standards under which appropriate personnel must operate. While the relatively small Cattle National Bank of Seward, Nebraska, demonstrated a proactive attitude toward community reinvestment according to the examiners, it did not have a formal CRA program with written goals, objectives, and review procedures.

Citibank of New York City discusses the results of its self-assessment in its expanded CRA statement. Citibank (New York State) of Pittsford, New York, conducts an annual self-assessment with semiannual updates. Their self-assessment mirrors the assessment factors, with programs that the bank has in place and those that need to be developed. The self-assessment is reviewed by that bank's board.

Expanded CRA Statements— No Excuses Here

Most outstanding banks have developed expanded CRA statements in accordance with recommended regulatory guidelines. There is really no excuse for any bank, especially outstanding ones, to be without an expanded CRA statement, considering the relatively nominal cost that is involved. Still though, there are even some outstanding banks (such as Denali State Bank of Alaska) that have not adopted an expanded CRA statement.

Some banks with expanded CRA statements may be criticized for their content. The expanded statement of Boatmen's First National Bank of Kansas City, Missouri, did not address the results of any self-assessment activity or summarize the bank's method of documenting CRA efforts. The examiners criticized that same bank's written CRA program as lacking a formal plan for conducting self-assessments. Lakeside National Bank of Denver was criticized because the material in its expanded CRA statement did not fully describe the results of the bank's self-assessment efforts.

Many of the banks with annual reports to their community on CRA activities, which are in effect expanded CRA statements, include the results of self-assessment activities. Bank One, Akron prepares an expanded CRA statement and issues a *Report to the Community* of its CRA activities on an annual basis. These annual reports are also useful for compliance with the previous assessment factor.

Outside Directors in Hawaii Hand Out Loan Brochures to Employees and Others

Board members of outstanding banks, including outside members, are thoroughly aware of the bank's CRA responsibilities. The CRA examiners at one very large outstanding bank reportedly visited some of their outside directors at their place of employment to discuss CRA. Such an action should not bother truly outstanding banks, as their directors are fully informed of the bank's CRA responsibilities.

Board members at really outstanding banks are personally involved in community activities, often in a leadership role. Several outside directors of Territorial Savings in Hawaii have taken brochures on their

"E-Z Qualify" loans to employees, associates, and others in the community who may not qualify for other types of mortgages.

President of First National Bank of Chicago is the CRA Officer

The First National Bank of Chicago has a Corporate and Community Affairs Department that manages the bank's CRA program on a day-to-day basis. However, that bank's president is the CRA Officer which the examiners noted "facilitates active oversight and input from the highest levels of the bank." The CRA Oversight Committee at the Dominion Bank of Middle Tennessee consists of nine senior managers, including the President, Vice Chairman of the board, and the bank's Compliance Officer.

All bank directors are involved in some type of community organization whether it be charitable, religious, or business. Outstanding banks are careful to document all of these activities. First Wisconsin National Bank of Milwaukee conducts an annual survey of board members to document involvement in community organizations and activities. That survey also asks directors to comment on the bank's CRA performance and requests suggestions for improvement.

Florida Bank Board Makes Annual Tour of "Low-Mod" Areas

The extent of board involvement at some outstanding banks is unique. The board of SunBank in Naples, Florida, which was commended for making CRA an integral part of the bank's daily operations, takes an annual tour of low- and moderate-income ("low-mod") census tracts to "increase their sensitivity to the areas." Representatives of Northern Trust Bank/O'Hare in Chicago conducted a "drive-by assessment" of the low- to moderate-income areas of its community during 1990.

Fair Lending Reviews at Citibank and Boatmen's

An increasing number of outstanding banks have developed procedures for the reevaluation of denied loans in low- to moderate-income neighborhoods. Citibank's Economic Development Banking Center, which specializes in community reinvestment financ-ing in low- to moderate-income areas, re-reviews individual loans initially denied by other lending departments.

Boatmen's First National Bank of Kansas City, Missouri, has a semiannual fair lending review process by bank personnel who do not make loans. The reviews determine whether bank staff treat potential consumer borrowers fairly and in a nondiscriminatory manner with respect to the bank's lending guidelines.

The Greater New York Savings Bank, also with an outstanding rating, was criticized for the "lack of a board inspired analysis." Such an analysis should study whether or not potential borrowers are treated in a fair and nondiscriminatory manner by reviewing loan application data, according to the examiners.

Videotaping the Chairman in California

Outstanding banks have board members who actively support CRA training. The minimal training found at most outstanding banks includes the distribution of basic CRA educational material plus the required viewing of one of several available videotapes by bank personnel. Great Western Bank of Beverly Hills took this approach a step beyond by producing its own videotape where the bank's chairman stressed to all staff the importance of CRA and the institution's commitment to it.

The most outstanding banks provide a basic level of CRA training to all personnel with customer contact, not just those directly involved in CRA. That is, any employee asked a question about CRA, whether over the phone or in person, should at least know what "CRA" stands for other than providing a puzzling response where someone else has to be asked.

It is so easy for an examiner, or anyone for that matter, to call a bank to ask about its CRA statement or public performance evaluation. The response can be graded in terms of the time elapsed and the number of people spoken to before you find someone who really knows what CRA is and is able to intelligently respond to your question. Of course, all outside board members should know the basics of CRA, especially if they are "caught off guard" by being interviewed outside the bank.

In-House CRA Educational Seminars and More Videotaping in California

Many outstanding banks use different types of internal seminars, which may be conducted by in-house or outside parties. Seminars are often held at different levels to reflect the audience make-up such as those for board members, senior management, and branch managers and personnel.

Great Western Bank conducts quarterly training sessions for its retail banking staff. Home Savings of America holds Fair Lending Community Reinvestment Seminars for all lending personnel nationwide. These seminars were designed to reeducate staff on compliance issues and to reinforce the association's commitment to equal housing, fair lending, and community reinvestment. Those seminars likewise featured videotaped introductory remarks from the chairman of the association.

CRA Training by Computer in New York and Texas

Citibank of New York City has a computer-based self-tutorial on CRA which all branch staff are required to take and pass. Citibank also requires all appropriate employees to attend CRA presentations and seminars. The Bank of Commerce of Auburn, California mandates that every member of the board, management team, and staff (even including janitors) receive CRA training and pass a bank test on the subject.

Texas Commerce Bank of El Paso has also implemented a comprehensive computer-based CRA training program. There are various computer software available on the market designed to assist banks in their CRA training efforts.

"Testers" in Chicago and Incentives in California

A few outstanding banks have developed "tester" programs to evaluate the effectiveness of their CRA training. We expect to see many more banks using internal or external testing programs, especially with increased use of government testers to detect loan bias. First National Bank of Chicago has tested for disparate treatment of applicants using minority individuals posing as applicants. Additionally, the internal audit function at that bank tests for discrimination.

Some outstanding banks have developed branch incentive programs to reward employees for outstanding CRA efforts. Bank of America has a branch incentive program for branch officers for meeting retail credit product goals. Some of the branch managers' goals include sourcing home mortgages in low-income census tracts and making CRA credit needs assessment and marketing calls.

Examiners Praise Innovative Underwriting Criteria and Loan Products

The most outstanding CRA programs are those that result in new or modified loan products to better meet the community's credit needs. Board members at outstanding banks consistently support prudent but innovative underwriting criteria in this regard.

For example, The Bank of Commerce in Auburn, California, developed innovative underwriting criteria for starter home rehabilitation by young, lower-income individuals. These individuals, who might not otherwise qualify for a loan, sometimes have property which does not fit conforming collateral standards.

The First National Bank of Chicago developed an unsecured line of credit product for applicants who have difficulty in obtaining credit due to lack of credit history. Also, that bank's first-time home buyers program relaxes debt service/income ratios and considers untraditional income sources to develop a credit history for an applicant.

As would be expected, outstanding banks clearly document their board CRA participation. The examiners at Citibank of New York City noted that its efforts were well documented through internal memoranda on civic activities, policy and procedure manuals (including training and branch closing manuals), results of studies and surveys, special marketing plans, geographic analyses of mortgages, and other retail lending products as well as the CRA public file.

II. Marketing and Types of Credit Offered and Extended

Marketing Programs for Credit Awareness (Assessment Factor B)

Outstanding banks generally have outstanding marketing programs in which advertising is just one element. Most examiners use the terms *marketing* and *advertising* interchangeably. Actually, advertising is but one type of promotional strategy in a bank's overall "marketing mix."

Marketing Plans at the Bank and *Branch Levels*

Most marketing-minded banks have marketing plans that are approved, reviewed, and monitored by the board and senior management. Many outstanding banks have specific CRA marketing plans, and some also have branch-oriented plans.

The First National Bank of Chicago has a CRA marketing plan which describes the bank's various marketing efforts, including mass media advertising, direct mailings, mortgage representatives, special presentations, and a touring "Bankmobile" (see discussion below). National Westminster Bank of New York City develops an annual CRA advertising plan prepared by the bank's marketing division.

Bank of America utilizes a branch marketing call program, whereby branch managers regularly call on local civic officials, business organizations, and community groups to market special credit products and banking services. Each branch at the First Interstate Bank of California may develop its own advertisements to appeal to their specific local clientele.

An effective marketing plan will include input from other departments of the bank, including compliance and lending. The Bank of Perryville in Missouri was commended for the coordination between its marketing and loan departments. For example, the bank advertises IRAs from January through April, credit cards just before summer and the Christmas season, and agricultural loans in the early spring and fall seasons. While other banks may follow such a credit advertising schedule, the documentation of it may be lacking.

First National Bank of Chicago's "Bankmobile"

Beyond the traditional print, radio, and TV media used by banks to inform all segments of the community about their services offered, outstanding banks often utilize nontraditional and innovative media. The "Bankmobile" of First National Bank of Chicago, noted above, was introduced in 1990. It is an innovative delivery system used to reach areas where the bank does not have a branch. The Bankmobile staff distributes pamphlets on the bank's products and assists people in understanding the bank's services. Low- and moderate-income areas have been specifically targeted for the Bankmobile.

World Savings and Loan Association of California uses a "Telefinancing Program" that enables prospective borrowers to apply for credit over the telephone. That program, which includes bilingual representatives, allows personnel to provide special assistance with loan applications.

First City, Texas in Houston opened a toll-free phone line to take consumer loan applications. Several banks have toll-free 800 numbers for general information, as well as specifics about different types of loans. Officer call programs, which are also used to ascertain community credit needs, represent a unique one-on-one opportunity to market credit products.

All Types of Loan Seminars Offered by Outstanding Banks

One of the most popular methods used by outstanding banks to inform all segments of their credit services is the use of general or specialized seminars. These are sometimes offered to specific groups (e.g., classes at school) but more generally are open to the public.

In addition to making presentations to senior citizens groups and classes at the local high school, Kansas State Bank of Ottawa, Kansas, sponsored free informational seminars on small business loans in one case and estate planning in another. Columbia National Bank of Chicago has not only been active in credit counseling but also provides seminars on student loans and home equity loans.

City National Bank of Fort Smith, Arkansas, holds several seminars for area high schools and others on basic banking services and how to apply for credit. That bank also cosponsors five different seminars with the continuing education department of a local community college. Delaware Trust Company, which conducts several types of presentations and sponsors different events, developed a program titled "CRA and Its Impact on Housing."

First Wisconsin National Bank of Fond Du Lac conducts public seminars on assistance to first-time home buyers and student loan applicants. First-time home buyer seminars are especially useful when a bank provides "how-to" material with actual examples.

Discount Coupons for Closing Costs in Massachusetts

Eastern Savings Bank of Lynn, Massachusetts, frequently offers first-time home buyers seminars, which include a ten-booth process that takes a consumer through a mortgage financing transaction on a step-by-step basis. That ten-step program is also available on a computer program to offer more privacy. Attendees at these seminars receive a coupon for a discount on closing costs if they use Eastern Savings Bank for their mortgage. This incentive to complete the program benefits both the consumer, who has become more educated on the credit process, and the bank if they receive the business. Thus, such an innovative approach may satisfy both CRA and corporate business objectives.

Some banks use exhibits at home builder shows or housing fairs to market their credit products. First of America Bank in Michigan's Upper Peninsula disseminates information on its credit and other services at home and builders shows. Besides using seminars to promote its consumer credit products, Boatmen's First National Bank of Kansas City promotes its lending services at major local trade fairs like the annual "Homes Show."

Getting the Word Out in Hawaii Despite a Ban on Billboard Advertising

Direct mail is a useful promotional technique, but it should be directed at all segments of the community, rather than just the existing customer base. The First National Bank of Chicago expanded the use of direct mailing to noncustomers with the marketing of a pre-approved line of credit. The mailing was targeted at two low- to moderate-income areas which the bank had identified as having a significant volume of rejected applications. Although no results of the campaign were available, the response rate was reportedly high.

First City, Texas in Houston conducts a statewide student loan program. Loans are generated through a direct mail solicitation to the parents of every graduating high school student in Texas.

Restrictions on certain types of advertising may affect the bank's choice of marketing media. For example, billboard advertising is prohibited in Hawaii. Territorial Savings therefore uses traditional print media and promotional techniques such as distributing brochures to community groups and others. SunBank of Naples, Florida, developed the "story board" which is on display at a local apartment complex to educate its residents about credit.

Benefiting from Free Publicity

Many outstanding banks disseminate information about their services through the use of free publicity. Western State Bank of St. Paul, Minnesota, occasionally receives publicity from news reports praising the bank for its community reinvestment efforts and awards. The willingness of First Gibraltar Bank of Texas to be involved in innovative housing programs has resulted in much media attention and focus on it. Firstier Bank of Lincoln, Nebraska, sponsors a biweekly "Money Sense" column, which discusses credit related products in a local newspaper. The bank also prints brochures on its CRA lending programs and mails a newsletter addressing farm credit related issues to small farms.

Some outstanding banks obtain publicity on their community reinvestment efforts by sending out material to various parties. Boatmen's National Bank of St. Louis publishes a report detailing the successes of its community reinvestment program. Bank management sent the report to various community groups; local, state, and national political leaders; all employees; and the local press.

Trilingual ATMs—English, Spanish or Chinese

While almost all banks use some type of advertising, outstanding banks use special advertising media aimed at particular segments of the community. Of particular interest is the extent to which a continuing and meaningful outreach is made to low- and moderate-income areas and residents.

Banks with non-English-speaking customers in their community often use bilingual or even a trilingual staff. Many of these same banks print brochures and even the CRA statement in the relevant language. Some even have ATMs designed for use by non-English-speaking residents. All of Citibank's 53 ATMs in the New York City area are trilingual, permitting customers to do their business in English, Spanish, or Chinese. Such ATMs also exist in California. Minority banks in ethnic areas, however, must be careful not to market so exclusively to one group that they give the perception of excluding other members (especially other minorities) of its community.

Wells Fargo Bank uses a special Hispanic marketing program consisting of Spanish marketing brochures and advertisements in bilingual newspapers and other minority publications. Home Savings of America advertises in more than sixty minority-owned publications and radio stations in nine markets. Minority borrowers are featured in television advertising, and minority-owned agencies are used to develop advertising for the Hispanic and Chinese communities. Home Savings also conducted research studies in Spanish and various Chinese dialects to better formulate marketing strategies for those communities. Home Savings also offers ATM screens in Spanish and is developing them in Chinese.

Using Minority Ad Agencies, Actors, and Media

Great Western Bank has retained minority-owned agencies to develop advertising for the Spanish-speaking community. In addition, several brochures have been translated into Spanish and Chinese. That bank advertises in major circulation newspapers as well as smaller ones aimed at minorities.

INB National Bank in Indianapolis uses minority actors in its advertisements. These ads are placed with minority print, radio, and television media. That bank also holds meetings at all branches in low- and moderate-income neighborhoods to discuss the bank's products and services and provide an opportunity for community residents to express their views.

Comerica Bank in Detroit uses several hundred radio ads promoting revolving credit and home equity loans with stations targeting minority interests. That bank also distributes a brochure which advertises its residential loan products in Spanish.

Bus Ads in Tennessee and "Door Hangers" in Denver

Dominion Bank of Middle Tennessee advertises for basic checking on buses that route through minority and low- and moderate-income neighborhoods. Lakeside National Bank of Denver distributes "door hangers" which advertise the bank's FHA "no equity" home improvement loan in low- and moderate-income neighborhoods. Also, they conduct officer calls targeting individuals and businesses in those neighborhoods.

Many banks target senior citizens in their advertising, especially when they fall into the low- and moderate-income categories in a community. Senior citizens may have a relatively low income (e.g., Social Security), but this frequently is not the case in terms of net worth. Most banks have special or no-charge checking accounts for senior citizens as well as other benefits. Because senior citizens are infrequent users of credit, with the exception of some credit card loans, the emphasis is usually on deposit products, which really does not meet the spirit of CRA.

Banks may be criticized for not using special advertising media aimed at particular segments of the community. The examiners at Washington Trust Bank in Spokane, Washington, which used general advertisements, noted that the nature of that marketplace made "targeting specific products and groups difficult." That is the exception rather than the rule, as most outstanding banks have advertising programs which target credit products.

Examiners Cite "Inconsistent" Advertising Strategy at Chemical Bank

Outstanding banks may conduct different types of advertising but almost always have a significant a-mount of credit advertising relating to loans in general or for a specific loan promotion. Banks with general image ads or those focused on deposit gathering services are usually downgraded in this regard.

Chemical Bank, which was rated as having only a "satisfactory" marketing effort, provided an interest-ing perspective because of its assertion that "image-oriented advertising is the most productive strategy." Chemical primarily promotes its image, home-owner loan products, and customer relationship products. However, management there considers other prod-uct-specific advertising, such as for home mortgages, to be "ineffective." The examiners noted that "man-agement was unable to substantiate these conten-tions on the basis of market research or studies." The examiners then noted that Chemical's own consumer advertising data indicated a larger volume of deposit and home-owner product advertising compared to image advertising. This, according to the examiners, appeared to be "inconsistent with management's stat-ed strategy to emphasize image-oriented advertising."

Outstanding banks maintain complete records on their advertising and marketing programs. Also, they routinely review them for effectiveness and compli-ance. Fleet National Bank of Rhode Island, which was cited for a well-documented marketing program, sub-scribes to a competitive spending tracking report, which shows that it consistently uses the media more than any of its competitors. Marketing effectiveness there is measured through outreach efforts, customer surveys, and analysis of product response. The Cattle National Bank of Seward, Nebraska, regularly re-views its advertisements for compliance, but was noted as not formally reviewing its advertising pro-gram for effectiveness.

Shared Credit Counseling Centers in California and Cincinnati

Outstanding banks use different approaches to providing routine assistance to individuals and groups applying for credit. Great Western Bank participates in a shared home loan counseling program with other banks. The home loan counseling centers are located in minority and/or low-income areas. These centers educate the public on credit matters and increase the accessibility of loans. Home Savings of America is also involved in the same counseling centers in California plus one in Cincinnati. Such loan counseling centers provide an excellent example of a shared resource that may best be provided by a group of local banks organized themselves or through a trade association.

"Mortgages Made Easy Kit" in New York

Citibank (New York State) of Pittsford, New York, has developed product kits for mortgages and other equity based offerings, such as the "Mortgages Made Easy Kit," which allow potential customers to better understand these products, the application process, and anticipated closing costs. That bank was respon-sive to the needs of the hearing impaired in its community by offering special telecommunication devices for the deaf.

Reaching Out to the Business Community in Milwaukee and Pittsburgh

First Wisconsin National Bank of Milwaukee pub-lishes two packets to aid the business community in applying for and obtaining credit. These packets, "Starting a Business" and "Arranging for a Business Loan," are available at each bank location.

In addition to general media, Pittsburgh National Bank has call programs and newsletters that reach local businesses, realtors, and community organi-zations. That bank distributes its monthly *Perform-ance* newsletter to 3,500 local businesses and its quarterly *Equity* newsletter to 4,000 realtors. This is another example of an innovative approach to not only meeting CRA goals but also business ones.

Available Credit Services (Assessment Factor I)

Once the bank has ascertained community credit needs, it must proceed to meet them. Outstanding banks undertake significant efforts to affirmatively meet a substantial portion of identified community credit needs through both originating and purchasing loans.

Lending on Mobile Homes in Maine and Nevada

Most banks offer a similar menu of loan types. Outstanding banks will modify their loan mix to create new credit products or change existing ones to better meet identified credit needs in the community.

One example is seen in those banks that provide credit for both new and used mobile homes in addition to traditional single or multifamily housing. The need for mobile home financing was identified as a pressing credit need in certain portions of Maine. Fleet Bank of Maine responded, and at the time of its exam had a $34 million mobile home loan portfolio, representing 2,406 such loans.

Valley Bank of Nevada addressed a major need for mobile housing in rural communities by introducing a mobile home loan program offering lower fixed interest rates and longer repayment terms. That same bank developed a nonequity home improvement loan to finance drought-tolerant exterior landscaping, an important need in that community's dry climate.

Most banks don't think twice about lending money on a used home, but many do not lend on used mobile homes, an important source of housing for low- and moderate-income residents. A few banks have met this important need. Likewise, most banks finance new cars but many are less aggressive when it comes to used cars, which again may be more important for low- and moderate-income residents. Manufacturers Hanover Trust Company financed used automobiles up to four model years old, but according to the examination increased the minimum loan for new or used automobiles from $5,000 to $7,500.

CRA Credit for Selling to the Secondary Market

Banks that originated loans and then sold them in the secondary market were commended for this turnover, which made more loanable funds available. The Bank of Commerce in Auburn, California, which sells most of the mortgage and SBA loans it originates, was complimented for "leveraging loan dollars through loan sales." The examiners concluded that "loan volume in relation to the bank's resources, exceeds expectations."

Fleet Bank of Maine, which sells its mortgages to a holding company affiliate, was noted as helping to increase the amount of money available for mortgage borrowers through this activity. Eastern Bank of Lynn, Massachusetts, was also commended for selling its residential mortgages on the secondary market for this same reason.

Banks which purchase loans can also obtain CRA credit, but that depends to a great degree on the location of the collateral relative to the bank's delineated community. First Wisconsin National Bank of Milwaukee generally does not make direct residential mortgage loans, but it does make home improvement loans. However, that bank purchases a significant volume of mortgage loans from a holding company affiliate. The bank then turns around and sells a significant volume of these loans in the secondary market, thus making available more funds to purchase more mortgages from its holding company affiliate. The examiners noted that this procedure allows the bank to "affirmatively address a substantial portion of the residential mortgage needs of the community," even though that bank generally does not make direct residential mortgage loans.

Some outstanding banks do not make certain types of loans because of their specialization or market. Territorial Savings of Hawaii does not provide small business or small farm loans, but is very active in the residential loan market with some consumer lending. This is the case for many thrifts.

Affordable Housing Programs—Most Individual but Some Shared

Outstanding banks are exceptionally responsive to the most pressing community credit needs, especially those in low- and moderate-income areas. Several outstanding banks have special programs to meet such credit needs.

Bank of America has developed several special loan products through its CRA program. Their low-income housing program offers construction, rehabilitation, and term financing for multiunit rental properties for low- and very low-income tenants. Neighborhood Advantage is a home mortgage loan with relaxed underwriting standards for houses within low- and moderate-income census tracts. Their BASIC program is a mix of consumer loan products with relaxed underwriting standards for low-income customers. Bank of America also offers business lending for minority-owned and start-up businesses through smaller, specialized programs.

United Jersey Bank/Central has developed its own low-cost mortgage program as well as a low-cost home improvement loan program. Society National Bank's Home Assist Program for low- and moderate-income residents, which has a 75% loan application approval rate, was responsible for 600 loans totalling $19 million.

Boatmen's National Bank of Belleville, Illinois, is one of four banks participating in a local Housing Acquisition Program. The bank has lent nearly $3 million to finance owner-occupied home purchases (all of which cost $45,000 or less), which represents 58% of the total loans outstanding in the program.

INB National Bank in Indianapolis established a special CRA mortgage program where it has purchased or committed to purchase 108 CRA mortgages amounting to $4.8 million in a year and a half.

First National Bank of Louisville has a Neighborhood Home Loan program for low- to moderate-income borrowers in addition to a "Ready Line" revolving account. This credit product, which is designed for individuals without established credit records, has resulted in over 4,000 such accounts totaling $1.7 million. That bank has also allocated mortgage funds at 1% below the market rate for individuals being displaced by the local airport expansion.

Chittenden Trust Company of Burlington, Vermont, developed the Chittenden Affordable Real Estate (CARE) program for low- and moderate-income groups. This program provides for a 5% downpayment from any source, reduced closing costs, and a stepped interest rate for the first two years of the mortgage.

Texas Bank of Weatherford, Texas, is the only financial institution in its home county to participate in a regional housing finance corporation's low interest first-time home buyers program by purchasing $1.5 million of these funds.

No Minimum Loan Amounts at Outstanding Banks

Many banks have minimum loan amounts, which CRA examiners may interpret as a factor that can discourage credit. Bank One, Akron was noted for having no minimum loan amount for residential mortgage loans. First Citizens Bank of Elizabethtown, Kentucky, also has no minimum loan amount. The absence of a minimum loan amount is especially beneficial for low- and moderate-income individuals who generally seek smaller loans.

A few outstanding banks were criticized for not having special loan programs for low- and moderate-income housing. This was the case for Bank Independent in Sheffield, Alabama, which only recently developed a conventional mortgage program. Home Savings of America, the nation's largest S&L, does not directly offer loans for rehabilitation, home improvement, small business, or farms. However, the examiners noted that the majority of their mortgages contained open-end provisions which allow for future advances to be used for any purpose.

"Country Living Program" in Kansas

Rural areas generally served by smaller community banks have unique credit needs, many of these related to agriculture. Kansas State Bank is the only local financial institution to participate in the Farm Credit Service's "Country Living Program," which provides interim residential construction financing in rural areas. First Wisconsin National Bank of Fond Du Lac is the most active lender to farmers within its community. Many large banks have a farm lending tradition such as Wells Fargo Bank, one of the largest agricultural lenders in the country.

75%-80% Loan-to-Deposit Ratios

Most outstanding banks have a substantial majority of loans within their delineated community. Smaller banks often have all or nearly all of their loans in their local community. Many outstanding banks have 90% or more of their loans in their community, but this percentage may go down to the 70%–75% range. Of course, a bank delineating an unreasonably large local community would have a greater percentage, but most outstanding banks have reasonably delineated areas.

Loan volume at outstanding banks often exceeds expectations in relation to the bank's resources and the community's credit needs. The most common ratio calculated by examiners to gauge this assessment factor is the simple loan-to-deposit (or loan-to-asset) ratio. This ratio is compared to other local banks and perhaps a peer group in a larger region or state. Most banks have fairly high loan-to-deposit ratios, often 75% – 80% and sometimes more, but there are wide variations.

A loan-to-deposit ratio for a small bank with all of its offices in a given community is meaningful, but this is not the case for a large bank with offices in many different markets. A large bank may have a high loan-to-deposit ratio because of the main office, but the loan-to-deposit ratio for a given market may be quite low. Also, such ratios must be reviewed relative to a bank's charge-off and nonperforming asset history to help to determine whether a low ratio is the result of excessively conservative lending practices or just low loan demand.

Outstanding Banks are Leaders, Not Followers

Many large banks are therefore evaluated on different standards, depending upon the situation. For example, First National Bank of Chicago is one of 39 financial institutions in the Community Investment Corporation, which attempts to revitalize older neighborhoods through development of low- and moderate-income housing. First National Bank took a leadership role in the creation of that corporation and furthermore is responsible for the largest portion of its financing.

Also in Chicago is the Illinois region of Citibank of Oakland, California. That bank's Illinois region originated more conventional single- and multifamily loans than any other lender in 65 of Chicago's 77 neighborhoods.

CRA "Megapledges" in California

Major CRA commitments by some of our nation's largest banks have also been noted under this assessment factor. For example, Wells Fargo Bank announced a commitment to lend $1 billion over seven years to community and economic development activities. Another outstanding bank, Bank of America, was responsible for the largest such commitment to date after its acquisition of Security Pacific Bank. A case study in the following chapter reviews these and other CRA "megapledges."

Texas Bank Had Net Loan-to-Deposit Ratio of Only 11%

A few banks with outstanding ratings were criticized for relatively low loan-to-deposit ratios. Loan volume at the Dominion Bank of Middle Tennessee exceeds expectations for all six of its communities combined, but not for some individual communities. The examiners noted that there was no documentation or analysis to indicate the reason for the "low level of loans to deposits at some communities."

First City, Texas in Kountze, Texas had a net loan-to-deposit ratio of only 11%, compared to the peer ratio of 65%. Examiners noted that members of the local community felt that the bank had become "too conservative" in its lending criteria, thus "squeezing out" some consumers in need of credit. The examiners (not management) suggested that the low loan-to-deposit ratio may be due to economic conditions and/or loan demand.

The CRA statements at most outstanding banks meet all of the technical requirements, including a correct listing of all credit products. Several of the larger outstanding banks incorporate their CRA statement into a glossy community reinvestment brochure or report to the community where credit products are not only listed but are also described, usually with examples and photographs. Community banks can accomplish most of the same education and communication objectives in a more cost-efficient manner through an expanded CRA statement.

Government Loan Programs (Assessment Factor J)

The most outstanding banks take a leadership role in affirmatively meeting identified community credit needs through several different governmentally insured, guaranteed, or subsidized loan programs. A surprisingly large number of banks with outstanding ratings, however, did not participate in any type of government loan program.

Government programs may involve loans for residences, housing rehabilitation, home improvement, small businesses, small farms, or for other purposes. There are numerous federal and state programs meeting these different types of objectives, and the most outstanding banks are usually involved in more than one. Housing loans are probably the most common government loans at outstanding banks involved in such programs.

Number One SBA Lender in California and Nevada

Of special interest to many outstanding banks is the SBA program. Many outstanding banks have obtained a certified or preferred lender status at the SBA. Valley Bank of Nevada is the leading SBA lender in the State of Nevada, with an entire department devoted to the processing of SBA applications. Bank of America leads the major banks in California with a 2.5% market share of all SBA lending there in 1989. National Westminster Bank in New York City is the third largest SBA lender in New York State.

Government Home Loans Account for One-Half of Portfolio at Large Texas and Montana Thrifts

Government loan programs at some outstanding banks represent a significant portion of their total portfolio. One-half of the mortgage loans originated in 1990 by First Gibraltar Bank of Texas were governmentally insured, guaranteed or subsidized. That bank offers FHA and VA loans as well as loans under state and county bond programs.

First Federal Savings Bank of Montana made 49% of its 1990 loans through the FHA and VA programs. Territorial Savings of Hawaii reported 28% of its portfolio in FHA, VA, or FHLMC products.

Only a few outstanding banks were involved with HUD programs. Dominion Bank of Middle Tennessee is a certified lender bank and affiliate participant with HUD. Chittenden Trust Company of Vermont was selected by HUD to participate in a reverse mortgage pilot program.

Number One Student Lender in U.S.

Some outstanding banks were very aggressive in the guaranteed student loan program. Citibank (New York State) of Pittsford, New York, is the largest student loan lender in the nation. That bank extended $616 million in student loans in 1990 to more than 214,000 students nationwide, with 23% of the loan amount in New York State. Lakeside National Bank in Denver has a relatively significant volume of governmentally insured student loans.

"Bank of the Year" in Maine

Many outstanding banks focus their efforts more on state government programs. Denali State Bank in Alaska is one of only two banks in that state qualified to originate loans guaranteed by the Alaska Industrial Development Authority. Cattle National Bank of Seward in Nebraska is one of the state's top participants in the Nebraska Investment Financing Authority farm loan program.

Probably one of the best examples of a leader in state lending programs is Fleet Bank of Maine. Because it had the highest level of commercial lending through the Finance Authority of Maine of any bank in the state, it was named Bank of the Year in 1989 by that authority. According to Fleet, it is the state's leading participant in the Maine State Housing Authority. The bank is also active in the SBA with eight SBA certified lenders on its staff and is involved in other federal and state loan programs as well.

Many outstanding banks are involved in government lending through state bond programs. Pacific First Bank in Seattle participates in both the Washington and Oregon Mortgage Revenue Bond Programs. Boatmen's National Bank of Belleville, Illinois, is involved in a first-time home buyers bond issue program. First National Bank of Louisville is one of 23 lenders in that state funding a Kentucky Housing Corporation program to assist first-time home buyers, and the bank committed $5 million for this $20 million program.

Many of the largest outstanding banks are also involved in several city loan projects. The Dime Savings Bank of New York is heavily engaged in various New York City programs to finance the rehabilitation and construction of abandoned or foreclosed low- and moderate-income projects. First Wisconsin National Bank of Milwaukee has participated in every program offered in that city designed to encourage home ownership. That bank is also a substantial purchaser of long-term debt issued by local municipalities in its delineated community.

Delinquent Tax Loans in Delaware

Some outstanding banks are involved in fairly innovative government programs. The Delaware Trust Company participates in a program designed to provide delinquent city taxpayers an opportunity to finance past-due taxes or utility bills at a lower rate and for a longer term. The bank has approved nearly 100 of these city-guaranteed loans, representing total outstandings of $180,000.

SunBank of Naples, Florida, has made a loan in the local area that is the first SBA loan in Florida to be structured as an import/export line of credit. That bank is also actively involved with the Service Corps of Retired Executives, an SBA sponsored agency. The bank provides free office space, professional guidance, client counseling, and other support to this agency.

Avoiding Government Programs but Keeping an Outstanding Rating

Some outstanding banks may become involved in government loan programs but be criticized for their relatively low level of participation. International Bank of Commerce of Laredo, Texas, makes FHA and VA loans. However, the examiners noted that applications for such loans are few, due to the bank's policy of only writing variable rate loans with 15-year amortizations.

A surprisingly large number of banks with outstanding ratings had little or no involvement whatsoever in any type of government loan program. Sometimes the examiner would attempt to justify that situation by noting other product alternatives that a bank offers that might be a substitute for a government loan program.

The nation's two largest savings and loans were criticized in this regard. Home Savings of America received a needs improvement rating under this assessment factor since it is not involved in any government lending programs with the exception of offering

FHA loans on a test basis in limited markets. Great Western Bank, the nation's second largest savings and loan, did not offer any government loan programs. Great Western's examiners noted that the bank does offer conventional mortgage products with 90% loan-to-value ratios "which are frequently a viable alternative to the various government programs available." The bulk of that bank's home mortgages, however, are adjustable rate ones. This is also true for Home Savings.

American Savings Bank of California has not participated in traditional government-backed programs such as FHA and VA because it "does not perceive a benefit to low-income families." That bank has developed a 95% loan-to-value mortgage product with purchase-money loans as a substitute.

First City, Texas in Kountze, Texas, does not participate in any government loan programs but forwards completed FHA and VA loan applications to its holding company affiliates. INB National Bank in Indianapolis has infrequent participation in government loan programs, primarily because of the significant efforts it devotes to working closely with local community organizations. Manufacturers Hanover Trust Company's participation in government loan programs was primarily limited to student loans. RCB Bank in Claremore, Oklahoma, does not participate in any government housing or farming loan programs but has participated in one SBA loan.

III. Geographic Distribution and Record of Opening and Closing Offices

Reasonableness of Delineated Community

The delineated communities for most of the outstanding banks analyzed here were considered to be reasonable. A community delineation is one of the few areas where a bank has considerable leeway and flexibility because the CRA guidelines in this regard are quite general.

The larger the area delineated, the larger the proportion of loans that will be encompassed within it. However, if an area is too large, considering the distribution of a bank's offices and its loan customers, then it may be criticized. Anytime low- and moderate-income areas are just outside of a delineated community, questions will likely be raised as to the area's reasonableness.

Unique Delineations—From a 50-Mile Radius to a One-Mile Radius

Some of the larger banks utilize an entire state for their community areas, such as Bank of America in California and Fleet National Bank in Rhode Island. Many large savings and loan associations with multi-state operations have several different non-contiguous communities throughout the country.

The delineated community would appear to be obvious for banks surrounded by geographic barriers, as is Territorial Savings in Hawaii. Even in that case, however, they only took one entire island with eight of its branches, but equal mileage radii around its four remaining branches on three other islands.

Some banks may change their community delineation following a new analysis. For example, City National Bank of Fort Smith, Arkansas, reduced its delineated community from a 50-mile radius to just the immediate city and a part of a county near another community.

Some outstanding banks take an affirmative role in reaching out to low- and moderate-income neighborhoods that may be outside of their delineated community, and this can result in "CRA credit" for the bank. Columbia National Bank of Chicago's delineated community is a roughly one-mile radius around its main office and facility. Since there are no low- or moderate-income neighborhoods within that area, management has expanded its affirmative efforts beyond its delineated community by meeting with groups which represent low- and moderate-income credit needs outside its area.

Examiner Criticism on Both Long Island and Staten Island

Dominion Bank of Middle Tennessee was criticized because one of its six delineated communities excluded a low- and moderate-income area, an army base. The bank was unaware of this omission, apparently since an outside firm was hired to make the map of the community.

Delaware Trust Company was criticized for one of its three delineated areas because 79% of the loans made by the bank within an 18-month period were located outside of that area. Although the examiners did not label the area as an "unreasonable" one, it noted that it "should be reviewed by management."

The delineated communities of the Greater New York Savings Bank did not appear to have been defined on a consistent basis according to the examiners. Some delineations appear "unjustifiable in the absence of supporting documentation." One office on Long Island used the delineation of the entire island, which was apparently too large. The "most curious community delineation" was all of Staten Island, where that bank doesn't even have an office.

Eastern Bank in Lynn, Massachusetts, had a delineated community that "appears somewhat broad" according to the examiners. They requested the bank to analyze its lending patterns and review the current delineation for reasonableness.

New York City's Dime Savings Bank Not Criticized for Community Delineation Based on Deposits Rather Than Loans

One of the recommended approaches to delineating the community is to use the "effective lending territory." While the distribution of deposits can be reviewed, the focus must be on loan distribution. It was therefore puzzling to learn that the delineation of the lending communities by Dime Savings Bank of New York City "placed greatest emphasis on the distribution of its deposits." Some subsequent adjustments were made to form contiguous communities and political boundaries, but the emphasis apparently was on the distribution of deposits rather than on loans. This delineation methodology was not criticized but was surprisingly noted as being "in accordance with the CRA." Importantly, low- and moderate-income areas and minority districts were not arbitrarily excluded.

Chittenden Trust Company of Burlington, Vermont, used a 15-mile radius around its offices for its local community. The bank did not arbitrarily exclude any low- or moderate-income areas. The result was a community made up of two noncontiguous areas described in the CRA statement. With two noncontiguous areas "but only one CRA statement," the examiners stated that the bank must "either develop a second CRA statement or revise the delineation of one local community to ensure all boundararies are contiguous." This apparent requirement of a contiguous delineated community or one statement per noncontiguous area represented a unique interpretation of CRA. Most banks that use equal mile radii about their offices for their local community do in fact result in noncontiguous areas (and one CRA statement).

Geographic Distribution of Credit (Assessment Factor E)

Outstanding banks conduct regular and well-documented analyses of the geographic distribution of credit extensions, applications, and denials. This type of geocoding analysis is often done concurrently on the deposit side, but the focus is always on the loan side. In addition to conducting a geocoding analysis, an outstanding bank will be able to document a reasonable penetration of all segments of its local community, including low- and moderate-income neighborhoods. Outstanding banks, because of specialized credit programs, often have a level of penetration in low- and moderate-income neighborhoods which exceeds expectations.

Geocoding at Citibank and Community Banks

Many large banks have comprehensive and formal geocoding systems in place as part of normal operations. A geocoding analysis for outstanding banks is not a special event, as it can be run at any time.

Citibank in New York City established geocoding committees to periodically review lending patterns in low- and moderate-income census tracts for all of its Northeast Division's products. The CRA Committee of National Westminster Bank of New York City created a geocode subcommittee to monitor and review the loan and deposit distribution by census tract on a quarterly basis. First Gibraltar Bank of Texas designed and implemented a special computer-based information system that tracks mortgage transactions from application through processing, pipeline, funding, denial, or withdrawal. That system provides HMDA data by metropolitan area, county, branch, etc.

While larger banks have more resources than smaller ones for geocoding analysis, size is no excuse for a small bank not to complete a geocoding analysis on an in-house basis. In fact, many community banks that have received outstanding ratings have developed their own internal geocoding systems that are accepted by CRA examiners.

Zip Code Analysis—An Acceptable and Economical Approach

Most banks have the capability, either in-house or through their service bureau, of creating a printout showing both the number and dollar volume of loans (and deposits) by five-digit zip codes. The analysis can be done only for a select group of zip codes representing the local community or for all zip codes, eliminating those out of state as well as those with very small balances.

One Valley Bank of Summersville, West Virginia, documents monthly the geographic distribution of all loans extended and denied by zip codes, and the information is analyzed quarterly by the bank's CRA committee. International Bank of Commerce of Laredo, Texas, maintains detailed files on the distribution of loans by type and amount within four designated zip codes in its metropolitan area. That bank also keeps files of credit applications and denials on hand. Magnolia Federal Bank in Mississippi made a detailed study of mortgage loans, installment loans, demand deposits, and savings accounts by zip codes.

Use of areas broader than a zip code, such as a county, have limited value except for general comparisons. First American Bank and Trust of Louisiana analyzes parish (equivalent to a county) statistical data in its mortgage geocoding analysis. Bank management, however, indicated that they are considering utilizing the zip codes to "more adequately determine" the distribution of credit applications and denials.

Zip codes have the advantage of easy recognition and data availability. However, very broad zip codes, which cover many different heterogeneous communities, may be of limited value for a geocoding analysis. Some cities and most towns are represented by one zip code, which also covers the surrounding area, and there is no way to determine where in a given zip code the relevant activity is occurring.

Loan Plottings for Even the Smallest Banks

One way for small banks to get around this problem is to plot out a random sample of loan extensions, applications, and denials on a local map. Deposits can also be plotted. This pinpointing process, which is actually more accurate than the use of census tracts or block numbering areas, often reveals valuable marketing information for a bank. All states have county highway or equivalent maps, and highly detailed U.S. topographic maps of varying scales cover the entire country.

The Cattle National Bank of Seward, Nebraska, maps the location of residential real estate, commercial, and light manufacturing loans on a city map and plat maps for the surrounding county areas. That bank is in the process of plotting loan applications and denials as well.

Texas Bank of Weatherford, Texas, has a loan monitoring program where the following loans are plotted on a map of the bank's delineated community: consumer loans under $2,000, all home improvement loans, all business loans under $25,000, all agricultural loans under $25,000, and all residential mortgage loans. That map is reviewed by senior management in conjunction with local demographic data.

Census Tract Analysis—The Preferred Approach

An increasing number of community banks are geocoding loans and deposits by census tracts or block numbering areas where census tracts are not available. Several CRA vendors offer different types of loan-tracking software for this purpose. Some banks, however, manually geocode each loan extension, application, and denial through use of a census tract/ street address cross-reference directory. These directories usually are available in all markets where census tracts exist. The most sophisticated such systems track all deposit and loan activity on a real-time basis by census tract and/or block numbering area with regular tabular and graphic reports.

Sunwest Bank of Roswell, New Mexico, manually tracks the geographic distribution of its credit extensions, applications, and denials by census tract. These data, along with withdrawn applications, are logged on a monthly summary sheet that is reviewed by the CRA specialist and the compliance officer.

City National Bank of Fort Smith, Arkansas, now geocodes all loans and denied applications by census tract. Using census data, the bank has identified five low- and moderate-income areas within its community and tracks loan activity including denials within them.

Forgetting to Geocode Non-Consummated Loans

It is important for banks to geocode not only loan extensions but also applications and denials. Loan extensions plus denials are usually less than the total number of applications. This is because of "non-consummated loans" that were withdrawn or otherwise removed from the application process. Banks that only focus on outstanding loans without considering declines or non-consummated loans may be criticized.

Dominion Bank of Middle Tennessee prepared a documented analysis of credit extensions by plotting loans according to zip codes (and by census tracts where required by HMDA). However, the examiners noted that declined application data had not been completed in a manner to adequately determine its geographic distribution (again with the exception of HMDA data plotted for its metropolitan areas). The examiners made this criticism even though the bank plots a sample of declined applications on a map each quarter to determine if any unfair credit patterns exist. Bank One, Akron periodically reviews denied applications to determine geographic distribution, but currently does not review withdrawn applications.

Lending 70% – 75% Locally

One of the most common calculations made by CRA examiners under this assessment factor is the percentage of loans outstanding within the delineated community. These ratios are usually quite high for most community banks, and often in the 70% – 75% range or higher for most outstanding banks. Many times this calculation is not made in a CRA examination, which again raises the issue of inconsistency.

Any CRA analysis using that ratio is only as good as the community delineated. In other words, if a bank has an unreasonably large delineated community, the resultant percentage of loans within it will be quite high; but meaningless to a great extent. Many small banks with fairly compact delineated communities have high in-community lending ratios because of their concentration on local credits.

Artificially High Local Lending Ratios Due to Unreasonably Large Community Delineations

Previous regulatory analyses of lending patterns at The Greater New York Savings Bank disclosed a strong level of in-community lending. However, the questions surrounding the reasonableness (i.e., inconsistencies) of its delineated community caused the examiners to note that "the relative importance of these results is diminished."

Eastern Bank of Lynn, Massachusetts, was criticized because its delineated community appeared somewhat broad. The examiners concluded that the high percentage (93% and 96%) of in-community lending in 1988 and 1989 according to that bank's HMDA statement "support the observation that the delineated community is somewhat broad." The examiners felt that the delineation appeared to "spread the bank's resources too thin" to adequately service community credit needs.

Post Office Boxes Can't Be Geocoded

First City of Kountze, Texas, geocodes loans and applications by both census tract and zip code within the delineated community of its home city. However, the bank was criticized because no efforts were made to determine the geographic distribution of activity outside its delineated community. This was important considering the fact that at least half of the applications received by the bank come from the area surrounding the city. The examiners at that bank did not geocode the sample loans and denials because most of the applicants had post office boxes or rural route addresses. Although rural route addresses present difficulties, they often can be overcome through labor-intensive plotting procedures with bank management and the local postmaster or rural carrier. Unless post office box customers are known to management, geocoding would not be possible.

Should Downtown Banks Geocode Employment or Home Addresses?

At the other extreme, many banks in downtown or business areas, with delineated communities limited to them, will most likely have low in-community lending for most residential mortgages and installment credits (but not for business loans). Western State Bank of St. Paul, Minnesota, made loans in all segments of its delineated communities, including numerous low-income areas. The examiners noted that a number of the bank's loans were made outside of its delineated communities, but the majority were to people who worked inside the communities but lived outside of them. Geocoding downtown employment addresses might give "CRA credit" but suburban home addresses might not. Banks in these or similar situations, such as a shopping mall bank drawing loan customers from distant areas, must have geocoding customer data for both addresses to explain and document these unique situations.

Geocoding by Examiners in Nebraska Verify Bank's Own Analysis

Most geocoding analyses are conducted by the banks themselves or in conjunction with outside vendor support. Even though a bank may have conducted a geocoding analysis, CRA examiners may conduct their own sample analysis. Firstier Bank of Lincoln, Nebraska, had a documented analysis showing its loans, applications, and denials being reasonably distributed throughout the delineated communities. The CRA examiners completed their own analysis by plotting on local maps the locations of small business, real estate, and home improvement accepted and rejected loans for the first six months of 1990. The examiners' analysis likewise concluded that the bank is reaching all areas of the community.

Geocoding for a Community Group

Some banks may be the subject of geocoding analyses by outside community groups or others using readily available HMDA data. A few local community groups and some legislators had requested expanded reviews of HMDA data for select communities by Citibank of New York City. Those studies showed that the bank made significant loans in those areas. As a result of the community groups' concerns, the bank established the previously mentioned geocoding committees.

Massachusetts Bank Criticized for Not Going Beyond HMDA

HMDA data are limited in the sense that they have not always been required for all banks and also because the data only cover home loans. Also, regulators do not reach any conclusions in the published HMDA reports, other than what may be gleaned from this part of the CRA evaluation. Many CRA examiners will base their evaluation of this assessment factor primarily on HMDA data analysis, when it may represent only a portion of a bank's total lending. If a bank has not geocoded other loans besides those covered by HMDA requirements, examiners will have to rely on their own sample analyses when they are made.

Worcester County Institution for Savings in Massachusetts was criticized because its geographic distribution of loans other than home mortgages covered under HMDA was not documented. Although the analysis of credit extensions and denials using HMDA data showed an adequate geographic distribution, the bank was recommended to conduct a more comprehensive geocoding analysis as part of its internal CRA assessment process.

Incentives for "Low-Mod" Lending in California

One of the most important considerations under this assessment factor is the extent to which a bank reasonably penetrates low- and moderate-income ("low-mod") neighborhoods in its local community. Columbia National Bank of Chicago, which did not have any such low- and moderate-income neighborhoods in its local community, expanded its ascertainment and affirmative credit efforts beyond its community to include low- and moderate-income residents.

Some outstanding banks have specific plans which outline their affirmative efforts in low- and moderate-income neighborhoods. Bank of America attempts to bring home mortgage lending levels in low- and moderate-income census tracts up to the bank's overall market share for the county in which those tracts are located. Branch managers are given incentives to

meet those goals and continually track lending performance in that regard. That goal program was successful, since the bank's 1989 HMDA data found that no low- to moderate-income area was excluded.

SunBank of Naples, Florida, developed an "action plan" to try to increase applications and loans from/to some neighborhoods. Senior management at Boatmen's First National Bank of Kansas City places a primary focus on their penetration in the low- and moderate-income census tracts throughout its delineated community. That bank has used its geocoding analysis to revise its lending policies, products, and services. For example, that bank offered a "target" mortgage program providing for more liberal qualifying guidelines in low-income neighborhoods; it removed the floor for mortgage loans; it offered VA and FHA mortgage loans; and it attempted to qualify credit applicants who didn't have a standard credit history.

First or Second in "Low-Mod" Penetration in Rhode Island

Senior management at Fleet National Bank of Rhode Island places a primary focus on penetrating the low- and moderate-income census tracts in the state. The bank is almost always first or second in market share in low- and moderate-income and minority areas in terms of home purchase and home improvement lending. Fleet made more than 50% of the total number and dollar amount of home purchase loans in low- and moderate-income neighborhoods of Rhode Island's metropolitan statistical areas in 1987 and 1988. The comparable percentage for home improvement loans was more than 80%. Fleet also provides 39% of all student loans in Rhode Island, and 29% of those loans benefit borrowers in low- and moderate-income areas.

10% "Low-Mod" Market Lending Share in Chicago

A market research analysis commissioned by the First National Bank of Chicago indicated that it had a 10% market leading share among low- and moderate-income consumers with accounts at financial institutions. That bank has a sophisticated geocoding and mapping system that identifies areas of low and nonexistent loan penetration. That bank made a direct mail solicitation to two areas of low credit penetration, using a preapproved line of credit. The bank's geocoding analysis concluded that it has loans in all but 14 of the more than 800 census tracts in Chicago.

Different Approaches to Measuring "Low-Mod" Penetration

CRA examiners often make a number of calculations regarding the penetration of lending in low- and moderate-income areas. The percentages may be based on the number of loans but more often on the dollar amount outstanding. The usual comparison is the quantity within the subject area relative to the total at the entire bank. Although it is more difficult, a ratio may also be calculated to show the market share of lending in the subject area relative to other financial institutions. Also, the percentage of lending in low- and moderate-income areas may be compared to the proportion of low- and moderate-income residents in the entire community. Furthermore, the number of bank branches in low- and moderate-income areas may also be noted.

The focus of CRA is usually on low- and moderate-income neighborhoods. Statistics may also be calculated for very low-income areas. Likewise, some CRA examiners calculate statistics for those areas that are predominantly or substantially minority (usually 50% or more), although this is not the primary focus of CRA.

The 1990 analysis of HMDA data at Wells Fargo Bank showed that its 19% of home loans in low- and very low-income census tracts was reasonable. Another analysis of that bank showed that approximately 48% of new credit card commitments during the second half of 1990 were granted to low-income customers. That bank distributes *Branch Market Area Performance* handbooks that break down the demographics and income levels by census tracts for branch officers to target areas for lending.

Some Outstanding Banks Criticized for Low Level of "Low-Mod" Penetration

A zip code analysis at the Fleet Bank of Maine favorably concluded that low- and moderate-income areas received 21% of that bank's consumer loans and 30% of its business loans, although low- and moderate-income households represented only 17% of all

statewide households. The bank did a geocoding analysis of two of the three metropolitan statistical areas, using 1988 HMDA data. The examiners replicated the findings for the third area on their own and even updated the analysis to 1989. Surprisingly, the examiners unfavorably concluded that the percentage of lending in low- and moderate-income areas in that third metropolitan statistical area was lower than the comparable statewide percentage, unlike the other two areas that were higher than that percentage.

Mapping of loan activity at Territorial Savings in Hawaii indicated the overall denial rate was low, but the rate was the highest in areas where the largest number of loans had been granted. One-third of the total residential loans originated by them in the first half of 1991 were in low- and moderate-income census tract areas.

The loan denial and withdrawal rates for low- and moderate-income borrowers at Pacific First Bank in Seattle were significantly higher than the corresponding rates for middle- and upper-income applicants. The examiners noted, however, that a review of rejected loan files indicated that loans were denied solely for economic reasons, and in no case was the location of the property deemed to be the reason for denial. The percentage of loan originations at that bank's Washington and Oregon operations paralleled the deposit distribution within the delineated communities. The examiners found that there was an uneven distribution of the deposit base and loan originations in California, due to the location of its loan centers relative to its retail branches.

Examiners Conduct Seven-City Analysis of "Low-Mod" Lending at Great Western

Great Western Bank, which also operates in three states, made 42% of its 1990 loans in California in low- and moderate-income and minority areas, a percentage which approximated the proportion of low- and moderate-income census tracts in that state. However, the examiners noted that "the ratios fall short" for Florida (loans of 27% compared to 43% of the population) and Arizona (loans of 24% compared to 50% of the population). The bank responded that these 1990 statewide data may be distorted because agricultural and commercial property is typically clas-

126

Chapter 4

sified as low-income, but this is also true in other states.

The examiners then conducted their own detailed lending analysis targeting seven cities served by that bank for the twelve months ending June 30, 1991. That analysis concluded that Great Western's lending efforts in the low- and moderate-income and minority areas in Miami "fell short," especially compared to the other cities reviewed (five in California and one in Florida). Bank management again responded that a significant portion of census tracts without loan activity were commercial and industrial areas, but this would likewise be true in all of the sample cities. The examiners' analysis was based upon the percentage of low- and moderate-income and/or minority census tracts which that bank lent in. That ratio was only 41% in Miami compared to ratios of between 84% and 100% in the six other cities in that analysis.

Examiners Excuse Cleveland Bank from Geocoding Loan Denials

Only in one case did we note where examiners placed a smaller emphasis on geocoding of denied loans. This was because the bank involved, Society National Bank of Cleveland, Ohio, has sufficient controls in its mortgage lending area to ensure that "all available avenues are explored before an application for credit is denied." The examiners then concluded that this review process has "mitigated the need for a formal geographic review of credit denials." Although earlier analyses had indicated some lack of penetration in low- and moderate-income areas for housing-related credits, that bank's Home Assist Program has increased the volume of lending to low- and moderate-income customers.

Office and Service Record (Assessment Factor G)

Outstanding banks by definition have readily accessible offices, tailored and convenient business hours and services, a favorable record of opening and closing offices, and a formal procedure for assessing the potential adverse impact of office closings. All of these activities, but especially the branch-closing impact assessment, are very important in terms of their impact on low- and moderate-income areas.

The accessibility criterion is particularly subjective to evaluate. For example, what is the difference between "readily" accessible offices at outstanding banks and "reasonably" accessible ones at satisfactory banks? Offices with difficult or limited accessibility, the criteria for below-average rated banks, often become "problem branches" that may be closed unless the subject office is the only available one in a given area. Even the most outstanding CRA-rated banks will have some branches that are not as accessible as others because of site factors or constraints, such as parking, ingress and egress, and so on. Consequently, this assessment factor is usually rated more in terms of the other criteria mentioned above.

A Retail Loan Officer at Most Branches

Many outstanding banks have unique or innovative methods for delivering services. Many branches, satellites, or limited facilities, which are primarily deposit-gathering outlets, are generally not as desirable from the CRA perspective as those facilities offering loan services. Even banks with such limited facilities should have personnel at these branches who can answer basic questions about lending and can distribute loan applications. All facilities should have brochures or other material available that at least describes credit products in the absence of a true credit function. Some banks only maintain full-service offices. For example, all 210 retail branches in the 11 states in which First Nationwide operates are full service offices, with most having a retail loan officer on site.

24-Hour Banking at the ATM or at Home

The most popular alternative delivery system besides the traditional brick and mortar is the ATM. While these are most commonly used for cash dispensing, certain credit-related activities, such as loan payments, can often be made through ATMs. Even banks without ATMs may issue ATM cards that "piggyback" onto ATMs of other banks or systems.

Banking from home using a personal computer is an even more sophisticated electronic delivery system, but it offers the advantage of allowing potential loan customers to better understand different credit products at their leisure. However, because this delivery system is so limited in its potential market, only a few banks have adopted it. For example, Wells Fargo Bank offers at-home computer banking as well as a 24-hour customer service line. That bank, which has the most ATMs per branch of any major California bank, has also opened branches in grocery stores. Again, these are primarily deposit-gathering outlets, although some supermarket branches have limited credit functions.

100,000 Calls per Month in New York

Several large outstanding banks offer 24-hour banking by making available an 800 toll-free customer service line that can be used with the credit function. Citibank (New York State) of Pittsford, New York, has such a service and now receives an average of over 100,000 calls per month, including an average of over 70,000 calls per month from its delineated communities. That bank also offers a telephone service responding to the needs of the hearing impaired in its communities. Pittsburgh National Bank offers a telemarketing department that allows the public to apply for all deposits and consumer loan products over the phone five days a week.

American Federal Bank in South Carolina maintains the "Anytime Answer Line," an automated information dispensing center customers can call for account information and interest rates 24 hours a day, seven days a week. In addition to that information center, the bank maintains extended office hours on certain days while keeping several of their branches open during lunch hours, in contrast to some of the competition. Even though mortgage loan officers are not located in each branch of the bank, loan applications are accepted and loan underwriting guidelines are provided to consumers upon request at all offices. Additionally, the bank arranges for mortgage loan officers to visit branch offices in their respective geographic areas to meet with applicants who request an appointment.

Getting around Illinois' Restrictive Branch Banking

A unique and innovative delivery system is the Bankmobile of the First National Bank of Chicago. Staff at the Bankmobile, which was introduced in 1990, distribute pamphlets explaining the bank's products and assist people in understanding the bank's services. The Bankmobile specifically targets low- and moderate-income areas. Because the bank's branching powers are limited by restrictive state laws, it aggressively pursues alternative delivery systems. Examples include both on- and off-premise ATMs (the latter category being limited to ten by state law) as well as 34 point-of-sale terminals limited in function to cash dispensing.

Now Open on Sunday

Office hours are one of the easiest items for CRA examiners to evaluate. Many outstanding banks not only offer extended lobby hours during the week but also on Saturday and sometimes even Sunday. Business hours must be regularly reviewed to the extent to which they are serving customer needs, and this often means changing them, sometimes more at certain branches than others.

Lakeside National Bank, a unit bank in Denver, is open from 7:00 A.M. to 7:00 P.M. during the week in addition to being open on Saturdays. Bank Independent in Sheffield, Alabama, is open until 8:00 P.M. during weekdays at four of its nine offices and on Saturday at two offices. City National Bank of Fort Smith, Arkansas, keeps its mall branch open from 9:30 A.M. to 9:00 P.M., Monday through Saturday. The lobbies at its other four offices close at 4:00 P.M. during the week and 6:00 P.M. on Friday, but the drive-ins are open from 8:00 A.M. to 6:00 P.M., Monday through Friday.

Boatmen's First National Bank of Kansas City, Missouri, has Saturday hours at 25 of its 33 facilities. Those closed on Saturday have a full-service facility open nearby. All offices of The Greater New York Savings Bank provide extended hours on at least one evening weekly, and many are open on Saturdays or Sundays. RCB Bank of Claremore, Oklahoma, stays open late every night of the week and also offers Saturday morning services.

A handful of outstanding banks have experimented with Sunday office hours. To the extent that there is little or no demand for them, they may be rolled back or eliminated as part of an ongoing review of business hours. Bank One, Akron offers extended evening and Sunday hours at one of its branch offices. Columbia National Bank of Chicago, which selectively surveys its customers through the tellers, decided to expand its hours to provide teller services on Sundays. First National Bank of Omaha was the first bank in that metro area to offer Sunday banking hours. Valley Bank of Nevada extended its business hours to include Saturdays at its offices in addition to Sunday hours at selected locations. Pacific First Bank in Seattle offers extended hours, including Sundays at those branches located in retail and grocery stores.

"Appointment Banking" in Kentucky, California, and Iowa

An innovative and cost-effective approach to offering convenient office hours is the use of "appointment banking." For example, customers at First National Bank of Louisville, Kentucky, may meet bank employees at the nearest branch office for banking services by appointment. One branch, which was converted to an appointment banking facility, had no adverse impact on customer service according to the CRA examiners.

The Bank of Commerce in Auburn, California, is open to customers any time by appointment, and this feature is regularly used by loan customers. Also, that bank has a courier service for customer convenience. One of the offices at First Security Bank & Trust of Charles City, Iowa, makes appointments to meet with customers during nonbanking hours for those unable to conduct business when the bank is open. Also, Firstier Bank in Lincoln, Nebraska, makes its bank offices available by appointment to meet with customers after hours if needed.

Bank of America's Commitment Not to Close Unprofitable Branches in Some Low-Income Areas

Probably the most important concern by CRA examiners under this assessment factor is whether or not offices have been closed in low- and moderate-income areas. Many outstanding banks have closed such offices but conducted a detailed assessment prior to the closing, including consultation with community members.

The branch closing process at Bank of America includes a thorough study with an action plan which involves communications with affected groups in the community. CRA examiners have pointed out that Bank of America has kept branches open in some

low-income areas, where other banks have reduced their presence, "even though these branches may no longer be efficient or profitable." Bank management has stated that it intends to keep those offices open as part of its community commitment. Senior management at First Gibraltar Bank in Texas has made a commitment that it would search for buyers in order to maintain a banking presence in a community if a proposed branch closing would leave it without other financial institutions. It is indeed ironic that the first of these two outstanding banks with similar branch closing philosophies purchased the second.

Citibank Averages only 1.2 Complaint Letters per Branch Closing

Chemical Bank's written branch closing policy states that prior to any determination of a closed branch, discussions should be held with community representatives, including elected officials, community groups, and merchant associations. Customers, who are notified of branch closings by direct mail and branch posters, are given the option of having their accounts automatically transferred to a designated consolidated branch or to any other branch of their choice. Internal bank studies are conducted not only on the unprofitability or marginal profitability of closed branches but also on the level of financial services in the affected areas.

Citibank's branch closing manual outlines procedures for notifying customers and working with community leaders before a final branch closing decision is made. Management tracks all complaints related to branch closings, and the public file at Citibank revealed that there were only 1.2 complaint letters per branch closing on average. National Westminster Bank of New York City also has a branch closing manual which describes procedures whereby community needs are factored into each branch closing decision.

Finally Closing a Branch—After 20 Years of Unprofitability!

Recent branch closings by Fleet Bank of Maine have "resulted in lower accessibility in certain segments of the local community, particularly in small towns," according to the examiners. However, they concluded that the branch closing decisions can be reasonably supported by the bank's financial analysis. Certain branch closings were not subject to review during that exam because they were considered to be consolidations with offices located nearby. Some of the closed offices in small towns were only open two days a week, and none of the offices were close to being profitable.

One of that bank's offices that was closed "consistently operated at a loss even after 20 years of operation." This statement brings into question the branch performance evaluation techniques previously used by that bank. Another branch of that bank which is located in a mobile home was profitable there but not anticipated to be profitable at another more permanent location. Nonetheless, the proposed closing of that branch was denied by the state, which has a branch closing application procedure for state banks.

Massachusetts Bank Spends over $250,000 in Branch Consolidation Plan

Lakeside National Bank of Denver closed its only branch located near a mall because the facility was not profitable. The bank solicited comments from the community and mall merchants prior to the closing.

At the time of its exam, Eastern Bank of Lynn, Massachusetts, had plans to close one of its branches while keeping another one in the same community open. In anticipation of the consolidation, the bank invested over $250,000 by adding safe deposit facilities, an extra drive-up window, increased parking, and an indoor ATM at the surviving branch. The bank also applied for approval to sell food stamps out of the consolidated branch. State bank branch closings in Massachusetts (like Maine) must be approved by the state bank commissioner.

74% of Wells Fargo Branches in "Low-Mod" Areas

Wells Fargo Bank has a detailed methodology for any decisions to close, consolidate, downsize, or relocate branch offices. Recent acquisitions of other financial institutions have enabled it to improve services in low- and moderate-income neighborhoods in certain parts of the state. The examiners noted that 37% of their branches are located in low- and very low-income areas, and another 37% are located in moderate-income areas.

Dominion Bank of Middle Tennessee assesses the potential impact of a closing by among other things consulting with members of the community. However, the CRA examiners noted that "such consultation is not always documented." The bank established a revised policy which requires documentation of such consultations. The CRA examiners also noted that the bank had "no policy to be followed to open an office," although such a comment is the exception rather than the rule.

Many banks that open branches in or near senior citizen complexes do so to generate deposits, because loan demand is usually quite low from elderly residents. Boatmen's National Bank of Belleville, Illinois, was nonetheless commended for opening a full-service facility at a senior citizens apartment community.

IV. DISCRIMINATION AND OTHER ILLEGAL CREDIT PRACTICES

Credit Application Practices (Assessment Factor D)

The two assessment factors in this performance category are probably the most important in many respects because they deal with the issue at the core of CRA, namely discrimination.

Charges of discrimination by banks in general have been at an all time high beginning with the October 1991 publication of the expanded HMDA data by the FED. Subsequently released data, FED studies, and actual and planned Justice Department investigations have resulted in even more publicity in this area. Racial, ethnic, or other illegal discrimination in lending can be direct or indirect. It may exist before or during the loan application process or even after approval, if a loan is made under discriminatory price or nonprice terms. It is quite difficult to detect specific instances of discrimination. Even if a CRA examiner suspects it, the write-up of it in a public CRA evaluation report would probably be quite general and guarded.

Many of the other assessment factors overlap here. For example, affirmative efforts to structure business hours, offices, and services to be readily accessible and convenient to the community can encourage credit applications (assessment factor G). Likewise, affirmative efforts under assessment factors regarding community ascertainment efforts (A) and specific products developed to meet unique credit needs (I) can likewise encourage loan applications.

"Make the Loan" Philosophy at World Savings

Outstanding banks affirmatively solicit loan applications from all segments of its community, often with an emphasis on low- and moderate-income neighborhoods. Many outstanding banks have innovative and comprehensive procedures to assure discriminatory practices do not exist.

An affirmative "CRA spirit" or philosophy at the bank detected by a CRA examiner is an important finding. For example, World Savings of Oakland, California, stresses a "make the loan" philosophy among its loan agents, appraisers, and loan origination personnel, according to its examiners.

Columbia National Bank of Chicago was found to have an excellent record in this regard. That bank offers an introductory rate for home equity loans through a minority group, even though it has no low- or moderate-income neighborhoods in its delineated community.

No Minimum Loan Amount in Arkansas but $1,000 Minimum in Oklahoma

The removal of a minimum loan amount is very important in encouraging loans to low- and moderate-income individuals. City National Bank of Fort Smith, Arkansas, does not have a minimum loan amount, and it has numerous loans under $2,000. By contrast, RCB Bank of Claremore, Oklahoma, has a minimum loan amount of $1,000. Customers needing small loans are referred to the bank's Overdraft Protection Plan, which helps fill small credit needs on a short-term basis. However, according to the examiners, "the needs of the small creditors who do not have accounts at the bank are not being serviced by the bank." Also, since that bank is primarily a consumer and small business lender, local home owners must go to nearby Tulsa to get financing for their home purchases.

Citibank's "Second Review" Rule on Denied Loans

An increasing number of banks are establishing internal review committees for loans denied in low- and moderate-income neighborhoods. No loan application at Citibank, FSB of San Francisco, California, may be denied without a "second review and the concurrence of a senior credit officer." That bank also modifies various loan characteristics (e.g., maximum loan-to-value ratios and loan amounts) on a regional basis on the basis of relative lending risk. The examiners found no indication of post-approval loan discrimination, since regional differences were properly administered and equitably applied.

First Nationwide Bank of San Francisco, California, established an antidiscrimination review committee from senior management to conduct a quarterly examination of a sample of denied loan applications for any consumer violations. American Federal Bank of South Carolina also conducts a secondary review of rejected mortgage loan applications from minority applicants and others in low-income areas.

More on CRA Incentives and "Testers"

A few outstanding banks provide incentives to encourage applicants from low- and moderate-income areas. Citibank, FSB in Oakland, California, has developed various compensation and incentive programs to encourage and reward employees referring potential loan applicants from targeted low- and moderate-income and substantially minority communities. Wells Fargo Bank likewise has a system of incentives to encourage loan officers to actively solicit credit applications from all segments of its community.

There has been considerable debate regarding the use of "testers" by the government to identify discriminatory practices. At least one outstanding-rated bank has embarked on its own internal testing procedure. First National Bank of Chicago tests for disparate treatment of applicants using minority individuals posing as applicants.

Internal CRA Audits at the Most Outstanding Banks

Many outstanding banks conduct internal CRA audits as part of a self-testing compliance check. Citibank in New York City has an "effective compliance management" system which includes regular testing for compliance with bank policies and procedures as well as a corrective follow-up on any exceptions. Society National Bank has an ongoing compliance testing system as part of an overall compliance program. These and other outstanding banks have developed complete written policies, procedures, and training programs to assure there is no illegal discouragement or prescreening of applicants.

Boatmen's First National Bank of Kansas City, Missouri, utilizes independent personnel to conduct semiannual fair lending reviews for the bank. These reviews, which are conducted by bank personnel who do not make loans, verify the adequacy of fair lending policies, procedures, and training. The reviews include all types of approved and denied direct and indirect consumer loans, including real estate, home improvement, and personal types.

National Banks in Nebraska Criticized for Inadequate Compliance Review Procedures

Some outstanding banks were criticized for their lack of formalized compliance review procedures. None of these banks, however, were cited for any discriminatory practices. For example, The Cattle National Bank of Seward, Nebraska, had effective policies and procedures to ensure compliance, but they were not written. Also, that bank did not have formal internal reviews to assess the effectiveness of its training for this program. Firstier Bank, N.A., also a national bank in Nebraska, was likewise criticized for the lack of a formalized review process to ensure that its compliance practices were effective. The Greater New York Savings Bank was noted as having no formal internal reviews or management reporting mechanisms in place to regularly examine the adequacy of the bank's implemented policies, procedures, and programs.

Illegal Credit Practices (Assessment Factor F)

This "F Factor" significantly broadens the scope of CRA, since a bank is rated in terms of its compliance with a large number of antidiscrimination laws and regulations. Thus, this factor provides us with a "window" to view other non-CRA consumer compliance violations of a bank that would not be disclosed elsewhere.

Truly Outstanding or Just "Good"?

One of the most important conclusions reached in our analysis of outstanding banks is the fact that more than one-fourth of all such rated banks had some type of compliance violation. Specifically, 22 of the 83, or 27%, of the outstanding CRA performance evaluations reviewed in detail revealed some form of antidiscrimination law or regulation violation. By comparison, just under half (46%) of the needs improvement and substantial noncompliant banks had such violations, although many of those were of a more serious nature.

We would argue that a "truly outstanding" bank has a preeminent, excellent, or remarkable compliance record with no such violations, even of a technical or procedural nature. Thus, such an interpretation would reduce by at least one-fourth the number of rated outstanding banks and lend support to the view that "grade inflation" exists.

We believe that this situation verifies the need for a fifth or "good" CRA rating between outstanding and satisfactory. Additionally, there are probably many banks in the satisfactory category that could logically be upgraded into this new category to set them apart from their peers in that present "category of the masses" with four out of five of all ratings.

Wanted: Full Disclosure of All Violations

An outstanding bank, according to CRA, is in "substantial compliance" with all provisions of the anti-discrimination laws and regulations. This is in contrast to a satisfactory bank, which is in compliance with the "substantive provisions" of those laws and regulations.

Truly outstanding banks under this assessment factor had a full disclosure statement by their CRA examiners to the effect that the bank was in compliance with *all* provisions of antidiscrimination laws and regulations. This was the case, for example, with Mellon Bank (MD) in Rockville, Maryland. Unfortunately, many examiners of banks with outstanding ratings were not as forthcoming in their disclosure of these findings. Alternatively, they may not have completed as extensive a review of all antidiscrimination laws and regulations to enable them to make that full disclosure statement.

The disclosure by an examiner that an outstanding bank was in compliance with the "substantive provisions" of antidiscrimination laws and regulations is really only consistent with a satisfactory rating. Does this mean that there were nonsubstantive violations that weren't disclosed? After all, why would an examiner giving an outstanding rating disclose a nonsubstantive violation which could bring that rating into question?

Worse yet, some examiners of outstanding-rated banks only disclosed compliance with a few specified laws and regulations, thus bringing into question whether others were looked at and not found in compliance or just not looked at all. Obviously, we would prefer a full disclosure of a complete review such as was the case with Mellon Bank (MD), especially for outstanding banks.

"Substantive Noncompliance" at the Outstanding First National Bank of Chicago

The examiners at Eastern Bank of Lynn, Massachusetts, noted that a sample of denied applications was taken as part of the review for ECOA compliance. Although no evidence of discriminatory or other illegal credit practices was found, no other discrimination laws and regulations were mentioned. Another FDIC-examined savings bank in Massachusetts, Worcester County Institution for Savings, was noted as having no credit practices inconsistent with the substantive provisions of Fair Housing and Fair Lending laws. Again, there were no other disclosures by those CRA examiners.

Over half of the specified violations at outstanding banks were technical or procedural. Surprisingly, one outstanding bank, First National Bank of Chicago, actually was cited for substantive noncompliance. This substantive noncompliance violation pertained to sections of the ECOA involving "notices of adverse action supplied to applicants denied credit, offered credit under terms different than applied for, or who submitted incomplete applications." That substantive noncompliance did not result in discriminatory treatment of applicants. The examiner further noted that the bank was required to take "remedial corrective action for applicants affected within six months of discovery of the noncompliance." Senior management at the First National Bank of Chicago reportedly took immediate action to correct the problem.

Multiple Compliance Violations and Some Inaccurate HMDA Reports at Great Western

By far the most common technical and procedural violations for outstanding banks were with provisions of the ECOA. Next were violations of the Fair Housing Act, and several other regulations and laws were mentioned but a few times.

A few banks were mentioned in conjunction with the violation of multiple regulations and/or laws under this assessment factor. For example, Texas Bank of Weatherford, Texas, was noted as having violations of "several consumer regulations," but there were no specifics.

Great Western Bank was found to be in noncompliance with various requirements of the OTS's General Nondiscrimination Regulations and the ECOA and Regulation B. According to that examination, the bank had deficiencies in the area of "recordkeeping, reporting and documentation." The CRA examiner's loan review also disclosed that Great Western's loan application register contained "numerous errors." The examiners therefore concluded that the HMDA report filed for 1990 "contains some inaccurate information."

Repeat HMDA Violations in Hawaii Despite New Computer System

First National Bank of Omaha was found to be in compliance with the substantive provisions of antidiscrimination laws and regulations. The examiners did, however, note some technical and procedural violations of the ECOA, the Fair Housing Act, and HMDA. Another outstanding bank, First American Bank & Trust of Louisiana, was likewise found to be in noncompliance with procedural provisions of the

Fair Housing Act and ECOA regulations, but those deficiencies were noted as "widespread."

Territorial Savings of Hawaii was recommended to revise its loan standards to incorporate the relatively new Fair Housing Act requirements, which now specifically prohibit discrimination on the basis of familial status or handicap. Technical HMDA violations were also noted. Management there chose to correct previously noted errors in its loan application register in 1990 through use of a new computer system. However, the recent examination noted that management monitoring of the accuracy of information put into the register has been "minimal," thereby resulting in "repeat HMDA violations."

Technical Violations at Chemical and Other Big Banks

About half of the outstanding banks that were cited for violations were large banks. For example, Chemical Bank of New York City was cited for technical violations of the ECOA and HMDA that were due to "inadequate procedures and clerical oversight." Ironically, the bank it later acquired, Manufacturers Hanover Trust Company, was likewise cited for isolated technical violations of the same two regulations which were noted as being "exceptions to established bank procedures" and which affected few applicants.

Fleet Bank of Maine was noted as being in compliance with the majority of the provisions of ECOA, the Fair Housing Act, and HMDA. The examiners stated that any violations noted were "limited," but there were no specifics. The examiners were less specific yet in the case of Pittsburgh National Bank, which was in compliance with the substantive provisions of antidiscrimination laws and regulations. The examiners only noted that "violations noted are easily corrected through procedural changes and increased training."

Additional large banks cited for technical violations included Valley Bank of Nevada (isolated violations of ECOA), Delaware Trust Company (unspecified but nonsubstantive violations), Dominion Bank of Middle Tennessee (limited technical violations of ECOA and the Fair Housing Act), Texas Commerce Bank of El Paso (technical violations of

ECOA), and Northern Trust Bank/O'Hare in Chicago (technical violations of ECOA).

V. COMMUNITY DEVELOPMENT

Local Community Development and Redevelopment Participation (Assessment Factor H)

Outstanding banks are not only thoroughly aware of community development programs but often take a leadership role in establishing them. Sometimes they are the sole participants, and other times they may serve as the catalyst in bringing in other banks.

Community Development since 1982 in Milwaukee and Indianapolis

First Wisconsin National Bank of Milwaukee was one of the first institutions in the country to establish a community development corporation in 1982. The First Wisconsin Community Investment Corporation has established several public/private relationships resulting in numerous residential and commercial projects benefiting Milwaukee's central city. One residential project involved a $400,000 conversion of a vacant warehouse into a ten-unit apartment building for lower-income residents. On the commercial side, another project involved the renovation of a vacant former bank building into both commercial space as well as 41 apartments for low- and moderate-income persons. This corporation has also provided equity financing to two minority-owned businesses in lower-income neighborhoods. According to the examiners, these projects are "excellent examples of the efforts being taken by the bank to meet the spirit of the CRA."

The holding company for INB National Bank of Indianapolis, Indiana, also established its INB Neighborhood Revitalization Corporation in 1982 to promote the revitalization of low- and moderate-income neighborhoods. This Community Development Corporation was the fourth such one in the nation. Many banks contribute to or join community assistance organizations, but a truly outstanding bank takes a leadership role in the organization of one.

Federal, State, and Local Recognition in Massachusetts

Eastern Bank of Lynn, Massachusetts, has been involved in several community development projects. That bank received a Certificate of National Merit from the U. S. Department of Housing and Urban Development for its participation in the Point Neighborhood Housing Program in Salem, Massachusetts. Additionally, that bank was presented with the 1989 Recognition Award for its outstanding participation in the Massachusetts Guaranteed Student Loan Program by the Massachusetts Higher Education Assistance Corporation.

Worcester County Institution for Savings in Massachusetts received a "Certificate of Achievement" from the City of Leominister for its leadership role in funding the construction and development of local housing projects. That bank also works closely with the local housing authority and a housing rehabilitation program.

Chemical and Boatmen's Take a Leadership Role

Comerica Bank of Detroit was instrumental in the development of the Detroit Neighborhood Investment Corporation, in conjunction with the city of Detroit and eight or nine other local lenders. Comerica Bank was also instrumental in the start-up of the Housing Initiative Program of the United Way of Oakland County. That program in turn supports the Pontiac Neighborhood Housing Services, which is involved in housing development in a predominantly minority neighborhood of Pontiac.

The parent holding company of Boatmen's National Bank of St. Louis formed a Community Development Corporation (CDC) in 1989. The bank, through the CDC, became the founding member in the St. Louis Equity Fund, a not-for-profit corporation which spurs low-income housing development. The bank has also taken a leadership role in establishing a multibank CDC to fund minority business development and contractor needs. Moreover, the bank took a leadership role in contacting the Missouri State Treasurer's Office to expand the state-sponsored "Mo-Bucks" program, which provides funds for low-interest rate loans to farmers, small businesses, and businesses that use the funds to create jobs.

Boatmen's First National Bank of Kansas City, Missouri, another holding company affiliate, is also involved in that program. Boatmen's National Bank of Belleville, Illinois, still another holding company affiliate, is the leading lender in the Belleville Area Housing Acquisition Program, which encourages owner-occupied purchases of older housing stock in and around downtown Belleville.

Small Banks and Thrifts Also Take a Leadership Role

First Federal Savings and Loan Association of Waterbury, Connecticut, played a major role in the establishment of the Local Neighborhood Housing Services. In addition to having a representative on its board since its inception, it has made $5.0 million in pledges to help that agency meet inner city needs.

Firstier Bank of Lincoln, Nebraska, helped design and implement the Home Improvement Loan Program and Year-Round Energy Savings Program for the city of Lincoln. The bank committed one loan officer solely to those projects for several months and also handled their accounting and administration.

Territorial Savings of Hawaii is an example of a much smaller institution taking an affirmative effort by seeking out community groups to find projects that would suit the institution's budget. One such project involved working with a nonprofit foundation that will provide both temporary and longer-term benefits to the homeless.

Community Development from California to New York

Bank of America has taken a leadership role in the formation of the California Community Redevelopment Corporation, a state-sponsored equity fund to originate special incentive loans for the development of low-income housing. Bank of America has the largest equity share in the fund of all participating California banks. It is also the leader in terms of the percentage of loan funds to finance specific deals. Furthermore, one of the bank's senior officers serves as chairman for that corporation. Bank of America is also a leader nationwide in terms of its establishment of a multibillion dollar CRA lending fund over several years. The CRA examiners noted that the bank will likely meet its $50 million annual low-income housing development goal for the second year.

Citibank in New York City holds a 10% share of the $100 million revolving loan pool of the Community Preservation Corporation, which was created by several New York banks to finance rehabilitation and preservation of New York City homes. Citibank also has a 10% share in the Neighborhood Housing Services' $5 million small multifamily loan pool. Chemical Bank established Chemical Community Development in 1987 to supply credit for affordable housing.

Pooling Funds through Loan Consortiums

Many outstanding banks are involved in loan consortiums with other lenders, even though they may not have taken a leadership role in their formation. There are many examples of outstanding banks that have pooled funds with other local financial institutions for community development projects.

One Valley Bank of Summersville, West Virginia, is one of 15 local banks in a four-county area participating in a community development corporation which provides loans and equity investments to small businesses or low-income housing developments. The Dime Savings Bank of New York is one of many members of the Community Preservation Corporation, the consortium of New York City lending institutions referenced above.

American Federal Bank of South Carolina is one of eight financial institutions in a residential development corporation which funds home purchase loans up to $40,000 each for low-income persons. First American Bank & Trust of Louisiana is involved with other local institutions in the economic restructuring of a local downtown area by providing a pool of funds to enable local businesses to relocate in or improve the surrounding area.

Historical Renovation Lending that
Others Turned Down

Many outstanding banks participate in individual community development projects rather than become involved through formal organizations, government programs, development corporations, or loan consortiums. Many outstanding banks will do both, that is, work on individual projects and also participate in group ones.

The Bank of Commerce of Auburn, California, took a leadership role in forming the Nevada County Fair Lenders' Action Group in 1990. The group, which was initially formed to raise funds to support a city-wide housing study, later evolved into a comprehensive study for a much larger area. A member of the bank's senior management is the founding chairman of that group. Another member of senior management is a founding director of the Sacramento Home Loan Counseling Center, which is designed to help first-time and low-income home buyers.

In addition to other community development projects, the bank provided acquisition and restoration financing for the renovation of a local post office building, an important historical landmark in the downtown area. Although other lenders turned down the loan package, management at the bank worked with the borrowers to make restoration funding possible. Boatmen's National Bank of Belleville, Illinois, which is also a leader in a local housing program, helped finance a local public library.

Model Lending, Donated Land,
and a "Team City"

Citibank, FSB of Oakland, California, has been involved in both private and public community development projects. That bank's California region is administering a model community lending program. It provides long-term, low-cost financing for low- and moderate-income housing projects of non-profit developers. The bank also received subsidized funding to work with a local housing and redevelopment agency in a unique mortgage program to assist low-income first-time home buyers with closing costs and minor rehabilitation using tax increment funds.

The Community Development Association at the First National Bank of Louisville, Kentucky, allows the bank to provide zero and low-interest rate financing in return for investment tax credits that allow the bank to earn a market rate of return over the loan's life. The realization of tax credits at the bank is dependent upon the project's success over a 15-year period.

First Security Bank & Trust of Charles City, Iowa, donated land to a local city for the purpose of community development. First Gibraltar Bank of Texas has also participated in community development programs by donating real estate and providing financial services and technical assistance.

RCB Bank of Claremore, Oklahoma, is actively involved with the local county industrial authority to provide loans to local businesses in need of special financing. The bank, which created an endowment to a local college, has also extended credit to the college and aided it in other ways.

First City of Kountze, Texas, revitalized an effort, previously abandoned by the local chamber of commerce, to complete the needed documentation to qualify as a "Team City" sponsored by a local utility. That project will enable the city to be marketed on a computerized network throughout North America to firms wishing to locate there. This bank has also taken a leadership role in sponsoring seminars on small business development through a local university.

Developing a State Housing Bond Program in Delaware, Not Just Investing in It

Most banks invest in municipal bonds. Several outstanding banks were noted in this regard, particularly if the financing affected local development projects. Delaware Trust Company, in conjunction with three other financial institutions in 1989, helped to design and initiate a state residential mortgage revenue bond program. The bank also works closely with the local government in a program which rehabilitates and sells abandoned homes to low-income citizens; the bank provides permanent mortgage financing after the local government subsidizes the borrower's down payment. This program was recognized in both 1988 and 1989 by FNMA as one of its approved low- and moderate-income housing efforts. The bank has also deposited $100,000 in a local minority federal development credit union that helped improve its lending capabilities.

First Interstate Bank of California worked with city officials in Pomona to develop a bond program to provide funding for affordable housing to first-time home buyers there at a favorable rate. That bank also worked with a city government agency and eight other financial institutions to implement a pilot program for extending small business loans in amounts of up to $10,000.

All banks make donations, but those that are directed toward community development groups are usually noted under this assessment factor. United Jersey Bank/Central in Princeton, New Jersey, participates in low- and moderate-income housing programs in several towns through loans and/or outright grants.

Limited Criticism of Outstanding Banks

Only a few outstanding banks were criticized for their community development participation. American Savings Bank in California has substantial investments in a financial institution loan consortium. Beyond that involvement and another proposed project, the examiners noted that there has been "limited" direct lending for community development and/or redevelopment activities.

The examiners raised the issue of the extent of participation in the six different delineated communities at Dominion Bank of Middle Tennessee. They stated that there was more awareness in some communities than others. Also, there was a high level of participation in some programs, often in a leadership role; but in others the bank "only participates if requested."

Ability to Meet Credit Needs (Assessment Factor K)

A bank's CRA rating is based on its performance in a manner "consistent with its resources and capabilities." This assessment factor evaluates an institution's ability to meet credit needs based on any financial, size, regulatory, economic, or other constraints which may exist.

This assessment factor sometimes involves a discussion of economic development projects which may also be described in the previous assessment factor (H). Also, a bank's working relationships with public and private sector representatives may also be covered in previous ascertainment (A) and director involvement (C) assessment factors.

Leadership in Economic Development in Akron and Omaha

Some outstanding banks have taken a leadership role in certain projects involving both public and private partnerships. Bank One, Akron established a community advisory council in 1990. This council is made up of local political and community leaders.

First National Bank of Omaha was instrumental in the development of the Greater Omaha Community Support Center formed in response to the closing of a local credit union and its affiliated financial counseling service. That bank has also been involved with a nonprofit organization working to develop a small business incubator program in South Omaha. Furthermore, the bank was instrumental in the passage of legislation providing funds to assist development projects in North Omaha.

"Cleaning Up Neighborhoods" in St. Paul

A wide variety of constraints which might affect an outstanding bank's ability to meet community credit needs were mentioned under this assessment factor. First National Bank of Chicago, although the largest financial institution in Illinois, is limited by state branching and ATM restrictions in terms of its ability to provide convenient access to its services.

Heartland Federal in Oklahoma is somewhat limited in its ability to ascertain and meet various types of credit needs because it is an Oklahoma Plan institution. The CRA efforts of American Federal Bank of South Carolina were "limited slightly by certain regulator constraints" according to the examiners.

The main office of Western State Bank in St. Paul, Minnesota, is located in a relatively low-income, high-crime area with a large minority population, according to the examiners. Bank management is well known in the area as being one of the driving forces behind "cleaning up and revitalizing neighborhoods," according to those examiners.

The 1990–91 recession has acted as an economic constraint to many institutions in their lending function. The downturn in the New York City real estate market has "substantially hampered" the ability of The Greater New York Savings Bank to maintain the significant volume of home-loan originations of previous years.

High Unemployment and Low Income in Small Communities in Texas and West Virginia

First City in Kountze, Texas, is located in a low- to moderate-income community with a large portion of the households receiving some type of government

assistance. Even with that community's increasing unemployment rate, the examiners noted that there is no evidence to indicate the bank is hindered in meeting community credit needs. One Valley Bank of Summersville, West Virginia, operates in a community with an unemployment rate of approximately 14%, roughly double that for the referenced community in Texas. However, that factor is not mentioned as a constraint to the bank's credit activities in any way.

Mississippi's Largest Thrift Specializes in "Low-Mod" Market

Magnolia Federal, the largest thrift in Mississippi, has designated its primary market as the average Mississippi family making less than $25,000 annually. The examiners noted that the bank's average loan and deposit balances reflect that it is serving low- and moderate-income residents throughout its community. For example, the average balance in its "Lifeline Checking" is less than $400. Also, its average mortgage balance was just over $33,000. Furthermore, that bank is a major lender on mobile homes, which are particularly important to low- and moderate-income families.

Other Factors (Assessment Factor L)

All other relevant factors that can affect a bank's CRA performance are placed here. Often it appears that CRA examiners may mention a positive development at a bank (possibly at their request) which may have little or no bearing on CRA performance.

Getting "CRA Credit" for 40% of Charitable Contributions

All banks make charitable contributions of one type or another. It appears, however, that CRA credit primarily is given to donations to housing groups, community organizations, and the like, which have a direct or indirect CRA benefit.

At least one bank has made its preference clear in this regard. Citibank, FSB of Oakland, California, which has three regions around the country, allocates approximately 40% of its donations to housing and community development organizations. The Community Affairs Committee in each of the three regions oversees corporate donations.

Pacific First Bank of Seattle targeted approximately one-fifth of its annual half-million dollar corporate contributions into its affordable housing program. Washington Trust Bank in Spokane established its own foundation, which is involved in various community projects and organizations. The foundation is administered and funded by the bank and plays an integral part in its CRA activities.

Award-Winning Banks

Certain outstanding banks that receive awards or recognition for community service are often noted under this assessment factor. Western State Bank of St. Paul, Minnesota, has received numerous local and national awards and praises for the bank's community development performance. Lakeside National Bank of Denver has also received numerous awards for community program participation. That bank recently was named "Business of the Year" by a local industry council for the bank's outstanding training and employment efforts for high school dropouts.

The Greater New York Savings Bank received the "Employer of the Year" award in 1990 from a local service organization for providing job opportunities to the elderly, immigrants, and students. The bank also received an award from the local electric utility for the bank's efforts in helping to rebuild Brooklyn neighborhoods.

Pittsburgh National Bank was commended for its efforts in participating in paint and fix-up projects that benefited elderly and low-income community members. World Savings of California established the "Paint-a-World" project, where bank employees of all levels paint homes in low-income neighborhoods to maintain property values and encourage investment. Citibank (New York State) of Pittsford, New York, provided a grant and supplied employee worker hours to help build low-income housing. Bank personnel there are also active in raising funds for low-income housing causes.

20% of Chicago Bank Purchases from Minorities

Some outstanding banks have active minority purchasing programs. For example, First National Bank of Chicago's program resulted in over 20% of 1990 bank purchases being made from minority owned businesses. Citibank, FSB in Oakland, California, also has a minority vendor program which resulted in business for 37 different minority- or women-owned businesses through its California region in 1990. Wells Fargo Bank participated in $5.5 million worth of minority vendor contracts in 1990.

Citibank, FSB also has a unique Shared Executive Program. Members of middle and senior management serve on the boards or provide technical expertise to hundreds of community and other organizations throughout the bank's delineated communities.

Assisting Customers, Non-Customers, and Even Other Banks

Many outstanding banks have seminars and workshops for customers and noncustomers alike on different credit topics (e.g., first-time home buyers). Some banks, such as Firstier Bank of Lincoln, Nebraska, provide meeting rooms to community organizations. National Westminster Bank of New York City donates business equipment and furniture to community development groups. Bank One of Appleton, Wisconsin, established a small business lending reference center in its downtown office. This center includes information on obtaining loans, making business plans, and other information of interest to small businesses.

A bank officer at First Security Bank & Trust of Charles City, Iowa, helped organize a marketing club to better educate and inform area farmers on marketing their products.

Some banks provide CRA assistance to other banks and are so noted under this assessment factor. INB National Bank of Indianapolis provides assistance to other banks in developing a program for meeting community credit needs. Boatmen's First National Bank of Kansas City provided technical assistance to another bank located in and serving a low- and moderate-income neighborhood.

Forbearance after Andrew

Some banks that provide special services to their customers and others affected by major unforeseen events are also noted under this assessment factor. Wells Fargo Bank was one of the first banks extending special credit considerations to members of the reserves called up during the Gulf War.

World Savings offered forbearances and advances to borrowers in the San Francisco Bay area whose properties were damaged by the 1989 earthquake. Home Savings of America in California also has an aid program for natural disasters which was used in both earthquakes and fires in California and a hurricane. Customers were primarily assisted by deferring loan payments and providing insurance information. Hurricane Andrew victims have likewise been assisted in numerous ways by banks, with some clearly doing more than others.

Special Services for Minorities and the Handicapped

Several banks which offer multilingual ATMs are often mentioned in this section as well as under a previous assessment factor (B). Tri-lingual Atms (English, Spanish, and Chinese) are available at American Savings Bank in California, First Nationwide Bank, and Citibank in New York City, among others.

Eastern Bank of Lynn, Massachusetts, which learned of many of the needs of its Spanish-speaking customers in a customer satisfaction survey, translated many of its brochures into Spanish. That bank also strategically placed bilingual employees in certain branches. Furthermore, the bank offered a 14-week Spanish class to all employees who wished to enroll.

A few outstanding banks have provided special banking services to aid the handicapped. For example, First National Bank of Louisville offers audio statements for visually impaired customers. Worcester County Institution for Savings in Massachusetts and Citibank (New York State) of Pittsford, New York, both offer a special device to allow hearing impaired residents to communicate with the bank.

Lifeline Checking—A "Dime-a-Check" in Arkansas

An important service that has been debated in Congress is free government check cashing at insured financial institutions. Some outstanding banks have been offering this service for some time now. These include the First National Bank of Louisville, First National Bank of Omaha, and Bank One, Akron.

Also discussed quite frequently is the "lifeline" or "basic banking" checking account. Many outstanding banks offer this service in one form or another. City National Bank of Fort Smith, Arkansas, has a "Dime-a-Check" program requiring no minimum deposit balance and a dime for each check written plus a $1.00 service charge per deposit. First National Bank of Louisville offers a lifeline checking account for customers with annual household incomes below $20,000. Citibank, FSB of Oakland, California, also has a basic banking service at minimal cost for low-income individuals.

Eastern Bank of Lynn, Massachusetts, has a low cost economy checking account plus free checking for senior citizens. Delaware Trust Company has a "Thrifty-Checking Account" for low- and moderate-income customers, senior citizens, and students. Bank One, Akron, also has an economy checking program. Bank of America offers low cost banking services to state teachers in addition to a limited checking program for low-income customers and another one for senior citizens.

The "lifeline" checking account at Manufacturers Hanover Trust Company had a $5.00 monthly fee with no minimum balance, allowing for eight free checks per month and unlimited free ATM usage. There was a charge of $0.75 for each additional check and teller transaction. That bank also offered a no-minimum balance savings account free of charge with a $400 minimum balance.

Free Checking in the South

Many banks offer senior citizens no-charge or low-charge accounts. However, they do not appear to offer the same CRA credit as free government check cashing or lifeline accounts, which more directly benefit low- and moderate-income individuals. Of course, many seniors fall in the latter group, but most of these programs are open to all senior citizens regardless of income or net worth.

Those banks that offer outright free checking clearly benefit all groups regardless of income or age levels. For example, Magnolia Federal in Mississippi was the first financial institution there to provide a totally free checking account. That account, which was designed for low- to moderate-income families, amounts to two-thirds of all that bank's checking accounts. The average account balance of only $375 in those checking accounts is considerably less than the $1,100 average checking account balance there.

American Federal Bank in South Carolina and First Citizen's Bank in Elizabethtown, Kentucky, also offer free checking accounts with no minimum balance required. The Greater New York Savings Bank offered the lowest monthly checking account fees in the New York area, according to surveys published by a local newspaper. That bank also finished fourth overall in those surveys in terms of reasonable service fees and attractive deposit rates.

5. CASE STUDIES OF OUTSTANDING BANKS

INTRODUCTION

Eight case studies of outstanding banks are included in this chapter. The first case study considers the question of "grade inflation" involving banks with outstanding ratings. The second case study discusses America's highest CRA-rated banks. The third and fourth case studies concern banks that have been upgraded to an outstanding rating from one of the lower ones.

The fifth case study involves the nation's second largest thrift, Great Western, which was upgraded to an outstanding rating from a satisfactory one. The sixth case study is about our recommended shared bank branch concept. The seventh case study concerns CRA "megapledges." The final case study details the step-by-step procedure utilized by a community bank to turn around a CRA rating from a likely failure to outstanding in approximately one year.

GAUGING GRADE INFLATION AT OUTSTANDING BANKS

Accepting the outstanding ratings at face value, there were 587 banks in America with the highest CRA rating, representing 8.7% of all ratings through year-end 1991, and 1,249 such banks (10.3% of the total) through year-end 1992. However, to the extent that there is any "grade inflation" or other factors that would dilute the value of an outstanding rating, the number of *truly* outstanding banks would be fewer.

Truly Outstanding Banks Overstated by 77%

One of the most important conclusions in our evaluation of individual assessment factors was the fact that 26.5% of the outstanding banks in our analysis, which includes most of the largest ones and a broad spectrum of others, had some type of consumer compliance violation. A strict interpretation of an outstanding bank as being a truly remarkable one in *all* respects would remove these 26.5%. Even though it can be argued that most of these were technical and procedural violations, it can also be argued that a "truly" outstanding bank would have an internal CRA audit and self-assessment function to ensure that no such violations existed.

A deduction of the 26.5% for this reason applied to the base of all 587 banks receiving an outstanding rating as of year-end 1991 would reduce the ranks of the truly outstanding to 431 banks, or just 6.4% of all banks instead of 8.7% of them.

A further strict interpretation of a truly outstanding bank would likewise remove those outstanding-rated banks that were criticized on one or more assessment factors other than the "F Factor" of consumer violations. Our detailed analysis of a broad-based sample of 83 outstanding evaluations through year-end 1991 concluded that 14 additional ones beyond those with consumer compliance violations had received some type of criticism in one or more assessment factor. This represents an additional 16.9% of the sample. Added to the 26.5% with consumer violations results in a total of 43.4% of outstanding rated banks with some criticism.

Applying this percentage to the total 587 outstanding ratings as of year-end 1991 would reduce that amount to only 332 banks or just 4.9% of all approximately 6,700 rated banks. Thus, the strictest interpretation of a truly outstanding bank would reduce their number by 43.4%. Rather than representing 8.7% of all rated banks, truly outstanding ones under this strict interpretation would represent but 4.9% of the total as of year-end 1991. Thus, truly outstanding banks in 1991 were overstated by approximately 77%. The comparable strict grade inflation adjustment would reduce year-end 1992 rated outstanding banks from 10.3% of the total to just 5.8% truly outstanding ones. Our grade inflation analysis in Chapter 4, however, was based upon 1991 evaluations.

A Case for a Fifth CRA Rating of "Good"

This strict approach to rating banks as outstanding suggests the existence of grade inflation by regulators in their current outstanding ratings. Additionally, we would interpret this finding as indicating the need for a fifth rating category of "good" between satisfactory and outstanding where these less than truly outstanding banks would be placed. This would be similar to the original FHLBB system of five ratings.

Under this proposed five-tiered system only 5% of all rated banks would be truly outstanding as of year-end 1991, and probably a much larger percentage would be in the good category. These would include the nearly 4% adjusted downward from the outstanding category as noted above plus an undetermined but probably large proportion of satisfactory rated banks that are really better than average CRA performers. Creating such a five-tiered system would be analogous to adding a "B" to a system that previously only had an "A," "C," "D," and "F."

Determining Grade Inflation with Individual Assessment Factor Ratings

There is another approach to determining the extent of grade inflation in outstanding ratings. This approach would first require regulators, as we recommend, to assign gradings for the individual assessment factors. Some regulators (notably the FED and

the West Region of the OTS) previously provided 13 separate ratings (for the 12 assessment factors plus the reasonableness of the delineated community) in addition to an overall rating. The regulators quickly backed away from this approach. They now reach conclusions using various adjectives (other than those defining the four CRA ratings) for each of the assessment factors.

We believe that the regulators avoid individual assessment factor ratings because the disclosure of so much information provides too much insight into their subjective weightings of different assessment factors and the final rating. We understand that the regulators also make individual ratings for each of the five performance categories, but these, likewise, are not made public.

We feel it would be in the public interest to not only require individual assessment factor ratings on the basis of the four CRA categories but also those for the five performance categories. Thus, an outside assessment of a bank's CRA performance, and most importantly its improvement over time, could be judged by both assessment factor and performance category using this information.

Even more importantly, individual assessment factor or performance category public ratings would allow a more objective analysis of what would and would not constitute grade inflation for outstanding ratings. This is the second approach referenced above.

Under this approach a truly outstanding bank would be defined as one with outstanding ratings for *all* performance categories. A stricter approach yet would require such ratings for *all* assessment factors, because it is possible to have an outstanding rating for each of the five performance categories but not for all of the assessment factors. *Any* compliance violation in the "F Factor" would disallow an outstanding rating for it or that performance category under this approach.

Our analysis was an attempt to replicate this recommended approach using a strict interpretation of a truly outstanding rating by assessment factor. Our findings indicated that the proportion of outstanding ratings would fall by approximately 43%. Thus, the percentage of truly outstanding banks as of year-end 1991 would fall from 8.7% to 4.9%. The same inflation adjustment applied to year-end 1992 data would reduce the proportion from 10.3% to 5.8%.

AMERICA'S HIGHEST CRA-RATED BANKS

There are several approaches to defining the highest CRA-rated banks in America. One approach, as described in the previous section, would be to use a strict interpretation of "truly" outstanding banks as those with outstanding ratings in all assessment factors, or more liberally, in all performance categories. Because of the lack of disclosure of these individual ratings, such an approach is not feasible. However, an individual review of each evaluation by assessment factor, similar to the type we conducted in the previous chapter, would provide an approximation of those likely individual ratings.

Multiple Outstanding Ratings

A second approach to defining the highest CRA-rated banks is to focus on those that have received *multiple* outstanding ratings. Even though the same examination team at the same regulator may be involved in the second compliance exam of a bank, there is usually a different head examiner. Even if this is not the case, the ability of a bank to maintain an outstanding rating in the face of multiple compliance examinations over time would clearly define it as being exceptional.

As pointed out in our previous analysis, only about 2% of all rated banks have received multiple exams as of year-end 1991, and most of these were by the FED, the FDIC's Dallas Region, and the OTS's West Region. According to our analysis, only five banks received multiple outstanding ratings at that time. These were the First Nebraska Bank in Valley, Nebraska (FED); Kanabec State Bank in Mora, Minnesota (FED); Bank of Romney in West Virginia (FED); Dayton State Bank in Dayton, Texas (FDIC); and First Nationwide Bank of San Francisco (OTS). By year-end 1992 many more banks received double outstanding ratings, and some such as the Dayton State Bank received triple outstanding ratings. There may have been others in this category as of year-end 1992, but complete data are not yet available.

Upgrading to an Outstanding Rating

A bank that significantly improves its CRA performance to upgrade itself into the outstanding category from a below-average one could also be categorized as truly outstanding. As of December 31, 1991, only two banks have upgraded themselves from needs improvement to outstanding, and each of these will be the subject of a separate case study.

The first of these, Bank of Commerce, N.A. of Auburn, California, was double upgraded from a needs improvement rating to an outstanding rating in one examination. The other bank, Security State Bank of Stockdale, Texas, was upgraded from needs improvement to a satisfactory rating in its second examination and then further upgraded to outstanding in its third examination. The latter case study will, however, raise questions on the outstanding rating given to the bank in Texas. Therefore, we would not consider it a truly outstanding one like the Bank of Commerce, N.A. Additional banks were upgraded from needs improvement ratings to outstanding ones in 1992, such as the First Bank and Trust of Groves, Texas, which received FDIC evaluations of needs improvement, satisfactory, and outstanding in 1990, 1991, and 1992, respectively.

An upgrade from satisfactory to outstanding, while more common, is not as dramatic, and there were many such upgradings in 1992. As of year-end 1991, eight banks were upgraded from a satisfactory rating to an outstanding rating during their second examination. Five of these were upgraded by the FDIC's Dallas Region, the source of most multiple evaluations: Commerce Bank of Aurora, Colorado; Red Oak State Bank in Red Oak, Texas; Commercial State Bank in Garrison, Texas; Carmine State Bank in Carmine, Texas; and First City, Texas in Sour Lake, Texas. The West Region of the OTS was responsible for three such upgradings: Citibank FSB in Oakland, California; Great Western Bank, FSB of Beverly Hills, California; and Pacific First Bank, a FSB of Seattle, Washington.

These ten banks, which worked themselves into an outstanding rating as of year-end 1991, clearly represent an exceptional group. This is because most banks upon their second examination receive the same rating. Most satisfactory banks that have been examined a second time received a satisfactory rating. The previously presented analysis provides the details in this regard. Most of the upgrades are from needs improvement to satisfactory, but only the two banks noted above took it a step further to upgrade themselves to an outstanding rating, as of year-end 1991. As would be expected, there were many more upgradings to outstanding in 1992, but complete data on such multiple ratings are not yet available.

An Outstanding CRA Rating for Citicorp

Another approach to defining America's highest CRA-rated banks is whether or not a bank received outstanding ratings from different regulators, especially multiple outstanding ratings. Bank holding companies are not provided CRA ratings. The rating of a one-bank holding company would essentially be that of its only bank. However, larger, multibank holding companies may receive a wide spectrum of CRA ratings from as many as four federal bank regulators plus state CRA regulators when relevant.

Citicorp, our nation's largest bank holding company, provides an example of a holding company which would likely receive an outstanding rating based upon the favorable ratings received by its largest subsidiaries. Citicorp would therefore qualify as one of America's highest CRA-rated financial institutions based on its published CRA ratings. As noted in Table 5-1, 11 of its 13 banking subsidiaries listed received CRA ratings from three different federal bank regulators plus the New York State Banking Department as of year-end 1992.

Eight of the 11 Citicorp bank subsidiaries receiving public CRA exams were rated satisfactory. The three others were rated outstanding, and these include the lead bank, which has approximately three-fourths of

Table 5-1   Citicorp CRA Ratings, 7/1/90–12/31/92

Bank	City	State	Regulator	Date of Exam	Rating
Citibank (Arizona)	Phoenix	AZ	FDIC	2/91	S
Citibank (Delaware)	New Castle	DE	FDIC	3/91	S
Citibank (Florida), N.A.	Dania	FL	OCC	3/90	S
			OCC	1/91	S
Citibank (Maine), N.A.	S. Portland	ME	OCC	1/91	S
Citibank (Maryland), N.A.	Towson	MD	OCC	10/91	S
Citibank (Nevada), N.A.	Las Vegas	NV	OCC	1/91	S
Citibank, N.A.	New York	NY	OCC	12/90	O
Citibank (New York State)	Perinton	NY	FDIC	3/91	O
			STATE	12/90	O
			STATE	8/91	O
Citibank (South Dakota), N.A.	Sioux Falls	SD	OCC	N/A	N/A
Citibank, F.S.B.	San Francisco	CA	OTS	7/90	S
			OTS	6/91	O*
Citibank, F.S.B.	Miami	FL	OTS	11/92	S
Citicorp Savings and Industrial Bank	Denver	CO	FDIC	N/A	N/A
DeAnza Bank	Sunnyvale	CA	FDIC	9/92	S

*Second evaluation after consolidation of Chicago and D.C. banks into San Francisco bank.

N/A — Not Available
Source: Citicorp

the holding company's assets, and its third and fourth largest bank subsidiaries. Its second largest bank subsidiary, the credit card bank in South Dakota, was not yet evaluated as of December 31, 1992, but it is possible that it could even receive a satisfactory rating, which is no easy task for a credit card bank.

Citibank (New York State) received an outstanding rating from the FDIC and multiple outstanding ratings from the New York State Banking Department. Citibank, FSB, based in San Francisco, with operations in Chicago and Washington, D.C., was one of the above-mentioned banks being upgraded by the OTS from a satisfactory to an outstanding rating. That bank's unique "second review" rule on denied loans as well as its CRA incentive program was cited in Chapter 4.

Counting the outstanding rating given by the OCC to the lead bank, Citicorp has received outstanding ratings from all federal bank regulators (except the FED) and from the New York State Banking Department. Furthermore, a detailed analysis of the evaluations of those three banks indicated no criticism whatsoever on any assessment factors which would prevent them from being designated as truly outstanding CRA-rated banks.

And an Outstanding CRA Rating for BankAmerica

Our nation's second largest bank holding company, BankAmerica Corporation, also provides an example of a bank holding company that would likely receive an outstanding rating. Our analysis of the public evaluation of the lead bank, which also represents three-fourths of the holding company's assets, characterized it as truly outstanding one in all respects. Of particular relevance is their commitment not to close unprofitable branches in some low-income areas (see Chapter 4). We should point out, however, that some community groups have challenged Bank of America's outstanding rating based on the community groups' evaluation of the bank's lending record, among other things.

BankAmerica Corporation's second largest subsidiary, Seattle–First National Bank, received a satisfactory rating from the OCC. The Arizona affiliate, the third largest bank subsidiary, received a satisfactory rating from the FDIC, but Bank of America State Bank in Concord, California, a very small community bank, received an outstanding rating from the FDIC. Two small bank affiliates likewise received satisfactory ratings from the FDIC. While other bank affiliates were not rated as of year-end 1992, it is interesting to note that Bank America's newly-acquired Valley Bank affiliate in Nevada received back-to-back outstanding ratings from the FED.

Most notable regarding BankAmerica's CRA performance is the very substantial CRA pledge it made both before and after its purchase of Security Pacific Corporation. Although these will be discussed in a subsequent section, BankAmerica Corporation's $12 billion postmerger pledge over a ten-year period is the largest on an absolute basis. BankAmerica Corporation also set a precedent prior to the merger by announcing a huge $5 billion CRA pledge over a ten-year period when it was evaluating the possible purchase of Bank of New England in April 1991. Thus, on the basis of its precedent-setting CRA pledges alone, BankAmerica Corporation would be considered one of America's highest CRA-rated financial institutions.

Our focus here on Citibank and Bank of America, our nation's two largest banks, by no means is meant to imply that only the largest banks can be the highest CRA-rated ones. In fact, most of the outstanding banks analyzed in this book were smaller ones. Again, by applying the same criterion above for a truly outstanding bank, the largest proportion of them would be community banks on the basis of numbers alone.

ONE BIG STEP FROM NEEDS IMPROVEMENT TO OUTSTANDING

The previous section identified a subset of truly outstanding banks as being two that were upgraded from a needs improvement rating to an outstanding one. Most upgradings upon a second examination were from needs improvement to satisfactory. However, one bank jumped all the way from needs improvement to outstanding in its second evaluation, the Bank of Commerce, N.A. of Auburn, California.

The other bank to upgrade itself from needs improvement to outstanding did so after three compliance exams. The Security State Bank of Stockdale,

Texas, was upgraded from needs improvement to satisfactory on its second exam and to outstanding on its third exam.

These two banks, which were both upgraded from needs improvement to outstanding, will be the subject of this and the following studies. Both made significant improvements in their CRA performance, one doing so in one large step, and the other doing it in two smaller ones.

The Bank of Commerce, N.A. is a $54 million dollar well-capitalized community bank. The bank, which was established in 1983, operates out of its main office in Auburn and branch offices in Grass Valley and Folsom. These three communities are located in north central California just northeast of Sacramento.

Bank of Commerce received a needs improvement rating during its first public examination on August 10, 1990. They applied for a new branch location, which necessitated a second exam because of their needs improvement rating. Less than nine months later, on April 30, 1991, they had their second public exam, whereupon they received an outstanding rating.

21 Areas of Improvement over a Nine-Month Period

The following items, in order of assessment factor, identify specific areas of *improvement* during that nine-month period which led to the outstanding rating at the Bank of Commerce:

1. The bank established a formal program, with affirmative guidelines, to ascertain community credit needs where no such program existed before. According to the CRA officer, this program was formed "from the board on down."

2. The bank went from a passive role to a leadership role in its communications with its three communities, especially in the area of helping to form groups to analyze the housing needs of low- and moderate-income households.

3. Management and board had always been in monthly contact with a large range of community representatives. Rather than being involved on just a limited basis, as was sometimes the case before, the bank actively "searched out" leaders from local, city, and county governments to discuss the bank's role in meeting community needs. An example is the bank's involvement as a reference source with the small business assistance center of a local college.

4. Management developed its own questionnaires for bank officers and the public to ascertain and document specific community credit needs, where no such documentation existed before. These questionnaires are sent out every six months. The board's CRA Committee reviews the survey results to tailor the terms of loan products to meet identified needs. One example was the bank's changing of terms relating to home improvement and home equity loans. We understand from the bank that these terms involved adding flexibility to the loan evaluation process to take into account circumstances that may not have been considered before.

5. The bank went from a situation of not using published local demographic or economic data to installing a program which analyzed it and used the results to address the needs of low- and moderate-income and minority individuals. Bank management purchased current data on average household income and the minority population from an outside vendor. This was the bank's only use of an outside vendor.

6. The board went from a situation of not dedicating adequate effort in formulating CRA policies and performance reviews to one where it dedicated "sufficient time and effort" to those activities. The board's CRA Committee completes a documented monthly review and discussion of the bank's CRA activities. The board's Vice Chairman became chairman of the new CRA Committee.

7. Bank management and the board developed a formal written CRA program, with goals and objectives for each assessment factor, compared

to the previous situation where it did not have an articulated program.

8. The bank developed two CRA self-assessment tools, a periodic geographic analysis of lending patterns and branch-level customer surveys on the effectiveness of the bank's CRA program. There was not even a written methodology for CRA self-assessment prior to this change.

9. The bank developed an annual program to analyze the disposition of loan applications where there was no such program before.

10. The bank provided for increased employee training to ensure borrowers are treated in a fair and nondiscriminatory manner where no such system existed before. The bank further mandated for the first time that every member of the board, the management team, and the staff (even including janitors) receive CRA training and pass, with a minimum 75% grade, a bank test on the subject. This contrasted to the previous situation where the board provided little, if any, support to CRA training.

11. The board's increased involvement in CRA activities by the time of the second exam ensured all regulatory requirements were met. Further, the bank now provides expanded information in the public file, including material on the bank's CRA program, the results of management's self-assessment, and copies of recent CRA committee minutes. This current substantial effort in documentation is contrasted to the previous situation where the board was cited as being "lax" in ensuring compliance with CRA technical requirements. For example, the first examination noted that the bank's public file did not even contain the required CRA statements for the past two years.

12. The bank began a formal marketing outreach program to low- and moderate-income areas through its personal assistance to and contact with housing groups and civic organizations within them. The bank previously had not instituted such a formal outreach program. Still,

though, the bank's marketing and advertising program at the time of its second examination was recommended to be revised or expanded "to inform all segments of the community" of specific credit services. In other words, there was improvement in this area, but there was still room for more.

13. The bank developed a system to review advertising compliance with applicable laws and regulations, where no such system was in effect before. Actually, the original exam revealed a number of Truth in Lending Act inconsistencies involving required disclosures, but these problems were apparently resolved by the time of the second exam.

14. The bank improved from an "adequate" to a "good" record of originating mortgage and small business loans. No specific changes in the bank's lending policies were noted. While the first evaluation noted that the bank may discourage applications by charging "above market rates" on home improvement and home equity loans, this factor was not even mentioned in the second public evaluation. We understand that the bank did *not* change its criticized loan pricing. Management made a firm decision not to follow what it felt was "loss-leader" pricing on these loans by certain competitors.

15. The bank utilized the same ten-mile radii around each of its three offices as its delineated communities in both examinations. While the first exam criticized the bank for not maintaining support for the delineation, the second examination noted that the bank's methodology was adequately supported. Reference in the latest exam was made to a geographic distribution of credit to develop and analyze the delineated communities, where no such analysis existed before.

16. The bank was not only criticized in its original examination for not performing a loan geocoding analysis, but even more so since the examiners determined that the bank's computer system at

that time had the "ability to track loans by census tract." By the time of the second exam, the bank had prepared a well-documented census tract analysis of credit extensions showing that 96% by number and dollar volume were within the delineated communities. Because outside sources could not assign a census tract to all addresses within the three local communities, the bank developed its *own* internal mapping system to do this task!

17. The bank prepared written guidelines concerning the opening or closing of branches, whereas such a formal policy was previously not available.

18. The first public examination identified four specific practices which may have discouraged loan applications. By the time of the second exam, the bank had corrected two of these with new outreach programs to low- and moderate-income neighborhoods and formal training programs. However, the two other practices *not*mentioned during the second exam included the bank's charging of higher than market rates on certain loans and the lack of an internal system to assess or ensure compliance with antidiscrimination laws and regulations.

19. The first public exam noted substantive violations of the ECOA and fair housing regulations, which in some cases demonstrated a "pattern or practice." The bank was found to comply with the substantive provisions of relevant laws and regulations during the second exam, but there was reference to the fact that any violations that were disclosed were "nonsubstantive" in nature. Thus, this bank was granted an outstanding rating even though it had some nonsubstantive violations, which the examiners noted were promptly corrected by senior management.

20. The bank's second exam reported that there was a high level of participation in community development projects, often in a leadership role. While the bank was aware of and involved in some projects according to the first exam, these contacts were not documented. Three new ex-

amples of community development projects were given in the second exam. First, a Fair Lenders' Action Group was formed in the bank's home county under the leadership of the bank with a member of senior management being the founding chairman. That group was initially responsible for a study of low- and moderate-income housing needs in one city, but under the bank's leadership the study was expanded to include the entire western portion of the county. That group has been responsible for approximately $1.7 million of affordable housing in the local community. Second, a member of senior management was noted as being a founding director of the Sacramento Home Loan Counseling Center, which helps first-time and low-income home buyers through special programs and seminars. Third, a member of bank management was appointed as one of two private sector representatives of a county economic development district.

21. The bank improved from a passive to an active role in developing or implementing specific projects to meet community credit needs and promote economic revitalization.

In summary, the most important difference between the bank's first and second public examination was the development of an affirmative CRA spirit from the top to the bottom. We understand from the bank that the same head examiner was involved in both evaluations, so there was no question as to an "easier grader" being involved the second time around.

A CRA In-House Turnaround for $50,000

Significantly, the bank did not change its basic loan products, although it did make an unspecified change adding flexibility to the underwriting terms of its home improvement and home equity loans, probably to the betterment of both the community and the bank. Even though the bank was criticized for its above-market rates on certain loans in the first exam, it refused to offer lower rates to match what it felt was "loss-leader" pricing by certain competitors.

The bank did not change many of the things it was doing, including its office hours and community delineations. Importantly, the bank's CRA program was mainly an internal effort as the only use of outside resources was the purchase of updated income and minority population demographics, a fairly nominal expense. The questionnaires were developed and analyzed in-house, as was also the case with the bank's revised and new CRA programs and systems.

We understand from the bank's CRA Officer that the estimated total direct and indirect costs to the bank of this CRA turnaround were approximately $50,000. This is less than the $60,000 reportedly paid by Harris Bank of Chicago just for a credit needs ascertainment survey! Harris Bank was upgraded from a needs improvement rating to a satisfactory one.

"CRA Can Be Profitable"

With the major change in the CRA spirit at the Bank of Commerce, the board, senior management, and the entire staff became actively involved. This involvement, often in a leadership role, was an important difference. It would be difficult to argue that these positive CRA changes were not good business decisions for this bank, as its increased exposure in the community in a positive way could only be helpful. This would also be the case with the publicity associated with the bank's new outstanding rating. In the CRA Officer's own words, "CRA can be profitable."

A further indication of the outstanding nature of the Bank of Commerce is the fact that on August 15, 1991, after its second public examination with an outstanding rating, this bank released a "CRA Public Response." This 23-page document was apparently prepared on a word processor and stapled together without any fancy binding. It provided all of the relevant background on the bank's CRA efforts and a detailed discussion of each of the individual assessment factors. Each of the bank's CRA goals and the progress made toward the achievement of them were mentioned in this detailed document, which was made public by the bank. This highly useful and informative document was prepared internally without substantial out-of-pocket costs.

Setting a New Standard for Community Banks in the OCC's Western District

A strict interpretation of a truly outstanding bank as being one without any consumer compliance violations or other criticisms would eliminate this bank from that category, primarily because of its non-substantive violations. As noted in a previous section, over one-fourth of all outstanding banks had some such violation, which would likewise remove them from the ranks of the truly outstanding. Still, though, the Bank of Commerce must be singled out for its exceptional turnaround in less than nine months, and for that reason alone should be considered a truly outstanding bank.

Another indication of the exceptional CRA performance of this bank is that it reportedly was the OCC's first outstanding rating for a community bank in that district. The head examiner, upon presenting the recommendation for an outstanding rating to his supervisors, was reportedly asked to carefully think about it in terms of "setting a standard" as the district's first of this type (and as we now know the nation's first and only double upgrade to an outstanding rating). The head examiner reportedly thought about it carefully over a weekend and reported back to his supervisors that this bank had in fact "set a new standard." "There was not one more thing I could ask that bank to do for CRA" was reportedly his conclusion.

STEPPING UP FROM NEEDS IMPROVEMENT TO SATISFACTORY AND TO OUTSTANDING—TOO HIGH TOO QUICKLY?

The second bank to be upgraded from a needs improvement rating to outstanding did so not in one step after its second public examination but in two steps after three public examinations. This is the case of the Security State Bank of Stockdale, Texas.

This bank initially received a needs improvement rating from the FDIC on September 28, 1990. Just over five months later the bank was reexamined and received a satisfactory rating on February 4, 1991. Then, seven months later, on September 3, 1991, this bank received an outstanding rating. Thus, this bank received three CRA evaluations in under one year.

The Security State Bank was established in 1932 and operates as a unit bank from its one office in Stockdale. This community is located in the southeastern portion of Texas just west of San Antonio. The bank is an approximately $25 million bank with just "average" financial ratios.

CRA "Swat Team" of 12 Compliance Examiners Surprise $25 Million Community Bank

The circumstances of the three CRA exams at that bank differ significantly. We learned from bank representatives that they were quite surprised to see 12 examiners show up for the first compliance exam in September 1990! It was obvious that many of the FDIC examiners were there for training purposes, a scenario many bankers experience as they provide on-the-job training experience for the "rookie regulators." Bank representatives were quite cooperative, although they were disappointed when they later received a needs improvement rating. We (but not the bank) surmised that the low rating may have been the result of the on-site "CRA training seminar," where perhaps the bank was used as an example to teach the neophyte examiners a lesson on how to be "tough" on a bank?

The bank was surprised to see the examiners show up roughly five months later in early February 1991. However, only two examiners showed up this time. The examiner in charge, a different one from the previous exam, was specializing in compliance as a career path. The bank was pleased to receive a satisfactory rating the second time around, which they felt they had deserved all along.

Their third exam came in conjunction with a safety and soundness review. This compliance exam again involved just two examiners, but a different head examiner once again. The bank maintained regular correspondence with the regulators throughout these different exams and was pleased to receive the outstanding rating the third time around.

All three exams resulted in typically short FDIC public evaluations. Each of them was only about three pages long, about as short as they come.

Eight Modest Improvements Result in Outstanding Rating

Our comparative analysis of these three CRA evaluations over roughly a one-year period indicates some improvements, but not anywhere near the depth or breadth of those made by the Bank of Commerce in Auburn, California, during a nine-month period. In fact, an argument can be made that the Security State Bank would be an ideal candidate for a fifth "good" category between satisfactory and "outstanding."

This conclusion is based on the following major differences among Security's three exams. Again, as in the previous case study, these comparisons roughly follow the order of assessment factors and emphasize what improvements were made by the bank in each case:

1. The first public evaluation criticized the bank for a lack of documentation of ascertainment efforts. The second exam noted a local newspaper article on the bank's ascertainment efforts, but still no further documentation was available. By the third exam bank management had developed a "tracking tool" to document community contacts and implemented an internal "survey program," which was only described in general terms. The third exam noted that responses to the surveys were "evaluated and documented," but no specific modified or new loan products were mentioned as a result of this effort.

2. The first examination noted management's awareness of local demographics but criticized the bank since "such data has not been used to analyze the bank's lending activities." Neither the second nor third exam mentioned this factor again, which could mean nothing was done about it. It would be logical to assume that if this deficiency was corrected, the second and/or third set of examiners would want to note this improvement to further justify their upgraded rating. Thus, the absence of a possible improvement may indicate that it was never done.

3. The first exam criticized the board's limited involvement in CRA, which only included the required annual review and approval of the CRA statement. The second exam of February 4, 1991, refers to a new CRA policy approved on January 19, 1991, a few weeks before the second exam. That policy was 3½ pages long and dealt with the assignment of responsibilities, including the naming of a CRA officer and committee, technical compliance requirements, methods of ascertaining community credit needs, CRA audits, complaint review procedures, and relationships with community groups. The third exam was identical to the second one on this topic, as it referred to the same adopted CRA policy.

4. The first examination also criticized the bank since no CRA audits had been conducted, even though they were referred to in the bank's adopted CRA statement. The second examination noted that the newly adopted CRA policy required an annual internal CRA audit. Again, the third exam was identical in this respect.

5. The bank's marketing efforts were criticized in the first exam because there was no documentation of any claimed credit contacts with civic groups and leaders. This criticism is not mentioned in either the second or third exams. Also, advertisements at the time of the first exam were primarily institution and deposit oriented. The second exam had the same basic criticism, but the third exam noted for the first time that the bank "has recently begun" to market credit-related products through the local newspaper.

6. The first two exams identified the bank as participating in the Farmers Home Administration guaranteed loan program. The third exam additionally noted the bank's participation in the Federal National Mortgage Association. No specifics as to the extent of involvement were noted.

7. The first two exams criticized the bank since no geographic distribution analysis of its credit extensions, applications, and denials was completed. The third exam, however, noted that management developed a system of analyzing the geographic distribution of credit extensions and denials (applications were not mentioned) to ascertain that no areas of their delineated community are being discriminated against. There were no further specifics on this system or the results of any geographic analysis.

8. The first exam criticized the bank because no review procedures had been implemented to assure that the bank does not inadvertently discourage or prescreen applicants. The second and third exams referred to the internal CRA audit function described in the bank's CRA policy but provided no specifics on that audit.

Additional Evidence for a Fifth CRA Rating of "Good"

What is most unusual about this case is the small number of relatively modest improvements made by this bank as its rating was improved each time. The improvements that were put into place, all of which were apparently internal, probably resulted in few out-of-pocket expenses, such as for the local newspaper credit advertising begun before the third exam. Even though this bank did make some improvements, it would be difficult to argue that it would be in the same category as the Bank of Commerce, N.A. of Auburn, California, which is only twice its size. That is, we do not believe that this Texas bank is a truly outstanding one.

Thus, we believe this case is evidence that there should in fact be a fifth category for "good" CRA ratings between satisfactory and outstanding. More than likely, that is where this bank would fall; although, a strict interpretation might recategorize this bank as a satisfactory one considering the relatively few and modest changes that occurred in the short seven-month time frame between its second and third exams. This latter interpretation suggests that there may have been grade inflation at this bank.

GREAT WESTERN OR GREAT SOUTHERN?—THE CASE FOR STATE-BY-STATE RATINGS FOR INTERSTATE BANKS

Bank holding companies with multistate operations don't receive CRA ratings. However, each of the bank subsidiaries receive CRA ratings from at least their respective federal bank regulator and sometimes from state regulators with applicable CRA statutes. Those banks with grandfathered interstate branches likewise receive one rating.

Some of our nation's largest savings and loans represent true interstate operations. Most of these are headquartered in California with operations in selected deposit-rich states, and these franchises are usually obtained through acquiring failed thrifts. The resultant multi-state savings and loans, however, receive only one CRA rating, although they may be operating in several different states and be meeting local community credit needs quite differently.

CRA Ratings May Be Meaningless for Large Interstate Banks

The purpose of this case study is to examine the CRA record of our nation's second largest thrift, Great Western Bank, in terms of its CRA performance in its second largest state of operations, Florida. This analysis is important not only because of the growing interstate network of the largest thrifts, but because the major bank holding companies would like to consolidate their sprawling multistate operations into one bank. A few very large holding companies (e.g., NationsBank Corporation) have been especially aggressive in pursuing this objective, noting significant economies of scale that would result for one combined and very large operation. One such economy would be preparing for and going through one CRA exam, rather than multiple ones.

The first and most obvious argument against single CRA ratings for multistate operations is found in examining the wide disparity of ratings being given to individual banks within large bank holding companies. Very few extremely large multibank holding companies have completely consistent CRA ratings.

To force one rating on a diverse multistate operation would be to dilute the value of the CRA rating and threaten the integrity of the CRA rating procedure. This is especially important considering the rapid pace of nationwide bank consolidation and the "anything goes" bank merger attitude that has existed in Washington.

Chemical Banking Corporation Receives All Four CRA Ratings

There are many examples of multi-state bank holding companies receiving different combinations of outstanding, satisfactory, and even below-average ratings.

For example, Chemical Banking Corporation of New York has subsidiaries with each of the four CRA ratings. Putting aside the outstanding ratings of the holding company's lead bank, Chemical Bank, and its acquired crosstown rival, Manufacturers Hanover Trust Company, we see examples of four ratings just through its Texas Commerce subsidiaries. Some of the Texas Commerce banks received outstanding ratings; most received satisfactory ratings; some received needs improvement ratings; and Texas Commerce Banks, the bank's credit card affiliate in Newark, Delaware, received the lowest substantial noncompliance rating. Another credit card affiliate, Chemical Bank Delaware, received a satisfactory rating.

Clearly one CRA rating for Chemical Banking Corporation or even its Texas Commerce affiliates would be of little value with such significant individual differences among bank holding company subsidiaries. Even if all of the ratings were somehow averaged into a satisfactory one, this approach would be fruitless because most big holding companies with a mix of CRA ratings probably would average into a satisfactory rating. What would be the purpose of even making CRA ratings if nearly everyone receives the same (satisfactory) one? It can be argued that the present situation—with four out of five ratings being in that category—is not far from that extreme.

CRA Ratings for Large Statewide Banks May Be of Little Value

Another argument against single ratings for large multistate operations is seen in the fact that single CRA ratings for large statewide banks are probably somewhat deficient themselves in reflecting individual differences throughout the state. For example, in Florida some large statewide operations are combined into one centralized bank, such as First Union National Bank of Florida and NationsBank of Florida, N.A. Others, such as the Florida operations of Sun-Trust Banks and Barnett Banks, are decentralized through numerous community banks all over the state. First Union National Bank of Florida received a satisfactory rating for its entire Florida operation. However, the many SunBanks of Florida received a mix of outstanding, satisfactory, and needs improvement ratings.

Obviously, we can learn much more about the community credit records of individual SunBank operations in this manner than we could if all of them were grouped into one large "SunBank of Florida" with a more than likely satisfactory rating. It would appear that banks would prefer the latter consolidated approach not only for CRA exam economies but also because the likelihood of a satisfactory rating increases, and the likelihood of a below-average one decreases.

Considering that the intent of Congress in disclosing CRA ratings and public evaluations was to encourage a dialogue between a bank and its community on CRA matters, CRA ratings for large banks with multistate operations and even big statewide ones leave much to be desired. Disclosure critics will obviously push for consolidated ratings at the state and national level for multistate operations and perhaps even at the holding company level. Again, the consolidated ratings approach means less disclosure of relevant CRA information and a much greater probability of satisfactory ratings, which lessen the value of the entire CRA ratings process. If our nation's banking structure ever shifted from a very large number of small banks as we have today to a small number of very large banks, as we see in most other countries, then what would we learn from a handful of satisfactory ratings?

Great Western—from California to Florida Plus 29 Other States

This particular case study focuses on Great Western Bank, FSB based in Beverly Hills, California. This bank was upgraded from satisfactory to outstanding. This case study will show that while such an upgrading may be justified for that bank's California operation, this certainly is not the case for Florida where a needs improvement rating would have been appropriate.

The parent Great Western Financial Corporation, with approximately $40 billion in assets, operates more than 1,100 mortgage lending, retail banking, and consumer finance offices in 31 states. Its principal branching networks for its mortgage-oriented consumer bank are in California, Florida, Washington, and Arizona.

Florida has become the second largest base of operations for Great Western, where it has acquired more failed thrift branches than anyone else. Not only did Great Western rapidly expand its market share in deposit-rich Florida through this approach, but it did so in the most inexpensive way through buying the franchises of Florida's two largest failed thrifts (CenTrust and AmeriFirst) at RTC fire-sale prices.

Upgraded CRA Ratings in Colorado and California

One of Great Western's subsidiaries is the Great Western Consumer Finance Group based in Cordova, Tennessee. This group owns the First Community Industrial Bank of Lakewood, Colorado, which received a needs improvement rating from the FDIC on September 7, 1990. That rating noted that the bank's CRA activity is "less than satisfactory" given the size and financial condition of the bank's parent company. That bank was upgraded to a satisfactory rating on August 30, 1991. Another subsidiary, First Community Industrial Bank of Longmont, Colorado, received a satisfactory rating from the FDIC on December 28, 1990. The FDIC had not released the public rating on the Great Western affiliate in Washington as of year-end 1992.

Great Western Bank, FSB, the parent company's lead bank in California, received a satisfactory rating from the OTS on July 23, 1990. After that exam Great

Western Bank prepared a five-page "Public Response," in which it stressed its positive efforts and areas of improvement while questioning some of the findings of that exam.

Great Western Bank put forth a significant effort to improve its rating, and its board adopted a specific policy and action plan in this regard. The bank was rewarded for its efforts on July 9, 1991, when it received an outstanding rating. Thus, Great Western Bank became one of the few banks nationwide to have been upgraded to the highest rating as of year-end 1991.

Individual Assessment Factor Ratings on the First Exam

The first exam on July 23, 1990, by the West Region of the OTS provided individual assessment factor ratings. Unfortunately, the OTS discontinued this desirable practice, and no such individual assessment factor ratings were disclosed during the second exam of that bank.

Great Western Bank's first exam had outstanding ratings on two assessment factors, satisfactory on eight, and needs improvement on three (counting the unreasonably large delineation for one of its three communities as a needs improvement rating). Applying a score of 4.0 for the outstanding ratings, 3.0 for the satisfactory ones, and 2.0 for the needs improvement ones results in an average score of 2.92 for the 13 assessment factors. This would be rounded up to 3.0 for an overall satisfactory rating, which is what the bank received. Disclosed assessment factor ratings provide this added advantage of being able to calculate an average rating for the entire bank. In this case we weighted all 13 assessment factors equally, although the preferred approach would be to weight certain assessment factors (primarily F) more than others.

The bank received outstanding ratings in its first exam on the assessment factors pertaining to loan originations and "other items." The bank's three needs improvement ratings were received for assessment factors pertaining to board involvement, government lending, and the delineated community. Although a rating was not given to this latter factor, Great Western's delineated community within Arizona was determined to be unreasonably large (it used the entire state although it only had one branch there).

Florida Has 44% of Branches and 29% of Deposits, but None of Bank's Directors

Great Western's outstanding CRA rating during its second exam reflected numerous improvements in these and other assessment factors. Our focus will be on the bank's CRA performance in Florida compared to the other states in which it operates.

The bank conducted three credit needs ascertainment surveys during 1990. All three surveys covered California, but only two of the three related to Florida. One of the groups mentioned that receives continued support from the bank was a development corporation in Florida. However, bank officials were noted as only having met with local community leaders in Phoenix and government officials in Los Angeles and Oakland.

Great Western made significant improvements in the level of CRA board participation, one of the assessment factors previously cited as needing improvement. Not mentioned in the CRA evaluation, however, is the relative composition of Great Western's board. Although board composition is a matter of shareholder determination, we found it of great interest that *none* of Great Western's 11 directors are from Florida, although Florida contributes 44% of their branches and 29% of their deposits.

We are not suggesting any directorate quotas. However, this apparent imbalance in terms of board representation may be perceived as contributing to a credit imbalance involving that bank's deposits and loans in Florida (see below). Also, several banks with below-average CRA ratings have been criticized for nonlocal directors, but there was so such criticism here.

Other Cases of Nonlocal Boards Are Criticized but Not Here

CRA public evaluations rarely comment on the place of residence of board members, probably because most live in the local community. However, in the case of Metropolitan Savings Bank of Cleveland, Ohio, which received a needs improvement rating, five of that bank's ten-member board live in New Jersey, and another director lives in New York. The examiners therefore concluded that they are "not actively involved in the institution's delineated community."

Security Trust Federal of Knoxville, Tennessee, which is a subsidiary of an institution in Jackson, Mississippi, also received a needs improvement rating. Security Trust Federal has only one local director, with the remainder residing in the Jackson area. According to the examiners of the Knoxville institution, their board's annual review of CRA statements and lending policies is "for all practical purposes" the extent of their local involvement.

Arvada 1st Industrial Bank of Arvada, Colorado, is located in the greater Denver area. This bank, which also received a needs improvement rating, was cited as having a limited degree of involvement in the CRA process by its board. The examiners noted that "this limited involvement can be partially attributed to the fact that none of the board members live or work in the Denver metropolitan area." Because the majority of the board live in the Salt Lake City area, the examiners concluded that "this geographic separation limits the communication channels between the bank's board and the bank's community."

Using this same logic, the fact that none of Great Western's 11 board members reside in Florida, which represents a significant and rapidly growing portion of that bank's operation, greatly limits the extent of their involvement in the bank's delineated communities in Florida. Again, the examiners never even raised this board issue.

Two of Great Western's Four Primary Markets Are in Florida

Great Western's management, according to the examiners, have identified L.A., San Francisco, Miami, and West Palm Beach as its four primary markets for advertising. Great Western was noted as being one of several financial institutions participating in home loan counseling centers in minority or low-income areas in L.A. and San Diego. Although no such activities were mentioned in either of the two markets in Florida, Great Western has contributed financial support to Neighborhood Housing Services, which has chapters in both California and Florida. The examination also points out that Great Western's CRA Officer

is the cochair of the Los Angeles Neighborhood Housing Services.

Error of Omission by Examiners

Probably the most important fact in this analysis is the relatively low level of lending by Great Western Bank in Florida compared to the bank's retail branches and deposits there. The public evaluation noted that the bank funded an "impressive volume" of loans during the year ending June 30, 1991. The only statistics provided in the examination on this topic were the percentage of the bank's in-state lending that was within its delineated community.

For example, 83% of the bank's California lending in 1990 was within its delineated community there, and the ratio was approximately 86% for the first six months of 1991. The comparable percentages for Florida were quite close at 78% and 83%, respectively. However, no absolute lending numbers were noted, and no loan-to-deposit ratios were calculated. We believe this was a major oversight and error of omission by the examiners.

Taking Deposits from the Sunshine State to Lend in the Golden State

Great Western Bank is now the number one thrift in Florida by a wide margin. It ranks in the top five in the state in market share, even after counting all of the largest banks. Real estate loans at Great Western Bank account for 98% of all their loans. A quick check of lending data made available by Great Western itself shows that only 5.1% of the $18 billion in real estate loans they made in 1990 and 1991 were in Florida. The comparable percentage for the first six months of 1992 was just 4.4%, down from 5.7% for the first six months of 1991. The lion's share (about 80%) of their lending in the two-and-one-half years ending June 30, 1992, has been in California.

According to that bank's June 30, 1992, financial reports, only $2.0 billion, or 6.6%, of their real estate loans outstanding then were in Florida. Again, the bulk (77.7%) were in California.

Of particular interest is the funding of these loans in terms of Great Western's deposit base. Great Western has acquired the branches of seven Florida institutions since June 1990. Great Western, after its AmeriFirst Bank acquisition during the first quarter of 1992, had $9.2 billion in retail deposits in Florida, or 29% of Great Western's total. This number is bound to grow, since 44% of all of that bank's retail branches are in Florida.

Accounting for a Less Than 25% Loan-to-Deposit Ratio and a $7 Billion Credit Imbalance in Florida

In summary, Florida is being used as a source of deposit funding primarily for California lending. For every dollar of deposits taken out of Florida, Great Western Bank is lending back less than one-fourth of it in Florida. We define this less than 25% loan-to-deposit ratio as a major credit imbalance, but these facts were totally absent from the bank's outstanding CRA evaluation.

To be fair to Great Western, it takes time to develop loan business. Deposits can be purchased overnight, as we have seen on so many Friday evenings. Great Western generally chooses not to purchase the loans but only the deposits.

Great Western has been operating in Florida since early 1990, and only 5% of their new loans since then were made in Florida. Clearly, there is room for some improvement here. With $9.2 billion in Florida deposits and just over $2 billion in loans, this would mean there is a roughly $7 billion credit imbalance.

We are not suggesting that Great Western change its name to "Great Southern." And we are not suggesting or recommending any directorate or loan-to-deposit quotas. We are merely suggesting that this very significant $7 billion credit imbalance reflects on this bank's performance in meeting the credit needs of its Florida community. Also, the fact that none of the bank's 11 board members are Florida residents may have a bearing on this significant credit imbalance.

From South Central to South Dade

We received personal correspondence and telephone calls from a Great Western senior vice president and later from a P.R. representative regarding this particular concern. The bank acknowledged that they were well aware of these numbers and that one of the bank's "most important objectives is to improve Great Western's success as a home mortgage lender in Florida." We are hopeful that the bank will make improvements in this area as there is considerable room for them. We trust, for example, Great Western devoted the same relative resources to aid victims of south Dade County's Hurricane Andrew as it did to aid victims of the riots in south-central L.A.

The fact that the outstanding CRA public evaluation for this bank failed to mention any of the above-cited relevant statistics supports our argument that state-by-state CRA ratings should be made on banks with multi-state operations. Great Western should receive a "needs improvement" in our opinion for its loan performance in Florida, at least for the assessment factor on loan activity.

Lending in "Low-Mod" and Minority Areas "Falls Short" in Florida

Under the assessment factor pertaining to geographic distribution of lending, the examiners noted the proportion of lending in low- and moderate-income and minority areas for the three states where Great Western operates. The proportion of such "low-mod and min" lending was 42% for the eighteen months ending June 30, 1991, in California. However, this ratio was only 27% in Florida during 1990 and 31% during the first six months of 1991.

The examiners noted that the ratios for Florida "fall short" compared to the total level of low- and moderate-income neighborhoods in Florida (approximately 43%). The examiners noted a "positive trend" in these percentages, and bank management explained that statewide data may be distorted because agricultural and commercial property is typically classified as low-income. This, however, would be true for California as well.

"Low-Mod" and Minority Lending in Miami "Fell Short" Compared to Six Other Cities

To the examiners' credit, they selected seven cities for a detailed lending analysis to evaluate the bank's efforts in serving the credit needs of the low- and moderate-income and/or minority members of those communities for the year ending June 30, 1991. Five of the cities were in California, and the other two were West Palm Beach and Miami. The examiners' analysis calculated the percentage of "low-mod and/

or min" census tracts in each city where Great Western made loans during the subject period.

Great Western lent in 100% of the low- and moderate-income and/or minority census tracts in two of the California cities, and the percentage in the other three cities there ranged from 84% to 96%. The comparable percentage in West Palm Beach was 84%, but the lowest ratio of 41% was recorded for Miami. That is, Great Western made loans in only 49 of Miami's 119 census tracts (41%) that were categorized as low- and moderate-income and/or minority.

The examiners concluded that "on the surface, it would appear that the institution's lending efforts in the low- and moderate-income and minority areas in Miami fell short, especially when compared to the other cities reviewed." Bank management again intervened to provide explanations for these results, and these explanations were again reproduced in the public evaluation. It is not always the case that management's rebuttal gets included in the official evaluation, but it was in this instance in a few places.

Management at the bank provided data to show that a significant portion of census tracts in Miami without loan activity were actually commercial and industrial areas. However, the examiners did not note the relevance of this factor for any of the other six cities, where these same types of areas exist. In any case, bank management admitted that it was "aware of the need to increase its penetration in the Miami area." This was evidenced by its recent relocation of its district lending office to a more central location in Miami to better serve the community, according to the examiners.

The examiners' evaluation of Great Western's community development efforts cited eight specific examples. Three of these pertained to California alone, two to Florida alone, and three to both California and Florida.

Compliance with Consumer Laws Deteriorated Rather Than Improved

Although not relevant to California or Florida in particular, we found it of interest that the bank's compliance with the "F Factor" pertaining to con-

sumer compliance violations actually deteriorated since the last exam.

The bank's first public evaluation, where it received a satisfactory rating, found it to be in compliance with the substantive provisions of federal laws and regulations. The exam noted a "few exceptions" which were deemed to be "nonsubstantial" in nature.

We were surprised to learn that the bank's second public exam, where it received an outstanding rating, had many more such violations. The exam noted that the bank was "not in compliance" with various requirements and regulations but that the deficiencies were due to "recordkeeping, reporting, and documentation." The examiners also noted that the bank's loan application register "contained numerous errors" and that, therefore, the bank's 1990 HMDA report "contains some inaccurate information." Considering all of the improvements the bank made in other assessment factors since the first exam, these compliance violations were indeed surprising.

A "Needs Improvement" Rating for Florida Operations and a "Good" Rating Overall

As noted in a previous section, a truly outstanding bank would not have any violations under the "F Factor," and this would eliminate Great Western for the above violations. Putting aside that strict interpretation, this present analysis has concluded that any outstanding rating for Great Western Bank should have been limited to its California operations. Although we did not do an analysis of the bank's small (one branch) presence in Arizona at the time of the exam, there is a significant difference between the bank's CRA performance in California and Florida. For this reason, we would rate the bank's CRA performance in Florida as "needs improvement." Thus, the concept of a composite rating for a multistate operation, which may be tantamount to grade inflation in one or more states, is not a preferred one based upon this analysis. If we were to assign a composite rating for Great Western Bank, it would clearly be in our recommended fifth "good" category between outstanding and satisfactory.

Bank "Colonization" and "Carpet-bagger Banking" in Florida

Although the Florida legislature recently considered the idea of adopting its own CRA regulations similar to many other states, it did not do so. With the increased "colonization" of Florida banking, whereby the majority of its assets are controlled by out-of-state lenders, increased attention may be devoted to a state CRA system. This likelihood may be increased to the extent Floridians perceive giant out-of-state operators as "carpetbagger bankers" only there to siphon deposits from this deposit-rich state but not to lend them back on a commensurate basis.

If the federal system was amended to provide state-by-state ratings for multistate operations as we have recommended here, then this would appear to eliminate the need for such duplicating regulations that may be considered at a state level. To the extent that heavily "colonized" states such as Florida and Arizona are increasingly dominated by out-of-state banks, there is likely to be increased attention paid to the extent of community involvement, particularly related to credit, by these out-of-state operations.

CRA'S MOST COST-EFFECTIVE DELIVERY SYSTEM—THE SHARED BANK BRANCH

The purpose of this section is to describe the specifics of our shared bank branch concept and how and why it would be a feasible one. Specifically, we believe that a shared branch in a low- and moderate-income area is the most cost-effective delivery system strategy to benefit both the community and bank CRA ratings.

Competition versus Cooperation Tradeoff

The increasing number of joint venturing and related collaborative efforts by financial and nonfinancial firms alike are driven by operational efficiency considerations. Each of these efforts explore new points on the competition vs. cooperation tradeoff. Public policy has become increasingly accommodative to more and more cooperative ventures in numerous industries in recent years.

We have been long-time advocates of the shared branch concept for financial institutions on the basis of both operational *and* allocational efficiency crite-

ria. Today's environment provides both an opportunity and a challenge for financial institutions to implement this concept.

Cooperative Efforts in Banking

Cooperative arrangements among independent banks to provide services have been around as long as banking and the concomitant need for check clearinghouses. Since joint efforts involving pricing decisions imply collusion, sharing has occurred in the major nonprice areas of banking.

Banks routinely link in the provision of loan products via participation and frequently on the deposit side with the pooling of CD offerings through brokers. Banks often affiliate in promotional matters, such as joint sponsorship of community functions or even the cooperative advertising of a new product. During the last decade we have observed the successful widespread sharing of ATMs, one of the components of the bank's service delivery or distribution system.

Shared Bank Delivery Systems

Banks have experimented with different types of delivery system sharing arrangements with many nonfinancial and financial firms alike over the last decade. Banks with excess office capacity have sublet lobby space to both financial firms (e.g., insurance companies, stockbrokers, and financial planners) and nonfinancial firms (e.g., travel agencies and real estate brokers). Although each party to these shared delivery system transactions benefits from the customer traffic generated by the other, the host firm obtains some experience with a broadened product line as well as earning a return on the leased space.

The firms involved in these affiliations are not generally competitive with the basic deposit and loan business of banks in the same way as their competitors. However, even the strongest of local rivals are taking advantage of the scale economies and risk reduction advantages of the sharing of ATMs. While we witnessed a proliferation of linkages among banks via shared networks of this important *electronic* delivery system, we have not seen similar sharing efforts with a bank's office and drive-ins, its key *conventional* delivery system.

Proprietary versus Generic Shared Offices

A bank office, like an ATM, can be shared with competitors on either a *proprietary* or *generic* basis. A proprietary shared office is owned and operated by one bank, and other competitive banks "piggyback" on it for a fee. This contrasts to a generic shared office, which is jointly owned and operated by a group of banks.

A shared branch system can have both types of offices. We believe that both the proprietary and generic shared branch concepts are feasible on all relevant economic, marketing, operational, and regulatory bases.

Like an ATM in a shared system, the bank in a proprietary shared system that owns the delivery point is paid a per-transaction fee based on the type of transaction by the "foreign" bank in the system. A portion of every fee is typically collected by the shared system sponsoring group, the organizational body that develops and coordinates shared system activities.

The per-human transaction fee, which normally would be expected to be higher than a comparable ATM transaction fee, can be completely absorbed by the user bank or passed along, in part, to the customer, as is done today in many shared ATM systems. However, rather than having access to a network of automated tellers in kiosks, outside walls, or vestibules, the bank's customers can now transact their business with human tellers inside a much larger number of offices that are identified as shared branch system members.

A Tradition of Branch Sharing

It is generally thought that proprietary bank branches would not be suitable for such sharing because they have little or no excess capacity as compared to ATMs with substantial excess capacity. However, many branches that were "overbuilt" relative to their actual market potential and others that have displaced substantial routine lobby traffic to ATMs would be suitable for sharing. Indeed, sometimes there is more excess capacity at a bank's drive-in lanes than at the inside teller windows, and this concept potentially could be applied to one or both of these delivery service points.

Branch sharing has roots in this country as well as abroad. In the mid-nineteenth century many mutual savings banks here would routinely operate in the same offices as, and through the offices of, a commercial bank with whom they were not generally competitive. The savings bank balances kept with the commercial bank would compensate them for the slight inconveniences and services rendered. Cooperative efforts have existed for many years within many European and other countries, where customers of any branch of any bank can cash checks at or transfer funds to any branch of another. These reciprocal arrangements, although nationwide and multinationwide in scope, are generally for check cashing and are often without charge.

Personnel and Transaction Fees at Generic Shared Branches

The generic shared branch concept is similar to an off-premise ATM owned and identified jointly by the shared system's sponsoring group rather than an individual member under the proprietary approach. These generic or "sterile" bank branches are banking service centers staffed by "neutral" personnel of the sponsoring group. The shared branch personnel transact requested banking functions upon being presented verifiable identification by a customer of any one of the system's participating banks. Again, member banks are charged on a per-transaction basis, with all revenues accruing to the system for service maintenance and enhancement.

Neutral personnel make available bank-provided deposit, loan, and other product information as well as requested applications on a nondiscriminatory basis. Those questions on these competitive products that cannot be answered there can be directly handled through bank personnel staffing individual telephone "hot lines" located in the generic branch.

Generic Shared Branches in Inner Cities or Small Communities

Generic shared branches could be established anywhere on a *de novo* basis, but they would more than likely be targeted for areas without any proprietary branches. These areas are often without branches because no one bank could economically justify a branch investment. But, like an off-premise shared ATM, the generic shared branch might be economically feasible because of the economies of scale in dealing with customers of several banks.

While a branch closing in an inner-city area or a small community may be the optimal course of action from the perspective of a given financial institution, this is usually not the case from a public policy perspective—especially if the closed branch was the last depository financial institution in the affected area.

The author has publicly advocated the generic shared branch concept in these types of situations beginning in the 1980s. For example, a February 1985 *Savings Institution* article contained a section titled "Shared Branches May Serve Inner Cities and Small Communities." That article and an unpublished research paper on this topic were forwarded to and discussed at the October 1986 meeting of the FED's Consumer Advisory Council. Also, the Branch Administration Division of the American Bankers Association likewise investigated our submitted proposal in 1987. Unfortunately, neither organization ever got back to us to pursue discussions about our shared branch proposal.

Feasibility of the Generic Shared Branch for an Inner-City Area

Just because the shared branch concept is a timely one, it does not necessarily follow that banks will adopt it. Like all capital investments, it must first be shown to be feasible. Both the proprietary and generic shared branch concepts are feasible in our opinion. However, the stronger case can probably be made for the establishment of a generic shared branch by larger banks in an inner-city area.

The generic shared branch is feasible from an *economic* perspective: economies of scale would result from several banks sharing fixed and variable expenses at a common distribution point. Also, this branch would be in an area where each bank has a customer base with the potential for additional business. In fact, a generic shared branch would be feasible in a very high rent district (such as New York's Upper East Side), where lease costs at prime corner locations have become prohibitive even for some of our biggest banks.

The generic shared branch is feasible from a *marketing* view: inner-city residents represent a large market that wants and needs competitively priced regular and basic banking services offered through convenient offices with both human and automated tellers. Also, the continuation or expansion of services in the inner city enhances a bank's image with not only customers and noncustomers but also with consumer groups, regulators, and legislators.

The generic shared branch is *operationally* feasible: the jointly-owned sponsoring group is responsible for the neutral personnel and banking service center. Adequate technology exists for the necessary customer identification, verification, and on-line data processing and switching procedures. In fact, many operational set-up problems and expenses would be minimized by using previously (or soon-to-be) closed branches of one of the participant banks as the banking service center facility.

In addition to satisfying the most relevant concerns of the market, consumer groups, and the banks themselves, the generic shared branch should certainly meet with legislative and regulatory approval, even if state and/or federal laws have to be changed to accommodate this worthwhile concept. The many social benefits of this proposal would outweigh perceived social costs: the restoration, maintenance, and even expansion of banking services in inner-city areas could be accomplished on a procompetitive basis in much the same way as is being done with most shared ATM networks.

Generic Shared Credit Union Branches in Michigan since 1975

The best evidence documenting the feasibility of the generic shared branch concept is the existence of one. The fact that the Service Centers Corporation, which is jointly owned and controlled by approximately 120 credit unions in southern Michigan, has been in operation since 1975 proves that this concept is a workable one. The motivating force in this case was the desire of individual credit unions to provide convenient and staffed off-premise locations in an affordable manner. No one credit union could financially justify such branch expansion but all could benefit from it through the generic shared branch concept.

Today there are 14 "credit union family service centers" offering extended office hours and ATMs. In addition to normal account deposit, withdrawal, transfers, and check-cashing transactions, these generic facilities offer limited customized loan services (i.e., taking applications, closings, and disbursements). Credit union members can choose their own product mix, and they are billed on a weighted per-transaction basis. The initial investment for a given credit union consists of a nominal fixed fee plus a variable one based upon the number of its members living near each service center.

Generic Shared Credit Union Branches Now in California and Indiana

Considering the growth in membership, number of service centers, and billable transactions, the generic shared branch concept has been an overwhelming success in this time-tested case. Probably the best proof of their success is the fact that a group of credit unions in California have recently replicated this concept with four generic branches, and another group of credit unions in Indiana just opened their first such branch in February 1993. We believe that this experience documents that the shared bank branch as described above would be CRA's most cost effective delivery system.

"MEGAMERGER CRA MEGAPLEDGES"

Can an outstanding CRA rating be bought? In other words, can any bank throw enough resources at CRA to "guarantee" an outstanding rating? Critics of CRA who contend there is a relationship between outstanding ratings and size of banks, because large banks have the resources to document their efforts, might answer in the affirmative.

Big Banks Don't Get the Best CRA Ratings

As pointed out in Chapter 3, our research has indicated that the biggest banks and thrifts alike receive a mix of ratings, primarily outstanding or satisfactory ones. Importantly, not all big banks and thrifts get outstanding ratings, and a few have even received needs improvement ratings. Further evidence to support this finding is the wide spectrum of ratings given to banks that are members of the same holding company, all of which presumably would have access to the parent's resources to document a good rating. In fact, our nation's third largest bank holding company, Chemical Banking Corporation in New York, has subsidiaries with all four CRA ratings.

In summary, our answer to this question is that money alone cannot buy a good CRA rating. Probably the best evidence of this is to view the variety of ratings given to those banks which have made CRA "megapledges."

Fifty Basis Point per Year Rule of Thumb

A 50 basis point per year CRA commitment on assets is a rule of thumb used by many community groups as a guideline for an "appropriate" annual commitment by a bank. A handful of banks have made substantial CRA commitments at or above this level in the last few years. The largest of these contributions occurred at or near the time when these banks were involved in major mergers, the point when they would have been most vulnerable to CRA protests. Even with these pledges some of these bank mergers were still criticized on CRA and other grounds.

The CRA megapledges discussed in this section are not meant to be a list of all CRA pledges. Many other banks have made CRA pledges to finance home lending in low- and moderate-income neighborhoods. Our focus was on megapledges in the billion dollar range or more, resulting from recent megamergers. We also included a CRA pledge of $0.75 billion in this category but not those at or below $0.5 billion (although two of those are discussed here).

The First CRA Megapledges in California

Our analysis included one megapledge by a large bank not involved in a megamerger. Wells Fargo Bank, which received an outstanding rating, was the first bank to make a CRA megapledge. As noted in Chapter 4, that bank announced a commitment in March 1990 to lend $1 billion over seven years to community and economic development activities. That translates into $143 million per year, or approximately 25 basis points on their year-end 1990 assets.

The second megapledge came approximately one month later by Security Pacific Corporation when it announced that it would spend $2.4 billion over a 10-year period on community involvement efforts.

The majority of that program was to be used for affordable-housing loans. This commitment amounted to $240 million per year, or roughly 28 basis points relative to year-end 1990 assets. Thus, on an annual relative basis this contribution was quite similar but a little greater than that made by Wells Fargo. It should be noted that Security Pacific, whose lead bank received a satisfactory rating, was in the process of attempting to buy a 20% share of Mitsui Manufacturers Bank then and was the subject of CRA protests by community groups.

BankAmerica's Noncontingent CRA Megapledge

It was not until a year later that the next CRA megapledge was made by BankAmerica Corporation, in April 1991. Bank of America, the lead bank, received an outstanding rating. The company's $5 billion community lending pledge over a ten-year period converted to the largest annual pledge ($500 million) on an absolute basis and also on a relative basis at that time. Specifically, based upon year-end 1990 assets, this amounted to an annual CRA commitment of approximately 45 basis points. These percentages would be somewhat higher using previous year assets or those for the lead bank alone. However, they have been calculated here in a consistent manner for the holding company for the same period.

BankAmerica's CRA pledge was made in the midst of its negotiations to acquire the failed Bank of New England. Community groups in California filed formal CRA protests, attempting to block the proposed purchased of that bank. BankAmerica's CRA pledge was not contingent upon a successful bid, which is important because they ultimately did not win the bid. The fact that it was not a contingent pledge speaks well of BankAmerica's CRA spirit. Bank of Boston, which also made a bid on the failed Bank of New England, reportedly made a $600 million CRA pledge over a five-year period contingent on their bid being accepted. That bank's bid was also rejected.

NationsBank Contingent CRA Megapledge

The next CRA megapledge was in fact contingent upon what was to be the first of several megamergers among our largest banks. NationsBank Corporation, the result of the marriage between NCNB Corporation and C&S/Sovran Corporation, made a $10 billion pledge over a ten-year period in August, 1991. This pledge was contingent on the approval of the merger. It was well known that there were several CRA protests planned to be filed against this merger, and their huge pledge would hopefully allow the merger to proceed. The lead banks at both of these corporations received satisfactory ratings.

The $10 billion over ten years translated into what then became the largest absolute pledge of $1 billion per year or 84 basis points on combined year-end 1990 assets of the resultant NationsBank Corporation. Thus, this was not only the largest absolute total and annual commitment to date but also the largest relative one. While the BankAmerica annual contribution was quite close to the 50 basis point commitment sought by community groups, the proposed NationsBank pledge of 84 basis points significantly exceeded it.

The Largest Absolute CRA Megapledge

The following CRA megapledge was again associated with the next, and actually the biggest, megamerger to date between BankAmerica Corporation and Security Pacific Corporation. The combined pledge of the resultant merged bank of $12 billion over a ten-year period became the largest absolute pledge on a total and annual basis. The resultant annual pledge of $1.2 billion per year represented approximately 61 basis points of the combined year-end 1990 assets of those two holding companies.

At the time of the October 1991 announcement of this pledge, BankAmerica referred to its original ten-year goal of $5 billion and a $4 billion goal of Security Pacific over a ten-year period in seven western states. Thus, Security Pacific's CRA pledge was apparently increased from $2.5 to $4.0 billion. Rather than representing 28 basis points, this higher pledge represented 47 basis points, almost identical to the 45 basis point pledge of BankAmerica Corporation.

According to BankAmerica, this new $12 billion commitment represented a 33% increase over the combined goals of the two corporations. This commitment was contingent upon the proposed merger, which was also being challenged on CRA grounds by various community groups.

The Smallest Absolute and Relative CRA Megapledge

The next big megamerger in the country was announced the following month. Chemical Banking Corporation and Manufacturers Hanover Corporation agreed to merge in November 1991 to create what would become the third largest banking organization behind Citicorp and BankAmerica Corporation. With a year-end 1990 combined asset level of approximately $135 billion, a 50 basis point annual contribution would have amounted to approximately $675 million per year. Using the 61 basis point CRA pledge from the BankAmerica Corporation merger of the previous month would have resulted in a $821 million per year pledge. The highest annual pledge of 84 basis points from NationsBank would have resulted in an annual pledge for Chemical Banking Corporation of $1.1 billion, just shy of the annual absolute pledge of BankAmerica Corporation but just over that of NationsBank.

Considering these various possible scenarios and the fact that this merger came not before but after the others, it was indeed most surprising to learn the amount of the combined annual CRA commitment for the Chemical Banking Corporation and Manufacturers Hanover Corporation merger. It was not in the $675 million to $1.1 billion range suggested above but just $150 million per year!

Chemical's CRA pledge was for a $750 million total commitment over five years. This amounted to just 11 basis points on combined year-end 1990 assets, clearly the lowest of all CRA pledges for megamergers. Chemical Bank and Manufacturers Hanover Trust Company received outstanding ratings from both federal and state regulators. The proposed merger was to be protested by various community groups, but this pledge, which, surprisingly, was made in conjunction with one of the community groups, eliminated that obstacle to the merger.

The Largest Relative CRA Megapledge

Of our nation's five largest bank holding companies as of year-end 1991, three have been involved in megamergers, and all have made CRA megapledges. These differ significantly on the basis of annual relative contributions, ranging from a low of just 11 basis points at Chemical Banking Corporation to a high of 84 basis points at NationsBank Corporation on year-end 1990 assets.

The most recent megamerger and CRA megapledge was announced in June 1992 by Barnett Banks after its proposed acquisition of First Florida Banks. The megapledge announcement did not stipulate any merger approval condition or for that matter even mention the proposed combination. Their megapledge of $2 billion over five years ranks as the third largest as does the average annual pledge of $400 million. What is unique about this pledge is that it represents the highest annual relative pledge to date, at 104 basis points based on year-end 1991 post-merger assets.

CRA Megapledges Average 57 Basis Points

Table 5-2, "Megamerger CRA Megapledges," is based on post-merger, year-end 1991 assets. Because most of these bank holding companies reported somewhat decreased combined asset sizes as of year-end 1991, the annual relative pledges per dollar of assets increased over the 1990 data cited above. Of greatest interest in this table is the calculated average of 57 basis points for the four megamergers (excluding Wells Fargo, which was not involved in one). This average, which was pushed downwards because of Chemical Banking Corporation, is still somewhat above the 50 basis point rule of thumb cited above.

Smaller ($0.5 Billion) CRA Pledges

This table doesn't show CRA pledges of $0.5 billion or smaller. For example, a November 1992 CRA commitment of $0.5 billion for three years by First Fidelity Bancorp of Newark, New Jersey, which was made shortly before its announced purchase of Connecticut's Northeast Bancorp, Inc., amounted to 50 basis points of post-merger assets. The more recent January 1993 minimum $0.5 billion CRA commitment over ten years by Sumitomo Bank of California,

TABLE 5-2   Megamerger CRA Megapledges

Bank Holding Company	Post-Merger Assets 12/31/91 (Billions)	CRA Megapledge Amount (Billions)	CRA Megapledge Years	Annual Pledge Amount (Billions)	Annual Pledge Per $ of Assets (%)
NationsBank	$110	$10.00	10	$1.00	.91
BankAmerica	192	12.00	10	1.20	.63
Chemical	139	.75	5	.15	.11
Barnett	39	2.00	5	.40	1.04
TOTAL, 4 MEGAMERGERS	$480	$24.75	—	$2.75	—
AVERAGE, 4 MEGAMERGERS	120	6.19	7.5	.69	.57
Wells Fargo (NO Megamerger)	54	1.00	7	.14	.26

Note: Banks involved in megamergers without CRA megapledges through December 31, 1992:

(1)	Banc One	(6)	Commercial
(2)	First Union	(7)	Wachovia
(3)	Fleet/Norstar	(8)	Key
(4)	NBD	(9)	National City
(5)	Society	(10)	Others

Source: K.H. Thomas Associates

whose Japanese parent was seeking permission to maintain partial ownership of Hawaii's Central Pacific Bank, amounted to a minimum of $50 million per year or 95 basis points of Sumitomo's assets. This relative CRA pledge was just above that of Nations-Bank but below that of Barnett. The Sumitomo commitment included a 20 to 25% ethnic minority contracting goal; a paid five-member minority advisory board; minority representation on the board; and a 2% of net income pledge to philanthropic groups, with two-thirds of the money going to CRA-type inner city economic development. The fact that Sumitomo's ten-year CRA plan was voluntarily filed with the FDIC suggests a meaningful commitment, because there is the implied regulatory oversight which will monitor progress with the plan and possibly even condition upgrades of that bank's existing needs improvement rating on it.

Banks without CRA Megapledges

There are two groups of banks conspicuously absent from Table 5-2. First are other large banks like Wells Fargo that have yet to be involved in a megamerger. These include Citicorp, J.P. Morgan & Company, Chase Manhattan Corporation, Bankers Trust New York Corporation, and First Chicago Corporation among the ten largest bank holding companies, as of year-end 1991. The lead banks at all of these companies, except for Chase and J.P. Morgan & Company, received outstanding ratings.

Even more conspicuous in their absence from this table are major super-regional banks involved in recent megamergers and other large failed bank/thrift acquisitions. This list includes Banc One Corporation, First Union Corporation, and Fleet/Norstar Financial Group, most notably. Others are NBD Bancorp, Society Corporation, Comerica, Wachovia Corporation, KeyCorp, and National City Corporation. Most of the lead banks at these companies have received outstanding ratings. This second list is growing rapidly.

Money Alone Can't Buy an Outstanding CRA Rating

It is of interest to point out that large CRA contributions alone will not "buy an outstanding rating." Although the lead banks at both NCNB and C&S/Sovran were rated before their merger and huge CRA pledge, those two banks received satisfactory ratings. Most other bank subsidiaries of NationsBank Corporation have received satisfactory ratings since that time. This was also the case with both Barnett and Security Pacific Banks. And, subsidiaries of Chemical Banking Corporation received all four CRA ratings.

A more vivid example is Farmers and Merchants Bank of Long Beach, California, the third bank in the nation to receive a substantial noncompliance rating but the first to work its way out of it into a needs improvement rating. According to their first needs improvement evaluation, that bank made CRA loans (not commitments) equivalent to an annual rate of 42 basis points. Although this was only half of the annual 84 basis point pledge of NationsBank, the first represented actual loans and the second was a commitment over time. Even with this substantial level of CRA lending, Farmers and Merchants Bank was later hit with a cease and desist order from the FED primarily on CRA grounds, and this was followed by a $100,000 civil money penalty and a branch denial (see Chapter 9).

CRA "Megapledge Inflation"

One of the biggest questions surrounding these megapledges is the extent to which these banks are meeting them with true CRA loans rather than counting every retail, business, or other loan normally made in a low- and moderate-income area or granted to low- and moderate-income individuals who may not live in those areas. After all, 40% of all U.S. households are low- and moderate-income, according to the 1990 census. Under this reasoning almost any very large bank could make a CRA megapledge.

For example, NationsBank's $10 billion community development lending program will include consumer and mortgage loans to low- and moderate-income customers as well as such loans in low- and moderate-income neighborhoods. Small business loans, among others, will be included. Their 1991 Annual Report notes that "much of the loan fund" will be for affordable housing but no specifics are provided. Representatives of that bank informed us that some report would be forthcoming in the future, but there was no information available on their progress in this regard as of late 1992.

There is no required reporting mechanism, public or otherwise, to measure a bank's real progress in meeting these megapledges. Because they are made over several years, a bank's progress in a given year may not necessarily meet the annual averages calculated above. They should be, however, fairly close over time in keeping with the CRA spirit in which these megapledges were made. Banks that make such megapledges benefit from the considerable positive publicity associated with them, not to mention a merger approval in most cases. We therefore believe that these banks have a responsibility to provide a regular (at least annual) progress report with specific data on how they are meeting their stated goals to assure that there is no "megapledge inflation."

CASE STUDY OF A CRA TURNAROUND— FROM LIKELY FAILURE TO OUTSTANDING IN ONE YEAR

A highly profitable and well-capitalized community bank was informally told by their examiner in early 1990 that they would likely not pass their next Community Reinvestment Act (CRA) exam. To make matters worse, their next exam was to be under the new CRA guidelines after July 1, 1990, and the results would be publicly disclosed for the first time.

Going Beyond the *Status Quo*

A banker facing the likelihood of a below-average CRA rating has basically two choices—do something or do nothing. The *status quo* alternative can be appealing to those bankers who view CRA as a misdirected government effort to allocate credit. This is especially the case for banks that do not foresee any branching, merging, holding company, or other corporate activities that may be adversely affected by a CRA protest or bad rating. They may believe that, because most banks have good relations with their communities, the odds of a formal CRA protest are remote anyway.

This "tough it out" approach to a CRA exam is a mistake for several reasons. First, it sends the wrong message to all of your examiners, not just the compliance ones. Second, you never know when some type of unexpected expansion opportunity (e.g., buying a failed thrift branch) or other corporate activity will develop that may be derailed by a bad CRA rating.

Third, it is quite likely that going through the "CRA exercise" will uncover some hidden or overlooked business opportunities as you learn more about your market vis-à-vis your deposit and loan customer base.

Fourth, how will the public perceive a "community bank" that has failed its *community* reinvestment exam?

Fifth, and most importantly, CRA is the law, and bankers must get used to the idea that they likely are going to see more, not fewer, proconsumer laws and regulations in the future.

The "Bandaid" Approach to a Needs Improvement or Even a Satisfactory CRA Rating

Most bankers facing the possibility of receiving one of the two below-average CRA ratings (substantial noncompliance or needs improvement) will do something. In many cases even the most CRA-deficient banks can receive a needs improvement rating by making a sincere effort to document their past CRA efforts and implementing a basic CRA strategy. A substantial noncompliance rating awaits those banks profiled above that really don't care for one reason or another.

The subject community bank is located in a small town on the urban fringe of a large city where it has a few branches. Its previous CRA efforts were the basics to meet the requirements: the published notice, a no-frills CRA statement with a map, and the board's annual review of it. On being notified of its likely failure, it purchased a few CRA publications which were helpful as overviews but lacked the "nuts and bolts" needed to help this bank.

Everyone in the bank agreed that *something* had to be done. One view was that a committee could be put together to patch up the holes in the CRA effort and do enough to at least get a needs improvement rating—maybe even a satisfactory one if they were lucky. This approach would involve the least time and cost outlay. Also, it would get the bank through the exam until a more professional approach could be taken later.

"Overkill" by Going Outside the Bank?

The chairman of the board of this well-managed and conservatively run bank disagreed and said, "if we do anything, we'll do it right." He made a sincere commitment to receive nothing less than an outstanding rating, which he felt the bank deserved. He would not accept a below-average rating because this was an above-average bank. The bank therefore retained our firm to develop a comprehensive CRA program, even though there were some in the bank then who felt that bringing in an outside CRA consultant was "overkill."

CRA Audit Results in Good and Bad News

Our first step was to complete a CRA audit to determine the state of the bank's CRA affairs. Our CRA audit concluded two things. First, we found that the bank was doing a *good* job of ascertaining and meeting community credit needs, including those of low- and moderate-income residents. Second, we found that the bank was doing a *poor* job of telling its story and documenting its CRA efforts.

It became clear to us why the bank could have received a below-average CRA rating. It also became clear that the bank would have to make some major changes in its CRA documentation efforts and procedures. Our recommended CRA strategy was adopted in full by the bank's board, and it was promptly implemented. The CRA examiners showed up near the end of 1990, and the bank was notified in early 1991 that it had received the highest outstanding rating. This was one year after the informal notification of a likely failure.

Eight Steps to an Outstanding Rating

The following is a summary of the major steps that represented our recommended CRA strategy for this bank. Not all of these steps would be relevant for all banks, and some additional steps might be needed for others. It all depends on the existing state of a bank's CRA affairs, which can obviously differ widely.

Step #1—Basic CRA Education and Awareness Training

We conducted a series of in-house CRA training seminars at the bank at three levels: the board, officers, and branch staff. The purpose was to inform individuals at each level of their minimum responsibilities under CRA and the extra steps that were necessary to receive an outstanding rating. The following publications available from the FDIC's Office of Consumer Affairs were summarized and provided: *Uniform Interagency Guidelines for Disclosure of CRA Evaluations and Revisions to Rating System* and *Expanded CRA Questions and Answers.* Both of these handouts have since been revised and are included as Appendices 2 and 3.

Step #2—Analysis of Deposit and Loan Geographic Distribution

The use of an outside vendor for an expensive CRA geocoding procedure for deposits and loans was not advisable in this case because of the large size of many census tracts and our need for geographic pinpointing. We utilized broad zip code summaries that were available on an in-house basis and refined those with actual plottings of a random sample of accounts on local maps. Applications, approvals, and denials by type of loan were plotted as well as deposits by type of account. This analysis was critical to delineate the CRA local community.

The map plottings were overlayed on a separate map showing low- and moderate-income neighborhoods. We paid careful attention to loan denials by examining whether or not they represented present or past customers and what type of credit was involved.

This analysis of loan volumes and loan approval rates concluded that the bank clearly emphasized credit extensions within its delineated CRA local community. The loan denial rate for out-of-area applicants was significantly higher than for local ones. Also, loan denials both in and outside of the local community were geographically well distributed among all types of neighborhoods with no significant concentration in low- or moderate-income ones.

We found that the highest rate of loan denials were of indirect auto loan applications, which were faxed directly into the bank (as well as many other banks at the same time) from auto dealers around town. Therefore, we conducted a separate analysis and plotting of this type of loan. We concluded that there were significant denials of this type both within and outside of the delineated CRA local community. Loan denials within it, however, were found to be fairly well distributed throughout all segments, including low- and moderate-income neighborhoods.

Step #3—Narrowing of the Delineated CRA Local Community

Many banks regularly use their county or metropolitan area as their CRA community because it is convenient for data and mapping purposes. Also, such political boundaries do not give the appearance of any "gerrymandering" to include or exclude certain neighborhoods.

Such broad areas are in fact reasonable for some banks but not for many community banks. This is because many smaller banks simply do not have the resources or delivery system to effectively serve the credit needs of such large areas. What is often required in these cases is a narrowing of the CRA local community, and care must be taken that it is modified in a uniform and reasonable manner.

In the subject case the bank previously used various mile radii about each office, and there was some overlap of the areas. Our approach resulted in a narrowing of the CRA local community from several large overlapping circles to one contiguous area.

The areas that were included had a substantial concentration of both deposit and loan business about each branch and the main office. We found that actual deposit and loan plottings were not only necessary for this purpose with the large number of rural routes and boxes but also more exact than broad census tracts or even housing blocks.

Step #4—Collection of CRA Statements and Publicly Available Completed Exams for All Competitive Banks and Thrifts

CRA statements and performance evaluations for competitors contain a wealth of useful information for CRA purposes. These documents, which are regularly updated, went into the banks' newly created "CRA Library."

All competitors have CRA statements, but not all have publicly available evaluations at this time. CRA statements, especially expanded ones, provide information on types of credit available and methods to ascertain and meet local community needs.

The delineated CRA local communities of nearby and/or similarly-sized competitors may even be used by CRA examiners themselves in evaluating the reasonableness of a delineated CRA area for a given bank. If your delineated CRA area is the exception rather than the rule for a reasonable peer group, then your documentation must be convincing.

The publicly available CRA performance evaluations can be very helpful in suggesting specific ideas and tips that may be directly applied to your bank. In fact, we have found that the highest and lowest CRA ratings (outstanding and needs improvement/ substantial noncompliance) CRA ratings yield the most useful information. The companion volume contains nearly 200 such evaluations.

In cases where a banker may feel uncomfortable in requesting this information from competitors, a third party may be used for this data-gathering effort. Although multiple written requests and nominal charges are often required to receive this information, this type of research should be undertaken as part of a comprehensive CRA analysis.

Step #5—In-House Evaluation of Existing Product Mix

This phase of the analysis involves an examination of all deposit, loan, and other products, with a description of relevant conditions, minimum balances, fees, and so on. Particular emphasis is placed on credit products, as this is the focus of the CRA.

For every credit product we evaluated we asked who uses it, for what purposes, and under what terms and conditions? Conversely, who doesn't use it and why? How, where, and to whom is it being directly and indirectly marketed? What credit products have been designed especially for low- and moderate-income residents?

In the subject case the banker was surprised to learn that their home census tract was designated as a "moderate income" one simply because the 1980

median family income was less than 80% of the countywide median. In fact a surprisingly large percentage of the entire CRA local community was either low- or moderate-income based on the 1980 census. These percentages have been revised since 1990 census small-area income data became available.

Further research into this bank's loan mix revealed that it has been not only an active lender to low- and moderate-income residents but also an innovative one. For example, they are one of the only banks in its market that considers loan requests of at least $300 to accommodate the borrowing needs of such individuals. Also, the bank was one of the first to extend credit for used mobile homes, a type of credit very important to such households.

On the deposit side this bank has its own version of a "basic banking" account requiring a new account deposit minimum of only $100 and a minimum balance of only $1 to avoid service charges. The account offered free checking with unlimited check writing and a monthly detailed statement. There was a similar but separate account package for seniors.

Other services that increase office accessibility and convenience to existing and potential customers were also evaluated. For example, the subject bank offered extended lobby hours compared to the competition. Also, customers closing accounts were surveyed as to the reasons why, and how service could be improved.

Step #6—Adoption of an Expanded CRA Statement

The bank's board adopted an expanded CRA statement as described in the above-referenced FDIC "guidelines" publication. The FDIC clearly states there that an expanded statement is "not required, but is encouraged by regulation."

Our review of hundreds of CRA statements since the law was enacted in 1977 has shown tremendous variety in format and content. However, we can not understand why so many banks today fail to make the modest effort to expand their statement in the recommended format.

It is obviously one of the first and easiest assessment items anyone, but especially examiners, can spot. Examiners who do not see expanded statements must feel like the teacher who has offered "extra credit" take-home work to improve a student's grade to later find out it wasn't even attempted.

The expanded statement prepared in the subject case contained all of the required information in a user-friendly and professional format (e.g., the map of the CRA local community could actually be read rather than being a fifth-generation fax copy). The list of specific types of credit available was comprehensive, organized, and in lay terms.

The three recommended areas of expansion for a CRA statement include separate sections on how the bank's current efforts help meet local credit needs, with specific examples, not glowing generalities; a periodic report on the bank's record of helping to meet community credit needs, again with specifics and hard nonproprietary data on the bank's lending record; and a specific description of the bank's efforts to ascertain local credit needs showing actual past and on-going meaningful activities.

The expanded statement was written with the employees and examiners in mind. However, the bank's existing and prospective customers were the real target audience for the statement. The actual statement was put on a word processor with an easily readable typeface so new data and activities could be added for board approval and branch distribution.

Unlike some bank personnel who give the "third degree" to anyone asking for a CRA statement (or worse yet the public evaluation), the employees at this bank actually encourage distribution of these documents. In fact, employees are trained to use the statement as a customer education and marketing tool. Of course, the outstanding public evaluation which is now available with it enforces the bank's sincere CRA concerns.

Step #7—Adopt a Formal Written CRA Plan

This plan, like other formal written plans in the bank, was prepared as not only an internal self-assessment tool but also as an aid to be used in the compliance examiners' evaluation. This plan is for the bank's internal use only, and it is regularly updated and modified.

This plan not only detailed where the bank's CRA program was, much like a comprehensive audit, but also where it was going. All elements of the bank's

CRA polices and procedures are described in this plan, including documents in the CRA Library.

It is the responsibility of the CRA committee and compliance officer to maintain the plan. Bank management and employees have direct input into the plan, and it is approved and regularly reviewed by the board.

We structured this plan in five major sections to correspond to the five CRA performance categories: ascertainment of needs, marketing and credit offered, business distribution and office record, illegal credit practices, and community development. These five sections were further subdivided into the 12 CRA "assessment factors," plus one for the delineated area, which represent 13 subsections in the plan.

The document concludes with a "plan for action," which contains a time-line for CRA activities. For example, *monthly* activities include a CRA update at board meetings; *semiannual* activities include CRA employee training meetings; *annual* activities include board review of the expanded statement and plan, update of geographical deposit and loan analyses, and revised demographics on the local community; and *ongoing* activities include collection of local community information (especially 1990 Census and updated data), CRA statements and public evaluations, as well as input on new CRA ideas gleaned from articles or other banks.

Step #8—Full Cooperation during the CRA Exam

Some CRA examiners may be fairly new in their functions, but they become quickly aware of a bank's "CRA spirit" during the compliance exam. The quality and quantity of documentation (yes, the examiners know the difference) and the degree of awareness of various CRA provisions by management may quickly mold the examiners' impression of a bank's CRA performance.

Many examiners may be on the fence between two ratings. We believe that subjectivities can make the difference, especially if the bank displays a sincere "we really care about CRA and are trying our best" attitude. Again, the *perception* of this attitude by examiners is what counts.

The CRA exam at the subject bank was preceded by a CRA questionnaire from the regulator which closely followed the required assessment factors. The questionnaire is a bank's opportunity to let the examiner know of all of the "good stuff" that may not be brought up during the exam.

This questionnaire was completely filled out by reference to the specific sections in the expanded CRA statement and CRA plan. Since all of the work was done in advance of the exam, this was just a formality. The bank was clearly prepared for the exam, and this was obvious to the examiners.

The examiners were knowledgeable and thorough. They were obviously pleased that the CRA plan was a virtual road map for them to go through each performance category and assessment factor one by one. This meant that the examiners could spend more of their time in loan sampling and other internal analyses. All supporting documentation, including map plottings, printouts of the samples, and denial files, were readily available for the examiners. This CRA exam was a "short and sweet" one.

Achieving the Goal of Bringing the CRA Effort In-House

A community bank that is truly committed to an outstanding CRA effort will make the *internalization* of a comprehensive CRA capability a top priority. The primary CRA corporate goal in the subject case was accomplished when the bank was notified of its outstanding CRA rating. The bank also accomplished its second CRA corporate goal of an in-house CRA capability.

This entire CRA effort was spearheaded by the board's hand-chosen CRA committee and compliance officer. Most of the deposit and loan plottings were done internally, and we were used as an outside CRA consultant in areas where there was no internal expertise, such as the CRA seminars and the development of the expanded CRA statement and plan. Now that all of these documents and written procedures are in-house, this bank has a complete internal CRA capability. We are only called in for periodic seminars.

Back-to-Back Outstanding Ratings

The bank's formal notification of its outstanding CRA rating came one year after their examiner had informed them of their likely failure. By doing something rather than nothing and making a sincere commitment from the top down, this bank met both of its CRA objectives: it received the highest CRA rating and has now internalized an outstanding CRA procedure to allow it to be prepared for future exams.

We have recently been notified by this bank that they received their *second* public CRA exam, which they totally prepared for on their own, using the newly internalized procedure without our assistance. Within the approximate year since they were notified of their first outstanding rating, our only major involvement with that bank, other than communicating with them on a regular basis to inform them of recent CRA developments, was to conduct a series of in-house CRA training seminars updating our previous ones. Neither the bank nor we were surprised to learn that the bank had just received its second outstanding rating.

6. THE LOWEST CRA RATINGS— PROFILES OF BANKS NEEDING IMPROVEMENT

INTRODUCTION

The purpose of this chapter is to review our analysis of the CRA evaluations of the lowest rated banks in America—those with needs improvement CRA ratings. Chapter 4 presented a comparable analysis for those banks receiving outstanding ratings. Chapter 8 contains profiles of banks with the *absolutely* lowest CRA rating, namely substantial noncompliance.

Banks with needs improvement ratings represent the next to the lowest level on the CRA rating system. Banks in this group need to improve their overall record of ascertaining and helping to meet the credit needs of its entire delineated community, including low- and moderate-income neighborhoods, in a manner consistent with its resources and capabilities.

Chapter 3 noted that 10.1% of all banks with public CRA ratings over the July 1, 1990—December 31, 1991, period received needs improvement ratings. Although the regulators made 675 such ratings during this period, only 578 of them were publicly released by December 31, 1991, according to federal bank regulators. The percentage of banks receiving this rating decreased to 9.6% by year-end 1992.

This chapter contains a detailed analysis of 108 needs improvement evaluations, reflecting a cross section of banks and thrifts nationwide through year-end 1991. This sample of evaluations includes most of the largest banks and thrifts with this rating as of year-end 1991 plus a stratified random sampling of smaller ones distributed throughout all states. This sample was designed to include banks and thrifts examined by all four federal regulators as well as by each of their different regions where possible. The name and location of the banks in this sample are mentioned throughout this chapter.

Our total sample size of 108 evaluations represented 19% of all available needs improvement public evaluations as of December 31, 1991. Considering that this sample represents a cross section of banks and thrifts, we believe it is representative of the entire universe of banks receiving needs improvement ratings as of that date.

The same type of individual assessment factor analysis completed in Chapter 4 on outstanding rated banks will be completed here. Again, the profile by assessment factor will not repeat the general profiles described in the appendix for this rating but rather focus on specific items and actual examples. The following profile should be reviewed in conjunction with the actual performance evaluations for the relevant banks whenever possible.

The profile of banks needing improvement is nowhere near as bad as the following one for those banks in substantial noncompliance. Still, much can be learned from banks with a needs improvement rating. That is, why weren't they good enough to receive the most common satisfactory rating four out of five banks received? Conversely, why weren't they bad enough to be placed in the lowest 1% of banks with substantial noncompliance ratings? As in the case of banks with satisfactory ratings, several of those with needs improvement ratings have developed some unique and innovative approaches to improving their CRA performance, and many of these will be mentioned in the following profile.

It should be noted that several of the banks with needs improvement ratings referenced in the following profile have since been upgraded to a satisfactory (and in two cases an outstanding) rating. Table 3–44 identifies those banks that have received more than one evaluation that was made public by the regulators as of December 31, 1991. While some of the upgraded evaluations are reproduced in the companion volume, most are not.

For this reason it is important that those banks which have been upgraded from a needs improvement rating also be evaluated in terms of their current rating and public evaluation. However, because we are preparing a profile of banks with needs improvement ratings, our focus is on why these and other banks received the lower ratings in their first public evaluation. That first evaluation is especially relevant since it may reflect undesirable conditions that existed at a bank for many years. Those conditions may have been criticized in previous confidential exams, but little or no corrective action may have been taken because the evaluations weren't public and/or enforcement was lax.

Many of the items specifically criticized by CRA examiners may have already been corrected by these banks, especially those with upgraded ratings. This fact should be kept in mind in the examination of the CRA activities of any particular bank mentioned in the profile below.

I. ASCERTAINMENT OF COMMUNITY CREDIT NEEDS

Activities to Ascertain Community Credit Needs (Assessment Factor A)

Banks with needs improvement ratings usually have not done a good job in their ascertainment of community credit needs. What contacts that may have been made in their community are often either limited in nature, too specialized to be useful to the entire community, or just plain unproductive in terms of a specific CRA benefit.

Community Bank in Texas Ignores Examiners' Past Recommendations Not Once But Twice

A very common criticism for banks in this category is that they have little or no documentation of their ascertainment efforts. The method of determining credit needs by Norstar Bank of Buffalo, New York, in its five delineated communities was found to be "inconsistent." Their community contact call program was active, but the quality of regional detail provided to the CRA department by the regions was deemed "inadequate." Certain regions more than others were noted as being especially lacking in their efforts.

The credit needs ascertainment efforts of First Interstate Bank of Oregon were found to be "inadequate." Their ascertainment procedures relied on a decentralized system. It was criticized because there was no process to ensure that input from branch, area, and regional managers flowed to that bank's CRA officers, senior management, and board. That bank was also cited for not maintaining adequate documentation of its ascertainment efforts.

Examiners at Alief Alamo Bank of Houston made numerous recommendations to that bank to improve its ascertainment efforts. The examiners noted that these same recommendations were included in the two previous CRA performance evaluations. That bank was found to need "substantial efforts" to adequately ascertain community credit needs.

Bell Federal's Low 6% Response Rate Because Survey Was Too Long and Too Late

Several banks with needs improvement ratings used different types of surveys to ascertain credit needs, although most banks did not even make such an attempt. Those banks with this rating that used surveys were often criticized for a less than scientific approach or the fact that they focused on customers to the exclusion of noncustomers.

Litchville State Bank of Litchville, North Dakota, conducted a mail questionnaire to bank customers regarding service satisfaction. Although the survey was done two years prior to the exam, the examiners noted that the information was "inconclusive and response was limited."

Bell Federal of Chicago sent out 250 credit needs surveys during the last three months of the review period. Most of the mailings went to 42 churches in low- and moderate-income neighborhoods plus 101 real estate agencies. At the time of the exam only 15 surveys (6%) had been returned, all of them from real estate agencies. The examiners indicated that surveys sent to the churches were not preceded by some preliminary contact. They also suggested that the low 6% return rate was probably due not only to the late mailing of the surveys but also their length (4 pages).

"High Profile" Community Group Snubbed by Chicago Bank

The Cole Taylor Bank of Chicago commissioned three credit needs surveys within approximately a one-year period. The bank developed an impressive list of contacts in its communities as a result of the surveys. While the examiners verified most of the contacts, they found "little evidence of actual ascertainment of credit needs being conducted." Some mail contacts resulted in "no significant communication" being established, and others resulted in "no communication at all." The examiners provided the following example of such a lack of communications: one "high profile low-income housing development group" in a low- and moderate-income and predominantly minority area near one of the bank's branches responded twice to a bank mail solicitation by telephone but had not been contacted by the bank.

Illinois Bank Can't Produce Survey That Disputes Community Contacts' Remarks

Senior management and other bank representatives at the Shelby County State Bank of Shelbyville, Illinois, were cited as being "unable to articulate the results of their activities in terms of ascertained credit needs." One of the many needs identified by outside community contacts made by the examiners was for a first-time home buyers program. Bank management "disputed the community contacts' remarks" at the final meeting with the examiners by stating that the bank had its own survey showing that there was no need for such a program. The examiners indicated, however, that the bank was "unable to provide specific information regarding this survey."

Pacific Valley National Bank of Modesto, California, which received a needs improvement rating on its first public exam, conducted customer surveys which were oriented toward improving services and convenience rather than identifying credit needs and concerns. The examiners reported that these surveys only reached existing customers.

Use of CRA Vendors Doesn't Guarantee Average or Better Rating

The use of outside CRA vendors and consultants does not guarantee an above-average or even average rating as evidenced by the fact that several banks with needs improvement ratings had used the services of outside CRA specialists. It can be argued, though, that without those outside experts these banks might have received a lower (i.e., substantial noncompliance) rating.

Allied Savings Bank in Santa Rosa, California, contracted with a public relations firm to help the bank identify specific credit needs within its delineated community. The examiners stated that those efforts were too recent to assess.

In the case of First Signature Bank and Trust of Portsmouth, New Hampshire, they had hired a consulting firm to ascertain credit needs two years prior to their exam. That bank's primary source of community credit need information is its membership in a local banking group representing 21 financial institutions.

Partially Neglecting "Low-Mod" Demographics at First Interstate of Arizona

Banks with needs improvement ratings usually consider or analyze published demographic data regarding lending activities on an occasional basis only. Some banks are criticized in their approach to using such data.

First Interstate Bank of Arizona uses demographics prepared annually by an external consulting firm. The bank is part of a syndicate using demographic information. Updated demographic data, however, has been primarily used to reshape some of that bank's deposit transaction accounts in contrast to lending products. The current demographic analysis at First Interstate Bank of Oregon was criticized because low- and moderate-income ("low-mod") areas were "partially neglected" according to the examiners.

Relying Too Much on Realtors

Some banks with needs improvement ratings may have adequate ascertainment methods, but they may be too limited in their focus to the possible exclusion of other interests. For example, many banks were looked askance at because their ascertainment efforts were limited to local realtors, just one of many possible sources of needs ascertainment. Realtors are an excellent source of housing market information, but they may not be the most objective source depending upon their business interests.

Metropolitan Savings Bank of Cleveland is involved in various local real estate-related groups. Although bank management believes that this involvement helps them to determine community credit needs, the examiners criticized them for not adequately documenting that involvement and failing to establish a method to measure the effectiveness of it.

Davy Crockett Federal Savings Bank of Crockett, Texas, ascertained community credit needs via contacts with local realtors. The examiners indicated that these contacts, which were done on an infrequent basis, did not involve the needs of civic, religious, neighborhood, minority, small business, or commercial groups or entities.

The majority of ascertainment contacts at Penn Federal Savings Bank of Newark, New Jersey, were with realtors, and none of those contacts resulted in low- and moderate-income neighborhood programs. The basic "outreach" activities at Gold River Savings Bank of Fair Oaks, California, were regular calls on realtors. Bank management did not document contacts with any community or civic organizations.

Another bank was criticized because its participation in civic organizations and community groups was minimal. The only civic organization participation by the Banyan Bank of Boca Raton, Florida, which received a needs improvement rating on its first public exam, was the local chamber of commerce.

Ignoring the Less Affluent in Beverly Hills

Banks in the needs improvement category are often viewed with disfavor if they don't consider low- and moderate-income neighborhood needs. World Trade Bank of Beverly Hills, California, was cited for inadequate credit needs ascertainment efforts. The bank documented involvement in various groups, but these represented the interests of the "more affluent areas" within the bank's delineated community, according to the examiners. Contrary to popular belief, even an area like zip code 90210 in Beverly Hills has a relatively substantial low- and moderate- income population.

Bell Federal of Chicago documented its officer calls to realtors for a five-month period. However, the examiners mentioned that less than 10% of their calls were in low- and moderate-income areas, and most were in Chicago's suburbs. Officer call programs at the First Interstate Bank of Arizona did not specifically target businesses established in low- and moderate-income neighborhoods, according to the examiners.

Overemphazing Ethnic Targeting

Many banks with needs improvement ratings that are primarily ethnic banks have been criticized because of their natural focus on a target ethnic group, which may result in the actual or perceived exclusion of other groups. United Savings Bank of San Francisco was commended for doing an effective job of serving the Asian community, but there was no general outreach to other members of the delineated community.

Pacific Valley National Bank, which initially received a needs improvement rating, attempted to reach out to Hispanics, the largest minority in its community, by periodically contacting the Hispanic Chamber of Commerce. That bank also advertised on a Portuguese radio station to reach that segment of the community, but its advertisements were noted as only promoting the bank's image.

Not Following Up on Officer Calls

Banks with officer call programs may be criticized if there is little CRA contact or follow-up. There are a few examples that fall in this category.

Harris Bank of Chicago has an extensive officer call program, but most calls were outside the bank's delineated community, and a large portion were generally "maintenance" calls. The needs ascertainment efforts of First Interstate Bank of Seattle, Washington, were indicated as being "very limited" in some areas with only limited contacts with public officials, minority groups, private nonprofit developers, and financial intermediaries.

Many banks with officer call programs do not maintain proper documentation or integrate them into the CRA program. First Executive Bank of Philadelphia maintains a monthly log of business development calls, but the CRA examiners recommended that this information and other outreach efforts be incorporated into the bank's CRA program as a method of community credit needs ascertainment.

BankAtlantic of Fort Lauderdale, Florida, has a call program where loan officers regularly contact real estate brokers. The bank, however, was criticized for not documenting how this activity identified a particular credit need or resulted in a product or service to help address that need. As will be noted later, this is a fairly frequent criticism of banks with a needs improvement rating.

Membership in Only One Organization in Puerto Rico

Many banks with this rating are criticized for their limited contacts with community groups, an important method of credit needs ascertainment. The CRA officer of Ponce Federal Bank of Ponce, Puerto Rico, was able to provide the CRA examiners with but one example of an organization in which he was a regular member on behalf of the bank. F&M Bank of Harrisonburg, Virginia, which received a needs improvement rating on its first public exam, "has not been assertive in initiating dialog and contact" with community groups according to CRA examiners.

InterBoro Savings of Cherry Hill, New Jersey, was reported to have a "lack of active involvement" with private, nonprofit community or development organizations. The extent of its involvement was through director and officer affiliations with various religious and civic organizations.

"For the President Only"

Beverly Bank of Lockport, Illinois, maintained a list of community organizations in its CRA files in which bank officers were involved. The examiners noted that membership in those organizations has been maintained only by the president, and in any case there was inadequate documentation to evaluate a meaningful involvement.

Virginia Commerce Bank of Arlington, Virginia, organized two advisory boards for its locations in two different areas. Because membership of these boards was made up exclusively of commercial and small business people, the examiners felt that there was not representation of the credit needs of the bank's entire area, including low- and moderate-income neighborhoods and individuals.

Ignoring "Uptown" in Des Moines

Some banks with needs improvement ratings which serve multiple areas were frowned upon because they emphasized one area more than another. SafraBank II of Pompano Beach, Florida, which received a needs improvement rating in its first public exam, centered its ascertainment efforts on one of its two delineated communities. The limited efforts in the other community were ineffective, according to the examiners.

Brenton Bank and Trust Company of Urbandale, Iowa, has four low- and moderate-income census tracts in its delineated community, all of which are located in the "uptown" area of Des Moines. The only apparent effort to ascertain credit needs in that community was a 1989 service questionnaire. In early 1990 the bank and its consultants from Drake University in Des Moines organized five focus groups. This effort, however, was met with criticism since commercial and residential real estate developers from that uptown community were not represented by any focus group.

River Oaks Bank of Houston, which received a needs improvement rating in its first public exam, made numerous ascertainment efforts in the greater Houston area, primarily with business organizations. Little attention, however, was given to the bank's local community within that larger area, according to the examiners.

Norwest Bank of Waupun, Wisconsin, defined its community as a 17-mile radius around the city of Waupun. The examiners' investigation of the bank's ascertainment efforts revealed that they were focused on the city, with only limited efforts outside of it.

Asking the Police Department about Lower Income Groups in L.A.

Bay Cities National Bank of Redondo Beach, California, was criticized in its first public CRA evaluation, where it received a needs improvement rating, because it limited city government contacts to only one city, Redondo Beach. According to the examiners, bank officers "meet regularly" with that city's police department, which "provides insight in identifying problems associated with lower income groups."

Being that Redondo Beach is a short distance from southwestern L.A., there are many who would argue that a police department would not be the best source of such information. It would be hard, for example, to imagine a bank in L.A. receiving substantial CRA credit for meeting with former Police Chief Gates to provide insight into problems of lower income groups in south central L.A.

That same bank's officer call program was criticized for not targeting any groups of minorities or low- and moderate-income neighborhoods to inform them of available credit. Further, senior management was generally aware of the large minority populations in certain portions of its delineated community, but the examiners mentioned that management did not identify one such city that includes 30% minorities.

Getting "CRA Credit" for Donations at Foreign Banks

Many special service banks, such as credit card and foreign banks, received below-average CRA ratings. In some cases there were little or no efforts to ascertain credit needs. For example, in the case of Mitsubishi Trust & Banking Corporation of New York, their ascertainment activities were limited to providing donations to a community-oriented organization. As previously pointed out, donations to such organizations and others that directly benefit the local community are preferred to those that do not in terms of CRA credit.

Louisiana Bank Did Not Respond to Three 1988 Comments on Bank Credit

Many banks with needs improvement ratings made little or no effort to offer more flexible lending criteria within safe and sound practices. The CRA file of Bank of Commerce and Trust of Crowley, Louisiana, contained three comments dated 1988 regarding the need for more liberal credit terms on housing loans. There was no evidence according to the examiners that the bank had responded to those requests. That bank's current loan policy, which includes a 20% down payment on residential mortgage loans and a maximum 10-year maturity, did not reflect any changes relative to those requests.

Small Mortgage Loans Referred to Other Banks at First Interstate of Denver

First Interstate Bank of Arizona "infrequently" offers loans with special features or more flexible lending criteria to make sound credit more widely available throughout its communities, according to its examiners.

Certain lending criteria for some loans at First Interstate Bank of Denver may restrict credit availability in low- and moderate-income neighborhoods, according to its CRA evaluation. The CRA examiners stated that "management could not explain why" it established policies requiring minimum loan amounts on conventional mortgage loans and minimum income levels for dealer auto loans. That bank reportedly refers customers with "small dollar requests" on conventional mortgage loans to other financial institutions.

"Last Minute" Ascertainment Efforts May Backfire

A fairly common criticism of several banks with needs improvement ratings was the "last minute" nature of many CRA compliance efforts, especially needs ascertainment. The ascertainment contacts at San Clemente Savings Bank in Irvine, California, were "too new to have produced any meaningful results at the time of review."

Regular calls on real estate professionals by staff loan agents at Surety Federal of Vallejo, California, were only "recently initiated." This was also true for another preliminary contact with local government officials. The first loan and deposit geocoding analysis at Norstar Bank of Buffalo, New York, which initially received a needs improvement rating, was "recently received by the bank" at the time of that first exam.

The fact that many community contacts were of a recent nature may limit a bank's ability to effectively respond to them in terms of meeting identified credit needs. In the case of the Commercial Bank of Bel Air, Maryland, which initially received a needs improvement rating, a number of organizations listed as contacts were only recently contacted at the time of the exam. The examiners concluded that the bank had not had time to effectively respond to identified credit needs.

23 Meetings with 14 Organizations Result in Three Loans in New York

Probably the most common criticism of banks with needs improvement ratings under this assessment factor is the lack of any meaningful results of ascertainment efforts in terms of meeting community credit needs, especially those in low- and moderate-income neighborhoods. In other words, a bank can do a good job in ascertaining credit needs but do a poor one in terms of effectively meeting them.

Several banks with needs improvement ratings made efforts to meet with various groups, but these banks were often criticized for a lack of results. IBJ Schroder Bank and Trust of New York, which initially received a needs improvement rating, documented 23 meetings with 14 organizations in 1990 to discuss

credit and other needs. Documentation was not available, however, to show what credit needs were identified as a result of these ascertainment efforts (although they resulted in three community development loans).

Golden Coin Savings of San Francisco has attended meetings with nonprofit developers, lending consortiums, and various community development seminars. The association, however, was criticized for not participating in any of the programs being made available by the organizations with which it has made contact.

HomeFed Bank of San Diego was involved with several community service organizations. There was no evidence, however, that these group contacts resulted in identifying any unmet credit needs that the bank could address in low- and moderate-income neighborhoods. Furthermore, the examiners determined that these activities were limited to that bank's home office area as compared to other parts of its community.

"Prison Banking" Service Commended, but Little or No Credit for Extensive List of Employee Community Involvement

Stockdale Savings of Bakersfield, California, listed involvement with various groups in its CRA statement. The examiners felt that while that association "may well have regular contacts" with some of those groups, there is no documentation, and more significantly, no resultant new loan products or targeted programs.

First Interstate Bank of Arizona has an extensive list of employee involvement in community groups. There is "no evidence," however, which shows this involvement has assisted the bank in determining community credit needs according to the examiners. That bank, however, designed an innovative service to permit the maintenance of accounts for prisoners located in correctional facilities.

Officers of the Boston Private and Trust Company are on the advisory board for a low- and moderate-income housing group as well as a homeless shelter. The bank, nevertheless, could not demonstrate to CRA examiners how this involvement resulted in wider credit availability in the community.

First Interstate Bank of Denver made a reasonable effort to ascertain community credit needs. Even though the bank responded to some identified credit needs by developing programs to offer new products, some of them were in the "developmental stage" at the time of the exam.

Glendale Federal of Glendale, California, has not translated its credit needs assessment efforts into new products or services which meet those needs. Glendale Federal is one of the four banks nationwide that was downgraded from a satisfactory to a needs improvement rating as of year-end 1991.

Board of Directors' Participation (Assessment Factor C)

The review of board minutes by CRA examiners at banks receiving needs improvement ratings usually reveals limited board participation and review of CRA activities. Often banks with this rating just have the wrong "CRA spirit." The most common criticism under this assessment factor concerns CRA technical violations, such as improper annual CRA reviews or incorrect material in the CRA statement or public file.

Alabama Bank's CRA Plan Meets Only One of Twelve Objectives

Few banks with needs improvement ratings have formal CRA programs, and many of those that do are frowned upon because of inadequacies within them. Pan American Savings Bank of San Mateo, California, did not have a formal CRA program, but it did have a recently approved strategic plan. The bank was criticized since CRA was not considered by management or the board in developing that strategic plan.

Union Federal Savings Bank of Brea, California, which likewise did not have a CRA program, was taken to task because its 1990 CRA Statement stated that the bank's board committed itself to implementing a CRA program. The examiners concluded that there was "limited evidence" that the board provided such support.

World Trade Bank of Beverly Hills, California, prepared a draft CRA program, including goals, objectives, and a self-assessment methodology. However, the program was not finalized at the time of the exam and was not reflected in bank policies, procedures, and training programs.

The board of the First National Bank of Florence, Alabama, approved a CRA action plan in early 1990 with 12 objectives. According to the examination in the latter part of 1990, "little effort has been exerted by the board" to achieve those objectives, with the exception of one of them.

Bell Federal's CRA Plan Missteps— 15 Month Delay, Shooting for Satisfactory, and Only 22% of Goal

Specific CRA objectives are usually more difficult to meet than general ones. A general objective might be to "increase" a bank's loan originations in low- and moderate-income or substantially minority neighborhoods. A specific objective would set an absolute or relative amount of such lending. Obviously, specific objectives leave a bank with much less flexibility in meeting them, although they provide greater credibility to a CRA action plan.

The board of Bell Federal of Chicago instructed senior management to prepare a CRA plan in October 1989. The plan was approved in October 1990 but did not become operational until January 1991, approximately 15 months after the board's original instructions. According to the CRA examiners, Bell's "delay in implementing its CRA plan indicates a lack of commitment by both the board of directors and senior management."

It would appear reasonable to assume that most banks would strive toward an outstanding CRA rating. In a unique disclosure by CRA examiners at Bell Federal, it appeared that the objective there may have been to receive just a satisfactory CRA rating. The examiners noted that beginning in May 1990 senior management provided reports to the board regarding "resource expenditures and activities required of Bell Federal in order for the institution to receive a satisfactory CRA rating."

Bell Federal's final CRA plan had for one of its specific goals that 10% of total originations be in low- and moderate-income neighborhoods. This goal "appeared practical and attainable" according to the examiners. Obviously, they were disappointed when the June 30, 1991, data indicated only 2.2% of loan originations were from those neighborhoods. The fact that Bell Federal could only meet 22% of its goal indicates that it may have been an overly optimistic goal in the first place. That, plus their apparent objective of striving for only a satisfactory CRA rating, may have contributed to their ultimate needs improvement rating.

"Vague" CRA Plan in St. Louis

First Exchange Bank of North St. Louis County in Florissant, Missouri, had a formal written CRA plan. This plan, however, was frowned upon by the examiners because it was "vague" in that it lacked goals, objectives, and a methodology for self-assessment.

Board and senior management at First Interstate Bank in Seattle, Washington, had "not dedicated adequate time and resources" to completely develop the bank's CRA program. In an apparent criticism of the program's objectives, the examiners noted that oversight by the board and senior management focused on "numbers of calls and loans made" rather than identification and meeting of credit needs.

$2 Billion Bank Needs at Least One Full-Time CRA Officer

One question facing many banks is when a full-time CRA officer is required. Examiners at Eureka Bank of Foster City, California, which initially received a needs improvement rating, provided some insight in this regard. The OTS examiners noted that a bank of this size (approximately $1.8 billion at the time of the exam) should "reasonably be expected to have at least the equivalent of one full-time employee devoted to CRA monitoring." Many banks with less than $1 billion and in some cases less than $500 million in size have full-time CRA officers. It would therefore appear that a bank in the $2 billion plus range is probably expected to have at least one full-time CRA officer, at least based on this case study.

$14 Billion Thrift with a "Last Minute" Part-Time CRA Officer

Regardless of size, most banks should have some type of CRA committee to provide input into CRA compliance from different areas of the bank. First Interstate Bank of Colstrip, Montana, which was involved in a merger denial because of its below-average CRA performance, formed a CRA committee. However, at the time of its exam, it had met on only two occasions. That bank was also taken to task

because its delineated community was not considered reasonable.

HomeFed Bank of San Diego, California, established a CRA committee, but it was not a committee of the board. The board's vice chairman was that committee's only director member, and there was "no indication" that he regularly presented CRA issues dealt with by the committee to the board, according to the examiners. This $13.9 billion thrift had only appointed a CRA officer on a part-time basis two months before its first public CRA exam. Board minutes at the bank did not include the directors' resolution ratifying the creation of the committee or the appointment of the CRA officer. A full-time CRA officer position was created during the examination. This thrift has failed since then.

Self-Assessments—Too Little, Too Late, and No Board Participation

Banks with needs improvement ratings most generally do not have self-assessment procedures. Those that do may be viewed with disfavor because of their general nature or the lack of board involvement in the process.

Security State Bank of Stockdale, Texas, one of only two banks upgraded from a needs improvement to an outstanding rating as of year-end 1991, was initially criticized in its first public exam on the topic of CRA audits. The bank's adopted CRA statement provided for an internal CRA assessment by its CRA officer. However, no such audit had been conducted at the time of their first public CRA exam.

F&M Bank of Harrisonburg, Virginia, had a CRA self-assessment presented to its board a few months before its first public exam. The self-assessment at this bank, which received a needs improvement rating on its first exam, was challenged as being "limited" since it did not include the results of a loan geocoding or needs assessment analysis.

SafraBank II of Pompano Beach, Florida, which received a needs improvement rating on its first public exam, prepared self-assessment analysis reports for its board. The examiners concluded that these reports "lack necessary detail" by reporting aggregate performance for both of its delineated communities rather than individually. By being grouped together, these reports "failed to detect the disproportionate lending patterns" between the two communities.

Senior management and other employees at the First National Bank and Trust Company of Nicholasville, Kentucky, performed a CRA self-assessment. The CRA examiners, however, objected to the fact that the bank's board did not participate in the self-assessment.

Not Using the Right Data

Banks with needs improvement ratings usually do not prepare anything more than a limited geocoding analysis of loan applications. Many such banks make no attempt at such analysis, and some that do may be questioned on their methodology.

The board at First Interstate Bank of Seattle, Washington, had not required an analysis of the disposition of loan applications. That bank relied on an analysis of deposits versus credits in local areas, according to the examiners.

The ability of the board of Virginia Commerce Bank of Arlington, Virginia, to review CRA performance is "inhibited by the use of limited geographic information," according to their public exam. "Informative data such as the location of low- and moderate-income areas and lending pattern data" were not used by that bank, according to its examiners.

Stale CRA Statements in Puerto Rico

Banks with needs improvement ratings infrequently if ever review CRA activities and performance beyond the required annual review of the CRA statement. The most recent such annual review at Ponce Federal Bank in Ponce, Puerto Rico, appeared to the examiners to have been "no more than a simple acknowledgment review." This is because major loans products (auto and equipment leasing and commercial lending), which were discontinued or suspended in July 1989, were still in that bank's current CRA statement adopted in June 1990.

The board at First Federal of Peekskill, New York, had reviewed a report of that institution's CRA activity. That institution, however, was nonetheless criticized because there was "no documented evidence of new policy initiatives" resulting from this review.

Examiners Cite Contradiction between Board Minutes and Management's Statements in New York

The only thing worse than a board not completing a review of CRA activities and performance is when they don't even complete the required annual review of the CRA statement. A review of board minutes for CRA issues and discussions is an automatic part of a CRA examination.

The CRA statement of Safra National Bank of New York had not been reviewed by their board in four years. The examiners' review of board minutes revealed a "lack of supervisory involvement." This was "contrary to management's position that CRA issues have been discussed at board meetings," according to their examiners.

The board of Allied Savings Bank of Santa Rosa, California, did not review that bank's CRA statement on an annual basis. Furthermore, their CRA statement did not comply with technical requirements.

"Last Minute" CRA Appointments May Result in Little or No CRA Credit

The compliance efforts of some banks with needs improvement ratings were of a "last minute" nature in terms of board involvement and oversight of the CRA function. As previously pointed out, HomeFed Bank of San Diego, California, appointed a part-time CRA officer just two months prior to its first public exam and created a full-time position during the examination.

A CRA officer for the $84 million First National Bank and Trust Company of Nicholasville, Kentucky, which is part of an approximately $500 million multibank holding company, appointed its CRA officer the month after their first public evaluation. The Community Affairs Officer of Beverly Bank of Lockport, Illinois, was appointed during the month of its first public exam.

First National Bank of Ipswich, Massachusetts, had a "newly formed CRA Committee," but there were no further specifics in the public evaluation. IBJ Schroder Bank and Trust Company of New York, which received a needs improvement rating on its first public evaluation, established a CRA committee one month after the date on its first public evaluation.

The CRA committee of Norstar Bank of Buffalo, New York, which initially received a needs improvement rating, formed its CRA committee during the month of its first public evaluation.

Nonlocal Directors Aren't Locally Involved

Outstanding banks generally have boards that are personally involved with CRA. By contrast, banks with needs improvement ratings have only a limited involvement. In those cases where some or most of the board live in distant areas, it is hard to argue that they could be involved in the local community in any meaningful way if they are usually not there. The increasing trend toward multistate operations will likely witness additional nonlocal board members.

Arvada 1st Industrial Bank of Arvada, Colorado, is a subsidiary of a bank holding company in Utah. None of the board members of this bank live or work in the greater Denver area, which includes Arvada, as the majority live in the Salt Lake City area. The examiners stated that "this geographic separation limits the communication channels between the bank's board and the bank's community."

Because five of the ten board members of Metropolitan Savings Bank of Cleveland lived in New Jersey (and another lived in New York), the examiners concluded that they were "not actively involved" in the local community. This was also the case for Security Trust Federal of Knoxville, Tennessee, a subsidiary of a Jackson, Mississippi, institution. Since Security Federal had only one local director (all of the others were from the Jackson area), this resulted in a limited degree of local involvement by that board.

EurekaBank of Foster City, California, which received a needs improvement rating on its first public evaluation, was found by the examiners to have only one of its six directors with a "documented record of local community involvement." There were no further specifics provided as to the basis for that finding.

CRA Training for Everyone but the Board, Senior Management, and the Community Affairs Officer in Illinois

Banks with needs improvement ratings usually provide only limited support to the CRA training of personnel. When there is training at such banks, board members and senior management are often not involved. In the case of Beverly Bank of Lockport, Illinois, they completed a CRA training program with the bank staff and marketing officer. According to the examiners, the register of attendance at the training sessions did not indicate that board members, senior management, or the bank's Community Affairs Officer received training.

Banks with needs improvement ratings generally perform little if any analysis of loan applications to check fairness and nondiscrimination compliance. Typical of such a bank would be the First Community Industrial Bank of Fort Collins, Colorado, where the board did not review denied loan applications to determine compliance with loan policy.

Getting CRA Credit for Two Bilingual Employees Who Had Left the Bank

The most common criticism by far of banks receiving needs improvement ratings was their laxity in insuring that CRA technical regulatory requirements are met. Most, but not all, of these have to do with the bank's CRA statement and public file.

Only in a few cases were there outright discrepancies between what management said and what CRA examiners found in their examination. As previously noted in the case of Safra National Bank of New York, management's position that CRA issues had been discussed at board meetings was found to contradict the findings of CRA examiners. They concluded that directors' minutes revealed a lack of supervisory involvement.

Board members at Stockdale Savings of Bakersfield, California, documented their involvement with various "housing and community organizations." According to the examiners' findings, the organizations in some cases are "not housing related" and/or "the link to housing is uncertain." Also, that bank's current CRA statement referenced bilingual staff members. According to the public evaluation, both of the bank's only two bilingual employees had left the bank.

Another example of an inconsistency in a CRA statement involves World Trade Bank of Beverly Hills, California. A previous CRA statement at that bank "conveyed inaccurate information" implying that the bank had already committed funds to a nonprofit mortgage banking consortium, "when only an expression of interest had been made." The CRA statement of Gold River Savings Bank of Fair Oaks, California, was found to be "outdated" and to "not accurately reflect the institution's current credit products or activities."

Kansas City CRA Statement Not Updated since 1979

The CRA statement of Inter-State Federal of Kansas City, Kansas, was also found to be "outdated" and include types of loans "no longer offered by the institution." This was one of the few banks we reviewed that was criticized for not updating its CRA statement in a long time. That statement, which "remained unchanged since 1979," may have been the first and only one that association ever completed, since the implementing regulations for CRA did not come out until November 1978.

There were other technical violations involving CRA regulations there. For example, that institution's map delineating the local community was inadequate due to the "lack of clarity caused by copy reduction." Furthermore, that institution failed to recognize that its delineated community should include portions of adjoining Missouri, which accounted for 30% of loan originations during the year.

San Jose National Bank of San Jose, California, which received a needs improvement rating on its first public evaluation, was found to have an inadequate CRA statement because it described loans the bank "does not market to all members of its community." BankAtlantic of Fort Lauderdale, Florida, was found to have a CRA statement that inaccurately identified the types of loans offered by that bank.

Public File Problems—Inaccessible, Incomplete, and Missing Correspondence

Some banks were viewed in disfavor because of technical errors in the public CRA notice. This was the case with First Community Industrial Bank of Lakewood, Colorado, which received a needs improvement rating on its first public evaluation.

Some banks were chastised because the CRA statement failed to contain a copy of the CRA notice. This was the case at both the Cornerstone Bank of Mission Viejo, California, and Tracy Savings and Loan of Tracy, California. Also, both of those banks were

taken to task because their CRA statement did not list all types of credit offered.

Some banks with needs improvement ratings encounter problems because of incomplete CRA public files. The Bank of Commerce of Auburn, California, which received a needs improvement rating on its first public evaluation, did not have the required past two years' CRA statements in its public file. The public file of the Bank of Alabama in Fultondale, Alabama, was "not readily accessible" and did not contain the required copies of the bank's CRA statements in effect during the last two years.

The public file of First Interstate Bank of Oregon did not contain a community group's correspondence on a cooperative lending program. According to the public evaluation, senior management was going to place the required correspondence in the public file after the issue was resolved.

First Interstate Bank of Denver was criticized because its CRA statement "does not accurately describe the bank's actual practice of extending conventional mortgage loans." The bank's statement says that conventional mortgage loans will be offered to all customers. In practice, however, "the bank refers customers with small dollar requests to other financial institutions," according to CRA examiners. Although that bank's Community Relations and Compliance Policy Committee oversees the CRA program, the committee minutes were found to be lacking. Specifically, the minutes did not show that the committee had formal approval authority over the CRA program or participated in developing strategies to meet credit needs.

California Miscues—Not Knowing Your Regulator and Overdoing the Paperwork

Bay Cities National Bank of Redondo Beach, California, which received a needs improvement rating in its first public evaluation, had an unusual inaccuracy in its CRA statement. According to the CRA examiners, that bank's board "erroneously allowed the Federal Reserve Bank to be disclosed as their regulatory authority on their public notice rather than the Comptroller of the Currency." Also, that bank's CRA statement indicated the availability of residential real estate mortgages, but they are only offered as "mini-perm" loans until conventional financing becomes available. That bank's statement was revised to reflect these changes.

With the emphasis on so many technical requirements and the attendant paperwork required, we found the criticism of Glendale Federal of Glendale, California, to almost be ironic. This was one of the four banks to be downgraded from a satisfactory to a needs improvement rating as of year-end 1991. Rather than compliment the bank for a CRA statement that meets regulatory requirements, the CRA examiners criticized it for being "voluminous and inappropriate as a tool to inform the public" of their CRA performance.

II. MARKETING AND TYPES OF CREDIT OFFERED AND EXTENDED

Marketing Programs for Credit Awareness (Assessment Factor B)

The marketing and advertising programs at banks with needs improvement ratings have limited oversight by senior management and the board. Many times there is no marketing or advertising program. As was the case with outstanding banks, many banks with needs improvement ratings (and their examiners) incorrectly used the terms *advertising* and *marketing* interchangeably, when the former is but a subset of the latter.

Getting By on Referrals and Walk-In Business in New Jersey

In the case of Inter-State Federal of Kansas City, Kansas, there was a "lack of a marketing program." There were no formal marketing programs at South Bergen Savings of Wood Ridge, New Jersey, which depends upon "personal references and walk-in business."

When Pacific Valley National Bank of Modesto, California, received a needs improvement rating on its first public examination, it did not have a formal marketing program. The bank was marketed primarily through referrals from directors, management, and existing customers. The bank used call programs and advertising, but both were criticized as being limited in terms of their subject and the various targets.

Banks with needs improvement ratings that do have marketing strategies may be criticized for their lack of focus or effectiveness. The First National Bank in Dolton, Illinois, did not have a "focused marketing strategy," according to its CRA examiners. Bay View Federal Bank of San Mateo, California, did not coordinate its marketing efforts with its overall CRA efforts.

Is Poor Loan Response Due to Poor Product or Poor Marketing?

A bank's marketing program may also be looked askance at if it is perceived to be ineffective by the examiners. We cannot imagine why any bank would continuing running an ineffective marketing program. Measuring the effectiveness of marketing efforts is much more of an art than a science, even for trained marketing professionals as compared to compliance examiners.

Security Bank of Commerce of Hamtramack, Michigan, received a "minimal response" to an advertised government-related lending program. The public's "unresponsiveness" to that program, according to the examiners, could be because the bank was offering products that "do not appeal to community residents." Another reason, according to the examiners, may have been the "bank's failure to adequately market the products through community groups and housing organizations."

CRA examiners at Norwest Bank in Waupun, Wisconsin, concluded from interviews that it appeared that members of the community were "not aware" that the bank offered small business loans. The examiners thus concluded that the bank had not made a "significant effort" to market its business loans. It also reached this conclusion regarding the bank's residential mortgage loans, as its only advertising for them "consisted entirely of brochures available in the bank's lobby."

Thrifts Cut Back Credit Advertising Due to Budget Cuts

Farmers and Merchants Bank of Long Beach, California, which received a needs improvement rating on its second public evaluation, was criticized for having no formal marketing program or strategy. The bank's marketing efforts, which rely largely on officer calls, "lack focus or direction or review by senior management." That bank received a "substantial noncompliance" rating for this specific assessment factor.

Some banks cut back on their marketing and advertising programs in recent years as a cost savings measure. These activities did not go unnoticed by the CRA examiners. In the case of Gold River Savings Bank of Fair Oaks, California, credit services were not advertised or marketed except through direct real estate contacts. This was done "in an attempt to reduce operating expenses" there. BankAtlantic of Fort Lauderdale, Florida, discontinued advertising its residential mortgage loan products, again probably as part of a cost-cutting effort.

Targeted Marketing Questioned at Specialty Banks

The most common criticism of banks with needs improvement ratings under this assessment factor is their lack of effective advertising of loan products, especially in low- and moderate-income neighborhoods, as compared to advertising the bank's image or deposit services. This objection may apply to special purpose or wholesale banks but especially applies to retail banks.

Specialty banks, such as those for credit cards or foreign operations, often receive below-average CRA ratings because of their narrow purpose and market. For example, bank marketing efforts at Mitsubishi Trust & Banking Corporation of New York City are for its pension trust and other trust-related services as compared to loans.

American Liberty Savings Bank of Oakland, California, "relies entirely" on wholesale mortgage brokers for credit applications, according to its CRA examiners. That bank advertises in trade and/or professional publications to promote its corporate image.

United Savings Bank of San Francisco, which received a needs improvement rating on its first public exam, solicits loans "almost exclusively" on the wholesale side through mortgage brokers and on the retail side through real estate brokers. Its marketing efforts are primarily for deposit gathering.

Focus on Image and Deposit Advertising Criticized Compared to Loan Advertising

Most banks with needs improvement ratings focused their advertising efforts on their image. Product offerings were generally referred to in a generic form, and usually deposits were the only product mentioned specifically.

First Interstate Bank of Arizona has an extensive advertising program, but its focus is primarily on checking and savings accounts as well as name recognition. Brenton Bank and Trust Company of Urbandale, Iowa, primarily advertises to promote its image as a general financial services provider rather than for specific products or programs. Marketing strategies at the North Side Deposit Bank in Pittsburgh are primarily designed to promote the same objective.

GSL Savings Bank of Guttenberg, New Jersey, focused its advertising primarily on its recent name change. Advertising of the bank's general image rather than credit products was done because of the "minimal success" the bank reported it had with advertising of credit products.

Fidelity U.S. Depository Trust Company of Salt Lake City advertises nationally for deposits in newspapers. It did not offer loans in its local area at the time of its exam and therefore did not have any credit program or advertising for it.

New Bank in St. Louis Excused from Loan Advertising

Advertising at the First National Bank of Ipswich, Massachusetts, has been "strictly deposit oriented" with no promotion of credit products. First Exchange Bank of North St. Louis County in Florissant, Missouri, primarily uses deposit-oriented newspaper ads. Because this was "considered typical of a de novo bank," it was "not viewed as a negative factor" by their examiners.

The majority of media advertising at First Interstate Bank of Oregon promotes the bank's image as a general financial services provider. That bank does, however, advertise some of its credit programs within its local community, but others such as real estate loans are not advertised. While senior management makes most major advertising decisions, branch managers at that bank can develop their own image advertisements and signs.

New Affluent and Business Banks Downgraded for Segmented Marketing

Several of the *de novo* banks formed in the 80s that were targeted at a specific market segment or niche may be taken to task if their marketing efforts are focused so much on one target group to the actual or perceived exclusion of others. In other words, a highly focused marketing strategy may be detrimental to a bank's CRA rating.

San Jose National Bank of San Jose, California, was criticized in its first public evaluation when it received a needs improvement rating because its advertising did not reach all members of its community. That bank primarily focused its marketing efforts on small businesses. This was also the case for the fairly new First Executive Bank of Philadelphia which marketed its products to the bank's chosen niche of "small businesses and professionals, particularly those in the health care industry."

Community Banks Must Consider All Advertising Media

Some banks with needs improvement ratings used only a limited menu of the several possible promotional strategies that are available to most banks. For example, a small bank may be frowned upon if its advertising is limited to only one part of its delineated community, especially if there are advertising media in other portions of it.

Litchville State Bank in Litchville, North Dakota, limited its advertising to its local paper but "not other media serving the entire delineated community." That bank usually uses "unspecific" advertising as compared to that mentioning specific services or types of loans.

Security State Bank of Stockdale, Texas, which received a needs improvement rating in its first public evaluation, communicated its credit services to the community through contacts with civic groups and leaders. There was, however, "no documentation of such communications," according to the examiners.

First Interstate Bank of Colstrip, Montana, utilizes local newspaper and radio stations for its advertising. That bank, which has been the subject of a CRA protest by a Cheyenne Indian community group, has held a number of community meetings. Attendance at those meetings by community members, however, has been "limited," according to the examiners.

Upscale Advertising at Boston Private Bank Challenged

The promotional strategies used by some banks meet with disapproval if they are too limited in their scope to effectively communicate information on a bank's credit services to its entire community. Advertising at the Boston Private Bank and Trust Company is limited to a weekly "rate sheet," which advertises both deposit and credit services mainly to "upscale" clients. The bank also uses direct calling programs and referrals to market its credit services. Because that bank specializes in "jumbo mortgages" of $150,000 and above, the examiners felt that this bank's marketing program "appears to preclude serving low- and moderate-income borrowers or depositors."

Advertising Limited to Statement Stuffers, In-Lobby Material, and Yellow Pages

Landmark Bank of Kansas City, Missouri, does not use newspaper or radio advertising. Its credit marketing is limited to statement stuffers and lobby brochures which are mainly for existing customers. The current customer base of Union Bank and Trust Company of Lincoln, Nebraska, is informed of credit services through direct mail and statement stuffers.

Kearny Federal of Kearny, New Jersey, does not advertise its credit products with the exception of "an occasional poster placed in the branch offices." The Guaranty Bank & Trust Company of Tulsa, Oklahoma, advertises in the yellow pages and has an "informal officer call program" according to its examiners.

Examiners Hint to Bank—Change Prime Billboard Advertising

Alief Alamo Bank of Houston, Texas, was recommended to expand its marketing efforts because members of the community contacted by CRA examiners were "not sufficiently aware of the credit products and services the bank has available." Community contacts interviewed by the examiners noted that the bank's billboard at the intersection of two major streets was one of the most visible means of marketing used by the bank. The examiners added that the subject billboard was used to promote local functions as opposed to credit services. The implication was clearly that this bank should use that highly visible billboard for advertising loans. Although CRA is about lending, this experience shows that it can sometimes be about other things such as hints about changing billboard advertising.

Advertising to Customers Excludes Noncustomers

As noted above, marketing to existing customers through direct mail, statement stuffers, in-lobby efforts, or other means is subject to criticism if noncustomers are not being reached. While statement stuffers go only to current customers and in-lobby brochures are mainly seen by existing customers, this does not have to be the case with direct mail. While a bank's existing customer base is often the first group selected for direct mail, banks should consider targeting representative groups of noncustomers in its local community to assure broad representation.

San Clemente Savings Bank of Irvine, California, which generally focuses on image and deposit advertising, offered a low-cost loan refinancing program only to existing customers through direct mail. Thus, all members of its community were not made aware of that credit service, according to examiners.

Little to No CRA Credit for "Philosophical" Ads in The Wall Street Journal

The marketing efforts of Harris Trust and Savings Bank of Chicago mainly focused on various calling programs and selective direct mailings. Its direct mail efforts, with the exception of student loans, were limited to "existing customers, bank employees or highly selective pre-qualified credit card solicitations."

Credit card direct mail solicitations accounted for 97% of Harris Bank's media marketing efforts since its previous exam. The focus of the bank's call programs were either "so broad" that they are generally outside its community or "so narrow" that they only covered small areas within it.

Little mass media that would reach the entire community was used, and 1990 newspaper advertisements by Harris Bank for real estate loans were canceled. "Philosophical" advertisements that year in *The Wall Street Journal* about deregulation or management techniques "were aimed at the business owner, and were not product specific or credit related." The examiners concluded that the bank's overall program "does not stimulate awareness of bank products to meet identified needs" throughout the community, especially in the case of real estate loans.

$25,000 Minimum Deposit in Beverly Hills

Many banks with needs improvement ratings that have adequate marketing or advertising programs may be criticized because they are not directed to low- and moderate-income neighborhoods within their local community. As noted in a few previous examples, private or upscale banks are particularly susceptible to this criticism because their marketing explicitly solicits affluent individuals to the actual or perceived exclusion of low- and moderate-income ones.

World Trade Bank of Beverly Hills, California, maintains memberships in organizations in the affluent areas of Beverly Hills and Century City. Because a CRA focus "appears lacking," management is "unexposed to the special credit needs of the low- to moderate-income areas" within its community. The bank's marketing efforts, which are focused on sophisticated borrowers, consist mainly of customer referrals and officer contacts. Advertising there is "virtually nonexistent," with the only ad being for a deposit with a $25,000 minimum.

Safra National Bank in New York City feels its expertise lies in "wholesale banking and lending to high net worth individuals." Deposit programs there are "geared toward the higher income individuals, making it difficult for the less affluent to benefit from such products," according to CRA examiners.

A 1988 self-assessment by First Federal Savings of San Gabriel Valley in West Covina, California, led it to conclude that it should focus its marketing efforts on "only one segment of its delineated community" rather than on all of it. The examiners did not specify that segment. The fact that the association received a "substantial noncompliance" rating for this assessment factor coupled with the conclusion that the bank's single segment strategy "does not meet the purpose and intent of the CRA" leads us to believe that it was likewise an affluent target market segment. Also, the association did not advertise in minority publications or in those targeted to low- and moderate-income ("low-mod") areas.

A Modest Start to Credit Advertising in Chicago's "Low-Mod" Areas—1% of Budget

The majority of the population in the communities of Ponce Federal Bank in Ponce, Puerto Rico, are low- and moderate-income. Yet, that bank "has not attempted to target specific low- and moderate-income communities in its advertisements."

The holding company of First Interstate Bank in Seattle, Washington, controls 28% of that bank's advertising budget. Advertisements directed to low- and moderate-income neighborhoods have only been limited, and they are primarily of an image type.

Pacific Valley National Bank of Modesto, California, which received a needs improvement rating on its first public evaluation, was challenged then because neither its call programs nor its advertisements were specifically directed at low- and moderate-income neighborhoods within its community.

Bell Federal of Chicago was likewise criticized for not placing any advertisements with media specifically directed to low- and moderate-income areas in 1989 and 1990. This changed to a small degree in the quarter preceding its first public examination when credit advertisements, representing less than 1% of its annual advertising budget, were placed in two Chicago newspapers directed to low- and moderate-income neighborhoods.

EurekaBank of Foster City, California, which received a needs improvement rating on its first public evaluation, ran three credit-related advertising campaigns in general circulation newspapers in 1990. None of them, however, were targeted to low- and moderate-income or minority populations.

Southern California Criticism of Foreign-Language Advertising— Two Languages Not Enough

Banks with non-English-speaking residents in their local community must likewise be sensitive to their needs in the marketing of credit products. In the case of EurekaBank's first public evaluation, they were cited for failing to modify its "product pamphlets, advertising, or applications packages" to serve the non-English-speaking portions of its communities.

Two large thrifts in southern California provide examples of banks that were taken exception with by their regulators in this regard—one for doing no foreign-language advertising and the other for not doing enough.

HomeFed Bank of San Diego, California, had a significant portion of its residents with a primary language other than English. That bank therefore met with disapproval as they were doing *no* advertising in any foreign language. Also, its advertising was not carried by media directed to low- and moderate-income and minority neighborhoods or individuals.

Glendale Federal of Glendale, California, serves a similar market with a large Spanish-speaking population. While that bank has made progress in using Spanish-language advertisements in its communities, it was recommended that the bank use special advertisements targeted toward "other ethnic groups" within its delineated communities.

No Plans to Run Spanish-Language Ad in CRA File

DuPage National Bank of West Chicago, Illinois, has a substantial Spanish-speaking population in its delineated community. That bank was therefore questioned for not having run any ads in Spanish.

Some of the pictorial savings advertisements for Stockdale Savings of Bakersfield, California, include both women and minorities, according to the examiners' review. No minority or targeted advertising has occurred, however, at that association. A "media review" conducted by the institution resulted in a listing of Spanish-language radio stations and newspapers along with a proposed Spanish-language advertisement. This advertisement, which was in the association's CRA file, was never run. Management advised the CRA examiners that there were "no pending plans to run it or any other foreign language advertisements." As previously noted, that association's current CRA statement referenced bilingual staff members who had since left at the time of the exam.

Even if a bank is a minority-owned and/or operated one in a primarily minority area, it can be looked askance at if it has an exclusive focus on its target segment to the actual or perceived exclusion of others in the local community. United Savings Bank of San Francisco directs much of its marketing efforts at deposit gathering from the Asian community. Even though it has programs assisting many Asian low- and moderate-income individuals, the examiners reported that there were "no similar efforts directed to other groups within the delineated communities."

Officer Call Program in Chicago Excluded Branch in Minority Area

A bank is subject to criticism if it does not market its credit products in all of its delineated communities. Bay View Federal Bank of San Mateo, California, which has a full service branch in Orange County, did not market its credit products there.

Cole Taylor Bank of Chicago uses a commercial and real estate loan officer call program which is equally divided between calls to present customers and new prospects. The examiners expressed concern for a lack of solicitations around one of the bank's offices that has some low- and moderate-income and predominantly minority neighborhoods near it. The specific calling officer responsible for that branch (and two others) noted to the examiners that no calls were made in the vicinity of the subject branch "due to the volume of applications for loans being generated elsewhere." The examiners concluded that this apparently left that branch "without service" for at least the scope of the examination.

Advertising Criticized for Incomplete Records and Compliance Reviews

Banks with needs improvement ratings usually maintain limited documentation of their advertising. Records of the marketing and advertising efforts of the Bank of Alabama of Fultondale, Alabama, were found to be "limited." CRA examiners during the first

public examination of SafraBank II of Pompano Beach, Florida, concluded that its advertising records were "incomplete": they did not consistently include media used, run dates, and/or copy of the advertisements. That same evaluation also criticized the bank's marketing strategy for not making members of one of its two communities aware of its credit programs and services.

Banks with needs improvement ratings infrequently review advertising for compliance with applicable laws and regulations or overall effectiveness in meeting marketing goals. Norstar Bank of Buffalo, New York, which received a needs improvement rating on its first public evaluation, was found to have "limited" documentation of its marketing and advertising programs. Furthermore, the examiners found "no evidence" of review or analysis of the effectiveness of those programs.

First Federal Savings of Morgantown, West Virginia, participates in a FNMA program for low- and moderate-income borrowers. However, "little is done" to make the public or bank employees aware of the program, the "results of which are not tracked."

Truth in Lending and Disclosure Violations in Advertising

Advertising programs that are infrequently or never reviewed for compliance with appropriate laws and regulations are common at banks with needs improvement ratings. Golden Coin Savings of San Francisco does not "regularly" review its advertising for compliance with federal laws and regulations. That bank also advertises primarily to the Chinese communities of San Francisco and Oakland for deposits or image purposes. Therefore, it was also criticized for not advertising in media targeting other minority groups or the low- and moderate-income neighborhoods within its "diverse" territory.

The Bank of Commerce of Auburn, California, which received a needs improvement rating on its first public evaluation, had "no real system" at that time for reviewing advertising for compliance. The examiners' review of advertising copy revealed a "number of advertisements" not consistent with Truth in Lending Act requirements. These violations pertained to the lack of required disclosures in those advertisements.

First Interstate Bank of Denver has "established but not enforced" policies regarding the compliance review of proposed marketing campaigns. The examiners there concluded that the bank's marketing department "failed to submit some advertisements to the compliance officer" for the necessary review.

The examiners at Bell Federal of Chicago concluded that advertisements require additional review to ensure compliance. The examiners noted that their review of radio advertisement transcripts revealed that Bell Federal was not providing the required "equal housing lender" disclosure.

Limited or Nonexistent Credit Counseling

Banks with needs improvement ratings were also characterized as having a limited, if any, effort by bank personnel to assist individuals and groups applying for credit. When banks did make such an effort, it usually was not for the bank's entire community, especially low- and moderate-income neighborhoods. The previously referenced limited attendance at community meetings sponsored by the First Interstate Bank of Colstrip, Montana, indicated an effort in this regard, but not a particularly successful one.

Officer call programs used by certain banks could also attain this goal of credit application assistance. Many of these programs, however, were criticized for being limited to a certain part of the community rather than all of it.

Available Credit Services (Assessment Factor I)

Banks that have received needs improvement ratings are only marginally involved in addressing identified community credit needs through loan originations and purchases. Absolute and relative lending levels and the menu of available loans at those banks reflect only a marginal responsiveness to the most pressing community credit needs.

SunBank of Orlando, Florida, which received a needs improvement rating on its first public evaluation, had a volume of loans which the examiners felt was "marginal in relation to the institution's resources." South Bergen Savings of Wood Ridge, New Jersey, was noted as taking a "passive approach" to implementing credit services. That institution, like

many traditional thrifts, only makes one- to four-family residential mortgages and home equity loans.

15–25% Loan-to-Deposit Ratios
Too Conservative

Banks with very low loan-to-deposit or loan-to-asset ratios are susceptible to below-average CRA ratings, unless these ratios can be justified by loan demand, competitive, or other relevant factors. A very low ratio compared to competitive and peer banks, coupled with relatively low charge-off and nonperforming trends, may indicate an excessively conservative bank.

The 22% loan-to-deposit ratio at The Citizens State Bank of Choteau, Montana, was in the lowest (first) percentile compared to its year-end peer group. Banks in surrounding communities had ratios two to three times as high. As low as that ratio was, it was actually up from 16% at the bank's previous exam. This improvement prompted a minor commendation from the examiners that the bank had been "moderately successful" in increasing the loan portfolio.

The 23% loan-to-deposit ratio at Litchville State Bank in Litchville, North Dakota, falls to only 18% when nonlocal loans are subtracted. The examiners concluded that the bank's "financial condition and resources allow for a higher loan volume." The examiners attributed the low volume to "conservative lending practices" as well as "lack of marketing and delineated community involvement."

Marquette Bank of Golden Valley, Minnesota, had a loan-to-asset ratio of just 15%. A majority of that bank's loans are outside of its delineated community. While 91% of total deposits come from that bank's community, only 31% of loans come from it. The examiners referred to this as a "disproportionate" volume of lending activity outside the local community compared to the activity inside it.

One fairly new bank with a needs improvement rating had a low loan-to-asset ratio, but it was apparently acceptable in that situation. This was the case at the First Exchange Bank of North St. Louis County in Florissant, Missouri. Its unspecified low volume of loans relative to assets was concluded as being "typical of a de novo institution in existence for less than a year." That same reasoning was used by that bank's examiners to excuse the bank from loan advertising.

When a 100% Loan-to-Deposit Ratio in a "Low-Mod" Area Isn't Enough

Only in one unusual case did CRA examiners actually question the concept of measuring loans relative to deposits. This was the case at First Inter-state Bank of Oregon, where the bank was using its loan and deposit penetration to evaluate the "fairness of lending patterns" within its community. According to the examiners, that approach "deemphasizes the credit needs of low- and moderate-income areas," which the bank apparently considered to have a fair distribution of loans relative to deposits.

In other words, under this interpretation loans in a low- and moderate-income area, which are approx-imately equal to deposits from it (i.e., a 100% loan-to-deposit ratio), may not be enough, as that area's need for credit may exceed available deposits. According to CRA examiners, this type of analysis is based "solely on existing loan and deposit customers rather than the actual population base." We would think most examiners would be impressed with a loan-to-deposit ratio in the 100% range for a "low-mod" area, but this was not the case here.

Criticized for Not Making the "Right" Type of Loans

Many banks with needs improvement ratings may be criticized for little if any lending of a certain type, which the examiners may feel is an important credit need in the delineated community. Farmers and Mer-chants Bank of Long Beach, California, received a needs improvement rating on its second public evalu-ation. It was criticized for an overall loan volume in regard to both home purchase and home improve-ment loans (especially in low- and moderate-income areas) that was "very low in relation to its resources."

The Bank of Alabama of Fultondale, Alabama, doesn't offer home purchase loans because the bank feels it does not have the "deposit base to fund long-term asset growth." The bank had not made any home improvement loans since its last exam. The bank explained this on the basis of customer unwill-ingness to secure loans with their homes as compared to the more popular unsecured personal loans.

San Jose National Bank of San Jose, California, received a needs improvement rating on its first

public exam. The bank focused on a business niche which, according to the examiners, means that "lim-ited funds are available to offer consumer products to the general community." For example, the bank does not make residential mortgage loans.

InterBoro Savings of Cherry Hill, New Jersey, did not make any small farm or rehabilitation loans during its review period. Bank management stated that it did not have the expertise to underwrite small farm (or business) loans, and that there was "very little de-mand" for home improvement loans. Most of that institution's offices are in urbanized areas. This was in contrast to the previously mentioned San Jose National Bank. It did not make small farm loans, but this was apparently of little concern to its examiners. They stated that "small farm loans are not needed within the bank's delineated community due to its geographic location."

Exclusive Use of Adjustable Rate Mortgages O.K. in California but Not Kansas City

A bank may offer a certain type of loan, such as home mortgages, but be criticized if that type of loan is not offered on a flexible basis. For example, many large California thrifts will only write adjustable rate mortgage loans, but they are usually not criticized for that practice. In fact, several of the largest California thrifts that exclusively or primarily make adjustable rate mortgage loans have received outstanding CRA ratings.

By contrast, one of the facts supporting the con-clusion that Inter-State Federal of Kansas City, Kan-sas, is only making a "limited effort" to meet local credit needs is that it only offers adjustable-rate mort-gages. Another savings association, Gold River Sav-ings of Fair Oaks, California, only offers fixed-rate mortgages because of "market resistance" to adjusta-ble-rate products. That institution, however, stated that it is prepared to once again offer adjustable-rate loans "if supported by market demand."

$5,000 Minimum Passbook Loan in Chicago Criticized

Some banks with needs improvement ratings were criticized under this factor for having loan terms that CRA examiners may have perceived as discouraging credit originations. The Bank of Commerce of Auburn, California, which received a needs improvement rating on its first public evaluation, made only a limited number of home improvement and home equity loans at the time of its first exam. The examiners concluded that applications may have been discouraged because the bank charges "above market rates" on these loans. As the case study in the previous chapter pointed out, bank management there did not want to compete with the "loss-leader" pricing being offered on these loans by certain competitors.

Bell Federal of Chicago restricts savings account loans to those with a $5,000 minimum balance. Also, first and second lien mortgage loans there are restricted to one- to four-family owner-occupied properties. The examiners concluded that both of these restrictions "excluded a significant portion of the local community as credit customers." These and related criticisms are also found under assessment factor D.

New York Foreign Bank—No Retail Loans (Except to Employees)

It is a fairly frequent criticism of special purpose banks that they are only marginally or minimally involved in meeting local credit needs because of their focus on their target market segment. For example, IBJ Schroder Bank and Trust Company of New York City predominantly serves an international corporate and institutional client base. This wholesale-oriented bank, which received a needs improvement rating on its first public evaluation, does not originate retail types of loans.

Banco Bilbao of Vizcaya, also of New York City, does not offer consumer or mortgage loans. The bank has, however, granted unsecured personal loans to its employees, according to the examiners. The bank also made available funds for housing development projects, but for high income rather than low- and moderate-income ones.

To the extent that a bank makes loans of a certain type only to employees, it has the appearance of an exclusionary and discriminating practice. This is also the case, but to a lesser extent, when the bank only makes certain types of loans to important (usually affluent) customers.

Korea First Bank of New York in New York City makes an "extremely limited" number of residential mortgage loans, and these are made "primarily to accommodate commercial loan customers." That bank will finance residential units, but only if the loan proceeds are used for the borrower's business needs.

Small Business and Private Banks Questioned for Targeted Lending

San Jose National Bank of San Jose, California, which received a needs improvement rating on its first public evaluation, focuses on the small business segment. That bank makes both home improvement and home equity loans, but they are "primarily a service for established relationship customers." Neither of those loans are marketed on a community-wide basis, according to the examiners.

As long as a certain type of loan is listed in the bank's CRA statement, it is presumed to be available to all members of the community on an equal basis, unlike some of the examples above. Otherwise, there may be a problem.

Virginia Commerce Bank of Arlington, Virginia, is devoted to a niche strategy of focusing on small businesses. Their CRA statement lists "first and second mortgages on residential structures" and "real estate acquisition loans." Even though this may be interpreted to mean traditional lending on owner-occupied residences, the bank really makes these loans for investment/business purposes (e.g., rental property and purchase for resale). That bank has made only three consumer-related home loans in more than two years.

Beverly Hills Bank Lends to Entertainers and "Low-Mod" Syndicators and Financiers

World Trade Bank of Beverly Hills, California, focuses on the affluent market, including that community's entertainment sector. The bank has lent $3.5 million to "low-income housing developers and syndicators" and a "low- to moderate-income financier." Also, the bank has not made residential mortgage loans, according to its examiners.

The CRA statement of First Interstate Bank of Denver, Colorado, states that the bank offers conventional mortgage loans to all customers. In practice, according to the examiners, the bank refers "small-dollar requests" to other financial institutions. Small business and home improvement loans, which account for just 1% of all loans at that bank, are "low in relation to the bank's size," according to its examiners.

CRA Statement Contradiction in Minnesota— "Desirable" Loans Not Made

Several banks with needs improvement ratings had inaccuracies in their CRA statements. Sometimes the CRA examiners were not specific and noted only that a bank's current statement did not accurately identify the types of credit offered. This was the case at BankAtlantic in Fort Lauderdale, Florida, and Fidelity U.S. Depository Trust Company of Salt Lake City, Utah. The CRA statement of Davy Crockett Federal of Crockett, Texas, listed credit products that the institution did not have available.

Although not listed on a previous CRA statement of River Oaks Bank of Houston, Texas, the bank makes some one- to four-family residential loans on a one-year renewable basis. The bank received a needs improvement rating on its first public evaluation. Certain government-guaranteed loans offered by El Capitan National Bank of Sonora, California, were not listed in its CRA statement until the CRA examiners alerted management.

In what appeared to be a statement of contradiction, the loan policy of one bank described first real estate mortgages as a "desirable" type of credit. Their CRA statement, however, stated that the bank does not generally make mortgage loans to purchase or refinance residential properties. This situation at Marquette Bank of Golden Valley, Minnesota, which received a needs improvement rating on its first public evaluation, was changed a few months prior to its first exam when it began referring home loan applicants to a nearby affiliated bank.

Significant Nonlocal Lending Criticized

The results of loan geocoding are usually included under assessment factor E. However, banks with needs improvement ratings and a significant volume of lending outside of their delineated community may be criticized under this assessment factor.

American Liberty Savings Bank of Oakland, California, reports the "majority" of its lending activity outside its delineated territory. Only one-third of the loans originated in the year before the first public exam of South Bergen Savings of Wood Ridge, New Jersey, were within its delineated community. The majority of bank loans at First Exchange Bank of North St. Louis County in Florissant, Missouri, were outside its delineated community. This fairly new bank purchased a substantial mortgage portfolio from a failed institution. Over 81% of the dollar volume and over 55% of the number of loans originated and purchased by Bell Federal of Chicago during its review period were not in its delineated community.

Disproportionately Low Lending in a Local Community

Even if a bank primarily lends within its community, CRA examiners may take exception with the loan distribution if it appears there is a disproportionate lending pattern. Bay View Federal Bank of San Mateo, California, did not make any loans in Orange County, even though it had a full service branch there.

SafraBank II of Pompano Beach, Florida, which received a needs improvement rating in its first public evaluation, adequately served one of its communities but "disproportionately" served the other. The first public examination of that bank concluded that its Broward County community received a "disproportionately small share" of many types of loan products, including auto loans and unsecured credit.

Union Bank and Trust Company of Lincoln, Nebraska, "effectively" does not make residential mortgage loans. Real estate loan inquiries received in Lincoln are referred to another financial institution. The bank, however, was looked upon unfavorably because this referral process was not available to applicants at its "remote branches," presumably those outside of Lincoln.

Disproportionately Low Lending in a "Low-Mod" Area

Any type of procedure which provides an actual or perceived preference to one group over another can obviously be questioned. This problem would probably be most severe if the excluded group is located in a low- and moderate-income ("low-mod") and/or substantially minority area within a bank's local community.

The overall loan volume of Farmers and Merchants Bank of Long Beach, California, was found to be "very low in relation to its resources" in regards to both home purchase and improvement loans, especially in low- and moderate-income areas. The number of mortgage loans in low- and moderate-income areas declined 50% in 1990 compared to 1989, although the number of loans made in both years was comparable. The percentage of home improvement loans in such areas declined from 18% to 9% between 1989 and 1990.

Loan volume in low- and moderate-income areas by Bell Federal of Chicago was found to be "limited" in relation to its resources and community credit needs. Bell Federal reinvested 17% of the deposits from Chicago's low- and moderate-income zip codes in 1990 back into those communities. While 39% of the delineated community consisted of low- and moderate-income areas, only 10% of Bell's applications and loans were associated with those areas. This indicated "disparate lending patterns" in those low- and moderate-income communities, according to the bank's examiners.

California Bank with 65% Minority Loan Approval Rate and 15% of All Loans to Minorities Criticized for Nonlocal Lending

It appeared that San Clemente Savings Bank of Irvine, California, was being commended when the examiners noted that nearly half of its mortgage loans reported in its 1989 HMDA report were in low- and moderate-income and/or minority census tracts. However, the bank was not commended on this conclusion but was criticized because only 18% of its loans were within its local community. Approximately 15% of all loans made by that bank were to minorities, but the bank was criticized, because this was considerably less than the estimated 25% of the total community's population made up by minorities. Even though that bank approved 65% of all minority loan applications compared to a 77% overall approval rate, it was still criticized because minority applications and loans were "not reflective of the minority population within the delineated community."

No "Low-Mod" Home Loans at Bank in Iowa

No residential mortgage or home improvement loans whatsoever were granted to residents in low- and moderate-income areas by Brenton Bank and Trust Company of Urbandale, Iowa, according to its 1989 HMDA report. First Interstate Bank of Colstrip, Montana, which was denied a merger after a protest on CRA grounds, has made only a "nominal" number of housing-related loans on the nearby Northern Cheyenne Reservation, an identified low- and moderate-income area. The reasons for the low lending are "perceived legal obstacles" that, according to the bank, prevent it from perfecting a security interest on land held in trust by the Bureau of Indian Affairs. The bank is pursuing an alternative method to remove this obstacle to enable it to address the housing needs of that portion of its community.

Government Loan Programs (Assessment Factor J)

Banks with needs improvement ratings sometimes become involved in governmentally insured, guaranteed, or subsidized loan programs. The performance evaluation under this assessment factor is usually made relative to a bank's resources and capabilities. For this reason, year-end 1990 assets, which most closely approximate the exam period for most of the banks reviewed here, will be provided for comparative purposes.

Cleveland Bank Had the People but Not the Involvement

Large banks with little or no involvement in such government programs are often looked upon unfavorably. The participation in such programs by Bell Federal of Chicago was termed "virtually nonexistent" by its examiners. Within a year of its first public examination, the $1.9 billion Bell Federal became involved in four different government lending or subsidized programs. By the time of the exam, however, no loans were made through two of the programs, and only one loan each was made in the other two programs.

Given the size and resources of First Interstate Bank of Denver, Colorado, ($1.5 billion) as well as the "many opportunities" in the Denver area, the examiners of that bank felt it was involved in a "relatively limited" number of government loan programs. The $214 million Metropolitan Savings Bank of Cleveland did not participate in FHA, VA, or other government loan programs at the time of its first public exam. This was apparently a matter of concern for the examiners because one of the bank's vice presidents was an approved FHA direct endorser, and another bank employee was an approved FHA underwriter.

The $2.4 billion Union Federal of Brea, California, participated in government loan programs through 1989 when management terminated them due to the "lack of interest" within the delineated communities. Such lending amounted to 6% of total originations in 1989. Also, that bank acquired branches during the latter half of 1989 that the examiners felt were in communities which would "benefit from FHA and VA loan programs." Even though they had discontinued such programs, the bank's CRA statement incorrectly stated that they were offering governmentally insured loans.

The $1.8 billion EurekaBank of Foster City, California, did not offer government loan programs at the time of its first public evaluation, when it received a needs improvement rating. Senior management felt that the bank did not have the "necessary expertise" for this type of lending.

Examiners Don't Criticize New or Fairly Small Banks

Relatively new or fairly small banks that were not involved in government lending programs often were not criticized for these reasons. For example, First Executive Bank of Philadelphia, a new and fairly small ($65 million) bank then, did not participate in any government programs due to its "asset size and limited staff." Davy Crockett Federal of Crockett, Texas, was somewhat smaller ($54 million), and the reason it gave for its lack of participation in such programs was "primarily due to staffing limitations."

Banks Claim Government Programs Not Feasible in California

While it is difficult to defend a $1 billion plus bank for lack of involvement in any government lending program, this may not be the case with smaller institutions, especially independent community banks. Still, though, many banks with a few hundred million dollars in assets may not become involved for different reasons.

The $314 million Pan American Savings Bank of San Mateo, California, did not offer government lending programs. Bank management cited "lack of qualified personnel" and the "unsuitably low loan limits" given the bank's delineated community. The $185 million Golden Coin Savings of San Francisco likewise did not offer such programs because they believed they "would not be successful in the majority of its market area" due to the high median housing costs, which exceed the upper loan limits in those programs.

Some banks with needs improvement ratings were involved with government loan programs in a modest way. The very small $13 million Litchville State Bank of Litchville, North Dakota, had only one FmHA guaranteed loan on its books that was mentioned under this assessment factor. The very large $6.7 billion First Interstate Bank of Arizona actively participates in governmentally insured housing programs but not in small farm lending and only minimally in SBA lending.

Kansas City Thrift Questioned for Purchasing Nonlocal FHA Loans

Some banks with needs improvement ratings are more active in government programs in certain geographic areas within their delineated communities than in others. The $2.4 billion Homestead Savings of Millbrae, California, qualified for two mortgage credit certificate programs, which provide first-time home buyer tax credits. This program, however, was limited to that institution's Northern California communities, as compared to those in Southern California.

Inter-State Federal of Kansas City, Kansas, does not offer government-insured loans. That $240 million institution was questioned, however, because it purchased FHA-insured mortgage loans from outside its local community. That institution had "not documented the lack of demand" for government-insured loans within its community, according to its examiners.

No SBA Loans in Four Years at Kansas City Bank

Several banks with needs improvement ratings offer SBA loans. However, many banks with needs improvement ratings found out that being an SBA lender is not enough if the bank is not actively putting such loans on the books.

The $20 million Landmark Bank of Kansas City, Missouri, which is part of a $1.9 billion bank holding company, apparently did not make any SBA guaranteed loans for the more than four-year period prior to its first CRA public examination. The bank advertises other types of loans under this category, but it appears that "very few loans" of those types were extended either.

The $21 million FirstBank at Arapahoe/Yosemite in Englewood, Colorado, which is part of a $1.1 billion bank holding company, participates in the SBA loan program. The bank, however, did not have any such loans booked at the time of its first public examination. BankAtlantic, a $1.9 billion savings bank in Fort Lauderdale, Florida, had only originated two SBA loans prior to its first public examination.

The $4.6 billion SunBank of Orlando, Florida, is an approved lender for both the SBA and student loan programs. The volume of those loans, however, is "marginal," according to the examiners, because each type represented less than 1% of total loans.

The $56 million Norwest Bank of Waupun, Wisconsin, which is part of a very large bank holding company, originated only one SBA loan since its previous exam. This was primarily due to a "minimal marketing effort," according to its examiners.

L.A. Area Bank Argues Community "Not Knowledgeable" on Government Housing Loans

The $1.4 billion Farmers and Merchants Bank of Long Beach, California, in the L.A. area does not offer most government-guaranteed housing loans, which is "consistent with its policy of not extending long-term residential mortgage loans." Furthermore, the community is "not knowledgeable" concerning these government-guaranteed housing loans, according to bank management. That bank has three SBA loans in its portfolio, and has extended only one such loan

since the previous exam. SBA loans are not marketed nor listed on the bank's CRA statement, according to its examiners.

The $51 million Bay Cities National Bank of Redondo Beach, California, which received a needs improvement rating on its first public examination, made 34 SBA guaranteed loans at the time of its first public exam. Because only 20% of those were within the bank's delineated community, the examiners did not consider this to be a "good indicator of the bank's efforts to service its community."

The $18 million Citizens State Bank of Choteau, Montana, originated one SBA loan and two FHA loans since the time of its last exam. That bank no longer makes guaranteed student loans but refers such applicants to area banks that do.

New Jersey Bank Offers PMI Alternative to Government Programs, but No Loans Made

Some banks with needs improvement ratings that do not make government loans may not be criticized if they offer alternative programs that are legitimate substitutes. The giant $21.5 billion Glendale Federal of Glendale, California, does not participate in any government loan programs. It has, however, certain loan products, such as its first-time home buyer program, which represent "potentially viable alternatives" to government programs.

The $115 million GSL Savings Bank of Guttenberg, New Jersey, likewise does not participate in government loan programs. Three years ago it began offering low down-payment mortgages with private mortgage insurance (PMI). This bank, however, "did not actively market this program" and made no loans with PMI during the approximate year and one-half before its first public exam.

III. GEOGRAPHIC DISTRIBUTION AND RECORD OF OPENING AND CLOSING OFFICES

Reasonableness of Delineated Community

Banks with needs improvement ratings are often characterized by unreasonably delineated communities, most of which are too large to be effectively served. The most severe criticism under this assessment factor would be for a "gerrymandered" community which was delineated so as to exclude low- and moderate-income or substantially minority areas. Some banks in this category may have a reasonable area, but it may not be properly documented or shown on the required map in the CRA statement.

CRA Officer Confused on Community Delineation in Puerto Rico

There was "some confusion among institution personnel" at Ponce Federal Bank of Ponce, Puerto Rico, as to what their actual community delineation was, according to the CRA examiners. The CRA officer stated that it was the entire Island of Puerto Rico, while the CRA statement clearly identified 23 local communities surrounding Ponce and San Juan. As it turned out, the 23 delineated local communities were considered reasonable, but the confusion on the part of bank personnel was apparently of enough concern to the examiners that they described it in detail in the public evaluation.

Using Both a Primary and Secondary Community without Being Criticized

A few banks with needs improvement ratings utilized the unconventional approach of having both primary and secondary delineated communities. Although these approaches surprisingly were not criticized by the examiners, CRA requires only one community to be delineated. Actually, much of the CRA evaluation process can break down if there is uncertainty as to the appropriate delineated community. For this reason we do not recommend this dual community approach.

United Savings Bank of San Francisco, which received a needs improvement rating on its first public evaluation, delineated its community into primary and secondary markets. The primary market consisted of six counties where it has branches, and the secondary market included nine counties where it had loan production offices. The examiners considered this to be a reasonable delineation.

Virginia Commerce Bank in Arlington, Virginia, used a portion of northern Virginia as its delineated community. The bank further defined a "secondary service area" of Washington, D.C., and a portion of adjacent Maryland. Again, this bank's delineation was considered to be reasonable.

Guaranty Bank & Trust Company of Tulsa, Oklahoma, defined a 20-mile radius as its primary community and up to a 50-mile radius as a secondary one. The examiners in this case considered the delineation, without specifying which radius, to be "large" based on the nature and geographic distribution of the bank's customer base. The examiners did not, however, criticize the dual community approach.

39% of Delineations Unreasonable— The U.S. as a "Local Community"?

Approximately 39% of the 108 needs improvement evaluations that were evaluated in detail in this analysis were found to have unreasonably delineated areas. Almost all of these cases had areas that were too large to be effectively served based upon the bank's size, nature of business, distribution of loans, location of offices, or other factors.

The largest delineated community by far was the entire United States defined by Fidelity U.S. Depository Trust Company of Salt Lake City, Utah, which provides its financial services on a national basis. Although the CRA examiners did not take exception with this definition, they noted that the boundaries of its community "must, of necessity, be somewhat arbitrarily set" because of the bank's unique business. It is interesting to note that some of the credit card banks based in Delaware that used multistate or other large areas were criticized for not defining a local community in the vicinity of their offices. This was not done in the case of Fidelity; its delineation was not criticized by its examiners. This may have been why the public evaluation also noted that Fidelity "recognizes a special obligation of service" to the entire state of Utah with emphasis on the metropolitan Salt Lake City area. Thus, the examiners, for all practical purposes, accepted a primary (metropolitan area), secondary (state), and tertiary (U.S.) "local" community.

Banco Bilbao Vizcaya of New York City considered its local community to be the New York metropolitan area plus the states of New Jersey and Connecticut. With one-third of its loans in Manhattan and the other two-thirds distributed around the country, this bank was "encouraged to re-evaluate its present local community in order to reflect the bank's actual lending patterns."

Small Banks Claiming Up to Nine-County Area as Local Community

Most banks with needs improvement ratings that were criticized for an excessively large community included too many counties in a multicounty delineation, included the entirety of a county when it should only have taken a portion, or used an excessively large mile radius that could not be justified. Several examples of each situation will be provided here. All bank size totals will refer to year-end 1990 assets as before to most closely approximate the exam review periods.

Davy Crockett Federal of Crockett, Texas, a fairly small ($54 million) institution with only one office, was concluded to have "over-extended" its delineation by taking in a nine-county area. A fairly similar case involved Iowa Savings Bank of Des Moines, which received a needs improvement rating on its first public evaluation. The eight-county delineated community used by that bank appeared to be "too large" with respect to the bank's small asset size of only $16 million.

The $118 million Birmingham Federal of Birmingham, Alabama, delineated its community as a five-county area. Because 95% of its residential loans granted in the year preceding the exam were in two of the five counties, the examiners felt the area should be redefined to "more reasonably reflect the areas it actually serves or intends to serve."

Penn Federal Savings Bank of Newark, New Jersey, delineated six separate local communities around its offices, but five of them encompassed entire counties. The delineation appeared to be "too broad," according to the examiners, based on the distribution of deposits, branches, and loans. This was one of the few evaluations that used deposit in addition to loan distribution data for this purpose.

Some Banks Criticized for Delineating Entire County

A bank may be criticized for including all or most of a county in its delineated community, if the entire county cannot be effectively served by the bank. First Federal Savings of San Rafael, California, defined its local community as the three counties which contained all of its offices. However, because it only had one branch near the tip of Alameda County, the inclusion of all of it was deemed to be unreasonable by the CRA examiners.

The one branch $56 million Cornerstone Bank of Mission Viejo, California, identified all of Orange County as its delineated community. The examiners determined that this was not a reasonable delineation because the bank was "not able to effectively ascertain and/or meet the credit needs of the entire community."

South Bergen Savings of Wood Ridge, New Jersey, defined its community as the southern part of Bergen County, which includes ten municipalities. The CRA examiners deemed this delineation unreasonable because lending patterns disclosed only "limited service" to that community and also because the delineation had not been reevaluated on an "ongoing basis."

BankAtlantic of Fort Lauderdale, Florida, delineated a three-county community in South Florida. The bank, however, was questioned for including all of Dade County. This was because that bank had only six branches in this large county, which encompasses all of greater Miami and its surrounding area. The delineation of that entire county was also felt to be unreasonably large because of the bank's relatively limited lending activities there over the past two years.

Community Banks in Boston and Denver Can't Effectively Serve Entire Metropolitan Area

Some banks with needs improvement ratings were criticized for considering their entire metropolitan area to represent their delineated community when the bank did not have the resources to effectively serve such a large area. The $105 million Boston Private Bank and Trust Company considered the entire Boston metropolitan area to be its delineated community. The CRA examiners considered this large area to be unreasonable. They stated that a reduction in the size of the delineated community is "imperative" so that the bank can better serve community credit needs.

The fairly small Resources Industrial Bank of Denver, Colorado, defined its community as the greater Denver metropolitan area plus two additional counties. This designation was deemed unreasonable considering the size of the bank ($16 million) and its ability to serve such a large area.

30-Mile Radius O.K. in Montana but Not Colorado or South Dakota

Besides using political or statistical boundaries such as those of a city, county, or metropolitan area, the next most popular delineation approach used specific mile radii about each office. In the case of banks with needs improvement ratings, these radii ranged from as small as two miles to as large as thirty miles and even fifty miles in one case. Most banks with needs improvement ratings that used mile radii preferred a five- or ten-mile radius. The determination of the reasonableness of the radii depended upon the nature of the individual market, the bank, the relevant customer base, and related factors.

For example, in some cases a thirty-mile radius was considered unreasonable, while in others it was not. The $18 million Citizens State Bank of Choteau, Montana, which is located on the eastern slopes of the Rocky Mountains, used a 30-mile radius as its community, which was determined to be a reasonable one. This was not the case, however, for the same sized $18 million First Community Industrial Bank of Fort Collins in Fort Collins, Colorado, or the larger $69 million Farmers State Bank of Parkston, South Dakota. Both of these banks were criticized for using a thirty-mile radius because of the relatively small size of each bank and their inability to service such a large area.

Even though the bank in Montana was also small, this was not a concern. Several of the small towns within a thirty-mile radius of Choteau, Montana, including one larger one, have banks. The city of Fort Collins is a much larger and more urbanized community, and there are several cities within a thirty-mile radius of it. Parkston, South Dakota, a small town of the same approximate population size of Choteau, also has several small communities and one larger city with several competitors within a thirty-mile radius.

Banks Urged by Examiners to Redefine Area as 5–10 Mile Radius

The 17-mile radius used for the community delineation by Norwest Bank of Waupun, Wisconsin, was considered unreasonable. This finding was based on the fact that the examiners' sample concluded that nearly all loan applicants reside within the immediate city of Waupun and that marketing efforts did not include any communities outside a five-mile radius of that city. The implication was clearly that the bank should reduce the 17-mile radius to a much smaller one, probably no larger than a five-mile radius, which would cover the area of its marketing efforts.

First Federal Savings of Morgantown, West Virginia, delineated its community as the central portion of its home county, which includes the city of Morgantown and surrounding areas. The examiners concluded that this area was too large to be serviced by the institution and should be reduced to an approximately ten-mile radius of the city. This radius would coincide with the institution's effective lending territory as defined by management.

"20 Mile Egg" Delineation in North Dakota Labeled "Unreasonable"

Litchville State Bank of Litchville, North Dakota, defined an "egg-shaped" community stretching twenty miles north and south but only six miles east and west. This delineated community was determined to be an "unreasonable" one by CRA examiners because most of the bank's credit activity was in and around the town of Litchville.

The $8 million Arvada 1st Industrial Bank of Arvada, Colorado, expanded its original five-mile radius to a large circle covering the majority of the Denver metropolitan area as a result of mergers with two other fairly small banks. However, the sample of loan applications confirmed that the majority of the bank's business was in the northwest portion of the metropolitan area including Arvada, which management indicated was the focal point of its service efforts. Considering these reasons and the merged bank's still relatively small size, the examiners concluded that the very large radii was unreasonable.

Local Community Includes Some of Pacific Ocean

The radius approach can be criticized if the resultant delineation doesn't reflect customer traffic patterns. Bay Cities National Bank of Redondo Beach, California, which received a needs improvement rating on its first public evaluation, is only two blocks from the ocean. Most of the bank's customers are scattered around a highway which runs parallel to the beach. Thus, the use of an undisclosed mile radius, which included some of the ocean and other uninhabited areas, was deemed "unreasonable" since bank customers obviously were not located throughout the radius.

Banks with needs improvement ratings may be criticized for including an area where they have no branches or, conversely, failing to include an area where it does. GSL Savings Bank of Guttenberg, New Jersey, delineated local communities around its branches plus another community in western New Jersey. While the first delineations were considered reasonable, the western New Jersey delineation was not. This was because the bank doesn't have any facilities in that area nor does it market its loans or other banking services there.

Bank's Delineation Omitted Area Surrounding Branch in Southern California

The opposite case existed at Bay View Federal Savings Bank of San Mateo, California. That bank delineated eight counties as its local community where it has twenty of its twenty-one branches. However, the omission of the area surrounding its remaining full service branch in Orange County was the problem. That bank neither ascertained credit needs nor marketed its credit products in that county, which further added to the problem.

Gold River Savings Bank of Fair Oaks, California, has a main office in Fair Oaks and a branch in Rancho Murieta. The bank's delineated community included the area surrounding the main office but not the branch. Furthermore, the bank's guidelines for defining its community were found to be "inconsistent."

Although specifics were not provided, First Interstate Bank of Seattle, Washington, was likewise challenged because it had "not established a consistent

methodology" for its delineations. The delineations of some local communities at that bank were not reasonable, others had "conflicting multiple delineations," and a few were "not supported by penetration data."

Chicago and Minneapolis Banks' Two- and Three-Mile Radii Exclude "Low-Mod" Areas

A few banks with needs improvement ratings were criticized because their delineated communities were too small rather than too large. The biggest problem here would be if the delineation was done in such a way to exclude low- and moderate-income ("low-mod") areas or substantially minority ones.

First National Bank in Dolton, Illinois, in the Chicago area used a two-mile radius for its community delineation. The CRA examiners, however, determined this delineation to be unreasonable and narrow. This was because it "excludes several areas including low- to moderate-income ones located south and west of the bank where lending activity occurs," according to the bank's own zip code analysis.

Marquette Bank of Golden Valley, Minnesota, which is part of the greater Minneapolis area, received a needs improvement rating on its first public evaluation. The bank delineated a three-mile radius around its main office and another one around its one branch as its local community. The delineation was determined to be unreasonable for two reasons. First, there was a disproportionate volume of lending *outside* of the community (69% of the dollar volume and 58% of the number of loans). Second, low- and moderate-income census tracts located "just beyond the three-mile radius" were excluded from the delineated community.

Gerrymandering in Montana?

First Interstate Bank of Colstrip, Montana, delineated an "irregular-shaped" area consisting of all of one school district and a portion of another. This apparently gerrymandered area, which extended outward from 11 to 28 miles in different directions, was deemed to be unreasonable not only because of the results of a loan geocoding analysis but also because a "significant portion of an identified low- and moderate-income area is excluded from it."

EurekaBank of Foster City, California, which received a needs improvement rating on its first public evaluation, delineated six entire and four partial counties as its communities based upon the effective lending territories of its offices. According to the examiners, portions of several counties, including low- and moderate-income and/or minority areas, were excluded from the delineation, which was therefore considered to be unreasonable.

The $73 million First Exchange Bank of Florissant, Missouri, delineated a community which its examiners deemed to be unreasonable and quite large given the bank's asset size. Although the delineation was not spelled out in the public evaluation, the examiners felt that it might have excluded some low- and moderate-income areas that "the bank may reasonably be expected to serve."

Examiners Urge Banks to Change Outdated Delineations

Although the delineated community at some banks with needs improvement ratings may not be deemed unreasonable, it may be recommended for revision by the examiners. This is often the case where few if any revisions to the delineated community have been made to reflect changing times.

Inter-State Federal of Kansas City, Kansas, apparently never changed its delineated community since its first CRA statement in the beginning of 1979. Because nearly one-third of applications in a recent twelve-month period were located outside of the delineated two-county area, it was recommended to be "altered to include those areas in the MSA which are consistent with lending distribution."

This was also the case with the North Side Deposit Bank of Pittsburgh, Pennsylvania, which did not change its delineation for "several years." According to the bank's own zip code analysis, 39% of its loans were located outside of its delineated community, which included portions of two counties. That community and its defining guidelines should be reviewed for revision, according to its examiners.

Delineation Revisions O.K. but Not the Lack of Documentation

Some banks with needs improvement ratings have revised their community delineations to reflect lending activity. For example, Bell Federal of Chicago eliminated two of the eight counties from its community during the year before its exam. The reason given was the lack of credit activity and branches in those two counties. The examiners expressed no concern over that deletion.

Landmark Bank of Kansas City, Missouri, also revised its delineated community, but there was no indication whether it was expanded or contracted. The examiners, however, did criticize the bank since no documentation was available to justify the new delineation or the "reasoning behind the change." Thus, even if a bank's delineated community is considered reasonable, it may be criticized because of a lack of documentation justifying it.

Surety Federal Savings Bank of Vallejo, California, delineated four "asymmetrical areas" in the vicinity of its offices as its community. While the community was deemed reasonable and didn't exclude any low- and moderate-income areas, the examiners noted that the resultant community was "arbitrary in size and shape."

Norstar Bank of Buffalo, New York, which received a needs improvement rating on its first public evaluation, had a reasonable delineation but no documentation of the supporting methodology. The delineated communities for both DuPage National Bank of West Chicago, Illinois, and World Trade Bank of Beverly Hills, California, were both accepted but criticized for a lack of supporting documentation justifying the boundaries of the delineation.

Illegible and Incorrect Maps in California

Some banks with needs improvement ratings may have had reasonable communities and supporting documentation but were criticized for problems in their presentation of the maps depicting the delineated communities in the CRA statements. For example, the maps in the CRA statement of Glendale Federal of Glendale, California, "do not effectively identify" its delineated communities. Worse yet was the case of the CRA statement of El Capitan National

Bank of Sonora, California, which had a map presentation that the examiners felt was "illegible and inadequate to provide the public with a basic understanding of the bank's primary service area."

The community delineation boundaries of Beverly Bank of Lockport, Illinois, were not shown on the required map in its CRA statement. The map in the CRA statement of Union Federal Savings Bank of Brea, California, was criticized because it did not "adequately identify" the delineated community.

The delineated community of San Jose National Bank of San Jose, California, which received a needs improvement rating on its first public evaluation, was considered reasonable. The narrative within the CRA statement, however, mistakenly excluded the local community of Cupertino, which the examiners hastened to point out was not a low- or moderate-income community.

Geographic Distribution of Credit (Assessment Factor E)

Many banks with needs improvement ratings had no procedure for geocoding loans, much less applications and denials. When that was the case, the CRA examiners either used available HMDA data, which is limited to certain banks and types of loans, or conducted their own sample analysis during the examination.

Disproportionate Lending Patterns at 41% of Banks

A total of 44, or approximately 41%, of the 108 needs improvement public evaluations we reviewed were characterized as having an unjustified, disproportionate, or otherwise unreasonable pattern with respect to lending activity. This disproportionate lending pattern often manifested itself totally within the community if certain areas were being excluded from lending. Alternatively, such a pattern could be evident inside versus outside the community if an extraordinarily large percentage of lending occurred outside the delineated area. The most significant disparity involved lack of lending in low- and moderate-income areas or substantially minority ones relative to other areas within a bank's delineated community.

Banks that were criticized for having an unreasonably large delineated community were more likely to be cited for disproportionate lending patterns. This would be the case if most of the bank's lending was within its local area, but its delineated community was much larger.

How One CRA Problem Can Cause Another

Management at Litchville State Bank of Litchville, North Dakota, plotted outstanding loans on a local map and concluded that there was a concentration of credit activity in and around the town of Litchville. That bank's egg-shaped delineated community, which stretched 20 miles north and south and six miles east and west around this small town, was deemed to be an unreasonable one. The examiners, therefore, concluded that the local concentration of credit in the immediate Litchville area represented a "disproportionate lending pattern" with respect to the rest of the delineated community. Thus, one problem (an unreasonably large community) compounded itself into a second one (a disproportionate lending pattern within it).

The State Bank of Springfield, Minnesota, which used an unreasonably large three-county area as its local community, has most of its customers within a 20-mile radius of Springfield. The examiners' geocoding showed only 10% of the bank's loans were in the towns surrounding Springfield that were within the delineated community. The examiners then concluded that the bank's credit distribution was "an unjustified, disproportionate" one within the various towns in the community.

Big Chicago S&L Lends 81–90% Nonlocally

There were several examples of banks being criticized for having a disproportionately high percentage of nonlocal lending. During the 27-month review period for Bell Federal of Chicago, Illinois, it was determined that over 81% of the dollar volume of originated and purchased loans was outside of its delineated community. This percentage jumped to 90% for the last ten months of the review period. This was the primary reason for the examiners concluding that there was a disproportionate pattern of lending inside of the community as compared to outside it. That bank was also criticized because lending to low-

and moderate-income and/or minority areas reflected "disparities" when compared to the opposite type of areas. Overall lending activity within its community was deemed "unacceptable" by its examiners "considering the institution's available resources and capabilities."

New Jersey Bank with 73% Nonlocal Home Loans Not Criticized by Examiners

GSL Savings Bank of Guttenberg, New Jersey, had 73% of its housing-related loan activity during the review period outside its delineated communities. Surprisingly, GSL's lending activity was *not* deemed disproportionate by its examiners. Rather, they attributed it to the large amount of purchased mortgages and participations as well as senior management's claim that there was "very little demand for credit in the community." The public evaluation did not contain any documentation by the examiners or management supporting that claim.

But, Banks with 39%–69% Nonlocal Loans Criticized for "Disproportionate Patterns"

Banco Bilbao Vizcaya of New York City, with two-thirds of its loans outside of its delineated community, was deemed to have a disproportionate lending pattern. Marquette Bank of Golden Valley, Minnesota, with 69% of the dollar volume of its loans outside its community, was likewise found to have a disproportionate lending pattern.

The delineated community of Brenton Bank and Trust Company of Urbandale, Iowa, was accepted as reasonable. The examiners' sample of loans revealed 48% of the portfolio to be outside that delineated community. The examiners, however, reached no conclusion as to whether or not that represented a disproportionate pattern.

This was not the case, however, for the North Side Deposit Bank of Pittsburgh, Pennsylvania, which had 39% of its loans outside its delineated community. The examiners determined that this constituted a disproportionate lending pattern.

Lending in Boston's Affluent Suburbs

The most troublesome type of disproportionate lending activity from a public policy perspective involves the lack of penetration in low- and moderate-

income and substantially minority neighborhoods of a bank's local community. This would be tantamount to "redlining" in its most extreme form.

Banks using a target market strategy with a private banking focus are more likely to be questioned under this assessment factor. Boston Private Bank and Trust Company specializes in serving "upscale" clients through a private banking relationship, and that focus drives its lending activity. Their 1989 HMDA data showed that 44% of their loans within the Boston MSA were in the City of Boston, none of which were in low- and moderate-income areas. The majority of remaining loans were located in Boston's "affluent suburbs." That bank was criticized for its focus on lending to the affluent.

Harris Bank Targets High-Income People in Low-Income Areas

The examination loan sample and HMDA statements at Harris Trust and Savings Bank of Chicago, Illinois, revealed 72% of applications were from within its delineated Cook County community, with 20% residing in low- and moderate-income areas. The examiners' further analysis, however, revealed "several unusual patterns." Their real estate loans were found to be concentrated in a "small upscale portion" of Chicago and Cook County's northwest suburbs. There was limited penetration in the low- and moderate-income areas of south and west Chicago or southern Cook County.

The analysis further revealed that the real estate loans made in low- and moderate-income areas appeared to be made to borrowers in those areas whose incomes are "clearly not low or moderate." That is, 68% of approved loans within such "low- and moderate-income areas" were to borrowers with incomes other than low and moderate ("low-mod"). In fact 37% of the loan recipients in these areas were upper-income individuals. Conversely, fewer than one third (32%) of approved loans in "low-mod" areas were going to truly "low-mod" individuals.

According to the examiners at Harris Bank, these findings appeared to be a "reflection of the bank's marketing effort." The same findings, but to a lesser extent, existed regarding installment approvals within low- and moderate-income areas. This case study indicates the importance of distinguishing between low- and moderate-income residents and areas. CRA was meant primarily to benefit the former and not necessarily the latter Nonetheless, banks generally get CRA credit for lending in low-mod areas, even if the loan recipients are upper-income individuals as was the case at Harris Bank..

Management in California Couldn't Explain Why "Zero Applications" Received from "Low-Mod" and/or Minority Areas

In the case of Birmingham Federal of Birmingham, Alabama, only one of its 1989 home mortgage loans was in a moderate-income census tract while none were granted in low-income or substantially minority census tracts, according to HMDA data. This constituted a "disproportionate pattern," according to its examiners. Similarly, analysis of the geographic distribution of lending by the examiners of Union Bank and Trust Company of Lincoln, Nebraska, suggested a "disproportionate concentration in middle- and upper-income neighborhoods."

The delineated communities of Tracy Savings of Tracy, California, contained "a number of low- and moderate-income and/or minority areas." According to the examiners, "management could not explain why zero applications were received from these areas." "Less than 1.0 percent of its credit applications were received from Black applicants," although the institution has an "overall reasonable record" of lending to minorities, according to the examiners. While the institution's performance under this assessment factor was rated as needing improvement, the institution's loan distribution was not cited as being disproportionate.

Examiners, however, did not consider the penetration of First Federal Savings of San Rafael, California, to be reasonable. This is because "no credit applications have been received, approved, or denied" from the several low- and moderate-income and/or minority neighborhoods within its delineated communities. Cornerstone Bank of Mission Viejo, California, did not have a reasonable penetration of all segments of its community, because its lending was primarily in areas of southern Orange County that were not predominantly low- and moderate-income or minority.

L.A. Area Bank Strong Lender to Hispanics but Weak to Blacks and Asians

As long as a bank's delineated community contains low- and moderate-income and substantially minority areas and there is little or no lending within them, there is a likelihood that the bank will be criticized for having a disproportionate lending pattern or at least an unreasonable penetration of those areas. Sometimes the finding on the reasonableness of penetration is made in terms of the percentage of total bank applications or loans in such areas. This is compared to the proportion of total population represented in those areas or the percentage of census tracts represented by those areas to the total number of tracts in the community. Also, HMDA approval rates can be used as a basis of comparison.

First Federal Savings of San Gabriel Valley in West Covina, California, had an overall minority loan application rate comparable to the minority population in its effective lending territory. That is, 39% of applications were received from minorities which constituted 40% of the population of its effective lending territory. Most (33% of the 39%) of their minority loans were to Hispanics. Because loans to Blacks and Asians were only 2% and 4% of all applications, respectively, the bank was criticized because those percentages were "below the respective minority group populations." Thus, even though the overall relative level of minority lending may be adequate, the *mix* of such lending must be representative of the different minority groups based upon this experience.

What Counts? Minority Residents or "Low-Mod" Areas?

An alternative approach to using the proportion of such residents in the total population is to use the number of low- and moderate-income or substantially minority census tracts as a percentage of all census tracts in the area. Again, this raises the issue of the appropriateness of measuring the number of such *residents* as compared to the number of such *areas* where they may live.

Sometimes the results under the two approaches are the same. For example, Union Federal Savings Bank of Brea, California, had 23% of its applications come from low- and moderate-income census tracts.

However, approximately 43% of the census tracts within its community are low- and moderate-income neighborhoods. The comparison using the population rather than area proportion was almost identical. That is, while 24% of that institution's applications were received from minorities, the minority population in its community stood at about 42%. Thus, in this case the proportion of relevant census tracts designated as low- and moderate-income and the proportion of the population designated as minority were about the same. This is not always the case. The examiners at this institution noted the above "disparities" but did not label them as disproportionate lending patterns.

Nearly half of the branches of the failed HomeFed Bank of San Diego, California, were located in low- and moderate-income areas. The bank's distribution of lending was rated as needing improvement because only 15% of all loans on homes and small apartment buildings were in such neighborhoods. Further, only 7% of loans were in substantially minority census tracts, although "many" parts of its community were so designated. Again, the examiners referred to these patterns as "disparities."

65% Minority Loan Approval Rate
Not High Enough for Examiners

Many examiners utilize loan approval rates in their evaluation of this assessment factor. This trend is bound to increase because of the visibility and proliferation of widely accessible and expanded HMDA data. The high minority loan approval rate of 65% for San Clemente Savings Bank of Irvine, California, was previously noted as being quite close to its overall 77% application approval rate. That bank, however, was criticized because the number of applications and loans for minorities were "not reflective" of its community's minority population. The examiners supported this statement by pointing out that loans to minorities by that bank represent only 15% of all originations, "considerably less" than the estimated 25% minority population in the delineated community. This bank was also criticized because of a low (18%) local lending rate.

Apple Bank's Disproportionate Lending
in Manhattan and the Bronx

Many banks with needs improvement ratings were criticized for disproportionate or unreasonable lending patterns only for a specific portion of its community, certain loans, or specific branches. Such lending patterns could, of course, be cited for more than one of these reasons.

The first public evaluation of SafraBank II of Pompano Beach, Florida, which resulted in a needs improvement rating, cited a "disproportionate" pattern involving one of its two delineated communities. The majority of the bank's deposits were from its Broward County community, while the majority of the bank's loans were in its Marion County community. This resulted in a disproportionately low level of lending in its Broward County community. This same "disproportionate" logic can be applied to large interstate networks that use branches in one state (e.g., Florida) to fund loans in another (e.g., California).

Apple Bank for Savings in New York City defines its community as all of Manhattan and the Bronx plus portions of surrounding counties. The bank was cited for having a disproportionate lending pattern based on 1988 and 1989 HMDA data. While 51% of Manhattan's census tracts are considered low- and moderate-income, only 11% in 1988 and 24% in 1989 of the bank's real estate lending there was in such areas. In the case of the Bronx, where 63% of all tracts are low- and moderate-income, Apple Bank had 20% in 1988 and 45% in 1989 of its real estate loans in low- and moderate-income areas. The proportion of such lending in some of the other counties exceeded the countywide averages but, for the most part, was below them.

Management at First Interstate of Denver
Couldn't Explain Disproportionate Lending

Some banks with needs improvement ratings were criticized because of lending patterns involving only certain types of loans. For example, First Interstate Bank of Denver, Colorado, was noted as having disproportionate trends in low- and moderate-income areas for indirect auto dealer and home improvement loans. Even though the bank had a slightly higher approval rate for indirect dealer auto loans in low- and moderate-income areas, it received relatively fewer applications from them. The examiners concluded that the bank's policy of requiring minimum income levels for dealer loan applicants may "reduce the availability of this type of loan in low- and moderate-income areas." The bank's HMDA data showed that the bank's 18% approval rate for home improvement applications in low- and moderate-income census tracts was half of the bank's overall approval rate for these types of loans. The examiners questioned bank officers on this finding but "management could not provide an explanation for this trend."

Discouraging Loan Applications in The South

A bank may be criticized for a disproportionate pattern within a given area for a certain type of loan. Security Trust Federal of Knoxville, Tennessee, has both a Kentucky and a Tennessee division. The latter division was deemed to have an "unsatisfactory distribution of mortgage loan originations" due in part to a loan referral procedure involving a Mississippi affiliate which "discourages applications" in certain areas, according to the examiners.

SunBank of Orlando, Florida, had an overall reasonable penetration of lending. Its HMDA data, however, revealed a disproportionately low level of home mortgage and home improvement lending in several census tracts in Orange and Brevard Counties, two of the five counties in its delineated community.

Only Three Home Loans per Year at Three Large Branches in Puerto Rico

Some banks may be criticized for the lending patterns of a few of its offices. Examiners at Farmers and Merchants Bank of Long Beach, California, found an "inconsistency" in the geographic distribution of lending. Whereas some branches had a reasonable distribution of applications and loans, others "received few applications and made very few loans" in their community's low- and moderate-income neighborhoods.

The examiners' analysis at Cole Taylor Bank in Chicago, Illinois, demonstrated a "lack of distribution" of loans northwest and east of one of the branches of that bank. These results were consistent with the bank's lack of ascertainment and effective marketing in that same branch area. This branch has

a low- and moderate-income and predominantly minority census tract located near it.

Ponce Federal Bank of Ponce, Puerto Rico, had an "unequal" distribution of mortgage loan originations in its communities. Three of the bank's five largest branches had made only nine mortgage loans over three years. This led the examiners to conclude that "there has not been the same commitment to provide for credit services throughout all of the institution's delineated communities."

Surety Federal Savings Bank of Vallejo, California, has four offices. The "combined loan- to- deposit ratio at the institution's two smallest branches is very small," according to the examiners. This was one of the few instances where this ratio was calculated for branches. Furthermore, that bank made "very few loans" in the last two years in the substantially minority census tracts of its home office community.

Justifying a High Loan Denial Rate on the Reservation

Some banks more than others maintain information supporting loan denials. CRA examiners at the First Interstate Bank of Colstrip, Montana, found a higher ratio of loan denials to residents of the Northern Cheyenne Reservation, an identified low- and moderate-income area. The reasons for those denials, however, were "adequately supported in the bank's files." That bank was nonetheless looked upon unfavorably because its board was unaware of this apparent pattern and had not reviewed loan policies and practices related to it.

Certain banks with needs improvement ratings had analyzed the geographic distribution of their loans but not applications or denials. River Oaks Bank of Houston, Texas, completed a zip code analysis of its loans but not of its applications or denials. This was also the case at Virginia Commerce Bank of Arlington, Virginia.

Alief Alamo Bank of Houston, Texas, plotted all home purchase and improvement loans on a census tract map. The examiners encouraged the bank to plot a sample of other approved consumer loans as well as denials for a particular time period, such as a quarter. The examiners then noted that this same recommendation regarding an analysis of the geographic distribution of approved and denied appli-

cations had been made at the previous exam. Furthermore, the examiners indicated there was "no evidence" that the bank's board or management reviewed or analyzed the geographic distribution of
those loans that were plotted.

"Geocoding from Memory" Doesn't Work at Community Bank in Alabama

The methodology used by banks with needs improvement ratings for analyzing the geographic distribution of loans is often a subject of criticism. As noted
in the above case, a bank may plot certain data but
not take the time to review or analyze the resultant
lending patterns. The examiners are particularly critical when management has not taken corrective action on previously identified recommendations, as
also was the case at the Alief Alamo Bank in Houston.

The Bank of Alabama of Fultondale, Alabama, did
not perform a formal geographic distribution analysis
at the time of its first exam. Management felt that due
to the bank's small size ($8 million), its lending
officers could "recall and outline the distribution from
memory." The examiners' review of accepted and
rejected consumer loan applications concluded there
was a "disproportionate pattern" within the community and in relation to activity outside it, but no
specifics were provided to support that conclusion.

The Bank of Commerce of Auburn, California, was
questioned on its first public evaluation, where it
received a needs improvement rating, because it had
not made a reasonable effort to analyze its lending
geographic distribution. The bank's computer system
had the ability to track loans by census tract, according to the examiners, but management did not use
this tool at the time of its first examination.

Marquette Bank of Golden Valley, Minnesota,
which also received a needs improvement rating on
its first public evaluation, had purchased new software at that time to help them identify the geographic
distribution of its lending. This information, however,
was not used by the bank in establishing policies or
plans at the time of its first exam.

Loan Denial Sample "Not Statistically Sound" at First Interstate of Seattle

The loan geographic distribution at the First Interstate Bank of Seattle, Washington, showed a reasonable penetration of low- and moderate-income areas.
The public evaluation reported that the bank's loan-
to-deposit ratio in low- and moderate-income areas
was higher than that for its delineated communities,
with the exception of a small group of low- to moderate-income areas. This may sometimes be the case
if a low level of deposits is being generated from such
areas. Credit applications and denials were not geographically identified by that bank. A planned credit
denial sample was determined as being "not statisti-
cally sound," according to the examiners.

Borrowers' Place of Residence Versus Place of Employment Becomes Issue in Colorado

There was a disproportionate lending distribution
outside the delineated community of the FirstBank at
Arapahoe/Yosemite in Englewood, Colorado. The
examiners reported that this disproportionate distribution "may be skewed" because the bank is located
in an office complex area where many of its borrowers
work but don't live. Even though that bank's three-
mile radius local community was considered reasonable by examiners, a larger area encompassing more
of the residential areas where its borrowers lived may
have represented a more reasonable community.

This case study raises the issue as to the relevant
location of a borrowing customer. While most analyses focus on the place of residence of the borrower,
they may conduct their lending activity near where
they work, shop, or otherwise frequently visit for
purposes of convenience. Whereas deposits are considered more of a "convenience" item, loans are
considered more of a "shopping" item, with convenience secondary. Still, though, any loan geographic
distribution analysis should consider these other factors in identifying customer lending patterns.

Examiners Prefer Census Tracts over Zip Codes

There were some instances where examiners criticized specific aspects of a bank's methodology in
analyzing the geographic distribution of its lending.

It appears that the general preference among CRA examiners is that the analysis be conducted in terms of census tracts because of the ready and more widespread availability of demographic data on that basis. However, demographic data are also available on other geographic levels such as zip codes.

Many banks prefer using zip codes because most loan and deposit files are readily available on this basis. However, zip codes have the disadvantage of being frequently changed and do not always reflect a homogenous composition as compared to census tracts. Furthermore, five-digit zip code maps, especially in rural areas, are much more difficult to come by than in a city where they can be found in most yellow pages. Census tracts maps, by comparison, are readily available from government agencies. While all areas have zip codes, this is not always true for census tracts, especially in rural communities. The 1990 census, however, has complete coverage with either census tracts in metropolitan areas or block numbering areas (BNAs) in nonmetropolitan areas.

Zip Code Analysis is Better
Than No Analysis at All

While a census tract analysis may be preferred to a zip code analysis, a zip code analysis is preferred to no analysis at all. In general, CRA examiners are critical of the use of zip codes, especially in cases where census tract data are also available.

Cole Taylor Bank of Chicago, Illinois, conducts an annual zip code analysis of loan extensions and denials. The bank recently began geocoding and plotting loans and denials by census tract. The examiners considered this a "more effective method" than using zip codes, which "hampered" the bank's geocoding efforts.

The geocoding analysis by Virginia Commerce Bank of Arlington, Virginia, was considered "very limited" because it used zip codes rather than census tracts, according to the examiners. The examiners concluded that census tract data are preferred because the bank can obtain information on the "population makeup" of an area. Again, while census data are more readily and quickly available by census tracts, demographic data are also available for five-digit zip codes and many other geographic units through the Census Bureau and other sources.

Examiners in California Conduct Own
Census Tract Analysis Rather than Use
Banks' Zip Code Analysis

Management at San Jose National Bank of San Jose, California, used a "manual analysis" of loan distribution by zip codes at the time of its first public evaluation when it received a needs improvement rating. The bank was looked askance at for not being aware of the distribution of loans by census tract. The examiners plotted a sample of fifty approved consumer loans and concluded that only two of them were in low- and moderate-income census tracts.

Stockdale Savings of Bakersfield, California, conducted a zip code analysis of its loan portfolio. "Reasonable conclusions could not be drawn" from that analysis, according to examiners, because it lacked information showing low- and moderate-income and/or minority census tracts. The examiners' own analysis of applications concluded that only two of the 18 census tracts designated as low- and moderate-income and/or minority in Bakersfield generated applications. Again, while it is possible to categorize zip codes as well as census tracts as being low- and moderate-income and/or substantially minority ones, there is a distinct preference by examiners for a census tract analysis because of readily available data and maps on this basis.

Community Bank in Montana Collected
Data but Didn't Analyze It

It is bad enough for a bank to be singled out for not completing any geographic analysis or perhaps a limited analysis, according to the examiners. But, it is even worse when the examiners feel they must conduct their own analysis. The worst situation occurs when the examiners conduct their own analysis and find a disproportionate or unreasonable penetration of low- and moderate-income and/or substantially minority areas. Even if a bank limits its analysis to using zip codes, it should make an effort to identify which ones would be low- and moderate-income and/or substantially minority. Because census tracts are usually much smaller than zip codes, especially in metropolitan areas, they provide a better and more consistent picture of small area demographics.

As noted previously, it is not enough for a bank to geocode loans by census tracts. The Citizens State Bank of Choteau, Montana, kept a register of credit extensions and denials by census tracts. However, the bank was criticized for not analyzing the distribution of the data collected. The examiners' own analysis of that data showed a reasonable distribution, with 86% of the loans within the delineated community.

Virginia Bank's Analysis Using Voting Districts Termed "Weak" and "Very Limited"

In one case a bank conducted a loan geographic distribution analysis by voting districts rather than zip codes or census tracts. F&M Bank of Harrisonburg, Virginia, which received a needs improvement rating on its first public evaluation, was cited as having a "weak" and "very limited" analysis. The primary reason given by the examiners was that census tracts provide information on the demographic make-up of an area. Again, the Census Bureau does in fact make demographic information available by districts, but it is not the approach preferred by examiners. The examiners at F&M Bank conducted their own census tract analysis of loan denials and approvals and concluded that the results were "positive" in terms of the bank's distribution of credit.

California Loan Brokers Result in Lending "Gaps" in "Low-Mod" and Minority Areas

Institutions that operate as mortgage bankers often have disproportionate loan geographic distributions. United Savings Bank of San Francisco, California, which received a needs improvement rating on its first public evaluation, had numerous lending "gaps," many of which were in low- and moderate-income and minority areas. The examiners concluded that the gaps may have been the result of that bank's use of loan brokers to obtain applications through the bank's mortgage banking division.

American Liberty Savings Bank of Oakland, California, acts as a mortgage banker. Its 1990 HMDA data showed only 2% of its applications emanating from its delineated community of the city of Oakland. The examiners moreover noted that the bank had "numerous errors" in its HMDA report and that it was "not accurately tracking loan activity."

Office and Service Record (Assessment Factor G)

Very few banks are criticized for having offices that result in difficult accessibility for certain segments of the local community. Special purpose banks that are located in nontraditional locations, such as in the upper levels of an office building, are prone to criticism here.

Salt Lake City Bank Not Open to the Public

Fidelity U.S. Depository Trust Company of Salt Lake City, Utah, provides an example, since its only office provides no public access. All business there is conducted through the postal service or its affiliates, according to its CRA examiners.

Foreign banks are also subject to criticism because their offices often are not accessible to the entire community. Banco Bilbao Vizcaya of New York City was apparently an exception because its office was deemed to be "reasonably accessible" to bank customers in midtown Manhattan. Foreign bank offices located on the upper floors of major New York City office buildings are quite common. For example, Mitsubishi Trust & Banking Corporation of New York City has its banking office on the 39th floor of an office building.

No Visible Teller Windows in Boston

Many private banks have offices that are difficult for all members of the local community to access. Often these offices are designed to be exclusive and appeal to the affluent market segment. Boston Private Bank and Trust Company, which has its only office located in a small facility in a prestigious office building in the downtown financial district, has "no visible teller windows." The examiners therefore concluded that low- and moderate-income communities probably cannot be adequately served by that bank.

Each of the many banks with needs improvement ratings that were criticized for an unreasonably large delineated community can likewise be criticized for lack of accessibility in its most distant areas. For example, the Broward County offices of SafraBank II of Pompano Beach, Florida, which received a needs improvement rating on its first public evaluation, were found to be "not reasonably accessible" to the entire Broward County delineated community. That community was deemed to be unreasonably large because the bank had neither the branch network nor the financial resources to adequately serve such a sizable and densely populated area.

Pittsburgh Bank Survey: Cut Back Office Hours and Use ATMs

Business hours at banks with needs improvement ratings may be inconvenient in terms of the needs of the local community, especially low- and moderate-income neighborhoods. Furthermore, business hours are infrequently reviewed for effectiveness in terms of customer surveys or comparative surveys involving other banks.

Pacific Valley National Bank of Modesto, California, which received a needs improvement rating on its first public evaluation, conducted a customer survey in 1989. That survey indicated that business hours "may be inconvenient." The bank's hours were, however, consistent with other commercially oriented banks in the community, according to the examiners.

The North Side Deposit Bank of Pittsburgh, Pennsylvania, conducted a lobby and use survey. The bank determined that business hours should be cut back at the main office, where the bank's ATMs could provide essential services when the offices were closed.

Bank hours and services at the Bank of Kansas in Lawrence, Kansas, appeared to be convenient, according to examiners. Nonetheless, the bank was questioned because of the lack of formal surveys documenting whether or not banking hours and services at the bank are desirable or needed by customers in the local community.

Bay Cities National Bank of Redondo Beach, California, which received a needs improvement rating on its first public evaluation, has not received any requests to extend evening hours or offer Saturday hours. Normal hours of operation for that bank are from 9:00 A.M. to 4:00 P.M., Monday through Thursday, and 9:00 A.M. to 7:00 P.M. on Friday. Loan officers are available by appointment on other evenings during the week.

Closing Branches without Considering the Consequences

Banks with needs improvement ratings are often criticized for performing an inadequate assessment of the potentially adverse impact of branch closings or ways of minimizing that impact on the local community. CRA examiners are more sensitive when the affected community is a low- and moderate-income neighborhood and/or a substantially minority one, particularly if the closed branch is the last branch left in that neighborhood.

Ponce Federal Bank of Ponce, Puerto Rico, closed six branches during the review period without formal procedures in place to determine the feasibility of those closings and their potential impact on the affected communities. Bay View Federal Bank of San Mateo, California, closed four branches during its review period. It likewise had no documentation supporting those closings or their potential impact on the affected communities. First Community Industrial Bank of Lakewood, Colorado, did not review the impact of the recent closing of "several" affiliated bank offices at the time of its first public evaluation when it received a needs improvement rating.

Large Bank Acquired 50 Branches, Opened 13, and Closed Four without Policy or Impact Study

HomeFed Bank of San Diego, California, acquired fifty branches, opened thirteen, and closed four during an approximate year-and-a-half period prior to its first public evaluation. Because that bank's policy on opening and closing branch offices was only "recently adopted" at the time of the first CRA evaluation, the examiners found no evidence that any impact study of office closings and openings was conducted prior to that time. That bank has since failed.

First National Bank of Ipswich, Massachusetts, "recently" drafted a branch closing policy according to CRA examiners. Management at Norstar Bank of Buffalo, New York, developed a written policy on branch closings at the time of its first public evaluation and was in the process of receiving board approval at that time.

Examiners Don't Criticize Bank for Closing a Branch in a High-Crime Area of Seattle for Safety Reasons

Many banks with needs improvement ratings closed branches but were not criticized by their examiners. For example, Glendale Federal of Glendale, California, consolidated or closed twenty-six offices in California and Florida during the 18-month period prior to its second public evaluation, but it opened only one office. The branch closings were not disproportionately located in low- and moderate-income neighborhoods, according to the examiners.

In one case a bank with a needs improvement rating closed a branch in a low- and moderate-income neighborhood which did have an adverse impact on the local community, according to examiners. First Interstate Bank of Seattle, Washington, closed a branch "for safety reasons" because the area's high crime rate had an "adverse affect on the bank's customers and employees." Even though the closure adversely impacted the local community, that bank worked with community and neighborhood representatives to minimize the impact of the closing. The bank, however, was not criticized for that closing.

Bank Surveys Justify Closing of Ten Branches in South Florida

Most banks that close a branch routinely track the "deposit retention rate." This is the proportion of deposits of the closed branch retained by the bank through other branches or delivery systems (e.g., bank by mail or ATMs). If the bank expands this type of internal survey to question affected customers on their reaction to the closings, this may lessen any potential criticism by CRA examiners. BankAtlantic of Fort Lauderdale, Florida, closed ten branch offices in the approximately two-year period prior to its CRA examination. Although the bank did not have written policies or procedures which assessed the impact of the closings, it conducted surveys to determine customer reaction to account transfers to nearby offices. The bank's surveys concluded there was no adverse impact of the branch closings.

Examiners' Use of Customer Satisfaction Surveys May Lead to Criticism

This assessment factor not only deals with the bank's record of opening and closing offices but also the provision of services at those offices. The evaluation of the level of services being provided by a bank is a very broad and difficult area to assess, even for large banks. Although many banks conduct customer satisfaction surveys throughout the course of business operations, bank management may feel uneasy about sharing the results of these studies with CRA examiners. First, these studies are usually expensive and proprietary in nature, and banks likely would not want any of the confidential results to be disclosed in public CRA evaluations. Second, there may be weaknesses in certain aspects of a bank's service or product mix, which may be the subject of criticism by CRA examiners if disclosed to them. As long as a bank is taking corrective action to improve such problems, there may be little or no criticism.

Few Banks Criticized for Poor Customer Service

Most CRA public evaluations are not really critical of the level of bank services provided. These are mainly business decisions at the bank. If a bank is not providing needed services in a competitive environment, then it will most likely be penalized by the market.

There are, nonetheless, a few examples of banks with needs improvement ratings that were criticized in terms of the level of service being provided through their offices. In the case of Pan American Savings Bank of San Mateo, California, the CRA examiners noted that all branches are "primarily deposit taking facilities" since there are "no loan agents permanently assigned to any branch."

Kearny Federal of Kearny, New Jersey, was noted as not offering checking accounts at any of its offices. There are obviously many types of accounts and services not being made available by many savings and loans and community banks. As noted above, criticism under this assessment factor for this reason is more the exception than the rule.

IV. DISCRIMINATION AND OTHER ILLEGAL CREDIT PRACTICES

Credit Application Practices (Assessment Factor D)

There are many practices which can discourage loan applications directly or indirectly. Banks with needs improvement ratings have been cited for numerous such activities. It is the exception rather than the rule, however, for a bank in this category to be criticized for illegal discouraging or prescreening of loan applicants.

There is considerable overlap between this assessment factor and several others. Banks that are criticized for poor CRA performance under certain other assessment factors may likewise be criticized here. That is, certain activities under almost every other assessment factor can be categorized as directly or indirectly discouraging loan applications.

A bank, for example, may discourage loan applications either directly or indirectly through poor credit ascertainment efforts (assessment factor A), lack of innovative underwriting criteria (assessment factor C), inadequate marketing or advertising for credit (assessment factor B), low loan volume relative to bank resources and community needs (assessment factor I), disproportionate lending patterns excluding certain neighborhoods (assessment factor E), closed or inaccessible offices and inconvenient hours (assessment factor G), and illegal or discriminatory credit practices (assessment factor F).

Criticizing Loan Application Practices in California without Ever Specifying Them

Some banks with needs improvement ratings were criticized under this assessment factor, but no specifics were provided as to the basis for the concern. Bay View Federal Bank of San Mateo, California, which received a needs improvement rating on its first public evaluation, had certain unspecified practices "that would have the effect of discouraging" a loan applicant. The examiners noted that those practices were being eliminated and affected personnel were being trained to avoid this unspecified problem.

Another instance of an unspecified type of credit practice of concern to examiners involved United Savings Bank of San Francisco, California, which also received a needs improvement rating in its first public evaluation. The examiners simply noted then that there was concern regarding that bank's "application-taking process" and that corrective action was promised by management.

Loan Applications Discouraged or Not Accepted at Specialized Banks

Most instances of credit practices that examiners believe discourage loan applicants are spelled out in the public evaluation, at least in general terms. Otherwise, the examiners are put in the uncomfortable position of making public an important conclusion without supporting documentation or at least reasoning.

Certain practices involving prescreening, high minimum loan amounts, and very restrictive terms may directly discourage applicants. Loan applicants, however, can be indirectly discouraged through certain bank practices.

For example, special purpose banks that clearly target one segment to the actual or perceived exclusion of others, may discourage the latter group. Some special purpose banks do not even make traditional loans, and they would clearly fall under this category. For example, Fidelity U.S. Depository Trust Company of Salt Lake City, Utah, does not accept applications or originate loans. Rather, loans are generated by a bank affiliate and then offered as investments in the form of participations.

Foreign banks are another type of specialized operation that indirectly discourage traditional loan applicants because they generally don't offer retail loans. For example, Banco Bilbao Vizcaya of New York City does not offer consumer loans or mortgage loans as it is primarily a wholesale bank involved in facilitating foreign trade. Their CRA examiners, however, noted that this bank has "granted unsecured personal loans to its employees."

Boston Private Bank Offers to Cash Welfare Checks, but No Takers Expected

One of the best examples of a bank that may indirectly discourage loan applications is a private bank or one that caters to the affluent market. The exclusive locations, sophisticated marketing promotions, clearly upscale product mix, and the like can have the unintended affect of intimidating low- and moderate-income individuals or at least making them feel uncomfortable. Thus, they may be unlikely to apply for or even inquire about a loan at such a bank.

The original goal of the Boston Private Bank and Trust Company was to cater to the affluent community. The bank specializes in jumbo mortgages of $150,000 and above. Marketing is directed primarily toward upscale clients, and it "appears to preclude serving low- and moderate-income borrowers or depositors." Furthermore, the bank is located in a small office in a prestigious building in Boston's downtown financial district. The office is not "readily identified as a bank, and is not designed to attract walk-up business." Although the bank's CRA statement lists loans available to all individuals of its community, these and related factors combined may discourage credit applicants from Boston's low- and moderate-income areas.

To the extent that a private bank catering to affluent individuals may intimidate or lessen the likelihood of low- and moderate-income individuals utilizing it, any services the bank offers to benefit those groups may be limited in their use. For example, Boston Private Bank and Trust Company, in conjunction with the Massachusetts Bankers Association, arranged to cash welfare checks for non-customers. After considering the prestigious and exclusive location of the bank, the examiners concluded that "it is unlikely that such a service would be used."

World Trade Bank of Beverly Hills, California, likewise specializes in its community's "more affluent areas." That bank has high initial deposit ($25,000) and minimum balance requirements for customer accounts as well as minimum loan amounts. The "extremely limited focus of the bank's marketing strategy does not encourage application for credit from all segments of the bank's local community," according to its examiners.

Poor Marketing Efforts at Community Banks in California May Discourage Loan Applications

Banks with limited marketing programs or those not directed to low- and moderate-income ("low-mod") neighborhoods within their community may indirectly discourage credit applications by those residents. San Jose National Bank of San Jose, California,

which received a needs improvement rating on its first public evaluation, did not advertise in media specifically directed to low- and moderate-income neighborhoods in its local community. The bank's "weak marketing efforts to some segments of the population also limit accessibility to credits offered," according to examiners.

EurekaBank of Foster City, California, which received a needs improvement rating on its first public evaluation, did not market all consumer products listed as being available in its CRA statement at that time. The examiners concluded that this may have the "indirect effect of discouraging applications for credit" since the community would not be aware of these products. That assumes, of course, that the community reads those statements.

Farmers and Merchants Bank of Long Beach, California, has no formal marketing program or strategy, and its credit marketing efforts were deemed to be in "substantial noncompliance." The examiners concluded that the bank's "inadequate marketing methods" among other things may have an "indirect effect of discouraging applications."

Pacific Valley National Bank of Modesto, California, received a needs improvement rating on its first public evaluation. That bank's marketing program was cited for lacking an "affirmative effort to market its credit services throughout its delineated community" at that time. It is not surprising, therefore, that management was criticized for not reviewing its marketing efforts "to assure that practices do not, in effect, discourage applicants."

Low Minority Loan Application Rate Causes Concern in Northern California

An examiner's finding of disproportionate lending practices, especially those involving low- and moderate-income areas, may suggest the possibility that loan applications are being discouraged there. SafraBank II of Pompano Beach, Florida, which received a needs improvement rating on its first public evaluation, had a disproportionately small share of lending in its Broward County community as compared to its Marion County community. The "marginal loan volume" in the former community "indicates the possibility of isolated, illegal discouraging, or prescreening of applicants," according to its examiners at that time.

While no lending practices which clearly discourage credit applications by Placer Savings of Auburn, California, were noted, "the low level of applications from low- and moderate-income and minority applicants causes concern," according to its examiners. The "very low application rate for various minority groups within its delineated community" was likewise noted under this assessment factor for Golden Coin Savings of San Francisco, California.

"Very Conservative" Lending Practices at Community Bank

A frequent complaint by examiners under this assessment factor for many banks with needs improvement ratings is the lack of flexible lending policies, which can discourage loan applications. Sometimes the public evaluations are specific in identifying particular loan terms or minimum amounts that represent the basis for this concern. Many times, however, CRA examiners are quite general in their reasons for dissatisfaction with lending policies in this regard.

The underwriting standards at El Capitan National Bank of Sonora, California, reflected "very conservative lending practices," according to its examiners. First Interstate Bank of Phoenix, Arizona, "infrequently offers conventional lending products with special features or more flexible lending criteria." Glendale Federal of Glendale, California, offers a variety of standard real estate loans including variable-rate, fixed-rate, and combination fixed-rate and variable-rate step loans. However, "none of these products feature flexible underwriting criteria" specifically for low- and moderate-income credit needs.

Not Lending in Kansas' 100-Year Flood Plain

There were a few instances where banks were criticized for specific credit application practices that may have discouraged applications. For example, certain loan policies and procedures at Glendale Federal "imposed more onerous terms based on the location of the property," which violates federal nondiscrimination regulations. Inter-State Federal of Kansas City, Kansas, has a policy of "not originating mortgage loans on properties which are located in a 100-year flood plain," and this was an item of concern by its examiners under this assessment factor.

Management Scolded for Designation of "Savings Office" in Minority Area

Stockdale Savings of Bakersfield, California, maintains a full service office plus a "savings office" in northeast Bakersfield. Management views the area surrounding the latter office as "requiring primarily savings services as opposed to credit." This view raised concern by the examiners, "particularly given the large number of low- and moderate-income and minority census tracts" in that area. Management's "attempt to distinguish this community so as to provide a different level of service and outreach" resulted in a policy position that "may discourage credit applications" from that community, according to the examiners.

The CRA statement of the Shelby County State Bank of Shelbyville, Illinois, indicates that "only loans secured by real estate in Shelby County (preferably within Shelbyville) are desirable real estate loans." Because that bank's delineated community also includes portions of two other counties, the examiners concluded that this statement "could be interpreted to mean that the bank will not make real estate loans in these areas," according to its CRA examiners.

Homestead Savings of Millbrae, California, reported very low application rates from those counties within its delineated community where it did not maintain a branch or lending office. This lack of presence may have acted as a "barrier to potential applicants" in those counties, according to its examiners.

Home Loans Offered "Only if Inquired About" in Virginia

There were many examples of specific lending terms that were cited as possibly discouraging credit applications. Farmers and Merchants Bank of Long Beach, California, offers residential mortgage loans with a 5-year maturity and 15-year amortization period. Customers requesting long-term mortgages are referred to local savings and loans. Although not specified, that bank's "low loan-to-value ratios," among other things, may have an "indirect effect of discouraging applications."

Stockdale Savings of Bakersfield, California, has a requirement of a six-month cash reserve on any loan with a loan-to-value ratio of greater than 90%. This practice "may tend to discourage applicants," according to its CRA examiners.

Consumer real estate loans at Virginia Commerce Bank of Arlington, Virginia, are offered "only if inquired about" on a five-year balloon payment term, generally not subject to rate reductions and/or renewal. This practice is due to the bank's adherence to "narrow market and strategic planning goals" rather than any discriminatory practices, according to its public evaluation.

Exceptions to Minimum Loan Amount on "Case by Case" Basis—But Only Two Exceptions and One Turn Down in a Year

A fairly common criticism under this assessment factor is the imposition of minimum loan amounts that could clearly and quickly discourage credit applicants. As previously noted, Boston Private Bank and Trust Company specializes in jumbo mortgages of $150,000 and above.

The underwriting guidelines at Stockdale Savings of Bakersfield, California, contain minimum loan amounts. The examiners' review of real estate listings in that bank's local community revealed "numerous homes selling for less than the minimum loan amount required for first trust deed loans." Management advised the examiners that it makes exceptions to this minimum loan amount policy on a "case-by-case basis." The examiners found only two such exceptions in all of 1990 and, in fact, found "at least one instance where the minimum amount was enforced."

Loan Policy Revised During Exam

Homestead Savings of Millbrae, California, had minimum loan amount requirements for first mortgage loans and refinanced loans in its policy manual. These minimum loan amounts, which reportedly were not being used, were "eliminated from the manual during the course of the examination."

Minimum loan amounts at San Jose National Bank of San Jose, California, may "discourage lower income applicants from applying for some products," according to that bank's first public evaluation where it received a needs improvement rating. Metropolitan Savings Bank of Cleveland, Ohio, likewise established minimum loan amounts for several types of its loans.

Its examiners concluded that these limitations may "discourage low- and moderate-income persons from applying for these types of loans."

Loan Referrals Discourage Applications in Tennessee

An alternative practice to minimum loan amounts is a bank's referral of smaller loans to other financial institutions. A few examples were previously cited. The CRA statement at First Interstate Bank of Denver, Colorado, claims that they are willing to extend mortgage loans to all creditworthy customers. This is not consistent with that bank's practice of "encouraging only large-dollar conventional real estate loans," according to its examiners. This practice "places the low- and moderate-income neighborhoods at a disadvantage" in obtaining this type of credit. The examination noted that the bank refers customers with "small-dollar requests" for conventional mortgage loans to other financial institutions.

Bank practices involving referrals to affiliates or other banks that may be inconvenient to potential customers could likewise represent a credit discouraging practice. Security Trust Federal of Knoxville, Tennessee, maintains both a Tennessee and Kentucky division. The Tennessee division doesn't originate residential mortgage loans but refers interested customers to its mortgage company parent which has an office in Knoxville. The examiners noted that two geographically separated counties in east Tennessee where the bank (but not the parent mortgage company) has offices had few loan originations.

The examiners attributed this finding to the fact that customers in those counties must deal with personnel in the mortgage company affiliate's office in Knoxville located approximately fifty miles away. Customers are provided with a toll-free telephone number, and personnel from that mortgage company will meet with prospective borrowers who don't have to travel to Knoxville. Nonetheless, this referral process was concluded to discourage mortgage and refinancing applications from those areas. This referral practice was further noted as being contrary to that association's CRA policy, which stated that they made these types of loans.

Rare Criticism of Higher Than Market Loan Rates in Virginia and California

Nonprice loan terms can directly or indirectly discourage credit applications. Price terms, on the other hand, can have a more direct impact. Only a small number of banks were criticized for what examiners perceived to be above-market loan rates. Criticism of a bank's loan pricing by examiners is fairly unusual because of the view that competitive markets rather than regulators should dictate prices. CRA critics citing the "credit allocation" argument feel that telling a bank where to or not to lend is bad enough, much less suggesting how much to charge for the loan.

Banks faced deposit pricing restrictions in the past, and this is still true today for brokered deposits for weaker banks. There are, however, a few examples today of regulatory involvement in loan pricing. The only fairly recent examples that come to mind are general "jawboning" efforts by the former Bush Administration and other politicians to encourage banks to lower credit card rates and even price and nonprice terms on some other loans to ease the "credit crunch" in certain areas. More recent Clinton Administration efforts to ease the "credit crunch" are focused on nonprice factors..

Virginia Commerce Bank of Arlington, Virginia, made only three consumer related home loans in a more than two-year period prior to its public examination. According to its examiners, that bank "discourages owner-occupied consumer home loans" by offering "high rates which are normally one and one half percent above market rates." The Bank of Commerce of Auburn, California, which received a needs improvement rating on its first public evaluation, was found to "discourage applications" for home improvement loans by charging "higher than market rates." As a previous case study pointed out, the "market rates" were "loss-leader" pricing by certain competitors, according to bank management.

"Inappropriate Language" in Loan Underwriting Guidelines in San Francisco

A variety of other unrelated types of practices were cited by examiners as discouraging credit applications. For example, in the case of Home Federal of San Francisco, California, its publicly available underwriting guidelines contained "inappropriate language," according to its examiners. There was no further elaboration as to what that meant, but it was included under this assessment factor involving practices which may discourage loan applications.

EurekaBank of Foster City, California, which received a needs improvement rating on its first public evaluation, was also questioned on the basis of the language in its written loan underwriting guidelines. According to the examiners, the guidelines contained language that "improperly addresses the age and location of the collateral property." Management told examiners that this standard was not used, and it was removed from the guidelines. The examiners pointed out that no denials based on that standard were detected during the loan review period.

Visit with Loan Officer Required for Mortgage Application at Community Bank in Louisiana—All Other Applications Available from Receptionist

The Bank of Commerce and Trust Company of Crowley, Louisiana, was looked upon with disfavor by its examiners because residential mortgage loan applications were not as accessible as other ones. Examiners interviewed bank employees and learned that all loan applications can be obtained from the bank's receptionist. However, residential mortgage loan applications "must be obtained from a loan officer." According to the examiners, "this may be construed as a discouraging factor." No further explanation of this unique situation was provided in public evaluation.

Does Texas Community Bank Make Mobile Home Loans or Not?

CRA examiners at the Community Bank of Waco, Texas, reported the "possibility of isolated discouraging of applicants." The specific instance noted involved an applicant denied credit based on the statement that "Community Bank does not finance mobile homes." That bank does in fact provide mobile home financing, and it is specifically listed in the bank's CRA statement as one of the types of loans offered. No further specifics were available regarding that instance. For example, it was not made clear whether the quoted statement was a verbal or written one, but it appears that it was written.

Substantive Violation at First Interstate of Denver

Many banks subscribe to "credit scoring" models and services to help control risk exposure on certain types of loans. This often involves the use of legal prescreening criteria. Some types of prescreening criteria are illegal and would be criticized under the following assessment factor F. Many of the prohibited discriminatory or other illegal credit practices discussed under the following assessment factor may directly discourage credit applicants. In most cases such violations are also mentioned under this assessment factor.

For example, First Interstate Bank of Denver, Colorado, was cited for a substantive violation of Regulation B for implementing policies and practices which "discourage members of a protected class from filing applications." That violation was limited to a specific area of consumer lending (such as credit cards), according to the examiners. Management took corrective action on that problem.

The same bank was previously noted for its practice of encouraging only large conventional real estate loans while referring small ones to other financial institutions. Moreover, the bank had a policy of requiring minimum income levels for dealer auto loan applicants which "may reduce the availability" of such loans in low- and moderate-income areas, according to the examiners.

Union City Savings Bank of Union City, New Jersey, was found to be in violation of various non-discrimination regulations, which resulted in "discouraging applications." Although these unspecified violations were "widespread and of significant supervisory concern," there was no evidence of discrimination, according to the examiners.

Mortgages for Investors, Not Homeowners in Virginia

Some banks with needs improvement ratings were criticized because of inconsistencies between what is stated in the bank's CRA statement and actual lending practices. In some cases, a specific type of loan is listed

as being available when in fact it is not. In other instances a bank may be making certain types of loans that are not included in its CRA statement. Both of these practices could discourage credit applications, according to examiners.

The CRA statement of Virginia Commerce Bank of Arlington, Virginia, indicates that "loans are made on first and second mortgages or residential structures." This would be interpreted to mean that the bank lends money to purchase owner-occupied residences. Rather, the intent of this bank, which targets small businesses, is to only make first and second residential mortgages for "investment/business purposes, i.e., rental property, purchase for resale."

The CRA statement of Beverly Bank of Lockport, Illinois, identifies various types of available mortgage loans. The examiners' review revealed that certain types of mortgage loans are no longer being offered by the bank. Because that bank's loan policy has changed since the previous exam, "the types of mortgage loans no longer offered by the bank should be deleted from the CRA statement."

There are also examples of banks that make certain types of loans that are not listed on the CRA statement. The Shelby County State Bank of Shelbyville, Illinois, offers special loans through its participation in government-related loan programs. However, those loans were not listed in the bank's CRA statement, according to its examiners. River Oaks Bank of Houston, Texas, makes some one- to four-family residential loans on a one-year renewable basis. These loans were likewise not listed in that bank's CRA statement.

Illegal Credit Practices (Assessment Factor F)

46% of Both Needs Improvement and Substantial Noncompliance Banks Have Violations

Nearly half of the banks with needs improvement ratings that we evaluated had some type of substantive, technical, or other violation of compliance laws or regulations. Specifically, 50 of the 108 banks, or 46%, of those with needs improvement ratings evaluated in this analysis had such violations.

It is curious that the 46% of needs improvement banks with such violations is identical to the percentage of banks with substantial noncompliance ratings that have such violations. This suggests that the difference between the two below-average categories may be one of degree not kind. This raises the question as to whether or not some of the banks with such violations in the needs improvement category should have been downgraded into substantial noncompliance. In other words, if precisely 46% of the banks in each of the two lowest categories had such violations, this may suggest the existence of grade inflation.

Of the 50 banks with needs improvement ratings that had some type of compliance violation under this assessment factor, 16 or 32% of them had "substantive" violations, the most serious type. This percentage is about half of the 60% of substantial noncompliant banks with compliance infractions that had substantive violations. This suggests, as would be expected, that the nature of violations at substantial noncompliant banks is more serious.

The 16 needs improvement banks with substantive violations represent 15% of all needs improvement banks in our sample. If, for example, 15% of all banks with needs improvement ratings were downgraded to substantial noncompliance, this lowest category would have about 2.4% rather than 0.9% of all banks as of year-end 1991. Besides that lowest category nearly tripling in size, the percentage of banks needing improvement would drop from 10.1% to 8.6% under such a scenario. Applying this same 1991 grade inflation adjustment factor to year-end 1992 data would lower the proportion of needs improvement banks from 9.6% to 8.1% and raise the proportion of substantial noncompliant banks from 0.9% to 2.3%.

ECOA Violations Most Common

The majority of compliance violations by needs improvement banks were technical and nonsubstantive ones, including several that were not specified. Only a handful of banks with this rating were cited for "widespread" violations, and a few were of "significant supervisory concern." Banks with substantive and widespread violations that are of significant supervisory concern, and were repeated from previous exams without corrective action, represent the worst-case scenario under this assessment factor.

Our evaluation of the types of violations by needs improvement banks concluded that the most common violations were those involving ECOA (Regulation B). The next most common violations were those of general antidiscrimination laws and regulations, the Fair Housing Act, and HMDA.

Substantive Violations at Three out of Four First Interstate Banks

Some of the largest banks with needs improvement ratings were chastised under this assessment factor. Most notable in this regard were the four large First Interstate Bank affiliates with needs improvement ratings as of year-end 1991.

First Interstate Bank of Arizona was cited for a substantive violation of the ECOA, which was a "general practice and widespread throughout one department" of that bank. Such violations are of "significant supervisory concern," according to the examiners. The unspecified practice in question was discontinued by management.

First Interstate Bank of Denver, Colorado, likewise had a substantive violation of Regulation B, which discouraged members of a protected class from filing loan applications. This violation was likewise limited to a specific area of consumer lending, and management has taken corrective action.

First Interstate Bank of Oregon was also charged with substantive ECOA violations limited to a single division within the bank. This bank had an additional substantive HMDA violation also limited to a single division, which apparently resulted in HMDA "reporting omissions." These violations were matters of "significant supervisory concern," according to the examiners at that bank.

First Interstate Bank of Seattle, Washington, was the only one of the four large First Interstate affiliates not cited for a substantive violation. Any violations disclosed by the examiners at that bank were "nonsubstantive" in nature, and senior management promptly took corrective action. Thus, there were nonsubstantive violations at one of their four large banks with needs improvement ratings and substantive violations at the other three. As of year-end 1992, all four of these First Interstate affiliates were upgraded to satisfactory ratings, which presumably means that all of these violations were corrected.

Radio Ads in Chicago Forgot Required "Equal Housing Lender" Tagline

Glendale Federal of Glendale, California, one of the largest thrifts in the nation, was found to be violating substantive provisions of various antidiscrimination laws and regulations. Violations of the ECOA, the Fair Housing Act, and OTS nondiscrimination regulations were cited by the bank's examiners. Furthermore, that bank was not in compliance with "various recordkeeping, reporting, and disclosure requirements." The unspecified substantive violations were limited to particular divisions of that bank.

Bell Federal, one of the largest thrifts in Chicago, violated a substantive provision of the OTS nondiscrimination regulations. Specifically, Bell Federal failed to state in its radio advertisements that it was an equal housing lender. The omission of this required text from the radio ads was considered to be "serious and a matter of supervisory concern." This was because radio represented a significant percentage of Bell's marketing budget and also because little advertising was placed by them in low- and moderate-income media.

All Four Downgraded Banks Cited for Compliance Violations

There were numerous instances of banks with needs improvement ratings that were cited for multiple violations. The Bank of Commerce of Auburn, California, which received a needs improvement rating on its first public evaluation, had substantive violations of the ECOA and fair housing regulations. Although no cases of discriminatory practices were found in that first examination, the examiners noted that there was a "pattern or practice of these substantive violations" in some cases.

Bay View Federal Bank of San Mateo, California, was cited for various substantive and technical violations of the ECOA, the Fair Housing Act, and federal antidiscrimination laws and regulations. The review at Ponce Federal Bank of Ponce, Puerto Rico, disclosed one substantive and a number of more widespread technical violations of the ECOA and related nondiscrimination regulations. Alief Alamo Bank of

Houston, Texas, was identified as having "several violations" of various consumer protection laws and regulations, but these were not specified in the public evaluation.

It is of interest to note that each of the four banks that were downgraded from satisfactory to needs improvement ratings during their second examination were cited for some type of compliance violation. These are the previously mentioned Glendale Federal, Alief Alamo Bank, Bay View Federal Bank, and the State Bank of Springfield, Minnesota. These banks are the subject of a case study in the following chapter.

Violations of All Types at Community Bank in Springfield, Minnesota

The State Bank of Springfield probably represented the greatest number of consumer compliance violations of different types and degrees. In each case the CRA examiners at that bank hedged themselves by noting that these were "apparent" violations. This hedging is unusual because most examiners are able to determine whether or not a violation occurred. In any case, the following listing of "apparent" violations at that bank was unique:

1. Substantive violation of ECOA's Reg. B on a widespread basis.

2. Technical violation of Reg. B on a widespread and limited basis.

3. Substantive violation of the fair housing regulations on an isolated basis and a technical provision on a limited basis.

The substantive violations of both Reg. B and the fair housing regulations were matters of "significant supervisory concern," according to that bank's examiners. Thus, this bank provided an example of violations that were substantive, technical, widespread, limited, isolated, and of significant supervisory concern.

Few banks with substantial noncompliance ratings had this mix of violations. As noted above, more than half of all banks with substantive noncompliance ratings don't even have violations under this important assessment factor. As will be pointed out in the case study in the following chapter involving this bank, its CRA problems were probably the least of its worries as it failed on July 17, 1992.

Age Discrimination in the Credit Card Department in Long Beach

Several banks with needs improvement ratings were cited for repeat compliance violations, meaning that corrective action previously recommended by the examiners was not taken. Farmers and Merchants Bank of Long Beach, California, was cited for being in substantial noncompliance with antidiscrimination laws and regulations, including the ECOA. Applicants in the bank's credit card department were "treated differently on a prohibited (age) basis," and this was deemed to be a "discriminatory practice." Management at that bank "has not been sufficiently responsive to previously cited violations of this nature, which permitted the practice to continue," according to the examiners. Furthermore, that bank's 1990 HMDA report was apparently filed late and contained "significant factual inaccuracies."

Brenton Bank and Trust Company of Urbandale, Iowa, was not in compliance with sections of the ECOA and the Fair Housing Act. The procedural violations of the Fair Housing Act were "repeated from the previous examination, with insufficient attention having been devoted by management to correct them."

Community Bank in Oklahoma Inadvertently Obtained Prohibited Information about a Customer

Any violations of consumer compliance laws and regulations are of "supervisory concern." However, CRA examiners apparently use this terminology with discretion, saving it for more serious cases. For example, Stockdale Savings of Bakersfield, California, was noted as having substantive violations of nondiscrimination laws and regulations. These various recordkeeping, reporting, and disclosure violations raised "supervisory concern," according to that bank's examiners.

The few cases where violations are more serious may result in a finding of "significant supervisory concern." This was the case with Farmers State Bank of Parkston, South Dakota, which had systemwide substantive violations of the ECOA and a systemwide

technical violation of the fair housing regulations. In some cases violations were noted but not specified. For example, in the case of Guaranty Bank & Trust Company of Tulsa, Oklahoma, "prohibited information has been inadvertently obtained by the bank about a customer." There was, however, no evidence that discrimination occurred, according to the examiners.

Loan Data Disparities and Deviations in Southern California and South Florida

Banks found to have substantially disproportionate or unreasonable lending patterns are usually criticized under assessment factor E. However, a few banks with needs improvement ratings were cited for this same reason under this assessment factor. However, disproportionate lending patterns by themselves may not represent illegal credit practices, unless there has been some type of compliance violation.

For example, HomeFed Bank of San Diego, California, was only noted as having record keeping exceptions regarding HMDA and the related OTS regulation. The examiners then pointed out that "unexplained and unaddressed disparities exist in the institution's data on the number of loan applications received from and denied to minority compared to non-minority applicants." The examiners did point out, however, that no instances of "overt prohibited discrimination" were identified during the examination.

BankAtlantic of Fort Lauderdale, Florida, was only cited for a procedural violation of OTS loan application reporting requirements. The examiners pointed out, however, that "statistical deviations" existed in that bank's lending patterns among certain segments of its community. Again, the examiners pointed out that no instances of prohibited discrimination were noted at that bank.

V. COMMUNITY DEVELOPMENT

Local Community Development and Redevelopment Participation (Assessment Factor H)

Banks with needs improvement ratings generally have only a limited awareness of any community development and redevelopment programs within their local community. Even if they are aware of such programs, there may be little, if any, effort to participate within them.

Community Bank Officer in Minnesota Was Member of "Inactive" Council

Many of the banks cited for inadequate ascertainment efforts involving local community groups or government agencies were often criticized under this assessment factor for a limited awareness of community development programs. There were, however, some banks with needs improvement ratings that were not only aware of such programs but participated in them, many times on an irregular basis.

Community Bank of Waco, Texas, is involved in local community development, but its involvement is "primarily limited to projects initiated in prior years." That bank "rarely seeks out community development projects," according to its examiners.

The 1990 CRA statement of Stockdale Savings of Bakersfield, California, lists various redevelopment projects undertaken to meet the credit needs of the community. A review of the bank's 1988 CRA statement "showed the same projects," according to the examiners. They concluded that "in essence, there has been no current activity in this regard."

One bank official of Marquette Bank of Golden Valley, Minnesota, was noted as being on the Valley Square Council. That group, however, was "reportedly inactive," according to the CRA examiners. Bank management has made other efforts to discuss community development needs. This information was taken from that bank's first public evaluation, where it received a needs improvement rating.

Glendale Federal's Activities Limited in Florida Compared to California

Some banks with needs improvement ratings were involved in community development projects, but they may have been too limited in geographic scope to benefit the bank's entire local community. For example, the level of participation in community development and redevelopment programs by Glendale Federal of Glendale, California, is "limited" in its Florida communities as compared to those in California. Part of the reason is that the bank has been unable to successfully identify a statewide housing

consortium in Florida which operates in its delineated communities there.

Participation in community development/redevelopment activities by Norstar Bank of Buffalo, New York, which received a needs improvement rating on its first public evaluation, is considered good in its Buffalo and Rochester communities. Management, however, has "not adequately demonstrated" such participation in the bank's other communities.

SafraBank II of Pompano Beach, Florida, which received a needs improvement rating on its first public evaluation, was criticized for a lack of involvement in one of its two communities under a number of different assessment factors. While the bank was aware of community development projects in its Marion County community and actually had an investment there, this was not the case in its Broward County community. According to its examiners, it had "limited awareness" of community development activity there. Since its efforts to participate there were "unduly limited," it had no such investments at the time of its first public evaluation.

Being Criticized for Community Development in the Cities

Some banks with needs improvement ratings with delineated local communities that cover their home cities and the surrounding areas were challenged under this assessment factor if all community development activities were in the city portion of the communities. Then again, most community development and redevelopment projects are usually in the central city of an urban or rural area.

Harris Trust and Savings Bank of Chicago, Illinois, includes the City of Chicago plus over ninety incorporated municipalities in its Cook County delineated community. Although the bank's community development efforts were extensive, "much of the activity is limited to Chicago" and excludes the suburban areas. This was particularly true for that bank's neighborhood banking center's loans, call activities, and its Harris Foundation grants.

First Commercial Bank of Asheville, North Carolina, which received a needs improvement rating on its first public evaluation, considers all or portions of four counties as its delineated community. The bank's redevelopment efforts, however, have been primarily confined to projects within the City of Asheville.

Norwest Bank of Waupun, Wisconsin, was considered to have an unreasonably large delineated community, which included a 17-mile radius around the City of Waupun. All of the community development projects which the bank has participated in are located in that city. That bank subsequently reduced the size of its delineated community.

Nonlocal Community Development in Southern California

It is clearly better to participate in a nonlocal community development project than to participate in none. Nonetheless, the greatest CRA credit comes from projects within a bank's local community. Still, though, a bank may receive some CRA credit for community development projects located outside of its delineated community.

Cornerstone Bank of Mission Viejo, California, participated with another financial institution in financing the construction of a senior citizen development. Even though that project was located outside of that bank's local community, the examiners praised the project. They, however, concluded that the bank needed to improve its performance under this assessment factor, most likely because it did not participate in such projects within its local community.

Joining a Loan Consortium but Not Making Any Loans

Many banks are involved in shared loan consortiums, an ideal approach to sharing both costs and risks associated with any project. Some banks with needs improvement ratings were questioned if their involvement did not result in any actual lending. Lake Savings of San Francisco, California, is a member of a shared credit program, but it had not participated in the financing of any projects during the review period, according to its examiners. It received a needs improvement rating under this assessment factor.

EurekaBank of Foster City, California, which received a needs improvement rating on its first public evaluation, did not participate in any community development projects at that time. The only exception was a commitment to a shared program representing about one percent of its originations of one- to four-family residential loans during the previous six-month period. Management focused on shared rather than individual participation in such projects because of the "limited availability" of programs involving one- to four- single family residences, the bank's primary area of expertise.

Big Chicago Thrift Should Be Doing More

Larger banks are held to a higher standard in terms of their participation in community development projects. Bell Federal of Chicago, Illinois, was involved in only four community redevelopment programs during a 27-month review period, and only "nominal benefits" resulted from those programs, according to the examiners. "Bell Federal has the ability to do more" in the area of community redevelopment considering "available resources and financial condition," according to its examiners.

Many smaller banks with needs improvement ratings were not taken to task on this assessment factor because of size or other constraints that may have limited their ability to participate in such programs. Iowa Savings Bank of Des Moines, Iowa, made no direct investments in local development or redevelopment programs "due to size and staff limitations." That bank did, however, make contributions to local housing organizations. That small bank had $16 million in assets as of year-end 1990.

The $65 million First Executive Bank of Philadelphia, Pennsylvania, has been "limited" in its ability to become involved in any substantial community development projects due to its "de novo status and lack of profitability," according to its examiners. Still, though, that bank made some contributions and loans to unspecified nonprofit organizations.

Commercial Lending Prohibited or Limited at Certain Banks

First Signature Bank and Trust Company of Portsmouth, New Hampshire, is prohibited from commercial lending activities according to the Competitive Equality Banking Act of 1987. That special-purpose credit card bank, however, is attempting to fulfill its community development obligations through membership in a shared loan consortium.

The $185 million Golden Coin Savings of San Francisco, California, was noted as being "limited" in its ability to participate in construction or commercial loans. They are therefore "unable to participate in any meaningful capacity" in community development lending, according to its examiners. No further explanation was provided. The association's performance under this assessment factor was "not rated."

Another much smaller savings institution in California which did not participate in any community development projects was rated as "needs improvement" under this assessment factor. Management at the $32 million Gold River Savings Bank of Fair Oaks, California, doesn't believe it has the "expertise or capacity to safely participate in projects of this type." While management has considered joining a shared credit organization, no decision was made at the time of its evaluation as to whether this activity would be "appropriate."

No Municipal Bond Purchases in Two-and-One-Half Years of Illinois Bank's Existence

Even if a bank does not get involved in community development or redevelopment projects, it can always invest in local municipal bonds. Surprisingly, some banks with needs improvement ratings had few or no municipal bonds.

The $15 million Beverly Bank of Lockport, Illinois, had not purchased any municipal bonds since it was opened some two and one-half years prior to its first public evaluation. That bank was not involved in any community development activities. Comments from members of the local community revealed a need for greater involvement in downtown redevelopment by the area's financial institutions, according to the examiners.

The $59 million Bank of Kansas of Lawrence, Kansas, has only a "limited" participation in local community development projects with "only a few" such loans on the bank's books. That bank does not have any local municipal bonds, according to CRA examiners.

The $134 million Marquette Bank of Golden Valley, Minnesota, which received a needs improvement rating on its first public evaluation, owns many municipal bonds. However, "none are investments in the local community," according to its examiners during its first public evaluation.

Admirable Goals but No Results

It is not enough for a bank to be aware of community development projects if the level of participation is limited or nonexistent. River Oaks Bank of Houston, Texas, which received a needs improvement rating on its first public evaluation, had a "limited" involvement in community development projects within its local community at the time of its first exam. Although management demonstrated a "desire to increase participation," the examiners reported that their "contacts have not resulted in any substantial action" as of that time.

The CRA plan of Cole Taylor Bank of Chicago, Illinois, called for an "increased bank presence in community neighborhoods" and "target loan programs for community improvement." There is "no indication" that these goals have yet "resulted in performance through an affirmative response," according to CRA examiners.

In a few instances, banks with needs improvement ratings were not rated under this assessment factor for one reason or another. One example in San Francisco was previously provided. Another example involves the First National Bank of Ipswich, Massachusetts. It maintained listings of a "limited" number of local community development projects showing management involvement and affiliations. However, the "level and extent of these activities could not be accurately determined," according to the examiners. Consequently, there was no conclusion reached regarding that bank's performance under this assessment factor.

Ability to Meet Credit Needs (Assessment Factor K)

Banks with needs improvement ratings play only a limited role in learning about and developing projects to encourage economic revitalization and growth. Such institutions rarely make community development contacts with government or private sector representatives.

Very Conservative Approach to Economic Development in Houston

River Oaks Bank of Houston, Texas, which received a needs improvement rating on its first public evaluation, was typical of such banks. It was characterized as only playing a "limited" role in economic development projects. While the bank demonstrated a "willingness to learn" more about such programs, the board has taken a "very conservative approach in actually becoming involved in such programs," according to the examiners at the time of their first evaluation.

This assessment factor, like the previous one, overlaps other factors in certain areas. For example, a bank with a poor record of ascertaining credit needs relating to community development projects (assessment factor A) and a limited marketing program to encourage discussions with community development representatives (assessment factor B) may be downgraded in their rating under this assessment factor. A case in point involves Farmers and Merchants Bank of Long Beach, California. It was cited under this assessment factor because its "lack of marketing efforts" may prevent awareness of the bank's loan programs by public and private entities.

Two Failing Thrifts Given Some Leeway

The intent of this assessment factor is to measure a bank's performance in meeting community credit needs relative to its financial condition and size, legal impediments, local economic conditions, and other factors. Banks with needs improvement ratings have been criticized on all of these bases.

The $118 million Birmingham Federal of Birmingham, Alabama, had a limited ability to finance community development projects due to "financial and regulatory constraints, and economic conditions affecting the thrift industry." The $54 million Davy Crockett Federal Savings Bank of Crockett, Texas, was deficient under this assessment factor due in part to that bank's "financial capacity" at the time of the evaluation. Both of these thrifts have since failed.

The most common criticism of banks with needs improvement ratings under this assessment factor was that they were not doing enough relative to their size. This was especially the case for a number of large

thrifts and some smaller ones that were subsidiaries of large holding companies.

Great Western Subsidiary in Colorado Not Doing Enough

The performance of Bell Federal of Chicago under this assessment factor was considered "inadequate" based on that institution's "financial condition and size." Given the resources and capabilities of this $1.9 billion institution, which is the fifth largest savings and loan in the Chicago area, "one would expect Bell Federal to do more" under this assessment factor, according to the examiners. Similarly, the $4.0 billion Apple Bank for Savings, one of the largest thrifts in New York City, had only a "limited" role in community development projects "in view of the financial resources available" to it.

SafraBank II of Pompano Beach, Florida, which received a needs improvement rating on its first public evaluation, had only limited community development efforts in one of its two communities. Its efforts in its Broward County community were "not reflective of the bank's size and financial condition." The bank's "less than satisfactory community development efforts" were due to a combination of factors, according to its examiners: a low loan-to-deposit ratio, disproportionate lending patterns, lack of community development investments, and limited community leader contacts.

First Community Industrial Bank of Lakewood, Colorado, which received a needs improvement rating on its first public evaluation, is a subsidiary of Great Western Financial Corporation, which also owns the nation's second largest thrift. The level of First Community's activity under this assessment factor was rated less than satisfactory "given the size and financial condition of the bank's parent company."

Management Change at Community Bank in Florida Limits CRA Efforts

At the opposite extreme of large banks that don't do enough are small and/or new banks that are limited in their ability to participate in community development projects. The $65 million First Executive Bank of Philadelphia, Pennsylvania, was subject to limitations on the level of its community development investments because it was a "start-up institution" in the highly competitive environment of center city Philadelphia.

Only a limited amount of resources are available for CRA activities at the $105 million Boston Private Bank and Trust Company. This is "due to an operation period of only three plus years and current budget constraints," according to its examiners. More resources and assets will be devoted to CRA activities "as profits increase," according to management.

Banyan Bank of Boca Raton, Florida, which received a needs improvement rating on its first public evaluation, was not active in community development programs at the time of its first evaluation. The fact that the $35 million bank was "small and relatively new" at that time precluded such participation, according to its examiners. The bank's CRA performance has also been affected because of a "recent change in senior management," who concentrated their efforts on internal operations rather than community credit needs, according to examiners.

Bank in Puerto Rico Faces Strong Competition and Weak Economy

Local economic conditions may have a bearing on a bank's ability to meet various community credit needs. First Interstate Bank of Denver, Colorado, was involved in several community development projects "despite difficult local and regional economic conditions."

Ponce Federal Bank of Ponce, Puerto Rico, is "strongly affected by the competition" from both commercial banks and small mortgage bankers as well as by "certain regulatory constraints." The examiners noted that Puerto Rico's economy is generally poor, with a large low- and moderate-income population. Even though it has a moderately priced housing stock, a large segment of Puerto Ricans are "still unable to acquire the funds needed" to purchase homes. This economic condition places a greater burden on financial institutions there to provide such credit.

Unequal Treatment of Different Communities by Small and Big Banks

Some banks with needs improvement ratings may be criticized under this assessment factor for an inconsistent or unequal treatment of its different communities. The case of SafraBank II of Pompano Beach, Florida, which was criticized on this basis in its first public evaluation, was noted above.

Glendale Federal Bank of Glendale, California, one of the nation's largest thrifts, has delineated communities in both California and Florida. While participation in community development projects in California is apparently adequate, this is not the case for Florida, where its activity is "less than expected considering its financial capabilities and resources." Even though that bank has met with nonprofit and government agencies about community development projects in both California and Florida, "actual participation has been limited."

Norstar Bank of Buffalo, New York, which received a needs improvement rating on its first public evaluation, has participated in economic growth and revitalization projects in the form of direct loans, contributions, and technical assistance. This participation, however, has been "inconsistent by region," according to its examiners.

"Nonbank Bank" Restricted from Commercial Lending

Legal impediments may represent a constraint for some banks in terms of the types of loans that may be offered. A few banks with needs improvement ratings were noted as being constrained by law to only offer consumer loans. For example, industrial banks chartered in Colorado are limited to savings and time accounts on the deposit side and consumer credits on the loan side. This constraint of only lending to consumer borrowers was relevant for the $18 million First Community Industrial Bank of Fort Collins, Colorado, and the $16 million Resources Industrial Bank of Denver. Both of these banks were identified by their examiners as being limited in their "size and financial capacity."

First Signature Bank and Trust Company of Portsmouth, New Hampshire, is a subsidiary of John Hancock Mutual Life Insurance Company. The bank was chartered in 1985 as a "nonbank bank" and is primarily engaged in issuing open-end credit extensions under its VISA credit card plans. One of the limitations imposed on nonbank banks by the Competitive Equality Banking Act of 1987 is that the bank can only make consumer loans. Because it is restricted from commercial lending, this bank cannot participate in certain government or community development lending programs.

"Management Deficiencies" Hampered CRA Efforts

There are other factors that may effect a bank's ability to meet community credit needs. For example, EurekaBank of Foster City, California, which received a needs improvement rating on its first public evaluation, was "hampered in its efforts to meet community credit needs due to past operating and management deficiencies," according to bank management. The examiners noted at that time that the bank had been operating under current management for about two years. Management also indicated that its CRA performance was further limited by its "shift from a wholesale business to a retail business" about fifteen months prior to its first evaluation.

The $377 million Safra National Bank of New York City considers "wholesale banking and lending to high net worth individuals" to be its area of expertise. According to examiners, the bank is located in an area "saturated with larger institutions, most of which possess greater name recognition, asset size and branch networks." The examiners concluded that the bank's "size, its location, and area of expertise has negatively impacted" its ability to meet community credit needs.

Boston Private Bank's Overall Record in Serving All Segments of Community Called "Failure"

Some banks specialize in a particular type of banking such as wholesale, foreign, credit card, and so on. Some retail banks target a specific segment such as the affluent, small businesses, or a certain ethnic group. These banks may be subject to such a self-imposed constraint in meeting the credit needs of the entire community.

For example, because the Boston Private Bank and Trust Company is primarily a private bank serving "upscale" clients, it is limited in its ability to comparably serve the other (low-, moderate-, and middle-income) portions of its community. Therefore, the bank must "demonstrate a superior CRA performance in other areas," such as community development or special credit programs, according to its examiners. In the case of that bank, its current level of participation in these other areas was "not considered adequate to offset its overall record of failure to service all segments of the community."

It goes without saying that a bank's participation in various economic revitalization and growth projects and contacts with public and private representatives regarding these must be documented. In the case of Bay View Federal Bank of San Mateo, California, the bank communicated its desire to participate in community development projects to developers and local government agencies. There was, however, "no documentation of this within certain areas of the delineated community," according to the bank's examiners.

Other Factors (Assessment Factor L)

Banks with needs improvement ratings generally have a limited degree of involvement in other activities that contribute to its efforts to help meet community credit needs. This assessment factor usually mentions positive factors that a bank may have to its credit that may not have fit neatly into other assessment factors.

Community Banks' Good Deeds Mentioned but Given Little or No CRA Credit

Many of these other factors may have little or no "CRA credit" but are nonetheless mentioned, if only to recognize the bank's efforts. Sometimes it appears that such CRA-irrelevant factors are only mentioned as a token gesture to assuage bank management and let them know that their good deeds were considered (although given little or no CRA credit).

The scope of this assessment factor depends to a great degree upon the examiners. For example, virtually all banks make charitable contributions; although, only a portion of them (e.g., those for housing groups) may be eligible for CRA credit. Some examiners will mention these contributions, and others will not.

For example, DuPage National Bank of West Chicago, Illinois, is typical in that it makes charitable contributions to various organizations and events. The bank also provides free parking for customers of downtown businesses in a large parking lot it owns and maintains. Even though the examiner mentioned these items, the extent of CRA credit for them became an issue when the examiners noted that "it is not documented how these activities help to meet or ascertain community credit needs."

The First National Bank of Florence, Alabama, is involved in a program where its employees perform services for local volunteer agencies. Although these programs are obviously very worthwhile and useful, the examiners noted that "these events are not utilized by management to help assess and determine community credit needs."

First Interstate's Community Efforts Cited but CRA Credit Questioned

Even if a bank provides some type of community service specifically designed to aid low- and moderate-income areas, the CRA credit may be limited if community credit needs are not ascertained or met in one way or another. First Interstate Bank of Seattle, Washington, engaged in only "minimal activities" which met community credit needs and are not covered under other performance categories. For example, that bank sponsored a contest for low- and moderate-income neighborhoods that resulted in a grant for a local project. The CRA examiners at that bank hastened to add that this activity was "not necessarily for community credit needs."

Most banks with needs improvement ratings express a willingness to participate in other activities which meet community credit needs only when specific proposals or requests are brought to the bank's attention. This was the case with both the Community Bank of Waco, Texas, and the DeWitt Bank and Trust Company of DeWitt, Arkansas.

This assessment factor also provides the examiners an opportunity to emphasize a positive or negative point made in another assessment factor. Because this is a "catchall" category, examiners have a wide degree of latitude as to what is included under this assessment factor.

For example, First Interstate Bank of Oregon in Portland, Oregon, was cited under this assessment factor for its lead role in starting its own community development corporation for financing small business. Although this corporation was briefly mentioned under a previous assessment factor, it was discussed in greater detail under this one. The examiners pointed out, however, that "only one loan" was made through this new program. The bank's marketing efforts, which was the subject of yet another assessment factor, were also mentioned under this assessment factor. Although First Interstate Bank of Oregon had made a number of different marketing initiatives, the examiner noted that these "were not all documented." This documentation criticism was not made under the marketing assessment factor.

Private Banking for the Affluent Called "Directly Contrary" to CRA

Many banks with needs improvement ratings have made important and worthwhile contributions of many different types, which were mentioned under this assessment factor. While there appears to be some inconsistency among CRA examiners as to what is and is not included, any material that bears upon a bank's "CRA spirit" is often cited here.

Whenever an examiner perceives the "wrong" CRA attitude at a bank, this assessment factor provides an opportunity to bring in additional material documenting this position. For example, while a number of banks with needs improvement ratings focused on specific affluent or small business groups, there was only one instance of a very strong statement by an examiner questioning the consistency of such market segmentation with CRA.

This was the case of Boston Private Bank and Trust Company, which targets affluent individuals. The examiners stated that such goals are "directly contrary to the purpose of the CRA regulation." Considering the examiners' strong view, it is not difficult to understand why that bank received a needs improvement rating.

7. CASE STUDIES OF BANKS NEEDING IMPROVEMENT

INTRODUCTION

This chapter contains three case studies involving banks with needs improvement ratings. The first case study will examine a unique situation, the only one of which we are aware, where a regulator upgraded (unjustifiably in our opinion) an evaluation after it was made public because one piece of "relevant" information had not been made available to the examiners. We believe there may have been some regulatory favoritism present in this unusual case study, which involved the acquisition of one of our nation's largest failed banks.

The second case study contains an anatomy of the only four banks and thrifts in the nation that have been *downgraded* in their CRA ratings as of year-end 1991. All these downgrades were from satisfactory to needs improvement.

The final case study compares two banks, one in New York's Chinatown and the other in L.A.'s Koreatown. Both probably should have received needs improvement ratings in their first public evaluations, but the result was a satisfactory rating in the first instance and a substantial noncompliance one in the second instance. This case study attempts to answer the question as to who really needs improvement, the regulated banks or the regulators?

CRA AND THE SALE OF THE BANK OF NEW ENGLAND—A CASE OF REGULATORY FAVORITISM?

Most Multiple CRA Exams Result in Same or Upgraded Rating

Chapter 3 reported that about 2% of all banks with public CRA ratings had received a second one as of December 31, 1991. About 15% of all ratings made as of year-end 1992 were multiple ratings.

Chapter 3 pointed out that over half or 55% of the 142 multiple bank and thrift ratings as of year-end 1991 maintained the same (usually satisfactory) rating. While there have only been four cases of downgraded ratings (see following case study), 42% of all multiple evaluations over this time frame have resulted in upgraded ratings. Almost all of these upgradings have been from needs improvement to satisfactory ratings. Conversely, the four downgradings (3%) as of year-end 1991 have been from satisfactory to needs improvement.

The Most Unusual CRA Upgrading Ever

Of all of the upgradings we reviewed from needs improvement to satisfactory, one stood out as being the most unusual by far. This was the case of Norstar

Bank, N.A. of Buffalo, New York, the third largest bank subsidiary of Fleet/Norstar Financial Group.

That bank's initial public evaluation was dated October 29, 1990, and resulted in a "needs improvement" rating. That document was marked "Preliminary Draft." It appears that the evaluation with that initial rating was transmitted to the bank on March 22, 1991. The actual rating was apparently to be made public 30 business days later, on May 3, 1991. Our review of that evaluation clearly indicated that a needs improvement rating was appropriate.

We were quite surprised to learn that a second evaluation for that same bank became public shortly thereafter but with the *same* October 29, 1990, date on it. This was highly unusual to say the least. In other words, it was as though the first evaluation never existed, and this was a revised version with the same date. There was no "Preliminary Draft" marking on this second one.

Two Nearly Identical CRA Evaluations with Different Ratings

The bank apparently received the results of this "second" evaluation on May 21, 1991, and it was made public on July 2, 1991. What was most surprising was that, with the exception of a few sentences under one assessment factor, the evaluations were identical. There was, however, one big change. The new evaluation carried a "satisfactory" rating as compared to the "needs improvement" rating on the first one. However, both of these evaluations still had the same examination date of October 29, 1990. Both of these evaluations are included at the end of this chapter, along with the accompanying cover letter for the second evaluation. (See Figures 7-1, 7-2 and 7-3.)

A comparison of the two evaluations side-by-side will show that they are in fact identical with the exception of the rating, the "Preliminary Draft" marking on the first one, and one paragraph contained under assessment factor E pertaining to the bank's geographic distribution of credit extensions, applications, and denials. Thus, this case study provides us with an almost perfect "control"; we are able to hold everything else constant (i.e., *ceteris paribus*) except for one change in one assessment factor and then associate a direct ratings improvement with it.

More importantly, this case study suggests the possibility of regulatory favoritism by the OCC in its handling of the second upgraded CRA evaluation. This involved the then proposed acquisition by that bank's parent, Fleet/Norstar Financial, of the failed Bank of New England franchise. This case study will first compare the contents of these evaluations and then relate them to the facts surrounding that acquisition.

"Last Minute" Geocoding in First Evaluation Too Late to Help "Unaware" Management

The first public evaluation of Norstar Bank, N.A. with a needs improvement rating stated under assessment factor E that management was "unaware of the distribution of loans, applications and denials" throughout its community. The first evaluation further noted that a report on the geographic distribution of the bank's loans and deposits (but not applications and denials) had "recently been completed." The report, however, had "not yet been thoroughly analyzed and utilized by the bank in establishing loan policies/products/services and marketing."

Thus, the first evaluation indicates that management was unaware of its loan distribution but made an effort to correct this deficiency just prior to or perhaps during the examination. The loan and deposit geocoding report had just been completed then, but because there was no thorough analysis or utilization of it, the bank apparently received little or no credit for it. This is typically the case for "last minute" analyses before or during an exam.

"One-Third Low-Mod" Statistic Key to Second Evanuation

The second evaluation with a satisfactory rating reversed the examiners' findings from the first exam by reporting merely one statistic from this new accepted geocoding report. Assessment factor E of the second evaluation for the bank states that "approximately one third of its total loans are in low to moderate income areas." This was the only new fact differentiating the two exams. The bank is apparently commended in the second exam because its primary market "tends to be a moderate income one" and also because the bank has "not aggressively pursued upscale customers."

This latter information regarding the bank's profile in its community and its market segmentation strategy was obviously known at the time of the first exam but was not mentioned there. It was probably only cited during the second exam because it supported the new "one-third low-mod" finding from the now available geocoding report and also supported the upgraded rating.

Still No Data on Loan Denials or Applications in Second Evaluation

The second evaluation goes on to state that "management is in the process of collecting data on loan denials." Thus, the only new data that was received during the second exam was information on total loan extensions by area. We don't even know if these were by census tract or zip code. This additional disclosure on the planned denial data is relevant because this bank apparently did *not* complete the recommended analysis of loan applications or denials but only of loan extensions. This is a frequent area of criticism for banks with needs improvement ratings (see previous chapter).

The second evaluation goes on to state that management "plans" to use the soon to be collected data on loan denials in conjunction with the recently collected loan data in "restructuring and refining loan policies, products, services and marketing." These were only "plans" with no actual implementation of the results of this "analysis" ever having been done. Furthermore, there was no mention of any effort to collect data on the geographic distribution of loan applications.

The first exam criticized management for being "unaware" of the "distribution of loans, applications and denials within various segments of its community." Thus, by the time of the second exam they had only gathered some information on one of these three items, namely the distribution of loans. Specifically, only one actual statistic (the one-third low-mod fact) was cited from this new report. At the time of the second exam the bank was "in the process of collecting data on loan denials," one of the other two original omissions, with no mention whatsoever of the third omission involving loan applications.

Vague "One-Third Low-Mod" Finding Not Unusual for Big City Banks

In summary, the only factual difference between the two evaluations was new information that approximately one-third of the bank's loans are in low- and moderate-income areas. This is not a surprising finding for many city banks, since about 40% of the nation's households are low- and moderate-income to begin with, according to the 1990 Census. This fact follows from the standard definition that low- and moderate-income households have incomes at 80% or less than the median income level. Thus, the one-third low-mod finding is likely to be the case for many large retail banks operating in big cities.

We don't know if all or most of those one-third of loans were in moderate- *or* low-income areas and whether or not they were in substantially minority areas. Also, we don't know if the loan recipients themselves were low- and moderate-income individuals, because individuals of any income category can reside in low- to moderate-income areas. We saw in the case of Harris Bank of Chicago that fewer than one-third of approved loans in "low-mod" areas were going to truly "low-mod" borrowers. Importantly, we don't even know if it's one-third of the dollar value of Norstar Bank, N.A. loans or the number of them, and there can be a big difference between the two.

Thus, the vaguely-stated fact that a large retail bank in a big city has approximately one-third of its number or dollar volume of loans in "low- to moderate-income areas," which may be true for many such banks, is apparently sufficient to justify an OCC rating upgrade from a needs improvement to a satisfactory, with everything else remaining constant. This is indeed a very important conclusion, as it provides great insight into the CRA examination process by the OCC, that bank's examiner. However, the relevance of this conclusion may be affected by other facts to be discussed below.

20 Reasons Why a Needs Improvement Rating Was Justified in Second Evaluation

A review of the bank's performance under other assessment factors indicates that it clearly deserved a needs improvement rating. That is, with the exception of assessment factors D, F, L, and E (in the second evaluation), the bank is criticized under every other assessment factor. Specifically, the bank is criticized at least once under assessment factors A, C, B, I, J, G, H, K, and on the reasonableness of its delineated community. Even counting the "improvement" in assessment factor E, with the one-third of lending in low- and moderate-income areas, we do not believe that the other factors in their totality justify a satisfactory rating for this bank by any stretch of the imagination.

The following items of criticism in both the first and second evaluations of Norstar Bank, N.A. document what we believe to be an overall needs improvement CRA performance regardless of one additional factual finding in assessment factor E during the second evaluation. The list below identifies 20 different criticisms by assessment factor. In cases where there is more than one criticism for a given assessment factor (e.g., A), they will be identified as A1, A2, and so on.

A1. Management's method of determining credit needs in their five delineated communities is "inconsistent."

A2. The quality of the detail in the call program provided by the regions to the CRA department is "inadequate."

A3. The depth of detail demonstrating community contacts and ascertainment efforts is "especially lacking" in three regions.

C1. Bank records "do not show meaningful participation" by the board in its CRA process.

C2. The bank formed its CRA committee in October 1990, the month of its public exam.

C3. There was "very little evidence" showing direct personal participation by the bank before October 1990, other than a list of organizations to which the directors belong.

B1. The CRA officer maintains "limited documentation" of the bank's marketing and advertising programs.

B2. There was "no evidence of review or analysis" by the CRA officer on the effectiveness of the programs.

B3. Demographics of media used, although available, are "not maintained" by the bank.

B4. Detailed demographic information on media used by the affiliated mortgage company is "neither maintained nor analyzed."

B5. Efforts to assist individuals and groups in understanding and applying for credit is "limited" to student loan products and SBA lending seminars.

I1. Management has "not analyzed" the extent of mortgage lending in its delineated communities.

J1. The bank has "not been consistent" in its involvement in helping to meet credit needs in all of its communities.

J2. The volume of government-guaranteed loans as it affects all regions is "indeterminable" based on a review of the bank's files.

J3. The bank's portfolio of farm loans is "limited" in contrast to the very large rural area considered to be the delineated community.

Area 1. Management's method used to determine the community boundaries "needs to be documented."

Area 2. The map displayed in the CRA statement needs only to reflect those portions of MSAs and counties that the bank reasonably may be expected to serve.

G1. The Board has "not approved" a written policy on branch closings and elimination of services to local communities.

H1. Management has "not adequately demonstrated" its participation in community development activities in other communities besides Buffalo and Rochester.

K1. Participation in economic growth and revitalization efforts has been "inconsistent" by region.

Profile of Other Banks Also Supports Needs Improvement Rating

We compared this performance evaluation to the profile developed in the previous chapter for banks with needs improvement ratings. Based on the above 20 criticisms of the Norstar's second "satisfactory" CRA evaluation plus other possible "errors of omission" that were not noted above, we have concluded that no more than a needs improvement rating could be justified in any case. This is true even after considering the new (one-third low-mod) fact under assessment factor E. The significant negatives noted above in almost every assessment factor outweigh the one new positive addition.

OCC's Likely Performance Category Ratings in Second Evaluation

We compared likely individual assessment factor and performance category ratings for Norstar Bank, N.A. for the first and second evaluations to reach this overall conclusion. Performance categories I and II would likely have been rated needs improvement, while categories IV and perhaps V would likely have been rated satisfactory. Thus, performance category III, which contains assessment factor E on the geographic distribution of credit, was the pivotal one.

The OCC probably justified its higher rating by noting that performance category III increased from a needs improvement to a satisfactory rating. However, we believe that the likely original needs improvement rating for performance category III would still be applicable, even with the new one-third low-mod fact. Both of the other factors (G and the Area) under this performance category were criticized.

The bank's performance under category V could be considered borderline. Also, there is a question that we raise below regarding possible technical and procedural compliance violations under category IV. In summary, we firmly believe that the bank should have received no better than an overall needs improvement rating, even after this new piece of information was allowed to be considered by the OCC.

OCC's Failure to Disclose Assessment Factor and Performance Category Ratings Shields Bank and CRA Examiners from Criticism

Comparison of the Norstar Bank, N.A. evaluation to those banks that have received satisfactory ratings would generally indicate a considerable disparity in most of the assessment factors. Thus, there is no question in our minds that the upgrade to a satisfactory rating for this bank was an improper and clearly questionable action, considering the facts of this situation. This is why we believe the above-mentioned *ceteris paribus* finding that a one-third low-mod finding will justify an OCC upgraded rating must be tempered by the facts of the situation.

Had the OCC provided individual assessment factor ratings in the first evaluation, they may have so constrained themselves that it would have been difficult to try to justify a higher rating. By refusing to disclose individual assessment factor or performance category ratings, the OCC (and now all other federal agencies) are able to shield themselves from this type of criticism for subjectivity and other questionable CRA examination procedures, as we have documented here.

If this situation were to be investigated more fully, a copy of the original confidential compliance examination would detail the performance category ratings and disclose whether or not there were compliance violations of a technical or procedural type by this bank. We believe that and other additional data would further document our position that Norstar Bank, N.A. never should have been upgraded to a satisfactory rating at that time.

Questions about OCC Regulatory Favoritism

Our comparison of these two evaluations raises more questions on regulatory favoritism than it answers. For example, why was this bank given a "second chance" when other banks are virtually never given this opportunity? Why was the first evaluation marked "Preliminary Draft" and then provided to the bank? Why wasn't this bank criticized for a "last minute" geocoding analysis? The fact that a geocoding analysis is done right before or at the time of an exam, when the results are not even available, is often a source of criticism for other banks. This bank not only was not criticized, but was actually rewarded with a higher rating!

Another question arises regarding the weighting of assessment factors in the overall CRA rating. In our opinion, performance category IV pertaining to discrimination and other illegal credit practices generally is and should be given the greatest weight. Why, therefore, was assessment factor E regarding the geographic distribution of credit apparently given so much weight in this instance?

Does this mean, as noted above, that any bank with a needs improvement rating should be able to receive a satisfactory rating just by documenting that one-third of its loans are in low- and moderate-income areas? If this is the case, then this truly sounds like a "credit allocation" interpretation of CRA performance, which should not be the case.

Both CRA and the December 17, 1991, FFIEC guidelines on geographic distribution (Appendix 4) emphasize the importance of knowing the distribution of not just loans but also applications and denials. Why, therefore, was this bank given credit and rewarded so well with an improved rating for just completing one of the three portions of the required analysis? In fact, at the time of the second evaluation, the bank had just been "in the process of" collecting data on loan denials, and no mention was even made of information on the geographic distribution of loan applications.

By agreeing to accept this "last minute" geocoding report for this bank, the OCC in effect granted the bank a second evaluation within a very short period after its first one. Most banks have to wait a year or longer for a second evaluation, but this one was almost done instantaneously.

OCC Disclosed Availability of Two Public Evaluations

Furthermore—and this is very important—the bank may have never reported that it received a needs improvement rating. This is because it can be interpreted that there was really only one evaluation for this bank. Consequently, this bank most likely did not have to suffer the potential adverse consequences of the publicity associated with a low rating.

The OCC put out a release dated November 25, 1991, identifying all public ratings of national banks in the state of New York during the July 1, 1990, to October 31, 1991, period. That bank only listed a satisfactory rating for Norstar Bank, N.A. and there was no indication that this bank had ever received a needs improvement rating.

The OCC monthly listing that was made available in early June 1991, identified the fact that a public performance evaluation of that bank became available for public review during the period of May 1 through May 31, 1991. This OCC disclosure, however, did *not* identify the fact that that bank had received a needs improvement rating at that time. Why would the OCC make this public disclosure of an exam's availability for a "Preliminary Draft"? Why not just wait for the final one?

As noted above, that first rating became "public" on May 3, 1991. However, the only people who would know about it were those such as us who obtained copies of it between the period of May 3, 1991, and July 2, 1991, the time when the second one became public. Thus, there was only a two month "window" in which the bank may have had to disclose the fact that it had received a needs improvement rating. Because it was marked as a "Preliminary Draft," the bank may have felt there was no obligation to make the first one public. We do not know whether or not the bank ever distributed any copies of the first "needs improvement" evaluation.

In early August 1991 the OCC disclosed that a public evaluation for Norstar Bank, N.A. had become available for public review during the July 1 through July 31, 1991, period. Because the second exam became public on July 2, 1991, this was the appropriate notification for it. Again, that notification did not disclose the actual rating. The only OCC release with a ratings disclosure was the above-mentioned November 25, 1991, one. The only indication that anyone would have that there were in fact two different public evaluations for this bank was the fact that both the May and July public listings from the OCC identified that public evaluations for that same bank had become available on each of those dates.

OCC's Confidential Cover Letter Raises More Questions about Regulatory Favoritism

When we obtained the second public evaluation, we noted with great interest the cover letter dated May 22, 1991, to the Board of Directors of Norstar Bank, N.A. from the Director for Regional Bank Supervision of the OCC's Northeastern District. A copy of this four-paragraph letter is found in its entirety as Figure 7-2.

The first paragraph of this four-paragraph letter noted that the letter was to be "treated with the same degree of confidentially [sic]" as the recently issued Report of Compliance Examination.

The second paragraph of the letter noted that the OCC had reviewed "certain factual information presented by senior management in response to certain areas of concern" noted in the Report of Compliance Examination. It appears that senior management at that bank took the initiative in presenting the new information on loan distribution. That paragraph went on to identify the additional information as the loan distribution.

The second paragraph concluded that "this documentation was not completely available to our examiners during the initial review." In other words, this bank was favored by receiving two reviews, the initial one and the present one. The first exam clearly stated that a geographic distribution of loans and deposits had "recently been completed," but that it had not been thoroughly analyzed or utilized by the bank. Therefore, management was in fact "unaware of the distribution of loans, applications and denials within various segments of its community," as stated in the first examination.

If the loan distribution documentation was not completely available to the examiners during the initial review, why did the OCC decide to have a second review to consider it? Was it only because senior management presented it to the OCC? This begins to raise the question as to whether some degree of favoritism or special treatment was provided to this bank for one reason or another.

The third paragraph of the May 22, 1991, letter stated that the new satisfactory rating was directly the result of the new loan distribution documentation.

The letter states specifically that "the documentation was sufficient to upgrade the rating" on assessment factor E to satisfactory. Thus, the change in rating on that one assessment factor, from what probably was a needs improvement rating, was enough to result in the bank's entire CRA rating being improved to satisfactory.

This information is important because it tells us that there was no other information made available to the OCC that could have been the basis for the improved overall rating. We know from this disclosure that the improvement in rating was justified solely on the basis of the new documentation. The rest of that third paragraph specified the information contained in the documentation regarding the one-third low-mod conclusion. This is basically a repeat of the information contained in the public portion of the second evaluation.

The fourth and final paragraph of the letter notes that the OCC fully expects the bank's board and management to "intensify their efforts to address the concerns remaining in the CRA Public Disclosure" (i.e., the second evaluation). This is the type of cover letter wording often accompanying a needs improvement rather than a satisfactory rating. It therefore appears that the OCC was cognizant of the bank's weak performance in the other assessment factors and may have wanted to make clear to the bank that it would have to "clean up" its performance in those other areas as well. As noted above, we believe that the relatively poor performance in the other assessment factors in their totality would still justify a needs improvement rating, even with this new piece of data.

Did the OCC Fail to Disclose Compliance Violations?

The last paragraph of that letter also requests that the bank provide a written response detailing its efforts to "correct the violations cited in the original Report of Examination and progress made in addressing the concerns noted." This is an important disclosure because it raises a new question as to the nature of the "violations" that were not reported in the public evaluations.

As noted above, assessment factor F in both evaluations only states that the bank is "in substantial compliance with fair lending and other credit laws." This is so general as to not rule out that the bank may have been in nonsubstantive, technical, or procedural noncompliance with some of these or other laws. As noted in the previous chapter, many banks with needs improvement ratings with violations of consumer compliance laws and regulations are solely of the technical type.

It therefore appears from this disclosure in this letter that there may have been some nonsubstantive, technical, or procedural violations at this bank, although they were not indicated in the public evaluations. If this were the case, this would be another example of the use of the "error of omissions" technique (i.e., purposely omitting an arguably irrelevant item) to justify grade inflation.

The last paragraph also requested that a copy of this information be forwarded to the Resident National Bank Examiner at Fleet National Bank in Providence, Rhode Island. Norstar Bank, N.A. is part of Fleet/Norstar Financial Group based there. This approximately $46 billion dollar bank holding company was the fourteenth largest such organization in the country as of year-end 1991.

Norstar Bank, N.A. Appealed Preliminary Needs Improvement Rating with Help of Top Compliance Consultant

We contacted the CRA manager at Norstar Bank, N.A. in Buffalo. The bank is now called Fleet Bank of New York, N.A. and is being merged into the FED-regulated affiliate Fleet Bank of New York. This bank representative stated that the bank had only one exam and one evaluation with a satisfactory rating. This was the "second" October 29, 1990, evaluation, an additional copy of which we received from them with the bank's current CRA statement. The CRA manager, who was not at the bank at the time of the original exam, did not think the bank had a geocoding system then but stated that improvements had been made since that time.

We also spoke with that bank's CRA Officer who managed the exam in question. We learned from him that the bank strongly disputed the needs improvement rating at the first exit interview and notified the examiners then that an appeal would be filed with the regional office. The bank then retained the ser-

vices of a very well-known and prominent compliance consulting firm that had authored the April 1990 *Examiner Manual* for the FFIEC and conducted numerous examiner training seminars for the FFIEC in this regard.

As it turns out, the principal of that firm, which bears her name, was a previous Deputy Comptroller of the Currency and responsible for OCC's enforcement of CRA during its first four years of existence. Moreover, we learned that the OCC's top CRA compliance examiner and spokesperson, who was also chair of the CRA subcommittee of the FFIEC's Consumer Compliance Task Force, left the OCC after 18 years there to join this same consulting firm in 1992.

We understand from the bank that it promptly pursued the appeal with the aid of this top consulting firm. The OCC's head examiner, who was an experienced regulator in this area, reportedly was "sent back" on site for another look at the bank. The bank's CRA officer did admit to the existence of a "Preliminary Draft" when we asked about it, but he felt it was not relevant as the appeal was successful in changing it.

Our Regulatory Favoritism Hypothesis

In our efforts to try to understand what happened during this unusual case, we first considered the possibility of this being just another subjective action by a regulator which, like much human behavior, we could not attempt to explain. As noted in other sections of this book, there are numerous instances of regulator subjectivities and inconsistencies regarding not just CRA ratings but also, in at least one case, the use of a cease and desist order primarily on CRA grounds.

We considered another hypothesis that could explain why these unusual events occurred at Norstar Bank, N.A. when they did. Our hypothesis, which can only be termed an allegation because of lack of additional corroborating evidence, is that the OCC took this unprecedented action and "flip-flopped" on its rating to facilitate Norstar's parent-winning bid for the failed Bank of New England at that time.

That is, we believe that if the original needs improvement rating had stuck at Norstar Bank, N.A., the federal bank regulators would not have been able to justify their selection of Fleet/Norstar Financial as the winning bidder for the Bank of New England franchise. Thus, our hypothesis is that regulatory favoritism, which benefited Fleet/Norstar Financial at the expense of the losing bidders, was at work. Our analysis described below suggests the acceptance of this hypothesis.

Bidding on the Failed Bank of New England

The Bank of New England Corporation's three subsidiary banks were declared insolvent by the OCC on January 6, 1991. Bidders instructions were mailed by the FDIC on February 11, 1991. These instructions were modified once on March 14 and a second time on March 22. On March 29, 1991, the FDIC received four bids on the failed Bank of New England franchise. Three of the bids on the entire franchise were from Fleet/Norstar Financial, BankAmerica Corporation, and Bank of Boston Corporation. The fourth bid, from New Maine Bank Associates, was only for the failed Maine National Bank portion of their franchise, but that bid was not pursued as it was not for the entire franchise. The FDIC was involved in an intensive period of bid analysis and negotiations with the three bidders. The winning bid was awarded to Fleet/Norstar Financial on April 22, 1991.

Bank CRA Ratings at Fleet/Norstar

Fleet/Norstar Financial had $32.5 billion in assets as of year-end 1990. Fleet National Bank of Providence was that holding company's largest bank ($9.8 billion), and the next three largest were all Norstar bank units in Albany ($4.8 billion), Buffalo ($4.2 billion), and Hempstead ($3.1 billion). For the reasons mentioned below, we believe that a needs improvement rating at this holding company's third largest subsidiary with $4.2 billion in assets or 13% of the total could have jeopardized the holding company's bid for the failed Bank of New England.

The other banks in the holding company had generally received favorable CRA ratings. Fleet National Bank, the holding company's lead bank, received an outstanding rating on October 29, 1990, the precise date as the rating for Norstar Bank, N.A. The Fleet rating was also completed by the OCC.

The FED gave the Fleet Bank of Maine an outstanding rating on July 16, 1990. The FED gave a satisfactory rating to Fleet Bank of New Hampshire on April 22, 1991. The FED had not completed an evaluation of the Norstar Bank, N.A. affiliates in Hempstead or Albany, New York, at that time. Similarly, the FDIC had not completed an examination of Fleet Bank of Connecticut as of that time.

Thus, at the time of the March/April 1991 bidding on the Bank of New England, Fleet/Norstar Financial had received two outstanding ratings for its first and sixth largest banks (one each from the OCC and the FED) and one satisfactory rating for its seventh largest bank from the FED. The rating in question by the OCC, which was changed from needs improvement to satisfactory, represented the fourth rating for the holding company's third largest bank. Had that rating been a needs improvement, this would have meant that one out of four of the holding company's bank ratings were below-average.

CRA Was an Important Issue in the Bidding

We believe that a needs improvement rating could have had serious repercussions on the bank's bidding for the failed Bank of New England. This is because the CRA performance of Fleet/Norstar Financial became an issue during the bidding negotiations. For example, there was well-publicized concern expressed over the alleged use of high-pressure tactics and foreclosures on inner-city homeowners in several cities by a holding company subsidiary, Fleet Finance. Fleet/Norstar Financial denied those allegations.

Also documenting the importance of CRA in this bidding process was the fact that two of the losing bidders, Bank of America and Bank of Boston, both made substantial CRA commitments at the time. While the Bank of America commitment was not contingent upon a winning bid, that was not the case at the Bank of Boston. Fleet/Norstar Financial itself announced a $100 million CRA planned investment contingent on a winning bid. Clearly, CRA performance was a prime concern for all parties.

One Weak Link in the Holding Company CRA Chain Can Derail a Merger

A needs improvement rating may be the basis for a merger denial on CRA grounds, as we saw in the FED's rejection of the merger application of First

Interstate BancSystem of Montana to merge with Commerce BancShares of Wyoming in October 1991. The First Interstate Bank of Colstrip, Montana (unrelated to First Interstate Bancorp in California), the smallest ($12 million) of the seven banks in that $687 holding company as of year-end 1991, received a needs improvement rating on October 26, 1990, from the FDIC. The other six banks in that company received satisfactory ratings. That FED decision, which was also in 1991, suggested that one weak CRA link in the holding company chain can derail a merger. In the Fleet/Norstar Financial case the needs improvement weak link was a much bigger link, actually that holding company's third largest bank.

OCC's Timing of Release of Original CRA Evaluation Was Critical

Fleet's winning bid was accepted on April 22, 1991. Thus, the timing of the release of the CRA public performance evaluation was critical. Had the original needs improvement evaluation marked "Preliminary Draft" become publicly known on a wide-scale basis on March 22, 1991, when it was made available to the bank, this could have caused a problem. However, the bank did not have to make that rating public until May 3, 1991. By that time Fleet had already won the bidding.

The needs improvement evaluation was transmitted by the OCC to Norstar Bank, N.A. on March 22, 1991. Actually, management had known about their first rating since the time of the exit interview in the fall of 1990. Thus, bank management and its outside consulting firm had considerable time to do something to try to get the evaluation changed. We know they were probably feverishly working on the loan geocoding report. This was a particularly critical period because the bids were received by the FDIC from the three bidders on March 29, just one week after the needs improvement rating was transmitted to Norstar Bank, N.A.

Did the OCC "Sit" on the Needs Improvement Evaluation to Delay Its Disclosure?

This raises the important question as to why it took so long for the original October 29, 1990, evaluation to be sent back to the bank by the OCC. Had they released it earlier in March or even in February or January, then the original needs improvement rating probably would have been made public during the bidding process.

We do not know if the OCC may have delayed sending the exam to Norstar Bank, N.A. so it did not have to make it public prior to its winning bid. This would have been a blatant act of favoritism. Since the original needs improvement evaluation was marked "Preliminary Draft," perhaps the OCC was going to delay the final one until the loan geocoding in question was done? This would justify the higher rating. But, why publish the existence of and transmit to the bank a "Preliminary Draft" in the first place? Also, the idea of a regulator possibly waiting for an examined bank to correct a cited deficiency for an immediate second review to justify a higher rating is unprecedented and suggestive of favoritism.

Similar Timing on Fleet's Rhode Island Evaluation

The public performance evaluation of Fleet National Bank of Providence, Rhode Island was dated October 29, 1990. This was the same date on the Norstar Bank, N.A. evaluation. The Fleet evaluation by the OCC was transmitted to the bank on March 18, 1991, for a publication date of April 29, 1991. These dates were quite close and only four days before the comparable needs improvement evaluation was transmitted to Norstar Bank, N.A.

Thus, if there was any effort to delay the transmission of the completed evaluation by the OCC to Norstar Bank, N.A., it would have also affected Fleet National Bank's evaluation, which was an outstanding one. However, public knowledge of an outstanding rating would have been helpful but not necessary, as long as it was satisfactory or better. Anything below satisfactory, such as the first needs improvement rating for Norstar Bank, N.A., could have been a big problem. Interestingly, the FED's July 1, 1991, order approving the acquisition pointed out the lead bank's outstanding rating and the fact that each of the other bank subsidiaries received a satisfactory or better CRA rating.

OCC's Five-Month Disclosure Delay for Norstar Bank, N.A. Was Unprecedented Compared to Peers

Delayed regulatory disclosure dilutes the value of the disclosed information. Nearly five months elapsed between the date of the initial Norstar exam and the transmittal of the completed evaluation to that bank. This was also the case for the evaluation for Fleet National Bank of Providence, Rhode Island, as noted above. Evaluations of banks in the same holding company are often completed at or near the same time.

Our comparison of the disclosure delays in three other large upstate New York banks by the OCC revealed significantly fewer delays compared to the Fleet/Norstar evaluations. For example, both Key Bank of Western New York, N.A. in Buffalo and Key Bank of Eastern New York, N.A. in Albany were evaluated by the same OCC regional office in New York on September 7, 1990. The completed evaluations were transmitted back to those banks on October 5, 1990, less than one month later. Both of these evaluations, which contained satisfactory ratings, were publicly disclosed on November 16, 1990. Key Bank of Buffalo is somewhat smaller than Norstar Bank, N.A. of Buffalo, but the Key Bank affiliate in Albany is somewhat larger.

Marine Midland Bank, N.A. is the largest bank in Buffalo. This bank, which also received a satisfactory rating, was similarly evaluated on September 7, 1990, by the same OCC regional office in New York. That completed evaluation was transmitted back to the bank on September 27, 1990, just three weeks later, and that evaluation was made public on November 8, 1990.

Thus, in all three of these cases involving large upstate New York banks that were examined by the OCC's same New York office that examined Norstar Bank, N.A. of Buffalo, the disclosure delays were approximately five times as short. That is, rather than the OCC's New York office taking five months to transmit the completed evaluation back to Norstar Bank, N.A., this was done within a month or shorter period at all three of these other large upstate New York banks that received satisfactory ratings. Again, the question remains as to why there was such a relatively unprecedented delay in the Norstar Bank, N.A. case.

The OCC's New York office that conducted these evaluations also examines banks in downstate New York, New Jersey, and Pennsylvania. The time between the CRA exams and the transmittal of the completed evaluations to the banks in those areas varied tremendously during this period. For the most part, these delays were considerably less than the one in the Norstar Bank, N.A. case.

More Research Needed on Our "Friendly Regulator Hypothesis"

Our preliminary analysis did not reveal a significant difference between regulatory disclosure delays and ratings. We were hoping to shed light on the hypothesis that banks with lower CRA ratings are granted longer disclosure periods by "friendly" regulators. This would better prepare the banks to handle public inquiries about their low ratings. For example, they would have time to make needed improvements to show that what happened in the "outdated" public evaluation is no longer relevant. More research is needed on our "friendly regulator hypothesis."

Neither the OCC's regional office in New York or the main one in Washington, D.C., to whom we were referred, would comment about this or any individual bank case. The OCC's representative in Washington, D.C., would only tell us that "a bank has a chance to correct misunderstandings or supply further information after it is given its preliminary CRA assessment and before it receives its final rating." No specific statistics on the number or disposition of such instances or CRA appeals were available from the OCC. Also, the only written material available on CRA appeals was the April 25, 1990, FFIEC Uniform Interagency CRA Final Guidelines, which basically states the above-mentioned general procedure with no further details.

Controversy over the Winning Bid— but Not on CRA Ratings Issue

There was considerable controversy over Fleet/Norstar Financial's winning bid for Bank of New England. In fact, several of the losers expressed considerable concern as to the basis for the winning bid selection. Also, important anticompetitive issues were raised, as this was an in-market merger for Fleet/Norstar Financial. However, none of these concerns had anything to do with the CRA ratings issue, which is being raised here for the first time.

As it turned out, the winning bid by Fleet/Norstar Financial was quite close to the second bid of Bank America Corporation. Many observers thought that BankAmerica was the winner and felt that Fleet/Norstar Financial was a "come-from-behind dark horse." Some observers questioned the Fleet bid because it was a joint one with takeover specialists Kohlberg, Kravis, Roberts and Company. BankAmerica Corporation took the unprecedented step of criticizing the latter bidder as a "speculative investor" and characterized the Bank of Boston Corporation as a "marginally capitalized" one. This was indeed a heated bidding battle.

Was the FED Aware of the Preliminary Draft of the CRA Evaluation?

The FED's final July 1, 1991, order approving the acquisition of the Bank of New England franchise by Fleet/Norstar Financial discussed the holding company's CRA performance. However, these discussions, as noted above, only stated that each of the bank subsidiaries received "CRA ratings of satisfactory or outstanding." There is no indication whatsoever in that final order that the winning bidder's third largest subsidiary had originally been given a needs improvement rating. It is in fact possible that the FED was not even aware that Norstar Bank, N.A. of Buffalo had received a needs improvement rating in the "Preliminary Draft" the first time around. We do know, however, from that final FED order that "the CRA record of an institution, as reflected in its examination reports, will be accorded great weight in the applications process." We learned from the 1992 LaSalle National Bank case that the FED can approve an acquisition by a bank with a needs improvement rating throught the troubled institution "loophole." There were no competitive bids being evaluated in that case, and the FED could argue that there were no ready alternatives to LaSalle's offer. This, however, was not the case with the Bank of New England.

Summary of Major Conclusions

The following summarizes the main conclusions we have reached from this case study:

1. The upgraded rating of Norstar Bank, N.A. from needs improvement to satisfactory was *not* justified on the basis of one additional piece of data (i.e., the one-third low/mod statistic). The bank's overall performance based upon what was disclosed (i.e., 20 different criticisms) clearly indicates that the original needs improvement rating should not have been changed. This would especially be the case if there were some technical violations of consumer compliance regulations and/or laws, which may have been the case.

2. If we accept the argument that the OCC's upgraded rating was justified, this sets a dangerous precedent as to what it takes to get out of the needs improvement category. Specifically, the OCC was clear in stating that the simple fact that one-third of this bank's dollar volume or number of loans (not approvals or denials) was in low- and moderate-income areas (and not necessarily to such individuals) was enough to justify an overall ratings improvement with all other items being held constant. This also supports the "credit allocation" approach to CRA and provides an unnecessarily high weighting to assessment factor E on loan geographic distribution. If any factor should be weighted more than others, it would be assessment factors F and D pertaining to discrimination and other illegal credit practices.

3. It appears that the OCC displayed favoritism toward Norstar Bank, N.A. and its parent Fleet/Norstar Financial on several counts. Why was Norstar Bank, N.A. allowed to submit "last minute" geocoding data which was not ready the first time around? Why wasn't the bank criticized for a "last minute" evaluation? Why wasn't the bank criticized for its failure to geocode applications (and denials for which it was just "in process")? Why was assessment factor E involving geocoding given so much credit? It is possible

that there were nonsubstantive, procedural, or technical consumer compliance violations that were not mentioned under assessment factor F. Why was this bank allowed the luxury of having a "Preliminary Draft" of an exam for two months with one rating, but get another one later with a better rating? Was this the only time the OCC ever granted an appeal where the protesting bank was successful in overturning the original examiners' findings? The OCC in effect granted Norstar Bank, N.A. a second evaluation almost immediately after the first one without making them wait a year or longer with a low rating, like many other banks. Favoritism may also have occurred regarding the OCC's long delay in returning the exam (see below).

4. It appears that the OCC may have delayed returning its completed October 29, 1990, evaluation to Norstar Bank, N.A. so it did not receive it until March 22, 1991. Thus, the bank did not have to make it public until May 3, 1991, but the FDIC had already accepted their parent's winning bid on April 22, 1991. In reality, no one knew that this evaluation was even available until the OCC's listing in early June 1991. That listing simply noted that an evaluation at that bank had become public, but there was no indication as to that bank's rating. This possible delay in returning the original evaluation and the public disclosure of it was critical, as this was the period in which Fleet/Norstar Financial was bidding on Bank of New England. This apparent delay caused the needs improvement rating not to become public during the course of the negotiations for the Bank of New England or at any time for that matter. The OCC's same New York office transmitted completed satisfactory evaluations of three other large upstate New York banks roughly five times as fast during this same time period.

5. It is our considered opinion that if the original needs improvement evaluation of Norstar Bank, N.A. of Buffalo became public during the bidding process for the Bank of New England Corpora-

tion, then Fleet/Norstar Financial could have lost the bid. This was a highly competitive bidding situation, and there was considerable controversy over the choice of Fleet/Norstar Financial as the winner. Their winning bid and the losing bid of BankAmerica Corporation were quite close, so much so that some observers believed that BankAmerica's bid should have been accepted. There were anticompetitive issues raised as well about allowing an in-market acquisition by Fleet/Norstar Financial. Because there was considerable scrutiny over the CRA performance of all three of the bidders, but especially that of Fleet/Norstar Financial, and because all of them made major CRA commitments during this time, CRA clearly was an important issue. We believe that the disclosure of this first needs improvement rating, which we believe was justified all along, could have caused Fleet/Norstar Financial to lose the bid. Thus, there appears to have been favoritism here by the OCC toward Fleet/Norstar Financial at the expense of BankAmerica and, to a lesser extent, Bank of Boston.

6. This case study once again documents the power of public disclosure. Had we never known about the original "Preliminary Draft" needs improvement rating and the conditions under which it was changed, we would have lacked this important insight into the resolution process of one of our largest failed banks. Subjectivity in any form by government regulators is undesirable, especially when it can be used to benefit one bank at the expense of another. To the extent that there was favoritism in this bidding process by the OCC, then this disclosure was very valuable, if we use this experience to make sure this does not happen again.

Fleet/Norstar's "Risk-Free" Acquisition of Bank of New England Was Immensely Profitable

Meanwhile, we should point out that this acquisition by Fleet/Norstar Financial, which expanded the size of that company by 40%, was very profitable for it and its investors, including takeover specialists Kohlberg, Kravis, Roberts and Company. Fleet/Norstar Financial's 1991 Annual Report stated that the acquisition, which was "structured to be substantially risk-free for the first three years," was expected to be profitable in 1992 and to "earn between $150 million and $200 million annually from 1993 to 1995." Updated financial data shows that this acquisition was immediately profitable and that actual profits are beyond expectations. The 1991 Annual Report also notes that "the FDIC's selection of Fleet/Norstar over several vigorous competitors was an important signal of that agency's belief in our company's underlying strengths. . . ." We know from this case study that the FDIC's selection of Fleet/Norstar over those vigorous competitors may also have been facilitated by favoritism on the part of the OCC, as documented above.

AN ANATOMY OF THE ONLY FOUR CRA RATING DOWNGRADES

Only 3% of Multiple CRA Exams Result in Downgraded Rating

Chapter 3 identified 142 banks and thrifts that had received multiple evaluations over the July 1, 1990 – December 31, 1991, time period. While 55% of those receiving multiple evaluations maintained the same (usually satisfactory) rating, 42% resulted in upgraded ratings (usually needs improvement to satisfactory).

Only 3% of all multiple ratings represented downgradings. These refer to just four banks, which were downgraded from satisfactory to needs improvement ratings through year-end 1991. Two of these downgradings were at California thrifts by the OTS, namely the large $2.8 billion Bay View Federal Bank of San Mateo, California, and the giant $23.4 billion Glendale Federal Bank of Glendale, California. The FDIC downgraded one bank, the $42 million State Bank of Springfield, Minnesota. Finally, the FED downgraded one bank, the $31 million Alief Alamo Bank of Houston, Texas. These assets are as of December 31, 1990, the approximate midpoint between both evaluations for most of these banks.

The "F" Factor as a Common Element in the Only Four Downgradings

The purpose of this case study is to analyze why these four banks were downgraded when virtually every other bank receiving a multiple evaluation either maintained the same rating or was upgraded. One possible answer to this question was cited in the previous chapter involving the discussion of assessment factor F on consumer compliance violations. Specifically, these four banks were among many that were cited for violations of various consumer protection laws and regulations. Each of these four was cited for both substantive and technical violations, with the exception of Alief Alamo Bank, which was noted as having "several violations" with no specifics given.

First and Second Evaluations at Four Downgraded Banks Differ Significantly in Length, Format, and Bank Response

There were some differences in the form of the public evaluations from the first satisfactory to the second needs improvement ones.

Alief Alamo Bank's first evaluation was completed on August 27, 1990, by the Federal Reserve Bank of Dallas, and their second was completed just over a year later on September 23, 1991. The first evaluation was seven pages long in its original form, but its second one was twelve pages. Neither one had specific assessment factor ratings, although the second one reached a conclusion at the end of each assessment factor. This was the only one of the four institutions that had separate bank and community profiles in each evaluation.

The West Region of the OTS assigned individual assessment factor ratings to the first evaluation of Bay View Federal Bank on August 13, 1990. That evaluation was seven pages long compared to the six-page evaluation they completed the second time around on May 13, 1991. That second evaluation contained neither individual assessment factor ratings nor specific conclusions for each assessment factor.

Bay View Federal Bank prepared a four-page reply on July 25, 1991, to its second needs improvement CRA evaluation. That document stated that the bank was "very disappointed" with the second rating. The bank felt it was "meeting the overall goals of CRA" but "failed to meet some of the technical requirements and documentation requirements." The bank further believed that the OTS was "incorrect" in its evaluation of "several" of the assessment factors. Surprisingly, this $2.8 billion bank concluded that its "limited size" and office locations represent "restrictions" on what they can accomplish in terms of CRA. Bank size obviously can be in the eyes of the beholder.

Because the same regulator completed the evaluation of Glendale Federal Bank, it followed a similar format. That is, the first evaluation on July 16, 1990, was eight pages long and had individual assessment factor ratings. The second evaluation of the same length on July 9, 1991, did not have individual assessment factor ratings or specific conclusions.

The Kansas City Region of the FDIC completed the CRA evaluations for the State Bank of Springfield, Minnesota. Their first evaluation on July 20, 1990, was six pages long and contained neither individual assessment factor ratings nor specific conclusions. The second evaluation of that bank on July 19, 1991, was seven pages long and likewise did not contain individual assessment factor ratings or specific conclusions.

Community Bank in Minnesota Refused to Send CRA Statement or Public Performance Evaluation

We should point out that the State Bank of Springfield was one of the few banks of the several hundred we contacted in this analysis that demonstrated a strong reluctance to send a copy of their needs improvement evaluation to us. That bank ignored our initial telephone requests for their CRA statement and the second public evaluation (along with any response to it).

Over two months later we made a second telephone request for the information, and we were told that a written request was required and that telephone requests "were not honored." Although we had not been informed of this requirement by the bank on the first calls, we complied and put our

request in writing. A week later, after not receiving this material, we requested and obtained a backup copy of the evaluation directly from the FDIC in case our written request was ignored.

This was fortunate because as it turned out the bank never sent us the requested CRA public evaluation but rather a copy of the confidential two page "Examiner's Comments and Conclusions" pertaining to that exam. As informative as that document was, it probably was not as interesting as that bank's recent safety and soundness exam, which we did not see. This is because that bank failed on July 17, 1992.

We were later informed by the FDIC (and we confirmed this with other federal banking agencies) that requests for CRA statements or evaluations need not be written but can be by telephone or fax. It didn't really matter in this case because we received the evaluation from the FDIC anyway, although much later than we had hoped for.

Downgrading Analysis Follows Performance Category and Assessment Factor Format

This analysis will follow the normal performance category and assessment factor approach. Our emphasis will be on those specific items that demonstrated a deterioration in performance. Again, because only 3% of all banks with multiple evaluations were downgraded, it is important to attempt to identify which particular factors are most likely to trigger a downgrading.

I. ASCERTAINMENT OF COMMUNITY CREDIT NEEDS

Activities to Ascertain Community Credit Needs (Assessment Factor A)

Alief Alamo Bank's credit ascertainment efforts appeared to be the same in both its first and second evaluations. Specifically, that bank relied upon personal contacts of its directors, management, and staff with various community members. While there was no criticism of this approach in the first exam, the examiners the second time around determined that there was not "sufficient documentation" on these contacts nor any credit/service information derived from them.

The second evaluation also stated that proactive ascertainment efforts at the bank appeared "infrequent." The bank was advised to broaden its contacts with additional segments of the community and to develop an appropriate "reporting mechanism." In summary, that bank needed "substantial efforts" to enable it to adequately ascertain credit needs.

The second evaluation noted that those recommendations were "included in the two previous CRA performance evaluations." Those recommendations were not in the *public* portion of the last performance evaluation. Therefore, these recommendations, which were critical of the bank, must have appeared in the confidential portion of the evaluation rather than the public portion. This immediately raises the question as to whether or not this relevant material was deleted from the public portion of the first satisfactory exam so as to better justify that rating.

Bay View Federal's credit ascertainment efforts were rated as needing improvement during its first exam. The second exam likewise concluded that there was a "less than adequate ascertainment" of credit needs, especially in two communities in the Bay area. Importantly, the second evaluation states that the bank made no effort to ascertain credit needs in Orange County, where it maintains an office. The bank was also criticized for not documenting efforts to target credit deficient areas through its mortgage broker system.

Although Bay View Federal was apparently being commended for a new "No Downpayment Loan" it offered during the review period, the examiners noted that a "very modest number" of loans were made under that program. The bank's reply to that evaluation disagreed by claiming their new program was "very successful" with 67 loans closed, representing almost $9 million in new credit in less than a year.

Glendale Federal's ascertainment efforts were rated as satisfactory during its first examination, and several examples were provided of different ascertainment activities. The second exam once again noted these various ascertainment contacts. The exam, however, criticized the bank for not developing an effective program to "identify and document specific credit needs" and translate these efforts into "new products or services" to meet those needs.

The bank was also questioned for the first time because it had "not effectively utilized or considered available demographic data" in its analysis of credit needs. This demographic data factor was not even mentioned in the first evaluation, although this deficiency most likely existed then. This raises the question of whether or not additional criticisms that could always be found (i.e., certain omissions) were not included in the first evaluation because it would not have supported a satisfactory evaluation.

The State Bank of Springfield mainly relied on daily customer contacts, participation in various local organizations, and "tenure in the community" to ascertain community credit needs. While the bank was not criticized at all in the first exam, the second one stated that the bank "maintains no documentation" of its community reinvestment activities. This deficiency was also "noted at the previous examination," but we could find no such reference in the public portion of the first exam. Again, our previous comments regarding the identical situation at Alief Alamo Bank are equally appropriate here.

In summary, it appears that the major weakness of downgraded banks under this assessment factor was the unresponsiveness of management to previously recommended (but not publicly disclosed) improvements dealing with the need to document credit needs ascertainment efforts. These cases support the view that documentation does in fact matter.

It appears that much of the criticism in the second evaluations could have easily been applied in the first ones but were just not made the first time. The fact that the conditions at many of these banks appeared to be quite similar during both exams supports the view that a much tougher approach was taken the second time around. This is especially true since management did not act on certain recommendations that were previously made for some of the banks.

These facts also indicate the possibility that some relevant criticism may have been omitted from the first exams with higher ratings, as they may not have been as easily justified. All of this suggests that CRA examiner subjectivity and inconsistency were at work here.

Board of Directors' Participation
(Assessment Factor C)

The first evaluation for Alief Alamo Bank had only one sentence under this assessment factor stating that the bank had not yet appointed a CRA officer, but another officer was "unofficially acting in that capacity." The second exam contained a one-and-one-half page verbose description of the requirements of CRA as well as several criticisms of the bank, which probably were equally as relevant during the first examination. This bank was criticized in the new exam for not implementing a CRA plan, inadequate participation by the board in CRA efforts, lack of a CRA employee training program, and failure to have an expanded CRA statement. It appeared that these FED examiners were going to throw the "CRA book" at this bank.

Bay View Federal received a satisfactory rating under this assessment factor during its first evaluation. The bank was commended then for various CRA reports and planning procedures, board CRA participation, an adequate CRA training program, and an expanded CRA statement. The bank was criticized only in the area of not having a formal system whereby directors could review the geographic distribution of loans. Their second evaluation did not mention these four positive items, which probably were still relevant, but rather contained a very general criticism pertaining to the lack of "established goals, objectives, or methodologies" for assessing CRA performance. That general criticism probably could just as well have been applicable during the first exam (and, in fact, for many banks). The only specific criticism contained in the second exam not contained in the first was the lack of improvement of CRA performance in two (East Bay and North Bay) communities. Also, various technical exceptions were noted in the second exam concerning the bank's CRA statement and public file.

Glendale Federal's rating under this assessment factor during its first examination was needs improvement. The first exam was critical in that board minutes did not reflect "active involvement" in the CRA process or related activities. This deficiency was apparently corrected by the second exam. However, the CRA statement was considered to be "voluminous

and inappropriate" as a tool to inform the public of the bank's CRA performance at the time of the second exam. Also, the maps and community description in the CRA statement were "not easily discernible."

The first evaluation at the State Bank of Springfield merely noted that the bank performed its required annual review of the CRA statement and that management relied upon its local board for knowledge of new community developments. The second exam also noted that the bank reviewed its CRA statement annually, but this time phrased it in a negative fashion. That is, board involvement "continues to be limited" to annual reviews. No mention was made of the use of the local board's community knowledge the second time around, although it probably was equally relevant. The same facts apparently were now being viewed through "needs improvement-colored glasses."

In summary of this assessment factor, it again does not appear that there were any significant adverse factors that occurred during the relevant review periods that affected this assessment factor for any of the four banks. Most of the new criticism in the second evaluations could have as easily been applied to the first ones, but this was not the case. It again appears that the examiners were inconsistent and exercised some subjectivities as to what was and was not included in the second exams, to better support their lower ratings.

II. MARKETING AND TYPES OF CREDIT OFFERED AND EXTENDED

Marketing Programs for Credit Awareness (Assessment Factor B)

Alief Alamo Bank used various advertising media and devoted one-third of its advertising to loans at the time of its first public evaluation. That evaluation also noted the bank's marketing efforts in various ethnic newspapers and its use of bilingual employees. The second evaluation, by contrast, failed to mention those positives, which were most likely still in effect. Rather, the new exam concluded that the bank's marketing efforts are only "marginally satisfactory and could be improved." The second evaluation noted that most advertising involves automobile loans, although the CRA statement lists other loan products. This was apparently meant as a criticism, but it is difficult to accept it as one unless the bank was advertising a specific credit service that was not appropriate for its market.

The bank was then advised to "expand its marketing efforts" based upon examiner contacts with "members of the community" who were "not sufficiently aware" of the bank's credit products and services. It is difficult to criticize an entire marketing program, which was not questioned in the first exam, based upon what may be random comments from unspecified members of the community. That is, we don't know if there was a representative or scientific sample used by the examiners.

The same "community contacts" commented that the bank's billboard at the intersection of two main streets is a highly visible means of marketing. The examiners then noted that the valuable billboard was "primarily used for promoting local functions as opposed to credit services." The implication clearly was that the bank should use its highly visible billboard for loan advertising. Could this be "advertising allocation" rather than credit allocation?

Bay View Federal received a satisfactory rating for its credit marketing programs in its first public evaluation. The bank's advertising programs were complimented during the first evaluation, and the only criticism was that there was not a significant effort placed on foreign language and other targeted advertisements.

The second evaluation was virtually a 180 degree turnaround highly critical of the bank's marketing efforts. The first one stated that the bank's advertising programs are "well-documented." The second evaluation, however, stated that the bank does not document efforts to assess marketing effectiveness or coordinate credit marketing throughout its community. There was additional general criticism that the bank's "marketing efforts are not coordinated with the institution's overall CRA efforts, nor are they targeted to low- to moderate-income areas."

It appears that each of these four criticisms, which could probably apply to many average or above-average CRA rated banks, just as easily could have been made during the first evaluation. The only specific new criticism was that the bank did not market its credit products in its Orange County community

where it has an office. But, as will be shown below, that office existed at the time of the first evaluation.

Glendale Federal received an outstanding rating for this assessment factor during its first evaluation. While the first evaluation complimented the bank for using Spanish-language advertisements, the second one criticized the bank for not targeting other ethnic groups within the delineated community. The first evaluation, however, complimented the bank for translating several lending brochures into Spanish and Chinese (and later into Korean and Vietnamese), but the second evaluation didn't mention these positives.

Rather than commend the bank for offering a new first-time home buyers loan program, the bank was criticized because its marketing efforts had "not been effective in informing the community of its availability." Again, general comments regarding overall advertising or marketing effectiveness are quite subjective and can be made for many banks.

The State Bank of Springfield's first evaluation contained only a fairly minor criticism about the bank's credit advertising, which represented about one-fourth of all that bank's advertising. That bank's second evaluation made a very general criticism that can be applied to many banks that there was no "formalized marketing program." This situation apparently existed the first time around, but it was not criticized then.

In summary, there were very few substantive changes for any of these banks during the review periods under this assessment factor. Again, most of the criticism toward these banks could also have been made during their first public evaluations but were not. Also, much of this criticism was so general and subjective that it could probably have been made against many banks, even some with average or higher CRA ratings. The use of unspecified and possibly unscientific customer contacts by examiners at Alief Alamo Bank is a matter of concern, considering the weight the examiners apparently placed upon that feedback.

Available Credit Services
(Assessment Factor I)

Alief Alamo Bank was not criticized under this assessment factor during its first public evaluation, even though it had a relatively low 38% loan-to-deposit ratio. Management was apparently able to justify that ratio on the basis of Houston's poor and volatile economy. That ratio had increased to 46% by the time of the second examination over a year later. However, this higher ratio was noted as being below the comparable 63% ratio for its peer group. But, such a peer comparison was not even made in the first exam when the bank's ratio was actually lower. Still, though, the bank's performance under this assessment factor was considered adequate at the time of the second exam.

Bay View Federal's first exam resulted in a satisfactory rating under this assessment factor. The only criticism under the second evaluation was the fact that the bank had not made any loans in Orange County, where it has a full service branch. The bank did, however, purchase a pool of loans there to offset the absence of loan originations.

Glendale Federal's performance under this assessment factor was rated as outstanding in its first public evaluation. This rating dropped to a satisfactory level by the time of the second evaluation. The bank was criticized at that time for failing to offer "flexible underwriting criteria specifically designed to meet the credit needs of low- to moderate-income individuals." It is quite likely that the same type of underwriting criteria existed for the bank's home loan products during both its first and second exams, but these were only criticized during the latter one. Also, the bank was criticized because it had "not identified the level of its lending activity" in its local community, although available documentation indicated a "substantial" volume of applications from within it.

The State Bank of Springfield was not criticized under this assessment factor during either the first or second evaluations. The second one contained specific information from the call report on the bank's 68% loan-to-deposit ratio and the composition of its loan portfolio. These statistics, which were not at all negative, were not included during the first evaluation but just as easily could have been.

In summary, none of the four downgraded banks had any major deteriorated condition under this assessment factor. The concern expressed by examiners at Bay View Federal Bank regarding the lack of lending in its Orange County community was only indicated in the second evaluation, although we will show below that this condition probably also existed at the time of the first evaluation.

Government Loan Programs
(Assessment Factor J)

Alief Alamo Bank's performance under this assessment factor was identical in both evaluations. That is, while the bank was an approved SBA lender, it had not yet originated any SBA loans.

Bay View Federal Bank received a needs improvement rating under this assessment factor in its first public evaluation. Although the bank did not participate in the VA or FHA loan programs, for which the bank determined there was "little demand" in its market area, it participated in several local government subsidized loan programs. The second evaluation made the same criticism regarding the lack of VA or FHA loans. This time the examiners failed to include the bank's stated justification for not participating. The second evaluation did, however, mention two of the bank's special credit programs.

The first evaluation for Glendale Federal rated the bank as needs improvement under this assessment factor. That bank offered SBA loans through one division and was involved in a subsidized loan program in a local community. The second evaluation does not mention either of these programs but rather criticizes the bank for not being involved in any government loan programs for housing. The examiners did, however, admit that certain loan products are "potentially viable alternatives," such as the bank's first-time home buyer program.

The State Bank of Springfield was involved in a number of different types of government loan programs, which were identified in the first evaluation. The bank's second evaluation lists a smaller number of such government programs, but it is not clear whether others were not listed or the bank no longer offered them. The second evaluation stated that the bank purchased "Farmer Mac" stock in 1988, but it had "not been involved with their programs." This same criticism would obviously have been appropriate during the first exam, but it was not made then.

In summary of this assessment factor, it appears that the performance of the four downgraded banks was quite similar at the time of the first and second evaluations. The main difference, however, was that CRA examiners were much more critical of the banks during the second evaluations in areas that could probably have been criticized just as easily during the first evaluations. This reinforces the subjectivities and inconsistencies previously referenced under the other assessment factors.

III. GEOGRAPHIC DISTRIBUTION AND RECORD OF OPENING AND CLOSING OFFICES

Reasonableness of Delineated Community

The delineated community for Alief Alamo Bank was considered reasonable in both evaluations. The first evaluation reported plans to plot credit extensions and denials and establish a loan monitoring program. By the time of the second evaluation, the bank only had plotted home purchase and home improvement loans on a census tract map. The bank was criticized for not reviewing or analyzing the results. The bank was then encouraged to plot a sample of other approved consumer loans as well as denied loan applicants for a particular period. The examiners noted that the recommended geocoding analysis of the distribution of approved and denied applications was made at the previous examination.

Bay View Federal Bank was deemed to have a reasonable delineated community consisting of eight counties in the Bay Area at the time of its first evaluation. This was not the case during the second evaluation because the bank failed to include Orange County, where it maintains a full service branch in its delineated community. The omission of the Orange County area in several assessment factors for this bank was probably its greatest source of problems.

We learned from this bank that their Orange County branch in southern California was purchased in October 1989. Thus, it existed at the time of the first public evaluation on August 13, 1990. Therefore, the examiners were just as guilty for not mentioning it when deeming the delineated community to be

reasonable at that time. The examiners' error of not catching this bank's mistake the first time around cost the bank dearly during its second exam. We were surprised that this point was not mentioned in the bank's reply to the second evaluation, as it was fairly critical of that examination.

The delineated community for Glendale Federal was considered reasonable in both of its public evaluations. The second evaluation, however, noted that the maps in the CRA statement did "not effectively identify" the delineated communities.

The State Bank of Springfield was considered to have a reasonable community defined as parts of three counties at the time of its first public evaluation. The delineation apparently was changed by the second exam when the local community included the entirety of those three counties rather than just portions of them. The new delineation was deemed to be "unreasonable due to its large size," according to the examiners during the second evaluation.

In summary of this assessment factor, two of the four delineated areas were deemed to be unreasonable. In the case of State Bank of Springfield, an expansion caused an unreasonable determination of that community. Importantly, Bay View Federal left out altogether the community surrounding one of its full service offices, but this same mistake was also made at the time of the first exam but just not caught by the examiners. The methodology used by Alief Alamo Bank was criticized for not containing the planned and recommended geocoding analysis.

Geographic Distribution of Credit (Assessment Factor E)

The evaluation of Alief Alamo Bank under this assessment factor in the first examination reviewed 1989 HMDA data. That analysis was limited because there was no indication as to how many of the loans were in minority or low-income areas. This analysis was conducted by the examiners (not the bank) at the time of the second evaluation. The examiners' analysis concluded that there was an "even distribution of lending" by the bank, with the "majority" of lending within the community. The bank was once again criticized for an "insufficient" geocoding analysis of its lending patterns.

Bay View Federal Bank received a satisfactory rating under this assessment factor in its first evaluation. Loans and applications were "evenly spread" throughout the community, and there was no evidence of "unusual gaps or obvious credit deficient areas within it." The bank, however, was criticized for not having a regular procedure to monitor the geographic distribution of applications, loans, and denials or the demographics of its community.

This criticism carried over to its second examination with particular emphasis on low- and moderate-income areas within one county where the bank was not receiving applications or making loans. The second evaluation raised the question as to whether or not there was a "reasonable distribution" of the bank's consumer credit applications, especially for low- and moderate-income and/or minority areas.

Bay View Federal's reply to the second examination noted that the bank made over $100 million in loans in low-income census tracts in 1990, representing almost one-fourth of all loans made that year. The bank's reply acknowledged, almost in a sarcastic tone, that it has "failed to track where each and every one of our loans are made."

Glendale Federal had a satisfactory rating under this assessment factor during its first examination. Both the first and second examinations noted that the bank monitors lending activity with respect to low- and moderate-income census tracts. Only the second evaluation contained the criticism that the bank had not identified the number of such tracts within its community. Both evaluations referred to minimum loan production standards or goals for low- and moderate-income census tracts, but only the second examination criticized the bank for not addressing the "reasonableness of the production standard." Finally, the second evaluation, but not the first, contained a very general criticism that the bank had not reviewed the "impact of its lending policies and procedures on the geographic distribution of its lending activity." Each of these criticisms could just as easily have been made during the first evaluation.

The State Bank of Springfield had approximately 70% of its loans and the "majority" of loan applications and denials within its community, according to its first examination. The loans were "evenly distributed" throughout the area. The examiners conducted their own geocoding analysis during the second examination, and they concluded that only 10% of the bank's loans were made in the several towns surrounding Springfield within the bank's three-county community. This constituted an "unjustified, disproportionate pattern" with respect to the bank's loan distribution throughout the various towns of its community. The examiners' review of denials, however, showed a "reasonable penetration" of the community.

The conclusion regarding the unjustified and disproportionate lending pattern during the second examination is in direct contradiction to the conclusion that extended credits were "evenly distributed" throughout the area during the first examination. The only change was an expansion of the delineated community, which picked up several small towns in the three-county area, where the bank probably had few or no loans. Also, the examiners conducted their own geocoding analysis this time. Considering that the examinations were only one year apart, the distribution of credit extensions probably did not change that much over this period. It appears that the examiners were displeased with the recently-expanded community delineation, which they previously referenced as "unreasonable."

In summary of this assessment factor, the basic geographic distribution of lending activity, when available, was reasonable for three of the four banks during both of the evaluations. Several banks were criticized for not having geocoded loan, application, and denial data even after it was recommended during previous exams. Some of the other criticisms could likewise have been made in the first evaluation but were not. Only in the case of the State Bank of Springfield did the examiners change their view on the reasonableness of lending patterns, although they probably did not change that much within one year.

Office and Service Record (Assessment Factor G)

There was no criticism of Alief Alamo Bank under this assessment factor in either their first or second exam. The much longer second evaluation noted detailed lobby and drive-in hours, but this was not the case in the first exam's discussion of this factor, which was only one sentence long.

Bay View Federal's performance was rated satisfactory under this assessment factor during their first examination. The second examination, however, criticized the bank for not having written policies for office openings and closings. However, this same criticism clearly would have applied during the first examination as well, but it was not made at that time. The difference probably was the fact that the bank closed four branches during the review period for the second exam, and no assessment was made of the impact of those closings. The bank's response to the second examination stated that there was "no negative impact" on any communities as a result of branch closings, since there were several other banking facilities nearby in each case.

Glendale Federal's rating under this assessment factor in their first examination was satisfactory. Many branches were closed or consolidated by the time of its second evaluation. But, there apparently was no problem since the closed branches were "not disproportionately located in low- to moderate-income neighborhoods."

The first examination of the State Bank of Springfield noted the bank's office and drive-up hours and the fact that no survey had been conducted on them. The hours were, however, believed to be "reasonable," according to that first evaluation. The same conclusion was reached during the second examination, which once again mentioned the fact that the bank had not performed a survey concerning banking hours.

In summary of this assessment factor, the substantive conditions were identical at the times of the first and second evaluations for three of the four banks. The only exception was Bay View Federal Bank, which closed four branches during the review period but did not have an impact assessment study made of those closings. The bank's reply after the second examination was to the effect that there was no adverse impact because there were other competitive facilities in those areas.

IV. DISCRIMINATION AND OTHER ILLEGAL CREDIT PRACTICES

Credit Application Practices (Assessment Factor D)

The performance of Alief Alamo Bank under this assessment factor was identical under both its first and second evaluations. The examiners only checked to ascertain that each of the nine types of loans listed in the bank's CRA statements were in fact being made during the relevant review periods.

Bay View Federal received a satisfactory rating under this assessment factor during its first evaluation. This was not the case at the time of its second evaluation when "various practices were observed during the review" that would have the effect of discouraging loan applications. Those practices, which were unspecified, were noted as being eliminated by the bank. Furthermore, credit training was being administered to affected personnel to assure that this unspecified problem was corrected. It is not clear whether these practices existed at the time of the first examination some nine months prior. The bank's response failed to address this assessment factor.

Glendale Federal received a satisfactory rating under this assessment factor during its first examination. The second examination, however, noted that certain loan policies and procedures "imposed more onerous terms based on the location of the property," which is a violation of a federal nondiscrimination regulation. Again, it is not clear whether or not this violation existed at the time of the first examination a year earlier and was either not discovered or reported by OTS examiners at that time.

The examiners expressed no concern under this assessment factor in either the first or second exams of the State Bank of Springfield. This was not the case, however, regarding the "F Factor," which is discussed below.

In summary of this assessment factor, two of the four banks had no changes in their performance. The two with observed changes were relatively significant ones representing practices that can discourage applications. It is not clear, however, whether these undesirable practices existed at the time of the first examinations at Bay View Federal and Glendale Federal.

They may have existed but were just not uncovered or reported in the public evaluations by the OTS examiners at that time.

Illegal Credit Practices (Assessment Factor F)

Both the first and second exams of Alief Alamo Bank revealed that there were violations of "several consumer laws and regulations," but none of these were specified as to type or severity. The second evaluation, of course, noted that the bank needed improvement under this assessment factor, especially since the same criticism was made in both exams.

Bay View Federal's performance under this assessment factor was rated as satisfactory during the first examination. This was not the case at the time of the second examination when various "substantive and technical violations" of the ECOA, the Fair Housing Act, and the federal antidiscrimination laws and regulations were identified. This represented a major deterioration of the bank's performance by the time of the second exam. Bay View Federal's reply to the second exam acknowledged that there were "several isolated documentation errors" but respectfully disagreed that they were "substantive or material."

Glendale Federal received a satisfactory rating under this assessment factor during its first exam. The first exam noted some technical violations that were corrected during the exam. The situation deteriorated considerably within the next year. The second exam concluded that the bank had violated "substantive provisions of anti-discrimination laws and regulations" including the ECOA, the Fair Housing Act, and OTS nondiscrimination regulations. The cited violations were limited to "particular divisions" of the bank, and there were additional "recordkeeping, reporting, and disclosure" violations.

The first examination of the State Bank of Springfield revealed no problems. This was not the case by the time of the second exam when it was found in apparent violation of both substantive and technical provisions of the ECOA and fair housing regulations. The apparent substantive violations were deemed to be matters of "significant supervisory concern."

According to the "Examiner's Comments and Conclusions" we received from the bank (instead of the public performance evaluation we requested), there were apparent systemwide violations of seven regulations. Two such violations involved the Real Estate Settlement Procedures Act where management did not give the customer a Special Information Booklet and a Uniform Settlement Statement. Two apparent systemwide violations of ECOA involved the failure to obtain supporting documentation for husband and wife signatures on a debt instrument and the failure to disclose the bank's name and address on loan denials. The other apparent systemwide violations included home ownership counseling, flood insurance, and the right to financial privacy.

Isolated exceptions at that bank involved truth in lending, fair housing, ECOA, fair credit reporting, and financial recordkeeping. These numerous systemwide infractions indicated "many deficiencies in the bank's compliance program which need to be addressed," according to the examiners. These infractions appeared to result from a "lack of familiarity with the requirements of the regulations and/or oversight," according to the examiners.

The above comparative analysis for these four banks, but especially the three last ones, substantiates our belief that assessment factor F is truly the CRA "death wish." In the last three cases the banks' performance deteriorated substantially in terms of this F factor by the time of the second exam. This factor and the previous one (D) are probably the two most important in explaining the downgrading of these four banks.

V. COMMUNITY DEVELOPMENT

Local Community Development and Redevelopment Participation (Assessment Factor H)

The performance of Alief Alamo Bank under this assessment factor was favorable during both exams. This was also the case for Bay View Federal Bank, which received a satisfactory rating under this assessment factor at the time of its first evaluation.

Glendale Federal had a satisfactory performance under this assessment factor at the time of its first examination. The second exam, while noting numerous positive developments at the bank, indicated it has experienced "limited success" in initiating community development programs without the help of a housing consortium. Also, the level of participation in community programs in Florida is "limited," probably because the bank was unable to successfully identify such a statewide consortium there. Furthermore, the bank's participation in self-initiated programs involving direct lending was limited in California. It is believed that all of these criticisms would have been equally as relevant at the time of its first evaluation, but they were not made then.

The performance of the State Bank of Springfield was considered to be favorable under this assessment factor for both of the public evaluations.

In summary of this assessment factor, there was little change in the performance of these four banks on the basis of their community development efforts. The only difference we could detect involved some general criticism of Glendale Federal's efforts, which just as easily could have been made at the time of its first examination.

Ability to Meet Credit Needs (Assessment Factor K)

Alief Alamo Bank received favorable comments under this assessment factor during its second examination. Management, but not the examiners, in the first examination indicated that the "bank's size is a hindrance" in their ability to meet credit needs due to the bank's low lending limits. These comments weren't made in the second exam, although the bank's size was virtually identical then.

Bay View Federal's performance under this assessment factor was rated as satisfactory during the first examination. The bank was criticized for a lack of documentation regarding its communications with public and private developers within certain areas at the time of its second evaluation. Documentation apparently was not a concern during the first examination.

Glendale Federal received a satisfactory rating for its performance under this assessment factor during its first evaluation. However, the bank's participation in development projects in Florida compared with California was "less than expected," considering the bank's financial capabilities and resources. Even though the bank has met with various agencies on these topics, "actual participation has been limited." Again, we believe this criticism could have just as

easily been applied in the first examination as the second one.

The Springfield State Bank was not criticized under this assessment factor in either its first or second examinations. Thus, this assessment factor, like the previous one, demonstrated few significant differences in any of the banks' performance between their first and second exams. The only exceptions were criticisms during the second evaluations, which probably were also relevant during the first examinations but were not made then.

Other Factors (Assessment Factor L)

Alief Alamo Bank's performance was considered adequate under this assessment factor in both of its exams. This was also the case for Bay View Federal Bank, Glendale Federal, and the State Bank of Springfield. Therefore, this assessment factor was not relevant in terms of differences between the first and second exams for any of these banks.

CONCLUSIONS

The CRA "Death Wish"

This comparative analysis of the four downgraded CRA ratings has confirmed some previous conclusions and documented some new ones. Probably the most important *tangible* conclusion which would explain why these four banks were downgraded involved the CRA "death wish," namely assessment factor F. Three of the four banks had a significant deterioration under this assessment factor in terms of both substantive and technical violations of consumer compliance laws and regulations. The fourth bank had several such violations, but they were not specified as to either type or severity.

This conclusion verifies what we already knew: that assessment factor F (and its related counterpart assessment factor D) are probably the two most important assessment factors in the overall CRA rating. This also means that performance category IV, dealing with discrimination and other illegal credit practices, is probably the most important one of the five in terms of a bank's overall CRA rating.

This conclusion is not a new one, and is in fact to be expected, considering the importance of compliance with consumer laws and regulations. However, this analysis provides us with an opportunity to document just how important these two assessment factors and this performance category are compared to others.

Broken Promises and Ignoring Examiners' Recommendations

The second important *tangible* conclusion as to why these banks were downgraded is that many of them simply did not make certain improvements that the banks themselves previously planned or promised or, more importantly, the examiners previously recommended. The latter type was clearly the more serious, and it was relevant for all of the four banks studied here except for Glendale Federal.

Hypothesizing the "CRA Examiner Subjectivity Range"

There were obviously many other differences between the first and second exams for each of the four banks. However, a great deal of these differences involved criticisms made in the second evaluations that probably could have just as easily have been made in the first evaluations but were not.

This leads us to an important *intangible* conclusion regarding this analysis, namely that there was a great degree of subjectivity and inconsistency on the part of the examiners in their CRA evaluations. We would hope this would not be the case with safety and soundness examinations, but we have no way to prove or disprove that because the results are not made public.

This problem of examiner subjectivity and inconsistency led us to hypothesize that a CRA examiner can probably move the rating of most banks by one notch in either direction from the "true" rating and be able to justify it in terms of the written evaluation. That is to say, we have hypothesized that the "CRA examiner subjectivity range" is plus or minus one rating around the "true" rating.

The fact that many of the assessment factors for the four banks covered in this comparative analysis were written so differently when many of the basic facts were the same provides support for our conclusion. We therefore believe that any two CRA examiners can look at the same set of facts indicating one

"true" rating and write significantly contrasting evaluations if desired, which could probably justify a rating either one notch above or below the "true" rating. The bank's "CRA spirit" and other subjective factors as perceived by the examiners most likely determine which direction this subjectivity "swing factor" will go.

Justifying CRA Grade Deflation

For example, if an examiner feels that a downgrading (i.e., grade deflation) in a bank's overall CRA rating relative to the true one is appropriate, each of the individual assessment factors in the evaluation can be written in such a way as to be critical of the bank. This is because there is always some type of analysis or plan or policy that a bank could have developed but did not, and the mention of it would be a criticism of that bank. This is the "error of omissions" technique. We noted several examples of this technique involving the four banks in this analysis. Also, positive CRA performance factors that may indeed be relevant may not be mentioned, and several examples of this were documented in the four banks reviewed here. This is also part of the error of omissions technique. We are not, however, suggesting that grade deflation occurred in any of these four cases. We are merely citing examples of how grade deflation can be justified.

Justifying CRA Grade Inflation

Conversely, if an examiner wants to upgrade a rating (i.e., "grade inflation") relative to the true one, then the selective "omission" criticisms would be excluded from the evaluation. All positive factors, regardless of how relevant, would be noted. Also, certain negative factual information (e.g., loan-to-deposit ratios, HMDA denial rates, etc.) may be excluded, because there is a great degree of subjectivity as to what is and what is not deemed to be relevant by the examiner under any assessment factor. An examiner can always argue that such (negative) factors were excluded because they were not relevant *or* that they were reviewed but not deemed important enough to include in the public evaluation. The following case study will provide two additional examples of evaluations and ratings at both extremes of this hypothesized CRA examiner subjectivity range.

Why Banks with Below-Average Ratings Should Prepare a Public Response

Another conclusion we have reached from this analysis is that all banks with below-average and especially downgraded ratings should prepare an immediate reply to the evaluation and distribute it with the requested public evaluation. Not only does the bank get to tell "their side of the story," but important missing facts, gaps, or explanations can be provided. Bay View Federal Bank's four-page reply was most helpful in this regard. Also, banks preparing such a response can be sure their next examination team will have read it in advance of their next public evaluation.

Three of Four CRA Downgradings Later Upgraded

This may have had something to do with the fact that Bay View Federal Bank's third evaluation on March 16, 1992, resulted in a satisfactory evaluation. Shortly thereafter on May 26, 1992, Glendale Federal was upgraded back to satisfactory, as was Alief Alamo Bank on August 3, 1992. Thus, three of the four banks in this case study were first downgraded, then upgraded back to their original ratings. The fourth bank, the State Bank of Springfield, failed on July 17, 1992.

Personal Experience Documenting "CRA Examiner Subjectivity Range"

We should mention in conclusion of this subjectivity topic that we have personal experience documenting the existence of the CRA examiner subjectivity range. The subject bank in this case was receiving its first *public* performance evaluation, but it had received a "needs improvement" rating on its previous one before they were made public. This bank spent more than a year and one-half significantly revamping and improving its CRA program across the board, with the help of the author acting as a consultant to the bank. By the time of the exam the bank felt that it might be able to receive an outstanding rating, which was its goal. The bank truly believed that it would not receive anything lower than a satisfactory rating.

When the CRA examiners came in and reviewed the bank, they were quite surprised as to the bank's previous needs improvement rating and unquestion-ably recommended a satisfactory CRA rating. Everything appeared to be going fine until the head examiner arrived to conduct the exit meeting. In attendance were the on-site examiners who had done the work, as well as senior bank management, and the author as the outside CRA consultant. The CRA examiner subjectivity range became very apparent with the head examiner's involvement.

The head examiner noted that the field examiners were recommending a satisfactory CRA rating. The head examiner also realized that the bank was strongly pushing for an outstanding rating. The head examiner then unilaterally pronounced that he felt the bank should receive no better than the needs improvement rating it had previously received. That head examiner then shocked everyone in attendance at the meeting, including his examiners, by stating to the author that if he wanted to he could probably "make a case with no questions from his office" for a substantial noncompliance rating!

Thus, we have a bank that spent more than a year and a half of work to improve its CRA performance to what it hopefully felt was an outstanding rating but certainly no lower than a satisfactory one, which the field examiners clearly agreed on. Then comes the head examiner who, for some reason or another, felt a needs improvement rating was appropriate but that the lowest possible rating could even be justified if necessary. Consequently, each of the four possible CRA ratings were on the table at the same time for the same bank!

As it turned out, logic prevailed, and the subject bank was later notified that it had received a satisfactory CRA rating and an overall outstanding compliance rating. However, the main lesson we learned from that meeting was that when it comes to CRA examiners, and especially the head examiner or other supervisors who have the final word, everything and anything is possible. This is one reason why we believe that the CRA examiner subjectivity range exists, and it is one rating on either side of the "true" rating.

WHO NEEDS CRA IMPROVEMENT— REGULATED BANKS OR BANK REGULATORS?

Grade Inflation in Chinatown and Grade Deflation in Koreatown

Community groups have long complained that grade inflation exists in CRA ratings by the regulators. Certain banks, on the other hand, may complain about "grade deflation" where they feel they were subjectively downgraded in their CRA examinations. The purpose of this case study is to present an example of probably the closest thing we could determine to be an example of grade inflation on one hand and grade deflation on the other.

Specifically, we have identified one bank in New York's Chinatown that received a satisfactory rating by the OTS where we believe a lower needs improvement rating would have been justified. We will compare this to a substantial noncompliance rating given by the OCC to a bank in L.A.'s Koreatown where we believe a higher (needs improvement) rating would have been justified.

On the surface this would appear to be an example of grade inflation (in Chinatown) and grade deflation (in Koreatown). Although neither bank was given a needs improvement rating, this would be the most appropriate one for each bank, in our opinion.

Many Similarities between Subject Banks in Chinatown and Koreatown

The subject bank in New York's Chinatown is the Abacus Federal Savings Bank, which received a satisfactory rating by the OTS on October 1, 1991. United Citizens National Bank in the Koreatown section of Los Angeles received a substantial noncompliance rating from the OCC on April 3, 1991.

Both of these banks are minority owned and operated. Both were (in 1991) approximately the same size—in the $43 – $62 million dollar range (the Koreatown bank is the smaller of the two). These banks were quite similar in their financial condition at the time of their exams in terms of being about average in most important financial ratios. Also, both banks were established in the 1980s, with the federal

savings bank in Chinatown opened in 1984 and the national bank in Koreatown opened in 1989.

OTS—the Toughest CRA Cop

The two regulators in this instance are unique because the OTS is generally associated with the lowest CRA ratings, and the opposite is true in some respects for the OCC. For example, the OCC has given out the second highest percentage of public outstanding ratings through year-end 1992, ranking only behind the FED. The OTS has given out the greatest number of substantial noncompliance ratings since 1982 and ranks second only behind the FDIC in terms of the number of such public ratings given out since July 1, 1990. The FED and the OCC, on the other hand, have given out the smallest number of substantial noncompliance ratings since July 1, 1990.

Method of Comparative Analysis

An obvious limitation of this type of comparative analysis is that we only have the information available in the public performance evaluations to go on. Any examiner can claim that there was additional relevant information not included in the public evaluation, but such a defense would be the subject of criticism in itself unless the undisclosed information was truly confidential.

We obtained CRA statements and other material when possible from both banks. We were able to interview the president of the bank in Koreatown. Officers of the Chinatown bank, however, would not speak to us over the telephone or answer any questions regarding their CRA examination despite telephone and written requests.

The remainder of this case study will point out specific examples of differences between the two banks in their public performance evaluations. As usual, we will follow the CRA's normal assessment factor rating scheme.

Unfortunately, neither evaluation contained individual assessment factor ratings (as we recommend). These separate ratings, which provide valuable insight into the evaluation process, are no longer made available by the regulators, possibly because such disclosed assessment factor ratings subjected the regulators to this type of public scrutiny.

Bank in Koreatown but Not Chinatown Had Written CRA Program

The bank in Chinatown was noted as having "no documented evidence" that they conducted any formal studies to ascertain credit needs. Furthermore, the examiners mentioned that the bank's ascertainment activities should reach a "broader range of the population."

The bank in Koreatown, by contrast, was specifically cited for poor ascertainment efforts, even though it had adopted a written CRA program requiring quarterly visits by officers and directors. There is no mention of such a written program for the Chinatown bank, and it is quite likely that none existed.

The bank in Koreatown was criticized for not researching the area's demographics. This factor, however, was not mentioned at all in the case of the Chinatown bank, which likewise probably had not done such research.

CRA Training in Koreatown but Not in Chinatown

The Chinatown bank was criticized since there was "no evidence" that the board regularly monitors its CRA program. The bank in Koreatown was also criticized on the topic of board CRA participation, although that bank had a board-approved, written CRA program as well as some CRA training for bank employees. There is no mention of any board-approved CRA program or CRA training for employees in the case of the Chinatown bank. Again, it is quite likely that neither of these CRA activities existed there.

Bank in Koreatown but Not Chinatown Criticized for Targeted Ethnic Advertising

The bank in Chinatown advertised in local newspapers "to make the Chinese community more aware" of its business. The examiners noted that "marketing opportunities which reach the entire delineated community and its diverse populations" should be investigated. Thus, it appears that the bank in Chinatown was advertising only or primarily to the Chinese community, but there was no direct criticism of this point.

By contrast, the bank in Koreatown was specifically criticized on this point since advertising was done in Korean, and only 14% of the bank's delineated community was Asian (not all Korean). Still, though, the bank in Koreatown had actually advertised credit products (i.e., credit cards), while there is no mention that the bank in Chinatown did any type of credit advertising.

The bank in Koreatown had a written marketing program (separate from the CRA program), but there is no indication whatsoever of such a program at the bank in Chinatown. Furthermore, the bank in Koreatown was actually commended for having adequate documentation of its advertising, but there was no mention of advertising documentation at all for the bank in Chinatown.

Significant Nonlocal Lending Defended in Chinatown but Criticized in Koreatown

The evaluation of the bank in Chinatown noted that a "low number" of mortgage loans were within its delineated community, and this was also true for consumer lending and loans to small businesses. Rather than criticize the bank in Chinatown for the low number of loans in its delineated community during the review period, the examiners actually attempted to *justify* these lending patterns on the basis of bank competition and the movement of Chinatown residents to the suburbs! Besides presenting no documentation to support these opinions, there were no statistics provided as to the proportion of residential or other types of loans by that bank inside versus outside of its delineated community.

By contrast, the bank in Koreatown was strongly criticized because examiner-conducted samplings showed that 69% of total loans were outside its delineated community. Whereas the bank in Chinatown is primarily a residential mortgage lender with some consumer lending and loans to small businesses, the bank in Koreatown doesn't make residential mortgage loans. The Koreatown bank, which is newer and smaller, however, offers commercial loans, construction loans, and secured and unsecured personal installment loans. This latter category includes automobile loans, home improvement loans, home equity lines of credit, credit card loans, and overdraft protection. Nonetheless, the bank in Koreatown was criticized for having no home improvement loans and only two construction loans, both of which were outside of community.

Identical Justification for High Nonlocal Lending Accepted in Chinatown but Rejected in Koreatown

The evaluation stated that management at the bank in Koreatown attempted to explain the high proportion of loans outside its community on the basis of customers with businesses inside it living in the suburbs. The examiner apparently did not accept this argument since the evaluation stated that "the bank had no documentation to support this claim."

This is in stark contrast to the case in Chinatown where the examiner (not bank management) attempted to justify the unspecified low number and percentage of loans inside its community. Ironically, the reasoning used by the examiner in Chinatown (i.e., former customers moving to the suburbs but still maintaining business ties with Chinatown) was identical to that claimed by bank management in Koreatown. Even though the situations apparently were identical, the bank in Chinatown was not criticized because their examiners justified without any documentation the same circumstances bank management in Koreatown claimed but couldn't document.

Little to No Government Lending in Chinatown or Koreatown

The Chinatown bank had four SBA loans and was approved for two other government housing programs, but it had originated no loans under either of them. The bank in Koreatown did not participate in any governmentally insured programs, but the examiners fairly noted that the bank was less than two years old and was "limited in its ability to participate in such loans." In fact, there are several fairly new banks less than two years old that have yet to even have their first CRA exam, much less participate in such programs.

Chinatown Examiners (Not Bank Management) Take Swipe at Local Competitors

The delineated communities for both of these banks were accepted by their respective examiners. We were particularly surprised to see that the examiners for the Chinatown bank editorialized as to why that bank was opened. That is, the examiners (not management) opined that the bank "was opened to address the credit needs of the local community in reaction to the failure of traditional lenders to extend credit in Chinatown." We are certain that the many banks and thrift institutions that have been serving Chinatown for many, many years would take exception to that opinion by federal CRA examiners.

Examiners Create New "Chinatown Suburban Community" to Justify Significant Nonlocal Lending

The evaluation of the Chinatown bank referenced a geographic distribution analysis of lending. (It was not clear from the evaluation, but we assume the examiner did this analysis.) This analysis indicated that the bank was "adequately serving all segments of its community, to include current and former residents of the Chinatown area." That is, the examiners unilaterally expanded the scope of this geographic analysis to not only include the immediate Chinatown area but also the suburbs (primarily the Bronx, Brooklyn, and north Jersey) where former Chinatown residents now live.

Rather than the customary procedure of evaluating the distribution of credit based upon the bank's actual community, a new "Chinatown suburban community" was created by the examiners. Does this mean that the bank in Chinatown was *not* adequately serving the immediate Chinatown area counting only current residents of that area?

The bank in Koreatown was not as fortunate with its examiners. Specifically noted as an examiner-conducted sample, it was determined that only 31% of all loans were within the local community, and these were primarily to one ethnic group of borrowers (obviously Koreans). Clearly the bank in Koreatown would have been found to be "adequately serving" its community if former as well as current residents were included, as was the case in Chinatown.

Needs Improvement Rating Could Have Jeopardized Branch in Chinatown

At the time of the first public CRA exam the Chinatown bank was seven years old, and the Koreatown bank was less than two years old. The Chinatown bank has a main office and a branch. We understand that at the time of the exam it had plans to relocate its branch to a prime corner location in Chinatown, an action that might not have been approved or even considered for a bank with a needs improvement rating. Since it did not receive that rating, the bank successfully relocated that branch in January 1993. The bank in Koreatown operates out of only one office. Both banks have reasonably similar office hours, and both are open on Friday evenings and Saturday mornings. The Koreatown bank, however, was criticized for not having a "policy for requiring analysis of the bank's business hours," but this factor was not even mentioned for the Chinatown bank (which likewise probably did not have one).

Widespread Consumer Compliance Violations of Supervisory Concern in Chinatown but Not in Koreatown

Without a doubt the most significant and disturbing distinction between the banks in Chinatown and Koreatown are the discrimination and other illegal credit practices that were cited for the bank in Chinatown but not for the bank in Koreatown. The bank in Chinatown "violated OTS Regulations resulting in potential loan applicants being discouraged from submitting loan applications." The examiners further noted that this practice is "widespread and of supervisory concern." These are strong and meaningful words when used by compliance examiners.

The bank in Koreatown had no such practices intended to discourage applications, since "policies and procedures have been developed" there to prevent such problems. The examiners for the Koreatown bank could only criticize a lack of certain discriminatory review systems (that much bigger banks usually don't even have) and the extremely limited focus of the bank's marketing strategy (which

was the subject of criticism under a previous assessment factor).

We were further surprised to learn that the bank in Chinatown was cited for "widespread violations of the technical aspects of the Equal Credit Opportunity Act as implemented by Regulations B and OTS Nondiscrimination Regulations." The examiners for the bank in Chinatown further noted that "management's failure to develop proper policies and procedures warrants supervisory concern."

This implies that there may have been a violation repeated from a past exam, but we have no way to prove this possibility. By contrast, the bank in Koreatown had no evidence of illegal credit practices or any such problems. It was found to be in compliance with antidiscrimination laws and regulations.

Chinatown Bank Surprisingly Escapes the CRA "Death Wish"

Violations under assessment factor F (and to a lesser extent D) in the "Discrimination and Other Illegal Credit Practices" performance category represent the CRA "death wish." It has been our experience that such violations, especially those noted as being "widespread" and of "supervisory concern," as was the case at the bank in Chinatown, often result in a substantial noncompliance rating but almost always a needs improvement rating.

This is probably the main reason why we were surprised to see a satisfactory rating for the bank in Chinatown, considering the nature and scope of these compliance violations. Conversely, there were no such problems at the bank in Koreatown, but it was cited as being in substantial noncompliance.

Koreatown Bank Actually Criticized for Sizeable CRA Commitment but Larger Chinatown Bank Excused by Examiners

Both banks' records regarding community development and redevelopment projects were quite similar. The bank in Chinatown apparently was involved in no such projects, although this was not clear from the exam. Rather, the examiners stated that smaller institutions such as that bank "have been constrained from active participation in large scale community development or redevelopment programs" because of "high property values and construction costs." This type of rationalization by examiners for a seven-year-old $61 million bank not becoming involved in local community development and redevelopment projects obviously could set a dangerous precedent for CRA compliance under this assessment factor.

L.A., like New York City, also has "high property values and construction costs." Nonetheless, the less than two-year-old and smaller bank in Koreatown was criticized for being "unaware" of local community development and redevelopment projects. This bank, however, actually committed a "sizeable amount of funds" to a statewide community reinvestment corporation.

Koreatown Examiners Question Statewide Community Reinvestment Concept

Rather than commend the bank on this voluntary and affirmative action, the examiners noted that no funds had been yet advanced under that program and, in any case, the bank "cannot control where the funds are used within California." We have never seen this latter type of criticism before, but it would be obvious for any such statewide shared program. These examiners, in effect, questioned the concept of a statewide community reinvestment corporation.

Thus, the bank in Chinatown, which apparently was not involved in any such projects, was provided with an excuse for not doing so by its examiners because of the bank's size. On the other hand, the smaller and newer bank in Koreatown, which had made a sizeable commitment to a statewide redevelopment program, was actually criticized in the above way for its efforts.

The Chinatown bank was noted as having the "ability" to participate in small scale projects, and management was "encouraged" to consider such projects. The bank in Koreatown was referenced as being "small in size and less than two years old and is somewhat limited by these factors in its ability to be innovative in meeting community credit needs." With the exception of government loan programs, it does not appear that the rest of this evaluation fully took account of that bank's obvious size and age constraints.

Bank in Koreatown but Not Chinatown Offers Low-Income Checking Account Program

No other factors were noted as being relevant in the case of the Chinatown bank. However, in the case of the Koreatown bank, it was commended for initiating a program to assist low-income households in opening a checking account. The evaluation noted that management (but apparently not the examiners) "felt this service met a community need and complied with the spirit of CRA." That bank was also noted for having made a small donation to a community senior citizens' group. No such donations or special low-income banking services were noted for the bank in Chinatown.

Further Documentation of the "CRA Examiner Subjectivity Range"

In summary, a comparison of the available facts in this case from the public performance evaluations suggests grade inflation in New York's Chinatown and grade deflation in L.A.'s Koreatown. Both of these subjective CRA rating processes are equally troubling in their implications.

Our CRA research in this case study as well as the previous one has led us to hypothesize that the "CRA examiner subjectivity range" can result in any CRA rating being one notch plus or minus what the "true" rating should be. In other words, a CRA subjectivity "swing factor" may exist which can go up ("grade inflation") or down ("grade deflation") by one rating. This swing factor is primarily based on the examiners' perception of a bank's "CRA spirit" and other subjective factors. In this case the bank in Chinatown was one rating above and the bank in Koreatown was one rating below their respective "true" ratings in our opinion.

"Errors of Omission" Technique in Cases of Grade Deflation and Inflation

The apparent grade deflation experience in Koreatown suggests that CRA examiners can justify at least one rating lower than the "true" rating by using the "error of omissions" technique. That is, by "going by the book" and listing a litany of admirable and affirmative CRA programs, analyses, plans, audits, and so on, that the most outstanding bank should have, virtually every bank can be criticized for omitting some or all of them. Considering the broad and subjective scope of CRA, there is always something (and usually several things) for which any bank can be criticized. Also, some positive relevant developments may likewise be omitted under this technique.

The culmination of these omissions, especially if there are several of them, as in Koreatown, can be used to justify grade deflation by one notch. Coupled with a few errors of commission, which in certain cases may be more relevant than others, either of the two lowest CRA ratings can be justified.

Of course, errors of omission are rarely if at all mentioned in cases of grade inflation, unless they are the stated basis for certain assessment factors, as was the case in Chinatown. Why would examiners raise a criticism that wouldn't justify their rating?

All CRA evaluations should be consistent in noting every relevant error of omission, but there is no way an outsider would know whether or not they were all included. In other words, was a certain desirable item not mentioned because the examiners didn't feel it was relevant or because it just didn't exist? The former situation can always be justified by the examiners. Examiners can justify many things, as we witnessed in the Chinatown case.

Chinatown Case Supports Our "Friendly Regulator Hypothesis"

What is particularly puzzling about this case is that the regulator for the bank in Chinatown, the OTS, typically has twice the proportion of low CRA ratings compared to the bank regulators. Therefore, if anyone would have been "tough" on a bank, especially one with widespread consumer compliance violations of supervisory concern, it would be logical to assume that it would be the OTS. This obviously was not the case for the Abacus Federal Savings Bank in New York's Chinatown. The fact that at the time of their exam it was known that the bank had branch relocation plans (which may have been derailed by a needs improvement rating) may have had a bearing on the OTS's inflated rating. This would lend support to our previously cited "friendly regulator hypothesis."

We must ask the question if that same OTS examination team from Jersey City, New Jersey, had examined the bank in L.A.'s Koreatown, would they have concluded that a substantial noncompliance rating would have been appropriate? Conversely, would the same examination team from the OCC's San Francisco office even have considered a satisfactory rating for the bank in New York's Chinatown? Of course, we must ask ourselves if Chinatown and Koreatown are isolated cases.

Is There a "Safety and Soundness Examiner Subjectivity Range?"

These unanswered questions are legitimate ones for which we will not receive answers. Yet, we must be thankful that, with the public disclosure of CRA evaluations, at least we have the opportunity to ask these important questions.

More importantly, we must wonder if safety and soundness exams were public, would we be asking these same questions about those examiners? Could there be such a thing as our hypothesized "plus or minus one" examiner subjectivity swing factor for CAMEL or MACRO ratings? Obviously, the banking and thrift industries are not the only groups that would oppose disclosure of safety and soundness ratings.

A "Needs Improvement" Rating for Both the Chinatown and Koreatown CRA Examiners

What we learn from this Chinatown/Koreatown case study is not that we should scrap or "gut" CRA because its ratings are inherently too subjective. We oppose all such recent proposals involving CRA exemptions, safe harbors, and "self certifications." (Can a self-certified safety and soundness exam be next?)

Rather than killing or crippling CRA, we would improve and make more efficient its enforcement. That is, we should look at this hopefully isolated situation and use it as a basis for further educating CRA examiners so they can become more objective and consistent. If it is true, as concluded here, that the "true" CRA rating for the banks in Chinatown and Koreatown should have been "needs improvement," then that rating should likewise apply to the CRA examiners for those banks.

Good News and Bad News in Koreatown

Meanwhile, Koreatown has been the site of both bad news and good news since the bank there received its substantial noncompliance rating. The obvious bad news was the damage Koreatown suffered in the adjacent south-central L.A riots. The good news is that a March 13, 1992, evaluation by the OCC upgraded the United Citizens National Bank to the rating we felt it deserved in the first place—needs improvement. It will probably be some time before the bank in Chinatown receives its second evaluation. We hope that it has made the needed improvements in its CRA program by then to justify the satisfactory rating it received in its first evaluation.

Figure 7-1   Preliminary Draft of October 29, 1990 CRA Performance Evaluation of Norstar Bank, N.A.

    3/22/91

Comptroller of the Currency
Administrator of National Banks

5/3/91

1114 Avenue of the Americas, Suite 3900
New York, New York 10036

PUBLIC DISCLOSURE

COMMUNITY REINVESTMENT ACT PERFORMANCE EVALUATION

October 29, 1990

Norstar Bank, N.A.
Charter No. 15080
10 Fountain Plaza
Buffalo, New York 14202

NOTE: This evaluation is not, nor should it be
construed as, an assessment of the financial
condition of this institution. The rating
assigned to this institution does not represent
an analysis, conclusion or opinion of the
federal financial supervisory agency concerning
the safety and soundness of this financial
institution.

Figure 7-1   Continued

GENERAL INFORMATION

This document is an evaluation of the Community Reinvestment Act (CRA) performance of Norstar Bank, N.A. prepared by the Office of the Comptroller of the Currency (OCC), the institution's supervisory agency.

The evaluation represents the OCC's current assessment and rating of the institution's CRA performance based on an examination conducted as of October 29, 1990. It does not reflect any CRA-related activities that may have been initiated or discontinued by the institution after the completion of the examination.

The purpose of the Community Reinvestment Act of 1977 (12 U.S.C. 2901), as amended, is to encourage each financial institution to help meet the credit needs of the communities in which it operates. The Act requires that in connection with its examination of a financial institution, each federal financial supervisory agency shall (1) assess the institution's record of helping to meet the credit needs of its entire community, including low- and moderate-income neighborhoods, consistent with safe and sound operations of the institution, and (2) take that record of performance into account when deciding whether to approve an application of the institution for a deposit facility.

The Financial Institutions Reform, Recovery and Enforcement Act of 1989, Pub. L. No. 101-73, amended the CRA to require the Agencies to make public certain portions of their CRA performance assessments of financial institutions.

Basis for the Rating

The assessment of the institution's record takes into account its financial capacity and size, legal impediments and local economic conditions and demographics, including the competitive environment in which it operates. Assessing the CRA performance is a process that does not rely on absolute standards. Institutions are not required to adopt specific activities, nor to offer specific types or amounts of credit. Each institution has considerable flexibility in determining how it can best help to meet the credit needs of its entire community. In that light, evaluations are based on a review of 12 assessment factors, which are grouped together under 5 performance categories, as detailed in the following section of this evaluation.

Figure 7-1   Continued

ASSIGNMENT OF RATING

Identification of Ratings

In connection with the assessment of each insured depository
institution's CRA performance, a rating is assigned from the
following groups:

Outstanding record of meeting community credit needs.

An institution in this group has an outstanding record
of, and is a leader in, ascertaining and helping to
meet the credit needs of its entire delineated
community, including low- and moderate-income
neighborhoods, in a manner consistent with its
resources and capabilities.

Satisfactory record of meeting community credit needs.

An institution in this group has a satisfactory record
of ascertaining and helping to meet the credit needs
of its entire delineated community, including low- and
moderate-income neighborhoods, in a manner consistent
with its resources and capabilities.

Needs to improve record of meeting community credit needs.

An institution in this group needs to improve its
overall record of ascertaining and helping to meet the
credit needs of its entire delineated community,
including low- and moderate-income neighborhoods, in a
manner consistent with its resources and capabilities.

Substantial noncompliance in meeting community credit
needs.

An institution in this group has a substantially
deficient record of ascertaining and helping to meet
the credit needs of its entire delineated community,
including low- and moderate-income neighborhoods, in a
manner consistent with its resources and
capabilities.

- 1 -

Figure 7-1   Continued

DISCUSSION OF INSTITUTION'S PERFORMANCE

PRELIMINARY DRAFT

Institution's Rating:

   Based on the findings presented below, this institution is
   rated: Needs to improve record of meeting community
   credit needs.

I.   ASCERTAINMENT OF COMMUNITY CREDIT NEEDS

   Assessment Factor A - Activities conducted by the
   institution to ascertain the credit needs of its
   community, including the extent of the institution's
   efforts to communicate with members of its community
   regarding the credit services being provided by the
   institution.

   Management's method of determining credit needs in their 5
   delineated communities is inconsistent. The call program
   (community contact) is now active, but the quality of the
   detail provided by the regions to the CRA department is
   inadequate. The depth of detail demonstrating community
   contacts and ascertainment efforts related to the bank's
   CRA program is especially lacking in the Niagara County,
   Southern Tier/Western and Finger Lakes/Eastern Regions.
   The first comprehensive geographic analysis of lending and
   deposit patterns was recently received by the bank.
   Management plans to analyze this information and utilize
   it in conjunction with its 1991 planning process.
   Management has recently shown response to outside input
   regarding credit needs by offering lines of credit to
   developers of low-to-moderate income housing in the
   Buffalo area. In order to meet perceived credit needs,
   the bank is willing to grant government insured loans such
   as SBA and student loans.

   Assessment Factor C - The extent of participation by the
   institution's board of directors in formulating the
   institution's policies and reviewing its performance with
   respect to the purposes of the Community Reinvestment Act.

   Bank records do not show meaningful participation by the
   Board in the CRA process. The CRA committee formed in
   October 1990 has four directors and represents Board
   participation. There was very little evidence presented
   during our examination showing any direct personal
   participation before October 1990 in planning or community
   activities other than a list of organizations to which the
   directors belong. The committee is advised on a monthly
   basis by the CRA officer who has addressed the full Board
   since his appointment and will address them quarterly.

- 2 -

Figure 7-1   Continued

II. MARKETING AND TYPES OF CREDIT OFFERED AND EXTENDED

Assessment Factor B - The extent of the institution's
marketing and special credit-related programs to make
members of the community aware of the credit services
offered by the institution.

The CRA officer maintains limited documentation of the
bank's marketing and advertising programs. The
advertising reviewed during the consumer portion of the
examination and inquiry of bank personnel indicate that a
wide range of media is used, including radio, TV and
newspapers. However, there was no evidence of review or
analysis by the CRA officer on the effectiveness of the
programs. Demographics of media used, although available,
are not maintained by the bank. Additionally, detailed
demographic information on media used by the affiliated
mortgage company to market mortgage products is neither
maintained nor analyzed. Efforts to assist individuals
and groups, in their delineated communities, in
understanding and applying for credit is limited to
student loan products and SBA lending seminars.

Assessment Factor I - The institution's origination of
residential mortgage loans, housing rehabilitation loans,
home improvement loans, and small business or small farm
loans within its community, or the purchase of such loans
originated in its community.

Management is generally responsive to community credit
needs. The overall consumer and commercial loan volume
continues to be adequate. Mortgage lending is done by an
affiliate of the holding company. However, management has
not analyzed the extent of mortgage lending in its
delineated communities. A geographic analysis of lending
and deposit patterns recently received by the bank
includes some of this information.

- 3 -

Figure 7-1   Continued

Assessment Factor J - The institution's participation in
governmentally-insured, guaranteed or subsidized loan
programs for housing, small businesses, or small farms.

The bank has not been consistent in its involvement in
helping to meet credit needs in all of the communities
that it serves. The bank is the number one SBA lender in
Western, New York. It is known that the mortgage
financing company does participate in FHA, FMHA, SONYMA
and VA guaranteed real estate loans. However the volume
as it affects all regions is indeterminable from review of
the bank's files. The bank has developed small credit
lines for the small business owner. The bank's portfolio
of farm loans is limited in contrast to the very large
rural area considered to be the delineated community.

III.   GEOGRAPHIC DISTRIBUTION AND RECORD OF OPENING AND CLOSING
       OFFICES

Reasonableness of Delineated Community

While the delineation of the communities is considered
reasonable, management's method used to determine the
community boundaries needs to be documented. The map
displayed in the statement needs only to reflect those
portions of MSA's and counties that it reasonably may be
expected to serve.

Assessment Factor E - The geographic distribution of the
institution's credit extensions, credit applications, and
credit denials.

Management is unaware of the distribution of loans,
applications and denials within various segments of its
community. A geographic distribution of loans and
deposits has recently been completed. The report has not
yet been thoroughly analyzed and utilized by the bank in
establishing loan policies/products/services and
marketing.

Assessment Factor G - The institution's record of opening
and closing offices and providing services at offices.

The bank's record of opening and closing offices is
generally satisfactory, and the offices are reasonably
accessible to the population of the delineated
communities. However, the Board has not approved a
written policy on branch closings and elimination of
services to local communities. Management has developed
such a policy and will remit it to the Board of Directors
for approval.

- 4 -

Figure 7-1   Continued

IV.   DISCRIMINATION AND OTHER ILLEGAL CREDIT PRACTICES

Assessment Factor D - Any practices intended to discourage
applications for types of credit set forth in the
institution's CRA Statement(s).

The bank is in compliance with this factor. There is no
evidence of any practice to discourage applicants for
credit. Training of employees effectively reinforces the
requirements of the fair lending laws. The bank's planned
analysis of the newly acquired geographic distribution
will serve to better test the banks compliance.

Assessment Factor F - Evidence of prohibited
discriminatory or other illegal credit practices.

The bank is in substantial compliance with fair lending
and other credit laws. No evidence of prohibited
discrimination or other illegal credit practices has been
noted.

V.   COMMUNITY DEVELOPMENT

Assessment Factor H - The institution's participation,
including investments, in local community development and
redevelopment projects or programs.

Documentation of participation in community
development/redevelopment in the Buffalo and Rochester
areas is considered good. Management has not adequately
demonstrated its participation in other communities.
Local/state investments are reasonable for this bank.

Assessment Factor K - The institution's ability to meet
various community credit needs based on its financial
condition and size, legal impediments, local economic
conditions and other factors.

Based on the institution's size and financial condition it
is making a reasonable effort to participate in economic
growth and revitalization in many of the communities that
it services. Participation, which has been in the form of
direct loans, contributions and technical assistance has
been inconsistent by region.

- 5 -

Figure 7-1   Continued

<u>Assessment Factor L</u> - Any other factors that, in the regulatory authority's judgment, reasonably bear upon the extent to which an institution is helping to meet the credit needs of its entire community.

Norstar Bank, N.A. has a good record of being engaged in meaningful civic and community service activities directed toward low-to-moderate income areas, such as financial assistance to nonprofit organizations providing human services and employees volunteer work.

- 6 -

Figure 7-2   OCC May 22, 1991 Cover Letter to Final Draft of October 29, 1990
                CRA Performance Evaluation of Norstar Bank, N.A.

Comptroller of the Currency
Administrator of National Banks

Northeastern District
1114 Avenue of the Americas, Suite 3900
New York, New York   10036

May 22, 1991

Board of Directors
Norstar Bank, N.A.
10 Fountain Plaza
Buffalo, New York   14202

Members of the Board:

This letter is supplemental to and part of the recently issued
Report of Compliance Examination. As part of that report, the
content of this letter is to be treated with the same degree of
confidentially.

This Office reviewed certain factual information presented by
senior management in response to certain areas of concern noted in
the aforementioned report. This information consisted of
additional materials documenting the bank's efforts in assessing
its geographic distribution of credit in its delineated
communities. This documentation was not completely available to
our examiners during the initial review.

Performance in meeting the credit needs of the community under CRA
is now considered satisfactory. The documentation was sufficient
to upgrade the rating on Assessment Factor E, the Geographic
Distribution of the institution's credit extensions, credit
applications, and credit denials, to satisfactory. The bank has
recently collected data on geographic distribution of its loans
which demonstrates that approximately one third of its total loans
are in low to moderate income areas. Our findings are consistent
in general with the bank's profile in its community. The bank has
not aggressively pursued upscale customers and its primary market
tends to be a moderate income one. Management is in the process of
collecting data on loan denials and plans to utilize the
information in conjunction with the geographic loan data in
restructuring and refining loan policies, products, services and
marketing.

Figure 7-2   Continued

It should be noted, however, we fully expect the Board and
Management to intensify their efforts to address the concerns
remaining in the CRA Public Disclosure attached to this letter.
The Public Comment must be included in your CRA public file. A
written response detailing the bank's efforts to correct the
violations cited in the original Report of Examination and progress
made in addressing the concerns noted should be forwarded, within
sixty days, to the above address with a copy to David D. Gibbons,
Resident National Bank Examiner, Fleet National Bank, 111
Westminster Street, Providence, Rhode Island 02903.

Sincerely,

Michael A. Carnovali
Director for Regional Bank Supervision
Northeastern District

cc: J. Terrence Murray
      Erland E. Kailbourne
      David D. Gibbons

Figure 7-3   Final Draft of October 29, 1990 CRA Performance Evaluation of
              Norstar Bank, N.A.

5/21/91   7/2/91

Comptroller of the Currency
Administrator of National Banks

1114 Avenue of the Americas, Suite 3900
New York, New York 10036

<u>PUBLIC DISCLOSURE</u>

COMMUNITY REINVESTMENT ACT PERFORMANCE EVALUATION

October 29, 1990

Norstar Bank, N.A.
Charter No. 15080
10 Fountain Plaza
Buffalo, New York 14202

NOTE: This evaluation is not, nor should it be
         construed as, an assessment of the financial
         condition of this institution. The rating
         assigned to this institution does not represent
         an analysis, conclusion or opinion of the
         federal financial supervisory agency concerning
         the safety and soundness of this financial
         institution.

Figure 7-3   Continued

GENERAL INFORMATION

This document is an evaluation of the Community Reinvestment Act
(CRA) performance of Norstar Bank, N.A. prepared by the Office
of the Comptroller of the Currency (OCC), the institution's
supervisory agency.

The evaluation represents the OCC's current assessment and
rating of the institution's CRA performance based on an
examination conducted as of October 29, 1990. It does not
reflect any CRA-related activities that may have been initiated
or discontinued by the institution after the completion of the
examination.

The purpose of the Community Reinvestment Act of 1977 (12 U.S.C.
2901), as amended, is to encourage each financial institution to
help meet the credit needs of the communities in which it
operates. The Act requires that in connection with its
examination of a financial institution, each federal financial
supervisory agency shall (1) assess the institution's record of
helping to meet the credit needs of its entire community,
including low- and moderate-income neighborhoods, consistent
with safe and sound operations of the institution, and (2) take
that record of performance into account when deciding whether to
approve an application of the institution for a deposit
facility.

The Financial Institutions Reform, Recovery and Enforcement Act
of 1989, Pub. L. No. 101-73, amended the CRA to require the
Agencies to make public certain portions of their CRA
performance assessments of financial institutions.

Basis for the Rating

The assessment of the institution's record takes into account
its financial capacity and size, legal impediments and local
economic conditions and demographics, including the competitive
environment in which it operates. Assessing the CRA performance
is a process that does not rely on absolute standards.
Institutions are not required to adopt specific activities, nor
to offer specific types or amounts of credit. Each institution
has considerable flexibility in determining how it can best help
to meet the credit needs of its entire community. In that
light, evaluations are based on a review of 12 assessment
factors, which are grouped together under 5 performance
categories, as detailed in the following section of this
evaluation.

Figure 7-3   Continued

ASSIGNMENT OF RATING

Identification of Ratings

In connection with the assessment of each insured depository institution's CRA performance, a rating is assigned from the following groups:

Outstanding record of meeting community credit needs.

> An institution in this group has an outstanding record of, and is a leader in, ascertaining and helping to meet the credit needs of its entire delineated community, including low- and moderate-income neighborhoods, in a manner consistent with its resources and capabilities.

Satisfactory record of meeting community credit needs.

> An institution in this group has a satisfactory record of ascertaining and helping to meet the credit needs of its entire delineated community, including low- and moderate-income neighborhoods, in a manner consistent with its resources and capabilities.

Needs to improve record of meeting community credit needs.

> An institution in this group needs to improve its overall record of ascertaining and helping to meet the credit needs of its entire delineated community, including low- and moderate-income neighborhoods, in a manner consistent with its resources and capabilities.

Substantial noncompliance in meeting community credit needs.

> An institution in this group has a substantially deficient record of ascertaining and helping to meet the credit needs of its entire delineated community, including low- and moderate-income neighborhoods, in a manner consistent with its resources and capabilities.

- 1 -

Figure 7-3   Continued

DISCUSSION OF INSTITUTION'S PERFORMANCE

Institution's Rating:

> Based on the findings presented below, this institution is rated: Satisfactory record of meeting community credit needs.

I.   ASCERTAINMENT OF COMMUNITY CREDIT NEEDS

Assessment Factor A - Activities conducted by the institution to ascertain the credit needs of its community, including the extent of the institution's efforts to communicate with members of its community regarding the credit services being provided by the institution.

Management's method of determining credit needs in their 5 delineated communities is inconsistent. The call program (community contact) is now active, but the quality of the detail provided by the regions to the CRA department is inadequate. The depth of detail demonstrating community contacts and ascertainment efforts related to the bank's CRA program is especially lacking in the Niagara County, Southern Tier/Western and Finger Lakes/Eastern Regions. The first comprehensive geographic analysis of lending and deposit patterns was recently received by the bank. Management plans to analyze this information and utilize it in conjunction with its 1991 planning process. Management has recently shown response to outside input regarding credit needs by offering lines of credit to developers of low-to-moderate income housing in the Buffalo area. In order to meet perceived credit needs, the bank is willing to grant government insured loans such as SBA and student loans.

Assessment Factor C - The extent of participation by the institution's board of directors in formulating the institution's policies and reviewing its performance with respect to the purposes of the Community Reinvestment Act.

Bank records do not show meaningful participation by the Board in the CRA process. The CRA committee formed in October 1990 has four directors and represents Board participation. There was very little evidence presented during our examination showing any direct personal participation before October 1990 in planning or community activities other than a list of organizations to which the directors belong. The committee is advised on a monthly basis by the CRA officer who has addressed the full Board since his appointment and will address them quarterly.

- 2 -

Figure 7-3   Continued

II. MARKETING AND TYPES OF CREDIT OFFERED AND EXTENDED

Assessment Factor B - The extent of the institution's marketing and special credit-related programs to make members of the community aware of the credit services offered by the institution.

The CRA officer maintains limited documentation of the bank's marketing and advertising programs. The advertising reviewed during the consumer portion of the examination and inquiry of bank personnel indicate that a wide range of media is used, including radio, TV and newspapers. However, there was no evidence of review or analysis by the CRA officer on the effectiveness of the programs. Demographics of media used, although available, are not maintained by the bank. Additionally, detailed demographic information on media used by the affiliated mortgage company to market mortgage products is neither maintained nor analyzed. Efforts to assist individuals and groups, in their delineated communities, in understanding and applying for credit is limited to student loan products and SBA lending seminars.

Assessment Factor I - The institution's origination of residential mortgage loans, housing rehabilitation loans, home improvement loans, and small business or small farm loans within its community, or the purchase of such loans originated in its community.

Management is generally responsive to community credit needs. The overall consumer and commercial loan volume continues to be adequate. Mortgage lending is done by an affiliate of the holding company. However, management has not analyzed the extent of mortgage lending in its delineated communities. A geographic analysis of lending and deposit patterns recently received by the bank includes some of this information.

Figure 7-3   Continued

    Assessment Factor J - The institution's participation in governmentally-insured, guaranteed or subsidized loan programs for housing, small businesses, or small farms.

    The bank has not been consistent in its involvement in helping to meet credit needs in all of the communities that it serves. The bank is the number one SBA lender in Western, New York. It is known that the mortgage financing company does participate in FHA, FMHA, SONYMA and VA guaranteed real estate loans. However the volume as it affects all regions is indeterminable from review of the bank's files. The bank has developed small credit lines for the small business owner. The bank's portfolio of farm loans is limited in contrast to the very large rural area considered to be the delineated community.

III.   GEOGRAPHIC DISTRIBUTION AND RECORD OF OPENING AND CLOSING OFFICES

    Reasonableness of Delineated Community

    While the delineation of the communities is considered reasonable, management's method used to determine the community boundaries needs to be documented. The map displayed in the statement needs only to reflect those portions of MSA's and counties that it reasonably may be expected to serve.

    Assessment Factor E - The geographic distribution of the institution's credit extensions, credit applications, and credit denials.

    The bank has recently collected data on geographic distribution of its loans which demonstrates that approximately one third of its total loans are in low to moderate income areas. Our findings are consistent in general with the bank's profile in its community. The bank has not aggressively pursued upscale customers and its primary market tends to be a moderate income one. Management is in the process of collecting data on loan denials and plans to utilize the information in conjunction with the geographic loan data in restructuring and refining loan policies, products, services and marketing.

    Assessment Factor G - The institution's record of opening and closing offices and providing services at offices.

    The bank's record of opening and closing offices is generally satisfactory, and the offices are reasonably accessible to the population of the delineated communities. However, the Board has not approved a written policy on branch closings and elimination of services to local communities. Management has developed such a policy and will remit it to the Board of Directors for approval.

- 4 -

Figure 7-3   Continued

IV.   DISCRIMINATION AND OTHER ILLEGAL CREDIT PRACTICES

<u>Assessment Factor D</u> - Any practices intended to discourage applications for types of credit set forth in the institution's CRA Statement(s).

The bank is in compliance with this factor. There is no evidence of any practice to discourage applicants for credit. Training of employees effectively reinforces the requirements of the fair lending laws. The bank's planned analysis of the newly acquired geographic distribution will serve to better test the banks compliance.

<u>Assessment Factor F</u> - Evidence of prohibited discriminatory or other illegal credit practices.

The bank is in substantial compliance with fair lending and other credit laws. No evidence of prohibited discrimination or other illegal credit practices has been noted.

V.   COMMUNITY DEVELOPMENT

<u>Assessment Factor H</u> - The institution's participation, including investments, in local community development and redevelopment projects or programs.

Documentation of participation in community development/redevelopment in the Buffalo and Rochester areas is considered good. Management has not adequately demonstrated its participation in other communities. Local/state investments are reasonable for this bank.

<u>Assessment Factor K</u> - The institution's ability to meet various community credit needs based on its financial condition and size, legal impediments, local economic conditions and other factors.

Based on the institution's size and financial condition it is making a reasonable effort to participate in economic growth and revitalization in many of the communities that it services. Participation, which has been in the form of direct loans, contributions and technical assistance has been inconsistent by region.

Figure 7-3   Continued

Assessment Factor L - Any other factors that, in the
regulatory authority's judgment, reasonably bear upon the
extent to which an institution is helping to meet the
credit needs of its entire community.

Norstar Bank, N.A. has a good record of being engaged in
meaningful civic and community service activities directed
toward low-to-moderate income areas, such as financial
assistance to nonprofit organizations providing human
services and employees volunteer work.

- 6 -

8. THE ABSOLUTELY LOWEST CRA RATINGS—PROFILES OF SUBSTANTIAL NONCOMPLIANT BANKS

INTRODUCTION

This chapter contains our analysis of the CRA evaluations of the absolutely lowest rated banks in America—those in substantial noncompliance with CRA. Chapters 4 and 6 presented comparable analyses for those banks receiving outstanding and needs improvement ratings.

A bank is deemed to be in substantial noncompliance in meeting community credit needs if it has a substantially deficient record of ascertaining and helping to meet the credit needs of its entire delineated community, including low- and moderate-income neighborhoods, in a manner consistent with its resources and capabilities.

OTS Gives Out Most Substantial Noncompliance Ratings

Table 8-1 shows that the OTS has given out more than three times the number of substantial noncompliance (or similar) ratings as all three bank regulators combined over the January 1, 1982–June 30, 1990, period. Over three-fourths of the 66 such ratings given over this pre-disclosure period were by the OTS. During the last two-and-one-half years of public CRA ratings, the number of such low ratings has increased dramatically to 106. Nearly two-thirds of those ratings in the last 11 years were made during

this two-and-one-half-year postdisclosure period (Table 8-1).

Table 8-2 lists the 88 banks that have received the absolutely lowest substantial noncompliance rating over the July 1, 1990 – December 31, 1992, period. Counting double and even some triple ratings of the same bank, those 88 banks received 99 substantial noncompliance ratings. Since 106 such ratings were made as of year-end 1992 (Table 8-1), there were seven substantial noncompliance ratings that were not yet made public by then. As of year-end 1991 there were 59 such ratings, counting multiple ones, for 54 identified banks which are analyzed in this chapter.

Substantial Noncompliance Banks are Big and Small, Strong and Weak

Table 8-2, which shows data on banks with publicly disclosed ratings as of year-end 1992, suggests that substantial noncompliant banks follow no particular size or financial condition pattern. These banks range in size from a few million dollars to five with assets exceeding $1 billion, the largest such one being the $3.3 billion Bank of New York (Delaware) of Wilmington, Delaware. These large banks skewed the asset size distribution of substantial noncompliant banks and resulted in an average size of such banks of just over $200 million. More meaningful, though,

Table 8-1   Number of Substantial Noncompliance CRA Ratings, 1982 – 1992

YEAR	BANKS (FDIC/FED/OCC)	THRIFTS (OTS)	TOTAL
1982	3	2	5
1983	2	1	3
1984	1	1	2
1985	0	8	8
1986	1	9	10
1987	1	11	12
1988	2	12	14
1989	3	7	10
1/1/90 – 6/30/90	2	0	2
SUBTOTAL:			
1/1/82 – 6/30/90*	15	51	66
7/1/90 – 12/31/92**	77	29	106
TOTAL	92	80	172

*   Predisclosure.
** Postdisclosure.

Source: Individual Regulators
          K.H. Thomas Associates

is the median size of $59 million, which also happens to be the mode of that size distribution.

The unweighted average overall financial rating for the banks using the IDC Financial Publishing rating system, which ranges from a low of 1 to a high of 300, was 159. This was also the median rating. This is representative of an average bank in the middle of the range. In fact, the two most frequent ratings in this bimodal distribution were the lowest possible rating of 1 (of which there were seven) and the highest possible rating of 300 (of which there were six). If we were to plot CAMEL and MACRO safety and soundness ratings against CRA ratings, it appears that the resultant scatter diagram would show little correlation between the two types of bank ratings. Thus, these data suggest no relationship between financial condition and CRA substantial noncompliance ratings on average.

150 Substantial Noncompliant Banks with $30 Billion in Assets?

Roughly 1% of all banks and thrifts received this absolutely lowest CRA rating. Projecting this to all of the nation's banks and thrifts would mean about 150 will ultimately receive this rating. Those 88 banks in Table 8-2 represent just over $17 billion in combined assets. Again, extrapolating to the others likely to obtain this rating reveals there may be as much as $30 billion in assets controlled by substantial noncompliant banks in the aggregate.

The OTS and FDIC rated three-fourths of the 88 banks reported in Table 8-2. The FDIC led with 46 such banks, and the OTS followed with 21 of them. The OCC and FED rated 12 and 9 banks, respectively, in this lowest category.

Table 8-2   Substantial Noncompliance CRA Ratings, 7/1/90 – 12/31/92

Name of Bank	City	State	Federal Regulator	Date of Exam	Rating	Assets (millions)	IDC Rating[a]
Allegiant Bank	St. Louis	MO	FDIC	3/25/91	SN	$ 20	88
				1/21/92	S		
American State Bank	Portland	OR	FDIC	7/22/91	SN	12	164
				6/1/92	NI		
Archer FS&LA*	Chicago	IL	OTS	11/1/90	SN	59[b]	270[b]
Austin State Bank	Austin	IN	FDIC	12/31/90	SN	6	148
AVCO National Bank*	Irvine	CA	OCC	6/21/91	SN	2[b]	261[b]
Avondale FSB*	Chicago	IL	OTS	7/30/90	SN	563	98
				9/8/92	NI		
Baltimore S&LA	Pikesville	MD	OTS	9/23/91	SN	37	207
Bank of the Eastern Shore	Cambridge	MD	FDIC	8/17/90	NI	63	190
				4/6/92	SN		
Bank of Fresno	Fresno	CA	FDIC	1/15/92	SN	400	168
Bank of Garber	Garber	OK	FED	9/10/90	NI	4	176
				8/31/92	SN		
Bank of New York (Delaware)	Wilmington	DE	FDIC	12/16/91	SN	3,276	225
Bank of North America	Fort Lauderdale	FL	FDIC	9/11/91	SN	523	135
Bank of Sardis	Sardis	MS	FDIC	6/12/92	SN	29	218
Bank of Walnut	Walnut	MS	FDIC	4/2/91	SN	12	255
Bannister B&T Co.	Kansas City	MO	FDIC	3/26/91	SN	89	107
				4/20/92	S		
Bay Financial Savings Bank*	Tampa	FL	OTS	10/15/90	SN	159	1
				2/3/92	SN		
Beneficial National Bank, USA	Wilmington	DE	OCC	5/29/92	SN	334	170
Bergen Commercial Bank	Paramus	NJ	FDIC	7/19/91	SN	43	150
Beverly Hills Business Bank, FSB*	Beverly Hills	CA	OTS	4/9/91	SN	1,208	211
				7/27/92	S		
Brookline Savings Bank	Brookline	MA	FDIC	7/8/91	SN	540	226
				9/8/92	S		
Brunswick B&T Co.	Manalapan Township	NJ	FDIC	8/31/90	SN	80	146
Butler Bank – A Cooperative Bank	Lowell	MA	FDIC	2/6/92	SN	22	107
California Business Bank, N.A.*	San Jose	CA	OCC	9/27/90	SN	59	182
				1/2/92	S		
Cambridge State Bank*	Cambridge	MN	FDIC	7/27/90	SN	66	192
				8/16/91	SN		
Capital B&T Co. of Clayton	Clayton	MO	FDIC	5/24/91	SN	68	184
				4/3/92	NI		

Table continues

Table 8-2 Continued

Name of Bank	City	State	Federal Regulator	Date of Exam	Rating	Assets (millions)	IDC Rating[a]
Cass B&T Company	Sunset Hills	MO	FDIC	3/6/92	SN	205	141
Cherry Grove S&L Company	Cincinnati	OH	OTS	7/28/92	SN	12	159
College Savings Bank	West Windsor	NJ	FDIC	9/9/91	SN	79	189
Colorado Savings Bank, FSB*	Denver	CO	OTS	11/20/90	SN	60	300
				12/2/91	S		
Conservative Bank, a FSB	St. Louis	MO	OTS	12/9/91	SN	72	89
Corporate Bank	Santa Ana	CA	FDIC	7/25/91	SN	93	80
Custom SB, a FSB	Pikesville	MD	OTS	2/13/91	SN	288	300
				3/30/92	SN		
Delta Bank & Trust	Drew	MS	FDIC	7/8/91	SN	8	114
				8/17/92	SN		
Delta National B&T Company	Miami	FL	OCC	6/30/92	SN	88	160
Embry National Bank*	Atlanta	GA	OCC	1/16/91	SN	40	96
				1/31/92	S		
Emerald City Bank	Seattle	WA	FDIC	12/26/91	SN	7	80
Enterprise Bank	Clayton	MO	FDIC	6/10/91	SN	81	121
Enterprise National Bank*	Atlanta	GA	OCC	2/28/91	SN	50	34
				4/2/92	S		
Enterprise S&LA*	Compton	CA	OTS	4/22/91	SN	11	1
Farmers and Merchants Bank*	Long Beach	CA	FED	8/6/90	SN	1,481	300
				4/22/91	NI		
				6/29/92	NI		
Farmers and Miners State Bank	Lucas	IA	FDIC	11/20/91	SN	4[c]	203[c]
First Bank of Jacksonville*	Jacksonville	FL	FDIC	8/16/90	SN	8	141
				10/21/91	NI		
First National Bank of Konowa	Konowa	OK	OCC	3/12/92	SN	14	293
First National Bank of Seiling	Seiling	OK	OCC	9/30/91	SN	59	195
Fountain Bank	Scottsdale	AZ	FED	3/18/91	SN	16[b]	1[b]
Gotham Bank*	New York	NY	FED	12/17/90	SN	87	258
				8/6/91	NI		
				8/17/92	S		
Guardian S&LA*	Huntington Beach	CA	OTS	11/5/90	SN	452	1
Haddon S&LA	Haddon Heights	NJ	OTS	9/9/91	SN	165	183
Hawthorne S&LA*	Hawthorne	CA	OTS	10/10/90	SN	1,035	231
				12/9/91	NI		
Hillcrest Bank	Kansas City	MO	FDIC	1/31/91	SN	34	55
				2/14/92	S		

Table continues

Table 8-2   Continued

Name of Bank	City	State	Federal Regulator	Date of Exam	Rating	Assets (millions)	IDC Rating[a]
Howard Savings Bank	Glenview	IL	FDIC	3/11/92	SN	43	300
Investors Thrift	Orange	CA	FDIC	7/16/91	SN	275	246
				7/29/92	S		
Key FSB*	Owings Mills	MD	OTS	3/4/91	SN	185	157
				6/22/92	NI		
Keystone FS&LA of Sharpsburg*	Sharpsburg	PA	OTS	3/14/91	SN	25	220
LBS Bank-New York*	New York	NY	FDIC	9/28/90	SN	173	155
Long Island City S&LA	Long Island City	NY	OTS	12/3/90	SN	344	300
Manufacturers Bank-Wilmington	Newark	DE	FDIC	1/28/91	SN	51	223
				1/30/92	S		
Marina State Bank	Marina Del Rey	CA	FDIC	4/29/91	SN	19	74
Maryland Permanent B&T Co.	Pikesville	MD	FDIC	8/23/91	SN	21	157
Mercantile National Bank	Los Angeles	CA	OCC	9/30/91	SN	396	68
Mercantile Savings Bank*	Southaven	MS	OTS	10/15/90	SN	22[b]	1[b]
Merchants National Bank*	Sacramento	CA	OCC	3/15/91	SN	70	250
Merrill Lynch B&T Co.*	Plainsboro Township	NJ	FDIC	12/11/90	SN	1,590	216
Missouri B&T Co. of Kansas City	Kansas City	MO	FDIC	1/10/91	SN	35	72
				6/12/92	S		
Missouri State B&T Co.	St. Louis	MO	FDIC	6/14/91	NI	38	1
				9/18/92	SN		
National Bank of Pakistan	Chicago	IL	FDIC	9/27/91	SN	N/A	N/A
Needham Co-operative Bank	Needham	MA	FDIC	2/11/92	SN	285	184
New River Bank	Oakland Park	FL	FDIC	4/30/92	SN	24	155
North Cincinnati Loan and Building Co.*	Blue Ash	OH	OTS	3/22/91	SN	59	132
Norwalk-Cumming State Bank	Norwalk	IA	FDIC	8/30/91	SN	16	147
Odebolt State Bank	Odebolt	IA	FDIC	3/13/92	SN	11	225
Okmulgee S&LA*	Okmulgee	OK	OTS	5/20/91	SN	5	271
				12/2/91	SN		
Parish B&T Co.*	Momence	IL	FED	10/23/90	SN	19	131
				12/30/91	SN		
				7/20/92	SN		
Premier Bank Rochester	Rochester	MN	FDIC	8/28/91	SN	79	128
				9/8/92	NI		
Public Service Bank, a FSB	St. Louis	MO	OTS	7/8/91	SN	64	167

Table continues

Table 8-2   Continued

Name of Bank	City	State	Federal Regulator	Date of Exam	Rating	Assets (millions)	IDC Rating[a]
Rancho Santa Fe Thrift & Loan Association	Encinitas	CA	FDIC	4/7/92	SN	26	230
Royal Savings Bank	Chicago	IL	FDIC	4/18/92	SN	84	176
Security Savings Bank, FSB*	Hillsboro	IL	OTS	1/22/91	SN	16	100
South Coast Thrift & Loan Association	Santa Ana	CA	FDIC	10/7/91	SN	80	71
State Bank of Coloma	Coloma	MI	FED	4/29/91	NI	28	126
				6/9/92	SN		
Standard Chartered Bank, LTD	Chicago	IL	FDIC	1/31/92	SN	N/A	N/A
Texas Coastal Bank	Pasadena	TX	FED	9/9/91	SN	14	156
				3/23/92	SN		
Texas Commerce Banks	Newark	DE	FDIC	5/6/91	SN	59	300
Tustin Thrift & Loan Association	Tustin	CA	FDIC	10/25/91	SN	27	150
UBAF Arab American Bank*	New York	NY	FED	1/22/91	SN	701	1
				1/6/92	S		
Uinta County State Bank*	Mountain View	WY	FED	10/30/90	SN	5[c]	234[c]
				9/16/91	SN		
				3/17/92	SN		
United Citizens National Bank*	Los Angeles	CA	OCC	4/3/91	SN	43	164
				3/13/92	NI		
Vinings B&T, N.A.*	Atlanta	GA	OCC	9/26/90	SN	39	8
				10/30/91	SN		

a/ Composite 12/31/91 financial rating of IDC Financial Publishing, ranging from high of 300 to low of 1; assets also as of 12/31/91.

b/ Last reported data for failed or merged bank; some other banks listed here have also failed or been merged.

c/ Data as of 9/30/91.

Rating: SN = Substantial Noncompliance
         N = Needs Improvement
         S = Satisfactory

*Complete CRA performance evaluation for one or more of these ratings included in companion volume.

N/A –   Not Available

Source: K.H. Thomas Associates
         IDC Financial Publishing
         Individual Regulators

Double and Triple Substantial Noncompliance Ratings

Table 8-2 contains information on the 36 substantial noncompliant banks receiving multiple ratings through December 31, 1992. The FDIC and FED downgraded two banks each from needs improvement to substantial noncompliance in 1992. Nine of the 36 multiple evaluations maintained the same substantial noncompliance rating. Interestingly, two of those were triple substantial noncompliance ratings by the FED given to the Parish Bank & Trust company of Momence, Illinois, and the Uinta County State Bank of Mountain View, Wyoming. The vast majority (23 of 36) of multiple ratings were upgrades with 14 to satisfactory (including one triple rating) and nine to needs improvement (including one triple rating). Eleven of the 23 upgrades were by the FDIC and five were in Missouri, with four of those 1992 upgrades to satisfactory. This could represent a significant turnaround in the CRA performance of FDIC-regulated banks in Missouri *or* the 1992 easing up on what may have been selective enforcement in 1991, *or* grade inflation.

L.A., Chicago and St. Louis Are Three Lowest CRA-Ranked Areas

The state outline map (Figure 8-1) shows the distribution of the 88 banks with substantial noncompliance ratings in 24 states throughout the country as of December 31, 1992. There are several concentrations of these banks that are apparent, most notably in the northeast, midwest, southeast, and especially southern California.

Specific concentrations are of special interest. The first and largest concentration by far with 13 banks or one in seven with such ratings is along and near L.A.'s I-405 (San Diego Freeway) corridor. This corridor also contains most of the largest banks with these ratings.

The second largest concentrations with seven banks each are in the greater Chicago and St. Louis areas. There are several areas with three to four banks in this category: northern Atlanta, midtown Manhattan, Kansas City, northwestern Baltimore, northern Delaware, central New Jersey, and south Florida.

Why "Chicagoland" is the Second Lowest CRA-Ranked Area

The greater Chicago area would be the second lowest-ranking area in terms of CRA behind L.A. in our opinion, with St. Louis ranking third. The "Chicagoland" area, which encompasses part of northeastern Illinois and northwestern Indiana, stands out for several reasons. First, this area was home to the very first CRA merger denial in 1979 involving a Gary, Indiana, bank owned by a Chicago corporation. Second, Chicago's Continental Illinois, in a landmark case, was denied the acquisition of an Arizona bank on CRA grounds ten years later. Third, a more recent 1992 merger denial on CRA grounds involved the denial of Gore-Bronson Bancorp, Inc. of Prospect Heights, Illinois to acquire the Water Tower Trust and Savings Bank in Chicago.

Thus, three merger denials on CRA grounds alone, representing the lion's share of all such denials, including the first and the biggest, were in the greater Chicago area. The FED had an opportunity to deny the acquisition of Chicago's Talman Home Federal through LaSalle National Bank on CRA grounds, but used the troubled institution "loophole" to approve it in February 1992. As noted in Chapter 3, Chicago's Harris Bank was the largest bank ever to receive a needs improvement rating. Counting LaSalle National Bank, two of the four of our nation's hundred largest banks ever receiving a needs improvement rating are based in Chicago. Moreover, Bell Federal, Chicago's fifth largest savings and loan, also received a needs improvement rating.

Missouri, with a total of 10 such rated banks (seven in St. Louis plus three in Kansas City), was second only to California with 17 in terms of banks with substantial noncompliance ratings. Illinois followed with eight such banks. These three states alone represented 40% of all banks with substantial noncompliance ratings. Florida, Maryland, and New Jersey followed with five such banks each.

Figure 8-1   Substantial Noncompliance Rated Banks, 7/1/90 – 12/31/92

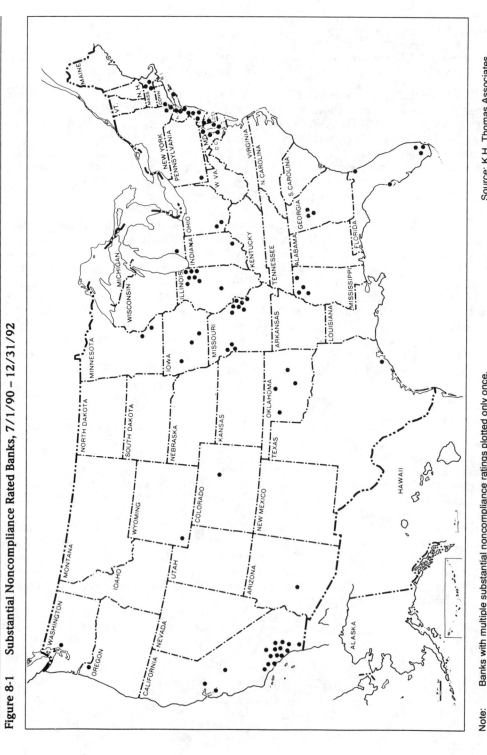

Note: Banks with multiple substantial noncompliance ratings plotted only once.

Source: K.H. Thomas Associates

Some but Not All Substantial Noncompliant Banks Have Been Upgraded

This chapter's analysis is in the form of a profile of substantial noncompliant banks categorized by CRA assessment factors, as was the case in Chapters 4 and 6. This profile is based primarily on the 54 banks that received substantial noncompliance ratings as of year-end 1991, even though several of these banks were upgraded since then. The profile that follows should be reviewed in conjunction with the actual performance evaluations of those 54 banks whenever possible.

It is important that those banks discussed here which have been upgraded from a substantial noncompliance rating also be evaluated in terms of their current rating and public evaluation. However, because we are preparing a profile of banks with substantial noncompliance ratings, our focus is on why these and other banks received the lower ratings. Many of the items specifically criticized by CRA examiners may have already been corrected by these banks, especially those with upgraded ratings. This fact should be kept in mind in the examination of the CRA activities of any particular bank mentioned in the profile below.

I. ASCERTAINMENT OF COMMUNITY CREDIT NEEDS

Activities to Ascertain Community Credit Needs (Assessment Factor A)

Substantial noncompliance banks have little or no involvement in activities that determine community credit needs. There are few if any contacts with community representatives at such banks.

No Intention to Expand Credit Services on Long Island

Long Island City Savings and Loan of Long Island City, New York, recently increased its efforts to ascertain community credit needs, but the examiners considered these recent efforts "inconsequential because the institution does not intend to expand its credit services regardless of the results of these efforts." In other words, that thrift was just going through the (ascertainment) motions.

UBAF Arab American Bank of New York, New York, a wholesale and international bank, asserted there was "no need to take an affirmative approach to ascertain the needs of the community" because of the bank's specialized nature.

Maryland's Key Federal Waits for Community Groups to Contact Branch Managers

An unusual view of this assessment factor was held by Key Federal Savings Bank of Owings Mill, Maryland, whose CRA statement encouraged community groups to contact branch managers. This is the reverse of the normal procedure of undertaking active community outreach efforts. Not surprisingly, the evaluation noted that no community groups had contacted the thrift.

Community Bank Employees Unknowingly Contradict Management

Many banks stated that they used different methods of credit needs ascertainment such as personal contacts of employees or call programs, but there was no documentation or results. Worse yet is where an examiner interviews employees who unknowingly contradict what management told them.

For example, in the case of Parish Bank & Trust Company of Momence, Illinois, management noted that an increased demand for automobile and student loans was identified through the bank's ascertainment efforts, although there was no documentation of these efforts. The examiners found, however, "through discussions with relevant bank staff," that the bank became aware of the increased demand or need for these products through "increased requests for and inquiries about these types of products during banking hours, and not as a result of any ascertainment efforts."

CRA as an "Afterthought"

Examiners sometimes interview members of the community who are often representatives of local groups or agencies. The evaluation of the Texas Coastal Bank of Pasadena, Texas, cited a local contact who was "curious" as to why another similarly sized local bank was so actively ascertaining and addressing credit needs in the community, while Texas Coastal Bank "made no effort at all." The examiners of that bank noted that its "board/management apparently chose to ignore" recommendations made in the previous exam to improve ascertainment efforts.

Vinings Bank & Trust, N.A. of Atlanta, Georgia, started a CRA "call program." The examiners, however, concluded that few calls were actually CRA-related, and that CRA was an "afterthought as opposed to being the reason for initiating the visit."

Denver Bank's Ascertainment Efforts Backfire

A bank's efforts to ascertain credit needs may backfire if initial contacts are made and interest is developed but there is no follow-through by the bank. Colorado Savings Bank of Denver, Colorado, initiated contact with the Colorado Housing and Finance Authority with a bank letter expressing interest in their credit programs. When these were met with various application forms, the bank did not respond by the deadline because of other pressing matters (i.e., a branch relocation, a computer conversion, and employee interviewing). This same bank, which has information on the local housing authority in its CRA file, is not actively involved in any lending program of the authority. The bank, however, did solicit and maintains its operating account and also bids on its jumbo deposits. The bank's ascertainment efforts were obviously sharply criticized by examiners.

"Last Minute" CRA Efforts Questioned

Ascertainment efforts should not be "last minute" before, or worse yet during, a CRA exam. Allegiant Bank of St. Louis, Missouri, obtained demographic information during the exam. Also, the Missouri Bank & Trust Co. of Kansas City, Missouri, obtained demographic data on a revised CRA area during the exam. Manufacturers Bank–Wilmington of Newark, Delaware, introduced its CRA management plan during the month of the exam. Texas Coastal Bank's president made "an attempt to track the bank's lending patterns . . . just prior to the examiner's arrival."

A few banks that had commissioned marketing surveys were criticized when the sample was limited to bank customers, because the needs of noncustomers were not being ascertained. Surveys may not be very useful under this assessment factor unless they specifically pertain to credit products directed at

a broad representative base. Colorado Savings of Denver, Colorado, was criticized since its holding company's marketing study did not state specific CRA goals or otherwise integrate the bank's CRA program.

Outdated Demographics in Southern California

One of the most glaring problems with this assessment factor involves banks that totally ignore or make little effort to collect and analyze relevant demographic data. There is really no excuse for this because a considerable amount of relevant data are available at little or no charge from several sources. Such sources include local, county, regional, and state chambers of commerce, planning departments, and other public and private organizations (e.g., utilities) that produce these data.

The largest provider of relevant demographic data on a small-area basis is the Bureau of the Census of the U.S. Department of Commerce. Many bankers are surprised to learn that a considerable amount of useful 1990 small-area census data are available directly from the Census Bureau or the relevant State Data Center at little or no charge (although private companies may charge handsomely for these same but repackaged data). It is therefore hard to defend a situation where a bank has little or no demographic data.

The collected demographic data must be relevant and updated. Hawthorne Savings of Hawthorne, California, was criticized for having outdated data not representative of its local community. Some banks with this rating did not even bother to collect demographic data (e.g., Archer Federal of Chicago, Illinois, and Merchants National Bank of Sacramento, California) or ignored its existence (e.g., Avondale Federal of Chicago, Illinois). This brings into question the mere existence of an effective marketing function at such institutions.

Board of Directors' Participation (Assessment Factor C)

The easiest test for an examiner to apply under this assessment factor is to merely review board minutes to ascertain participation, or more than likely the lack of it for substantial noncompliant banks.

Board Minutes on File in Karachi

The worst situation we saw in this regard was with the National Bank of Pakistan, a Chicago branch of the parent in Karachi, Pakistan, which did not even have a CRA statement. The examiners couldn't even see the board minutes since they were kept with the parent in Karachi.

Other bad situations are when there is no CRA notice or CRA public file (e.g., in the case of AVCO National Bank of Irvine, California); when board minutes reveal absolutely no discussions of CRA (for over two years in the case of Enterprise Savings of Compton, California); or, when there is no CRA statement approval (for one year for the Austin State Bank of Austin, Indiana, for two years in the case of Hawthorne Savings of Hawthorne, California, and the Bank of Walnut of Walnut, Mississippi, and not at all for the Enterprise National Bank of Atlanta, Georgia).

Texas Bank Board Mistakenly Approves Wrong CRA Statement

Board minutes about CRA right before or during an exam may carry little weight if they are the only relevant discussions of CRA. A very troubling situation is when the examiners conclude that recommended changes made in a previous exam were not implemented (as was the case for the California Business Bank of San Jose, California, regarding its previous 1989 exam). Also, the Texas Coastal Bank of Pasadena, Texas, approved its CRA statement but "the board failed to recognize that they were approving the same CRA statement that had been cited for violations" at the prior exam.

UBAF Bank had a CRA officer with a "wide range of responsibilities" that reduced the officer's ability to address CRA issues effectively. Both Beverly Hills Business Bank of Beverly Hills, California, and Key Federal Savings Bank of Owings Mill, Maryland, had a senior management committee involved in CRA decisions, but neither committee was formally established by a full board resolution.

Duplicating the Same CRA Statement for the Last 14 Years

The CRA statements that are approved by the board must be correct, and board minutes must be complete. For example, Enterprise Savings of Compton, California, did not have a CRA notice in its 1990 CRA statement. Colorado Savings of Denver, Colorado, revised their CRA statement, but the board minutes did not indicate any discussion of the impact of the changes.

Bay Financial Savings of Tampa, Florida, was criticized because the two most recent board CRA reviews "were neither timely nor accurate." AVCO National Bank's (Irvine, California) CRA statement was "inaccurate with respect to the types of credit the bank is willing to make available." The CRA statement of Merrill Lynch Bank & Trust Company of Plainsboro Township, New Jersey, failed to list the availability of a home mortgage program. The CRA notice of Manufacturers Bank–Wilmington of Newark, Delaware, included "misleading information," according to the examiner.

The Capital Bank & Trust Company of Clayton, Missouri, had not revised its CRA statement since the bank opened in 1985, and several "exceptions" concerning that statement were noted. Few changes in the CRA statement of Public Service Bank of St. Louis, Missouri, were made since 1977, the year CRA became law. The examiners further noted that the optional expanded section of it has "for the most part, been duplicated for the last 14 years."

The Board at Security Savings Bank of Hillsboro, Illinois, was criticized for being "lax" on CRA technicalities, since available loans listed in the statement are "not specific enough" and board minutes approving the CRA statement were not signed by board members. Security's board was also cited for not reviewing or adopting annual loan underwriting standards. These were not available to customers upon request nor were inquirers informed of their rights to file an application and receive these standards. Furthermore, Security did not maintain the required loan application register.

*CRA Manual at Baltimore Bank Called
"Confusing, Inadequate, Repetitive, and
Contradictory"*

All banks are recommended to have a CRA plan (see case study in Chapter 5). It can be counterproductive to have a CRA plan but then fail to implement it (e.g., in the cases of Enterprise National Bank of Atlanta, Georgia, Parish Bank & Trust Company of Momence, Illinois, or Security Savings Bank of Hillsboro, Illinois). Merchants National Bank of Sacramento, California, had a 1988 board-adopted CRA program calling for semiannual meetings (which were not held) and quarterly reports of director and officer contacts (which reports were not consistently provided).

Custom Savings Bank of Pikesville, Maryland, in the greater Baltimore area, had a CRA manual, but it was strongly criticized by the examiners for being "confusing, inadequate, repetitive, and contradictory." This reinforced the examiners' conclusion that the bank's board and management had "little understanding of the CRA and are generally not willing to respond to its requirements."

Worse yet were those banks that did not even have a formal CRA plan or policy, especially those that were criticized for this omission on a previous exam (e.g., Uinta County State Bank of Mountain View, Wyoming).

II. MARKETING AND TYPES OF CREDIT OFFERED AND EXTENDED

Marketing Programs for Credit Awareness (Assessment Factor B)

A review of a bank's advertising strategy, a part of its overall marketing program, is really the easiest and quickest means of examining compliance for this assessment factor.

*Community Bank Advertising Limited to
Calendars and Lobby Deposit Rate Board*

The worst situation is when a bank has absolutely no advertising or marketing program for any type of service, such as the Cambridge State Bank of Cambridge, Minnesota. They primarily advertise bank holiday closings and use miscellaneous advertising to thank the community and congratulate institutions on new construction or improvements.

Many banks were criticized for advertising focused solely on deposit products or image, with no reference to credit products. Some banks, such as the Gotham Bank of New York, New York, which uses referrals as its loan source, do no credit advertising anywhere. The Uinta County State Bank of Mountain View, Wyoming, primarily makes loans to applicants personally known to management. It does no credit advertising but advertises its image on calendars passed out to local businesses.

The only "disclosed bank advertising" by Premier Bank Rochester of Rochester, Minnesota, is "the lobby poster board that gives rates on deposits." Capital Bank & Trust Company of Clayton, Missouri, has run only three deposit-related advertising programs since the bank opened in 1985.

*Small Illinois Thrift Claims Radio and
Newspaper Advertising "Not Responsive
to Community Needs"*

Banks advertising their credit services should carefully choose the media to be representative of its market. Security Savings of Hillsboro, Illinois, told its examiners that radio and newspaper advertising was "not responsive to community needs" since competitors used them. Instead, that bank preferred "direct" communications.

In addition to advertising in the local general newspaper, banks should also select media which reaches low- and moderate-income residents in the bank's local community. If there is a local neighborhood paper or other media that is specifically directed to low- and moderate-income neighborhoods, it clearly should be utilized for advertising credit products. Many of the banks with this rating that did advertise ignored these special media (e.g., all three Atlanta banks).

*Being Criticized for Credit Advertising in a
Minority Publication in Kansas City*

We found one unusual case where the Hillcrest Bank of Kansas City, Missouri, was actually criticized for "use of a minority oriented publication for home improvement and general advertisements." The examiners felt that the use of such media "greatly limits exposure of the bank's credit programs to non-minorities and to lower-income individuals who may not read such a publication." This seemingly "reverse discrimination" argument regarding nonminorities was a first as best we could determine. After being criticized for credit advertising in a minority publication, management at Hillcrest Bank may have been thinking "Damned if you do and damned if you don't!"

The examiners at the Hillcrest Bank were apparently also concerned that only six of the 22 outside contacts made during the exam were aware of the bank or familiar with the types of credit programs offered. Yet, the examiners at the Texas Coastal Bank of Pasadena, Texas, noted that the two outside contacts made during that exam suggested specific media for loan advertisements, and one was a minority radio station. Most exams recommend the use of media to target low- and moderate-income or minority residents, but few make specific recommendations based on outside contacts. A sample of 22 is better than two, but nonrandom or unscientific samples are of little value to anyone.

Banks that are specialized lenders, such as LBS Bank (New York, New York), UBAF Bank (New York, New York), and Guardian Savings (Huntington Beach, California), are particularly susceptible to criticism under this assessment factor. For example, Guardian Savings advertises only to brokers, since that institution only accepts loan applications from its network of brokers. Merrill Lynch Bank & Trust Company of Plainsboro Township, New Jersey, limits its marketing to customers of its parent, Merrill Lynch & Company.

"Token" Advertising in Minority Publications in the Middle of the CRA Exam

Banks that attempt to remedy their deficiencies under this assessment factor *during* the exam may find that it backfires with the examiners. This is especially the case if it is perceived as a "token" gesture to please the examiners rather than forming the basis of a new program.

Although we don't know what the motivation or situation was, California Business Bank of San Jose, California, which does most of its advertising in the local business journal, placed one of its advertisements in a local Spanish language newspaper "during

the examination." The examiners noted that this bank used an external compliance consultant to review the bank's advertising copy.

Other banks had minimal advertising during the exam's review period. Credit marketing during a 26-month review period at the North Cincinnati Loan and Building Company of Blue Ash, Ohio, was limited to a one-day print advertisement in a local paper.

Archer Federal of Chicago, Illinois, was noted as running one advertisement for loan products during the exam's review period, as compared to advertisements that normally focus on services and image.

"Grossly Inadequate" Marketing in St. Louis—Aiming Only at Large Churches

AVCO National Bank of Irvine, California, was cited in 1991 for maintaining advertising brochures "from the last lending program which ended in 1989." Merchants National Bank of Sacramento, California, was criticized because it did "not actively promote" a unique credit program with low rates, fees, and a minimum loan amount. That is, the bank had a good credit program but was criticized for failing to actively promote it.

Allegiant Bank's (St. Louis, Missouri) marketing and advertising programs were characterized as being "grossly inadequate." Marketing efforts there were aimed only at larger churches in the area. Also, the bank was criticized since its name was not displayed on its building for "at least a three month period after the change in control and name change."

Available Credit Services (Assessment Factor I)

Many banks receiving a substantial noncompliance rating had very few or no loans of a particular type, such as residential mortgage loans.

Only One Savings Account Loan since Illinois Thrift Was Chartered

First Bank of Jacksonville, Florida, which was opened in August of 1989, had made no loans during its first full year of operations. It had received 10 applications though.

Allegiant Bank of St. Louis, Missouri, had made no loans in its delineated area since new management acquired the bank some six months prior to the exam.

Delta Bank & Trust of Drew, Mississippi, made only $1.8 million in new loans for the one year it was in operation prior to the exam. The bank purchased nearly three times that volume of loans from the RTC.

Security Savings of Hillsboro, Illinois, which offers only one-year adjustable rate mortgages and passbook loans, granted only one savings account loan "since the date of its charter." Rather, it purchased loans from the RTC as part of its "acquisition package."

Oklahoma Thrift Stopped Lending in 1985 since Two Local Banks Do the Job

Worse yet is the case of Okmulgee Savings of Okmulgee, Oklahoma, which "ceased offering credit services" in 1985, since management and the board claimed that the two competing local banks adequately served community credit needs. In fact, management of Okmulgee Savings arranged for the CRA examiners to interview loan officers at both local banks to support the thrift's claim. (Incidentally, one of the local banks' received a satisfactory CRA rating, and the other bank's rating was not available as of year-end 1992.) Even though both bank officers indicated a relatively small demand for home loan financing, the examiners noted that this does not exempt a bank from its CRA obligations.

Mercantile Savings Bank of Southaven, Mississippi, made or purchased no loans of any type in its local community except for savings account loans. It purchased most of its loans from a Texas service corporation subsidiary.

The Chicago office of the National Bank of Pakistan makes only export/import types of credit. Special purpose credit card banks headquartered in Delaware are limited by law to that one type of loan and are further restricted from competing with local banks. Not all such credit card or foreign banks, however, have received substantial noncompliance or even needs improvement ratings.

Baltimore Thrift Claims It Is "Impossible" to Geocode

Custom Savings Bank of Pikesville, Maryland, in the greater Baltimore area, has "not met any community credit need through the origination and purchase of loans." The bank does not originate loans but invests in mortgage-backed securities and blocks of

mortgage loans originated by others. Management states that it is "impossible to determine the locations of the properties that secure these loans."

Long Island City Savings and Loan of Long Island City, New York, has an "excessively low" loan volume, offering only passbook and guaranteed student loans. The vast majority of its assets are in mortgage-backed securities collateralized by property outside its delineated community.

Beverly Hills Business Bank of Beverly Hills, California, "merely acts in a brokerage capacity" and does not originate or purchase any loans. North Cincinnati Loan and Building Company of Blue Ash, Ohio, made only 35 first mortgage loans in the 26-month review period because it became a purchaser of adjustable-rate, mortgage-backed securities.

The Vinings Bank & Trust Company of Atlanta, Georgia, was unable to determine lending by type of loan because of an inadequate loan tracking system. The Enterprise National Bank of Atlanta, Georgia, made no residential mortgage loans.

Super Conservative Lenders—No "Walk-In" Business and 1% Loan-to-Assets

Many banks that did make all types of loans may have had very low loan-to-deposit or loan-to-asset ratios, which may have been related to unduly conservative credit underwriting standards. The Gotham Bank of New York, New York, makes residential mortgage loans to accommodate business customers only and has a policy "not to accept walk-in business in the area of credit products."

The Uinta County State Bank of Mountain View, Wyoming, had a loan-to-asset ratio of just 1%, virtually unchanged from that in the previous year! AVCO National Bank of Irvine, California, also had a 1% ratio. That bank had not extended credit since December 1989 and was liquidating its loan portfolio.

Premier Bank Rochester of Rochester, Minnesota, had a loan-to-deposit ratio of just 2.7%. The Austin State Bank of Austin, Indiana, had a loan-to-asset ratio of only 5%. It had but three mortgage loans and one large business loan in its portfolio with the rest being small consumer loans. The Cambridge State Bank of Cambridge, Minnesota, had a loan-to-deposit ratio of only 15% versus a peer average of roughly four times that amount. The comparable ratio of Merchants

National Bank of Sacramento, California, was only 21%.

No Home Loans since Kansas City Bank Chartered in 1987

Many examiners immediately focused their attention on the very low level of real estate loans at certain banks with this rating. Hillcrest Bank of Kansas City, Missouri, has made no home purchase or residential swing loans since the bank was chartered in 1987.

Colorado Savings of Denver, Colorado, made only one retail mortgage loan developed from just three applications over an approximately nine-month period. Keystone Federal Savings of Sharpsburg, Pennsylvania, granted only three mortgage loans over a three-year period, and only one of those loans was in its delineated community. Investors Thrift of Orange, California, made "virtually no residential mortgage loans."

Archer Federal of Chicago, Illinois, made only six loans in a roughly 16-month period. Embry National Bank of Atlanta, Georgia, made only one conventional home purchase money loan and one home improvement loan in an entire year. Again, this was better than those banks not making any of these loans at all.

Community Says 25% Ceiling on Adjustable Rate Loans at Chicago Thrift "Too Risky"

In cases where examiners find minimal lending, they may first question officers and then actual existing or potential borrowers. Archer Federal of Chicago, Illinois, which had only six loans in a 16-month period, had rejected only one loan application. Management's explanation was that the low level of lending was "due to competition," but that could not be documented, according to the examiners.

The evaluation notes, however, that "individuals from within Archer's delineated community that were contacted" gave other reasons. They said a 30-year fixed-rate mortgage loan was needed instead of the present 15-year one, and that adjustable-rate loan interest rates offered by Archer with a 25% ceiling were "too risky." The Uinta County State Bank of Mountain View, Wyoming, was cited under this assessment factor because its loan interest rates were "not competitive."

Government Loan Programs (Assessment Factor J)

Substantial noncompliant banks rarely or never become involved in government lending programs. Many banks with this rating in this analysis did not participate in any type of government loan program.

Government Loan Programs "Not Compatible" with Philosophy of Sacramento Bank

Merchants National Bank of Saramento, California, has not participated in any such programs because its board has determined that available programs are "not compatible with the bank's philosophy and products." The president of Texas Coastal Bank of Pasadena, Texas, stated that "these types of programs have historically had bad performance with other institutions;" therefore, the bank would "not consider participating in these programs."

Banks generally don't receive credit for enrolling in a program without making loans or at least making a reasonable effort. Also, loans outside a bank's delineated area may carry less weight, although regulator sentiment is changing on this issue.

Last SBA Loan by Minnesota Bank Was in 1977, the Year CRA Was Enacted

Those banks that did participate in government loan programs most often were involved with the Small Business Administration (SBA). Some banks said they considered SBA loans but none were made (e.g., Farmers and Merchants Bank of Long Beach, California). Vinings Bank & Trust Company of Atlanta, Georgia, made only nine SBA loans, with most of them being sold to investors.

The Cambridge State Bank's (Cambridge, Minnesota) last participation with the SBA loan program was in 1977, the year CRA became law. Investors Thrift of Orange, California, is a heavy user of the FHA Title I program, with 15% of its portfolio in this one product.

III. GEOGRAPHIC DISTRIBUTION AND RECORD OF OPENING AND CLOSING OFFICES

Reasonableness of Delineated Community

Approximately one-half of the substantial noncompliant banks were cited as having unreasonably delineated communities under this assessment factor.

$2 Million California Bank Claims Local Community Is Entire U.S.—Including Territories and Possessions!

Most delineated communities that were cited as being unreasonable were too large to be reasonably and effectively served by the resources of the bank. The most egregious example was the very small ($2 million) AVCO National Bank of Irvine, California, which delineated its community to be the entire U.S., together with its territories and possessions!

Delaware Bank Mistaken on Location of Its Headquarters

The Manufacturers Bank–Wilmington of Newark, Delaware, a special-purpose credit card bank, delineated two communities: a local area around its Newark office and another seven-state area including six contiguous midwestern states plus Florida. That bank was criticized not only for that seven-state area where it had no offices but also because the description of the smaller local area mistakenly referred to the bank being located in Wilmington, not Newark, Delaware.

Small Mississippi Bank Claims "Local Community" is 75-Mile Radius with 39 Counties in Three States

The small $13 million Bank of Walnut of Walnut, Mississippi, was criticized for an unreasonably large community of a 75-mile radius around its bank. This very large area included 39 counties in the three-state area of Alabama, Mississippi, and Tennessee.

Another example of a bank criticized for its delineated community was the relatively small $32 million Colorado Savings of Denver, Colorado, which used an excessively large seven-county area containing over 50% of the state's population.

Bank Management Confides to Examiner That Delineated Community Too Large

The similarly-sized Missouri Bank and Trust Company of Kansas City, Missouri, likewise used the seven-county, two-state area comprising the Kansas City metropolitan statistical area. Besides criticizing this area as being unreasonable for this bank, the examiners noted that management themselves indicated that a three-mile radius around the bank's two downtown facilities would be a "more realistic delineation." The examiners obviously agreed. If that was the case, why was the original large area used in the first place, one may ask?

One exception to the general tendency to overstate community areas was the very small delineated area of a local township in central New Jersey used by Merrill Lynch Bank & Trust Company of Plainsboro Township, New Jersey. This bank's credit product is offered to the employees and customer base of its parent Merrill Lynch & Company. Another exception was the California Business Bank of San Jose, California, which had an unreasonably small community of just a two-mile radius about its only office. Most of its loans were made outside that community.

Arizona Bank Management Can't Defend "Gerrymandered" Community

The greatest concern of a CRA examiner in evaluating the reasonableness of the delineated community is whether certain areas, especially low- and moderate-income and/or minority neighborhoods, are unreasonably excluded. This would be indicative of redlining. Fountain Bank of Scottsdale, Arizona, was deemed to have an unreasonable delineation, since it excluded the only low- to moderate-income area in that city. Furthermore, this apparently gerrymandered delineation contained "random irregular boundaries" and senior management was "unable to offer an acceptable explanation" for it. Moreover, the delineation ultimately used failed to represent the areas from which that bank originated most of its loans.

Capital Bank & Trust Company of Clayton, Missouri, was likewise criticized for an unreasonably delineated area, partially because it excluded identified low- to moderate-income areas "without the use of a reasonable method." That bank was also cited for using a map in the CRA statement that was a "poor copy (unreadable)" and did not include street names or other identifying boundaries.

"Community Activist Group" in St. Louis Delineated Overly Broad Community

In cases where the bank states that it conducted an analysis to delineate the community, it should be prepared to document it. Archer Federal of Chicago, Illinois, could not document the savings analysis it cited. Parish Bank & Trust Company of Momence, Illinois, described two different methodologies for its community delineation, but the examiners concluded that neither approach was justified.

Allegiant Bank of St. Louis, Missouri, which was criticized for an overly broad area, had used a community determined by former management. It turns out that former management relied on a "community activist group" to delineate the area rather than conduct their own analysis. This unusual approach to community delineation failed to shield that bank from regulatory criticism about the area's reasonableness.

The delineated community must be clear on the maps accompanying the CRA statement. This was not the case with the Farmers and Merchants Bank of Long Beach, California, since its CRA statement did not reflect its delineated communities.

The narrative description of the community in the CRA statement was inconsistent with the map for Merchants National Bank (Sacramento, California), North Cincinnati Loan and Building Company (Blue Ash, Ohio), and Beverly Hills Business Bank (Beverly Hills, California). The narrative description must be specific rather than a general reference to "adjacent communities" without naming them, as was the case with Texas Coastal Bank of Pasadena, Texas

Expansion of Local Community to 5-Mile Radius Not Enough

Guardian Savings of Huntington Beach, California, expanded the definition of its community from a local one to a multi-county area, which was acceptable to the examiners. Hillcrest Bank of Kansas City, Missouri, on the other hand, was questioned as to the appropriateness of expanding its community from a two and one-half to just a five-mile radius around its

bank, since the "substantive portion" (about three-fourths) of the bank's lending activity still was outside this larger area.

Incomplete and Obsolete CRA Statement in New Jersey

Cambridge State Bank of Cambridge, Minnesota, which was criticized for an overly large community, was noted for having the same delineated area since 1979 in the bank's first CRA statement. Bay Financial Savings of Tampa, Florida, was criticized since its current delineation "contains several areas in which the institution no longer has a presence."

Worse yet was the case of the Chicago branch of the National Bank of Pakistan, since they didn't even have a CRA statement (and obviously no delineated CRA local area). Brunswick Bank and Trust Company of Manalapan Township, New Jersey, received no evaluation of its delineated community, since none was discernible from its CRA statement. That statement was "incomplete in the presentation, obsolete in its content, and had not received any apparent attention from management in a number of years."

Geographic Distribution of Credit (Assessment Factor E)

This is one of the most important sections of a CRA evaluation because a bank either completed an analysis of the geographic distribution of credit extensions, applications, and denials or did not.

Examiners at St. Louis Bank Determine Its Computer Servicer Could Have Run Missing Zip Code Listing

A partial analysis of extensions but not applications or denials could represent grounds for criticism, as was the case with Enterprise Bank of Clayton, Missouri.

Allegiant Bank of St. Louis, Missouri, was criticized because bank officers were not utilizing zip code loan distribution data, which the examiners somehow determined were available from the "bank's computer servicer."

If a bank undertook a comprehensive analysis, it would have had to use an appropriate methodology. Assuming this was done, the results would hopefully indicate reasonable application, lending, and denial patterns inside and outside the delineated community.

Loan Analysis Meaningless if Local Community Unreasonably Large

Of course, to the extent the CRA local community was unreasonably delineated, this type of analysis would be of little value, or meaningless at worst. For example, the extreme case of using the entire U.S. as a delineated area (e.g., AVCO National Bank of Irvine, California) would render any analysis of the proportion of lending within or outside it meaningless. Actually, that bank had not analyzed its loan distribution since 1987.

At the other extreme of a very small delineated area of a local township for Merrill Lynch Bank & Trust Company of Plainsboro Township, New Jersey, the geographic analysis demonstrated an "extremely disproportionate pattern of lending outside the delineated community."

Most substantial noncompliant banks did not prepare the appropriate analysis. Some banks, like Texas Coastal Bank of Pasadena, Texas, had failed to develop a loan tracking system, even after a previous exam had recommended the establishment of one.

Community Bank in Mississippi Doesn't Require Loan Applications from "Known Customers"

A geographic analysis of loan applications can't be undertaken if there are no applications for some customers. This was the case with the Bank of Walnut of Walnut, Mississippi, where loan applications "are not required of known customers."

Even worse is the case of Custom Savings Bank of Pikesville, Maryland, where a geographic analysis of loans could not be done because that bank "does not originate loans." According to management, it is "impossible" to determine the locations of the properties that secure the blocks of mortgage loans and mortgage-backed securities it purchases. The National Bank of Pakistan had only one $65,000 loan on the books of its Chicago branch, and a "sample of one" obviously would prove nothing.

Most examiners in cases where there were no geocoding analyses used a few years of HMDA data when available and/or completed their own sample analysis of the data. The scope and methodologies of the examiner-conducted samples varied widely.

"Lopsided" Loan Distribution for Southern California Boat Lender

Well over half of all substantial noncompliant banks were found to have unreasonable lending patterns. This most often meant a large proportion of loans outside the community and/or some type of undesirable pattern relative to low- and moderate-income neighborhoods within or outside of the community. Some banks cited for unreasonable lending patterns (e.g., Avondale Federal of Chicago, Illinois) had no supporting details in the public evaluation. Others were more specific on this charge.

Archer Federal's (Chicago, Illinois) evaluation noted that only three of that bank's six loans, or 50% of the total number, made in a 16-month period were in its community. Only 25% of Gotham Bank's (New York, New York) loans were inside its community.

Marina State Bank of Marina Del Ray, California, had a "lopsided distribution" since it specializes in financing recreational boats, which draws customers from outside its community. Virtually all of UBAF Bank's (New York, New York) loans were outside its local Manhattan community because the bank is an international lender.

Revised Community Delineation Increases Local Lending Rate from 10% to 74%

Guardian Savings of Huntington Beach, California, had only 10% of its loans in its originally delineated community, but the number jumped to 74% in its recently expanded definition. Guardian Savings broadened its community (without any examiner criticism) from the local areas surrounding its offices to six counties in southern California. Bay Financial Savings of Tampa, Florida, was criticized for heavy and increased out-of-state credit extensions, with lending decreasing 87% in-state and increasing over 60% out-of-state.

Hillcrest Bank of Kansas City, Missouri, was cited for an unreasonable lending pattern since only 26% of its loans were within its community and 48% of all loans were purchased loan participations outside the community.

Vinings Bank & Trust, N.A. of Atlanta, Georgia, which was cited for having an unjustified and disproportionate pattern, had only 1.6% of the total number of loans in low- and moderate-income census tracts within its delineated community, compared to the 45% of such tracts in that community. The examiners were apparently concerned that "senior management have not taken appropriate corrective action" on the unreasonable lending patterns that were identified there.

Iowa Bank Cited for Disproportionate Lending Pattern Due to 9% – 16% Difference in Local Lending and Denial Rates

North Cincinnati Loan and Building Company of Blue Ash, Ohio, was criticized not only because it made only 35 first mortgage loans over the 26-month review period, but also for disproportionate lending —one nonspecified area had a disproportionate concentration of mortgage loans. Key Federal Savings Bank of Owings Mill, Maryland, made only 15 mortgage loans in its delineated community in 1989 and 1990, and none of these were in low- and moderate-income areas.

The Norwalk-Cumming State Bank of Norwalk, Iowa, had two delineated communities, one for each of its two offices. An examiner-conducted sample of one community showed 72% of credit extensions and 63% of denials within it, and this led the examiners to conclude there was a "reasonable penetration" of that community. The other community, however, with 63% of extensions and 47% of denials within it, was deemed to represent a "disproportionate pattern," yet the differences were only 9% and 16%, respectively.

"Ultra Conservative" Lender with a 15% Loan-to-Deposit Ratio

Banks with strict credit underwriting standards may also be cited in this assessment factor, especially if there is a low loan-to-deposit ratio. Cambridge State Bank of Cambridge, Minnesota, with only a 15% ratio, was cited for having "ultraconservative lending practices" that appeared to discourage loan applications.

Niche banks which target affluent customers, professionals, or small businesses may be criticized if

lending patterns are deemed to adversely impact loan availability in low- and moderate-income neighborhoods. This was the case for Capital Bank & Trust Company and Enterprise Bank, both of Clayton, Missouri, in suburban St. Louis.

Office and Service Record (Assessment Factor G)

Even the most substantial noncompliant banks had little difficulty under this assessment factor. This is because most offices are accessible to someone unless, of course, a bank has no office. This was, in fact, the case with AVCO National Bank of Irvine, California, which had no office open to the public and was therefore providing no services.

If a bank was cited for an excessively large CRA community, however, the bank would be subject to the automatic criticism of lack of accessibility. It is, however, usually difficult to criticize office accessibility in most cases with a reasonably delineated area. Also, there may be little a bank may be able to do about the criticism. Nonetheless, some banks were criticized for this reason.

Delaware Law Requires Credit Card Banks Not to Attract General Public—An Automatic CRA Criticism

LBS Bank of New York, New York, a wholesale bank with offices on the 30th floor of a Manhattan office building, was noted as having no teller windows to accept consumer cash transactions. Merrill Lynch Bank & Trust Company of Plainsboro Township, New Jersey, with its only office at its parent's headquarters, only provides cash advances for Merrill Lynch cash management accounts held by Merrill Lynch employees.

The National Bank of Pakistan's branch in downtown Chicago is restricted by Illinois banking law to a single office. Credit card banks such as Texas Commerce Banks and Manufacturers Bank–Wilmington, both of Newark, Delaware, are restricted by Delaware law from soliciting business (including deposits below $100,000) in that state. They are limited to one office that is located and operated in a manner that is "not likely to attract customers from the general public." Thus, by operating within Delaware law these specialty banks are subject to automatic CRA criticism under this assessment factor.

Offices Criticized for Lack of Visibility, Signage, Drive-Ups, and Parking

Enterprise National Bank of Atlanta, Georgia, and Bay Financial Savings of Tampa, Florida, were cited for difficult accessibility for certain segments of the local community because of the lack of a visible office. Bay Financial Savings was also cited for having no signs advertising that office's branch. Cambridge State Bank of Cambridge, Minnesota, was noted as not having drive-up facilities available. Keystone Federal Savings of Sharpsburg, Pennsylvania, was criticized because its "customer parking is limited."

Downtown Kansas City Offices Result in "Extreme Difficulty"

Missouri Bank & Trust Company of Kansas City, Missouri, with two offices in downtown Kansas City, has neither drive-up nor adjacent parking facilities. Even though this situation is common to many downtown locations, because of price and land availability constraints, the examiners noted that this "appears to greatly limit accessibility" to the offices. Further, the bank's only ATM, which was located inside one of its offices, was noted as being accessible only during business hours. This is often the case in downtown offices for security reasons. Coupled with the lack of Saturday hours (again typical for a downtown office) plus other office hours established "in consideration of downtown walk-in traffic," the examiners concluded this caused "extreme difficulty" for residents to transact business.

Tampa Bank Closed Two of Its Three Branches and Experienced Five Relocations since 1989

There was no criticism of branch closings by Enterprise Savings of Compton, California, and Guardian Savings of Huntington Beach, California, probably because of their weak financial condition (they both later failed). This was not the case however with Mercantile Savings Bank of Southaven, Mississippi, which closed its Memphis loan production office in 1988. The evaluation noted that since that time the "credit needs of the delineated community have not been served." That bank also failed.

Bay Financial Savings of Tampa, Florida, was singled out for a "continuing pattern of disinvestment outside the local community." Two of its three branch offices opened since 1984 have been closed, with one relocating three times in six years. The corporate offices were relocated twice over this period. Thus, there were five relocations. Also, three loan production offices of a subsidiary have both opened and closed since 1986.

Management's Claimed "Zero Impact" of Branch Closing Referred to Bank, Not Customers

Branch closings and even relocations should be discussed by the board in terms of their potential impact on a bank's CRA performance. Colorado Savings of Denver, Colorado, was criticized for a branch relocation on this basis. Also, because its delineated local area was so excessively large, it was subject to the automatic criticism that office accessibility within it was inadequate.

Fountain Bank of Scottsdale, Arizona, did not conduct an adverse impact study after closing one of its three offices, although "management confidently stated there was 'zero impact' to the community." The examiners, however, questioned this conclusion since the bank retained only 29% of personal accounts after they were "unilaterally transferred" to the main office some nine miles away. Management's response was that the "zero impact" really referred to the bank, not the community, since the majority of affected accounts had "small balances."

Examiners Criticize 3:00 P.M. Weekday Office Closings in St. Louis and Baltimore

Most of the criticism for substantial noncompliant banks under this assessment factor was due to the failure to review the effectiveness of business hours. Several banks were criticized in this regard. One bank that did a survey of bank customers to determine desired hours was criticized because the survey ignored noncustomers.

Most banks with this rating did no surveys to determine convenient office hours. Allegiant Bank's (St. Louis, Missouri) lobby (but not drive-up or walk-up) hours, which go to 3:00 P.M. on weekdays, except 6:00 P.M. on Friday with no Saturday hours, were noted as "somewhat restrictive." Custom Savings Bank of Pikesville, Maryland, in the greater Baltimore area, was criticized for hours which "do not assure accommodation" of all segments of the community, since branches closed at 3:00 P.M. on weekdays with no evening or Saturday hours. Further, none of their branches have drive-in or ATM facilities. Office hours at Capital Bank & Trust Company and Enterprise Bank, both of Clayton, Missouri, also in the greater St. Louis area, were noted as being "inconsistent with the needs" of the community, but no specifics were provided.

IV. DISCRIMINATION AND OTHER ILLEGAL CREDIT PRACTICES

Credit Application Practices (Assessment Factor D)

Mississippi Loan Customers Sent Away since No Loan Officer and Bank Not "Set Up" for Loan Processing

The most clear-cut example of loan application discouragement was at Mercantile Savings Bank of Southaven, Mississippi, where potential customers were told that the institution had no loan officer and was not "set up" to process mortgage loans.

AVCO National Bank of Irvine, California, had no offices open to the public, and Okmulgee Savings of Okmulgee, Oklahoma, ceased offering credit services altogether in 1985. At least potential borrowers could go into an office in the latter case and learn that no credit products were available. There was no office to go into in the case of AVCO National Bank.

Branch Personnel Quoted Loan Rates and Terms—But No Loans Made or Applications Taken

Custom Savings Bank of Pikesville, Maryland, "does not extend any loan nor does it accept applications for credit." Their examiners apparently were not pleased with branch personnel who would "quote rates and terms to potential credit customers" and direct them to call the corporate office for "further details," only to learn that the bank "does not take applications for such credit."

"The President Will See You Now"

Some banks will accept applications but approve them only under certain conditions. In the case of The Butler Bank – A Cooperative Bank of Lowell, Massachusetts, the condition for application approval is a personal interview with the bank's president. This interview reportedly assesses the applicant by their appearance and demeanor. The interviews have occurred both before and after written applications have been filled out. That bank's stated policy of generally lending only on single-family, owner-occupied homes with "substantial land on all sides" could also discourage certain loan applicants, according to the examiners. Based upon these and related practices the FDIC referred this bank to the Justice Department for review in October 1992..

Cases where banks extend little or no credit of the type listed in their CRA statement will often lead to a conclusion that loan applications have been discouraged. This was the case for Premier Bank Rochester of Rochester, Minnesota, a new bank that did not have a lending staff until two months before the exam.

Reliance on Loan Referrals Viewed as Discouraging Loan Applicants

AVCO National Bank's (Irvine, California) practice of "not soliciting or accepting applications from any segment of its community" was in conflict with its CRA statement. Parish Bank & Trust Company of Momence, Illinois, was mentioned as having two loans listed on its CRA statement that were not available.

Some banks were cited for discouraging applicants because of their loan solicitation procedures. For example, Gotham Bank (New York, New York), Farmers and Merchants Bank (Long Beach, California), and Capital Bank & Trust Company (Clayton, Missouri), all of which relied on referrals for loan applications, were cited in this regard. Guardian Savings of Huntington Beach, California, was found to discourage applications through its exclusive use of a broker network.

Banks Downgraded for Minimum Loan Amounts, High Rates, and "Prohibitive Financing Terms"

Several banks were found to indirectly discourage loan applicants through strict credit underwriting standards. Security Savings of Hillsboro, Illinois, was criticized in this regard for both of its loan products. First, the $500 minimum on its savings account loan was viewed by the examiners as a "possible" deterrent to future originations. Second, the relatively high rates on its two one-year adjustable rate mortgages were believed to have the effect of "discouraging" applications.

North Cincinnati Loan and Building Company's (Blue Ash, Ohio) loan policy had a minimum mortgage loan amount limitation. Hillcrest Bank of Kansas City, Missouri, was cited for "prohibitive financing terms" on automobile loans, and their underwriting criteria for certain loans was noted as limiting access to them by lower income residents. Long Island City Savings of Long Island City, New York, was also criticized for lending restrictions which have a "significant adverse impact" on loan availability.

Banks using target or niche marketing strategies focusing on one market segment, where it appears that other segments represented in the local community may be ignored, risk criticism under this assessment factor. Capital Bank & Trust Company and Enterprise Bank, both of Clayton, Missouri, target small businesses, and this "in effect discouraged applications" from some segments of their respective communities. Yet, the Marina State Bank, of Marina Del Rey, California, with over 70% of its loans in the recreational boat target market segment, was not criticized under this assessment factor.

Two California Banks Cited for Prescreening Credit Card Applicants

Banks deemed to have inadequate credit marketing programs are likewise prone to being criticized for discouraging credit applicants. Austin State Bank's (Austin, Indiana) lack of credit advertising "could have the effect of discouraging applications by giving the impression in the community that the bank is not making loans." The examiners supported their position by noting that one interviewed community resident was "not aware of any programs the bank offered." The lack of marketing and early closing of the lobby at Allegiant Bank of St. Louis, Missouri, "may result in discouraging loan applications," according to their examiners.

Special purpose banks, like the credit card banks in Delaware, may be restricted from soliciting loan applications from the local community by state law. Both Hawthorne Savings of Hawthorne, California, and California Business Bank of San Jose, California, were cited as having either an indication of or isolated instances of credit discouragement via prescreening of credit card applicants.

Illegal Credit Practices (Assessment Factor F)

Prohibited discriminatory or other illegal credit practices represent the CRA "death wish." Violations can be of many types: substantive, nonsubstantive, procedural, technical, or not specified. They may be widespread, limited, or isolated in scope. Also, they may or may not be of supervisory or significant supervisory concern. Substantive and widespread violations of one or more compliance laws and regulations almost surely result in a low CRA rating, although this may not be the case for a few isolated technical violations. The worst situation is when substantive and widespread violations are of significant supervisory concern and have been repeated from previous exams without corrective action.

Compliance Violations at 46% of Substantial Noncompliant Banks

Twenty-five (or 46%) of the 54 substantial noncompliant banks analyzed here were found to have substantive, technical, or some other type of violation in this category. This is the same percentage of needs improvement banks with such violations. Nine banks with substantial noncompliance ratings had substantive *and* technical violations, six had just substantive ones, and ten had technical or unspecified violations. Therefore, 15 of the 25 banks, or 60% of the total, had substantive violations.

All three banks in Kansas City, Missouri, with substantial noncompliance ratings had substantive and/or technical violations. Hillcrest Bank was cited for various substantive and technical violations. Some were isolated and some widespread, some were of significant supervisory concern and some were not, and some were repeated from past exams and others were first-time violations. Bannister Bank & Trust Company had both substantive and limited violations, while Missouri Bank & Trust Company had repeated substantive violations.

Allegiant Bank, Bannister Bank & Trust Company, Capital Bank & Trust Company, Guardian Savings, Hawthorne Savings, Hillcrest Bank, Norwalk-Cumming State Bank, Premier Bank Rochester, and Security Savings were all cited as having both substantive and technical violations of at least one compliance law or regulation. Avondale Federal, Farmers and Merchants Bank, Fountain Bank, Key Federal, Missouri Bank & Trust Company, and Parish Bank & Trust Company violated substantive provisions of at least one compliance law or regulation. Fountain Bank and Missouri Bank & Trust Company were cited for some repeat violations.

The most common substantive violations were of the Equal Credit Opportunity Act (Reg B) followed by the Fair Housing Act and the Home Mortgage Disclosure Act (HMDA). The most common technical violations were of Reg B, HMDA, and the Fair Housing Act. Many compliance violations did not cite specific laws or regulations.

V. COMMUNITY DEVELOPMENT

Local Community Development and Redevelopment Participation (Assessment Factor H)

Long Island Thrift Just "Not Interested" in Community Development

Only a few banks with this rating were cited as having made any effort or progress in the area of community development. Most were unaware of such projects, and some were simply "not interested," as was the case with Long Island City Savings of Long Island City, New York, according to their examiners. Investors Thrift of Orange, California, doesn't participate in these programs and projects since they "do not meet their lending criteria."

Merchants National Bank of Sacramento, California, with $73 million in assets, felt it was "not large enough" to participate in government-sponsored community projects. The examiners criticized this view since they felt the board "failed to adequately explore available alternatives" within the bank's ability to participate.

North Cincinnati Loan and Building Company of Blue Ash, Ohio, was represented at local housing meetings by middle management, but the evaluation noted that no monetary investment in local community projects was made.

$50,000 Community Development Loan Participation Not Enough for Subsidiary of Michigan National Corporation

The $1.4 billion asset Beverly Hills Business Bank of Beverly Hills, California, a subsidiary of Michigan National Corporation, had a $50,000 loan participation in a local community project. However, the bank's past and present efforts were criticized as being inadequate and "not commensurate with the participation level expected" from an institution with its resources.

Key Federal Savings Bank of Owings Mill, Maryland, lent $3.2 million on six low- and moderate-income private development projects in Maryland. However, only one loan of $0.4 million "appeared to have been within the delineated community." Regulators have apparently changed their view on being critical of nonlocal lending, as long as it benefits low- and moderate-income neighborhoods or borrowers.

Five of the Seven Substantial Noncompliant Banks in Missouri Don't Even Own Muncipals

Most banks own municipal bonds, and a few of the evaluations noted this as a positive under this assessment factor. Several substantial noncompliant banks, including five of the seven in Missouri, owned no municipals. Other banks were criticized for holding mostly nonlocal bonds.

The Bank of Walnut of Walnut, Mississippi, was noted as having only three of its 45 municipal bonds in its community. All of Fountain Bank's (Scottsdale, Arizona) investments are out-of-state, "with no explanation from management as to why the investments were not made locally."

*President of Community Bank in Texas
"Grilled" by Examiner on Volunteer Effort*

The president of Texas Coastal Bank, of Pasadena, Texas, stated that he assisted in a city bond issuance by staffing telephones and preparing mail-outs to residents, but the examiners noted that this activity was "not documented." The seemingly argumentative examiners then made a point that the president was unaware of the current status of that issue.

Most banks had little or no participation in community projects except for donations to community organizations. UBAF Bank of New York, New York, made corporate contributions of over $5,000 in each of the last two years, but it was noted that no donations were to housing or economic development organizations.

*L.A. Bank Criticized for Sizeable Commitment
to Statewide Redevelopment Corporation*

California Business Bank of San Jose, California, joined a local loan consortium for an enterprise zone. The examiner, however, noted this program met with little success since there were no loan applications. United Citizens National Bank of Los Angeles, California, committed a "sizeable amount of funds" to a statewide redevelopment corporation. The examiners, however, noted that no funds were yet advanced under the program, and the bank in any case "cannot control where the funds are used" in the state. This was the only criticism of this type we have ever seen, and it therefore proves that just about anything can be criticized by examiners if desired.

*Community Bank in Illinois Ignores Request
for New Fire Station Loan*

Parish Bank & Trust Company of Momence, Illinois, was criticized for not getting involved in the community's only development project since that bank's last examination. The bank was approached about possible financing for the construction of a new fire station. The result? The bank "neither responded to the request nor suggested an alternative, and a local competitor ultimately made the loan."

Ability to Meet Credit Needs
(Assessment Factor K)

Most banks were unaffected by financial or other constraints in this area. The most common constraints noted were for wholesale, foreign, credit card, or other special-purpose banks.

The constraints may include federal laws such as the Competitive Equality Banking Act of 1987 and/or state laws such as those in Delaware, which is home to many credit card banks. The four-employee Chicago branch of the National Bank of Pakistan was constrained because all major policies and decisions are made in Karachi, Pakistan.

*Banks That Are Troubled, Small or
Reorganized Given Special Consideration*

Another constraint noted was financial condition. The two banks noted in this regard were Mercantile Savings Bank of Southaven, Mississippi, and Enterprise Savings of Compton, California. The latter bank was "subject to regulatory constraints" that limited its lending ability. Both of these substantial noncompliant banks plus at least two others (Guardian Savings of Huntington Beach, California, and Fountain Bank of Scottsdale, Arizona) have since failed. The capacity of the Marina State Bank of Marina Del Rey, California, to fund loans was restricted as it "reorganizes its balance sheet," but this was noted by the examiners as a "self-imposed restriction."

CRA performance is supposed to be evaluated relative to a bank's resources and capabilities. A bank's small size, therefore, may be noted as a constraint under this assessment factor. A more commonly cited constraint is the relative newness of a recently chartered or reorganized bank. United Citizens National Bank of Los Angeles, California, was referred to as being small in size ($42 million as of December 31, 1990) and less than two years old, both of which "somewhat limited" the bank's "ability to be innovative in meeting community credit needs."

The $15 million (as of December 31, 1990) Allegiant Bank of St. Louis, Missouri, changed ownership and management on September 1, 1990. Its CRA exam some seven months later noted that its "small size may be a detracting factor in its ability to meet the various community credit needs." Premier Bank Rochester of Rochester, Minnesota, opened in October 1990, and its CRA exam less than one year later did not mention this constraint under this assessment factor. The examiners did, however, note under another factor that the bank "did not have a lending staff" until two months prior to the exam.

No Excuses for Large Banks

A large bank (say in excess of a billion dollars in assets) usually is held to a higher standard, and this again is consistent with a bank being evaluated relative to its resources and capabilities. Of the four large substantial noncompliant banks, only two raised this issue.

Beverly Hills Business Bank of Beverly Hills, California, a subsidiary of Michigan National Corporation, was cited under the previous assessment factor for inadequate participation considering its resources. The substantial noncompliance evaluation of Farmers and Merchants Bank of Long Beach, California, stated that the bank's size and financial condition should "easily enable it to expand its participation in, and implementation of, community development programs."

Self-Imposed $4 Million Limit on Real Estate Loans at Community Bank in Illinois Criticized

Many banks that were criticized under this assessment factor had little if any outreach or marketing efforts. The Parish Bank & Trust Company of Momence, Illinois, was criticized because of its "self-imposed $4 million limit on outstanding real estate loans." Also, Security Savings of Hillsboro, Illinois, was cited here since its loan department was "basically inactive during the review period." Texas Coastal Bank of Pasadena, Texas, blamed its CRA deficiencies on "employee turnover."

Other Factors (Assessment Factor L)

This catch-all category was generally used to indicate the examiner's perception of a bank's "CRA spirit." Most banks cited here were criticized for not taking an affirmative stance on CRA.

St. Louis' "Public Service Bank" Not Interested in Public Service?

Public Service Bank of St. Louis, Missouri, virtually assured itself of a low CRA rating because of a statement made by management to the examiner in charge. According to the public evaluation, management "proclaimed that CRA is not of primary importance to the Board of Directors, as the directors have invested personally into the institution and are interested primarily in maximizing their return on their investment."

The examiners, not surprisingly, stated that management's attitude toward CRA was "perhaps the most significant factor" in their evaluation of Public Service Bank. The examiners stopped short of any possible editorializing on whether the bank's name was an oxymoron after management's proclamation as to the bank's primary interest.

Community Bank in Wyoming: Let Credit Unions and Others Do Community Lending

Another clear-cut example of the lack of the right "CRA spirit" was the Uinta County State Bank of Mountain View, Wyoming. It believes that the "credit unions and other local financial institutions should meet the majority of the community's credit needs."

The Board of AVCO National Bank of Irvine, California, placed full reliance for CRA activities on its large parent, AVCO Financial Services. The bank's board was criticized since compliance with CRA was its responsibility as a federally chartered bank, not that of its parent. The overall policy objectives of Long Island City Savings of Long Island City, New York, are "geared towards security investment principles with no emphasis on serving community credit needs."

Baltimore Bank Made Community Donations but Couldn't Document Them

This assessment factor also presented the examiners with an opportunity to identify positive contributions that may not have been cited elsewhere in the evaluation. Sometimes the lack of CRA complaints in the CRA public file is noted as a positive, as was the case with Investors Thrift of Orange, California.

Virtually every bank makes some types of dona-
tions, but those to housing or community groups
apparently carry more weight for CRA purposes.
Examples include donations to a housing organiza-
tion (Gotham Bank of New York, New York, and
Long Island City Savings of Long Island City, New
York) and a community senior citizens group (United
Citizens National Bank of Los Angeles, California).

Other worthwhile efforts include the forgiveness
of debt to a charity (by Farmers and Merchants Bank
of Long Beach, California) and the involvement with
a low-interest mortgage program for university pro-
fessors (by California Business Bank of San Jose,
California). Custom Savings Bank of Pikesville, Maryland, in the greater Baltimore area, stated that several
donations were made in its community, but "no
documentation was produced to support this statement," according to the examiner.

*Free NOW Account in Illinois Can Be Closed
by Bank if Average Monthly Balance Too Low*

Key Federal Savings Bank of Owings Mill, Maryland, was identified as offering free checking accounts
and credit cards with no annual fees within its community. Bank of Walnut of Walnut, Mississippi, offers
free checking to seniors. Security Savings of Hillsboro,
Illinois, apparently was being commended for offering a free NOW account with a minimum deposit.
The evaluation, however, then noted that the bank
can close such an account if the average monthly
balance falls below the stated minimum.

In a similar vein, United Citizens National Bank of
Los Angeles, California, offered a basic banking
checking account for low-income households which
bank management (but apparently not the examiners) felt "met a community need and complied with
the spirit of CRA." Management at Allegiant Bank of
St. Louis, Missouri, had reported a similar account
and a specialized mortgage loan for low- and moderate-income persons, but their examiners responded
that these services were "not being aggressively marketed or utilized."

9. CASE STUDIES OF SUBSTANTIAL NONCOMPLIANT BANKS

INTRODUCTION

Eight case studies of substantial noncompliant banks are included in this chapter. The first case study is about the nation's largest concentration of banks with this rating along the I-405 corridor of L.A. The second case study is of three banks with this rating in northern Atlanta.

The third case study is about what we have designated to be the absolutely lowest CRA-rated bank in America. This is the Mercantile Savings Bank of Southaven, Mississippi. Prior to being taken over by the government, this bank made history by being the first one to receive a cease and desist order primarily on CRA grounds. A fourth case study looks at the other lowest CRA-rated banks in America.

The fifth and sixth case studies are about the only bank to date that has upgraded itself out of the substantial noncompliance category. This bank, the Farmers and Merchants Bank of Long Beach, California, was one of 142 banks identified that received a second rating under the new system as of year-end 1991. For purposes of this analysis, we include an evaluation of both the original and updated rating. While the fifth case study is about their upgraded rating, the sixth one is about their cease and desist order mainly on CRA grounds and its implications as to regulatory consistency.

The seventh case study compares a bank with a recent substantial noncompliance rating to one with the same name which also had community reinvestment problems—more than 200 years ago! The final case study focuses on the FED and asks, "Is the FED undermining CRA enforcement?"

SUBSTANTIAL NONCOMPLIANCE ALONG THE I-405 CORRIDOR IN L.A.

The portion of Los Angeles along the I-405 corridor (the San Diego Freeway) from Beverly Hills to Irvine represents the largest single concentration of CRA substantial noncompliant banks in the country, with nine of the nation's 54 in this category as of year-end 1991. This proportion increased to one out of five through the first part of 1992, but dropped to one out of seven by year-end 1992.

Substantial Noncompliant Banks Represent Cross-Section of Bank Types, Sizes, and Communities

These nine institutions in L.A. as of December 31, 1991, included three of the nation's four largest (billion dollar plus) substantial noncompliant banks at that time. These nine thrifts and banks represented a true cross-section of bank types, sizes, and communities.

Four of these nine institutions were thrifts regulated by the OTS. The five banks include two each evaluated by the FDIC and OCC and one by the FED. Thus, each of the four federal bank regulators have placed at least one of these nine banks in this lowest CRA category.

One of these nine institutions, Farmers and Merchants Bank of Long Beach (F&M Bank), was the only bank in the nation as of December 31, 1991, that has worked itself out of the lowest rated category. F&M Bank is large, with $1.4 billion in assets as of year-end 1991, and an overall "superior" (actually the highest possible) financial rating, according to IDC Financial Publishing (all ratings noted here are from their *Bank Financial Quarterly* or *S&L-Savings Bank Financial Quarterly*.

Hawthorne S&LA is also a large institution ($1.1 billion in assets) with a superior rating. Guardian S&LA was a medium-sized thrift ($682 million in assets) which was placed into RTC conservatorship on December 6, 1991. Enterprise S&LA, on the other hand, was a very small thrift with only $14 million in assets, which also has since failed.

Beverly Hills Business Bank is a strong $1.4 billion federal savings bank, which is a subsidiary of Michigan National Corporation. Investors Thrift of Orange is a $209 million thrift company with an average financial rating.

AVCO National Bank, a very small ($2 million) bank, which is a subsidiary of giant AVCO Financial Services, is located in Irvine at the other end of the I-405 corridor. Marina State Bank of Marina Del Rey is a small ($18 million) bank with a below-average rating. Finally, United Citizens National Bank is a fairly strong but small ($42 million) bank located in the Koreatown district of L.A. This bank was the subject of a case study in Chapter 7.

In summary, the nine substantial noncompliant banks and thrifts along and near the I-405 corridor represented a wide spectrum of asset sizes and financial conditions. They included three of the four largest (billion dollar plus) substantial noncompliant banks in America as of year-end 1991. Our findings were different in this regard for the three banks in the following northern Atlanta case, which had a great deal in common.

CRA "Death Wish" in L.A.

Many communities in southeastern L.A. along and near the I-405 corridor have a substantial absolute and relative number of low- and moderate-income and minority residents, as does south central L.A. Four of the above nine substantial noncompliant banks in L.A. had violations of various consumer compliance laws or regulations. Further, all violations but those of Enterprise Savings were deemed to be substantive, not just technical, violations. Compliance violations, which represent the CRA "death wish," usually result in a needs improvement rating and many times a substantial noncompliance one when the violations are substantive, widespread, or repeated.

Enterprise Savings was unique in that the examiners could find no proof of CRA even being mentioned in board minutes for more than two years, thereby precluding the possibility of the required CRA board approvals. Hawthorne Savings likewise had not had its CRA statement approved within a two-year period.

Hawthorne Savings and Loan Association was the only one of the nine cited for having "disproportionate trends" for loan applications in various low- and moderate-income areas and substantially minority census tracts. The examiners concluded that this was an "unreasonable" situation in terms of the number of loans in those areas.

The silver lining in the L.A. situation is that already five of the seven surviving banks have removed themselves from this lowest ranked category as a result of improvements in their CRA performance (see Table 8-2). Hopefully, the banks in L.A. that received substantial noncompliance ratings in 1992 will follow their example

L.A.'s I-405 Corridor Represents between One out of Five and One out of Seven Substantial Noncompliant Banks in U.S.

We updated our analysis of the L.A. area after the riots there and released our study on May 5, 1992. Of the 64 substantial noncompliant banks spread out over 22 states as of March 31, 1992, 12, or 19%, of those banks were in the same I-405 corridor of L.A. Thus, the percentage of such banks in L.A. increased from 17% to 19% as three of the ten new substantial noncompliant banks in the first quarter of 1992 were from this area. Our updated analysis as of April 30, 1992, the night the riots began, showed the same pattern. One of the three banks receiving this rating from bank regulators was from this same corridor, keeping L.A.'s percentage of such banks at 19%, or 13 of 67. Since there were no more substantial noncompliant banks reported in this area through the remainder of 1992, the proportion dropped to 15% or 13 of 88 as of year-end 1992.

L.A.'s Substantial Noncompliant Banks— Part of the Problem or Solution?

Because these findings have been fairly consistent through the first part of 1992, they may be reflective of a troubling pattern that cannot be dismissed as irrelevant or just coincidental to what happened in L.A. Obviously more research is required on this important issue. The problems of our inner cities are complex, and a lack of meaningful and consistent private community investment is just one of the pieces of this seemingly unsolvable puzzle.

We prefer a positive view of L.A.'s banks and thrifts which deem them part of the solution rather than part of the problem. The upgraded ratings and affirmative efforts many of these banks and thrifts have made since they received these absolutely lowest CRA ratings are encouraging and supportive of such a positive outlook.

SUBSTANTIAL NONCOMPLIANCE IN NORTHERN ATLANTA

Another early concentration of substantial noncompliant CRA banks in the country was in northern Atlanta. The following three banks in the northern Atlanta suburbs received the substantial noncompliance rating: Embry National Bank, Enterprise National Bank, and Vinings Bank & Trust, N.A. These three banks were evaluated between September 1990 and January 1991.

More Similarities than Differences among Atlanta's Substantial Noncompliant Banks

Whereas the L.A. case represented a disparity of bank sizes and condition, the reverse is true in the northern Atlanta case. All three of the subject Atlanta banks are national banks, and they were rated by the Atlanta Region of the Office of the Comptroller of the Currency. All three banks are independent unit banks with no branches. All three banks were chartered by the OCC in 1987 in different parts of the fairly affluent northern Atlanta suburbs.

All three of these national banks are fairly small, with assets in the $33–$62 million range as of year-end 1990. All three have been unprofitable since their inception, for the most part. The main problem

in each case is substantial amounts of nonperforming loans and charge-offs well above acceptable levels. Their overall financial condition as of year-end 1990 and 1991 has been described as "below average" in each case, according to IDC Financial Publishing.

Many CRA Deficiencies and Violations Were Also Similar

There were many similarities among the reasons for the lowest possible CRA ratings. According to the performance evaluations, all three northern Atlanta banks made few, if any, conventional mortgage, home improvement, or rehabilitation loans. Rather, each of them focused on the same lending specialty, namely small business lending.

The Enterprise National Bank made no residential mortgage loans, and the Embry National Bank and Vinings Bank & Trust, N.A. made only one and eight mortgage loans, respectively, during an entire year. Also, there was little involvement by each of these banks in government lending programs, with the exception of some small business administration loans.

Importantly, each of the three banks were cited as having some type of "disproportionate" or "unreasonable" lending pattern inside and/or outside their delineated community. The Vinings Bank & Trust, N.A. was noted as having an "unjustified, disproportionate" lending pattern, since they made less than 2% of the number of loans in low- and moderate-income census tracts, while they comprised 45% of all tracts in their entire community.

Overall, board members of each of these three banks were noted as providing minimal or limited support to CRA activities. Senior management was noted as having "little interest" in this regard in two of the three cases.

No Pulitzer Prize for This CRA Story

Our findings regarding this northern Atlanta case were first made public in our news release dated May 22, 1991. This news release was provided on an exclusive basis to a reporter who published our findings (unfortunately without attribution) in the May 25, 1991, edition of *The Atlanta Journal/The Atlanta Constitution.* This story was then picked up by the

Associated Press (this time with appropriate attribution) and received nationwide attention.

Our follow-up analysis of these three banks revealed both good and bad news. The second public CRA evaluations in early 1992 of two of these three banks resulted in upgradings to satisfactory ratings. Unfortunately, the Vinings Bank & Trust, N.A. received the same substantial noncompliance rating upon its second exam in 1992.

Also of recent interest in Atlanta was the September 1992 complaint against Decatur Federal by the Department of Justice, alleging mortgage discrimination. That four-year investigation was settled with a consent degree requiring a $1 million payment and other stringent affirmative provisions. Of great interest to this case is the fact that Decatur Federal had received a satisfactory CRA rating from the OTS in the first half of 1990, probably representing one of the classic examples of grade inflation.

AMERICA'S LOWEST CRA-RATED BANK

We have determined that the lowest CRA-rated bank in America was the Mercantile Savings Bank of Southaven, Mississippi, which is located just south of Memphis, Tennessee.

In what was probably the strongest CRA action ever taken against a financial institution at that time, the OTS issued a cease and desist (C&D) order mainly on CRA grounds against the Mercantile Savings Bank.

Abysmal CRA Record Not Reason for Bank's Failure

This bank was seized by the government on April 19, 1991, and was operated as an RTC conservatorship. The bank had also received a safety and soundness C&D, and the bank's unsafe and unsound condition was the ultimate reason for its failure. The bank likely would have been seized regardless of its abysmal CRA record; it did nothing but bring additional regulatory and supervisory attention to this bank.

Mercantile Savings Bank was an approximately $38 million asset thrift based in a small town south of and part of the Memphis, Tennessee metropolitan statistical area. It had a branch in another small Mississippi town in a nearby county. Its CRA delineated community consisted of the two counties containing these offices. It also maintained a loan origination office in Memphis until 1988 through its wholly-owned Texas-based subsidiary, Mercantile Mortgage Corporation.

Classic Case of Loan Application Discouragement

The bank's CRA statement was typical of most "no frills" statements (i.e., more glittering generalities than specifics). The October 15, 1990, CRA performance evaluation which resulted in the lowest possible substantial noncompliance rating concluded, among other things, that

- There was no loan officer at the bank.

- No loans, other than savings account loans, were made in its local delineated community in approximately one year.

- No loans originated in its community were purchased by the bank.

- Loans purchased by the bank during the review period were from its mortgage subsidiary and were secured by properties in Texas, Colorado, and New Mexico.

- Potential customers were discouraged from applying for home loans in the delineated community in that they were told that the bank did not have a loan officer and was "not set up to process mortgage loans locally."

First C&D Order Ever Mainly on CRA Grounds

Since FIRREA mandated disclosure of enforcement actions, there have been a large number of them issued by the four federal financial bank and thrift regulatory agencies. The strongest and most formal action, short of removing deposit insurance, directors, or officers, is the issuance of a C&D order. The first safety and soundness C&D against the Mercantile Savings Bank on January 28, 1991, mentioned CRA compliance as one of many areas of concern. The second C&D on February 12, 1991, was mainly on CRA grounds and the first such C&D ever issued of its type according to representatives of the four regulatory agencies with whom we spoke.

The C&D ordered the Mercantile Savings Bank to

- File a revised CRA statement.

- Appoint an on-site CRA compliance officer at the main office.

- Establish a CRA "Action Plan" and have it approved by the board and reviewed quarterly by them.

- Establish a Loan Application System by appropriately trained personnel so that loan applications are maintained at both offices, along with a loan application register which is approved by the board and reviewed monthly by the board and management.

- Ensure that "the practice of discouraging loan applications ceases immediately."

Pitiful CRA Performance Put Another Nail in Bank's Coffin

Mercantile's CRA problems were very serious but so too were its safety and soundness problems. The bank was seized by the government roughly two months after the second C&D order. Mercantile's pitiful CRA performance did nothing but put another nail in its coffin and earn for the bank the distinction of being America's lowest CRA-rated bank. There is no doubt that the OTS and some other federal bank regulators are taking CRA enforcement more seriously, so much so that the C&D order is now part of their CRA regulatory arsenal. The consistency and frequency of use of this enforcement tool is another question that will be addressed in a subsequent case study.

AMERICA'S OTHER LOWEST CRA-RATED BANKS

Who are America's other lowest CRA-rated banks besides the absolutely lowest rated one, Mercantile Savings Bank of Southaven, Mississippi? Arguably, any of the other banks profiled in the last chapter with current substantial noncompliant ratings would qualify by the fact that they are in the lowest 1% of all CRA ratings. The only apparent exception would be the Koreatown bank, which was the subject of a previous case study in Chapter 7, and those that

upgraded themselves out of that category without the help of any grade inflation.

The "Worst of the Worst" —Double and Even Triple Substantial Noncompliance Ratings

We would argue, however, that certain banks more than others should be singled out for their very poor CRA performance. First would be those banks receiving *repeat* substantial noncompliance ratings, especially those where few if any improvements were made and where there may even have been some deterioration in CRA compliance. Table 8-2 reports that as of December 31, 1992, there were seven banks with *double* substantial noncompliance ratings plus two banks with *triple* substantial noncompliance ratings.

The seven banks with back-to-back substantial noncompliance ratings are: Bay Financial Savings Bank of Tampa, Florida; Cambridge State Bank of Cambridge, Minnesota; Custom Savings Bank, a FSB of Pikesville, Maryland; Delta Bank and Trust of Delta, Mississippi; Okmulgee Savings and Loan Association of Okmulgee, Oklahoma; Texas Coastal Bank of Pasadena, Texas; and Vinings Bank and Trust, N.A. of Atlanta, Georgia. Even worse were the two banks with back-to-back-to-back substantial noncompliance ratings and these are Parish Bank and Trust Company of Momence, Illinois, and Uinta County State Bank of Mountain View, Wyoming.

Four Community Banks Downgraded to Substantial Noncompliance

A second type of bank we would point to as having very bad CRA performance would be one dropping from needs improvement (or even a higher category) to substantial noncompliance. Only a handful of banks have actually been downgraded, but none to substantial noncompliance through December 31, 1991. This situation changed since then with the downgrading of four banks in 1992 from needs improvement to substantial noncompliance. These four banks are the Bank of Garber (Oklahoma), Bank of the Eastern Shore (Cambridge, Maryland), Missouri State Bank and Trust Company (St. Louis, Missouri), and the State Bank of Coloma (Michigan).

Minnesota Community Banker: "Too much easy credit kills people."

A third type of bank in this category would be one with a substantial noncompliance rating where senior bank officials publicly criticize CRA for some reason or another. For example, one of the more vocal and visible "CRA bashers" is the chairman of the Cambridge State Bank of Cambridge, Minnesota, who has openly criticized CRA several times in the media. For example, in an April 22, 1991 *American Banker* article titled "A Bank that Won't Bend to Meet CRA Standards," that banker, who with his brother owns about 85% of that bank, stated that "I'm not going to change to bend over backwards to those bastards." He was presumably referring to the FDIC and its CRA examiners. Regarding that bank's "extremely low" 15% loan-to-deposit ratio, the banker noted that "Too much easy credit kills people." Unfortunately for that bank, CRA substantial noncompliance kills expansion plans. That's exactly what happened in 1990 when the FDIC denied that bank's application for an off-premise ATM on CRA grounds. That bank's second public CRA examination by the FDIC, on August 16, 1991, not surprisingly resulted in a repeat substantial noncompliance rating.

CRA "Troublemakers"—People Requesting CRA Documents or Banks Refusing Them?

A fourth type of bank in this category would be those with any CRA rating, but especially low ones, who discourage access to their CRA statements or public evaluations. We contacted most of the substantial noncompliance banks and only experienced a few delays where phone requests were not accepted but written ones were demanded.

One of the only four banks to be downgraded on their second exam, State Bank of Springfield, Minnesota, was adamant about a written request, although our understanding of the regulations was that any type of request should be honored. After we complied with a written request, that bank inadvertently sent us the wrong CRA documents (the confidential portion of the exam).

The most uncooperative bank by far in this regard was Bayside Federal S&LA of Queens, New York; they ignored our three *written* requests for both their CRA statement and public performance evaluation (which surprisingly had a "satisfactory" rating). We obtained the latter document from the OTS.

Even "Scrooge" Will Promptly Send Requested CRA Material at No Charge

There is really no excuse for not dropping a CRA statement and/or public evaluation in the mail when requested. The main out-of-pocket cost is for the stamp. Even the most "penny-pinching" bank we've ever encountered, World Savings of Oakland, California, promptly sent us the requested CRA material via first class mail. Yet, that outstanding CRA-rated bank sent us requested annual and quarterly financial reports via "book rate" in August, 1991. That saved World Savings a whopping $1.77 in postage over first class mail but caused a significant delay in our receiving the material. If this bank, which contrary to its 1990 Annual Report apparently subscribes to the "Scrooge School of Management," will promptly send any requested CRA material via first class mail, then any bank should be able to do the same. Incidentally, World Savings did not charge us $5–$10 for copying costs as some banks (almost always smaller ones with low ratings) have done.

"Heavy CRA Artillery"

A fifth type of bank that would be among America's lowest CRA-rated would be those with cease and desist orders, application denials, civil money penalties, or other "heavy CRA artillery" totally or partially on CRA grounds. This includes the Farmers and Merchants Bank of Long Beach, California, the subject of the following two case studies.

IN AND OUT OF SUBSTANTIAL NONCOMPLIANCE WITHIN EIGHT MONTHS

There will likely be about 150 banks and thrifts in the country that will receive this absolutely lowest CRA rating. One question these institutions, as well as the other 99% of banks and thrifts not in this category, may ask is how subjective are substantial noncompliance CRA ratings? A more pressing and relevant question substantial noncompliant institutions should ask is, "what can we do to get out of this category?"

The purpose of this case study is to attempt to answer this question using the experience of the only bank or thrift as of year-end 1991 that had been in and out of CRA substantial noncompliance, and all within a relatively short eight-month period. Many more banks and thrifts have exited that category in 1992 (see Table 8-2).

Bank Prepared Public Response Protesting the FED's Findings

Farmers and Merchants Bank of Long Beach was one of the first banks in the nation to receive a substantial noncompliance CRA rating. The rating was made on August 6, 1990, by the Federal Reserve Bank of San Francisco (FED). F&M Bank is also one of the largest banks or thrifts to ever receive that publicly released rating. Another case study on this same bank follows this one.

The bank, in its public written response to the rating, strongly protested the CRA exam's contents and conclusions. This $1.4 billion family-owned bank with 16 branches is a very strong, highly profitable, and well-capitalized institution, actually the best-capitalized big bank in California. As noted in Table 8-2, this bank had the highest possible IDC overall financial rating. F&M Bank did more than just protest its very poor rating. It was able to make enough improvements in its CRA performance to justify an upgraded rating of needs improvement from the FED on April 22, 1991, less than eight months later.

The Federal Reserve System, with the smallest number of regulated banks of the four federal CRA regulators, has the shortest compliance exam cycle of generally 10 to 14 months on average. An even shorter six- to eight-month cycle is appropriate for substantial noncompliant banks such as F&M Bank. The fact that they had a *de novo* branch application pending before the Board of Governors since November of the previous year was obviously an item of concern to this bank.

Previous Public Ratings and Evaluations Not Public

CRA does not require a bank to maintain previous public performance evaluations and their accompanying ratings in the CRA public file. The past two years' CRA statements, however, are maintained there. Therefore, as far as this bank or any other bank in this situation is concerned, a previous lower "public" rating and evaluation is no longer a part of the public record.

In fact, a representative of SafraBank II of Pompano Beach, Florida, that was upgraded from a needs improvement to a satisfactory rating, refused to admit to us the existence of the previous lower rating and evaluation even when specifically questioned about it! Regardless of CRA regulations, we believe that past evaluations and ratings do count since they are quite informative, especially when compared with present ones. The comparative analysis that follows hopefully will make this point.

Same Exam Team but Different Chief Examiner

We can learn a lot from what F&M Bank apparently did and did not do to get the higher rating. A careful reading of both the old and new evaluations confirmed what we later learned, that a different chief examiner was involved in each exam; although, we understand the same examination team was utilized.

The second public CRA evaluation of nine pages is roughly twice as long as the first one. The second evaluation is also much more detailed and analytical. It is possible that the same analysis may have been completed the first time around but just not summarized in the public evaluation. But, that is all we have to go on from the FED.

$38 Million of CRA Loans since Last Exam

The comparison of the two evaluations shows that the most substantive positive change made by the F&M Bank was that it extended nearly $38 million in loans to "development projects and to nonprofit organizations" since the previous examination. These included loans for condos, apartment complexes, and mobile home parks in low- and moderate-income areas; a senior citizen housing project; and a nonprofit organization that helps homeless victims of domestic violence.

The first evaluation noted that the bank provided "extensive development and revitalization credits, primarily to local private developers" but gave no specifics. The bank's public response, however, noted that approximately 10% of its total loan portfolio then was for loans to nonprofit and charitable organizations.

A Dollar of Actual CRA Loans in Hand is Worth Two "Conditional" Dollars in the Bush

The $38 million of CRA loan extensions for community development and nonprofit projects identified in the second exam is quite large on both an absolute and relative basis. Those loans over an eight-month period are equivalent to $57 million on an annual basis, which in turn represents roughly 42 basis points of that bank's assets. These are actual CRA loans rather than commitments which may or may not ever be made over a five- or ten-year period.

The large California banks that have made commitments generally range from 25 to 50 basis points of assets per year. Many community groups consider a 50 basis point annual CRA commitment to be socially responsive.

The largest such CRA commitment at that time by NationsBank, which represented 84 basis points of its assets annually over 10 years, was to become effective after approval of a proposed merger. Assuming every dollar of an actual CRA loan extension in hand is worth "two in the bush" in the form of a conditional commitment, then F&M's CRA loans over that period are equivalent to the huge NationsBank pledge on an annual relative basis.

Hard Cash versus "Soft" CRA Improvements

F&M's substantial CRA loan extensions apparently got the attention of the FED examiners and may have been the most important determining factor in the upgraded rating. There were some other cited improvements as well that were "soft" in nature compared to the hard cash.

For example, the most recent evaluation states that the bank has "taken the first steps" in determining the geographic distribution of its credit extensions

and denials. This is in stark contrast to a previous bank effort that was discounted as providing no useful information because of "faulty methodology" used by the bank's staff.

The new evaluation revealed that the bank formed a "CRA/Compliance Committee," which had met twice since the last examination. However, the documentation of those meetings and other CRA efforts was found to be lacking.

Some past criticisms of the bank were not addressed in the new evaluation or only in a minimal way. For example, the bank was criticized before because it did not advertise or market its credit products. Now the bank advertises its home equity loans on ATM machines at its branches and also ran one advertisement for loans in a local magazine.

FED's Second Evaluation Provided Individual Assessment Factor Ratings

The format used by the FED in the second evaluation was an improvement in itself. The new evaluation provided individual ratings for each of the 12 CRA assessment factors in addition to the one overall rating, which was all that was provided in the first evaluation. This revised format, which was more the exception than the rule, is unfortunately not used anymore.

The most recent evaluation for the F&M Bank revealed four satisfactory, five needs improvement, and three substantial noncompliance individual assessment factor ratings. The latter ratings were for assessment factors pertaining to credit marketing, government loan programs, and prohibited credit practices.

Areas of CRA Performance Deterioration

There were a few areas in which the bank's CRA performance actually *deteriorated* since the last examination. For example, there was no indication of questionable geographic lending patterns in the first evaluation. The new evaluation, which compared 1990 and 1989 Home Mortgage Disclosure Act (HMDA) data, concluded that the bank's volume of home purchase and home improvement loans located in low- and moderate-income areas declined in 1990 compared to 1989. Although the number of mortgage loans made during the two years is comparable, those located in low- and moderate-income areas declined 50% in 1990.

FED Claims Credit Card Age Discrimination but Bank Denies It

We were very surprised to learn that the new evaluation once again found the F&M Bank in substantial noncompliance with the provisions of antidiscrimination laws and regulations, including Regulation B (the Equal Credit Opportunity Act). F&M Bank's original evaluation only noted that "a policy administered by the bank is in substantial noncompliance with the provisions of Regulation B." The bank in its public response "expressly, explicitly and absolutely" denied any such discrimination and contended it was in full compliance with Regulation B.

The FED apparently did not agree with the bank in this regard. The new evaluation was specific in pointing out that the bank's credit card department engaged in a discriminatory practice where "applicants were treated differently on a prohibited (age) basis."

What was surprising for a bank that was attempting to improve its record was the FED's finding in the most recent evaluation that "bank management has not been sufficiently responsive to previously cited violations of this nature, which permitted the practice to continue." Furthermore, the new evaluation pointed out that the bank failed to file its 1990 HMDA report in a "timely manner," and when it was filed, it contained "significant factual inaccuracies."

One Very Good CRA Deed Outweighs the Bad One

What have we learned from this case? One lesson is that apparently one very good deed may outweigh a bad one, even if the bad one has been around for awhile and may have gotten worse. In the F&M case it appears that substantial CRA loan extensions (the good deed) may have outweighed the FED's finding of a violation of antidiscrimination laws and regulations (the bad deed).

Another lesson learned from this case is that any bank with a CRA rating of needs improvement or especially substantial noncompliance is well advised to prepare a detailed public response to the performance evaluation. In addition to making the public

aware of its side of the story, it raises important issues and questions which the examiners likely will have to address the second time around. Also as part of an ongoing self-assessment program, it helps the bank monitor and improve its CRA performance.

How Subjective Was the Upgrading?

This situation forces us to revisit the controversial question as to subjectivity involving CRA ratings. How subjective was this decision to elevate F&M Bank's overall rating out of the lowest category? Would a group of examiners from another FED region have reached the same conclusion? What about another bank or thrift regulator?

The purpose of this comparative analysis is not to embarrass the examination team or the F&M Bank as a result of the most recent evaluation. Rather, we are merely attempting to demonstrate the inherent subjectivities in the CRA ratings process and the dilemma they pose for regulators and bankers alike.

The examiners apparently did their job in this case. The most recent evaluation was twice as long and more analytical and comprehensive than the first one. And, there is almost always additional relevant information not contained in the public evaluation of which we are not aware. The F&M Bank is likewise to be commended on their improved rating and CRA performance. Their sizable CRA loans place them among the top nationwide on a relative basis.

A Quadruple Weighting for the CRA "Death Wish?"

Bankers, community groups, and even regulators have criticized the present evaluation system because it does not contain a weighting mechanism among the 12 assessment factors and five performance categories to result in the overall rating.

The interagency CRA rating system in effect explicitly recognizes this. But, the system defends the examiner's need to be flexible and to take into account each institution's unique and sometimes complex factors on a case-by-case basis in the overall CRA assessment. The rating system, however, emphasizes that of all assessment factors and performance categories, "compliance with antidiscrimination laws and regulations, including fair lending and fair housing laws, has great significance in reaching the overall conclusion."

But how great is that significance? Does it mean a double, triple, or quadruple weighting? Assuming an equal weighting for each of the 12 assessment factors, the F&M Bank would receive an overall needs improvement rating, as it did. The one CRA "death wish" assessment factor F, on prohibited discriminatory or other illegal credit practices, would have to have been weighted not two or three but *four* times its normal weight to result in an overall substantial noncompliance rating for the bank, with everything else remaining the same.

The Positive Power of Public Disclosure

The F&M case study also teaches us something about the positive power of public disclosure of CRA ratings and evaluations. We do not know if this bank previously had received very poor "4" or "5" CRA ratings under the old system, but it is possible considering their first public substantial noncompliance rating. What we do know, however, is that once public attention was drawn to the substantial noncompliance rating at this bank, positive changes apparently took place very quickly.

There is no way to prove that this bank's CRA corrective action would have occurred anyway without the disclosure of the first public rating and evaluation. There is, however, a strong supposition that such public disclosure is a powerful catalyst for CRA improvements.

An $8 Million Silver Lining in the CRA Substantial Noncompliance Cloud

There was one unexpected and seemingly perverse side effect of the publicity the bank received over its initial very poor CRA evaluation. This was roughly $8 million in *new* deposits that according to the bank was attracted by its very strong and conservative reputation that was publicized with its poor CRA rating. Thus, there was actually a silver lining in this substantial noncompliance cloud! Importantly, there was no public confusion between that bank's good safety and soundness condition and its bad CRA rating.

Shining Light on Safety and Soundness

We believe this experience lends support to the view that CAMEL and MACRO ratings and a portion of the exams on safety and soundness should be made public. There is truth in the argument that public disclosure can work more quickly and strongly to accomplish certain public policy objectives than the regulator's existing arsenal of enforcement and other tools. If the social benefit of such disclosure does in fact outweigh the social costs, then we ought to give thought to shedding further light on the financial condition of our banks and thrifts.

DOES CRA MEAN CONSISTENT REGULATORY APPLICATIONS?

F&M Bank's "CRA Eye Chart"

The C&D order involving CRA compliance by the Farmers and Merchants Bank of Long Beach reads like an eye chart as it cites numerous violations of FED Regulations B, C, D, E, H, Q, Z, BB, CC, and The Fair Credit Reporting Act.

This C&D order involving CRA was not a "first" for federal bank regulators. The first C&D order issued mainly on CRA grounds was dated February 12, 1991, against the now defunct Mercantile Savings Bank of Southaven, Mississippi. A previous case study identifies that $38 million bank as the nation's lowest CRA-rated bank. While all of the federal regulators have issued C&D orders involving compliance issues, the Mercantile and F&M C&D orders are the only two to date primarily on CRA grounds, according to each of those regulators.

C&D Orders Can Be Short and General or Long and Specific

The F&M Bank C&D order was unique in both its length and specificity. It was 14 pages long, double spaced, with about 30% devoted to CRA, 40% to consumer compliance problems, and 30% to procedure (introduction and conclusion). The Mercantile C&D order, by contrast, was just over 2 pages long, single spaced, with about the same 30% being devoted to CRA, 20% to loan application problems, and 50% to procedure.

Mercantile's CRA requirements in its C&D order were fairly general: a revised CRA statement, an on-site CRA compliance officer, an "Action Plan" for CRA needs assessment and compliance, and quarterly board reviews of the plan. The C&D order also required loan applications be maintained at all offices and that the practice of discouraging loan applications cease. That C&D order and CRA in general were probably the last things on the minds of those board members, as that bank was seized by the government less than two months later.

The FED's First C&D Order on CRA Grounds

When F&M Bank was found in substantial noncompliance on August 6, 1990, it was the third, not the first, institution in the country to receive that CRA rating. The Cambridge State Bank of Cambridge, Minnesota, and Avondale Federal Savings Bank of Chicago, Illinois, were found in substantial noncompliance on July 27, 1990, and July 30, 1990, respectively.

However, F&M Bank was the only bank as of year-end 1991 to have moved out of substantial noncompliance after receiving a "needs improvement" rating in its second public CRA exam of April 22, 1991. F&M's C&D was issued by the FED's Board of Governors on March 23, 1992, less than one year after F&M Bank received a needs improvement CRA rating from the Federal Reserve Bank of San Francisco. This was not only the first compliance and CRA C&D order for the FED, according to them, but also the first by any regulator against a bank without the lowest CRA rating.

Who's Discriminating? F&M Bank or the FED?

Some specific violations cited in that C&D order from past exams of F&M Bank involved an age discrimination practice for elderly credit applicants that related age to required assets, a discriminatory practice of requiring credit card applicants under 25 to provide a guarantor for credit approval rather than collateral as was allowed for those over 25, the apparent closing of Money Market Deposit Accounts because of excessive activity, and the use of "unduly subjective review criteria" in evaluating credit card applicants.

After hearing F&M Bank's side of the story, it is clear that they believe it is the FED, particularly the Federal Reserve Bank of San Francisco, not F&M bank, that is guilty of using such "unduly subjective review criteria" in their CRA exams. That bank would probably also argue that if any discrimination took place, it was by the FED against them, not the bank against its existing or potential customers. To a great extent, discrimination is in the eyes of the beholder.

C&D Order Requires Quarterly Board Review, Documentation, and an Expanded CRA Statement

F&M's C&D order called for a written comprehensive CRA plan with 11 specific requirements, including at least quarterly board CRA reviews; the maintenance of documentation to ensure a "complete and accurate record" of CRA activities to provide "clear, measurable evidence" of CRA performance; and the development of an expanded CRA statement "in accordance with the provisions" of the March 21, 1989, joint CRA regulatory statement.

The first requirement, like the Mercantile one, suggests boards should discuss CRA compliance efforts at least quarterly but probably monthly as a regular agenda item, as we recommend. The second requirement, contrary to what a compliance regulator may say, verifies CRA Survival Rule #1: "If it wasn't documented, it wasn't done!" The third requirement of an expanded CRA statement, which we unquestionably recommend, is unusual because the cited provisions strongly encourage but do *not* require an expanded statement as this C&D does.

CRA Regulatory Inconsistency at the FED

The C&D order against F&M Bank raises several questions regarding CRA regulatory consistency. Why did the FED's second CRA exam of this bank grant them the distinction of being the only bank in America to rise out of substantial noncompliance? And why did the FED turn around less than one year later and impose the nation's second compliance and CRA C&D order, citing most of the same conditions that existed at the time of the second exam? It does not appear that the conditions that allowed the bank to move out of substantial noncompliance disappeared in less than one year. Perhaps the FED should have never upgraded that bank out of substantial noncompliance in its second exam? The previous case study on their upgrading raised some inconsistencies in this regard.

Does this mean that F&M Bank's third CRA exam *must* result in a substantial noncompliance rating? If the FED "flip-flopped" back to a substantial noncompliance rating the third time around, what would that say about CRA examination consistency? Assuming F&M Bank's CRA compliance efforts now are the same if not better than they were during their second exam (which is what the bank believes), would the FED give a needs improvement rating to the only surviving bank in America of which we are aware with a C&D order partly on CRA grounds? The answer is "yes," because that's exactly what the FED did on June 29, 1992

The FED Plays "Hard Ball" with a $100,000 Penalty and a Branch Denial

F&M Bank received bad CRA news in late 1992 and early 1993. On December 29, 1992, it was assessed a $100,000 civil money penalty by the FED for "alleged violations" of federal compliance statutes and regulations. This generally-worded allegation did not mention CRA, but the implication is clear, based on the C&D order. On February 9, 1993, the FED denied applications, this time specifically on CRA grounds, for F&M Bank to open a branch in Costa Mesa, California, and to make an additional investment in bank premises. And, all of this is for a bank without the lowest possible CRA rating!

Back-to-Back-to-Back Substantial Noncompliance Ratings and Still No C&D Order?

Speaking of consistency, under what conditions is a C&D order partly on CRA grounds justified? We have learned from this case of two banks that a C&D order can be issued against a bank with a substantial noncompliance *or* a needs improvement CRA rating. Also, the C&D order may be short and fairly general *or* very long and specific. Since written guidelines for specific public CRA ratings are available, shouldn't there be similar ones for C&D orders on compliance and especially CRA grounds, as these actions are also

public? For example, a C&D order on CRA grounds could be appropriate for any bank receiving two consecutive substantial noncompliance ratings, but required in the case of three such ratings. There are already two candidates (one in Illinois and the other in Wyoming) fitting that description identified in Table 8-2, and both of these are FED-regulated banks.

Two Banks with Similar CRA Ratings but Vastly Different Results

We are strong advocates of public disclosure of bank examination ratings and enforcement actions. This case study points out some of the problems such disclosure raises for regulators and banks alike. The issue of CRA enforcement consistency at the FED was raised again in a November 1992 controversial merger approval involving the Capital Bank of Clayton, Missouri. That bank's substantial noncompliance and needs improvement rating resulted in a merger approval by the FED. But, a substantial noncompliance and needs improvement rating at F&M Bank resulted in a C&D order from the FED as well as a subsequent $100,000 civil money penalty and a branch denial. All of this leads us to conclude that consistent regulatory applications of CRA do *not* exist, especially at the FED.

OVER 200 YEARS OF CRA SUBSTANTIAL NONCOMPLIANCE AT THE BANK OF NORTH AMERICA

The First "CRA Protest" in 1781

The Community Reinvestment Act wasn't around in 1781, but CRA-type protests certainly were. In fact, what was in effect our nation's first "CRA protest" was lodged against our country's first bank of a modern type. This was the Bank of North America founded in 1781 in Philadelphia.

The history of America's first bank is well chronicled in Bray Hammond's *Banks and Politics in America—From the Revolution to the Civil War* (Princeton University Press, 1957). Alexander Hamilton, serving under General George Washington, sought a permanent private bank not only to help finance the revolutionary war but also to represent the independence for which America was fighting. Financier Robert Morris, with the help of Benjamin Franklin (and the French Treasury), capitalized the bank as a new source of credit for both the public and private sectors.

The City Folk versus the Country Folk

The bank's first three years of operations in center city, Philadelphia beginning in 1782 were generally successful, so much so that it became a focal point of a heated controversy between those in the city and the country. That is, rather than a classic CRA confrontation between bankers and an inner-city community group, the order of that day was the "city folk versus the country folk."

The rural ("agrarian") majority in the Pennsylvania legislature felt that the aristocratic-like city bank's lending policies were of little help to the "country people." According to the above-referenced book, the bank's short-term loans with a 45-day maturity were a "discouragement to agricultural borrowing." Furthermore, the "drain of profits" back to European stockholders didn't sit well with bank critics. Thomas Paine, Pelatiah Webster, James Wilson, and others defended the new bank by noting, among other things, that credit for city merchants indirectly benefited farmers who brought their products to market. All charges of favoritism by the bank were vehemently denied.

Redlining the "Country People?"

The Bank of North America may likely have been found to be in "substantial noncompliance" in today's CRA parlance. That is, that bank may likely have been substantially deficient in ascertaining and helping to meet the credit needs of its entire community, including low- and moderate-income neighborhoods. We are not suggesting that the likes of Ben Franklin, Alexander Hamilton, Robert Morris, and other founding fathers associated with this city bank were guilty of redlining the "country people." Nonetheless, many of them probably felt discriminated against simply because they lived and worked in the country, unlike the merchants in the city. And, the Bank of North America, which was operated and partly owned by Philadelphia merchants, was located in center city. It therefore appears that it was not a question of alleged discrimination by race, religion, ethnicity, or the like, but just plain geography.

Financier Robert Morris of the Bank of North America was the first to admit that his bank couldn't meet all of the credit needs of the farmers. He was likewise probably one of the first to identify the need for specialized financial intermediaries. He suggested that banks be used for short-term credit in "favour of commerce" and that "loan offices" be used for long-term credit in "favour of the landed interest." According to the above-mentioned source, Robert Morris went so far as to state that he would submit to a tax to "establish a fund for the purpose of lending sums to farmers for the improvement of their lands," in other words, a federal farm financing agency.

The First CRA Enforcement Action Ever— A Charter Repeal in 1787

The agrarian CRA-type protest to the Bank of North America wasn't asking for revised loan policies, growth restrictions, or even a pledge for "country" lending. They wanted to repeal its charter! The first bank of a modern type in America would soon become the last if the protestants had their way. A two-year effort beginning in 1785 did, in fact, result in a charter repeal, a significant weakening of the bank, and a highly restrictive new charter.

Therefore, our nation's first CRA-type protest was a "success" in the political sense of the rural majority defeating the urban minority. But, there were really no winners until the political balance tilted toward the growing cities, *and* the new bankers of the age broadened their scope to serve a wider market. Besides that first bank in Philadelphia, others soon formed in New York (the same Bank of New York of today), Boston, and Baltimore. The original Bank of North America, which maintained its existence until 1929, was absorbed into other banks and ultimately into First Pennsylvania Bank, which is now owned by CoreStates Financial Corp.

The Bank of North America Reincarnated in South Florida

The Bank of North America lives on, not just as a memory on a plaque at an office in Philadelphia's historic Independence Hall area, but in sunny south Florida. Dr. M. Lee Pearce, a wealthy investor born and raised in Philadelphia, was the chairman of the former Miami-based AmeriFirst Bank, America's first federally chartered savings and loan. He later established a privately-owned commercial bank in Miami in June 1990, which he decided to call the Bank of North America. By buying the deposits of failed banks and thrifts at truly "fire-sale" prices from the government, it quickly became south Florida's fastest growing and one of its largest and most profitable big banks.

This bank's unprecedented growth through such purchases, which reached a half billion dollars in under two years, apparently came to an abrupt halt when it received a substantial noncompliance CRA rating dated September 11, 1991. It became the first bank in South Florida and just the third in Florida to receive this rating (the other two were in Jacksonville and Tampa) as of that time.

Similarities between South Florida and Southern California

There are many similarities between the first banks receiving this absolutely lowest CRA rating in south Florida and southern California. Farmers and Merchants Bank of Long Beach, the first southern California bank to receive this rating, is the best capitalized big bank in California and also one of the most profitable. The Bank of North America of Fort Lauderdale is one of Florida's most profitable big banks. Both banks are independent and privately owned. The $1.4 billion F&M Bank is family owned, and the $0.5 billion Bank of North America is owned by the wealthy investor Dr. Pearce.

1% Direct Community Reinvestment—A Commercial Bank or an Investment Bank?

Banks acting more like *investment* banks, which make investments and buy loans, rather than *commercial* banks, which make loans in their community, are susceptible to low CRA ratings. This is especially the case for any bank that doesn't do a good job of "reinvesting" deposits back into the community through loans. This is the essence of the Community Reinvestment Act.

In the case of the Bank of North America, most of its $350 million in loans were purchased from other institutions, and just 4.4% of them were made by that bank itself. But, only one-third of that small amount was made in the local communities surrounding its

ten offices in Dade, Broward, and Palm Beach counties. This means that only $5 million, or 1%, of the roughly $500 million taken out of those communities in the form of deposits was being reinvested back into them in the form of loans made directly by that bank. This percentage increases significantly if purchased loans made by other banks are included.

"Turning Down" Government Programs

Besides these "unreasonable lending patterns," that bank was also criticized by federal bank examiners for making few loans in the bank's low- and moderate-income neighborhoods, "turning down" opportunities to participate in government or public programs, failing to assess the community impact of branch closings, and displaying "little intent" of participating in community projects. There was, however, *no* evidence of any prohibited discriminatory or other illegal credit practices at that bank.

Crimping the Style of the "Very Little Bank with the Very Big Name"

What happens to the 1% of banks that receive this substantial noncompliance CRA rating? Besides the public disclosure of a federal bank regulator telling a *community* bank that it is not adequately serving *community* credit needs, there is a more serious implication. Federal regulators can and occasionally have denied branch, merger, and other expansion plans of banks with low CRA ratings. This is still a lot better than having a bank charter repealed, as was the case with this bank's namesake more than 200 years ago.

CRA growth restrictions are obviously very important to what was once a "very little bank with a very big name." Ironically, the same federal bank regulators who let this bank become south Florida's fastest growing and one of its largest banks almost overnight have been effectively limiting any major growth plans because of the bank's CRA rating.

For example, it was well known that the Bank of North America was very interested in buying all or portions of the failed half-billion dollar Professional Savings Bank of Coral Gables. The fact that the Bank of North America did not even bid on any branches of that failed bank (or AmeriFirst or others) in early

1992 leads us to believe that their expansion efforts have been hampered for the time being.

That is, until they are able to upgrade their rating to at least the next notch, which includes 10% of all banks nationwide. Some banks such as F&M Bank and the one in Jacksonville have already been upgraded as a result of their improved CRA performance. We understand from the Bank of North America that they have already hired outside CRA consultants and a new compliance officer. Hopefully, their efforts, along with a refocused lending strategy and other improvements, will likewise result in a better CRA program and rating.

Will There Be a Silver Lining to This Substantial Noncompliance Cloud?

Meanwhile, they shouldn't be terribly concerned over any adverse publicity they may receive with their very low rating, at least based on the seemingly perverse experience of F&M Bank, described in a previous case study. If south Florida depositors are anything like those in southern California in that respect, the Bank of North America may actually benefit from their CRA rating.

More than 200 years have passed, and we still have a Bank of North America, even with the Philadelphia connection. And, like the original Bank of North America, the present one has run into a roadblock within its initial few years of operations because of its substantial deficiency in helping to meet community credit needs. The new bank has already made several improvements in its CRA performance. Assuming it is upgraded in its next evaluation, it should resume its growth, just like the original Bank of North America came back after running into several roadblocks.

CRA—At the Top of Banking's "Hit List"

CRA was formally put on the books in 1977, but we know from this case study that it's been around in one form or another for over 200 years. What's remarkable about CRA is that it wasn't until 1977, nearly 200 years after our first bank of a modern type was formed, that this law was actually put on the books, primarily through the efforts of Senator William Proxmire of Wisconsin. It quickly became bank-

ing's least-liked law, never more so than in 1990 when CRA ratings were first publicly disclosed. Not surprisingly in 1991, just 14 years after CRA was born, the banking lobby nearly persuaded the House and Senate to effectively "gut" CRA. This effort continued in 1992, with the full backing of the Bush Administration, using the politically proper and undeniably popular "unnecessary regulatory burden" argument. The banking lobby has put CRA at the top of their 1993 "hit list," but this time they won't enjoy the same support of the White House, because the "anti-CRA" Bush is out and the expected "pro-CRA" Clinton is in.

America's CRA Spirit Will Not Die

America is no different than most other countries around the world in that there always has been and probably always will be *at least* two socioeconomic groups which, for lack of better terms, we will refer to as "rich" on one hand and "poor" on the other. As long as the credit granting process is primarily in the hands of the rich, the poor will likely not be satisfied that they're receiving their "fair share." Many country people weren't satisfied 200 years ago and neither are many inner-city inhabitants today.

What makes America different is that we have a large and mobile middle class that softens the sharp class difference existing in many other countries. Also, we are unique in that we have always had an unwritten (pre-1977) or written (CRA) law that attempts to make the credit-granting process as equitable as possible, so the 40% of all American households that are low and moderate income have a better chance of getting their fair share.

That is why we believe that this CRA spirit of equal access to credit by the entire community—city or country people, merchants or farmers, and suburbanites or inner city residents—will always be a part of the American tradition. Even if CRA is ultimately killed or handicapped, its spirit will not die.

IS THE FED UNDERMINING CRA ENFORCEMENT?

Three announcements by the FED over the December 1992–February 1993 period and the ensuing publicity they received suggested that the FED was stepping up enforcement of CRA. The first announcement in December 1992 was about the FED's imposition of a $100,000 civil money penalty on Farmers and Merchants (F&M) Bank of Long Beach, California, for violation of consumer compliance laws and regulations, including CRA. Within two months the FED announced its denial of a branch application of that same bank on CRA grounds. Also, during this period the FED's Inspector General announced an extensive review of FED CRA examinations.

If the truth be known, the FED is the furthest thing from a tough CRA enforcer. Our two-and-one-half years of research on CRA has led us to conclude that the FED is the most lax CRA enforcer of the four federal bank regulators. The FED's CRA enforcement record, especially the most recent of two 1992 relatively unnoticed merger decisions, further support this argument. In fact, we must question the FED's commitment to CRA and ask, "Is the FED undermining CRA enforcement?"

Why the FED is the Most Lax CRA Enforcer

If the FED's evaluation of CRA examinations is a comprehensive and objective one, it will conclude that the FED is the most lax CRA enforcer of all four federal bank regulators for the following reasons:

1. Of the 12,100 CRA ratings publicly disclosed from July 1, 1990, to December 31, 1992, the FED gave out the highest percentage (11.8%) of above-average ratings compared to the FDIC at 10.4%, the OCC at 10.8%, and the OTS at 8.2%. Over this same period the FED reported the second lowest percentage (9.0%) of below-average ("needs improvement" and "substantial noncompliance") ratings, ranking behind the FDIC (7.8%), but well ahead of the OCC at 13.9% and the OTS at 18.4%. Our research on CRA ratings has concluded that substantial CRA ratings variations among the FED, FDIC, and OCC primarily reflect differences among these bank regulators rather than among the banks' CRA performance. This, however, is not the case with the OTS, where we concluded that the thrifts themselves were as much if not more responsible than the OTS for the relatively low CRA ratings.

2. The FED gave out the absolutely lowest "substantial noncompliance" rating to only nine banks over this two-and-one-half year period, the fewest number for any of the four regulators. The above-referenced F&M Bank was the first of those nine banks to get that rating on August 6, 1990. While the FED has the fewest number of regulated banks compared to other regulators, the FED has relatively more examining resources. For example, it conducted 1.63 CRA exams per regulated bank as of year-end 1992, twice as many as all three other regulators combined. Thus, the most lax CRA enforcer also happens to be the most frequent CRA examiner. Importantly, the FED is in a unique position among all regulators because it oversees bank holding company activities which account for the bulk of the banking industry. Also, since the FED has had specialized compliance examiners since 1977 (the other agencies began in 1989 or later), the FED has assumed the leadership role among the other regulators in the area of consumer compliance.

3. All four federal regulators, but especially the FED, have been lax in "true" CRA enforcement in terms of branch and merger denials on CRA grounds, with only 20 of them out of nearly 70,000 applications filed over the last 15 years. The regulators prefer CRA "enforcement" through "conditional approvals," of which there have been several hundred over this period compared to but 20 denials. Only one denial out of every 3,500 applications doesn't represent bad odds for a bank, even one with a deficient CRA record. The FED has denied only *three* mergers on CRA grounds since the 1977 CRA, an average of only one every five years. The first of those denials was not until 1989, and it involved the then quasi-public Continental Bank of Chicago. The other two merger denials involved small banks in Montana in 1991 and in Chicago in 1992. The FED has denied only *one* branch application on CRA grounds since 1977, and this was the February 1993 F&M Bank decision. Thus, all four of the FED's denials were since

1989, hardly a sign of vigorous enforcement during CRA's first dozen years. By contrast the FDIC and OCC denied their first applications ten years earlier in 1979.

4. The four federal regulators have likewise been lax in "true" CRA enforcement through use of cease and desist (C&D) orders (only two to date), civil money penalties (only one to date), and Justice Department referrals (only one through mid-year 1992 and five to date) on CRA and related compliance grounds. Thus, there have been a total of eight such CRA enforcement activities to date according to data provided us by individual regulators. The FED has issued only one C&D order on CRA grounds since 1977, and this was also against the F&M Bank on March 23, 1992, *after* it was upgraded by the FED to a needs improvement CRA rating on April 22, 1991. Yet, the FED did not issue C&D orders on comparable CRA grounds to the Texas Coastal Bank of Pasadena, Texas, with back-to-back substantial noncompliance ratings from the FED or worse yet to the Parish Bank and Trust Company of Momence, Illinois, or the Uinta County State Bank of Mountain View, Wyoming, both of which received unprecedented back-to-back-to-back substantial noncompliance ratings from the FED. The FED has likewise assessed a civil money penalty in connection with violations of CRA and other consumer compliance laws and regulations in only one case, and this was also against the F&M Bank in the amount of $100,000 in December 1992. Thus, the FED has used three of the four toughest CRA enforcement tools (branch denial, C&D order, and civil money penalty), but in only one instance in each case. Of greatest interest is the fact that the FED's use of those three enforcement tools all involved the same bank which also happens to be the first one it publicly rated substantial noncompliance. This begs the question why the FED didn't refer the F&M case to the Justice Department, especially considering F&M Bank's alleged repeated discriminatory credit practices representing substantive viola-

tions of the Equal Credit Opportunity Act (ECOA). In the FED's defense it has been a strict CRA enforcer, but only in the case of the F&M Bank. It appears that the FED's primary CRA "enforcement" tools in dealing with other banks are "jawboning," the issuance of "politically correct" pro-CRA policy statements, and "conditional approvals" of mergers.

5. The FED approved two mergers in 1992 which just as easily *could* have been denied in the first case on CRA grounds and which clearly *should* have been denied in the second case on CRA grounds. The first case was the February, 1992 approval of the acquisition of Chicago's troubled Talman Home Federal through LaSalle National Bank, the only big bank with a current needs improvement rating. The second case was the FED's November 1992, approval of an acquisition by the parent of the Capital Bank and Trust Company of Clayton, Missouri, one of the lowest CRA-rated banks in America. The Capital Bank was a precedent-setting one in many ways, not the least of which was the dissent by two of the seven governors of the Federal Reserve Board in this controversial decision. Both of these merger approvals that could or should have been denials are discussed below.

6. The FED recently approved an acquisition of a bank holding company which involved banks that were denied to merge on CRA grounds by the OCC just four months earlier. On March 10, 1993, the FED approved the acquisition of the parent of First City National Bank of Memphis, Tennessee, by First Commerical Corporation of Little Rock, Arkansas, the parent of First Commercial Bank, N.A. of Memphis. Two of the seven governors (Kelley and Lindsey) of the Federal Reserve Board were "absent and not voting" on this decision. The FED's approval effectively overruled the OCC's November 1992 denial of the merger of those two Memphis banks, although there will still be the inconvenience of having to operate them as separate charters under the same parent. The OCC's

denial was primarily because of First Commercial Bank's back-to-back "needs improvement" ratings in August 1991 and May 1992. The FED, however, concluded there was "substantial improvement" in that bank's CRA performance during the intervening nine months, even though the OCC gave a second needs improvement rating. In an attempt to justify the effective overturning of the OCC's merger denial, the FED noted modest improvements at the bank, including extended office hours, and numerous commitments since the May 1992 second exam (not the November 1992 denial). If those improvements and commitments were as good as the FED's decision would lead one to believe, why did the OCC deny the merger application? The FED's decision, in an unusual disclosure, stated that the OCC "advised the Board" at the FED (probably after the FED contacted, but hopefully not pressured, the OCC) that the bank's proposed actions and commitments "should be sufficient when effectively implemented" to improve the bank's rating, presumably to a satisfactory one. Thus, the FED got from the OCC a public commitment for an upgraded rating contingent on the bank's own commitments. Would the OCC dare give that bank a third needs improvement rating, even if it truly deserved one? Because the FED has jurisdiction over bank holding company acquisitions involving banks and thrifts regulated by the OCC, FDIC, and OTS, the FED can use its regulatory muscle to pressure and effectively override CRA enforcement efforts by those other agencies. It is possible that those agencies will feel FED pressure to avoid giving below-average CRA ratings to banks like First Commercial of Memphis, if the FED has approved a bank holding company application involving them. If the "lender of last resort" is also the "CRA enforcer of last resort," then this case suggests that the FED's position as the most lax CRA enforcer is having an adverse impact much beyond the 7% of all banks and thrifts that are FED-member banks.

Using the "Loophole" in Chicago's "Loop"

Both of the FED's two most recent merger denials and most of the denials of other regulators on CRA grounds are because of at least one needs improvement rating. Banks with substantial noncompliance ratings don't even bother to apply, but this may now change considering the FED's recent CRA precedents (see below).

Of the nation's 100 largest banks (see Table 3-46), Chicago's LaSalle National Bank is the only one with a current needs improvement rating (none have a substantial noncompliance rating). The only other big banks to ever receive a needs improvement rating have been upgraded, and these include Chicago's Harris Bank and First Interstate Banks of Arizona and Oregon. LaSalle's parent ABN AMRO Bank of the Netherlands was approved by the FED to acquire Talman Home Federal on February 27, 1992, thereby giving LaSalle the second largest retail deposit base in Chicago. The FED's approval order noted that it took the unusual step of considering *commitments* to overcome LaSalle's deficient CRA record because Talman was "troubled." Thus, the FED might have denied this acquisition, had it not been for their use of the troubled institution "loophole."

Talman's troubled condition, however, was well known for over three years as it operated with negative tangible capital. It is possible that this *status quo* could have been maintained even longer to find an alternate investor, especially one that isn't the only large bank in the country with a needs improvement rating. Thus, if the FED really wanted to flex its CRA enforcement muscles, it could have easily denied the LaSalle acquisition.

The troubled institution loophole is apparently used at the FED's discretion, since it was not invoked in the August 13, 1992, denial of the application of Gore-Bronson Bancorp Inc. to acquire troubled Water Tower Trust and Savings Bank of Chicago. That bank and both banks representing the acquirer had needs improvement ratings, but the FED refused to consider commitments to overcome their deficient CRA records, even though the target bank was a troubled one.

Grade Inflation in St. Louis

Less than four months after the LaSalle approval, the FED had yet another chance to flex its CRA enforcement muscles on a merger decision. This was the November 30, 1992, approval of the acquisition of Magna Bank of Ozark, Missouri, by Capital Bancorporation, the parent of Capital Bank and Trust Company of Clayton, Missouri, a suburb of St. Louis. Instead of sending a "tough cop" message on CRA enforcement, the FED may have undermined it with a controversial approval that clearly should have been a denial on CRA grounds.

Capital Bank was one of only 88 banks in the nation to have publicly received a substantial noncompliance rating in the two and one-half years ending December 31, 1992 (see Table 8-2). Less than 1% of the 12,100 ratings made over this period were in this absolutely lowest CRA category. Our review of the FDIC's May 24, 1991, performance evaluation of Capital Bank, as well as a comparative evaluation of other banks with a substantial noncompliance rating, concluded that Capital Bank definitely deserved that lowest rating.

We were shocked, however, to learn that an April 3, 1992, reevaluation by the FDIC upgraded that bank to a needs improvement rating when there was little to no "real" improvement in their CRA performance. The bank, for example, conducted a study of its office hours and as a result kept its lobby open until 4:30 P.M. instead of 4 P.M. during the week. There were a few other broadly described improvements, but we could not obtain specifics from the bank as they would not respond to our telephone or written requests for further information in this regard.

Surprisingly, the bank's record of "prohibited discriminatory or other illegal credit practices" was as bad as before with substantive violations of the ECOA and the FDIC's Fair Housing Regulation among others. In fact, the most recent exam with the higher rating revealed "disproportionate lending patterns," but such a finding was not made in the first exam with the lower rating. Rather than reward Capital Bank with a merger approval for these and other questionable practices, the FED and FDIC should have considered referring this case to the Justice Department. Such a referral would have been appro-

priate under the provisions of the FDIC Improvement Act of 1991 because of that bank's repeated substantive violations of ECOA, which would appear to suggest a pattern or practice of discouraging or denying credit applications.

We concluded that the second CRA rating was a case of blatant grade inflation by the FDIC. The FED not only accepted the FDIC's inflated needs improvement rating at face value but also attempted to justify what was clearly a deficient CRA record by noting that management's emphasis on other matters "limited its ability" to strengthen its CRA program. Capital Bank did, however, begin to consider some real improvements in its CRA program but not until the merger application was filed. And, some of the bank's most notable "improvements" were commitments for the future rather than past performance.

FED Sets CRA Precedents in Capital Bank Decision

The FED's approval of this merger involving Capital Bank was precedent setting because:

1. It was the only bank of which we are aware to ever receive a substantial noncompliance rating (and arguably two of them excluding grade inflation) and gain a FED expansion approval of any type. There was no troubled institution "loophole" to bail out the FED this time as in the LaSalle case.

2. Capital Bank was one of only ten banks to ever be upgraded by any regulator from substantial noncompliance to needs improvement (excluding grade inflation) and then be rewarded with a FED merger approval. This is in stark contrast to being hit with a FED cease and desist order, a $100,000 civil money penalty, and a branch denial as was the case with F&M Bank, another one of those ten banks, against whom the FED has directed most of its "CRA firepower."

3. Contrary to what the FED and other regulators preach to bankers, the FED accepted CRA "promises over performance," especially last-minute promises, to correct Capital Bank's deficient CRA record. The FED also did this in the

LaSalle case, but the FED justified their action with the troubled institution "loophole."

4. Most importantly, Governors Kelley and La-Ware, apparently the only two pro-CRA FED Board members based on this decision, dissented from the approval because several of the initiatives to correct CRA deficiencies "were not put in place until well after this application had been filed" and there was no demonstrable record of improved performance.

FED Sends the Wrong Messages

The FED's LaSalle decision apparently tells us that being among the lowest 10% of banks with a needs improvement CRA rating is acceptable for expansion-minded bankers as long as they target a troubled institution. The FED may, however, use its discretion here in defining a "troubled" institution as in the Talman case or in applying this loophole in the first place as in the Water Tower case (where the FED rejected it).

The FED's Clayton decision goes even farther in potentially undermining CRA enforcement by suggesting that "CRA ratings don't matter," even if you are one of America's lowest CRA-rated banks, as was Clayton Bank. More importantly the FED board, save Governors Kelley and LaWare, has now proclaimed that even if you have a low rating, they will accept commitments to correct it. So don't even bother looking for a troubled institution if you have a below average CRA rating, because the FED apparently will accept CRA "promises over performance" in approving your application.

A "CRA Division" at the Justice Department?

This seemingly "anything goes" merger attitude involving CRA at the FED is painfully suggestive of their antitrust analysis. That is, the FED can always expand the definition of the relevant geographic and/or product markets to result in acceptable concentration measures or consider "other factors" to justify an approval where it otherwise would not be warranted. The Justice Department may have to set up a "CRA Division" like its antitrust division to provide a balanced view on CRA enforcement in merger decisions.

"Competition in Laxity" Revisited

It is ironic that we should conclude that the FED is the most lax of all federal regulators in terms of CRA enforcement. This is because it was former FED Chairman Arthur Burns who coined the phrase "competition in laxity" to refer to other regulators who eased up on banks to attract them to their respective folds. While the FED was traditionally thought of as the "toughest" regulator, we now know that this applies only to safety and soundness, and certainly not to CRA. The OTS and its FHLBB predecessor have long been criticized as being the "easiest" safety and soundness regulator, and the S&L crisis seems to bear this allegation out. Ironically, though, we have determined that the OTS is the toughest CRA compliance regulator on a relative basis. Thus, the OTS and FED are each at two ends of the extreme in the competition in laxity depending upon whether we are talking about safety and soundness or CRA compliance.

FED Board Chairman Greenspan reportedly indicated an interest in working with President Clinton's Administration to achieve certain public policy goals. It seems that CRA enforcement is not one of them, at least based upon the Clayton decision. It appears from that decision that only two of the seven FED board members are serious about adopting Clinton's expected pro-CRA viewpoint. This would suggest that someone will have to undergo a CRA "attitude adjustment," and it is our guess that it won't be President Clinton.

10. Conclusions and Recommendations

INTRODUCTION

The analysis in this book has resulted in two general conclusions and several specific ones. The first general conclusion is that CRA is needed and it works, but it can be improved and expanded into other areas. As it stands now, we would rate the CRA system itself as "needs improvement." The second general finding verifies the "positive power of public disclosure." That is, the disclosure of CRA ratings and performance evaluations has been an unqualified success, but such disclosure can be improved and also expanded.

This analysis has resulted in several specific conclusions regarding the regulators themselves, CRA ratings trends, the existing CRA rating structure, and methods by which banks can improve their CRA performance and ratings. These individual conclusions will be detailed in this chapter.

Our recommendations to both improve and expand CRA and its disclosure will also be included in this chapter. Our final recommendation will include a proposal for a complete restructuring of CRA involving an explicit CRA assessment in lieu of the extensive existing CRA documentation requirements. This chapter concludes with a review of popular myths as well as likely future trends involving CRA.

CONCLUSIONS

1. **CRA is needed and it works, but it can be improved and expanded into other areas.**

Our country has always had an unwritten (pre-1977) or written (CRA) law that attempts to make the credit-granting process as equitable as possible, so the 40% of all American households that are low- and moderate-income have a better chance of getting their fair share. The issue of equal access to credit by the entire community has been a controversial one since our first bank of a modern type was established in Philadelphia more than 200 years ago. We believe the CRA spirit will always be a part of the American tradition, despite continued efforts by the banking lobby to effectively "gut" CRA.

Banking is the most heavily regulated industry in America, and we believe that CRA is by far the least-liked law in banking today. Efforts by the banking lobby to partially repeal parts of CRA were nearly successful in 1991, and they continued full steam in 1992 with the backing of the Bush Administration. The anti-CRA effort continued in 1993, but this time without the apparent support of the expected pro-CRA Clinton Administration. Even if CRA is handicapped or ultimately killed, we don't believe that America's heritage of a CRA spirit of equal credit opportunity for everyone will die.

All businesses should have some type of corporate social responsibility, which may be a function of size, revenues, profits, or government benefits received. We don't believe that such a concept of a "corporate conscience" is inconsistent with capitalism. The primary goal for corporate managers under capitalism is to maximize the present value of shareholder wealth. This goal is primarily interpreted as meaning profit maximization. Rather than such an absolute goal of maximizing profits, we prefer a conditional goal of maximizing profits subject to some type of "corporate conscience" condition or social constraint. We refer to this as "Capitalism with a Corporate Conscience."

Many CRA participants, chief among them community groups, cite the "social compact" argument for CRA, namely, that banks have a social responsibility because of the wide variety of benefits received from the government such as federal deposit insurance, access to the "lender of last resort," protection from competition in certain areas, and so on. We believe this same argument can be applied to other financial industries but to a much lesser extent. In fact, it is counter to the "level playing field" argument and the basic theme of fairness that banks and thrifts should be the only financial institutions to bear a social responsibility such as CRA. What about other financial institutions of the depository type (credit unions and to a lesser extent money market mutual funds) and non-depository type (such as insurance companies)?

There is no reason why credit unions that benefit from federal deposit insurance, among other things, should be exempt from a CRA responsibility. Large depository-like money market mutual funds could be argued to have some type of social responsibility similar to CRA, even though they are not consumer lenders. Money market mutual funds are highly competitive substitutes for money market accounts offered by banks and thrifts and, in fact, represent the primary reason why they offered them in the first place (the "level playing field" argument). Also, it is possible that the largest such funds might benefit from the federal safety net in the event of a liquidity crisis (a weaker version of the "social compact" argument).

The social responsibility of some of the large nondepository financial institutions has been questioned recently. For example, in the wake of the L.A. riots, there have been renewed charges of redlining by insurance companies for property, auto, and casualty lines. More recently we have witnessed the apparent redlining of coastal and flood zone areas by major property and casualty insurers after the catastrophic losses of Hurricane Andrew. If a potential homeowner can't get insurance, the question of possible mortgage loan discrimination is irrelevant, as no lender will finance a home without property insurance. This "no insurance, no loan" situation spares a banker from possibly saying "no" to a potential inner city home loan applicant.

If there was a CRA type of requirement for the insurance industry, this problem would be nonexistent or greatly reduced. If banks were more involved in the insurance business, we doubt that they would practice the same alleged redlining techniques because of their corporate CRA culture. Even though a bank holding company's nonbank subsidiaries are not covered by CRA, they are often held to a higher CRA-like standard because of the "CRA halo" on bank subsidiaries. This has been the case for several mortgage banking and finance company affiliates of bank holding companies.

Nondepository financial institutions that are major lenders in the area of residential mortgages, installment loans, credit cards, small business loans, and the like presently have no CRA requirement. These firms include some of our largest nonfinancial companies as well as traditional mortgage banking, credit card, and consumer lending firms.

Even investment banking firms differ widely in terms of their demonstrated level of social conscience. For example, one New York firm (Muriel Siebert & Company) has been contributing half of its underwriting commissions from new municipal and corporate security issues to local housing groups and charities in an innovative arrangement. This program allows banks and thrifts to receive "CRA credit" through purchasing RTC mortgage and other securities through this firm.

Meanwhile, giant Merrill Lynch & Company recently offered 100% mortgage financing in its new "Mortgage 100" program, but the minimum mortgage amounts at preferred rates range from $100,000 to $250,000. Merrill Lynch, like some other security firms, also has introduced a basic brokerage $40 annual fee in addition to normal trading commissions. Some firms have a $50 annual "inactive fee" for infrequent traders and a $50 "transfer fee" for closed accounts transferred to competitors. If a bank had a minimum $100,000 preferred mortgage program and a basic banking privilege fee (or an inactive or transfer fee), all of which would have a more adverse impact on low- and moderate-income households, a CRA "red flag" would certainly be raised. But, this is not the case in the investment banking industry where some firms have a higher level of social consciousness than others. It is interesting to point out that a Merrill Lynch bank subsidiary received a substantial noncompliance CRA rating.

The best proof that CRA works is the more than $30 billion (according to the Center for Community Change) of actual and pledged investments that have poured into communities, especially low- and moderate-income ones, that most likely would never have been made without this law. Community banks, by their very nature, must serve their community to stay in business. This may not be the case, however, for banks operating in "one-bank towns," with little or no real competition, as they may have little or no incentive to emphasize such service.

Our research has shown that banks, including community banks, differ widely in terms of the extent to which they meet the credit needs of low- and moderate-income individuals. CRA has clearly been a success in this latter regard by raising awareness about both direct and indirect means of credit discouragement and discrimination and its effect on these groups.

For the first time ever, the largest banking trade association (the American Bankers Association) and one of the three federal banking regulators (the OCC) have admitted the existence of some types of discrimination in banking. Such an admission is the first step toward correcting a problem, and it is likely that we would not have come this far without the disclosure of CRA ratings and HMDA data. Both of these admissions were prior to the Federal Reserve Bank of Boston's landmark October, 1992 study ("Mortgage Lending in Boston: Interpreting HMDA Data"), which provided the most definitive evidence to date that racial discrimination in mortgage lending is widespread. The FED had little choice but to follow the OCC's lead and accept these significant findings of its bank in Boston.

It is not clear from our research that all CRA activities must be marginally profitable or even un-

profitable. We have documented numerous instances where banks can meet both their business goals and those of CRA in various ways through officer call programs, seminars, and the like. Yes, it requires additional work and often some innovation, but it can be done. No bank has yet failed because of CRA. On the other hand, some of our nation's most profitable banks, including both small and large ones, are truly outstanding in terms of their CRA performance.

The original argument against CRA was that of "credit allocation." The argument of the day against CRA is that it is an "unnecessary regulatory burden." Both of these arguments have some merit, but we are particularly sensitive to the latter argument, as we have documented numerous instances of what appears to be unnecessary and wasteful documentation with little or no direct benefit to the community. We believe that these CRA shortcomings are not reasons to "gut" CRA but rather to improve it. Our 10 most important recommendations in this regard will be discussed later in this chapter. Also, we have proposed a complete restructuring of CRA, which we believe is more consistent with its original goals, and responsive to the most important problems we have found with CRA.

2. **The disclosure of CRA ratings and performance evaluations has been an unqualified success, but the "positive power of public disclosure" can be strengthened even more through improvements in and expansion of the present disclosure system.**

The "positive power of public disclosure" has been well documented in our analysis of CRA. This represented the first time in which federal bank regulatory ratings or evaluations were ever made public in this country. There was and still is considerable opposition to such public disclosure, mostly by the banking lobby, but some even by the regulators themselves.

The claims by the banking lobby, and to a lesser extent some regulators, that CRA ratings would somehow be confused with safety and soundness ratings proved to be totally unfounded. In fact, experience has shown that the public could not only discriminate between the two types of ratings but actually make investment decisions based upon them, at least in one instance. Specifically, in the case of Farmers and Merchants Bank of Long Beach, California, the bank's well-publicized substantial noncompliance rating resulted in an inflow of $8 million in new deposits because the bank said that its low CRA mark signaled it was very strong and conservative. Had the worst CRA rating somehow been interpreted as a safety and soundness problem, the opposite reaction would have ensued. Clearly, the public is much more knowledgeable on financial matters than either the banking lobby or the regulators would have thought or might admit

What CRA disclosure did was in fact what it was supposed to do. That is, it shed light on previously confidential ratings and exams. Now that these ratings and performance evaluations have been made public, we have seen many positive results. Most of these pertain to improvements in the CRA performance of the banks themselves. Unfortunately, our first look through the window of regulatory examination processes has also documented some unfavorable conclusions regarding subjectivities, inconsistencies, and other problems in the regulatory process which will be discussed below. None of these insights would have been possible without public disclosure.

We have concluded that the likelihood of disclosure of CRA ratings in 1989 and the first half of 1990, and especially the actual disclosure of them beginning on July 1, 1990, have been associated with an increase in the percentage of below-average CRA ratings and a decrease in the percentage of above-average ones. This conclusion holds up not only for the approximately year-and-one-half period before and after the actual disclosure but also for the broader 11-year period for which data are available. The number of absolutely lowest (substantial noncompliant) rated banks in the two-and-one-half-year post-disclosure period was more than one-and-one-half times the number over the eight-and-one-half-year predisclosure period.

We believe that the public disclosure for the first time of the worst CRA offenders (those with below-average ratings) is in fact evidence that CRA public disclosure works. Many of the roughly 11% of all banks with below-average ratings probably were "repeat offenders" with similarly low ratings on previous nonpublic exams. However, we are now noticing that

many banks with disclosed low ratings are making serious attempts to improve their CRA performance, where they likely never would have had any motivation to do so before their ratings were made public. Public disclosure has resulted in such banks doing what the regulators could not (or in some cases would not) make the banks do.

Our analysis of multiple CRA ratings through year-end 1991 has concluded that 42% of all multiple evaluations have resulted in upgraded ratings. And, most of the upgradings were from needs improvement to satisfactory, with one being from substantial noncompliance to needs improvement. Only 3% of the banks were downgraded. We don't believe we would see this type of significant improvement in banks with below-average CRA ratings if their ratings and evaluations were not made public.

It is not, therefore, unexpected that some of the greatest opposition to CRA is by banks with actual or expected low CRA ratings. Public identification of the 1% of absolutely lowest CRA-rated banks and 10% of lowest rated banks may have indeed caused some embarrassment to the affected banks. No bank, but especially a small community bank, likes the idea of a federal bank regulator publicly telling them that they are not serving community credit needs properly. Many of these banks are working harder than ever before to improve their CRA performance and rating, and yet others have little concern over their low ratings because they don't plan to branch or merge. The fact that we can now monitor the results of multiple evaluations of these banks to gauge their progress is a further benefit of public disclosure.

We have concluded that the positive power of public disclosure may be more powerful than the federal bank regulators' current arsenal of tools, even including enforcement actions under certain circumstances. Virtually all of the predicted fears stated by the banking lobby and some bank regulators regarding the disclosure of CRA ratings and examinations proved to be unfounded. The fact that there is still so much opposition to CRA, probably now more than ever, suggests that CRA disclosure has had its desired effect. If the day ever comes when bankers drop this opposition and actually embrace CRA, then and only then might we say that CRA has done its job and is ready for repeal. Until that time, the positive power of public disclosure can be strengthened through the five recommendations to expand and improve CRA disclosure contained in a following section.

3. CRA has been and probably always will be representative of a series of tradeoffs among the elements of the "CRA triangle."

We have defined the CRA triangle in terms of three main interested parties: community groups representing consumer interests, regulators implementing and enforcing consumer legislation, and America's banks and thrifts.

There has always been conflict between community groups and banks on certain matters, to the point where regulators often acted as liasons attempting to reach a middle ground between the two views. Today there are often conflicts between bankers and regulators regarding CRA issues and sometimes even between community groups and the regulators themselves.

Many community groups feel that grade inflation exists in CRA ratings, which they believe may measure the level of documentation by a bank more than its actual CRA performance in the community. In other words, they may believe that bankers are more interested in their CRA ratings rather than their actual CRA performance. Bankers themselves are clearly interested in receiving an average or better rating, but they would also like to benefit the community if it can be done within the banks' resource and safety and soundness constraints. These are just some of the many tradeoffs involved in CRA.

We have determined that there is a difference between a good CRA rating and good CRA performance. That is, not all banks with outstanding CRA ratings are truly outstanding CRA performers. Chapter 5 estimated the extent to which we believe there is a difference between outstanding rated banks (8.7% of all banks) and those that are "truly" outstanding (only 4.9% of the total) as of year-end 1991. The comparable grade inflation adjustments as of year-end 1992 reduced the proportion of banks rated outstanding from 10.3% to 5.8% for those "truly" outstanding.

We believe that one of the reasons for this distinction is that a bank can undertake numerous actions

to mainly benefit its CRA rating but not provide a commensurate level of direct benefit to the community. It can be argued that any bank activity resulting in an outstanding CRA rating should also benefit the community. While this may be the case over the long term, it is hard to associate many specific activities designed to gain a high rating with actual community benefits. For example, the use of "testers" to identify whether overt or subtle discrimination exists within a bank results in many important and interesting conclusions. However, regardless of the conclusions, this would not directly benefit the community in the same way as using the funds spent on those testers at a specific housing project in a "low-mod" (low- and moderate-income) or "sub-min" (substantially minority) neighborhood.

This same argument can be extended to most of the paperwork requirements of CRA, which in reality form the basis for much of the banking industry's dislike for banking's most unpopular law. For example, the requirement to maintain an extensive CRA public file, which may never be opened by anyone but CRA regulators and researchers, may be counterproductive in the sense that no one in the community is really benefiting (unless bank employees who maintain those files happen to live there).

Taking this a step further, there is now an entire CRA support industry made up of vendors of software, survey and research firms, "tester" firms, and other consultants competing for assignments at banks. Interestingly, this new growth industry includes the government itself, through one Federal Home Loan Bank that has consulted with banks and thrifts (for a fee) to help them improve their CRA performance and ratings.

The Federal Home Loan Bank (FHLB) of Cincinnati has a CRA Consulting Services Group that has advertised credit needs assessment services, mortgage market mapping services, CRA program evaluation services, and CRA "comprehensive consulting services." A 1991 direct mail piece on this agency's letterhead to banks and thrifts advertised their $495 CRA video and workbook. The advertisement touted their CRA product as a way "to get a handle on the CRA monster" and notes the importance of a bank's CRA rating. Another advertising piece for that product notes that their CRA Consulting Services Group has "helped resolve eleven protests against financial institutions." It further stated that the FHLB of Cincinnati has become the "CRA Compliance Leader" as "banks, thrifts and savings banks are coming to us from all over the country for our consulting services." The 1991 advertisement for the agency's "CRA GEO-ANALYST" notes that it has a "proven trade record" and assures potential purchasers that "your federal examiners will have a great deal of confidence" in it.

The FHLB of Cincinnati's 1990 Annual Report stated that "for over 10 years, our staff worked with member lenders in analyzing, understanding and meeting the requirements of CRA . . . We now offer this unique experience to our members through a variety of CRA consulting services." Before reminding readers that "failure to pass a CRA exam could ignite a public relations crisis," that report notes that "assistance in the field of CRA was a natural development for the Bank," which prior to FIRREA was "actively involved in the review and adjudication of CRA cases."

Thus, one government agency is profiting from consulting to help banks and thrifts get good CRA ratings from another government agency. Thrifts formerly examined by the FHLB of Cincinnati, but since examined by the Cincinnati District of the OTS's Central Region, would appear to have been well advised to use these CRA consulting services to improve the likelihood of better CRA ratings. Actually, the top three officers at the current FHLB of Cincinnati were among the top officers of the old FHLB of Cincinnati, which was the S&L regulator before the OTS was established.

This gives new meaning to the "revolving door" phenomenon where former government employees become lawyers, accountants, or consultants for banks they regulated. In the case of this government-sponsored enterprise, a part of the staff effectively became a vendor competing with the private sector. The FHLB of Cincinnati's 1989 and 1990 Annual Reports ironically addressed the "potential perception of any conflict of interest between provider and judge of problem solving and operating strategies." The post-FIRREA removal of the regulatory function from the bank eliminated this potential perception, according to those reports.

Our most recent communications with the FHLB of Cincinnati revealed that they scaled back their CRA Consulting Services Group in January 1992, and many members of that group formed a private firm that now benefits from referrals from their old employer in many cases. The FHLB of Cincinnati, however, still offers community credit needs assessment and mortgage market mapping services for a fee, which can reach five figures for the former study. We learned that other FHLBs, like the one in Atlanta, offer geocoding and other CRA technical services for members, but those are offered generally at little or no cost.

The primary objective of a bank going outside to such public or private sector specialists would be to try to attain a higher rating, ideally an outstanding one. However, all of the resultant documentation and form created by these activities really don't directly benefit the community.

While it can be argued that in the long run local communities will benefit from these efforts, there may be little noticeable benefit in the short run. In our opinion, Congress and the president in 1977 did not intend CRA to benefit this new army of CRA vendors, especially if it included some government agency employees themselves. Rather, the stated intent was to benefit the entire community, including low- and moderate-income neighborhoods.

Faced with this dilemma, a banker will likely ask, "What activities can be done to not only benefit the bank in terms of a higher CRA rating but also the community?" In an attempt to answer this and related questions we developed the "CRA Cost/Benefit Matrix." This matrix, which is graphically portrayed in Figure 10-1, attempts to identify the tradeoff between bank costs associated with CRA and two categories of benefits. The first category on the left side of the graph refers to activities which primarily benefit the bank's CRA rating. Again, these can benefit the community over time, depending upon the resulting actions taken by the bank.

The second type of benefits are those that accrue directly to the community. By definition, any such community benefit should also directly benefit a bank's CRA rating. It would be quite troubling to learn of bank activities that are directly benefiting the local community, especially low-mod neighborhoods,

Figure 10-1   CRA Cost/Benefit Matrix©

OUTSIDE VENDORS

"Testers"
Outside CRA Consultant
External CRA Assessment
Outside Loan Geocoding Analysis
Outside Credit Needs Survey
Outside CRA Training
"Low-Mod" Advertising Agencies
"Glossy" CRA Brochure

PRIMARILY BENEFIT CRA RATING

HIGH COST ↑

INDIVIDUAL BANK EFFORTS

50 b.p./year CRA Commitment
"Low-Mod" Branch
"Low-Mod" Housing Project
"Low-Mod" Loan Product
"Low-Mod" Loan Counseling

PRIMARILY BENEFIT COMMUNITY (AND CRA RATING)

IN HOUSE EFFORTS

Extended Weekday/Saturday Hours
Extensive CRA Public File
In-House CRA Assessment
In-House Loan Geocoding Analysis
In-House Credit Needs Survey
In-House CRA Training
"Appointment Banking"
"Low-Mod" Advertising Media
Written CRA Policies and Plan
CRA Officer and CRA Committee
Regular Board CRA Discussions
Expanded CRA Statement
Affirmative "CRA Spirit"

HIGH DOCUMENTATION (FORM)

LOW COST ↓

SHARED EFFORTS

Shared "Low-Mod" Branch
Shared "Low-Mod" Housing Project
"Low-Mod" Loan Consortium
Shared "Low-Mod" Loan Counseling
Government Guaranteed Loans (or Pools) in "Low-Mod" Areas
Local Housing Mortgage Revenue Bonds
Deposits of Joint Investments in Community Development Credit Union or Bank

HIGH PERFORMANCE (FUNCTION)

"Low-Mod" = low- and moderate-income

where the bank was not receiving direct or indirect CRA benefit. The right side of the graph pertains to those activities which primarily benefit the community (and the CRA rating).

Another way to distinguish between the left and right side of the graph is that the left, or western, half pertains to activities involving high documentation. In contrast, the right, or eastern, half of the matrix pertains to activities relating to high CRA performance. In other words, the left half of the matrix relates more to form or process, and the right half relates more to function or performance.

Criticism by community groups and others that bank CRA ratings measure "form over function," "process over performance," or "style over substance" can be viewed in the context of this matrix. That is, to the extent that an individual CRA evaluation is primarily based upon items on the left side of the matrix compared to those on the right side, this would be a valid criticism.

We have reviewed many outstanding CRA ratings that would mainly be in either the form or function category. Most represent a combination of the two. Again, we would argue that a truly outstanding bank is one that received its rating on the basis of function, not form. For this reason there are probably some truly outstanding banks with a high level of CRA performance but only satisfactory ratings due to an average or low level of documentation. Thus, there is a difference between *actual* and *documented* CRA performance, both of which may differ from the examiners' *perceived* performance.

This situation would be indicative of the complaints of many community bankers who feel the regulators overemphasize documentation in their CRA ratings. We have identified several case studies which verify "CRA Survival Rule #1"—"If it wasn't documented, it wasn't done." A small community bank with a high level of performance may not have the resources to document it, and therefore the bank may only receive a satisfactory (or even lower) rating. The CRA Cost/Benefit Matrix can also be used to explain this concern.

The upper and lower halves of this matrix generally indicate high versus low cost activities in terms of the bank's total in-house and outside expenses. We would impute a value here to the time of management and other internal staff used to compile CRA materials to determine the true cost. The current discussion in Washington pertaining to the burden of various bank regulations often focuses on CRA because of the significant costs associated with its compliance. Many times these costs are estimates of in-house time devoted to these activities, but there may also be out-of-pocket expenses associated with CRA compliance.

An increasing number of banks are choosing to use outside vendors rather than conducting their CRA efforts internally. The upper, or northern, half of the matrix generally involves the use of outside vendors and individual bank efforts, both of which represent a high cost to the bank. By comparison, the lower, or southern, half of the matrix relies on in-house and shared efforts, which represent a lower cost to the bank. Of course, the experience and specialized expertise associated with outside vendors is usually not found in-house except at the larger financial institutions.

One of the most important conclusions from our research is that the most cost-effective way by which banks can meet CRA requirements, obtain a high rating, and also benefit the community is through the use of shared arrangements with other banks and thrifts. The use of a sharing mechanism, which has a widespread basis in American banking, not only reduces costs significantly but also provides a degree of diversification in terms of the risks associated with any particular activity. For this reason, the southeastern quadrant of the matrix has a preponderance of shared activities, compared to the northeastern quadrant which primarily focuses on individual bank efforts.

The several examples in the four quadrants of this matrix are meant to be illustrative of the literally countless number of possible activities that could benefit a bank's CRA rating and/or its community. The "low cost" approach to obtaining a high CRA rating would be demonstrated by the activities in the southwestern quadrant of the matrix. These would include in-house activities designed not only to meet CRA requirements but all recommended procedures relating to credit needs ascertainment, geocoding, training, and advertising. The least-cost method of attempting to improve a bank's CRA rating, besides having the "right" CRA spirit or attitude, is preparing an expanded CRA statement. This is one of the most basic affirmative CRA activities recommended by federal bank regulators.

The northwestern quadrant of the matrix would essentially "outsource" many of these and other activities to specialized vendors. For example, CRA consultants can prepare an expanded CRA statement for a bank or a detailed community report in the form of a "glossy" bound CRA brochure. Specialized vendors can prepare highly informative and useful computer-based tables and graphics as part of a sophisticated loan geocoding analysis. Some banks in the Chicago area have used outside marketing research firms to conduct credit needs assessment surveys. Harris Bank reportedly paid $60,000 for a survey research firm to conduct a credit needs ascertainment survey of local small businesses. Outside CRA consultants can manage most of a bank's CRA program, including external assessments as well as the use of "testers."

If a bank truly feels it is doing a good job of meeting its community's needs, or if it really doesn't believe in the need for CRA in the first place, then the southwestern quadrant, representing the low cost avenue to a high CRA rating, is the way to go. If that approach is not preferred, or if a bank is making a serious effort to upgrade its rating, then it may choose the northwestern quadrant, representing the high cost approach to a better CRA rating.

We believe that most banks would look at this analysis and ask what are the most cost-effective ways of not only benefiting the community but also receiving a high CRA rating. The recommended approach here would be illustrated in the southeastern quadrant of the matrix. Here the emphasis is on shared approaches that primarily benefit low-mod neighborhoods. Other cost-effective approaches here include participation in individual government guaranteed loans or pools of them that benefit such areas. Although CRA looks to benefit the entire community, the real emphasis where the most good could be done to the community and to a bank's CRA rating appears to involve low-mod neighborhoods. While the shared branch concept has other applications, we believe that this is an ideal one, especially in cases where there are no longer offices of federally-insured financial institutions in a specific neighborhood.

The northeastern quadrant in the matrix describes individual bank efforts, which are generally of a higher cost to a bank, that primarily benefit the community and the bank's CRA rating. Rather than becoming involved in a shared low-mod branch, housing project, loan consortium, or loan counseling center, a bank may decide to take on these efforts individually. Many large banks use this approach, as do some progressive community banks.

We should point out, however, that a bank currently cannot obtain a high CRA rating without meeting the various CRA paperwork requirements, including maintenance of a public file, loan geocoding analyses, and so on. Therefore, the most cost-effective way to benefit both the community and the bank's CRA rating would not only involve the activities in the southeastern quadrant but also those in the southwestern quadrant, which represent CRA requirements and other recommended activities.

The ideal situation, of course, would be that regulators would rate a bank solely on its CRA performance and look only at function rather than form. This approach would not only please community groups but also the banks themselves. There are probably few if any bankers who would rather put a dollar into CRA documentation rather than into a low-mod housing project or loan product. Until the CRA rating process is changed to measure function over form or performance over documentation, banks must continue to meet CRA requirements and recommendations to receive an average or better rating.

In summary, the real problem is not with CRA but with the implementation of it, whereby style is often emphasized over substance. A change in the CRA procedure to reverse the situation would likely be supported by all interested parties except the new army of CRA vendors, which ironically includes the government itself through the FHLB of Cincinnati. Our recommended approach to restructuring CRA compliance, which clearly emphasizes substance over style, is contained in a following section.

4. **The most important determining factor in the CRA rating of an individual bank or thrift is the makeup of the examination team and the chief examiner. In other words, CRA ratings and performance evaluations are quite subjective, and grade inflation (and sometimes deflation) exists.**

CRA always has been and probably always will be a highly subjective law. In many respects CRA, like the Constitution, must retain a degree of vagueness to allow the necessary flexibility to be modified over time as credit needs change. This vagueness necessarily results in subjectivity of which we have documented a considerable amount in our analysis.

We have hypothesized the existence of a "CRA examiner subjectivity range." In other words, we believe that the head examiner and the examination team in the CRA evaluation of any bank can always justify a CRA rating one level plus or minus the "true" CRA rating. In the Chapter 7 case of the banks in Chinatown and Koreatown, both of which should have received a needs improvement rating in our opinion, we substantiated this subjectivity range. The resultant ratings for the two banks in that case were one notch above or below what they should have been.

Another way of viewing the subjectivity range is our finding that grade inflation (and sometimes deflation) exists in CRA ratings. The significant differences between the percentage of above- and below-average ratings on a pre- and postdisclosure basis are indicative of grade inflation. This conclusion is based upon our analysis of 72,344 CRA ratings over the 11-year 1982 – 92 period.

During the eight-and-one-half-year predisclosure period the percentage of above-average CRA ratings was 11.8%. The comparable postdisclosure percentage of 8.7% during the one-and-one-half years since July 1, 1990, is only three-fourths of the latter number. More recent data through year-end 1992 show this postdisclosure above-average ratio increasing to 10.3%, apparently as a result of improved CRA performance in 1992. The percentage of above-average ratings was in the 13 – 16% range during the 1982 –

84 period, when grade inflation was probably at its greatest. In fact, in 1980 the FED doled out a whopping 40.2% above-average ratings, possibly one of the most outrageous examples of an inflated CRA ratings distribution.

By comparison, the percentage of below-average CRA ratings over the eight-and-one-half-year predisclosure period averaged only 3.3%. Postdisclosure below-average ratings totaled 11.0% through December 31, 1991, and 10.5% through year-end 1992. Thus, disclosure was associated with more than three times the percentage of below-average ratings, another indication that grade inflation existed, especially during the earlier years of predisclosure. Also, there were only 66 substantial noncompliance ratings made over the eight-and-one-half-year predisclosure period compared to 106 such ratings in the two-and-one-half-year postdisclosure period, a more than five-fold relative difference.

Our analysis of a representative sample of performance evaluations with outstanding ratings suggested that as many as 43% of them could be inflated based upon a fairly strict interpretation of a "truly" outstanding bank. Under this interpretation the proportion of postdisclosure outstanding ratings through year-end 1991 would be reduced from 8.7% of all banks to just 4.9% of them. The same grade-inflation adjustment for year-end 1992 data would reduce this proportion from 10.3% to 5.8%.

A comparable analysis of needs improvement evaluations as of year-end 1991 also indicated the existence of some grade inflation there. Under the strictest interpretation we determined that the proportion of needs improvement ratings would be 8.6% instead of 10.1% as of year-end 1991. This difference would increase those banks in substantial noncompliance by more than two-and-one-half times, from 0.9% to 2.4%. Thus, the proportion of banks that are truly in substantial noncompliance may be understated by as much as two-and-one-half times under the strictest interpretation. The comparable grade-inflation adjustment for year-end 1992 data would reduce the proportion of banks with needs improvement ratings from 9.6% to 8.1% and increase the proportion of banks with substantial noncompliance ratings from 0.9% to 2.3%. But, even these adjusted needs improvement percentages are artificially low because of grade inflation in the largest satisfactory category.

Based upon this grade inflation analysis, it is reasonable to assume that there is a fairly substantial proportion of banks with satisfactory ratings that should likely be downgraded into the needs improvement range. Assuming the "true" percentage of banks with needs improvement ratings was two-and-one-half times the actual number with that rating, as was the case with substantial noncompliant banks, the percentage of such banks with needs improvement ratings would jump from 9% to 23% as of year-end 1991 and from 8% to 20% as of year-end 1992. Conversely, the proportion of satisfactory banks (after adding inflated "outstanding" ratings) would fall from 84% to 70% of all banks as of year-end 1991 and from 84% to 72% as of year-end 1992. The inflation adjustment in the largest satisfactory category is based on the above-mentioned assumption, because we did not complete a detailed analysis of the 80% of banks with satisfactory ratings.

In summary, our analysis suggests that CRA grade inflation does exist. The postdisclosure grading distribution through year-end 1991 of outstanding, satisfactory, needs improvement, and substantial noncompliance stood at approximately 9%, 80%, 10%, and 1%, respectively. The most recent data as of year-end 1992 are quite similar at 10%, 79%, 10%, and 1%. Our analysis suggests that this rating distribution under a strict interpretation of CRA would change to at least 5%, 70%, 23%, and 2% as of year-end 1991 and 6%, 72%, 20%, and 2% as of year-end 1992, respectively.

Our analysis of CRA ratings by state and regulator revealed numerous apparent instances of "selective enforcement," defined as disproportionately high or low ratings by a given regulator or within certain regions or states of a given regulator. Selective enforcement may likewise suggest the existence of grade inflation or deflation. We identified numerous regions and states and the appropriate regulator(s) where selective enforcement likely existed. For example, the banks in Tennessee received some of the lowest ratings in the nation from the OCC's Southeastern District over the study period, but some of the highest from the FDIC's Memphis Region. This tells us that the problem here was more with the regulators than the regulated.

Because of the highly subjective nature of CRA, allegations of grade inflation or deflation are to a great extent in the eyes of the beholder. For example, the basic finding that the distribution of above-average, average, and below-average CRA ratings approximate 10%–80%–10% can be viewed in different ways. A banker may say that this distribution is "good" because 90% of all banks received average or above-average CRA ratings. A consumer group may take the opposite view that these results are "bad" because 90% of banks received average or below-average ratings. This is the familiar "half-full/half-empty" dilemma that suggests that interpretations of CRA data are a function of one's perspective.

In fact, the entire CRA effort may be positioned as an issue of consumer regulatory "compliance" by bankers versus one of consumer "protection" by community groups. Everyone is in favor of consumer protection, but most people are likewise aware of the significant costs associated with complying with government regulations and bureaucratic red tape.

To date, most of the controversy involving the CRA triangle has been between bankers and community groups. Our findings suggest that community groups should keep a more watchful eye on overall CRA ratings distributions by regulators to identify trends suggestive of grade inflation on a general basis or specific cases involving individual banks.

Various case studies in this book identified numerous instances of grade inflation. Probably the classic example of grade inflation was the "satisfactory" CRA rating given by the OTS to Atlanta's Decatur Federal in the first part of 1990 before ratings were made public. Decatur Federal was then in the midst of a four-year investigation by the Department of Justice, which resulted in a $1 million payment plus numerous stringent affirmative requirements. If roughly 90% of all banks receive a satisfactory or lower rating, would they likewise be candidates for such an investigation? The Decatur Federal example of grade inflation is particularly troubling, as we have identified the OTS as the "toughest" of the four bank regulators in terms of CRA enforcement.

Because we have also identified the phenomenon of grade deflation in certain cases, bankers themselves must be watchful that their CRA rating was not unnecessarily downgraded from what it should have been. If in fact a "CRA examiner subjectivity range" exists with a "swing factor" of plus or minus one rating, then this should be of concern to not just community groups and bankers alike but everyone, as it impacts directly on the integrity of the CRA rating system.

We believe that a regulator will always be able to defend any individual rating by noting that "other factors" of which we may not be aware affected their decision. Of course, because regulators never comment on individual cases, we don't even get to hear this defense. A very important factor, which is totally subjective in nature, is a bank's "CRA spirit." This may have an important bearing on the above-mentioned swing factor, especially in cases where examiners are sitting on the fence between two ratings.

We have concluded that there is a considerable amount of inconsistency in how different examiners deal with specialty banks, especially wholesale, foreign, and credit card banks, but also niche retail ones, such as private and ethnic banks. The approach taken by some examiners makes it all but impossible for niche banks to get anything better than a needs improvement rating and often a substantial noncompliance rating. It appears that some examiners more than others are more flexible in applying CRA criteria to the unique situations faced by specialty banks.

In summary, one of the unexpected dividends of disclosure of CRA ratings and evaluations has been the insight provided into the bank regulatory examination process. If CRA ratings and evaluations are as subjective as we suggest, then this has potentially serious implications in terms of what the situation may be with respect to safety and soundness ratings and evaluations. For example, what if there is a safety and soundness (CAMEL or MACRO) examiner subjectivity rating range similar to the CRA one hypothesized here? Additionally, if our "friendly regulator" and "selective enforcement" hypotheses are also applicable for safety and soundness exams, then past regulatory decisions to issue enforcement actions and even close certain problem banks but leave other ones untouched may be called into question. Without public disclosure of safety and soundness ratings, and portions of those exams, we will never know whether

the same level of regulatory subjectivity we have documented in CRA exists on a systemic basis.

In conclusion, the public disclosure of CRA ratings and evaluations may have taught us more about the regulators themselves than about the banks they regulate. The lesson learned here is that our concern over possible discrimination should not only be limited to banks' potential disparate treatment of any lending customers but also to regulators' potential disparate treatment of any banks.

> **5. We have uncovered at least one instance of what appears to be "regulatory favoritism," which occurred in part because of the unilateral power regulators have to delay timely disclosure of CRA ratings and evaluations. Regulatory favoritism may also occur in the regulators' decision on the timing of CRA examinations and reexaminations.**

Our above findings on grade inflation (and sometimes deflation) of CRA ratings by bank regulators is indeed an unfortunate side effect of the subjectivity inherent in CRA. The single most troubling incident we uncovered involving regulator subjectivity and inconsistency appears to have involved favoritism by a regulator.

Specifically, we are referring to the OCC and its handling of the CRA examination(s) of Norstar Bank, N.A. of Buffalo, New York, a subsidiary of Fleet/ Norstar Financial Group. This bank received a needs improvement rating on a public evaluation dated October 29, 1990, marked "Preliminary Draft." For an unknown reason the OCC decided to give this bank a "second chance" and consider one bit of additional information (the fact that one-third of that bank's loans were in low- and moderate-income areas) to justify an upgrading of its rating to a satisfactory one. There is no evidence of the needs improvement ratings as ever having existed except for a copy of the original "Preliminary Draft" we obtained.

The timing of this unprecedented ratings change was critical because Fleet/Norstar Financial was in the midst of bidding for the franchise of the failed Bank of New England Corporation. CRA became an issue during this heated and controversial bidding procedure which Fleet/Norstar Financial ultimately won.

Our analysis of the situation indicated that the needs improvement rating of Norstar Bank, N.A. in the preliminary draft should never have been changed in the first place. Even with the additional material submitted (the above-mentioned one-third low- and moderate-income fact), this was not enough to change the overwhelming amount of evidence substantiating a needs improvement rating, in our opinion.

We also concluded that because of the role CRA played in this closely contested bidding war, a needs improvement rating for Fleet/Norstar Financial's third largest subsidiary could have resulted in a denial of that application. Thus, the special treatment (i.e., favoritism) apparently afforded Norstar Bank, N.A., in the unprecedented and unwarranted upgrading of its CRA rating resulted in the approval of the acquisition of one of the largest failed banks in our country's history. This turned out to be an immensely profitable deal for Fleet/Norstar Financial and its investment partner, Wall Street takeover specialists Kohlberg, Kravis, Roberts and Company.

An important issue involving this case was the timing of the OCC's disclosure of the preliminary and revised ratings. Three similarly-sized banks in upstate New York also evaluated by the OCC at roughly the same time received their completed evaluations and ratings in one-fifth of the time it took the OCC to transmit the preliminary draft of its evaluation with the needs improvement rating to Norstar Bank, N.A. This unprecedented delay by the OCC did not require public disclosure of the original Norstar Bank, N.A. rating until May 3, 1991. But, Fleet/Norstar Financial's winning bid was accepted less than two weeks earlier on April 22, 1991.

This case study documents the tremendous leeway a regulator has in deciding when and when not to make a CRA evaluation and rating public. At the present time the only timing requirement is that banks must make the rating public 30 business days after it has been transmitted to them by their regulator. However, there is no such requirement as to the amount of time a regulator may "sit" on the exam before it transmits it to the bank (and it is therefore made public).

Thus, a regulator who may be "favoring" a particular bank can always come up with many reasons why the final evaluation is delayed for several months before a below-average rating is to be made public by the bank. The bank usually knows the result of the evaluation and the rating at the time of the exam's exit interview. The significant delay afforded to a bank by a "friendly" regulator not only allows the bank more time to prepare a public defense and correct noted deficiencies, but also enables a bank to question the relevance of an "outdated" evaluation and rating. Moreover, a friendly regulator can schedule an expedited reevaluation to hopefully result in a higher rating. Thus, the favored bank doesn't have to carry the stigma of a low rating that long. Importantly, such a bank can move ahead with corporate expansions that otherwise might be delayed or denied.

We have documented instances where it has taken upwards of eight months for a bank to receive its completed evaluation and rating by the OCC. Counting the 30 business day publication requirement, this is a delay of over nine months before the public is notified of a low CRA rating.

Thus, special treatment in delaying the transmittal of the completed evaluation and rating to a bank shields it from public scrutiny and criticism in the event of a below-average rating. In special cases where that below-average rating might call into question or even kill a proposed merger or acquisition, such as in the case of the Bank of New England Corporation, such an action would be extremely beneficial to the bank in question.

A preliminary analysis we conducted of the hypothesis that regulators may take longer to transmit below-average ratings compared to above-average ones did not result in any conclusive findings. However, in this one case involving Norstar Bank, N.A., it took approximately five months to receive its initial evaluation and seven months for its revised one. This was one of the longest delays we've seen. A review of the circumstances surrounding that case suggests that regulatory favoritism may have occurred, which handsomely benefited that bank, its parent, and its investors in the purchase of the Bank of New England Corporation.

Any act by regulators to delay unnecessarily the disclosure of a CRA rating and evaluation to benefit a bank in any way is indicative of "regulatory circumvention" of congressional intent. Congress intended the prompt disclosure of CRA ratings and evaluations, and there was considerable pre-FIRREA debate over the length of time between when a bank would receive its rating and evaluation and when it was to be made public. There was, however, no discussion of the amount of time that regulators might "sit" on an evaluation and rating. Now that we have the first window open into the regulatory examination process, we are able to witness some less than desirable processes which may have resulted in favoritism in at least this one case.

Time gone by reduces the power of public disclosure. Congress intended meaningful and prompt disclosure. It is especially distasteful when the delay is arbitrarily or capriciously caused by the regulators. A regulator may always be able to justify a delay on any individual case because the analysis was not yet complete, they were waiting for an additional piece of information, and so on. However, disclosure delays of upwards of a quarter of a year or more raise the question as to whether or not they are necessary. When these delays result in special action favoring a particular bank, they become unwarranted and unjustified.

Regulatory favoritism, as noted above, may also exist in the timing of a reevaluation where it is expedited hopefully to upgrade the previous evaluation's low rating. Regulatory favoritism can likewise surface in cases where a regulator may decide to hold off on a compliance exam, where it is fairly well-known in advance that the result would probably be a below-average rating.

For example, the OCC is the only one of the four federal bank regulators without a specialized compliance function, although we expect this will change. Their safety and soundness examiners, who also conduct compliance exams, may have determined in a recent safety and soundness exam that a bank would likely receive a below-average CRA rating, even though no formal compliance exam was conducted. Safety and soundness examiners often know that a bank may be planning to open a branch, merge, make an acquisition, or engage in some other corporate activity. Knowing that a below-average CRA rating might delay or eliminate the chances of approval of

such a corporate activity, a friendly regulator may decide to hold off on the compliance exam until after the approval of the corporate activity. Alternatively, such a regulator might expedite the approval of the former activity.

A friendly regulator, who is disposed to using "jawboning" and pro-CRA policy statements as the primary "enforcement" tools, will give a "conditional approval" rather than a denial and, if necessary, issue a confidential "informal enforcement action" rather than a public cease and desist order. Friendly regulators prefer the informal and private approach over the formal and public approach. The implications of this "friendly regulator" hypothesis are indeed troubling, considering that similar activities may occur on the safety and soundness side involving the timing of regulatory decisions to issue enforcement actions or even close troubled banks.

As long as there is no precisely published schedule as to when a CRA exam or re-exam has to be conducted, this leaves open the possibility of regulatory subjectivity which may deteriorate into regulatory favoritism. Exam and reexam timing is mainly a function of compliance resources at the various regulators. The FED has a large number of examiners relative to a small number of member banks. Specifically, the FED enjoys a ratio of only six banks per compliance examiner compared to an average of about 22 banks for all regulators combined. Almost all of the FED regulated banks had received a CRA exam as of year-end 1991, and many have since received a second and even third exam. The most recent data as of year-end 1992 shows that the FED had completed 1.63 evaluations per regulated bank, meaning that as many as one-half of its banks may have been evaluated a second time.

This is not the case, however, with the other three regulators who have completed a combined average of .81 CRA exams per bank, which is one-half the FED's average. The national total of about 639 compliance examiners, which includes a functionally-equivalent estimate for the OCC, are responsible for roughly 22 banks each, on average. This ratio ranges from a low of 6 banks at the FED to a high of 43 banks at the FDIC. The OTS at 20 banks and the OCC at an estimated 19 banks per "compliance examiner" equivalent were in the middle of the range.

The OCC had by far made the least progress in its CRA ratings by examining less than one-fourth of the national banks by year-end 1991 and less than one-half by year-end 1992. The OCC had completed only .46 CRA exams per bank as of year-end 1992, just over one-fourth the rate for the FED. Both the FDIC and OTS had examined roughly half or more of their respective banks as of December 31, 1991. The FDIC examination rate went up to at least 80% by year-end 1992, and the OTS had evaluated nearly all of its thrifts by that time.

Thus, it appears that the OCC would have the greatest opportunity out of the four regulators to adjust its scheduling of compliance exams because so many of its banks have not yet received their first CRA evaluation. As noted above, the OCC is also the only one of the four federal bank regulators that does not have a specialized compliance examination staff. And, unfortunately, the OCC was the regulator involved in the only case of apparent regulatory favoritism which we could document.

Our analysis of multiple ratings indicates a misallocation of CRA regulatory resources across regulators and also across regions for the same regulator. In the first case, as noted above, the FED is the leader and the OCC is clearly the laggard of the four regulators when it comes to CRA exam frequency. In the second case involving individual regions, we witnessed a very high incidence of double and even triple CRA ratings by the FDIC's Dallas Region, where there has been a large number of examiners due to safety and soundness problems. The opposite situation exists in their Atlanta Region where many banks have yet to have their first public CRA evaluation, much less a second or third one.

This is also true for the OTS's West Region with only 3.4% of all thrifts being unrated, compared to their Central Region with 32.8% of such thrifts, a nearly tenfold difference. Not surprisingly, the ratio of banks to compliance examiners in the West Region (10) is one-fourth the comparable rate in the Central Region (40). This misallocation of CRA regulatory resources has public policy implications. This is not only because of an uneven regulatory burden on banks but also because it is a disservice to local communities with nonrated banks who are poor CRA

performers; that is, the positive power of public disclosure is not allowed to work.

6. CRA ratings differ significantly by regulator, size, and area, but apparently not by bank financial strength.

The first conclusion we reached from this analysis regarding regulators is that thrifts are nearly twice as likely to receive below-average ratings as banks. This conclusion may reflect the fact that the OTS is the "toughest" grader or that thrifts themselves are below-average CRA performers. We believe that both factors are at work here.

The OTS has given out the lowest percentage of outstanding ratings (8.2%) and the highest percentage of below-average ratings (18.4%) as of year-end 1992. In fact, 27% of all substantial noncompliance ratings through year-end 1992 have been given by the OTS, yet it only regulates about 15% of all banks and thrifts.

The FED reported the highest percentage of outstanding ratings at 11.8% as of December 31, 1992. The FDIC had the lowest percentage of below-average ratings as of December 31, 1992 (7.8%), and the FED followed at 9.0%. One way to interpret these data, as noted above, is that the OTS is the "toughest" CRA grader and the FED is the "easiest." Still, though, we have identified cases of grade inflation at the OTS, including perhaps the most egregious example involving the "satisfactory" CRA rating given to Atlanta's Decatur Federal during the Justice Department's four-year investigation alleging racial discrimination in mortgage lending.

The FED had an opportunity to flex its CRA enforcement muscles by denying the February 1992 acquisition of troubled Talman Home Federal by the parent of Chicago's LaSalle National Bank, the largest bank with a current needs improvement rating. The FED approved the acquisition by using the troubled institution "loophole." We believe the FED could have just as easily found ample reasons for a denial, because it is possible that an alternate investor could have been found while Talman's status quo was maintained.

The best evidence we have to date that the FED is the most lenient enforcer is the November 30,

1992, merger approval involving Capital Bank and Trust Company of Clayton, Missouri. It received a substantial noncompliance and then a needs improvement rating. The FED's approval was precedent setting because it accepted CRA promises (including several last-minute ones) over performance. No troubled institution "loophole" was available this time to bail out the FED as was the case in the LaSalle case. Board of Governors members Kelley and La-Ware, apparently the only two pro-CRA board members, dissented from the FED's approval in the Capital case. These two 1992 merger approvals, but especially the second one, cause as to question the FED's commitment to CRA enforcement. Worse yet, the Capital case threatens to undermine CRA enforcement by sending the wrong message (i.e., such low CRA ratings don't matter).

It is of interest to note that earlier in the same month (November 1992) the FED approved the controversial Capital merger, the OCC denied one involving the First Commercial Bank, N.A. of Memphis, Tennessee, because it had back-to-back needs improvement ratings Yet, the FED turned around four months later in March 1993 and approved an acquisition by that bank's parent. Thus, the FED effectively overruled the OCC's merger denial and, worse yet, may have put undue pressure on the OCC to upgrade First Commercial Bank's CRA rating during its next exam. It is ironic that we should conclude that the FED is the most lax of all regulators in terms of CRA enforcement, because it was former FED Chairman Burns who coined the phrase "competition in laxity" to refer to other regulators who eased up on banks to attract them to their respective fold.

Another conclusion we reached regarding the relationship between regulators and CRA ratings is that the use of specialized compliance examiners results in a much more strict enforcement of CRA defined in terms of a higher percentage of below-average ratings and a lower percentage of above-average ones. We examined the proportion of below-average ratings made by the FHLBB and the OTS during the 15-month period both before and after the inception of a specialized compliance program. This resulted in a roughly sixfold increase in the percentage of below-average ratings. The decrease in the proportion of above-average ratings was much less dramatic. As

pointed out above, the OCC is the only one of the four regulators without a specialized compliance program at this time, but we expect that will change.

We have reached a few conclusions regarding the relationship between CRA ratings and size. Smaller banks generally receive the greatest percentage of below-average ratings. However, when the proportion of below-average ratings is related to the size distribution of banks, it becomes clear that small banks receive most of the poor ratings because most banks are small banks. Holding constant the size factor, there appears to be some evidence to support the view that small banks generally have lower CRA scores than larger banks. Small banks are getting less than their expected share of outstanding ratings but generally are receiving their expected share of low ratings. While this finding holds for banks of $100 million or less in size, we concluded that the very small banks of under $25 million were primarily responsible for this conclusion. Large banks, by contrast, are receiving more than their expected share of outstanding ratings (and below-average ratings in the $250 – 500 million asset size category).

Our analysis has not supported the view that size alone determines CRA ratings. Many banks in the larger size categories had a disproportionately high percentage in the two lowest CRA rating categories. In fact, we have documented the case of one bank holding company (Chemical Banking Corporation of New York City) where its subsidiary banks received all four ratings, ranging from outstanding to substantial noncompliance. Our analysis of the 100 largest banks and 50 largest thrifts determined that the proportions receiving outstanding ratings were 33.0% and 45.9%, respectively. Therefore, we have concluded that size alone does not determine CRA ratings. Thus the argument by many small banks and others that large banks receive outstanding ratings simply because they have the resources to better document their position is not supported by our analysis.

Our analysis of CRA ratings by area has concluded that there are significant differences by region and state. We have determined that the nation's highest CRA-rated state is Wisconsin, where all of the federal regulators are consistent in giving their lowest or near-lowest percentage of below-average ratings to banks there. Other indicators involving outstanding ratings and their relationship to below-average ones are consistent in this finding about Wisconsin. We have concluded that it is more the banks than the regulators responsible for this result. Wisconsin's top-ranking status is followed by Indiana, Kentucky, Michigan, and Washington state. The ratings in those states were not consistent by all regulators in all cases.

At the other extreme, we have concluded that Florida is our nation's lowest CRA-rated state, with all federal regulators consistent in giving banks there the highest or near-highest percentage of below-average ratings. Again, this suggests that the problem in Florida is more with the banks than the regulators. California and Missouri rank as the second and third lowest CRA-rated states overall, according to our analysis, followed by Illinois and Georgia. However, not all of the federal regulators were totally consistent in downgrading banks in those states as was the case in Florida.

As noted previously, we have expanded our analysis to examine regulatory patterns within each of the states. We have determined that certain regulators more than others have a disproportionately high or low percentage of certain types of ratings in certain regions or states. This led to the previously cited conclusion that "selective enforcement" likely existed in certain areas (e.g., by the OCC in Tennessee).

We did not develop any general conclusions regarding the relationship between a bank's CRA rating and its safety and soundness rating. We used a proxy for the safety and soundness rating, and concluded that in the case of the absolutely lowest-rated banks (those in substantial noncompliance), there was no relationship between that CRA rating and a bank's financial condition. We did not expand this analysis to banks receiving needs improvement or outstanding ratings. However, a casual analysis of available data suggested that the relationship between CRA ratings and financial condition would probably not be a strong one if any relationship existed. That is to say that both strong and weak banks are probably equally likely to receive good and bad CRA ratings. More research will be required to provide a definitive answer on the nature of this relationship.

Our analysis also identified America's highest and lowest CRA-rated banks. Chapter 5 identified five

banks receiving multiple outstanding evaluations as of year-end 1991 as well as the Dayton State Bank of Dayton, Texas, which received *triple* outstanding ratings as of year-end 1992. Also, two banks upgraded from needs improvement to outstanding as of year-end 1991 were singled out in Chapter 5, and the Bank of Commerce, N.A. of Auburn, California, was clearly the more outstanding. Our two largest bank holding companies, Citicorp and BankAmerica Corporation, were likewise identified in Chapter 5 as being among America's highest CRA-rated institutions.

At the other extreme we identified America's lowest CRA-rated bank as the failed Mercantile Savings Bank of Southaven, Mississippi. Chapter 9 singled out seven banks with back-to-back substantial noncompliance ratings as being America's remaining lowest CRA-rated banks. The worst offenders were two community banks with unprecedented back-to-back-to-back substantial noncompliance ratings: Parish Bank and Trust Company of Momence, Illinois, and Uinta County State Bank of Mountain View, Wyoming. Additionally, four community banks downgraded from needs improvement to substantial noncompliance would be among this lowest CRA-rated category. Finally, we considered banks with cease and desist orders, application denials, and civil money penalties primarily on CRA grounds in this category, and this would include Farmers and Merchants Bank of Long Beach, California, the subject of two case studies in Chapter 9. Also, any banks referred to the Justice Department for review in this area would likewise be in this category.

7. **The absolutely lowest rated CRA banks (those in substantial noncompliance) are spread out throughout the country with one major exception—between one out of five and one out of seven have been located in the L.A. area.**

Less than 1% of all banks and thrifts received the lowest possible substantial noncompliance rating. Most substantial noncompliance ratings have been given out by the OTS, but the number of such ratings by all regulators has increased dramatically during the postdisclosure period.

A total of 59 such ratings were made during the one-and-one-half-year period beginning on July 1, 1990. By year-end 1992 there were 106 substantial noncompliance ratings. The 54 banks that had publicly disclosed that rating as of year-end 1991 ranged in size from a few million dollars to four with assets of $1 billion or more. The largest one in the latter category was the $1.8 billion Merrill Lynch Bank and Trust Company. By year-end 1992 we identified 88 banks with this rating, the largest one being the $3.3 billion Bank of New York (Delaware) of Wilmington, Delaware.

We expect that about 150 banks and thrifts nationwide will receive this lowest possible rating based on the 1% that have received them to date. This means that as much as $30 billion in total assets may be controlled by all substantial noncompliant banks.

The FDIC and the OTS gave out roughly three-fourths of all substantial noncompliance ratings since July 1, 1990. These publicly disclosed ratings as of December 31, 1992, were made on 88 banks distributed throughout 24 states around the country. The largest concentration by far, with nearly one in seven banks receiving such ratings, is along and near L.A.'s I-405 (San Diego Freeway) corridor. Data through the first part of 1992 when the L.A. riots broke out substantiated the fact that roughly one out of five banks and thrifts receiving this lowest possible rating were in that corridor. It is not clear if this finding is indicative of a troubling pattern, but we could not dismiss it as a statistical coincidence because of its consistency over time.

Other concentrations of substantial noncompliant banks exist but to a much lesser extent. The second largest concentrations as of year-end 1992 with seven banks each are in the greater Chicago and St. Louis areas. We considered the greater Chicago area to be the second-lowest ranking metropolitan area behind L.A. This was not only because of these ratings but also because the lion's share of all mergers denied on CRA grounds, including the first and the largest, were in the Chicago area. Also, Chicago is home to two of the four among the country's 100 largest banks to get a needs improvement rating, including the largest ever.

There are several areas with three to four banks in the substantial noncompliance category, namely, nor-

thern Atlanta, midtown Manhattan, Kansas City, northwestern Baltimore, northern Delaware, central New Jersey, and south Florida. On a state-by-state basis, California led with 17 banks with substantial noncompliance ratings. It was followed by Missouri with a total of ten such banks (seven in St. Louis plus three in Kansas City). Illinois followed with eight such rated banks. Next was Florida, Maryland, and New Jersey, each with five such banks.

A previous conclusion on grade inflation indicates that the percentage of banks that are truly in substantial noncompliance may be as much as two and one-half times as what has been reported. This conclusion is based upon a strict interpretation of CRA. Specifically, we counted any bank with a needs improvement rating that had violated consumer compliance regulations or laws. Under this strict interpretation the proportion of all banks receiving such low ratings would go from just under 1% to nearly 2½%.

We have uncovered at least one incidence of grade *deflation* involving a bank that received a substantial noncompliance rating. Specifically, in the case of United Citizens National Bank of Los Angeles, California, we have determined that it should have received a needs improvement rating rather than the absolutely lowest one it did receive on its first evaluation. We do note for the record that a recent reevaluation of that bank resulted in a needs improvement rating, the rating we believe it truly deserved in the first place. Our review of all other banks with the substantial noncompliance rating as of year-end 1991 indicated that they were clearly deserved. Our only question, as mentioned above, concerns those banks that should have been included in this lowest category but were for some reason inflated into the next highest one.

We should also note that many of the largest nonbanks with bank subsidiaries (mainly credit card banks) have not received the most desirable CRA ratings. As long as some credit card and other special-purpose banks receive satisfactory or even outstanding CRA ratings, similar banks receiving below-average CRA ratings should follow their lead in improving CRA performance. This is especially true for our largest corporations.

As previously noted, a Merrill Lynch bank subsidiary is one of the largest banks ever to receive a substantial noncompliance rating. A very small California bank subsidiary of AVCO Financial Services also received a substantial noncompliance rating. Another bank subsidiary, AVCO Lakewood Industrial Bank in Colorado, received a needs improvement rating. Beneficial National Bank USA of Wilmington, Delaware received a substantial noncompliance rating, and that bank is a subsidiary of our nation's largest consumer finance company, Beneficial Corporation, also of Wilmington, Delaware. Also, Household Bank (Illinois), NA., a subsidiary of Household International, received a needs improvement rating.

Some of the bank subsidiaries of our largest insurance companies have likewise received below-average CRA ratings. Prudential Insurance Company of America, the country's largest, saw its Prudential Bank and Trust Company subsidiary in Atlanta receive a needs improvement rating. This was also the case for First Signature Bank and Trust Company of Portsmouth, New Hampshire, a subsidiary of John Hancock Insurance Company.

Even some of our largest corporate citizens with bank affiliates have not fared much better. General Motors' subsidiary, GMAC Capital Corporation of Salt Lake City, received a needs improvement rating, as did the Hurley State Bank (of Sioux Falls, South Dakota), a subsidiary of Sears Roebuck and Company. This was also the case with Monogram Bank USA in Cincinnati, a subsidiary of GE Capital Corporation, itself a subsidiary of giant General Electric. Finally, American Express had not one but two bank affiliates receive needs improvement ratings, and these were American Express Resource Corporation and IDS Deposit Corporation, both of Midvale, Utah.

8. The present four-tier CRA rating structure is inadequate and leads to suboptimal public policy results.

We have determined that the most glaring deficiency in the present CRA rating structure is the existence of four rather than five CRA rating categories as was previously the case. We believe that the approach previously used by the Federal Home Loan Bank Board involving five rating categories, with two above-average and two below-average, represents the ideal system.

Under the present system we have roughly 80% of all banks receiving a satisfactory rating. This rating could be interpreted as the grade equivalent in school of a "B" or "C," since the present system is now giving out A's (outstanding), D's (needs improvement), and F's (substantial noncompliance) ratings. Thus, we have a mixed rating in the case of satisfactory evaluations. Lumping B+ and C- grades in one large category removes the incentive to get a better grade.

The fact that approximately one-fourth of all banks with outstanding ratings have some type of compliance violation further suggests the need for a "good" rating category between outstanding and satisfactory. The original pre-FIRREA argument that five rating categories might somehow be confused with the five safety and soundness ones was shown to be as baseless as the argument that there could be confusion between compliance and safety and soundness ratings.

Another area of inconsistency involving the present CRA rating structure is the lack of individual assessment factor ratings. These were fairly commonplace early on by the West Region of the OTS and several Federal Reserve Banks. With but few exceptions today, individual assessment factors have been eliminated by all the regulators. We believe that the lack of this valuable information does a disservice to both the public and the banking community. We believe that the primary opposition to the use of such individual assessment factor ratings comes not from the bankers but from the regulators themselves who would otherwise be held accountable for specific bank CRA ratings. Considerable subjectivity in the granting of a bank's overall rating is lost when individual assessment factor ratings are publicly made.

Another problem with the current rating structure is the "spiked" distribution, namely the fact that 80% of all ratings are satisfactory. Also, almost all upgraded ratings are from needs improvement to satisfactory. This in effect results in a "quest for an S" situation where banks become more and more satisfied with a satisfactory rating. "If 80% of all banks get a satisfactory rating, then it can't be bad," a banker might think. Furthermore, "if we get an outstanding rating, the regulators and the community might expect too much from us, so we should be happy to be in the 'category of the masses' with a satisfactory rating."

344

Chapter 10

This type of thinking is counterproductive from a CRA perspective.

Besides the decreased incentive for an outstanding rating from a public policy perspective, there is another concern purely from a research perspective. That is, we lose much of the "richness" of the data when four out five of all rated banks are in one category. There really is no meaningful distribution, just one big spike. The use of five rather than four ratings would encourage a less spiked distribution.

As pointed out previously, it would be a matter of public policy to determine the ideal distribution among the four (or five) categories. This may or may not be a normally shaped distribution. Ideally, all banks should be outstanding, but this would not be a realistic distribution. We believe that the postdisclosure ratings distribution as of year-end 1991 of approximately 9%, 80%, 10% and 1% in the categories of outstanding, satisfactory, needs improvement, and substantial noncompliance, respectively, is suboptimal and also inflated. The year-end 1992 distribution of 10%, 79%, 10%, and 1% is quite similar. Public policy guidance in terms of the optimal rating distribution would enable us to better evaluate allegations of grade inflation.

For example, our analysis of the grade inflation issue indicated that a more appropriate distribution as of year-end 1991 using the current four ratings might be 5%, 84%, 9%, and 2%, *without* adjusting for any inflated grades in the 84% satisfactory category. Such an adjustment, based upon an assumption of grade inflation in the satisfactory category similar to that in the needs improvement one, would result in a 5%, 70%, 23%, and 2% distribution as of year-end 1991. However, public policy under our recommended five-tiered rating system might determine that the most appropriate distribution for banks in the outstanding, good, satisfactory, needs improvement, and substantial noncompliance categories would be 5%, 20%, 50%, 20% and 5%, respectively. If this were the case, the 70% in the "adjusted satisfactory" category would be reduced to 50%, with the remaining 20% being upgraded to the new "good" category. Again, the results for the year-end 1992 distribution would be quite similar.

There is another reason why an increasing number of banks seem to be "satisficed" with a satisfactory rating. Larger banks, especially statewide ones, may be able to "hide" below-average CRA performances with a satisfactory rating. That is, if one large statewide bank with 100 branches in 10 different banking markets receives one CRA rating of satisfactory, it is likely a weighted "average" of mainly satisfactory but also high and low ones. As a matter of public policy, we should be able to identify, at a minimum, which banking markets throughout that statewide system received the highest and the lowest ratings. The current system is suboptimal in that it does not allow that.

You can be sure that bank management at such large statewide banks have regular profitability performance reports by market (and even by office in many cases). If bank management wants to know profitability performance by market, then the public should have the right to know CRA performance by market. The movement toward consolidation, especially on an interstate level, further obscures this issue. As long as there is a "one rating per one bank" rule as we have now, the increasingly larger consolidated banks will be in a better position to "hide" underperforming CRA states and/or regions. Required CRA ratings by state and banking market would prevent this "loophole."

Another conclusion we have reached relative to the current CRA rating structure is the lack of more explicit guidelines for examiners on handling the most serious problem, namely violations of consumer compliance regulations and laws. We are referring to the two assessment factors under performance category IV pertaining to discrimination and other illegal credit practices. Our chief concern is with assessment factor F, the CRA "death wish."

There is a tremendous amount of inconsistency as to how CRA ratings are made with banks with different types of compliance violations. In the case of the First National Bank of Chicago, it received an outstanding rating but was cited for a "substantive" noncompliance violation of the ECOA. Over one-fourth of all outstanding rated banks received some type of criticism for an antidiscrimination law or regulation violation. By comparison, just under half (46%) of banks with needs improvement and substantial noncompliance ratings had such violations, although many of these were of a more serious nature.

There is clearly too much inconsistency in the handling of this critical assessment factor F, which is probably the most important one in terms of the overall CRA rating.

Cease and desist orders, civil money penalties, and referrals to the Justice Department on CRA and related compliance grounds are quite rare—you can count on one hand the total number of all such enforcement actions through mid-year 1992, according to individual regulators. By contrast, these enforcement actions are relatively common for safety and soundness and other violations.

We are particularly troubled by the fact that there has been but one fair lending discrimination case referred to the Justice Department through mid-year 1992, and this was by the OCC in the late 1980s against a small Montana bank, according to the OCC. The celebrated Decatur Federal investigation was not even based upon an OTS referral of that thrift but rather on the Justice Department's own initiative. OTS's involvement apparently was limited to giving Decatur Federal an inflated satisfactory rating during that investigation. The FDIC Improvement Act of 1991 amended the ECOA to place an affirmative obligation on the regulators to refer to the Justice Department any pattern or practice of discouraging or denying loan applications. Many banks with these types of activities were specified in the profiles and case studies in this book.

At the insistence of Congress the FDIC in October 1992 referred three cooperative banks in Massachusetts to the Justice Department for review of OCOA violations disclosed in public performance evaluations. These three banks are the Butler Bank – A Co-operative Bank of Lowell, the Needham Cooperative Bank of Needham in suburban Boston, and the Lowell Co-operative Bank of Lowell. The Butler and Needham banks received substantial noncompliance ratings and "informal enforcement actions" (in April and June 1992) from the FDIC, and the Lowell bank received a satisfactory rating from the FDIC. The most recent Justice Department referral was by the FED in February 1993 involving Boston's Shawmut Bank, N.A. This referral was reportedly based on the Federal Reserve Bank of Boston's mortgage discrimination study and the fact that Shawmut Bank is Boston's most active mortgage lender. That bank

received a satisfactory rating from the OCC. The former chairman of that bank's parent, Shawmut National Corporation is John LaWare, the current chairman of the FFIEC and member of the Federal Reserve Board. Of the five Justice Department referrals to date, four were banks in the Boston and surrounding areas. Two of those four banks had satisfactory CRA ratings like Decatur Federal.

Besides publicly disclosed CRA ratings and evaluations, real CRA enforcement to date primarily has been through branch or merger denials. We could, however, identify only 20 denials on CRA grounds out of nearly 70,000 applications filed with the four regulators since the 1977 CRA. In other words, only one of every 3,500 applications has been denied on CRA grounds. The OCC was responsible for 11 or over half of these 20 denials, and they were spread out between 1979 and 1992. In contrast, all of the FDIC's three denials were before 1981, the FHLBB's two denials were in 1985 and 1989, and the FED's four denials were since 1989.

The regulators' preferred CRA "enforcement" tool, besides "jawboning" and issuing "politically correct" pro-CRA policy statements, is the "conditional approval," not the denial. We have identified several hundred approvals by all four regulators conditioned on future improvements to correct CRA deficiencies. Most of these conditional approvals would have been denials if the regulators had adopted the "performance not promises" CRA philosophy that they preach to banks. We believe that an application approval of any type for a below-average CRA performing bank doesn't represent "true" CRA enforcement.

Conditional approvals remove any incentive for banks to impose CRA performance until after they have applied and received the conditions for approval. This approach not only fails to encourage consistently good CRA performance but also fails as a disincentive for bad performance, because the "friendly" regulator always gives banks a chance to "clean up their act" after the application. The conditional approval is indicative of the lack of true CRA enforcement and, worse yet, a way of potentially undermining the goal of CRA.

Besides publicly disclosed ratings and evaluations, we would define "true" CRA enforcement mainly in terms of denials, Justice Department referrals, C&D orders, and civil money penalties. The infrequency and, more accurately, rarity of these enforcement tools on CRA grounds point to the inescapable conclusion that true CRA enforcement has been lax at best and almost nonexistent over the last 16 years.

In summary, we have identified at least one example of each of the following ten CRA "pitfalls" for examiners and regulators that lead to suboptimal public policy results:

1. *CRA Examiner Subjectivity Range*—A CRA examiner can always "justify" a rating one category above or below the "true" rating

    a. *Grade Inflation*—In all rating categories (except substantial noncompliance)

    b. *Grade Deflation*—Few and far between

2. *Reevaluation Rating Inflation*—Grade inflation of CRA ratings upon reevaluation

    a. *Semiautomatic Upgrading*—In almost half of all cases—"Nearly everyone improves over time"

    b. *Aversion to Downgrading* (only 3% of all cases)—"When in doubt, keep the same rating" (the result in over half of all cases)

3. *Misallocation of CRA Regulatory Resources* among the four regulators *and* among regions of the same regulator

4. *Selective Enforcement* by certain regulators *and* by certain regions of the same regulator

5. *Underuse of CRA Branch and Merger Denials and Overuse of Conditional Approvals*—We identified a total of only 20 denials on CRA grounds compared to several hundred approvals conditioned on future CRA improvements; we believe the preferred tool of CRA enforcement "cops" should be denials, not conditional approvals (which are "copouts").

6. *Infrequent Justice Department Referrals*—(only one through mid-year 1992 and five to date) for pattern or practice of discouraging or denying loan applications in violation of ECOA

7. *C&D Infrequency and Inconsistency*—The use of cease and desist (C&D) orders primarily on CRA grounds is not only rare (only two to date according to the regulators) but also inconsistent; furthermore, the public disclosure benefits of C&D orders are circumvented by regulators who issue confidential "informal enforcement actions" or engage in other activities to shield banks from the scrutiny of public disclosure.

8. *Infrequent Civil Money Penalties*— (only a few to date) on CRA and related compliance grounds

9. *The "Friendly Regulator"*—Beyond the "revolving door" . . . "It's all in the timing" of exam dates and disclosures; the friendly regulator will give an inflated CRA rating, a conditional approval not a denial, an informal enforcement action not a C&D order, and never consider a civil money penalty or Justice Department referral.

10. *Regulatory Favoritism*—The extreme case of an arbitrary and capricious CRA examiner

These 10 pitfalls can be used as a basis for distinguishing between "strong" and "weak" CRA examiners and regulators. Borrowing terminology from the author's experience with Hurricane Andrew, we now distinguish between two types of CRA regulators and examiners (and their examinations). The "strong" ones are "CBS" types, standing for "concrete block and stucco," the most durable type of construction in south Florida. CBS construction is based on a strong foundation of concrete and steel that generally can withstand a major hurricane. This is not the case for "wood frame" construction, which gives the outside appearance of adequacy and permanence, but is relatively weak and "blown away" in a big storm like Andrew. This "CBS" versus "wood frame" analogy also applies to bankers and banks or anyone or anything, for that matter, that can be distinguished as "strong" versus "weak."

9. There are numerous low-cost and in-house efforts that banks can undertake to not only improve their CRA rating but also to benefit the community.

Figure 10-1, the CRA Cost/Benefit Matrix, identified the southwestern quadrant as being representative of low-cost and in-house efforts that can result in an improved CRA rating. By comparison, the southeastern quadrant involves shared efforts that reduce the costs and risks of any CRA activity.

Focusing first on the southwestern quadrant of the matrix, we have concluded that far too many banks are ignoring the easiest and most economical means of improving their CRA ratings (but not necessarily benefiting the community). Most of these techniques are not secrets but are in fact recommended in the CRA documents distributed by the regulators themselves.

The single most effective way and clearly the lowest-cost one to improve a bank's CRA rating is the development of an affirmative "CRA spirit." That is, if a bank truly "believes" in CRA, then this positive spirit likely will be picked up by the examiners. Unfortunately, the reverse is also true. This most definitely can make a difference in a bank's rating in cases where examiners are on the fence.

Those banks that display the "unnecessary regulatory burden," "costly paperwork," "we're too small," or "give me a break" attitude are more than likely to fall on the side of the fence with the lower rating. By contrast, those banks with the "we're doing the best we can" and "we'll improve if you show us how" attitude are likely to end up on the other side of the fence, with the higher rating.

Most CRA examiners today are trained to know the difference between form and function, style and substance, and process and performance. It is really not worth the effort to emphasize form over function when the time could be better spent on truly worthwhile efforts. For example, the creation of a CRA officer or committee that is nothing more than a title may hurt a bank if perceived by the examiners as a token gesture with the wrong CRA spirit. This is especially true when done on a "last minute" basis.

The most important exception here involves the issue of documentation. Our research has led us to reaffirm CRA Survival Rule #1—"If it wasn't documented, it wasn't done." The chief compliance representatives of some of the federal bank regulators have told us personally that this documentation emphasis no longer exists. This is the politically proper, on-the-record statement in Washington, D.C., with the efforts to reduce the regulatory burden on banks. Our response is that some of the top compliance people in the "beltway" just don't know what their examiners are doing out in the field. The fact of the matter is documentation still rules the day in CRA. The need to substantiate a claim makes good business sense. How is an examiner supposed to do the job without the appropriate documentation? What is an examiner supposed to examine? There is much more to an exam than just conducting a "windshield survey." Of course, there are extremes to this argument.

The least-cost approach to improving a bank's CRA rating besides an affirmative CRA spirit is the use of an expanded CRA statement. We are amazed as to the number of banks that do not use this recommended approach, since an expanded CRA statement is one of the first and easiest things that an examiner will check. Other activities that would fall into this category would include regular (preferably monthly) meaningful board CRA discussions, the appointment of a knowledgeable CRA officer, the formation of an active CRA committee, and the use of written CRA policies and a plan. The appointment of a bank's CEO as chairman of the CRA committee is not a bad idea.

One of the most unappreciated CRA "loopholes" for banks is the fact that they can delineate their own local community lending area. Since most of the CRA evaluation is a function of this delineated area, the definition of it is extremely important. Most banks are not criticized for unreasonable areas, but when they are it is usually because they are too large. Sometimes, however, these areas are "gerrymandered." This apparently was the case at Decatur Federal where their delineated area followed the railroad tracks in Atlanta, thereby excluding over 76% of Fulton County's black population, according to the Justice Department.

All banks should devote particular attention to delineating the most appropriate and reasonable area. The delineation may be more critical for some banks than others, as is the case where a bank's deposits emanate from local areas surrounding branches but loans are spread over a much larger area. One of the CRA delineation guidelines suggests the use of the effective lending territory if it is not inconsistent with other CRA guidelines. A bank using the smaller areas around the branches as the delineated community, probably to the delight of many examiners, will likely be criticized for an unreasonably low lending penetration of that smaller community. Such a bank should, therefore, consider using the larger effective lending territory for the CRA delineation in accordance with the guidelines. Banks that are specialized lenders, with the greatest demand for their lending products outside of their local branching area, must be particularly careful to document their delineation methodology, especially if the area is expanded without the addition of new offices.

We have determined that banks have made far too little use of shared efforts in meeting CRA obligations. The several examples in the southeastern quadrant of the CRA Cost/Benefit Matrix provide numerous possibilities in this regard. We are particularly optimistic regarding the feasibility of the shared branch concept, especially in low- and moderate-income and substantially minority areas. We feel that many bank trade associations and groups have come up woefully short not only in the area of acting as a clearinghouse for valuable CRA information and training but especially of being a facilitator of shared efforts. We would hope that many banking groups will devote more effort into these positive CRA activities rather than trying to lobby Congress on the need to significantly cut back CRA coverage. Leaders of these groups may think that it would appear inconsistent to be a facilitator of CRA compliance on one hand and be a "CRA basher" on the other. Actually, the regulators could also act as a facilitator of shared efforts.

We have concluded that it is in a bank's interest to "internalize" the CRA function as much as possible. Although there is an expanding army of CRA vendors, we believe that CRA examiners are more impressed by in-house efforts even though they may

not be as professional or "slick" as those of outside vendors. We believe that the best use of CRA "outsourcing" involves external CRA assessments because of the objectivity that would be brought to bear on the issue. The use of outside CRA experts for loan geocoding, credit needs surveys, and the like may not always be cost justified. Outside vendors are best justified in areas where the bank has little expertise or experience, and this differs widely by bank.

We feel that all banks should have an ongoing self-assessment program comprised, at a minimum, of a paper-based or "electronic" notebook with 13 index tabs, one for each of the assessment factors plus the reasonableness of the delineated area. All of the supporting information documenting the bank's performance under each of these assessment factors should be summarized in this notebook, and an honest rating should be applied to each of the factors. A truly objective assessment may have at least one "needs improvement" rating which may be upgraded over time. More detailed backup documentation can be maintained in separate files, but this one notebook will act as a map or guide for the CRA examiner to review the entire program. This reduces the likelihood that positive CRA developments that may benefit a bank's CRA rating will be left out of a bank's public evaluation. This internal self-assessment effort should be the responsibility of the bank's CRA officer and be overseen by the CRA committee.

A great degree of CRA training can be done on an in-house basis. All bank personnel who come in contact with the public should at least know what "CRA" stands for. Most bankers are shocked to "shop" some of their own branches and find that a significant portion of receptionists, tellers, or others with customer contact have to ask two or three people before they find out what the CRA statement is. If CRA examiners may randomly check customer contact personnel about this item, shouldn't it be a part of in-house CRA training?

Every bank should have a data base comprised of public performance evaluations of as many local and peer banks as possible. This database of evaluations, which should be continually updated, should also include those nonlocal banks of a similar size or business focus that would meet a peer criterion.

Banks, in our opinion, should become more assertive in dealing with regulators regarding their "rights" under the CRA examination procedure. First and foremost would be to understand the proper appeal procedure. Second, we believe all banks have a right to know specifically what their individual assessment factor ratings are as well as those for the five performance categories. Only in this way can a bank determine specific areas needing improvement as well has how the final rating was calculated. Banks that were involved in an examination where considerable subjectivity is suspected may be able to better document this problem with such individual ratings. Third, we believe that banks have the right to demand that all of the important positive factors relating to their CRA performance be included in their public performance evaluation. Even though a CRA examiner may not consider a particular development or fact to be pertinent, we believe that a bank should insist on having this material included, if nowhere else, under assessment factor L regarding "other factors."

In the event that a bank receives one of the two lowest ratings, we believe that it is absolutely critical that it provide a timely response that is fashioned in a constructive and positive manner rather than one that is critical of the regulator. A response provides a bank an opportunity to rebut particular items, including errors, that may exist in the performance evaluation. Also, because it becomes a part of the public file, the examiners on the next evaluation will be certain to see it and be more careful about possibly making any unsubstantiated or incorrect findings.

Community groups and others requesting a copy of the evaluation and receiving such a response with it will know that the bank receiving the low rating is serious about improving it. This is because they have already made the positive effort of acknowledging some of the problems and taking steps to improve them. We have seen many cases of banks with satisfactory ratings that have prepared such response documents, because the bankers felt they should have received outstanding ratings. As long as the bank feels there is room for improvement in their rating, and they are serious about wanting to improve it, then the preparation of such a public response is worthwhile

and indeed recommended. Even some banks with outstanding ratings have prepared such documents.

Banks that have received one of the two below-average ratings and have not developed a public response to it may be sending out the wrong signal to the regulators and/or community groups regarding their CRA spirit. That is, it may send a message of tacit approval of the low rating or, worse yet, a "we don't really care" attitude. A public response placed in the public file a substantial time after the completion of the exam may again send the wrong signal. Quickly sending the right message to regulators and community groups is especially important when we are dealing with an inherently subjective rating. (But, like everything else, better late than never.)

In summary, it can be argued that there is no excuse for a low CRA rating except an arbitrary and capricious decision on the part of a subjective regulator over which a bank has no control anyway. Because grossly subjective evaluations and ratings are hard to prove, and hopefully the exception more than the rule, a bank must accept the fact that a low rating was probably given to them because they deserved it. This is not always the case with an average or outstanding rating, because we believe the incidence of grade inflation greatly exceeds that of grade deflation.

A CRA examination is much like an "open book" exam in school where you have been given the test questions in advance and know exactly what will be required. For example, when so much emphasis is placed on geocoding and the FFIEC puts out a separate release on the importance of it, how can a bank expect to get anything better than a satisfactory rating when it completely ignores this issue? So many of the items noted in the southwestern quadrant of the CRA Cost/Benefit Matrix are low-cost, in-house efforts for which there is really no excuse for not doing, other than just having the wrong CRA spirit.

Banks must treat CRA as another cost of doing business in the increasingly pro-consumer environment of the 1990s. Efforts to attack it will more than likely be unfruitful. Therefore, it is better to spend that time preparing for the next open book exam, especially since we know the questions in advance.

In summary, the ten most common CRA "Pitfalls" for bankers that can adversely impact bank CRA ratings and/or community performance are as follows:

1. *Ignoring Low-Cost, In-House Efforts* that primarily benefit CRA ratings such as those items in the southwestern quadrant of the CRA Cost/Benefit Matrix (e.g., an expanded CRA statement, appointment of a CRA officer and CRA committee, regular board CRA discussions, and so on)

2. *Forgetting CRA Survival Rule #1*—"If it wasn't documented, it wasn't done," regardless of what bank regulators may say to the contrary

3. *Failure to Modify Local Community Boundaries* over time to reflect changing bank, community, or other conditions—just because examiners failed to object to a delineation doesn't mean it is the right one!

4. *Ignoring Shared CRA Resources* such as those in the southeastern quadrant of the CRA Cost/Benefit Matrix that can result in reduced costs and risks

5. *Over-Using or Under-Using Outside CRA Vendors*—The CRA compliance function should be internalized as much as possible with judicious use of CRA "outsourcing" in areas where a bank has little or no experience or expertise

6. *Not Learning From the Successes and Failures of Other CRA Programs* as described in the public performance evaluations of the highest and lowest CRA-rated banks

7. *Lack of Written Public Response to a Below-Average Rating* or even a satisfactory rating if an outstanding one is the bank's goal

8. *No Loan Geocoding Effort*—even the smallest bank can always run a zip code listing or at least plot a loan sample by hand for CRA credit

9. *Misconceptions as to How to Get "CRA Credit,"* especially involving certain charitable donations, volunteer work, or other "good deeds" for which a bank receives little or no "CRA credit"

10. *Wasting Time by "CRA Bashing" Rather Than CRA Compliance* and then making "token" or "last minute" preexamination efforts only to see many of them backfire; it is not easy to hide the wrong "CRA spirit" from the examiners

10. Considerable additional research is required in many areas of CRA.

There are many unanswered questions regarding CRA ratings and performance evaluations in addition to those raised above. We believe that an independent body such as the General Accounting Office, or even an FFIEC-organized team comprised of all four regulators, should devote time and effort to answering these important questions. The General Accounting Office or some other independent body would probably be most objective. The 25 most important questions we have raised are as follows:

1. How are CRA ratings related to bank financial condition? What about upgraded ratings?

2. Are CRA ratings related to the length of the public performance evaluations? In other words, do regulators use a longer evaluation to justify a good or bad rating or perhaps neither or both?

3. How important is the distinction between low- and moderate-income "areas" and "individuals"? Was the substantial difference witnessed in the case of Harris Bank of Chicago an exception rather than the rule?

4. Are some technical or nonsubstantive consumer compliance violations more serious than others? How serious is a "substantive" violation? Are there many cases of examiners failing to report nonsubstantive violations but only substantive ones?

5. Did those thrifts that paid for the CRA consulting services of the Federal Home Loan Bank of Cincinnati receive disproportionately better ratings from the Cincinnati District of the OTS? What about the relationship between the approval rate of Community Support Statements by the Federal Housing Finance Board and the use of purchased CRA services from that Federal Home

Loan Bank? More generally, what is the relationship between the approval rate of such statements (and action plans) and CRA ratings?

6. How rampant is grade inflation? Specifically, what is the extent of grade inflation among the 80% of banks with a "satisfactory" rating? How could the OTS justify a "satisfactory" rating for Atlanta's Decatur Federal during the four-year investigation by the Justice Department, which alleged racial discrimination in their mortgage lending? Was that OTS rating and evaluation pushed up to the first half of 1990 so it would not become public?

7. Are there other instances of regulatory favoritism besides the one we alleged? With reference to that case involving Norstar Bank, N.A., what really happened and why?

8. Do regulators use the timing of CRA exams, re-exams, or transmittals to benefit certain banks? How can regulators justify the significant differences in the transmittal times we observed? Is there any relationship between these delays and bank ratings? What about the possible relationship of timing delays to the size of the bank, type of bank, or area? In summary, we need a testing of the "friendly regulator" hypothesis in this respect.

9. What justification is there for a nonspecialized compliance function at the OCC? How has that affected their CRA ratings compared to the other regulators?

10. How many CRA ratings have been formally or informally appealed? What regulators were involved and what were the results?

11. Are banks that prepare public responses to CRA ratings more likely to receive an upgraded rating on a re-evaluation?

12. Would a market-by-market evaluation of a large statewide bank result in an overall rating that is a true "weighted average" of the individual ones?

13. How much of the "public" has ever requested a copy of a CRA statement or reviewed a public file? What about public performance evaluations?

14. Are CRA "megapledges" actually being fulfilled with true CRA projects? In other words, to what extent does "megapledge inflation" exist where large commitments are "padded" with non-CRA items?

15. Was our finding of the roughly 20% of all substantial noncompliance ratings in L.A. prior to the civil disturbance there just a coincidence or indicative of a troubling pattern?

16. What relevant CRA information is contained in the nonpublic compliance examination reports? How are the overall compliance ratings on those exams related to CRA ratings? Are the public reports "watered-down" and less critical versions of the private reports?

17. How are the different regulators' four CRA ratings distributed by state, metropolitan area, and major city? What about different neighborhoods within a large city? Are the examples of "selective enforcement" we witnessed (such as the case of the OCC in Tennessee) the result of just one or two examiners or an entire office of them?

18. What is the relationship between CRA ratings and HMDA results? Does the lowest decile of CRA-rated banks have the poorest HMDA results (e.g., trends in minority approval/rejection gaps and rates)? Is the highest decile reporting the best HMDA results?

19. What is the extent and impact of the alleged redlining of inner cities and flood zone and coastal areas by insurance companies?

20. Does the FED exercise too much discretion in its use of the troubled institution "loophole" to approve acquisitions of troubled institutions by banks with below-average CRA ratings, as in the February 1992 LaSalle case?

21. How committed is the FED to CRA enforcement in view of the LaSalle case and especially the November 1992 Capital Bank of Clayton, Missouri, merger approval? More generally speaking, is the FED capable of truly effective CRA enforcement in a manner comparable to its anti-inflation enforcement? Can our top inflation cop also be our top loan discrimination cop?

22. Are the OCC, FDIC, and OTS under any FED pressure to avoid giving below-average CRA ratings to banks (like First Commercial Bank, N.A. of Memphis, Tennessee) which have been involved in FED bank holding company approvals? How often and under what conditions has the FED contacted (or even pressured) these other agencies into a commitment for a satisfactory or better rating to help justify a bank holding company approval (as was the case with First Commercial)? In other words, is the "lender of last resort" also the "CRA enforcer of last resort?"

23. How widespread and effective has the regulators' frequent use of "conditional approvals" instead of denials been as a CRA enforcement tool? What about regulatory use of confidential "informal enforcement actions" instead of public cease and desist orders? Are there other examples of private and informal arrangements between regulators and bankers that should be disclosed as a matter of public policy?

24. What justification is there, if any, for the infrequent use of cease and desist orders and civil money penalties on CRA and related compliance grounds?

25. Why haven't more referrals been made to the Justice Department for ECOA violations involving the discouraging or denying of loan applications, especially considering that several specific examples of such activities are readily apparent in public performance evaluations?

RECOMMENDATIONS TO EXPAND AND IMPROVE CRA

1. Consideration should be given to selectively expanding a CRA-type of requirement to other financial institutions so that banks and thrifts are not the only ones subject to this this kind of affirmative legislation.

It is inconsistent with the "level playing field" and "social compact" arguments that credit unions and certain other financial institutions are exempt from CRA. Credit unions, while large in number but small in aggregate size, receive many of the same federal government benefits, including federal deposit insurance, that banks receive. A popular argument exempting credit unions is that they must be serving their local community well because it is a small, compact group with a common bond. But this is the same argument that many small community banks use as to why they should be exempt from CRA. We believe that credit unions, community banks, and all other federally insured depository institutions should be treated equally, especially when it comes to their affirmative obligation for important consumer laws such as CRA.

The nonbank financial institutions that are most like banks in their depository gathering function are money market mutual funds, and we feel that consideration should be given to some CRA type of affirmative responsibility for them. While it is true that they are not consumer lenders and do not have access to the same benefits as federally insured depositories, we believe that there may be an implicit guarantee of a federal safety net for the largest such money market mutual funds in the event of a liquidity crisis. This is a weak version of the "social compact" argument. This same argument of an implied federal safety net, where the FED could act as a "lender of last resort," might also apply to other very large financial institutions to prevent a widespread "contagion" effect. Money market mutual funds represent the most likely target in terms of the "level playing field argument," because they represent a highly effective and proven competitive force to the ability of banks to gather deposits. The imposition of a CRA type of requirement on them would be consistent with the general theme of fairness among competing financial institutions in the same retail market. As in the case of investment or nonlending investment firms, the money market mutual funds could meet a CRA type of requirement in nontraditional ways, such as investing in CD's or commercial paper of banks with outstanding CRA ratings, as compared to those with below-average ratings.

The nonbank financial institutions that compete directly with banks on the lending side of the business could also be argued to have some type of CRA requirement. These institutions would include lenders in the area of residential mortgage loans, installment loans, credit cards, small business loans, and other competitive products. Affected firms would include mortgage banking, credit card, and finance companies as well as corporate giants involved in such lending (American Express, AT&T, General Electric, General Motors, Sears, etc.) In fact, many of our largest bank holding companies have affiliates in these lending businesses. Such a CRA type of requirement could be justified on the basis of the above arguments as well as the need for consumer protection legislation in any major industry involving lending to the public. There will always be some relatively minor sources of legitimate lending (e.g., pawn shops) or financial services (e.g., check cashing outlets), which may be more frequently used by lower-income individuals, that would be more difficult to impose CRA types of federal regulations on.

Support for a CRA type of requirement in the insurance industry is found in the numerous recent allegations of redlining by insurance companies in property and casualty lines in many inner city and flood zone and coastal areas. To the extent that redlining does in fact exist by insurance companies, including those involved in private mortgage insurance, then this should be motivation enough for the serious consideration of this proposal. Insurance companies have long competed with banks in lending, but mainly on the commercial, not retail side, although life insurance policy loans have always been a popular retail product when interest rates increased. We have witnessed the failure of a few fairly large, junk bond-laden insurance companies, and there was no government effort to bail them out. However, the likely failure of one of our largest insurance companies,

with numerous subsidiaries including those in banking and other industries, might require the use of the federal safety net. In the wake of Hurricane Andrew's massive insurance losses, there has been talk of the insurance industry seeking federal help in the form of a government "hurricane fund" that would put a ceiling on the insurers' losses in such a catastrophe. This would be on top of other government benefits now enjoyed by the insurance industry. Thus, all of the above-cited arguments supporting such a CRA type of requirement would apply to the insurance industry.

The insurance industry has so far escaped widespread federal regulation, but this is what may be necessary to ensure the fair provision of insurance services to the entire community without any redlining. The October 1992 ruling by the Seventh Circuit Court of Appeals that the federal Fair Housing Act prohibits redlining by insurance companies may signal the beginning of aggressive federal regulation in this area.

The insurance industry today is reminiscent of where the banking industry was on consumer compliance issues in the seventies prior to the 1977 CRA, which was instituted by a proconsumer Democratic administration. The insurance industry may not only be brought under an expanding CRA umbrella in the current proconsumer Democratic administration but possibly even a broadening net of new federal regulations.

Many large banks have long been involved in the insurance business, and these and others want to become involved in a bigger way. Some of the largest insurance companies operate nonbank banks and compete directly with commercial banks in numerous areas. If our largest banks operated major insurance companies which practiced redlining in our inner cities or flood zone and coastal areas of the type alleged for insurance companies, this activity would not be tolerated. Why should insurance companies be held to any lesser of a standard in terms of their corporate social responsibility simply because they are not beneficiaries of federal deposit insurance? We therefore believe that any bank or thrift that is interested in operating in the insurance industry should have the full power to do so. This would not only provide additional competition but also inject a new and higher level of corporate social responsibility that apparently does not exist at this time.

We would be the first to point out that the argument of a possible federal bailout such as those involving Chrysler Corporation or Lockheed may indeed be too extreme of a possibility to justify a new layer of federal regulations for large nonfinancial companies. Yet we are reminded of the "invisible safety net" afforded to some of these large firms by Chrysler's 1992 solicitation of FED Chairman Alan Greenspan to help persuade German central bankers to provide vital financing for the troubled number three auto maker. As long as the possibility of such indirect or direct federal assistance exists for our largest companies, the weak version of the "social compact" argument would support the selective expansion of a CRA type of requirement.

It is our opinion that the entire business community, not just banks and thrifts, must become more responsive to important social needs, especially those involving the 40% of American households that are low- and moderate-income. We believe we are moving into an era where the pro-consumer environment will be stronger than ever, and that it would not be inconsistent with sound business practices to have this type of corporate conscience. That is why we feel that a vital theme for businesses in the 90s, whether they be banks or nonbanks, should be "Capitalism with a Corporate Conscience," especially in areas that benefit low- and moderate-income individuals.

We would hope that this CRA spirit of a corporate conscience would carry over into other nonbank financial institutions, such as mutual funds, pension funds, and even security firms. These firms can meet a CRA type of obligation, for example, through preferred treatment and purchases of debt and equity investments of outstanding banks and the opposite activities for below-average banks. Some firms in these industries, such as the previously-cited Muriel Siebert & Company, clearly have demonstrated a higher level of social responsibility than others. Ideally, these and other institutions can meet their social responsibility without the heavy hand of government intervention coming into play, but we have learned from CRA in the case of the banking industry that this is not always the case.

2. CRA performance evaluations should be much more objective, quantitative, and structured than they presently are.

CRA always has and probably always will have certain subjective elements. However, we believe that the level of subjectivity inherent in CRA examinations is far too high at the present time. We recommend that federal bank regulators require that all conclusions be substantiated with facts, numbers, examples, and the like to the greatest extent possible. In fact, the FDIC Improvement Act of 1991 required the regulators to include data supporting their conclusions in the CRA public performance evaluations. Unsubstantiated conclusions, and especially unneeded and irrelevant opinions, as we have found in too many cases, have no place in an objective examination process.

We feel that the CRA examination process should contain a minimum number of objective questions that must be answered in every evaluation. The precise criteria and minimum requirements would have to be determined. For example, the following ratios for a present and past period should be calculated at a minimum: loan-to-deposit ratios (relative to loan quality) for the overall bank and specific markets as appropriate compared to peers; the percentage of loans in the delineated community; and the percentage of loans in low- and moderate-income areas relative to the total bank and the total for all banks in those areas. Every evaluation should summarize basic past and present HMDA data denial rates with peer comparisons where appropriate. A HMDA analysis of a prescribed form with conclusions should be mandatory in all CRA evaluations, without exception.

Specific questions should be directed at whether or not loan application discouraging practices or subtle discrimination exists. For example, the following should be determined: minimum loan amounts, if any; special fees or other unfavorable terms on small loans, if any; and the average loan size by type of loan compared to the average deposit size. Notation should be made of any evidence of the "fat file" phenomenon, which refers to the discriminating practice of maintaining thicker loan files to justify the approval of marginal white as compared to the thinner files of equivalently qualified but denied marginal minority applicants. This discriminatory phenomenon, which involves "coaching" by bank officials to establish the thicker files for marginal white applicants, was well documented in the Federal Reserve Bank of Boston's mortgage lending study, as well as the Justice Department's investigation of Atlanta's Decatur Federal.

Every evaluation should specifically note whether or not a bank offers special services, such as lifeline checking, free government check cashing, and certain types of loans that may be especially appealing to low- and moderate-income households (e.g., used mobile home loans). Also, does the bank in question have an appointed CRA officer, an active CRA committee, or regularly discuss meaningful CRA matters at the board meetings?

Many CRA performance evaluations have most or all of these questions answered, but the problem is that far too many do not. When an outside party is reviewing a CRA evaluation, the facts presented by the examiners should document the assessment factor conclusions and ultimately the final rating. Far too many evaluations fail in this respect because there are no discernible conclusions for individual assessment factors. These "weak" evaluations emphasize the qualitative over the quantitative, "glittering generalities" over specifics, and rarely use an "exam plan" to prepare a "strong" evaluation. In other words, weak performance evaluations are long on process and short on performance, a criticism examiners usually associate with bankers' CRA efforts, not their own. The use of a more structured and streamlined approach by examiners, which would by necessity eliminate much of the flexibility they now employ, would reduce the amount of subjectivity in the current examination process. Also, bankers would better know in advance what to expect.

3. CRA performance evaluations and enforcement should be more consistent among the four regulators and among different regions of the same regulator.

The tremendous inconsistencies we have noticed in the type and style of evaluations suggests the need for greater consistency within and across banking agencies. The idea that one regulator may be an "easier"

grader than another brings back memories of what former FED Chairman Arthur Burns titled a "competition in laxity" among regulators. This refers to the possibility that a bank would switch its charter to be regulated by a different federal banking agency to receive "easier" treatment in one or more specific areas. Regulators, not banks, would compete among themselves for the most regulated banks, which translated into greater budgets and ultimately power.

There appears to be considerable room for improvement in the area of consistency, beginning with the basic length and style of the public performance evaluations. For example, we have noted in a sample of standardized retyped public evaluations several instances where they differ in length from as few as two retyped standardized pages (in a few cases for the FDIC and OTS) to as much as 22 pages (in two cases for the FED). The FED's April 6, 1992, evaluation of the Northern Trust Company of Chicago, which was not in our sample, was 33 pages long including a 10-page appendix made up of HMDA, call report, and examination sample tables. The FDIC had the shortest average length (3.8 pages), and the FED had the longest average length (7.0 pages) based on our sample.

Such significant differences in length, by over 10 times in our sample, clearly suggest disparities in the level of documentation supporting the conclusions. A public performance evaluation of just a few pages barely has enough room to state the required assessment factors and conclusions, much less any documentation supporting them. The average length of performance evaluations in our sample was about five pages. We cannot judge the quality of evaluations by their length. We do know, however, that there is a great deal of inconsistency in length, and that this issue should be addressed.

Many performance evaluations will start off or end with a brief profile of the subject bank and its community. We found these to be very helpful to outside readers, and regulators should be consistent in requiring this type of useful material rather than it being the examiners' prerogative. This is also the case for placing the bank name, city/state, date, and ideally, charter or docket number at the top of each numbered page of each performance evaluation.

Some evaluations contain boring and wasteful pages restating CRA requirements and guidelines that could apply to any bank in the country. Many evaluations will contain tables of HMDA data comparing approval or denial rates, but others will merely summarize this material in narrative form. A surprisingly large number of CRA evaluations for HMDA-covered banks don't even mention any HMDA data, and this is puzzling.

Some evaluations calculate total and market loan-to-deposit ratios and compare them to peers and past years. Because a basic concern in CRA has always been the possible failure of a bank to reinvest local deposits, we believe that such ratios are intuitively appealing and always should be calculated for the total bank and by market area with time and peer comparisons. A complete loan-to-deposit ratio analysis must use meaningful and effective loan and deposit totals and relate the resultant ratios to loan chargeoff and nonperforming asset ratios, again with time and peer comparisons. The CRA guidelines are almost silent on this important topic, probably because of fear over credit allocation implications. We would argue that this is a misguided fear because "reinvestment" is CRA's middle name. Again, there is very little consistency as to the level of quantitative support of many conclusions, and this should be changed.

Some performance evaluations don't even disclose the relevant delineated community area in performance category III. When so much of the evaluation is based upon this area, the specific disclosure of it should be mandatory. Another area where we believe public performance evaluations could be more consistent would be in specifying the appropriate review period for which the examinations are relevant. Many times these review periods are greater than one year, but the reader has no idea as to the relevant period because it is not mentioned. A requirement that this information be placed in all evaluations at a minimum would clearly make them more user-friendly.

One of our greatest concerns in terms of improper CRA examination procedures by bank regulators, besides subjectivity, friendly regulators, and regulatory favoritism, is the issue of "selective enforcement" by certain regulators or within certain districts or regions of the same regulator. The fact that a bank happens to be regulated by a certain examination team, head examiner, or agency or that a bank is located in a particular district of a certain agency should have no bearing on its final CRA rating. This would, in effect, be the counterpart of geographic discrimination or "regulatory redlining." Our research has provided several examples of apparent selective enforcement.

CRA public performance evaluations and ratings should be guided by a more consistent theme of fairness than is currently the case. We were able to identify at least one case of what appeared to be "regulatory favoritism," where a regulator made an unnecessary and unwarranted change in a bank's CRA rating that benefited its parent handsomely in terms of the winning bid of a major failed bank. We believe any incidents of regulatory favoritism are probably isolated and clearly the exception, not the rule.

Overall, there is considerable room for more consistent treatment of banks and thrifts in the enforcement of CRA. First and foremost, specialized banks, including wholesale, foreign, credit card, and related banks, should be treated under different CRA standards because they are not traditional retail banks. A strict interpretation of CRA would almost guarantee a needs improvement or worse rating for any such specialized bank. For this reason, we believe that bank regulators must apply a greater degree of flexibility in this area, but still do so in a consistent manner among all such financial institutions.

Niche banks, which focus on the affluent, a certain ethnic group, or small businesses, however, should be treated no differently than other traditional banks, in our opinion. This is because these are retail banks that have chosen to concentrate on one profitable segment to the actual or perceived exclusion of others that are obviously less profitable, in their opinion. Such niche banks compete with other retail banks, but the wholesale and other banks noted really represent a different industry. We believe that niche retail banks should be held to the same standard as traditional retail banks because it was a voluntary decision for the board of the niche bank to focus on a specific area. If they are able to profit more handsomely from that niche, then this is all the more reason why those banks should be subject to a social responsibility in serving non-niche members of their community. In the final analysis it is the entire community of tax-payers, including those with low and moderate incomes, that ultimately stands behind the federal deposit insurance system.

Another aspect of the issue of fairness involves the appeal process for banks receiving ratings that they do not feel were justified. The above-mentioned case of apparent regulatory favoritism was the only one we have determined in which a bank was granted an immediate appeal and the regulator overturned and upgraded a previous rating. Yet the OCC had no specific guidelines available on the appeals process, other than a general statement, when we asked them about this issue.

We have documented at least one case of grade deflation, and that is enough to indicate that a bank may receive an unnecessarily low rating for which an appeal process should exist. As long as a CRA examiner subjectivity range of plus or minus one notch above or below the "true" CRA rating may exist, as we have hypothesized, then there should be a clear and publicly known process for CRA appeals.

We recommend that a CRA public appeal process be clearly defined and consistent across all regulators. A review board of highly experienced appellate CRA examiners should exist at the federal level. This ideally could be established on a centralized basis (e.g., at the FFIEC) or, less desirably, on a decentralized basis (at the individual regulators). If the appealed evaluation results in the same rating, then the bank requesting the appeal should pay for all expenses associated with it. The government would absorb those expenses if a different rating resulted. Community groups and other interested parties would be advised of and have input into the appeal process.

There should also be a comparable process whereby community groups can appeal an alleged case of grade inflation to a regulator. This, however, may not be a feasible alternative because of the lack of funds of many community groups and the likelihood that grade inflation may be claimed on too many ratings. This results in the uncomfortable position that banks may be able to afford an appeal to get a higher rating in the case of alleged grade deflation because they have the resources, but community groups without

resources will not be able to get that same satisfaction in the case of alleged grade inflation.

In the event that a community group or any interested party felt there was a legitimate case of grade inflation, they would be required to present documentation supporting that view. It is possible that the above-mentioned appellate review board could examine the situation to determine if a formal review by them was necessary, in which case the government would foot the bill. This would be similar to a CRA protest to a merger being filed by a community group and then possibly resulting in a public hearing. At the very least, the views of any community group regarding an alleged case of grade inflation would be placed in a public file for review by the examiners at the next examination.

4. The CRA rating process should be restructured to include a fifth "good" rating and specific rating guidelines involving compliance violations.

Our most important recommendation in this area is the addition of a fifth CRA rating of "good" between satisfactory and outstanding. This would be similar to the original five-tiered system at the FHLBB (but not the three banking agencies).

Specifically, we believe that the appropriate rating system should have five rather than four specifically defined categories, with two above-average and two below-average ratings. Our specific recommendations in this regard were made in a series of articles between April and August 1991, wherein the author was interviewed. Such a system would be analogous to the academic grading system used in schools with an A, B, C, D, and F. The A and B would now represent above-average categories, and the D and F would represent those below-average.

Under the present rating system 10.3% of all banks are rated as outstanding or above-average. If those are assumed to be truly A-rated banks, then the next notch of B-rated banks have been lumped into the large average or satisfactory category. It would only seem fair to those banks that truly are above-average that they receive some special distinction. That is, why should B+ banks be rated together with C− ones, which essentially is what is happening with the current system? Also, five rather than four tiers may encourage more normally distributed ratings, rather than 80% being in just one category.

We would recommend as a matter of public policy that some general guidelines be established, and made public, as to the ideal distribution among the different rating categories. The current distribution of above-average, average, and below-average ratings is approximately 10%–80%–10%, but this is far from ideal because of the grade inflation built into it. A truly ideal distribution would be made up of all outstanding ratings, but this would not be realistic. Our grade inflation analysis suggested that a more realistic distribution would be 25%–50%–25%, which would also be a "bell-shaped" curved. The comparable distribution with the five recommended categories would be 5%–20%–50%–20%–5%.

We would also recommend that specific public guidelines be established pertaining to performance category IV, which contains assessment factors D and F. Because these categories are probably the two most important, especially the CRA "death wish" factor F, there should be guidelines set up regarding minimum or maximum ratings for banks with certain types of consumer compliance violations. Also, examiners should be required to fully disclose whether or not there were technical or procedural violations of any laws or regulations, rather than just covering these facts up by conveniently stating "there were no substantive violations" of one or more specific laws or regulations.

Under the present system, a bank with a substantive consumer compliance violation can receive any of the four ratings, and we have documented examples in each case. For example, the First National Bank of Chicago, which had a substantive ECOA violation, received an outstanding CRA rating. We would recommend that a *truly* outstanding bank be defined as one with *no* violations of consumer compliance regulations or laws under these assessment factors. A bank with a technical or procedural violation might receive a recommended fifth rating of "good," but that would be the highest such category under such a scenario. Under the present four-tiered rating system, banks with any type of violation should receive no more than a satisfactory rating. And, a satisfactory rating may even be an inflated one in some instances.

This apparently was the case at the Glenwood State Bank of Glenwood, Iowa, which received what we believe to be an inflated satisfactory rating from the FED on November 5, 1990. While the public evaluation only noted several technical and an isolated ECOA (Reg B) procedural violation, the confidential compliance exam of that date reported violations of Regulations B and Z, the Fair Credit Reporting Act, and the Real Estate Settlement Procedures Act. The FED examiners' omission of these relevant violations under assessment factor F helped justify the inflated rating. On September 26, 1991, the FED announced that both that bank and its president were hit with a $25,000 civil money penalty for these violations, which were detailed in a December 10, 1991 "written agreement" between that bank and the FED. The Fed got $50,000 and the bank got not only one satisfactory rating but a second one on December 2, 1991, less than three months later.

At the other end of the spectrum from technical violations would be those banks with substantive violations, especially repeated ones or those of significant supervisory concern. These banks would be rated substantial noncompliance, or needs improvement at best, but in no case satisfactory. The original FHLBB system reserved the lowest possible CRA rating for a bank with unresolved violations of nondiscrimination regulations or numerous repetitive violations of technical/procedural requirements. We believe that a return to the approach of the original FHLBB system, which did have specific guidelines in this regard, would clearly make CRA ratings more meaningful than they are today.

5. The OCC, like the other three federal bank regulators, should have specialized compliance examiners.

The fact that the OCC is unique among the four federal bank regulatory agencies as the only one without a specialized compliance examination force would indicate that it was doing something better than all of the other agencies or perhaps not as good. We believe that the latter description is the more appropriate one, and we would therefore recommend the use of specialized compliance examiners by the OCC. Actually, the OCC had separate compliance procedures and reports in 1982 and a "compliance program" since 1987 (but without specialized compliance examiners). The FED has had specialized consumer compliance examiners since 1977, the OTS since 1989, and the FDIC just since 1991.

The main benefit we see for a joint examination force is the strong safety and soundness background that OCC examiners have when conducting a CRA examination. Because of the concern among bankers about the trade-off between safety and soundness considerations on one hand and CRA activities on the other, it would probably provide a greater degree of comfort for bankers to know that their CRA examiners had a strong safety and soundness background. We believe it is desirable for this and other reasons to have compliance examiners with some safety and soundness knowledge. However, we believe that this same objective can be accomplished through additional training of a specialized compliance examination force. For these and related reasons noted above, we expect that the OCC will soon adopt such a specialized compliance examination force.

6. **We recommend that the FFIEC jointly and the four federal bank regulatory agencies individually embark on an aggressive program of training compliance examiners not just in CRA but in other areas, such as safety and soundness.**

As long as subjectivities and inconsistencies exist among CRA evaluations and ratings, as we have documented from our research, there will be a continuing need for better educated and trained examiners. A more objective and consistent examination process as recommended above would help eliminate some of the subjectivities. However, training to increase sensitivity to these issues is critical.

A requirement that examiners read public performance evaluations of other examiners within the same and different regions of their regulator as well as those of different regulators would be a step toward greater consistency. The diversity within and across regulators today is so great as to suggest that there has been very little effective training in the area of consis-

tency in CRA exams and performance evaluations. This is a definite area needing improvement.

One of the chief complaints of bankers is that compliance examiners at all federal bank regulators except for the OCC have little or no idea as to safety and soundness issues. As noted above, this is one of the few benefits of a joint examination force. We are strong advocates of specialized compliance examination personnel. We also believe, however, that training in the basics of safety and soundness of all CRA examiners should be mandatory. This can be accomplished by having CRA examiners accompany safety and soundness examiners on a rotating basis or probably more efficiently through special training sessions.

Bankers indeed have a valid complaint when one group of safety and soundness examiners come in and tell them one thing about loan quality and another group of compliance examiners come in later and may encourage them to do something that the bankers might perceive to be inconsistent with safety and soundness. CRA examiners trained in basic safety and soundness principles would not only broaden their view but become more sensitive to this valid criticism by bankers.

7. **The bank compliance examination process should be managed and centralized through a new federal bank compliance "super-regulator."**

This recommendation would supersede the previous one on the OCC's specialized compliance function. The merits of a federal bank "super-regulator" have long been discussed because of the wasteful and unnecessary duplication of bank regulation and supervision functions at the four federal banking and thrift regulatory agencies. We believe that an ideal beginning for such a super-regulator would be with the compliance function because it would ensure a highly specialized, consistent, and well-trained group of professional compliance examiners. They would lessen the likelihood of examiner subjectivity, selective enforcement, and regulatory favoritism. In other words, the "competition in laxity" argument would cease to exist with one federal super-regulator in the compliance area.

We recommend that the best starting point for such an initiative would be for the four federal bank regulators to establish a pilot CRA examination program through the FFIEC's existing CRA Subcommittee of its Consumer Compliance Task Force. This would involve a well-trained team of experienced CRA examiners from all four agencies (although the OCC does not yet have specialized ones) that would review a representative sample of public performance evaluations to determine the extent to which grade inflation and deflation exists.

Although such a group may not conduct such an examination as objectively as an independent research group such as the General Accounting Office, it would be a start toward a centralized compliance function. In addition to determining the extent to which grade inflation and deflation exists, such a pilot program could also examine the issue of selective enforcement and test our hypothesized CRA examiner subjectivity range. Other questions and areas of future research previously noted likewise could be investigated.

We would recommend that the proposed centralized compliance agency examine all of the banks and thrifts in a particular community or market at one time. Our CRA "swat team" approach, focusing on communities rather than banks, would not only result in economies of scale and scope from the examiners' perspective but would allow many functions such as public interviews to be conducted on a broader scale and a more efficient and scientific basis. The examiners could even hold CRA educational seminars for the bankers in the targeted community to encourage shared resources and other affirmative CRA efforts. Also, the CRA ratings of all banks in a community would be simultaneously published. Different examiners might become specialists in different areas or for different types or sizes of banks. For example, we would recommend that a specialized compliance team using flexible CRA standards be used for limited-purpose institutions such as wholesale banks, foreign banks, and credit card banks. More than likely, a specialized team could also be used for very large multinational or interstate banks.

A further advantage of a centralized compliance function would be that a regular compliance schedule of examinations would be published and known by the bankers and the public alike. This centralized agency could be the source of the previously recommended group to hear CRA appeals. Furthermore, this agency would be responsible for disseminating regular (weekly) listings of completed CRA ratings plus periodic (e.g., annual) cumulative listings with all past ratings. These listings would be available to all interested parties on a no-charge basis, unlike the FED's current policy of charging $35 per year for its weekly announcement of actions including CRA-covered applications and public CRA ratings. Moreover, we would recommend that this new agency have a toll-free "hotline" for customer questions or complaints on any CRA matter. The 800 number would be clearly visible on bank premises and possibly even loan documents and advertising.

Today, a FED member bank receiving a below-average rating would probably have to wait no longer than six months to a year to receive a second rating. However, if that same bank were regulated by the FDIC or OTS, the re-evaluation might not be for a year or longer. The OCC may go as long as seven years between CRA exams for community banks, although below-average rated ones are examined more frequently. Also, certain banks at any agency with below-average ratings may get a re-evaluation simply because they're applying for a branch or other corporate activity, while others not doing this must wait their turn. A centralized compliance function would eliminate these inequities in the examination process and treat all banks more fairly, regardless of their regulator. This is especially critical in the area of publicly disclosed evaluations and ratings. Just because an OCC regulated bank receives a needs improvement or lower rating, it shouldn't have to carry the burden of what it feels is an unwarranted rating for twice the length of time, or longer, as a bank regulated by the FED. The theme of fairness should exist throughout all aspects of CRA, including the regulatory side.

We should mention that we considered and rejected the concept of "audited self-certification." This would be similar to a regulator (e.g., the Securities and Exchange Commission) auditing a partially or totally industry-controlled organization (e.g., the New York Stock Exchange), which in turn supervises compliance within the industry (member firms).

Because none of the existing banking associations or organizations are truly "pro-compliance" and because of the unique position CRA holds as the least-liked law in banking, we dismissed this approach as not being feasible. This audited self-certification concept is significantly different from some of the unaudited self-certification CRA proposals that were made by the Bush Administration and others.

8. CRA implementing regulations should be more specific in emphasizing banks' affirmative responsibility toward low- and moderate-income ("low-mod") people rather than areas.

According to the 1990 census, low- and moderate-income ("low-mod") households comprised 40% of the nation. This statistic follows from the definition of low- and moderate-income households as being those with an annual household income of 80% or below the median. Because a median is one measure of a distribution's point of central tendency, often around the 50% midpoint, 80% of 50% is 40%. The 1989 median household income, according to the 1990 census, was about $30,000. Low-income households making $15,000 (50% of the median) or less made up 25% of all households. Low- and moderate-income households making $24,000 (80% of the median) or less made up 40% of our nation's roughly 92 million households.

CRA specifies that a bank should ascertain and help meet the credit needs of its *entire* community, *including* low- and moderate-income neighborhoods. We feel that this legal standard, which is written into every public performance evaluation, may not be consistent with the true spirit of CRA in two ways. First, we believe that the focus of CRA should be on low- and moderate-income *people*, not neighborhoods. This is due to the simple fact that individuals of any income level can live in a defined low- and moderate-income neighborhood.

We saw in the case of Harris Bank of Chicago that fewer than one-third of approved real estate loans in low- and moderate-income areas were actually going to low- and moderate-income borrowers. This important difference between areas and individuals can represent a major loophole that can pervert many of the intended benefits of CRA. Therefore, we believe

that CRA examiners should be trained to focus on low- and moderate-income individuals and households, not necessarily areas.

If data were available on net worth, that would be an even better indication of overall wealth and need. Many low- and moderate-income individuals, such as retirees, have substantial net worth in the form of accumulated assets. A census tract or neighborhood with well-to-do retirees may likely be designated a low- and moderate-income area. Thus, a focus on the "stock" of wealth at a point in time rather than the "flow" of income over a period of time would be preferred. Because net worth data are very difficult to obtain, the idea of focusing on a low- and moderate-income area was meant to capture such individuals, but this is not always the case. That is why we would change the focus to such individuals not areas.

One prominent CRA vendor has already capitalized on the emphasis on low-mod areas by offering a software program that, in their words, "alerts" bank personnel that the loan applicant or preapplicant is calling from a low-mod census tract. While the use of such real-time responses to address demographics may provide some useful information, the potential for prescreening of loan applicants using this possible "tele-redlining" tool may be a reason for concern. Incidentally, that same CRA vendor provides a written "warranty" with their CRA compliance program that client banks will receive a satisfactory or outstanding rating or receive a refund of the license fee. This is really not that big of a risk for that vendor considering that the *a priori* probability of one or the other of these two ratings for any bank is 90%!

A related concern is that there is a great degree of inconsistency among evaluations and their treatment of "substantially minority" areas, usually defined as 50% or more minority. Some evaluations equate a substantially minority area with a low- and moderate-income area, but this is not always the case. Even though many minorities may be low- or moderate-income persons, this is not a fair or accurate generalization. Therefore, we recommend that the emphasis be placed on low- and moderate-income individuals rather than minority ones, unless it has been documented in the evaluation that there is no difference.

A second area of concern in this regard is the use of the term "including" with regard to low- and moderate-income neighborhoods. We would recommend that the operative word for purposes of CRA implementation and enforcement be "especially." not "including," notwithstanding the actual wording of CRA. The intent of CRA in an affirmative sense should be to help that group in particular, not as one of many groups. Because we are talking about a group that represents 40% of all American households, we do not think that this is an unnecessarily narrow focus.

We believe there would be a difference in how an examination would be conducted if the operative words were "especially low- and moderate-income individuals" rather than "including low- and moderate-income neighborhoods." Such a recommended change would also signal to bankers what they probably already knew as to whom should be the primary beneficiaries of CRA activities.

9. Unnecessary and irrelevant CRA documentation and paperwork that results in an unjustified regulatory burden to banks should be eliminated.

Banking always has and probably always will be the most heavily regulated industry in America. Bankers have learned to live with all types of regulations, including the least-liked one, CRA. However, it is unfair from the point of view of bankers and unproductive from the point of view of society to require an unnecessary regulatory burden on banks to meet a social compact responsibility. Of course, what is "unnecessary" is in the eyes of the beholder.

We have documented many instances where banks maintain elaborate and extensive CRA public files where no one but the banker who put them together and the CRA examiner who reviews them ever looks at them. This is also the case with CRA statements. The only exception is probably an occasional CRA researcher, such as the author, who is reminded on a daily basis that "you are the only one outside of our examiner who has ever requested our CRA statement or asked about our CRA public file."

As pointed out in our CRA Cost/Benefit Matrix, we believe there is a major trade-off of significant public policy concern between those activities that primarily benefit a CRA rating and those that primarily benefit the community (but also the rating). We believe that those required activities that emphasize form over function and primarily benefit the CRA rating with little or no tangible proof of benefiting the community may be considered unnecessarily burdensome. As noted above, chief among these possibilities would be the requirement to maintain an extensive CRA public file and to maintain and post a CRA statement.

We would also recommend that the regulators themselves provide a greater degree of encouragement to banks to get involved in shared CRA efforts. Examples of such efforts that primarily benefit the community, but reduce both the cost and risk of CRA activities that would otherwise be done on an individual basis, are provided in the southeastern quadrant of that matrix. We believe that many banks have overlooked the shared approach to meeting CRA responsibilities. Importantly, we feel that many national and, especially, state banking associations have missed an important opportunity to benefit their membership in this area.

10. The existing CRA system requires a major restructuring to become more performance oriented and less process oriented, with incentives for good CRA performance and disincentives for bad CRA performance.

We recommend a complete restructuring of the existing CRA system to make it more performance oriented and less process or documentation based. This proposal will be explained in detail in a following section.

The CRA Cost/Benefit Matrix identifies most of the relevant trade-offs involving CRA. A major public policy problem is that much of the existing CRA system emphasizes documentation or process items over performance items. In many cases the real beneficiary of several aspects of the existing CRA system is the new army of CRA vendors themselves, rather than the communities it was the intention to help in the first place.

At least in one case, involving the Federal Home Loan Bank of Cincinnati, a CRA consulting service is a source of profit to that government-sponsored enterprise. We would recommend that such membership services be provided on a cost-recovery basis only, like most other FHLBs, rather than competing with the private sector as a "public vendor." Contrary to the claims of the FHLB of Cincinnati, we believe there is at least the appearance of a potential conflict of interest when one government agency consults with banks for a fee to improve their CRA ratings by another government agency.

Congress put teeth into CRA in 1989 when the public disclosure of CRA evaluations and ratings was required. Notwithstanding the positive power of public disclosure, there are still some bankers at below-average CRA performing banks who just don't care about their low CRA rating. Bankers at some of the banks that have received one or more needs improvement or substantial noncompliance ratings could not care less about them, because they don't have any plans to branch, merge, or otherwise expand their corporate activities in a way that the regulators might prevent them from doing so. Some of the smaller banks, which have received single and multiple substantial noncompliance ratings, have been especially vocal about the "credit allocation," regulatory burden, and other criticisms of CRA. Based on the FED's November 1992 merger approval involving the Capital Bank of Clayton, Missouri, which received a substantial noncompliance and a needs improvement rating, the 11% of banks with below-average ratings may have little to be concerned about even if they want to branch or merge.

We recommend that CRA should have even sharper teeth than it does now with public disclosure by including specific disincentives for below-average ratings that can directly take a bite out of a bank's bottom line. Any effort by a "friendly" regulator to attempt to be lenient on a below-average rated bank would be more difficult under this approach, especially if there is little or no regulatory discretion as to the application of these disincentives.

Conversely, we see little in the way of real incentives for a bank to strive for an outstanding rating other than putting out a press release that they are in the top 10% of banks with that rating. We likewise believe that banks that have received this highest rating, which places them in the top decile of all banks, should have some type of special bottom line benefit. Proposals to benefit banks with outstanding

or satisfactory ratings have little merit, as the latter group represents four out of five banks.

Probably the first major "greenlining" program at the New York State Banking Department between 1985 and 1988 tied a bank's permissible amount of investment in real estate equity to the bank's state CRA rating. The Bank Enterprise Act, passed in 1991, rewards banks offering loans, investments, or "lifeline" accounts in low-income areas by reducing deposit insurance premiums, regardless of their CRA ratings. Some Federal Home Loan Banks offer banks preferential rates for advances if the funds are used for qualifying community investments, again regardless of the bank's CRA ratings. The FHLBs of Boston and Des Moines provide a five and ten basis point discount, respectively, on such advances to members with an outstanding CRA rating and FHFB community support review. Our specific recommendations, which would contain real incentives for the highest and disincentives for the lowest CRA ratings, are contained in a following section.

RECOMMENDATIONS TO EXPAND AND IMPROVE CRA DISCLOSURE

1. **Disclosure of CRA ratings and performance evaluations should be expanded.**

We believe the positive power of public disclosure has made an unqualified success of the disclosure of CRA ratings and public performance evaluations. Our analysis also addressed the question of the possible disclosure of the complete compliance ratings and examination reports.

Our review of a small number of overall compliance examination reports and ratings relative to CRA suggests that there is some additional CRA-relevant information in the confidential portion of the examination reports, but probably not enough to justify their release. In many instances the examiners are far more critical of a bank's CRA performance in the private as compared to the public report. To the extent "friendly" regulators may be protecting certain banks from the scrutiny of public disclosure in this or any other way, these regulators are undermining CRA enforcement. Most of the information contained within these overall compliance evaluations are confidential items involving specific cases and names of individuals in numerous instances. There is really no public benefit in the disclosure of confidential information that could embarrass or otherwise put a particular individual in an uncomfortable situation.

Our only concern, however, is that there is some relevant information of a nonconfidential nature that should be included in the CRA public performance evaluation (especially assessment factors D and F) that is not presently included in them. In the case of Norstar Bank, N.A., we noted that there may have been nonsubstantive, technical, or procedural compliance violations. The very general finding that the bank was in "substantial compliance" did not eliminate this possibility. The only way we would know that would be to review its confidential Report of Compliance Examination.

Other than taking the large step of recommending the public disclosure of overall compliance ratings and evaluations, we recommend that an independent and objective body such as the General Accounting Office review a representative sample of CRA ratings and public evaluations, along with their accompanying confidential overall compliance ratings and examination reports, to determine if CRA-relevant information has been left out. Because we only reviewed a small number of confidential compliance examinations, we are not in a position to draw a conclusion or make a recommendation based upon our limited analysis.

If, however, a comprehensive analysis of this type suggests that there has been relevant information not contained in the CRA public performance evaluations, consideration should be given to additional disclosures from the present confidential compliance examination report as well as the rating within it. An alternative approach may be to publish the overall compliance rating with the CRA rating but not disclose any portions of the compliance examination report, but this approach may raise more questions than it answers. More research is required on this topic.

Another area of recommended disclosure is a published listing of the results of the evaluations of the Community Support Statements (CSS) of members of the Federal Home Loan Banks (FHLBs). The CSS reviews by the Federal Housing Finance Board (FHFB) were required by FIRREA. These reviews do not include an on-site exam. They include consideration of a bank's CRA rating, however, as well as its first-time home buyer programs and public comments from "community groups and other interested parties" directly solicited by a FHLB. Each CSS is approved or disapproved by the FHFB. Those that are disapproved are requested to prepare a community support action plan that may be approved or disapproved. The penalty for noncompliance according to FIRREA could be limited access to FHLB advances of greater than one year. A bank or thrift may receive a satisfactory or even outstanding CRA rating, which may be based upon its performance regarding non-housing related credit products, but conceivably be disapproved and required to improve its CSS. Conversely, the FHFB might reach the opposite conclusion for a bank with a below-average CRA rating, if improvements were made since the time of the rating or if the bank was not given credit for out-of-area activities.

Our repeated efforts with the FHFB to obtain a listing of the results of CSS and action plan reviews with names of member banks were unsuccessful. We understand that the FHFB maintains a FOIA public file for each member bank in Washington, D.C., which contains the reviewed CSS and the finding, any public comments, and any action plan with the finding on it. While such relevant information will be disclosed for any requested bank, there is no regular (i.e., monthly or quarterly) CRA-type listing giving these data by bank. Without such a public listing, a bank could have a disapproved CSS review and action plan, but no one but the regulator and the regulated would know about it unless a specific written FOIA request for these results for that bank was made to the FHFB. A regularly published listing of the banks that will undergo a CSS review is not enough. What is needed additionally is a regular listing with all relevant results after the review not just before it. The disclosure of such a list can be justified on the same grounds as CRA ratings, namely the positive power of public disclosure. Also, greater disclosure in this area will be helpful in assessing the social costs and benefits of this program and whether or not a similar program involving banks and their access to the FED's discount window should be considered.

The one area where we feel that serious consideration should be given is the disclosure of a nonconfidential version of safety and soundness examinations, including the overall safety and soundness (CAMEL and MACRO) rating. We believe that some day safety and soundness ratings and a nonconfidential version of those examinations will be available on a regular basis. However, it will take time to get to that point because of heavy opposition not just by bankers but also, at least based upon our CRA experience, by the regulators themselves. A good first step would be the full disclosure of risk evaluations for individual banks as part of the new risk-adjusted deposit insurance assessment system.

A final area of expanded disclosure we recommend is in the area of previous public performance evaluations. Presently banks are only required to maintain their current evaluation, although they must have the previous year's CRA statement if it was different. As documented in various case studies here, we believe we can learn much more from comparing a present and past public performance evaluation than a CRA statement. Therefore, we recommend that both the banks themselves and the regulators be required to maintain and make available if requested copies of all past public performance evaluations.

2. CRA performance evaluations should contain more comprehensive disclosure of relevant information, including individual assessment factor and performance category ratings.

We recommend that all bank regulators require examiners to disclose individual ratings for the five performance categories and the individual assessment factors (including the reasonableness of the delineated area). The former ratings are now prepared but not publicly disclosed, but the latter ratings aren't even made any more. The West Region of the OTS and various Federal Reserve Banks prepared individual assessment factor ratings for awhile, but this practice has been discontinued.

We feel that the lack of disclosed individual assessment factor and performance category ratings has been a great disservice to informing the public of the true nature of a bank's CRA performance. We believe that this recommendation would greatly reduce cases of grade inflation and deflation, as examiners would now be required to justify their overall CRA rating on the basis of the component performance categories and assessment factors.

A secondary recommendation is that disclosed information in performance evaluations be more complete. We have previously noted several areas of inconsistency involving specific items that should be required on all performance evaluations, such as the review period, nonsubstantive violations, the relevant community, and so on.

3. Disclosure of CRA ratings and performance evaluations by both regulators and bankers alike should be more timely.

Delayed disclosure is diluted disclosure. We have documented instances where not only banks have benefited by the delayed disclosure of low CRA ratings but also the regulators themselves. The more time that elapses between the date of the examination and the public disclosure of an evaluation and rating, the more diluted is the value of that disclosure.

We therefore recommend that regulators be required to transmit the completed CRA evaluation and rating to the bank within a specified time (such as 45 total days) after the exit interview. We assume that there would be no unnecessary delays in the scheduling of the exit interviews. We also recommend that the public performance evaluation and rating be released to the public at the same time it is transmitted to the bank. The bank is already familiar with the recommended rating from the exit interview, so it will have the benefit of preparing for the public disclosure of it while the final report is being prepared by the examiners. Even if the complete compliance examination and rating is not available by that time, the CRA evaluation and rating should be returned to the bank within the above-mentioned time frame.

This approach would eliminate the problem of unnecessary and unwarranted delays in the disclosure of CRA ratings. The one case of apparent regulatory favoritism we identified had an unnecessarily long delay between the time of the exam and the time the evaluation and rating were finally made public.

Any potential favoritism whereby a "friendly" regulator could protect a bank from having to make a low rating public by delaying the return of the evaluation and rating to the bank would be eliminated under this approach.

The disclosure of CRA ratings should be more widespread than it is presently. Under the present disclosure system, a bank can receive its public performance evaluation and rating and make it public 30 business days later. In reality no one may know about it unless they just happen to ask about it. The only "official notification" that such a rating and evaluation has been made public and is available is when the regulators on a weekly, monthly, or quarterly basis publish such a notice listing all banks or those in a region. These regulatory releases are generally read by interested bankers, regulators, consultants, community groups, and the media, but very rarely by the general public. In the case of the quarterly releases by the OTS, a thrift may have a few more months of "nondisclosure" because of the delay between their releases.

We therefore recommend that banks be required to publish a notice of the availability of a public evaluation and the actual CRA rating similar to a branch application announcement. Banks would be required to publish these notices in a local paper of wide circulation in each of the respective markets in which the bank operates within a short period (such as five business days) from when the bank receives the public evaluation and CRA rating.

We believe that the benefits of public disclosure would also be enhanced if banks and their regulators were required to publish a schedule as to when individual banks would be receiving their next compliance exams. Many banks don't even have this information themselves. Therefore, we recommend that the regulators be required to publish and stick to a fairly strict schedule as to when their banks will be examined for CRA compliance. This schedule could be a function of CRA ratings as it is today but on a consistent basis, such as every six months for banks with substantial noncompliance ratings, nine months for needs improvement, one year for satisfactory, and one-and-one-half years for the recommended "good" rating, and every two years for banks with outstanding ratings. This type of rating-based exam scheduling

is in itself an incentive for above-average CRA ratings and a disincentive for below-average ratings. Also, interested members of the public will have a better idea of the examination process and how and when to become involved in it if desired. The previously recommended compliance super-regulator would not only have a more consistent examination schedule but also be responsible for disseminating a no-charge, regular (weekly) list of completed CRA ratings.

4. CRA ratings and performance evaluations should be made and disclosed for individual banking markets.

The fact that four out of five CRA ratings are "satisfactory" limits our ability to distinguish among different banks' CRA performance. The increased consolidation and centralization of banks tends to result in more satisfactory ratings because it happens to be the most convenient average of both good and bad ratings alike. It is the CRA rating of least resistance by all parties and clearly the regulators' choice in most cases.

The problem of proliferating satisfactory ratings is especially acute in the case of large interstate banking operations that may have vastly different CRA performances in different states. The idea of assigning one CRA rating to a multistate operation is almost inconsistent with the concept of evaluating how a bank is serving its local community. For this reason we recommend that at a minimum interstate banking operations receive separate performance evaluations and ratings for each of the individual states in which they operate. The Great Western case study documented the need for this minimum requirement.

We believe that this line of reasoning should be taken a step further, not only for interstate banks but also for large statewide banks that operate in many different markets around a state. Because their CRA performance may not be equal in all of those areas, the preferred approach is to have individual performance evaluations and ratings by banking market. We believe that this approach should only be applicable to very large statewide banking operations with a minimum market share in a given market. For example, the five largest banks in a given banking market (based upon readily available, mid-year FDIC deposit market share data) may be required to have a separate performance evaluation and rating for that market.

Thus, instead of most large statewide banking operations receiving a satisfactory rating for a combination of good, bad, and mostly average CRA performances around a state, we would now know exactly how they are meeting their CRA obligations in the major markets in which they operate. Large statewide banks would no longer be able to "hide" their poor CRA performance in a particular market with an all-encompassing satisfactory rating, and this form of grade inflation would be eliminated. We believe that the increased regulatory burden of this recommendation would mainly fall upon the regulators themselves rather than the banks, especially if our recommended approach of a streamlined and more objective examination is adopted.

5. **There should be publicly-disclosed written guidelines on the conditions for issuing CRA-related informal versus formal enforcement actions, conditional approvals versus denials of branch and merger applications, civil money penalties, and Justice Department referrals.**

Just as we have written guidelines for specific public CRA ratings, there should be similar ones for cease and desist (C&D) orders, application denials, civil money penalties, and Justice Department referrals on compliance and especially CRA grounds.

The post-FIRREA disclosure of C&D orders has been a success, but not a total one until all of the conditions of their issuances are likewise public. Of particular concern is regulatory circumvention of public disclosure through use of confidential "informal enforcement actions" that are not publicly reported. What are the conditions under which these informal actions are issued? Two case studies described here showed that C&D orders wholly or partly on CRA grounds could be issued against a bank with a substantial noncompliance *or* needs improvement rating.

A specific guideline on C&D order issuances or other enforcement actions on CRA grounds may be related to consecutive substantial noncompliance ratings. For example, a C&D order could be appropriate for any bank receiving two consecutive substantial noncompliance ratings but required in the case of three such ratings. Table 8-2 identifies two small banks (one in Illinois and the other in Wyoming) that would fall in the latter category. If three consecutive substantial noncompliance ratings over three years won't activate a C&D order on CRA grounds, what should?

This same question could be asked regarding branch and merger denials, civil money penalties, and Justice Department referrals on CRA and related compliance grounds. It appears that regulators have tremendous discretionary powers in these CRA enforcement areas. Particularly troubling is the regulators' unilateral discretion over when to issue an application denial in contrast to their preferred approach of issuing conditional approvals. At least in the case of Justice Department referrals, the FDIC Improvement Act of 1991 has specified conditions which would trigger such a referral. However, there had been only one such referral through mid-year 1992, and five to date, three of which were referred by the FDIC only at the repeated insistence of Congress.

A PROPOSAL FOR A RESTRUCTURED CRA SYSTEM WITH A "CRA ASSESSMENT"

One of the most important public policy issues involving CRA is whether or not all banks have a CRA obligation. We believe this to be the case. We are opposed to scaling bank coverage of the CRA umbrella to just bigger banks (greater than $100 million in assets) as has been proposed by both the banking lobby and the former Bush Administration. We would argue alternatively, that the coverage should be *expanded* to other nonbank financial institutions now exempt from CRA, such as credit unions at a minimum.

Assuming that all banks have a CRA obligation, the next important public policy issue involves the most efficient allocation of funds directed towards CRA. In other words, how can CRA expenditures best benefit the local communities, *especially* targeted low- and moderate-income ("low-mod") individuals? That is, how can CRA be structured to encourage form over function, substance over style, or performance over process rather than the opposite, which is often true today?

Another way of viewing this tradeoff is with reference to the CRA Cost/Benefit Matrix (Figure 10-1). That is, what is the most efficient approach to reaching the right hand side of the matrix representing high performance (function), which primarily benefits the community, versus the left hand side representing high documentation (form), which primarily benefits a bank's CRA rating? The southeastern quadrant involving shared efforts represents the most efficient solution from the perspective of individual banks spreading both operating costs and risks. The northeastern quadrant involving individual efforts is not as efficient.

The Clinton Administration approach to community development will reportedly include a nationwide network of 100 community development banks funded by nearly $1 billion in federal aid. This approach is encouraging, but it would be even better to improve the CRA performance of our roughly 14,000 existing banks in *all* communities throughout our country rather than just at 100 new banks in certain hand-picked communities. CRA was meant for all banks serving their entire community, not just special-purpose ones in certain communities. Any emphasis on the latter approach may be perceived as detracting from the former one. Moreover, it would probably be 1995 or 1996 before a new network of community development banks could make a difference in lending in these 100 selected communities, and Clinton's present term will have ended by then. If there is going to be real change in our communities in the Clinton presidency, it must come through our existing banking network, not a new one. The proposal below is our recommended approach for a truly effective and restructured CRA system.

Our recommended approach includes the imposition of an explicit assessment or "CRA tax," the proceeds of which directly benefit local communities, especially low-mod ones. This is an outright annual assessment by a federal regulatory agency rather than a CRA pledge or commitment by a bank to make a certain type of loan.

A banker may look at this proposal and say, "What's new about a CRA tax? We already have one!" In other words, all of the documentation and other CRA compliance requirements today effectively represent an implicit CRA tax. This proposal is about making a portion of this implicit tax explicit, but at the same time removing most costly procedural tasks that really don't benefit local communities.

Just as a bank's deposit insurance premium represents a certain explicit cost to banking operations, so too could CRA compliance. The *quid pro quo* would be that one lump sum amount (i.e., the explicit CRA tax) would replace most of the significant management time and expenses associated with CRA compliance (i.e., the implicit CRA tax).

These costs are not trivial. The American Bankers Association (ABA) conducted a comprehensive survey of all bank compliance costs in June 1992. That study concluded that commercial banks spent $10.7 billion in 1991 on direct and indirect costs for all regulatory compliance, not just CRA. The Independent Bankers Association of America (IBAA), which represents community banks, completed a January 1993 study titled *Regulatory Burden: The Cost to Community Banks*, wherein it estimated that 1992 compliance costs for 13 regulations were $11 billion. Of course, both of these industry studies are silent on the *benefits* of such regulations in terms of consumer protection and even assistance to the banks themselves in certain areas. A December 17, 1992, *Study on Regulatory Burden* by the FFIEC estimated that 1991 regulatory costs for the banking industry could be between $7.5 billion and $17 billion.

We will use the ABA's $10.7 billion estimated cost of regulatory compliance. This total represented 40 basis points of the $2.7 trillion in average 1991 commercial bank deposits. Applying this same percentage to the $3.6 trillion of average 1991 deposits of all commercial and mutual savings banks and private savings and loan associations yields an estimated $14.5 billion in 1991 total compliance costs. This averages about $1 million for every bank and thrift in the country, although the biggest institutions pay the lion's share of these costs. However, it is well known that there are economies of scale in these costs, meaning that bigger banks have a relative cost advantage over smaller banks in this area.

Although no specific compliance cost for CRA was calculated, the ABA study hastened to point out that seven in ten survey respondents cited CRA as their "greatest regulatory concern." That study also reported that 40% of all banks cited CRA as "giving CEOs the most headaches." Also, 34% of all banks cited CRA as the "most time consuming regulation" for CEOs, and the comparable percentage for compliance managers/officers was 42%. Moreover, several "examination time" summaries of compliance exams by bank regulators we reviewed suggested that CRA represents between 25% and 40% of total compliance examination time.

Let us conservatively assume from these findings that CRA represents 30% of all compliance costs. There was no such specific finding in that ABA study, but this assumption doesn't appear to be a terribly unreasonable one based on these survey results. In fact, the recent IBAA study estimated that CRA represents 31.8% of all compliance costs and 30.4% of all compliance hours expended for community banks. Applying this 30% assumed factor to the 1991 total compliance cost for all banks and thrifts of $14.5 billion results in an estimated $4.4 billion CRA compliance cost.

That is, all banks and thrifts spent an estimated $4.4 billion, representing approximately 12 basis points of 1991 average deposits, to comply with CRA. Since all or most of these direct and indirect compliance costs did not directly benefit local communities, as CRA originally intended, this obviously represents a significant public policy concern. This is especially true considering the adverse impact on bank productivity and competitiveness the CRA regulatory burden may have.

According to the same ABA survey, most (55%) of total bank compliance costs are "indirect," including hardware/software costs and noncompliance staff time. The rest is attributed to the compliance staff (15%), outside compliance vendors (13%), employee training (10%), and training materials (7%). Assuming this cost breakdown is also appropriate to the estimated $4.4 billion CRA compliance costs, the bulk of this money is going everywhere but in the local community (unless compliance personnel or vendors live there).

Thus, a CRA assessment would result in a shift of wealth from these compliance and documentation sources to the local community. This would literally represent a "reinvestment" of current dollars for such compliance and documentation activities back into the local community—the original intent of CRA. Our proposal would substitute an explicit assessment for the implicit cost of CRA compliance.

We would not repeal or "gut" CRA in lieu of an assessment but greatly streamline it to focus on function over form. We would not require *any* of the documentation items on the left side of the CRA Cost/Benefit Matrix. That is, banks would no longer be required to maintain a CRA public file, statement, plan, geocoding analysis, training program, and so on. All such documentation, which mainly benefits the CRA rating today, would just not be required.

Rather, the streamlined CRA exam would be based strictly on performance in meeting community credit needs, *especially* (not just "including") those of low-mod individuals. Banks would be judged by such items as those on the right side of the CRA Cost/Benefit Matrix (Figure 10-1).

The exams would be much shorter and more objective than today, with the focus on quantitative, not qualitative factors, as detailed in a previous recommendation. Examiners would now look for how community credit needs are being met, not how they're being ascertained. Examiners, not bankers, would conduct any desired loan geocoding analysis to determine the proportion of local lending, low-mod lending, average loan size by type, and loan-to-deposit ratios (relative to loan quality). Examiners would calculate these and other basic statistics for the examiner-defined local community and other relevant areas and then compare them to peers and past periods. The calculation of certain basic HMDA denial rate trends and a complete assessment of all compliance violations by the examiners would be mandatory, as these items would play an important role in the final ratings.

We would propose a much more objective rating system, with public written guidelines which would suggest certain ratings under certain conditions. For example, as previously suggested, *any* substantive compliance violation would require a below-average rating, and cases of multiple and repeated such violations would trigger a substantial noncompliance rating. Other factors that could result in a below-average rating would be persistent and unjustified very low loan-to-deposit ratios (such as 15% – 25% or less) and repeated significant HMDA "gaps" measuring differences in minority and nonminority loan denial rates.

Banks would know exactly what would and would not get CRA credit. For example, CRA credit would be given for charitable contributions to low-mod housing and related groups, but not for general charities. CRA credit would be given for CRA loans anywhere, even outside the local community. CRA credit also would be given for lifeline accounts, free government check cashing, branches maintained in low-mod areas (especially where other banks have left), low or no minimum loan amounts, special or flexible terms for low-mod loans, participation in government lending programs, or other special credit projects benefiting low-mod individuals. The exam would be more of a quantitative, streamlined "checklist" type, with certain ratios and yes/no or numerical answers rather than lengthy narrative ones, which are inherently more subjective. All assessment factor and performance category ratings would be public.

Banks would receive public ratings (ideally including a fifth "good" category) and a written public evaluation, as is the case today, but it would be more objective, streamlined, and standardized. The substantial savings to banks as a result of this significantly reduced compliance burden would form the basis for the required CRA assessment. It would average 6 basis points of average deposits and be a function of a bank's CRA rating. We chose 6 rather than 12 basis points to recognize the likelihood that banks might still be incurring some of the "built-in" CRA compliance costs under the new program. Also, in the event that some of those costs were overstated in the original estimates, the impact on banks would be lessened. Finally, use of half of the estimated average cost for the recommended program would result in a more politically acceptable alternative.

This new approach to CRA compliance would be analogous to the new and long overdue risk-adjusted deposit premiums where riskier banks pay more and less risky ones pay less. In our case, below-average CRA performers pay more, and above-average ones pay less, so the assessment acts as an incentive for good ratings and a disincentive for bad ones.

Under our proposal, banks with a satisfactory rating would pay the average 6 basis point annual assessment on average deposits. Outstanding-rated banks would not be required to pay any assessment, the ultimate incentive for truly exceptional CRA performance. Those banks with the recommended fifth, "good," rating would be assessed 3 basis points. Banks with needs improvement ratings would pay 9 basis points, and those with a substantial noncompliance rating would be assessed a 12 basis point rate.

The CRA examinations and assessments would be administered by the previously recommended newly created, centralized, and specialized federal compliance agency rather than the current four individual bank regulators. CRA assessment receipts would have approximated $2.2 billion in 1991 alone, assuming a normal ratings distribution. These receipts would be returned by the new agency on a pro-rata basis through governmental agencies to the originating communities, *especially* (not including) low-mod ones. Annual FDIC and OTS deposit data as of June 30 each year are already readily available by originating state, metropolitan area, and county to expedite the administrative side of this annual CRA funds distribution process. Guidelines would be established to make certain the ultimate beneficiaries of these funds are low-mod individuals, so there is no Harris Bank type of misallocation.

Obviously, one advantage of this compliance-adjusted CRA assessment is that something in addition to the positive power of public disclosure would be working to encourage banks to improve their CRA performance and rating. Namely, the *added* penalty or disincentive (3 basis points for needs improvement and 6 basis points for substantial noncompliance) for a below-average rating.

Those bankers with below-average ratings who have no plans to branch or merge and could not care less about the current public disclosure of their ratings would now have a new motivation to improve their compliance efforts. CRA would have real "teeth" that would take a bite out of the earnings of a below-average CRA performing bank. Conversely, there would be a new motivation (i.e., no assessment) for banks to seek an outstanding rating and a 3 basis point incentive for those with the recommended fifth, "good," rating.

This recommended assessment structure could be changed depending on public policy. The average 6 basis point assessment, for example, could be gradually increased to the fully phased-in CRA cost estimate of 12 basis points over time. The rating differentials representing incentives/disincentives would be changed under this more motivating alternative (i.e., with "sharper" teeth) as follows: outstanding—0; good—6 basis points; satisfactory—12; needs improvement—18; and, substantial noncompliance—24.

Another advantage of this CRA assessment proposal is that it explicitly recognizes that compliance costs are here to stay. The proposed assessment represents a cost of doing business in what is an increasingly pro-consumer banking environment of the 90s. Banks could now associate a range of annual costs for CRA compliance, much the same as is the case with the FDIC insurance assessment, so they could spend their time on more productive areas. There would no longer be any uncertainty as to what type of documentation would be required for a good rating, as performance, not process, would be the basis for the rating.

In summary, we believe our concept of a compliance adjusted CRA assessment deserves serious consideration as an alternative to the current CRA system. We are not suggesting that CRA be eliminated but be restructured to benefit local communities, especially low-mod ones. This approach would stress form over function, substance over style, and performance over process. It would work within the structure of our existing banking system rather than a newly created one. Banks, regulators, and community groups alike may consider this an equitable approach to the trade-offs inherent in the CRA Cost/Benefit Matrix.

CRA MYTHOLOGY—THE 25 MOST POPULAR MYTHS ABOUT CRA

It is not surprising that a number of myths about CRA would develop over time, considering how misunderstood this law is by so many people and how unpopular it is with bankers. Some of what we label as myths are really misunderstandings and misinterpretations, but others are nothing more than lore or outright untruths that are unsubstantiated by the facts. Some CRA myths are more widespread than others, and some are more shocking than others. None of them, however, are correct based upon our research, and that is why we refer to them as myths.

1. CRA is for poor people and minorities, especially African Americans in the inner cities.

CRA is for the *entire* community, including (not especially or exclusively) low- and moderate-income areas. According to the 1990 Census, low- and moderate-income households represent 40% of America. Thus, CRA is for 100% of America, including that 40%.

2. CRA means "credit allocation"—the government is trying to tell banks where to make loans.

CRA is about *ascertaining* and *helping to meet* the credit needs of a bank's entire community. Since lending is the "basic business of banking," CRA is just reaffirming what most banks have been doing all along. CRA was written, implemented, and enforced in such a way as to specifically avoid credit allocation, although CRA critics probably will never accept this argument. CRA critics may view the idea of reinvesting deposits taken out of a community back into it as credit allocation, but "reinvestment" is CRA's middle name. Because certain low- and moderate-income areas may have been redlined and unfairly denied credit in the past, the CRA initiative to treat all areas (i.e., the entire community) fairly is often perceived as a government effort to "force" banks to lend in those affected areas.

3. CRA is just more "red tape" by Big Government bureaucrats who are strangling bankers in a sea of endless regulations.

Banking always has been and probably always will be America's most heavily regulated business. But there are several good reasons for many of these regulations, especially important consumer protection legislation such as CRA. Yes, regulations have their costs to bankers, but regulations also have benefits to the public and even the banks themselves in some cases.

4. CRA is anticapitalistic and borders on socialism.

All banks, and nonbanks for that matter, should have a "social conscience." This is especially true when they directly or indirectly benefit from the government in such areas as federal (and previously underpriced) deposit insurance, access to a "lender of last resort," and regulations that help insulate a bank from competition in certain areas. We believe bank and nonbank companies should maximize profits but subject to some social constraint. We call this "Capitalism with a Corporate Conscience." Capitalism can have a social conscience and still be a far cry from socialism. Many social good deeds have nothing to do with socialism except for sharing the same root word.

5. There was never a need for CRA in the first place. It was an unprecedented government intrusion into an industry that was doing fine without it.

The problem was that the banking industry was not doing fine for everyone. The Bank of North America case taught us that the CRA spirit of equal opportunity for credit for everyone has been around for over 200 years, since that first bank of a modern type was established in Philadelphia in 1781. But not all banks operated in that spirit. Alleged redlining and other discriminatory practices in banking resulted in various pro-consumer regulations and legislation in the mid-1970s, including the 1977 CRA. The perceived failure of the market to fairly allocate loanable funds, especially in our inner cities and other low- and moderate-income areas, is what precipitated CRA in the first place. Whenever the marketplace's invisible hand is perceived as inefficient or failing in its economic goals, government's heavy hand of regulation is not far behind.

6. Community activists and others who support CRA are "trouble makers" looking for publicity, confrontation, and especially money for their causes if they can "extort" it from bankers.

CRA is the law and has been since 1977. Community groups are the most likely supporters of this pro-consumer law. There would be no reason why bankers or their lawyers, consultants, lobbyists, trade associations, or the like would defend CRA, when most of them probably feel the law is directed against banks. Interestingly, though, the Independent Bankers Association of America attempted to use CRA to its benefit when it requested a CRA investigation of NCNB Texas National Bank on behalf of its members, much like a community group would do on behalf of its members. Sure, there are probably some questionable community groups with separate agendas, just as there are some problem banks. But most community groups, like banks, probably act in the public interest.

7. Discrimination, like redlining, has only been alleged but never proven in banking.

Discrimination, like redlining, is to a great extent in the eyes of the beholder. And, it is not unexpected that someone with dark skin and brown eyes sees more discrimination than someone with light skin and blue eyes. Bankers are quite unlikely to view any lending action or lack thereof as discrimination, while a denied loan applicant will often take the opposite position. Surprisingly, the American Bankers Association and the OCC have taken the unprecedented step of admitting the existence of some types of discrimination in banking. Also, several specific acts of lending discrimination have been identified in the public performance evaluations and cease and desist orders of banks with below-average ratings. The October 1992 Federal Reserve Bank of Boston's landmark study documented that racial discrimination in mortgage lending is a widespread phenomenon, and such a conclusion was also alleged in the Justice Department's investigation of the Decatur Federal case in Atlanta. There will likely be more studies by the government and other organizations that will reach similar conclusions about racial discrimination.

8. **It's just a matter of time before CRA goes away. The continued lobbying by the banking industry, which had the full support of the Bush Administration, is certain to be successful in rolling back and ultimately "gutting" CRA.**

First of all, the Bush anti-CRA policy has been replaced by what is expected to be the Clinton pro-CRA policy. The CRA spirit of equal opportunity for credit has been around for over 200 years, not just since the 1977 law. The pro-consumer movement in banking is too strong to allow a repeal or significant weakening of CRA, especially with a pro-consumer Democratic congress and administration. If banks and their lobbies can kill or handicap the least-liked law in banking, the removal or weakening of any other pro-consumer law or regulation would be relatively easy. CRA is almost a "sacred" consumer protection law in the sense that it stands for the basic right of equal opportunity for credit by the entire community. If CRA is "gutted" or killed, the major line of defense of the pro-consumer movement in banking is gone, and it probably would just be a matter of time before there were more pro-consumer casualties.

9. **CRA loans are risky loans.**

No bank ever failed because of CRA. In fact, CRA specifically states that any activities should be consistent with the safe and sound operation of the institution. If loans to low- and moderate-income areas are considered "CRA loans," then all of these certainly can't be risky. After all, 40% of American households are low- and moderate-income, and loans to 40% of America can't all be risky. All loans have some risk, and the risk inherent in "CRA loans" like others is manageable. Also, there is some evidence that the risk experience on some "CRA loans" has been much more favorable than expected. This is especially true compared to some other loan categories, such as those involving lesser developed countries (LDCs), leveraged buyouts (LBOs), commercial real estate, and the like. Also, the favorable loan-loss experiences of the few community development "CRA banks" in

existence further support this claim that "CRA loans" aren't necessarily risky loans.

10. **CRA can't be profitable. It can only cost a bank money.**

The basic and most profitable business of banking is lending. CRA is about a bank's affirmative obligation to help meet credit needs in its entire community, which is nothing more than this basic business. Ascertaining these credit needs, the other part of CRA, is a basic marketing function. The marketing concept is about understanding and satisfying customer needs in a manner consistent with corporate objectives. Yes, a proper interpretation of CRA would indicate that it is not inconsistent with profitability. Actually, some of our nation's most profitable small and large banks are truly outstanding CRA performers. And, as noted above, "CRA banks" such as the few community development banks in existence have survived and made money.

11. **The disclosure of CRA evaluations and ratings only confuses the public. In fact, below-average CRA ratings may be confused with safety and soundness ratings.**

This myth, which the banking lobby pushed to prevent those FIRREA disclosures, was shattered shortly after the July 1, 1990, release of CRA evaluations and ratings. With two and one-half years of experience under the new system, we have not documented one such instance of confusion between CRA and safety and soundness ratings. To the contrary, the Farmers & Merchants Bank case study taught us that the public can not only discriminate between the two types of ratings but can actually make investment decisions based upon this distinction. The public disclosure of CRA ratings and evaluations since 1984 by the New York State Banking Department has likewise not resulted in any such major confusion problems, according to that department.

12. **CRA contributes to the "credit crunch."**

The ABA has gone so far as to claim that there would be an additional $86 billion for credit *if* Congress reduced the regulatory burden of such laws as CRA.

CRA is about *expanding* credit, not *contracting* it! The credit crunch primarily has been an economic phenomenon associated with the 1990–1991 recession and the very gradual recovery. We had many credit crunches before the 1977 CRA, and we will certainly have more in the future. To make CRA a "whipping boy" for economic or other maladies is unfair but not unexpected for banking's most intensely disliked law.

13. CRA is not needed for community or other small banks. If they weren't adequately serving their community, they would be out of business.

Most banks, roughly three-fourths by numbers, are small banks. To exempt small banks from CRA, as has been repeatedly proposed, would effectively "gut" this law. Actually, small banks of $100 million or less (and especially $25 million or less) in assets have a disproportionately low percentage of above-average ratings. Just because a bank is a "full service" one making a profit doesn't necessarily mean it's adequately ascertaining and helping to meet community credit needs. Many small banks are in one-bank towns where there is little or no effective competition, which often reduces the incentive for such banks to be innovative and aggressive in serving customer needs. CRA is needed for all banks and even some nonbanks.

14. Only big banks, with their resources to document and meet other paperwork requirements, can get outstanding ratings.

This myth was easily and quickly disproved with the earliest CRA ratings distributions by size. Outstanding ratings have been fairly well distributed by size, with the exception of the smallest banks, which have received less than their expected share. Many small banks that are part of and have access to the resources of the largest bank holding companies have received below-average ratings. Bank subsidiaries of Chemical Banking Corporation of New York, for example, have received all four CRA ratings. Also, our analysis of the CRA ratings of the 100 largest banks and 50 largest thrifts revealed that the proportion of outstanding ratings was only 33.0% and 45.9%, respectively.

15. Any bank can get an outstanding rating if it's willing to spend the money for CRA "megapledges," consultants, surveys, geocoding software, and the like.

Many banks that are part of giant bank holding companies (e.g., NationsBank Corporation) which have made CRA megapledges have received only satisfactory ratings. Likewise, many banks that have expended substantial sums for CRA consultants or other vendors have received average and below-average ratings. It is not clear, however, whether or not those banks would have received even lower ratings without such outside assistance. Conversely, many community banks with outstanding ratings earned them through internal efforts with nominal out-of-pocket expenses. These and other experiences suggest that an outstanding rating can't be "bought."

16. CRA documentation doesn't matter. If a bank is an average or above-average CRA performer, the examiners will determine this on their own without documentation.

Our research has verified the continued relevance and truth of "CRA Survival Rule #1"—"If it wasn't documented, it wasn't done." Regardless of what regulators or examiners say, documentation always has and probably always will rule the day for CRA under the present system.

17. All banks strive for an outstanding CRA rating.

There is a small fraction of banks that could not care less about CRA or any such evaluation or rating. Most banks who do care about their disclosed evaluation and rating would probably state their goal as an outstanding rating. We believe, however, that an increasing number of banks are following a "satisficing" objective where their real unstated goal is just a satisfactory rating, which four out of five banks receive. Bell Federal of Chicago, which received a needs improvement rating, reportedly made a satisfactory rating their goal. Some bankers may feel an outstanding rating may be "impossible" to obtain or at least not worth the cost or effort trying for it. Even if they get that rating, some bankers may believe that the positive publicity associated with it may require a bank to do "too much" to maintain that rating for the next examination.

18. The best way for a bank to perform a good "CRA deed" is to do it by itself.

"CRA credit" may be maximized when a bank takes on a CRA project by itself, but the risks and costs of the project are borne totally by the bank. The ideal approach from both a private and public perspective in many respects is to *share* CRA projects with other banks. Those banks acting in an originating or leadership role should receive more CRA credit than other participants. Shared loan consortiums are quite common today, but other shared arrangements, such as credit needs ascertainment surveys, loan counseling centers, and even shared branches, are much less common.

19. The subjectivities, inconsistencies, and other problems with CRA examination procedures mean CRA isn't working and should be scrapped.

CRA is working, but it can be improved. This is especially true in the area of examination procedures, which must become more objective and consistent. We don't need *lesser* CRA enforcement. What we need is *better* CRA enforcement.

20. "The reason our bank got a below-average CRA rating was because of documentation problems. Government bureaucrats felt we didn't dot our i's and cross our t's."

This myth represents the most common rationalization by far for a below-average rating. Few banks will accept all of the criticisms in the public evaluation. Many, therefore, conveniently shift the blame for their low rating to the evaluation and rating process itself. Because the documentation factor is the most common, well-known, and easily understood criticism, it is the CRA excuse of choice by bankers with low CRA ratings.

21. CRA examiners are young, inexperienced, and only in compliance because they "couldn't handle" safety and soundness exams.

Bankers displeased with their evaluations or ratings may not only use the documentation excuse (see above) but also blame their CRA examiners. After all, any subjective evaluation or rating such as CRA can easily be criticized by anyone, but especially those who feel victimized by a below-average rating. Public CRA evaluations and ratings are a first in banking, and there was bound to be a long learning curve. Compliance is a real growth area in banking regulation, and new compliance examiners are being continuously hired and trained. Many new CRA examiners are young and inexperienced, but so is the idea of public CRA evaluations and ratings. Yes, the current system needs to be improved, but this will take time. We believe most CRA examiners likely have chosen compliance as a long-term career path because they believe it is a vitally important area, not because they weren't "safety and soundness types." It is likely that bankers displeased with their safety and soundness evaluations and ratings privately voice a similar criticism against those examiners, but there is much less at stake when the government's veil of secrecy prevents any disclosure.

22. Bankers are the only ones opposed to the public disclosure of confidential bank examinations and ratings.

The disclosure of CRA evaluations and ratings has taught us that regulators have as much if not more vested interest in discouraging further disclosure of confidential bank examinations and ratings as do the bankers themselves. We have documented specific cases of grade inflation and deflation as well as a case of apparent regulatory favoritism. We have to wonder if these subjective and inconsistent examination procedures are unique to CRA or are also the case with safety and soundness examinations and ratings. We will never know the answer to this question without the positive power of public disclosure.

23. **Banking is a private business. The government has already made too much bank information public, like CRA ratings and evaluations and cease and desist orders. All of this publicity is bad for banking!**

Public disclosure is bad for bad banks but good for the others. We need more, not less, disclosure, not just in CRA but in other areas like safety and soundness. Our research has shown that the discipline of public disclosure makes good bankers better and bad bankers mad. Likewise, good regulators become better and bad regulators, who are too "friendly" with or protective of banks, are forced to change for the better.

24. **The FED plays the smallest role in CRA enforcement of the four federal regulators because only 7% of all banks and thrifts are FED-regulated member banks.**

The FED was the first regulator to have specialized compliance examiners, some 12 years before the other regulators. The FED has the smallest number of member banks of any regulator but the largest compliance examination force relative to member banks, with only 6 banks per compliance examiner compared to a national average of 22 for all regulators. The FED has a unique role as overseer of all bank holding company activities, which account for the bulk of the banking industry. It therefore has the opportunity to use its regulatory muscle to pressure and effectively override CRA enforcement efforts of the FDIC, OTS, AND OCC. This opportunity apparently became a reality recently when the FED effectively overruled an OCC merger denial involving First Commercial Bank, N.A. of Memphis, Tennessee. Thus, the FED, the "CRA enforcer of last resort," actually plays the biggest role in CRA enforcement of the four federal bank regulators.

25. **The FED always has and always will be the "toughest" of the four federal banking regulators, whether in safety and soundness or in compliance.**

While the FED has always been thought of as the toughest regulator, our research has shown that this

would apply only to safety and soundness and certainly not to compliance, especially CRA. In fact, we have determined that the FED is the most lax CRA enforcer of all four banking regulators, based on past and present relative CRA ratings and the infrequency and near-rarity of "true" CRA enforcement activities. The FED's primary CRA enforcement tools are "jawboning," pro-CRA policy statements, and "conditional" approvals. Only in one instance has the FED rolled out most of its heavy CRA artillery (cease and desist orders, application denials, and civil money penalties); but, they were all fired at one bank, the Farmers and Merchants Bank of Long Beach, California. Thus, the FED, like many of the banks it criticizes, is itself long on process and short on performance when it comes to true CRA enforcement.

CRA TRENDS IN THE 90s.

This concluding section will summarize 15 recent and likely trends involving CRA that we believe will dominate much of the direction of CRA in the 90s. Many of these trends are based upon "gut" feelings and practical experience in CRA rather than specific facts from the present analysis.

1. *We believe there will be repeated efforts by the banking lobby to kill or handicap CRA during the 90s, but none of these will be really successful because of the increasingly proconsumer environment of the 90s, and especially the expected pro-CRA position of the Clinton Administration.*

2. *We believe that the "Corporate Conscience of Capitalism" will become more evident than ever before during the 90s. We believe there will be new efforts to expand the scope and concept of CRA to nonbank and other financial institutions.*

3. *We believe that each of the three elements of the CRA triangle—community groups, regulators, and banks—will become larger and more powerful. We further believe that the past adversarial relationships that existed among these elements of the CRA triangle will continue. We believe, however, that regulators in the expect-*

ed pro-CRA Clinton Administration will become somewhat more closely aligned to the goals of community groups than with bank goals.

4. We expect "CRA duality," which consists of both federal and state CRA regulations, will continue stronger than ever. We believe more states will enact CRA and related compliance laws, especially with the increasing "colonization" of certain states (Arizona and Florida), increased concentration of market power, loss of local control because of the elimination of head offices, and the exporting of local deposits out of state. If individual states do not develop their own CRA regulations, we believe we will see an increasing number of states and even large municipalities requiring banks to make certain CRA disclosures or perhaps to maintain a satisfactory or better rating for certain government business. The possibility of a state deposit assessment (tax) on all local deposits "exported" out of state to be lent or invested elsewhere by the holding company would be most appealing in large "banking colonies" like Arizona or Florida.

5. We expect to see stricter CRA enforcement by federal regulators, partly enhanced by an expanded and specialized compliance examination force at the OCC. More stringent CRA enforcement will be seen in the issuance of additional branch and merger denials and cease and desist orders on CRA and related grounds. Additionally, we expect to see more rigorous sanctions against banks with below-average CRA ratings. We have already seen the Federal Housing Finance Board impose a requirement tying access to their long-term advances at the Federal Home Loan Banks to a member's community performance. The regulatory penalty system will likely result in more monetary damages in extreme cases, such as the FED's December 1992 $100,000 civil money penalty against the Farmers and Merchants Bank of Long Beach, California. This would be the case especially with increased referrals to the Department of Justice, which we also foresee as being more commonplace. The September 1992 Justice Department's case alleging racial discrimination by Atlanta's Decatur Federal, which resulted in a $1 million consent decree payment plus numerous other stringent affirmative requirements, likely will be the first of several such cases brought by them. The role of the Justice Department in CRA and related matters likely will increase, especially if the FED and other bank regulators are perceived as being lax enforcers of CRA. We also foresee a greater role for other federal agencies in fair lending enforcement, such as HUD, which will continue to expand its use of loan bias "testers." Based on the Decatur Federal case, it is clear that the Justice Department is the "CRA Regulator from Hell," and we expect it to live up to that reputation in the 90s.

6. We believe that we will see some large mergers, acquisitions, or other corporate activities denied on the basis of CRA considerations. We believe that these denials will be the result of not just substantial noncompliance but also needs improvement ratings, especially if these are repeated ratings with little or no improvement in CRA performance. We expect the FED to gradually reverse its position of approving mergers involving banks with below-average CRA ratings as it did in the LaSalle of Chicago case, the First Commercial of Memphis case, and especially the controversial November 1992 case involving Capital Bank of Clayton, Missouri.

7. We believe we will see greater use of CRA ratings by more people, businesses, regulators, and institutions to benefit banks with good ratings and penalize those with bad ratings. For example, banks with outstanding ratings may benefit from jumbo CD or commercial paper purchases by money market mutual funds, stock and bond purchases by institutional investors, loan participation by insurance companies, and

new and expanded banking relationships and referrals by attorneys and others.

8. *We expect to see a closer tie-in between CRA ratings and HMDA results. We expect the annual HMDA data to be more visible and more widely distributed than ever. Also, we believe HMDA will be further expanded to cover all major areas of consumer and small business lending and even additional lenders now exempt from HMDA. Banks with substantial HMDA gaps (e.g., the difference between minority and nonminority rejection rates) will be more frequently examined or required to verify that no illegal discrimination was present. Using the relatively new Federal Reserve Bank of Boston and Justice Department (Decatur Federal) examination procedures, regulators will be increasingly searching for evidence of the "fat file" phenomenon and related "coaching" efforts. Since we believe that the increasingly visible and publicized HMDA data may have a greater influence on CRA ratings, banks with substantial HMDA gaps may find it more difficult to receive above-average or even average CRA ratings. Conversely, we expect that the lowest decile of banks with below-average CRA ratings will receive the greatest scrutiny of their HMDA data. Banks with below-average CRA ratings and a pattern of substantial HMDA gaps will be in the most difficult position of justifying their compliance record.*

9. *We expect CRA to play a greater role in efforts to rebuild our inner cities, especially after our unique finding regarding the inordinately large concentration of banks with substantial noncompliance ratings in L.A. Whether or not banks were part of the problem, they must be part of the solution. Without such private investment, we will likely see more civil disturbances in our inner cities, not just those in L.A.*

10. *We expect that a new senior-level banking title of the 90s will be "Chief Compliance Officer" as we move into an increasingly proconsumer environment. This function will be more fre-*

quently centralized at the holding company level, especially as we move towards a more consolidated banking system. Banks will realize more than ever that the costs of compliance will probably increase and must be treated as just another cost of doing business. Relatedly, we expect to see an increased number and variety of CRA vendors, survey researchers, testers, and other consultants to satisfy the increasing demand for outsourcing of the compliance function among banks of all sizes.*

11. *We expect to see more CRA "megapledges" by larger banks. And we expect that banks that have made these will increasingly provide at least an annual accounting of their progress in meeting their stated goals. Otherwise, there will likely be allegations of "megapledge inflation" where the stated goal was not met or perhaps questionably met with non-CRA loans. Banks may also file more of their megapledge and CRA plans with their regulators, who would not only impose regulatory oversight but possibly condition CRA ratings or upgrades on a bank's progress in meeting their goals.*

12. *We expect to see increased sharing efforts by banks in the area of CRA compliance as they realize the tremendous benefits of reduced cost and risk exposure by joining with other banks in their CRA compliance efforts.*

13. *We expect to see greater competition among banks for the "preferred" loan customers in low- and moderate-income areas to get the greatest "CRA credit" per dollar of CRA lending.*

14. *We expect many more studies of racial discrimination by government and private researchers alike. These studies will cover all walks of life, not just banking, and be more quantitative and definitive in documenting racial discrimination than previous studies. The results of these studies probably will lead to more, not less compliance regulations and enforcement.*

15. *We expect that the Clinton Administration will reverse the anti-CRA course taken by the Bush Administration and encourage the pro-CRA environment envisioned by the Democratic national platform. The proposal for 100 new community development banks is encouraging, but a Clinton-encouraged and rejuvenated CRA spirit at our roughly 14,000 existing banks would be even better. A truly pro-CRA Clinton Administration could be one of the best things that has happened to our cities and rural communities in the last 16 years since CRA was created. Conversely, the maintenance of the status quo of little to no true CRA enforcement will be a major setback to our communities and especially to the 40% of low- and moderate-income Americans within them.*

TABLE OF APPENDICES

Appendix 1

"A Citizen's Guide to the CRA"

Federal Financial Institutions Examination Council

A Citizen's Guide to the CRA

June 1992

Published by the Federal Financial Institutions Examination Council for use by those who want to know more about the Community Reinvestment Act, the regulatory process, and the role the public can play.

Table of Contents

About This Guide

A Citizen's Guide to the CRA is designed to help people understand the Community Reinvestment Act (CRA) and the responsibility it gives to the federal financial supervisory agencies to encourage financial institutions to reinvest in the local communities where they do business.[1] This guide describes the origins of the CRA, the policies and procedures the agencies use to enforce it, and the important changes to the CRA that took effect in July 1990. It explains how members of the public can be involved in the "CRA process" by communicating with their local financial institutions and with the agencies that regulate them, and how public input is considered when certain types of applications are filed.

Banks and savings associations are supervised by one of the four agencies below. These agencies enforce the CRA as well as consumer protection laws and many other laws governing the financial services industry.

- Federal Deposit Insurance Corporation (FDIC)—supervises state-chartered banks that are not members of the Federal Reserve System.

- Federal Reserve System (FRS)—supervises state-chartered banks that are members of the Federal Reserve System.

- Office of the Comptroller of the Currency (OCC)—supervises national banks. Often the word "National" appears in the bank's name, or the initials "N.A." or "N.T.& S.A." follow its name.

- Office of Thrift Supervision (OTS)—supervises federally and state-chartered savings associations as well as federally chartered savings banks. The names of these institutions generally identify them as savings and loan associations, savings associations, or savings banks. Federally chartered savings institutions have the word "Federal" or the initials "FSB" or "FA" in their names.

If you are uncertain about which agency supervises a financial institution, you can call the FDIC toll-free at 800–424–5488.

This guide is published by the Federal Financial Institutions Examination Council (FFIEC), which is an umbrella group for the agencies.[2]

---

[1] The federal financial supervisory agencies will be referred to simply as "the agencies" in this guide.

[2] The National Credit Union Administration, which supervises federally insured credit unions, is a member of the FFIEC, but it does not participate in the CRA supervisory process. See the paragraph, *Who is covered?*

Background

The history of the Community Reinvestment Act (CRA) really began long before it was enacted in 1977. Traditionally, financial institutions in the United States have had an obligation to serve the public because of the privileges they receive from the government—which other businesses do not. For example, financial institutions have charters to do business, obtain federal deposit insurance, and borrow money under special arrangements from the Federal Reserve discount window and the Federal Home Loan Banks. These privileges gave rise to the principle, found in our banking laws as far back as the 1930s, that financial institutions should serve the "convenience and needs of their communities."

In the years leading to passage of the CRA, there was considerable concern about ensuring fair access to credit, especially in the inner cities. Community groups spoke out against redlining—the perceived practice of drawing red lines around disfavored neighborhoods where money would not be lent, regardless of the creditworthiness of individual loan applicants. Many people felt that the visible economic decline of urban areas was aggravated by financial institutions, which were seen as taking deposits out of the neighborhoods from which they came and investing them elsewhere. Against this backdrop, the attention of the Congress was turned to the problem of revitalizing neighborhoods and the role financial institutions could play in that effort.

The CRA: What it does and does not do

The CRA affirms that financial institutions have an obligation to help meet the credit needs of their entire communities, including low- and moderate-income neighborhoods. It requires that the agencies (1) use their authority to encourage them to do so; (2) regularly assess the CRA performance of the institutions they supervise; and (3) take CRA performance into account when deciding whether to allow institutions to expand their businesses in certain ways.

The law recognizes that financial institutions should address their CRA responsibilities in keeping with safe and sound banking practices. The CRA does not require financial institutions to make loans that could jeopardize their safety nor dictate the type, amount, or terms of the loans they make. The Congress believed that precise requirements, representing credit allocation, should be avoided.

Who is covered?

The CRA applies to federally insured commercial banks, savings banks, and savings associations that are in the business of providing credit to the public—whether their operations are retail or wholesale. Exempted are those institutions which serve solely as correspondent banks, or as trust companies or as check clearing agents and do not extend credit to the public for their own account. Credit unions are not subject to the CRA.

The CRA policy framework

In March 1989, the agencies issued a Joint Policy Statement on CRA. Based on more than ten years' experience with enforcement of CRA, the statement addresses key questions that bankers and the public have raised.

The Joint Statement outlines what the agencies expect from financial institutions in fulfilling their CRA responsibilities. The agencies firmly believe that CRA efforts should be part of an ongoing *process* that involves specific steps

3

to determine the credit needs of the community (including those of low- and moderate-income neighborhoods) and to help address those needs through prudent lending. The management of a financial institution should be involved in the CRA process and oversee it, just as with other business plans and operations. A major element in making the process work is establishing a dialogue with all segments of the community—local governments, businesses, neighborhood organizations, and civic, consumer, minority, and religious groups, as well as those concerned with housing and other community matters.

The Joint Statement also makes clear that the dialogue with the community should be two-way, involving an ongoing effort by members of the public to make their concerns known. Just as financial institutions are expected to communicate with people in the communities they serve, community groups are urged to raise CRA-related issues with an institution's management and with the appropriate supervisory agency as soon as possible.

Financial institutions have considerable latitude in which to develop their own CRA programs and to offer the loans and services best suited to their expertise, their business objectives, and their community's needs. By way of guidance, the Joint Statement provides examples of the kinds of initiatives the agencies have found in effective CRA programs.

Important changes to the CRA

Amendments to the CRA, included in the Financial Institutions Reform, Recovery, and Enforcement Act of 1989 (FIRREA) and effective as of July 1, 1990, laid the groundwork for a greater degree of public involvement in the CRA process.

As a result of the amendments, the agencies prepare a written assessment, including the assigned rating of the CRA performance of each institution they examine. These assessments, called CRA Performance Evaluations, are available to the public. They describe the activities the institution has undertaken under each of twelve assessment factors (presented on page 6) and the conclusions examiners have drawn from them.

In assigning a CRA rating, examiners take into account several considerations, including an institution's size, expertise, financial strength, the type of community it serves (for example whether it is urban or rural), local economic conditions, and the nature of the institution's competition and business strategy. With these considerations in mind, examiners make judgments about the institution's CRA performance under the twelve assessment factors.

The purpose of the CRA Performance Evaluation is to help the reader understand the overall level of the institution's CRA performance.

It is important to remember that the ratings and the CRA Performance Evaluations do not in any way represent the financial condition of the institution.

The CRA rating system identifies four levels of performance that may describe an institution's record of meeting community credit needs:

- Outstanding

- Satisfactory

- Needs to improve

- Substantial noncompliance

4

The guidelines that examiners use in rating an institution incorporate much of the guidance that the Joint Statement provides to institutions.

While not changing the basic thrust of the CRA, the amendments in FIRREA gave the agencies an important new task—making public their assessments of an institution's performance, to open the CRA process to more informed public discussion and involvement.

Other changes to federal law in FIRREA also aimed to put more information about financial institutions' lending efforts, notably in the housing area, in the public domain. Amendments to the Home Mortgage Disclosure Act (HMDA) expanded the scope of information that covered lenders must report every year about their housing-related loan activity. Such information now includes the race, sex, and income of all applicants, not only of those who were granted credit. The new HMDA requirements give interested members of the public more information about the way financial institutions are serving the needs of their neighorhoods for housing credit and should suggest the areas in which greater efforts may be needed.

The CRA assessment factors

1. Activities conducted by the institution to ascertain the credit needs of its community, including the extent of efforts to communicate with members of its community regarding the credit services being provided by the institution.

2. The extent of the institution's marketing and special credit-related programs to make members of the community aware of the credit services offered by the institution.

3. The extent of participation by the institution's board of directors in formulating the institution's policies and reviewing its performance with respect to the purposes of the Community Reinvestment Act.

4. Any practices intended to discourage applications for types of credit set forth in the institution's CRA Statement.

5. The geographic distribution of the institution's credit extensions, credit applications, and credit denials.

6. Evidence of prohibited discriminatory or other illegal credit practices.

7. The institution's record of opening and closing offices and providing services at offices.

8. The institution's participation, including investments, in local community development and redevelopment projects or programs.

9. The institution's origination of residential mortgage loans, housing rehabilitation loans, home improvement loans, and small business or small farm loans within its community, or the purchase of such loans originated in its community.

10. The institution's participation in governmentally insured, guaranteed, or subsidized loan programs for housing, small businesses, or small farms.

11. The institution's ability to meet various community credit needs based on its financial condition and size, and legal impediments, local economic conditions, and other factors.

12. Other factors that, in the agency's judgment, reasonably bear upon the extent to which an institution is helping to meet the credit needs of its entire community.

CRA Requirements

What the agencies must do

CRA examinations are the main vehicle for the agencies to evaluate financial institutions' CRA activities and, at the same time, to encourage them to do better. Examiners from all the agencies follow uniform CRA examination procedures, which focus attention in a methodical way on each of the twelve assessment factors. Based on examination findings, ratings are assigned in accordance with the interagency CRA rating system. To help ensure a balanced perspective, examiners may also conduct interviews with representative individuals and groups from the local community, outside the institution, to hear their views on the community's credit needs and the performance of local financial institutions.

Examiners' findings are orally communicated to institution management at the end of the examination, and a written examination report and CRA Performance Evaluation are sent later. After the examination, institutions receive continued supervisory attention through correspondence, follow-up visits, and subsequent examinations.

Besides conducting examinations, the agencies may undertake outreach efforts to educate financial institutions about the range of opportunities and techniques for community development lending. Government agencies, private and nonprofit developers, national financial intermediaries, and others often participate in this effort. The emphasis is on helping build public–private partnerships that can effectively address community reinvestment needs.

The agencies must take CRA performance (and other factors) into account when evaluating applications by the institutions they regulate to engage in certain activities. The applications process and the way citizens can participate in it are discussed later in this guide.

What financial institutions must do

Institutions must adhere to substantially identical regulations adopted by the agencies to implement the CRA (Appendix C provides citations for these regulations and pertinent application provisions). The regulations specify the twelve factors that examiners use in assessing institutions' performance under the CRA. They also set out three specific technical requirements, which follow.

1. A Community Reinvestment Act Statement for each local community the institution serves. Each CRA Statement must be updated and approved annually by the institution's Board of Directors. It must contain the following:

   • a map showing the local community that the institution serves

   • a list of the types of loans the institution is willing to make within its community

   • a notice of the process by which the public can comment on the institution's CRA performance (The contents of the notice are discussed in detail below.)

In addition, the agencies—through the CRA regulations and the Joint Statement on the CRA—strongly encourage institutions to include in their CRA Statements a description of their CRA efforts. Such an "expanded" CRA

Statement would, for example, tell the public how the institution has identified community credit needs and has communicated with people in the community about them, steps it has taken to market and advertise its services, and any special credit-related programs it offers.

The CRA Statement must be readily available for the public to review, on request, at an institution's principal office and at each branch office in the local community delineated in the statement. An institution may charge for copies, but it may not charge more than the cost of reproduction and mailing, if applicable.

2. A file that contains written comments from members of the public about the institution's CRA performance. The "CRA Public File" should also contain the following:

   - any responses the institution has made to the public's comments
   - the institution's CRA Statements for the past two years
   - the most recent CRA Performance Evaluation prepared by its regulatory agency, which must be placed in the file within thirty business days after the institution receives it. If the institution chooses, it may also include any response it has made to the Performance Evaluation.

The CRA Public File must be available for the public to inspect at the institution's principal office and at least one office in each local community (if the institution serves more than one community). No fee may be charged for public inspection of the contents of the file but, as with the CRA Statement, a fee (not to exceed the cost of reproduction and mailing, if applicable) may be charged for copies of the Performance Evaluation.

The agencies also maintain files of comments received from the public on the performance of the institutions they regulate. To review these files, members of the public should contact the agencies' district or regional offices (see appendix A for the addresses).

3. A notice, posted in the lobby of each of the institution's offices, which lets the public know the following:

   - where it can get copies of the institution's CRA Statement
   - where, and to whom, it may send comments about the institution's CRA performance
   - where to locate the institution's public file(s)
   - the address of the appropriate supervisory agency to which the public may send comments about the institution's CRA performance
   - the fact that the CRA Performance Evaluation is available for public inspection (once the first one has been received), and where it is located
   - whether the institution is owned by a holding company
   - how to obtain announcements from the supervisory agency of any applications, for which CRA is considered, filed by the institution.

You may call, write, or visit your local financial institution to get a copy of its most recent CRA Performance Evaluation. You should not be charged more than the cost of duplicating and mailing it (if applicable). Check the CRA notice posted in the institution's lobby for the location of the institution's offices where the CRA Public File, including the CRA Performance Evaluation, is available.

CRA and the Applications Process

The CRA requires that CRA performance be considered with other factors when the agencies evaluate certain types of applications by financial institutions and their parent companies, known as holding companies. This requirement provides a powerful incentive for financial institutions to meet their CRA obligations should they intend to expand their business. Adverse findings about an applicant's CRA performance can result in denial of an application.

What kinds of applications are covered?

The types of applications covered are those asking the agencies for permission to do the following:

- obtain federal deposit insurance (includes start-up or "de novo" institutions and conversions from a state to national charter and vice versa)

- establish a branch or other facility authorized to receive deposits, or relocate a main office or existing branch (including federally insured branches of foreign banks)

- merge, consolidate, or acquire another financial institution, or acquire deposits from another financial institution

- form a bank or savings association holding company.

Applications for these activities are filed with and handled by the applicant's supervisory agency. All applications for savings association holding companies are evaluated by the Office of Thrift Supervision. All applications filed by bank holding companies are evaluated by the Federal Reserve, even though their subsidiary banks may be supervised by one or more of the other agencies.

How the agencies review CRA performance

In considering applications covered by the CRA, the agencies routinely review the applicant's performance in helping meet the credit needs of its entire local community.[3] Great weight is given to the findings of CRA examinations, although sometimes the agencies may need to obtain additional information to update the examination record or to clarify any questions about how well institutions are actually performing.

The agencies must evaluate more than CRA in the applications process. They must assess also the financial capacity of the applicant institution and the competency of its management, the effect of the proposal on competition, and any legal constraints or considerations the proposal may entail.

The agencies believe that institutions should address their CRA responsibilities and have the necessary policies in place and working well **before** they file an application. In fulfilling their responsibilities under the CRA, institutions may initiate programs for future action to ensure a strong CRA record or to resolve CRA issues. Commitments for future action are not viewed as part of the CRA record of performance of the institution, but they may be given weight as an indicator of potential improvement in the institution's performance. The agencies can use commitments for such improvement to address

---

[3] Where the applicant is a bank or savings association holding company, the CRA performance of all subsidiary financial institutions is reviewed. Holding companies, *per se*, do not have CRA responsibilities, but the financial institutions they own or control do. Thus, the agencies expect that holding companies will oversee the CRA performance of their subsidiaries and be accountable for it.

specific problems in an otherwise satisfactory record or to address CRA performance when a troubled institution is being acquired. In some cases, these commitments have an important bearing on the determination that CRA considerations are consistent with an approval of the application. In general, institutions cannot use commitments made in the applications process to overcome a seriously deficient record of CRA performance. Commitment for improvements in an institution's performance can be used to address specific problems in an otherwise satisfactory record. The agencies monitor the fulfillment of commitments made to the agencies in the applications process and may use their supervisory authority to enforce them. Where appropriate, the agencies may, by granting conditional approval of an application, also require financial institutions to take specific actions to improve CRA performance; the approval becomes final only after the conditions have been satisfied.

Opportunity for public input

An important feature of the applications process is the opportunity for the public to comment, in writing, on any or all of the factors the agencies must consider in acting on an application—including CRA performance. Public comments may help provide a more complete or more current picture of CRA performance than is indicated by examination records alone. Written comments, which may express either support for or opposition to the application, become part of the record, which the agencies carefully examine in making their decision. Comments regarding an application that are critical of an applicant's CRA performance are commonly referred to as "CRA protests."

The comments need not be submitted in a legal brief or any other particular format. However, they should be supported with facts about the applicant's performance and should be as specific as possible in explaining the basis for the protest. For example, they could discuss any information that the commenter believes shows an institution's poor lending performance or illegal discrimination in its lending or a failure to comply with the technical requirements of the CRA (such as an improper delineation of its local community or an inaccurate listing of loan products in its CRA Statement). Stating whether the issues raised in the protest have previously been brought to the attention of the institution's management is also helpful to the agencies.

When to submit comments

Anyone wishing to comment on an application should do so in a timely fashion, to give the agencies time to analyze the issues raised and any responses to them from the applicant. The length of the period for comment varies somewhat from agency to agency and by type of application. The following chart provides basic information about the length of this period; the agencies' district or regional offices can provide further guidance.

Length of public comment period for applications subject to CRA

FRB	30 days for most applications
FDIC	15 days for most applications; 21 days for office relocations; 30 days for mergers[4]
OCC	30 days for most applications; 10 days for Customer–Bank Communication Terminal branches
OTS	10 days for most applications; a 7-day extension is granted on written request

[4] Periods are counted from the date of the publication of the last notice or receipt by the FDIC Regional Office, whichever is later.

How to find out when an application has been filed

The agencies' administrative rules set out procedures for notifying the public when applications subject to the CRA are received. You can find out if an application has been filed with one of the agencies through the following:

- bulletins published by each agency. Nonprofit community or civic organizations may ask to be placed free of charge on the mailing list for bulletins, issued by the agencies' district or regional offices, that list applications received based on the geographic area served by the agencies' offices.

- a newspaper notice published by the institution. Generally, institutions must publish the notice in a local newspaper that is distributed in the community served by the institution's principal office and in any new location in which the institution proposes to do business.

- a notice posted in the lobby of an office that the institution proposes to move to a new location.

- an announcement in the *Federal Register* (for bank holding company applications).

The agencies' district or regional offices maintain files on the applications they receive. These files contain the application, materials supporting the application, and any comments received from the public. Information such as financial data or trade secrets must be kept confidential, but the public may see the other contents of the file by arranging a visit to the agency's office. Copies of the nonconfidential part of the file will be provided for a reasonable fee.

Role of private meetings

The agencies believe that financial institutions and protestants can benefit by meeting informally to discuss the matters at issue and to resolve any misunderstandings or differences. The agencies sometimes facilitate such private meetings and may attend them, but they maintain a neutral role.

Private meetings sometimes result in the parties settling their differences and reaching a formal agreement, which may entail specific lending or other initiatives by the financial institution. Any decision to enter into a formal agreement is completely at the discretion of the parties involved; the agencies do not require or enforce such agreements. Moreover, the agencies do not suspend the processing of pending applications simply to allow the parties time to conclude their negotiations. Because they have an obligation to process applications in a timely manner, the agencies will act on an application once they have enough information about the CRA issues raised to make a well-supported determination.

Public meeting, hearing, or oral argument

The agencies may supplement the written information pertaining to the CRA performance of applicant institutions by convening a meeting. The agencies use different terms for these events—public meeting (FRB), hearing and informal proceeding (FDIC), public hearing (OCC), and oral argument (OTS). The agency usually has the prerogative of deciding whether or not to hold such a meeting.

The purpose of the meeting is to obtain additional information for developing a complete record on which the agency can base its decision. The purpose is not to promote a reconciling of differences. Because the agencies follow different administrative procedures for such meetings, the district or regional office of the agency involved should be contacted for details.

The Role Citizens Can Play

The CRA provides a framework for productive interaction between financial institutions and all those who make up a community—representatives of local government, businesses, civic and consumer organizations, trade associations, the religious community, and many others. It can help bring together their resources and expertise to address concerns and needs regarding community development. The CRA works best when it is the basis of an ongoing dialogue and is not associated exclusively with pending applications by financial institutions.

The CRA process is strengthened by the public availability of CRA Performance Evaluations prepared by the agencies. The public is encouraged to contact the institution directly to obtain a copy of the CRA Performance Evaluation. To facilitate public access to CRA Performance Evaluations, the agencies regularly publish listings of the institutions that have CRA Performance Evaluations, and their corresponding CRA ratings, available for public review.

You can be kept informed of which institutions have publicly available CRA Performance Evaluations, and their CRA ratings, through a listing published at least quarterly by each agency for the institutions it supervises. Contact the agency's district or regional office to be placed on the mailing list.[5]

The CRA Performance Evaluations are an important source of information about the CRA activities of local financial institutions. They explain how the agencies have judged the institutions' efforts to help meet community credit needs. However, the Performance Evaluations represent the agencies' judgments, based on information available at the time of examination. The agencies hope that members of the public will present their own observations about an institution's CRA performance, especially in light of changes in community credit needs and the opportunities these changes present for involvement by financial institutions. The public is encouraged to write letters to the institution for inclusion in the CRA Public File or directly to the agency, at any time.

[5] For institutions supervised by the FDIC, please write the FDIC's Office of Corporate Communication at 550 17th St., NW, Washington, DC 20429.

Appendix A: Maps and Addresses of Supervisory Agencies' District and Regional Offices

Districts of the Federal Reserve System

Federal Reserve Banks

FEDERAL RESERVE BANK OF BOSTON 600 Atlantic Avenue Boston, Massachusetts 02106	(617) 973-3000
FEDERAL RESERVE BANK OF NEW YORK 33 Liberty Street New York, New York 10045	(212) 720-5000
FEDERAL RESERVE BANK OF PHILADELPHIA 10 Independence Mall Philadelphia, Pennsylvania 19106	(215) 574-6000
FEDERAL RESERVE BANK OF CLEVELAND 1455 East Sixth Street Cleveland, Ohio 44114	(216) 579-2000
FEDERAL RESERVE BANK OF RICHMOND 701 East Byrd Street Richmond, Virginia 23219	(804) 697-8000
FEDERAL RESERVE BANK OF ATLANTA 104 Marietta Street, N.W. Atlanta, Georgia 30303	(404) 521-8500
FEDERAL RESERVE BANK OF CHICAGO 230 South LaSalle Street Chicago, Illinois 60604	(312) 322-5322
FEDERAL RESERVE BANK OF ST. LOUIS 411 Locust Street St. Louis, Missouri 63102	(314) 444-8444
FEDERAL RESERVE BANK OF MINNEAPOLIS 250 Marquette Avenue Minneapolis, Minnesota 55480	(612) 340-2345
FEDERAL RESERVE BANK OF KANSAS CITY 925 Grand Avenue Kansas City, Missouri 64198	(816) 881-2000
FEDERAL RESERVE BANK OF DALLAS 400 South Akard Street Dallas, Texas 75222	(214) 651-6111
FEDERAL RESERVE BANK OF SAN FRANCISCO 101 Market Street San Francisco, California 94120	(415) 974-2000

Regions of the Federal Deposit Insurance Corporation

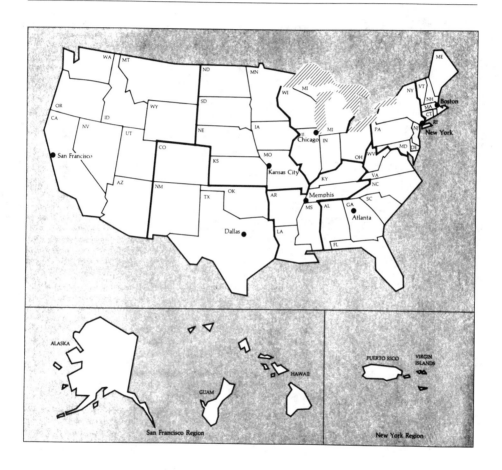

Federal Deposit Insurance Corporation Regional Offices

ATLANTA
Marquis One Building, Suite 1200
245 Peachtree Center Avenue, N.E.
Atlanta, Georgia 30303

(404) 525-0308

BOSTON
160 Gould Street
Needham, Massachusetts 02194

(617) 449-9080

CHICAGO
30 South Wacker Drive, Suite 3100
Chicago, Illinois 60606

(312) 207-0210

DALLAS
1910 Pacific Avenue, Suite 1900
Dallas, Texas 75201

(214) 220-3342

KANSAS CITY
2345 Grand Avenue, Suite 1500
Kansas City, Missouri 64108

(816) 234-8000

MEMPHIS
5100 Poplar Avenue, Suite 1900
Memphis, Tennessee 38137

(901) 685-1603

NEW YORK
452 Fifth Avenue, 21st Floor
New York, New York 10018

(212) 704-1200

SAN FRANCISCO
25 Ecker Street, Suite 2300
San Francisco, California 94105

(415) 546-0160

District Organization of the Office of the Comptroller
of the Currency

Office of the Comptroller of the Currency District Offices

NORTHEASTERN DISTRICT   (212) 819-9860
1114 Avenue of the Americas
Suite 3900
New York, New York 10036

SOUTHEASTERN DISTRICT   (404) 659-8855
Marquis One Tower
245 Peachtree Center Avenue, N.E.
Suite 600
Atlanta, Georgia 30303

CENTRAL DISTRICT   (312) 663-8000
One Financial Place
440 South LaSalle Street
Suite 2700
Chicago, Illinois 60605

MIDWESTERN DISTRICT   (816) 556-1800
2345 Grand Avenue
Suite 700
Kansas City, Missouri 64108

SOUTHWESTERN DISTRICT   (214) 720-0656
1600 Lincoln Plaza
500 North Akard Street
Dallas, Texas 75201-3394

WESTERN DISTRICT   (415) 545-5900
50 Fremont Street
Suite 3900
San Francisco, California 94105

Regions of the Office of Thrift Supervision

Office of Thrift Supervision Regional Offices

NORTHEAST REGIONAL OFFICE 10 Exchange Plaza Centre, Floor 17 Jersey City, New Jersey 07302	(201) 413-1000
SOUTHEAST REGIONAL OFFICE 1475 Peachtree Street, N.E. Atlanta, Georgia 30309	(404) 888-0771
CENTRAL REGIONAL OFFICE 111 E. Wacker Drive, Suite 800 Chicago, Illinois 60601	(312) 565-5300
MIDWEST REGIONAL OFFICE 122 W. John Carpenter Freeway Suite 600 Irving, Texas 75039	(214) 281-2000
WEST REGIONAL OFFICE Pacific Telesis Center One Montgomery Street, Suite 400 San Francisco, California 94120	(415) 616-1500

Appendix B: Federal Register Citations for Important CRA-Related Documents

Joint Statement on the CRA	54 FR 13742 April 5, 1989
Uniform Interagency CRA Final Guidelines for Disclosure of Written Evaluations and Revised Assessment Rating System	55 FR 18163 May 1, 1990
Final Rule to CRA Implementing Regulations	56 FR 26899 June 12, 1991

Appendix C: Citations for CRA Procedures and Applications

Board of Governors of the Federal Reserve System	CRA Procedures Applications	12 CFR 228 12 CFR 262 & 265 12 CFR 208 12 CFR 225 12 CFR USC 1828 (c)
Federal Deposit Insurance Corporation	CRA Procedures Applications	12 CFR 345 12 CFR 308 12 CFR 303
Office of the Comptroller of the Currency	CRA Application Procedures	12 CFR 25 12 CFR 5
Office of Thrift Supervision	CRA Procedures Applications	12 CFR 563e 12 CFR 543 12 CFR 543 12 CFR 545 12 CFR 546 12 CFR 563

Appendix 2

FFIEC Updated Statement on CRA Requirements and Revised CRA Examination Procedures and Checklist

Federal Financial Institutions **Examination Council**

2100 Pennsylvania Avenue, NW, Suite 200 · Washington, DC 20037 · (202) 634-6526 · FAX (202) 634-6556

Press Release

For immediate release

June 17, 1992

The Board of Governors of the Federal Reserve System, the Federal Deposit Insurance Corporation, the Office of the Comptroller of the Currency and the Office of Thrift Supervision, in an effort to simplify and streamline compliance supervisory processes and pursue reduction in regulatory burden, are issuing guidance regarding recordkeeping and documentation under the Community Reinvestment Act of 1977 (CRA).

This guidance clarifies the agencies' expectations regarding documentation that financial institutions should maintain to support their performance efforts under the CRA. It emphasizes that the agencies base their evaluation of CRA performance primarily on how well an institution helps meet the credit needs of its community or communities, not on the amount of documentation it maintains. It also indicates that a lack of documentation is not sufficient basis on which to grant a poor rating if an institution's performance can otherwise be determined to be satisfactory or better.

Board of Governors of the Federal Reserve System, Federal Deposit Insurance Corporation, National Credit Union Administration, Office of the Comptroller of the Currency, Office of Thrift Supervision

-2-

The CRA contains a Congressional finding that regulated financial institutions are "required by law to demonstrate that their deposit facilities serve the convenience and needs of the communities in which they are chartered." It also directs the agencies to assess the institution's "...record of meeting the credit needs of its entire community, including low- and moderate-income neighborhoods."

In the March 21, 1989 Statement of the Federal Financial Supervisory Agencies Regarding the Community Reinvestment Act, the agencies stated that they expect depository institutions to have a well-managed program in place to address their responsibilities under the law. A well-managed CRA program involves (1) ascertaining community credit needs, (2) developing products and services responsive to those identified community credit needs, (3) affirmatively marketing those products to ensure that they are available equitably throughout the community served, including low- and moderate-income areas, and (4) monitoring and evaluating the effectiveness of the program, including the geographic distribution of credit applications, extensions, and denials.

The documentation expected by the agencies is primarily that which is useful to the institution's own management needs. In a well-managed CRA program, a financial institution's board of

-3-

directors and management use relevant documentation to make sure their programs are working as planned. The regulatory agencies can use this documentation in their assessment of the institution's CRA performance and to make sure that a proper level of management oversight of the institution's CRA program is in place.

In so doing, the agencies and their examiners are mindful that CRA-related documentation will generally be less formal and less extensive in small and rural institutions than in larger, urban institutions. Documents such as the minutes of board of directors meetings, program plans, marketing plans, advertising scripts, geographic analyses and other information that the institution prepares and maintains for its own management use should demonstrate the level of CRA performance. The agencies do not expect detailed documentation of every contact or finding to effectively demonstrate performance.

Agency examiners will use this guidance, along with the attached updated Uniform Interagency Community Reinvestment Act Examination Procedures in assessing performance under the CRA. In addition, the agencies, working through the FFIEC Consumer Compliance Task Force and the interagency groups working on the Regulatory Burden Study prescribed by section 221 of Federal Deposit Insurance Corporation Improvement Act and the Regulatory Uniformity Project,

-4-

will continue to review additional ways to simplify and clarify compliance expectations and requirements appropriately.

Although these examination procedures are being issued in final form at this time, interested parties may comment on these or other issues and aspects of the Community Reinvestment Act by writing to the Federal Financial Institutions Examination Council, Attn: Consumer Compliance Task Force, 2100 Pennsylvania, NW, Suite 200, Washington, D.C. 20037.

#   #   #   #

COMMUNITY REINVESTMENT ACT

Requirements and History of the Act

The Community Reinvestment Act (CRA)(12 USC 2901 et. seq.) is intended to encourage certain regulated financial institutions to help meet the credit needs of their entire communities, including low- and moderate-income neighborhoods, consistent with safe and sound operations. Each of the four supervisory agencies, (the Board of Governors of the Federal Reserve System, the Comptroller of the Currency, the Federal Deposit Insurance Corporation, and the Office of Thrift Supervision) is required to:

- use its examination authority to encourage an institution to help meet the credit needs of its entire community, consistent with safe and sound operation of the institution;

- assess, in connection with its examination, an institution's record of helping to meet the credit needs of its entire community; and

- take that record into account in evaluating an application for a charter, deposit insurance, branch or other deposit facility, office relocation, merger, or holding company acquisition of a regulated financial institution.

Proponents of the CRA were concerned, among other things, with situations in which local lenders reportedly exported local deposits to other areas despite sound local lending opportunities. Such disinvestment was considered a threat to community and neighborhood vitality. The Act, therefore, encourages lenders to give particular attention to local housing and economic development needs in urban and rural areas. Increased lender sensitivity to such lending needs can help preserve, rehabilitate, and revitalize such neighborhoods. Moreover, even though the Act emphasizes credit for local housing and community development, it recognizes that other types of credit also provide for neighborhood vitality and, more generally, a healthy local community.

- 2 -

The CRA is not intended to inject hard and fast rules or ratios into the examination or application processes. Rather, the law contemplates an evaluation of each lender's record that can accommodate individual circumstances. The Act also does not require financial institutions to make high risk loans that jeopardize their safety. To the contrary, the law indicates that such lending should be done within the bounds of safety and soundness. Rebuilding and revitalizing communities through sound lending should benefit both the communities and financial institutions.

An institution's capacity to help meet community credit needs is influenced by its financial condition and size, as well as by legal impediments and local economic conditions. An examiner must take these considerations into account when assessing the institution's performance and encouraging improved CRA performance. Larger institutions, for example, would generally be expected to be doing more than smaller ones, especially those in rural areas and small towns.

Requirements of the Agencies' CRA Regulation

CRA Statement

The CRA regulations of each agency require the board of directors of each institution to adopt, and at least annually review, a CRA Statement. The institution must provide a copy of its current CRA Statement to members of the public upon request. The institution may charge a fee, not to exceed actual costs, for reproduction and mailing, if applicable. The Statement must include:

1. A delineation, on a map, of each local community served by the institution.

Each institution must identify the local community or communities that it serves. For instance, a statewide branching institution would serve a number of "local communities." Further, more than one office of an institution may serve the same local community. An institution with offices throughout a city and its suburbs, for example, may consider the entire metropolitan area to be the local community for those offices. Each community must, of course, include the contiguous areas surrounding each office or group of offices.

Because many factors influence the size and shape of a lender's community, the regulation provides guidelines to help each institution define its local community or communities.

- 3 -

The overriding concern, however, is to ensure that low- and moderate-income neighborhoods are not arbitrarily excluded from the delineated area.

The first guideline suggests that institutions consider using widely recognized existing boundaries, such as those of Metropolitan Statistical Areas (MSA) or counties, as a basis for delineating their local community or communities. Such boundaries are frequently a reasonable approximation . an institution's local community.

Generally, a local community based on existing boundaries should be no larger than an entire MSA, or a county in a non-MSA area. If an institution has offices in more than one such area, it should generally have more than one local community. However, when an institution has an office near the boundary of a MSA or county, it should include those portions of adjacent counties that it serves. In rural areas, a local community may sometimes encompass more than one county, but generally institutions should not use states or regions of states to delineate local communities. A small institution that serves an area smaller than a MSA or county may define its community to be a part of the MSA or county. An institution may adjust the community delineation when areas are divided by state borders, significant geographic barriers, or areas that are extremely large or of unusual configuration.

The second guideline indicates that institutions could delineate their local community based on their effective lending territory -- the local area or areas around each office or group of offices where the lender makes a substantial portion of its loans -- and all other areas equally distant from each office. If an institution uses its effective lending territory to define its local community, it should follow existing boundaries as much as practical.

This guideline does not mean that each office necessarily serves a separate and distinct local community because they typically have different, though possibly overlapping, effective lending territories. An institution that is represented throughout a trade or market area may use that entire area as its local community.

The final guideline allows institutions to delineate their communities using any other reasonably defined area. An institution thus has substantial leeway to specify its local community as long as the definition is reasonable. That is to say, the institution must be able to provide a sensible rationale for the delineation and to show that it has not arbitrarily excluded any low- and moderate-income neighborhoods.

- 4 -

2. A list of specific types of credit that the institution is prepared to extend within each local community.

While an institution must prepare a separate CRA Statement for each local community it serves, including a delineation of the relevant local community, it does not necessarily follow that the list of available credits will be unique for each community. A lender that serves several local communities may elect to prepare Statements that contain lists of credits which are similar or identical for all the local communities served. Since some credit needs are common to many local communities, such an approach would be consistent with the intent of CRA. However, if the institution does offer different types of credit in different communities, the institution's CRA Statement for each community must reflect the types of credit offered in that particular community.

3. A copy of the CRA Notice.

An institution must provide in each office a CRA Notice, the exact wording of which is prescribed in the regulation. This includes:

- The availability of the CRA Statement;

- That written comments on the Statement and the institution's community lending performance may be submitted to the institution or its supervisory agency;

- That a file of such comments is publicly available;

- That the public may request announcements of the institution's applications covered by CRA from the supervisory agency; and

- The availability of the CRA Performance Evaluation.

4. Encouraged Additional Information

The regulations also encourage each institution to include the following information in its CRA Statement:

- A description of how its current efforts, including special credit-related programs, help to meet community credit needs;

- A periodic report on its record of helping to meet community credit needs; and

- a description of its efforts to ascertain the credit needs of its community, including efforts to communicate with members of its community regarding credit services.

- 5 -

Public File

Each institution must keep a file that is readily available for public inspection. That file must include:

- All CRA Statements in effect during the past two years;

- A copy of the institution'ᵤ most recent CRA Performance Evaluation. At a minimum, the evaluation must be available at the home office and at a designated office in each local community; and

- All written comments received from the public within the last two years that relate to the CRA Statement, Performance Evaluation or the institution's record of helping to meet community credit needs.

CRA Performance Evaluation

After a CRA examination, each institution will receive from its supervisory agency a written, public CRA evaluation. This evaluation must be placed in the Public File within 30 business days of receipt by the institution. The institution must provide a copy of this evaluation to the public upon request, and may charge a fee, not to exceed actual costs, for reproduction and mailing. While the institution may include a response to the CRA Performance Evaluation in its Public File or may otherwise make such response available to the public, the format and content of the evaluation, as transmitted by the supervisory agency, may not be altered or abridged in any manner.

Review and Retention of Records

Each institution's board of directors must review each CRA Statement at least annually and must amend the Statement at its first regular meeting after a change in any of the information presented in the Statement occurs. Such changes may be, but are not limited to, a revision in the institution's community delineation, or the introduction of a new credit product. All CRA Statements in effect over the past two years and all written, signed CRA public comments received during that period must be maintained. Each current CRA Statement must be readily available for public inspection at the head office and at each office of the institution in the local community delineated in the CRA Statement, except off-premises electronic deposit facilities.

Examination Burden/Documentation

Section 802 of the CRA statute conveys the Congress's finding that financial institutions are "required by law to demonstrate that they serve the convenience and needs of the

- 6 -

communities in which they are chartered." It also directs the
agencies to assess the institution's "...record of meeting the
credit needs of its entire community, including low- and
moderate-income areas."

The examination process gives institutions the
opportunity to demonstrate how they are having a beneficial
influence on the local community or communities. The
documentation expected by the agencies is primarily that which
is useful to the institution's own management needs. In a
well-managed CRA program, a financial institution's board of
directors and management use relevant documentation to make
sure their programs are working as planned. The agencies can
use this documentation in their assessment of the
institution's CRA performance and to make sure that a proper
level of management oversight of the institution's CRA program
is in place.

The agencies are mindful that CRA-related documentation
will generally be less formal and less extensive in small and
rural institutions than in larger, urban institutions.
Documents such as the minutes of board of directors meetings,
program plans, marketing plans, advertising scripts,
geographic analyses and other information that the institution
prepares and maintains for its own management use should
demonstrate the level of CRA performance. The agencies do not
expect detailed documentation of every contact or finding to
effectively demonstrate performance.

CRA ratings should be based on an institution's
performance (primarily the granting of loans, but also
technical support for community development efforts, and other
activities that help make credit available to members of the
community), not on the amount of documentation it maintains.
The lack of documentation is not sufficient basis on which to
grant a poor rating if performance can otherwise be determined
to be satisfactory or better.

Judgmental Process/Regulatory Flexibility

In conducting a CRA examination, the examiner should
adjust the CRA procedures on a case-by-case basis to
accommodate institutions that vary in size, type, capabilities
and locale. Community credit needs often differ based on the
specific characteristics of a local community, and different
institutions may serve these local credit needs in a variety
of ways. Each institution should be evaluated based on its
efforts to ascertain the credit needs of its community(ies),
and on its performance in helping meet those needs.

There are a number of factors to be considered when
assessing an institution's record of helping to meet community
credit needs, including those of low- and moderate-income
neighborhoods. Institutions are not required to undertake
particular activities, because the regulation allows each

- 7 -

institution considerable flexibility in determining how it can best help to meet the credit needs of its entire community in view of its resources and capabilities.

In essence, the regulation encourages institutions to become aware of the full range of credit needs of their communities and to offer the types of credit and credit-related services that will help meet those needs. However, the regulation does not require institutions to offer particular types or amounts of credit.

Examiner Encouragement

As part of the examination process, the examiner should discuss with management the various ways in which identified weaknesses in CRA performance may be addressed and aspects of an institution's performance may be strengthened. The examiner should not, however, interfere with the institution's responsibility for establishing its policies and programs by insisting on any specific lending programs that involve the making of certain types or amounts of loans.

Balanced Viewpoint/Use of Outside Contact Information

An examiner should maintain a balanced perspective in conducting a CRA examination and, whenever possible, should consult sources other than the institution being examined to better understand the credit needs of a particular community. Many city and local governments have extensive information on economic and community development activities that are being undertaken or planned. Regional planning units and major universities sometimes can provide examiners with information to help them understand economic conditions in a particular area. Such contacts can help the examiner gain a more comprehensive understanding of an institution's community. The agencies have agreed that outside information should be routinely shared with the other agencies by means of the uniform Community Contact Form.

CRA Joint Policy Statement

On March 21, 1989, the agencies adopted a Joint Policy Statement that was designed to guide institutions and the public regarding the agencies' expectations with respect to the CRA and the policies and procedures the agencies apply during the applications process. It strongly encourages institutions to expand their CRA Statements to include information regarding their record of meeting obligations under the CRA. The Joint Policy Statement also addresses a number of other CRA-related issues, including the need for institutions to have a well-managed process for meeting their responsibilities under the law, including a periodic review of their own CRA performance and the basic components of an

- 8 -

effective CRA process. It also indicates some of the various
types of activities the agencies have found to be consistent
with an effective process for meeting CRA obligations.

Policy Statement on Geographic Distribution Analysis

On November 22, 1991, the FFIEC approved a Policy
Statement that stresses the need for institutions to analyze
the geographic distribution of their lending patterns as part
of their CRA planning process, indicates what the agencies
expect of the institutions they supervise, and gives them
guidance on how to meet these expectations. Examiners should
consider the Policy Statement when they assess the extent of
board participation and the geographic distribution of lending
activity (assessment factors (c) and (e)). Analyses by
institution management or agency examiners also should help
assess the reasonableness of an institution's community
delineation(s) and help form hypotheses to test during the
fair housing and fair lending phase of the examination.

As indicated in the Policy Statement, the extent and
sophistication of such analyses expected by the agencies will
depend on the size and location of the institution.
Obviously, institutions in small towns and rural areas,
especially small institutions, can perform this analysis in
relatively simple, unsophisticated ways. However, if an
institution's management does not know where its loans are
going, it is unlikely to be carrying out its responsibilities
under the CRA.

Communication, Community Development and Low- and Moderate-Income Neighborhoods

In assessing an institutions's record of performance,
the examiner should remember the emphasis placed on effective
communication and community development activities.
Communication is important because community needs that can be
met on a safe and sound basis are more likely to be met when
the community is aware of the types of credit available and
the lender is well informed about community credit needs. The
agencies encourage all efforts by institutions to ascertain
community credit needs and to publicize available credit
services. Those efforts include measures to identify the
credit needs of low- and moderate-income neighborhoods, and
targeted advertising in such neighborhoods.

The CRA also is concerned with activities that foster
development in the entire community, including low- and
moderate-income neighborhoods. Consequently, the agencies
look favorably on housing-related loans and investments,
participation in community development programs, and small
business financing, including loans to small farms. The
examiner should also give positive consideration to the
donation, sale on favorable terms, or making available on a

- 9 -

rent-free basis any branch located in a predominately minority neighborhood to any minority or women's depository institution.

Low- and Moderate-Income Neighborhoods

In determining whether a community delineation is reasonable, the examiner must be alert to situations where low- and moderate-income neighborhoods are arbitrarily excluded.

In most cases institutions and examiners can identify low- and moderate-income neighborhoods by the same approach HUD takes in administering the Community Development Block Grant Program. That program uses census tracts in a MSA where median family income is less than 80 percent of median family income for the entire MSA to approximate such neighborhoods.

Non-MSA areas, especially rural ones, present a particular problem in identifying low- and moderate-income neighborhoods. Beginning with the 1990 census, all counties of the United States are composed of either census tracts or block numbering areas (BNAs). For the BNAs of small, rural counties, the Census Bureau has demographic information similar to that available for the census tracts of MSAs. Even with that information, however, identifying low- and moderate-income neighborhoods in small, rural counties may still present a problem.

In assessing an institution's record, the examiner should focus particular attention on the lender's performance with respect to typical customers in low- and moderate-income neighborhoods within a local community. Examiners should supplement that information with knowledge gained from community contacts, physical inspection as necessary, and discussion with institution personnel.

Small Business Lending

The agencies believe small business lending is directly related to the purposes of the CRA. In considering small business lending the examiner should not be concerned with any hard and fast or precise definition of what constitutes a small business. Instead, the examiner should, in particular, consider any loans to local firms whose access to credit is limited to local sources. Loans guaranteed by the Small Business Administration are only one type of small business lending that an examiner should consider in assessing an institution's performance in this area.

- 10 -

EXAMINATION OBJECTIVES

1. To encourage the institution to help meet the credit
    needs of its local communities, consistent with safe and
    sound operations.

2. To determine if the institution has established and
    implemented policies and procedures to ensure that it
    serves the credit needs of the communities in which it
    is chartered to do business.

3. To determine if the institution is in compliance with
    the requirements of the Community Reinvestment Act's
    implementing regulation.

4. To assess the institution's record of helping to meet
    the credit needs of its entire community, including low-
    and moderate-income neighborhoods, consistent with safe
    and sound operations.

5. To assess, organize, and prepare information on the
    institution's CRA record to facilitate the assignment of
    a CRA rating and the preparation of examination report
    comments and the public Performance Evaluation.

- 11 -

EXAMINATION PROCEDURES

The procedures below should be used together with the Uniform Interagency Community Reinvestment Act Assessment Rating System. They should enable the examiner to gather the information necessary to form conclusions under the twelve CRA assessment factors that are grouped by five Performance Categories. In formulating conclusions, the examiner must weigh the information gathered in light of the institution's unique ability to serve credit needs.

I. ASCERTAINMENT OF COMMUNITY CREDIT NEEDS

Assessment Factor A - Activities conducted by the institution to ascertain the credit needs of its community, including the extent of the institution's efforts to communicate with members of its community regarding the credit services being provided by the institution.

1. Determine the extent to which the institution has included credit ascertainment efforts in a formal, written CRA program.

2. Determine the type and extent of contact the institution has with:

   a. Individuals and groups representing civic, religious, minority, small business, commercial and residential development, and neighborhood and fair housing interests, especially those based in or representing low- and moderate-income areas;

   b. Officials from city, county, state and federal governments;

   c. Public programs;

   d. Private, nonprofit developers or financial intermediaries that facilitate public/private partnership activities; and

   e. Trade associations and other business-related organizations.

   Such contacts should be readily described either verbally by the institution's management or through documentation maintained by the institution.

3. For 2a through 2e above, identify the steps or methods the institution undertook to determine community credit needs, including those of low- to moderate-income neighborhoods. Consideration should be given to:

- 12 -

a. Whether the institution uses a written and/or oral survey, a "call" program, or similar approach. If so, identify the members who undertook these efforts;

    b. The regularity and frequency of the effort or activities conducted;

    c. Whether specific community credit needs were identified through these contacts. If so, determine to what extent the institution responded and/or developed credit products to meet those needs. Review these credit products and the frequency of their use, particularly those designed for low- to moderate-income areas;

    d. The adequacy of management's data collection and credit needs ascertainment activities for purposes of CRA planning and management;

    e. The use of available demographic data; and

    f. The extent of participation by appropriate levels of management and staff in credit needs ascertainment.

4. Determine the extent to which the institution systematically and regularly reviews its own credit services in conjunction with community credit needs.

5. Form a conclusion as to the effectiveness of the institution's record in this area.

Note: Avoid considering social participation that results in no identification of credit needs or which is unrelated to CRA. Consider only those organizations and contacts that have actually provided information about community credit needs.

Assessment Factor C - The extent of participation by the institution's board of directors in formulating the institution's policies and reviewing its performance with respect to the purposes of the Community Reinvestment Act.

1. Determine how the board of directors and senior management use information obtained from outreach activities to review and reformulate CRA policies and performance.

2. Determine whether the board of directors has a plan for addressing its CRA responsibilities that contains measureable goals and objectives.

3. Determine whether the institution regularly analyzes the geographic distribution of its lending patterns, using available demographic information, and whether such

- 13 -

analyses are reviewed and considered by the board of directors and management, as part of the CRA planning process.

4. Determine the general role that the institution's CRA goals and objectives play in its overall business strategy.

5. Analyze how and the degree to which the board of directors and senior management are involved in the institution's CRA processes including:

    a. Exercising CRA policy oversight;

    b. Reviewing CRA activities and performance related to the institution's own lending goals and objectives;

    c. Performing periodic (at least annual) comprehensive review and analysis of the disposition of credit applications, extensions, and denials to ensure that potential borrowers are treated in a fair and nondiscriminatory manner and that all segments of the delineated community are appropriately served;

    d. Participating in activities designed to develop, improve, and enhance the local community;

    e. Developing prudent but innovative underwriting criteria that help address community credit needs;

    f. Supporting the CRA program by providing adequate, ongoing CRA-related training for institution personnel;

    g. Ensuring that the institution satisfactorily meets the supervisory agency's regulatory requirements, both technical and substantive; and

    h. Expanding the CRA Statement as suggested by the CRA Joint Policy Statement.

7. Form a conclusion as to the effectiveness of the board of director's role in CRA planning and performance.

II. MARKETING AND TYPES OF CREDIT OFFERED AND EXTENDED

Assessment Factor B - The extent of the institution's marketing and special credit-related programs to make members of the community aware of the credit services offered by the institution.

1. Determine how the institution makes members of its delineated community aware of the types of loans it offers:

- 14 -

    a. Identify each type of loan the institution offers and how it makes the community aware of that type of loan;

    b. Identify, if possible, market penetration from the various methods the institution uses (radio-listener profile, newspaper circulation, direct mail penetration, word-of-mouth or officer call programs);

    c. Identify efforts to direct credit products to low- and moderate-income neighborhoods;

    d. Identify any segments of the community that the institution's marketing methods have not reached; and

    e. Identify how the institution's staff helps individuals and groups understand the credit application process (educational activities, special financial analysis workshops, homebuyer workshops, one-on-one counseling and meetings) and apply for credit (help complete applications, referral to other financial sources, interpreters).

2. Review any geographic distribution analysis performed for purposes of Assessment Factor E. If it identified any unreasonable patterns in the distribution of the institution's credit products, determine the degree to which the institution's marketing practices contributed to the unreasonable distribution.

3. Determine the extent of the board's and management's involvement in the marketing activities of the institution as indicated by:

    a. Whether the board has approved the marketing program;

    b. Whether the board is adequately informed and aware of the institution's marketing activities and results; and

    c. Whether the board has taken appropriate follow-up action when deficiencies with the marketing are identified.

4. Form a conclusion regarding the quality and effectiveness of the institution's marketing activities and methods of making the community aware of the credit services the institution offers.

Assessment Factor I - The institution's origination of residential mortgage loans, housing rehabilitation loans, home improvement loans, and small business or small farm loans within its community, or the purchase of such loans originated in its community.

- 15 -

1. Identify the volume, both in dollars and number, of each type of loan the institution has made or purchased within its delineated community.

2. Identify the volume, both in dollars and number, of each type of loan the institution has made or purchased outside its delineated community.

3. Determine if the institution's CRA Statement is accurate:

   a. Whether the institution actually makes or purchases the types of loans it lists; and

   b. Whether the institution makes or purchases loans it does not list. If so, determine why they are not listed on the CRA Statement.

4. Form a conclusion regarding the volume and types of loans the institution has made or purchased, both within and outside its delineated community, considering its resources, the market demand for these types of loans, and the identified and most pressing credit needs of its community.

Assessment Factor J - The institution's participation in governmentally insured, guaranteed or subsidized loan programs for housing, small businesses and small farms.

1. Determine the extent of the board's and management's awareness of government-sponsored loan programs.

2. Identify the volume, both in dollars and number, for each type of loan program in which the institution participates that is within its delineated community.

3. Identify the volume, both in dollars and number, of participation in loan programs outside its delineated community.

4. Form a conclusion regarding the volume and the types of government-sponsored loan programs in which the institution participates, both within and outside its delineated community, considering its resources, the market demand for these types of loans and the identified and most pressing credit needs of its community.

- 16 -

III. GEOGRAPHIC DISTRIBUTION AND RECORD OF OPENING AND CLOSING OFFICES

Reasonableness of Delineated Community

1. Determine the institution's current community delineation(s), and review any changes since the previous examination. Note any problems that may be evident from an inspection of the maps, such as management's identification of an extremely large or small area as its community for CRA purposes.

2. Determine the method used to prepare and portray the delineation(s). Determine the extent and frequency of management's and the board's review of the delineation(s).

3. Determine whether the institution's community delineation is considered in the institution's planning process.

4. Determine the extent to which, in defining its community, the institution has considered the presence or absence of other providers of financial services, and the specific services that they provide.

5. Analyze the local community delineation(s) that comprise the institution's entire community.

    a. If the institution used the "existing boundaries" method, determine whether the area is of reasonable size for the institution, and whether significant political borders or geographic barriers used to adjust the boundaries improperly exclude adjacent low- or moderate-income areas. Analyze borders and barriers cited by the institution as reasons for adjustment and exclusion.

    Determine whether the board requested and/or management performed any other analyses to support the delineation(s).

    b. If the institution used the "effective lending territory" method, review the geographic distribution analysis performed by management, and determine whether that analysis is sufficient to identify an effective lending territory. Perform necessary validation and testing of management's analysis, and review any adjustments. Determine whether any adjacent low- or moderate-income areas have been excluded. Evaluate the reasons for such exclusion to determine whether the exclusions were proper. Determine whether any other analyses support the delineation(s).

- 17 -

    c. If the institution used "any other reasonable" method, determine whether the analysis performed by the institution supports its reasonableness.

    d. If the institution conducted "existing boundaries" or "effective lending territory" analyses before arriving at some other delineation, pay particular attention to a resulting delineation(s) that differs significantly from the results indicated by the other analyses. Analyze boundaries and excluded areas for the presence of low- or moderate-income areas.

6. Form a conclusion as to whether the community delineation is reasonable.

Assessment Factor E - The geographic distribution of the institution's credit extensions, credit applications and credit denials.

    If the institution performs its own analysis, complete steps 1 - 6; if not, or if the institution's analysis is inadequate, complete steps 7 - 9.

1. Review management's analysis or monitoring of the geographic distribution of credit extensions, applications, and denials.

2. Determine whether management's analysis includes all major product lines, but not necessarily each type of credit offered. Confirm that HMDA data (if HMDA is applicable) are used in performing the analysis.

3. Determine whether any geographic units selected other than census tracts (i.e., minor civil divisions, nine-digit Zip Code areas, etc.) are the most appropriate units available to allow meaningful analysis of loan penetration levels. Determine the adequacy of demographic information for those individual geographic units used in the analysis.

4. Determine whether management has sought explanations for any disparities and/or gaps in distribution, and whether these factors are consistent with the results of the fair housing and fair lending review and the outside contact interviews conducted.

5. Determine the extent to which the information obtained from management's analysis or monitoring is incorporated into the institution's planning process and marketing efforts.

- 18 -

6. Determine the extent to which the board of directors reviews the results of management's analyses and any action plan into which these results are incorporated.

7. If the institution is subject to HMDA or otherwise maintains a mortgage loan application log, review the distribution of home lending activity. For HMDA reporters, reports generated using the agencies' HMDA Analysis System should be utilized for this purpose. If home lending activity does not represent a major product line and the institution does not identify this activity as being particularly responsive to local credit needs, review the distribution of at least one major product line intended by management to address CRA responsibilities. These may include small business, small farm, multifamily housing purchase or rehabilitation, home equity, or other geographically significant loan programs. The use of limited judgmental samples of lending activity may be appropriate for the product line(s) selected, and the review should focus on low-and moderate-income areas.

8. Use available demographic information to identify low- and moderate-income areas. In small towns and rural areas, such identifications may be based upon information obtained from outside contacts, personal knowledge, or physical inspection.

9. Determine whether the distribution demonstrates reasonable penetration of all segments of the community. If the distribution demonstrates an unjustified, disproportionate pattern determine, to the extent possible, the causes of this pattern.

10. Form a conclusion about the appropriateness of the geographic distribution of credit, including applications and denials.

Assessment Factor G - The institution's record of opening and closing offices and providing services at offices.

1. Determine whether the institution has adopted a written policy concerning branch closings. Verify that the policy has been followed in closing any branches since the last examination.

2. Determine whether the institution evaluates the potential impact on its community of any opening and closing of offices, particularly the effect of any reduction in services provided to low- and moderate-income segments of the community.

- 19 -

3. Determine the nature and the extent to which
    representatives of the community, including the low- and
    moderate-income areas, have been consulted regarding
    proposed office closures, and the nature and extent of
    efforts by the institution to mitigate any adverse impact
    of such closings on community residents.

4. Determine whether the institution has provided timely
    advance notification of branch closures to customers
    (through a lobby notice posted at least 30 days before the
    proposed closure, and with a regular account statement or
    in a separate mailing at least 90 days before the proposed
    closure).

5. Determine whether the institution has provided at least 90
    days advance notice to the appropriate supervisory agency
    of any proposed branch closures, stating the reasons and
    statistical or other information supporting the decision.

6. Evaluate the accessibility of the institution's offices,
    including its full service business hours to all segments
    of the community.

7. Evaluate the appropriateness of services provided at
    institution offices, and of any mechanism the institution
    uses to evaluate their effectiveness.

8. Form a conclusion regarding the institution's record under
    this assessment factor addressing office opening and
    closings and the provision of services.

IV. DISCRIMINATION AND OTHER ILLEGAL CREDIT PRACTICES

Conclusions reached under factors D and F draw upon examination
findings pertaining to compliance with the antidiscrimination
laws and regulations, including the Equal Credit Opportunity
Act, Fair Housing Act, the Home Mortgage Disclosure Act, and
any agency regulations that address nondiscrimination in credit
or housing transactions. Information obtained from outside
contact interviews may provide additional insight regarding
performance under these factors.

These CRA examination procedures do not substitute for the
agency's fair lending examination procedures.

Assessment Factor D - Any practices intended to discourage
applications for types of credit set forth in the institution's
CRA Statement(s).

1. Based on work performed under the fair lending examination
    procedures and under the CRA examination procedures for
    other Assessment Factors:

- 20 -

a.   Assess the effectiveness of the institution's efforts
     to solicit credit applications from all segments of its
     community. Particular consideration should be given to
     any practices and activities that discourage or
     prescreen applicants or potential applicants on a
     prohibited basis;

b.   Assess the adequacy of written policies, procedures,
     and training programs that address illegal
     discouragement and prescreening;

c.   Determine the effectiveness of internal review systems
     and/or audit coverage with respect to the policies,
     procedures and training mentioned above;

d.   Determine the effectiveness of management reporting
     systems with respect to the policies, procedures and
     training mentioned above; and

e.   Form a conclusion regarding the effectiveness of all
     these efforts, as indicated by a review of consumer
     complaints received by the institution and the agency,
     advertisements, discussions with management and staff,
     and loan application patterns observed in HMDA
     disclosure statements or analysis reports, loan
     application registers and other lending records, and
     the results of outside contact interviews.

Assessment Factor F - Evidence of prohibited discriminatory or
other illegal credit practices.

1.   Based on work performed under the fair lending examination
     procedures and under the CRA examination procedures for
     other Assessment Factors:

a.   Determine the institution's level of compliance with
     the antidiscrimination laws and regulations, including
     the ECOA, the FHA, the HMDA and any agency regulations
     pertaining to nondiscriminatory treatment of credit
     applicants. Attention should focus on the presence of
     violations of the substantive provisions of the laws or
     regulations, and any violations that have been
     repeated;

b.   Evaluate the adequacy of action taken by management to
     avoid or correct any deficiencies and/or violations
     discovered, such as programs to ensure that potential
     denials of housing-related loans to minorities and low-
     and moderate-income applicants are reconsidered by a
     second party before denial; and

- 21 -

    c. Determine whether corrective actions were prompt, voluntary and comprehensive in scope.

2. Form a conclusion regarding performance under this assessment factor.

Note: Findings presented in the Performance Evaluation should convey the level of supervisory concern that an institution poses, as a result of its compliance (or noncompliance) with the fair lending laws. The write-up should indicate the substance and extent of any deficiencies noted that affect CRA performance, and the adequacy and timeliness of corrective action taken by management.

V. COMMUNITY DEVELOPMENT

Assessment Factor H - The institution's participation, including investments, in local community development and redevelopment projects or programs.

1. Determine the level of management awareness of opportunities for involvement in community development and redevelopment projects or programs.

2. Determine the nature of the working relationships the institution has established with government and private sector representatives to identify such opportunities, such as the frequency of contacts and the results obtained.

3. Identify the specific development and redevelopment projects or programs the institution has been involved with including:

    a. The community or communities they affect;

    b. The form of participation (direct loans or loans through intermediaries, technical advice or assistance, investment, financial or in-kind contributions);

    c. The duration of such involvement (whether ongoing or one-time);

    d. The amount of such support or participation; and

    e. Whether the institution has been a leader or follower in these projects/programs.

4. Evaluate the institution's use of nontraditional activities, such as those listed in the answer to Questions 29, 30 and 31 of the interagency question and answer document on CRA. This may be particularly applicable to limited purpose/limited service institutions.

- 22 -

5. Consider information provided by outside community contacts regarding the institution's involvement in development and redevelopment projects or programs.

6. Evaluate the extent to which these activities address the community credit needs identified through the ascertainment process.

7. Form a conclusion about the institution's awareness, and the role and scope of its involvement in community development projects and programs.

Assessment Factor K - The institution's ability to meet various credit needs based on its financial condition and size, legal impediments, local economic conditions and other factors.

1. Develop a brief profile of the institution and its community including, as appropriate, but not necessarily limited to, asset size, number of branches, business focus during the period under review (retail or wholesale, agricultural, housing, etc.), population, principal industries, and demographic information.

2. Identify any contraints on CRA performance posed by the institution's financial condition and size, legal impediments, local economic conditions and other factors.

3. Evaluate the role the institution has played in promoting economic revitalization and growth.

Note: The profile should be carried forward to the public Performance Evaluation under this factor. The Performance Evaluation may mention any formal enforcement action to which the institution is subject, if it has already been made public by the agency and is necessary to support a conclusion under this factor.

Assessment Factor L - Any other factors that, in the regulatory authority's judgement, reasonably bear upon the extent to which an institution is helping to meet the credit needs of its entire community.

1. Identify other activities which management believes have contributed to community development. Determine the extent to which such activities have a bearing on CRA performance.

2. Consider information provided by outside community contacts regarding any other CRA-related activities.

3. Determine the extent to which the institution has donated, sold on favorable terms, or made available on a rent-free

- 23 -

basis any branch of such institution which is located in any predominately minority neighborhood to any minority or women's depository institution. For purposes of this procedure "sold on favorable terms" indicates a sale at less than market value. The term "branch" indicates the physical premises and may include the assets and liabilities connected to the premises, as well. A "predominately minority neighborhood" is one that is greater than 50 percent minority.

4. Form a conclusion about the extent to which such activities have helped the institution address community credit needs.

- 24 -

EXAMINATION CHECKLIST   Yes/No

1. Has the board of directors:

   a. Adopted a CRA Statement for each local community?

   b. Approved any material change in each Statement at the first regular meeting after such change occured?

   c. Reviewed each Statement at least annually?

2. Does the institution maintain a "public file" as required?

3. Do the CRA public files contain:

   a. Signed public comments received in the past two years on the institution's CRA Statement or its community lending performance?

   b. Any responses to the comments that the institution elected to make?

   c. CRA Statement(s) in effect during the past two years?

   d. The current evaluation prepared by the supervisory agency?

4. Are public files readily available for public inspection?

5. Are all file materials maintained at the head office, and are file materials relating to each local community maintained at a designated office in that community?

6. Does the CRA Notice contain the required information and a disclosure of the availability of the evaluations to the public?

7. Is a notice provided in the public lobby of institution offices either as a part of the CRA Statement or separately?

8. Does each CRA Statement contain:

   a. A delineation of the institution's entire community, including local communities, if any?

   b. A list of specific types of credit that the institution is prepared to extend within the local community?

- 25 -

Yes/No

c. The required notice including a disclosure of the availability to the public of the evaluation and ratings, either as a part of the Statement or as an attachment?

9. Is the CRA Statement(s) readily available at the head office and at each office of the institution in the local community?

10. If a charge is made for copies of the CRA Statement or the CRA performance evaluation, do records indicate this charge does not exceed the cost of reproduction and any applicable mailing fees?

11. Does the CRA Statement contain the following additional information:

a. A description of how the institution's current efforts, including special credit-related programs, help to meet local credit needs?

b. A periodic report on the institution's record of helping to meet community credit needs?

c. A description of the institution's efforts to ascertain local credit needs, including efforts to communicate with members regarding credit services?

(Note: Inclusion of these items in the CRA Statement is not required, but is encouraged by regulation.)

12. Was the method used by the institution to define its community reasonable?

13. Does the institution's delineation of community include all low- and moderate-income neighborhoods?

14. Do the types of credit made by the institution correspond to the types of credit listed in the CRA Statement?

15. Do the types of credit the institution has made and is currently making appear reasonable?

16. Do any material changes in the types of credit the institution has made and is currently making appear reasonable?

17. Do the institution's procedures ensure that applications for listed credits are accepted?

- 26 -

Yes/No

18. Are credit and credit-related services at any offices in low- and moderate-income neighborhoods comparable to such services at other similar offices?

19. Does the institution originate or purchase residential mortgage loans, housing rehabilitation loans, and home improvement loans in the local community?

20. Does the institution originate or purchase small business loans or loans to small farms in the local community?

21. Does the institution's financial condition allow it to fully help meet community credit needs?

22. Is the institution aware of unmet credit needs in the community?

23. Does the institution consult with members of its local community about its plans and policies on available credit services?

24. Is the Board of Directors supportive of and involved in the CRA process?

25. Is the Board of Directors involved in approval, review and monitoring of marketing and advertising programs?

26. Are the institution's marketing strategies and advertising responsive to identified community credit needs?

27. Does the institution regularly perform and document analyses of the geographic distribution of its lending?

28. Are the results of geographic distribution analyses considered in establishing and evaluating the CRA program and lending policies?

29. Has the institution taken action to minimize the impact of branch closings?

30. Does the institution have policies in place regarding the closing of branches, and does it follow them?

31. Does the institution give adequate and timely advance notification to customers of any planned branch closures?

32. Does the institution participate in investment in local community development and redevelopment projects or programs?

# # #

APPENDIX 3

INTERAGENCY CRA QUESTIONS AND ANSWERS

Federal Financial Institutions **Examination Council**

2100 Pennsylvania Avenue, NW, Suite 200 · Washington, DC 20037 · (202) 634-6526 · FAX (202) 634-6556

Press Release

For immediate release   **February 16, 1993**

The Consumer Compliance Task Force of the Federal Financial Institutions Examination Council (FFIEC) today has adopted revised Interagency Questions and Answers Regarding Community Reinvestment. To help financial institutions meet their responsibilities under the Community Reinvestment Act (CRA) and to increase public understanding of the regulations and examination procedures, the staffs of the Federal Reserve Board, the Federal Deposit Insurance Corporation, the Office of Thrift Supervision, and the Office of the Comptroller of the Currency have prepared answers to the most commonly asked questions about community reinvestment. The Questions and Answers should not be regarded as official interpretations. Their purpose is to provide useful guidance to agency personnel, financial institutions and the public.

The document includes four new questions, which address the following:

o   The agencies' emphasis on lending and investment rather than documentation (23);

o   State CRA performance evaluations and the public file (13);

-over-

Board of Governors of the Federal Reserve System, Federal Deposit Insurance Corporation, National Credit Union Administration, Office of the Comptroller of the Currency, Office of Thrift Supervision

o   Outside activities and CRA performance (22); and

o   Institutions' targeting specific ethnic groups and CRA considerations (5).

The Questions and Answers are now organized by subject matter with the previously assigned numbers appearing in parentheses. Questions and answers previously numbered 4 and 5 were deleted because they were basically a reiteration of the regulation, and those previously numbered 11 and 19 were deleted because other questions and answers address the same issues. Other minor modifications were made as necessary to improve clarity.

The Interagency Questions and Answers will also appear in the Federal Register. General questions regarding this press release should be directed to Debra D. Clements, Compliance Analyst, FFIEC, (202) 634-6526.

Specific agency related questions should be directed to the following:

Federal Deposit Insurance Corporation - Office of Consumer Affairs (202) 898-3536 or Division of Supervision (202) 898-7155

Federal Reserve Board - Division of Consumer and Community Affairs (202) 452-2631

Office of the Comptroller of the Currency - Compliance Management (202) 874-4446

Office of Thrift Supervision - Specialized Programs (202) 906-6000

# # # #

INTERAGENCY QUESTIONS AND ANSWERS REGARDING CRA

SCOPE OF THE CRA'S COVERAGE

1. (26)   Are there any "regulated financial institutions" that are excluded from the scope of CRA?

In general, the CRA defines a "regulated financial institution" as one that meets the definition of an insured depository institution, under Section 3 of the Federal Deposit Insurance Act. However, the banking agency CRA "Interpretation 101" (12 CFR 25.101, 12 CFR 228.100, and 12 CFR 345.101) excludes from CRA requirements certain institutions that serve solely as correspondent banks, trust companies, or clearing agents. The banking agencies have also excluded from CRA certain financial institutions whose activities are limited to providing cash management controlled disbursement services. The rationale used in allowing certain financial institutions to be excluded from the scope of CRA is that these institutions are only incidentally involved, if at all, in granting credit to the public. The financial supervisory agencies periodically review the applicability of CRA to other types of financial institutions.

2. (1)   What does the term "office" mean as used in the regulation?

Office refers generally to a facility of an institution that accepts deposits, including an electronic deposit facility. It does not include purely administrative offices, agencies, loan production offices or facilities used, for example, only for the check collection process. In delineating a local community, an institution need not consider shared electronic deposit facilities, unless otherwise directed by the appropriate financial supervisory agency.

3. (24)   How are bank and savings association holding companies affected by the CRA?

The CRA applies to applications filed by holding companies to merge or to acquire banks and savings associations. When decisions on such applications are made, the Federal Reserve Board and the Office of Thrift Supervision will consider the CRA records of all the bank or savings association subsidiaries of the applicant holding company. The parent holding company need not prepare a CRA Statement or public notice, or maintain public comment files; but are encouraged to ensure that subsidiary financial institutions have expanded CRA

statements that include a description of the
institution's CRA performance. The holding company must
conform to the requirements of the applicable regulation
for media notices of corporate applications filed to
acquire a bank or savings association.

DELINEATION OF THE CRA COMMUNITY

**4. (2)   What is meant by "local community" and how detailed a map
should be used to portray it?**

The term "local community" refers to the contiguous area
surrounding each office or group of offices of an
institution. Although the geographic areas served by an
institution may vary with the type of service, only one
local community is to be delineated for a particular
office or group of offices. Any map which depicts an
institution's local community or communities with
reasonable clarity may be used. The map need not show
each street in the community, nor be prepared
professionally by a cartographer. Low- and
moderate-income neighborhoods should not be specifically
indicated on the map. The community delineation,
however, must not unreasonably exclude such
neighborhoods. An institution may delineate several
local communities on one map. However, each local
community, comprising the entire community, must be
delineated with sufficient clarity so that the areas
included in those local communities are obvious. If the
entire community is made up of more than a few local
communities, or the local communities are separated by
significant distances, it may be easier and clearer to
use a separate map for each local community.
Furthermore, the locations of the institution's offices
need not be shown on the maps.

**5. (new)   Can a financial institution identify a specific ethnic
group, rather than a geographic area, as its delineated
community; and can this financial institution target a
specific ethnic group in designing and marketing products
and services?**

As indicated in the answer to Question four of this
series, an institution must geographically delineate its
local community(ies) on the basis of the locations of its
offices. A delineation that does not have a geographic
basis would be inconsistent with the CRA and implementing
regulation. (The only permissible exception involves an
institution's ability to delineate a "military community"
in addition to the geographic communities surrounding its
offices.)

If an institution can maintain compliance with the Fair
Housing and Equal Credit Opportunity Acts (and this may

not always be possible), it may direct the marketing of its products and services to one or more specific ethnic groups. However, institutions that target a single ethnic group, while having offices located in multi-ethnic areas, often exhibit significant lending disparities and unsatisfactory CRA performance.

6. (3) **How should an institution deal with low- and moderate-income neighborhoods in its local community delineation?**

The CRA regulation requires that low- and moderate-income neighborhoods not be unreasonably excluded from a delineation of the local community. Institutions are expected to be generally aware of low- and moderate-income neighborhoods within their community, without undertaking extensive research. No attempt need be made to distinguish between low-income neighborhoods and moderate-income neighborhoods. If institutions desire further information about low- and moderate-income neighborhoods, they should consult such sources as state and local community development and planning agencies.

THE CRA STATEMENT

7. (6) **If an institution is prepared to offer particular types of credit only at some of its offices in a local community, should those types of credit be listed on the CRA Statements of all of its offices in that community?**

Yes. Because the institution is willing to extend that type of credit to any creditworthy borrower in the community, the institution should list the same types of credit on the CRA Statement available at each office within a particular local community even though a prospective borrower at one office may be referred to another when seeking to make application. The institution should recognize, however, that public complaints may arise because of such practices; and the financial supervisory agencies will have to decide whether the practice significantly discourages applications for such credit or otherwise adversely affects the institution's CRA performance.

THE CRA PUBLIC NOTICE

8. (13) **Are there any requirements relating to the size and placement of the Community Reinvestment Act Notice?**

The notice must be placed in the public lobby of the financial institution but the size and placement may vary. For example, if the notice takes the form of a poster, the poster must be placed within the lobby where

- 3 -

it will be seen by customers and be of sufficient size to
be easily read from a normal distance. If the notice is
provided in the form of a brochure, a supply of such
brochures printed in easily read type and placed where
they will be noticed will suffice.

THE CRA AND PUBLIC COMMENT

9. (14) **What information and avenues of communication are
         available to members of a community who are concerned
         about the CRA performance of financial institutions in
         their community?**

         Financial institutions are encouraged to communicate with
         members of their community. The CRA regulations require
         financial institutions to make their CRA Statement and
         the public CRA Performance Evaluation available to the
         public. The statement contains a copy of the Community
         Reinvestment Act Notice which must be placed in the
         offices of all financial institutions. The notice states
         that the public may write to the financial institution or
         the   appropriate   supervisory   agency   about   the
         institution's performance in helping to meet community
         credit needs.

         The public may also review letters received by the
         financial institution regarding its CRA performance and
         the public CRA Performance Evaluation prepared by the
         institution's   financial   supervisory   agency.
         Announcements of CRA-covered applications may be obtained
         by writing to the institution's financial supervisory
         agency.   Anyone   may   comment   on   the   filing   of   an
         application by writing to the appropriate financial
         supervisory agency listed either in the applicant's
         newspaper notice or its CRA notice. The financial
         supervisory agencies have varying comment periods for
         applications. Therefore, any questions about the comment
         period should be directed to the financial supervisory
         agency. Comments received within the appropriate period
         will be considered by the financial supervisory agency in
         the application process.

10. (9) **Are all signed, written CRA comment letters to be placed
         in the public comment file?**

         The regulations state that the institution must put into
         a public comment file, all signed, written comments
         relating to the CRA Statement or to the institution's
         performance in helping to meet community credit needs.
         The only exceptions are comments that reflect adversely
         on the reputation of any person, or which would violate
         a law. The institution must use its own judgment in
         deciding which comments should be placed in the public
         comment file. Signed, written comments which might harm

a person's reputation should be retained in a confidential file for inspection by the examiner.

Comments received by a financial supervisory agency will be on file at that agency. Those comments are also available to the public unless the Freedom of Information Act prohibits their disclosure.

11. (10)   **If a letter is addressed in part to an institution's overall CRA performance, but contains information which is harmful to an individual or violates a law, should the institution withhold the entire letter from the public file?**

The institution may do so. Alternatively, the statements which reflect adversely on an individual or violate a law may be deleted from the letter and the balance included in the public file. In any event, the entire original letter should be retained in a confidential file for inspection by the examiner.

12. (21)   **In assessing an institution's CRA performance, does an examiner consider and evaluate information outside of the institution being examined?**

Yes, an examiner should seek and consider any information that is necessary to complete a fair and accurate picture of the institution's CRA performance. Contacts will be made, for example, with persons who have commented on an institution's performance, local officials, local business owners, community residents, real estate brokers, or others who may be able to provide information concerning local financial institutions in helping to meet those needs. In addition, if the examiner believes that the institution's description of its community is unreasonable, the examiner may review the delineations of other, similar institutions in the community.

13. (new)   **May a State-chartered financial institution place a copy of a community reinvestment performance evaluation prepared by a State regulatory agency in the comment file(s) maintained for public inspection pursuant to Federal rules?**

A signed written comment, that addresses an institution's CRA Statement or performance in helping to meet the credit needs of its community, received from the public during the past two years should be placed in the public comment file. For the purposes of the Federal financial supervisory agencies' CRA implementing rules, any comment not prepared by the institution itself or its Federal financial supervisory agency may be considered to be from "the public." Institutions should consider the answers to Questions 10 and 11 of this series, if they are concerned that the disclosure of information received from a State regulatory agency or other source would violate Federal rules. Institutions are also advised to consult with their State regulatory agencies if they are unsure of what material received from the State is intended for public availability.

14. (12)   Must the institution respond to any or all comments received from the public?

There is no requirement that the institution respond. However, the institution may find it helpful to respond to certain comments to foster a dialogue with members of the community or to present relevant information to a financial supervisory agency. If any institution responds to a letter in the public comment file, the response must also be placed in that file, unless it reflects adversely on any person or violates a law.

15. (8)   How should past and current CRA Statements and public comment files be made available to the public in each office of an institution, particularly an institution that has offices in more than one local community?

An institution that has offices in more than one local community should maintain current CRA Statements for all its local communities at its head office and current CRA Statements for each local community in each office of the institution in that local community, except off-premises electronic deposit facilities. Any CRA Statements that were in effect during the past two years should be retained with the public comment letters in the public comment file. A comment file for the entire institution must be maintained at the head office, and a comment file pertaining to a particular local community must be retained at a designated office in that community. A copy of the most recent public CRA Performance Evaluation prepared by the institution's Federal financial supervisory agency must be maintained in each of the public comment files.

ASSESSING THE RECORD OF PERFORMANCE UNDER THE CRA

16. (17)   Will an institution's performance in helping to meet community credit needs be assessed even if an institution does not intend to make an application covered by the CRA?

Yes. While Congress directed that the approval or rejection of applications be used to encourage community reinvestment by banks and savings associations on a safe and sound basis, it also sought to have each financial supervisory agency use its examination process "to encourage" institutions to be sensitive to their responsibilities to help meet local credit needs.

17. (16)   Will activities in addition to lending be considered in the CRA assessment?

Yes.   Although the principal focus is on lending, the financial supervisory agencies recognize that other activities and efforts contribute toward the CRA's goals. The financial supervisory agencies will consider the extent to which an institution's activities foster local community revitalization. For example, the agencies will consider the institution's purchase of state or municipal bonds or involvement through investment or other contributions in a local community development project. The agencies also will consider activities such as:

o   Efforts to establish meaningful dialogue with community members concerning credit needs of the community;

o   The institution's record of opening and closing branches and offering services (including noncredit services);

o   Marketing and special credit-related programs to make community members aware of credit services offered at its offices;

o   The extent of participation by the institution's board of directors in formulating policies and reviewing its CRA performance.

18. (29)   In addition to traditional direct lending activities, what activities can financial institutions consider in meeting obligations and responsibilities under the Community Reinvestment Act?

The answer to this question is primarily designed to provide guidance to regulated financial institutions that are not "full service" providers.   The guidance herein can also be utilized by full service institutions as a means of augmenting their traditional lending activities as part of a comprehensive CRA program.   Some of these activities may require prior financial supervisory agency approval.

The following are some non-traditional activities that financial institutions may consider to help meet their responsibilities under the Community Reinvestment Act.

Debt Investments and Related Securities

o   Purchase of mortgage-backed securities or collateral trust notes from lenders or other community development finance intermediaries serving primarily low- and moderate-income areas or persons.

o   Purchase of housing, community and economic
    development loans, or participations in loans or
    loan pools from other financial institutions, state
    and local government agencies, nonprofit
    community-based development corporations, community
    loan funds, or other community development
    intermediaries originating loans to help meet the
    needs of low- and moderate-income persons or small
    businesses.

o   Purchase of government guaranteed loans (or
    participations in pools representing such loans)
    made to low- and moderate-income persons, or to
    small farm and small business owners, such as:

    --   SBA guaranteed loans or loan pools;
    --   FmHA guaranteed farm, business or housing
         loans;
    --   FHA insured loans;
    --   EDA (U.S. Economic Development Administration)
         guaranteed loans;
    --   State housing or economic development agency
         guaranteed loans.

o   Purchase of state and local government agency
    housing mortgage revenue bonds or industrial
    revenue bonds.

Equity Investments

Some activities to serve community credit needs may be
carried out through certain federal and state supervisory
agencies' programs to promote community development
investments. Such investments are required to serve
predominantly a public or community purpose. Activities
that might be carried out directly by an institution
under these programs include:

o   Purchase of limited partnership shares to provide
    the equity financing for public purpose projects
    such as construction of low- and moderate-income
    housing or provision of small business seed
    capital. General partners could be quasi-public or
    private, for-profit or nonprofit organizations;

o   Investment in the stock of a public purpose
    corporation, either for-profit or nonprofit,
    chartered to carry out activities to benefit low-
    and moderate-income areas and residents or small
    businesses.

For certain banks and holding companies, the formation
of, or investment in, a community development corporation

- 8 -

may, in accordance with applicable laws and restrictions, be a viable way to address certain credit needs in the communities of banks or holding company subsidiary banks.

Limited service or specialized banks in a holding company that owns a community development corporation operating in the bank's community could take advantage of the CDC's activities in planning and executing its own CRA responsibilities. Activities that could be carried out through a community development corporation subsidiary include, for example:

o   Acting as a general partner, joint venture partner and/or equity investor in projects that have a clear public purpose, particularly projects focused on assisting low- and moderate-income housing or small business, and on the redevelopment of deteriorating or blighted areas where private developers are not interested in the opportunities;

o   Carrying out a program to provide needed technical assistance on financial matters to small businesses or public-purpose organizations;

o   Financing and managing a public-purpose revolving loan fund to provide financing that cannot normally be provided through the private market. An example is a fund to lend monies for pre-development costs involved in evaluating and packaging projects for financing by financial institutions and/or public sector investors.

An activity that could be carried out by the institution, directly or through establishment of a separate corporation, is an investment in a wholly-owned or multi-bank/multi-investor Small Business Investment Company (SBIC) or Minority Enterprise Small Business Investment Company (MESBIC) licensed by the U.S. Small Business Administration.

Other Services and Activities

o   Letters/lines of credit to community-based organizations, private developers, nonprofit development corporations or other community finance intermediaries to support financing of low- and moderate-income housing or small business development.

o   Highly targeted corporate contributions (monetary and in-kind) to support the personnel, facilities, marketing and finance activities of community-based nonprofit organizations or other financial intermediaries that explicitly focus on helping meet credit needs of low- and moderate-income

- 9 -

persons or small businesses. Such organizations might include:

-- Nonprofit, neighborhood development corporations;
-- Housing and other credit counseling organizations;
-- Community foundations and loan funds;
-- Neighborhood Housing Services organizations;
-- SBA 504 Certified Development Companies.

o   Technical assistance to community-based nonprofit groups, state and local government agencies and community development finance and secondary market intermediaries which focus on helping to meet the credit needs of low- and moderate-income persons or areas, or small businesses. Examples of such technical assistance activities might include:

-- Serving on the board of directors or loan review committee;
-- Development of loan application and underwriting standards;
-- Development of loan processing systems;
-- Development of secondary market vehicles or programs;
-- Marketing assistance, including development of advertising and promotions, publications, workshops and conferences;
-- Training for staff and management;
-- Accounting/bookkeeping services;
-- Fund-raising, including soliciting or arranging investments;
-- Consumer education to broaden knowledge and use of credit and deposit services.

o   Assistance to community development credit unions in the institution's local community through, for example, provision of technical assistance or stable deposits to fund the credit union's lending.

19. (15)   **Must an institution document that is actually extending the types of credit listed in its CRA statement as being offered in the local community?**

The CRA regulations do not require the maintenance of any documentation other than the public comment files, CRA Statements and CRA Notices. However, an institution's level of CRA performance depends far more on its credit activities than it does on strict regulatory compliance. In assessing CRA performance, examiners will review:

o   Any analyses of the geographic distribution of the institution's credit extensions, applications, and denials prepared by the institution;

- 10 -

o   Disclosure statements, aggregation tables and Loan Application Registers, if the institution is subject to the Home Mortgage Disclosure Act;

o   Periodic financial reports filed by the institution with its supervisory agency;

o   Records such as credit files required to be maintained under Federal Reserve Regulation B implementing the Equal Credit Opportunity Act;

o   Other loan documentation that may be required under agency regulations and other information that the institution may have compiled for internal reporting and monitoring purposes;

o   Marketing materials such as advertising copy.

The documentation that the agencies expect to be maintained is primarily that which is useful to the institution's own management in administering a successful CRA program.

20. (30) **When assessing CRA performance, do the financial supervisory agencies consider a financial institutions' lending, investment, development and general support activities outside of the institution's delineated community?**

In general, the assessment of an institution's performance under CRA focuses on its record in helping to meet credit needs within its delineated community. The agencies are aware, however, that financial institutions may organize, support, or use a wide variety of programs, organizational mechanisms or intermediaries that help finance such things as low- and moderate-income housing, small and minority businesses and other community projects on a statewide, regional or even national basis. Although these programs or mechanisms may be available to support loans and investments within an institution's delineated community, they often provide the bulk of their financial support in other geographical areas.

Under certain circumstances, the agencies will give positive consideration in assessing CRA performance for active participation by a financial institution in such programs and mechanisms, even where most or all of the financing provided may ultimately benefit low- and moderate-income borrowers or neighborhoods located outside of the institution's delineated community. In determining whether and to what extent positive consideration will be given, the agencies assess the activities undertaken in the context of an institution's overall CRA program. Where such participation augments or complements an overall CRA program that is directly

- 11 -

responsive to the credit needs in an institution's delineated community, it will be considered favorably in reaching an overall CRA conclusion. However, such activities and involvements will be insufficient to compensate for an otherwise deficient record of addressing the credit needs of an institution's delineated community.

Examples of such programs or intermediary organizations (other than traditional direct lending) are:

o   Lending consortia or loan pools that provide community development financing and technical assistance for low- and moderate-income housing, small and minority business development, or other neighborhood revitalization projects;

o   Multi-investor community development corporations;

o   Limited partnerships that invest in low- and moderate-income housing;

o   Secondary market corporations and programs which explicitly target loans for low- and moderate-income housing, small and minority businesses, or small farms;

o   Quasi-public housing, community development or economic development finance corporations in which state or local government agencies participate, often with financial institutions or other contributors;

o   State bond programs for housing, community and economic development, or public infrastructure projects;

o   Public or private intermediaries which provide loan guarantees or other credit enhancements used by financial institutions to support community development lending and investment;

o   Capital investment, loan participation and other co-ventures undertaken with minority and women-owned financial institutions.

These and similar vehicles help institutionalize and support community development lending and investment. In general, they enhance the capacity of financial institutions to help meet community credit needs, including those of low- and moderate-income neighborhoods.

21. (20) **May an institution use a policy of making certain loans only to existing customers, without adversely affecting its CRA performance?**

In examining an institution, the financial supervisory agencies will pay particular attention to any restrictions placed on the availability of those types of credit that an institution has indicated on its CRA Statement that it would extend in its local community. Examiners will focus on whether any such restrictions have or would have a significantly greater impact on low- and moderate-income neighborhoods. In every case, examiners will consider:

o   The business rationale for adopting a particular policy;

o   Whether other policies would serve the same business purpose with less adverse impact;

o   The relative ease of becoming a customer eligible for credit under the restriction;

o   Whether the institution has adopted a policy of limiting certain loans to customers as a temporary response to tight money conditions or as a permanent policy.

Loans available on any restrictive basis should be listed on the CRA Statement with the restrictions noted. However, the agencies recognize that institutions occasionally make certain specialized loans to "good" customers. This type of spot lending activity need not be listed on the CRA Statement.

Any restrictive lending policies or practices found to be discriminatory on a prohibited basis will have a substantial adverse impact on an institution's CRA performance.

22. (new) **What criteria do examiners use to determine whether a director's, officer's or employee's outside activities contribute to an institution's CRA performance? What criteria do the examiners use to determine whether an institution's charitable donations contribute to its CRA performance?**

To contribute to an institution's CRA performance, an activity or charitable donation should fall into one of the following categories:

o   It resulted in the sharing of information about the institution's lending services;

- 13 -

o   Information was obtained regarding the community's
        credit needs;

o   Community members were informed about how to get or
        use credit;

o   The activity or charitable donation assisted in
        providing credit services or information to the
        community;

o   The activity or donation assisted a community
        development or redevelopment effort.

23. (new)   **Some parties have commented that the financial
            supervisory agencies emphasize assessment criteria
            relating to the CRA process over results such as lending.
            What is the current emphasis of the agencies in their
            supervisory efforts?**

            The principal focus of the financial supervisory agencies
            and the activity most encouraged through an examination
            continues to be lending and other activities within the
            community that result in extensions of credit that help
            meet identified credit needs. The answers to Questions
            20 and 30 in this series also address this issue. A
            conclusion that performance is satisfactory or better
            generally requires that the community delineation is
            reasonable; that credit extensions are consistent with
            the capacity of the institution and the identified needs
            of the community; and that lending activity reflects a
            reasonable penetration of all segments of the community,
            including its low- and moderate-income neighborhoods.

            When the above characteristics are not found to be
            present in an institution's reinvestment record, the
            underlying causes identified by the financial supervisory
            agencies' examiners are likely related to deficiencies in
            the institution's community reinvestment process. Agency
            recommendations for improving the institution's CRA
            performance usually involve:

            o   Oversight by the board of directors and management;
            o   The establishment of goals and objectives;
            o   Community outreach, product development and
                    marketing;
            o   Management and employee training;
            o   Regular monitoring of the institution's progress
                    and performance.

            Process-oriented corrective measures should be
            implemented to make the institution more responsive to
            local credit needs on a regular, ongoing basis. However,
            no level of emphasis by an institution on the CRA process
            can make up for a seriously deficient record of lending
            and investment in the community.

24. (7)   What is a "small" business or farm?

For CRA purposes, the term "small" refers to the absolute size of the business and farm rather than the relative size in their industries. Because a major concern of CRA is that all creditworthy borrowers have reasonable access to loans from banks and savings associations, small businesses and farms generally are viewed as those which do not have access to regional and national credit markets and must rely on their local lending institutions for credit.

25. (31)   What effect would an institution's selling loans it has originated within its delineated community have on the institution's CRA performance?

The agencies have found that the sale of loans in the secondary market enhances CRA performance where such sales enable an institution to recycle funds for origination of additional loans within its delineated community.

Where loans are part of a comprehensive CRA program designed to ascertain and help meet credit needs within the institution's delineated community, such loans clearly help demonstrate CRA performance, whether or not they are ultimately sold on the secondary market. To ensure that appropriate consideration under CRA is given for loans sold, however, institutions should consider retaining information concerning when and where the loans were originated.

26. (27)   To what extent will a "regulated financial institution" which is subject to statutory and/or regulatory constraints that prevent it from operating as a "full service" financial institution be expected to meet CRA performance requirements?

The institution has an affirmative obligation to seek out ways consistent with its permitted activities to assist, directly or indirectly, in helping to meet the credit needs identified in its local community, with appropriate attention to low- and moderate-income neighborhoods. As indicated in the answers to Questions 20 and 21 of this series, many services other than direct credit services can be developed to benefit the local community in a manner consistent with the intent of the CRA. Currently the financial supervisory agencies are reviewing the applicability of CRA to financial institutions that have statutory restrictions placed on their loan or deposit activities.

The CRA implementing regulations of the Federal financial supervisory agencies include twelve factors to be considered in assessing CRA performance. Every

institution's overall CRA performance record should
compare favorably, consistent with its resources and
capabilities, with the issues expressed through these
twelve factors. A financial institution's inability to
provide specific credit products or services because of
statutory or regulatory limitations does not preclude a
positive CRA performance evaluation.

An institution's board of directors should assure that
CRA performance is an integral part of the institution's
business strategy. Expected activities will include, at
minimum, meeting the basic obligations to define a local
community, to ascertain the credit needs within that
community, and to demonstrate responsiveness, directly or
indirectly, to the needs identified.

27. (28) **What do the financial supervisory agencies expect from
institutions that have <u>voluntarily</u> limited or specialized
their services to target particular markets?**

Such an institution has the same continuing and
affirmative obligation as a "full service" institution to
help meet the credit needs of its entire local community,
consistent with safe and sound operations. An
institution's self-imposed service or market limitations
may not be used as justification for a failure to define
its local community or to help, directly or indirectly,
meet the credit needs within that community, including
low- and moderate-income neighborhoods.

Whether or not an institution operates as a "full
service" entity is not a determining factor in evaluating
its CRA performance. Every institution should be able to
demonstrate that it is fulfilling its CRA
responsibilities, either within the context of its chosen
service specialties or in other ways. The final measure
of CRA performance is in the credit benefits accruing to
the institution's local community as a result of that
institution's activities, irrespective of the vehicle by
which those credit benefits are provided.

28. (18) **How will the agencies "encourage" institutions to help
meet the credit needs of their local communities?**

Encouragement will be provided in four ways. First,
within the limits of the agencies' resources, their
staffs will provide information and technical assistance
and will meet with representatives of industry and the
management of individual institutions to explain the CRA,
regulations, and examination procedures. This exchange
of information will help institutions understand the
purposes of the CRA and how the financial supervisory
agencies implement the act. Second, as part of each CRA
examination, financial supervisory agency staff will
discuss with management their findings about the

institution's CRA performance. Where appropriate, the financial supervisory agency staff may suggest ways in which the institution can improve its performance. Third, in decisions on applications, where CRA is a material factor, the agencies will publicly comment on an institution's record of performance. Fourth, the financial supervisory agencies believe that the availability the public CRA Performance Evaluations serve as an additional encouragement for institutions to help meet local credit needs on an ongoing basis.

THE EFFECT OF AN INSTITUTION'S CRA PERFORMANCE ON APPLICATIONS

29. (22) What sanctions are available to the financial supervisory agencies under the CRA?

A poor CRA performance record may result in denial of corporate application. The financial supervisory agencies may also use the full range of their enforcement powers to ensure compliance with the requirements of the CRA regulation, including preparing a CRA Statement, maintaining public comment files and making them available, and providing the CRA Notice. In addition, widespread, repeat/uncorrected, or otherwise substantive violations of anti-discrimination laws and regulations are significant adverse factors in an institution's CRA performance record, and they will prompt enforcement actions under the Equal Credit Opportunity Act, Fair Housing Act, or other applicable fair lending rules.

30. (23) Are applications for electronic deposit facilities covered by the CRA?

Generally, such applications are covered. The financial supervisory agencies have different rules regarding the processing of applications for electronic deposit facilities, and institutions should, therefore, consult their financial supervisory agency before filing.

31. (25) How does the CRA affect applications by banks and savings associations that are subsidiaries of holding companies?

Applications by a bank or savings association that is a subsidiary of a holding company will be treated by the financial supervisory agencies in the same manner as those filed by any bank or savings association. Only the CRA record of the applying bank or savings association and the activities of their subsidiaries will be taken into account. The bank or savings association may request, however, that the financial supervisory agency consider the contribution of any of the bank's or savings association's non-depository affiliates in helping to meet the credit needs of the community or communities of the applicant bank or savings association. For example,

- 17 -

if the applicant bank or savings association has an
affiliate community development corporation operating in
the same community as the applicant, the applicant may
ask that the contributions of that corporation in helping
to meet the credit needs of the particular community be
considered by the financial supervisory agency in
assessing the overall CRA record of the applicant.

# # # #

Appendix 4

FFIEC Policy Statement on Analyses of Geographic Distribution of Lending

Federal Financial Institutions **Examination Council**

1776 G Street, NW, Suite 850B · Washington, DC 20006 · (202) 357-0177 · FAX (202) 357-0191

Press Release

For immediate release

December 17, 1991

The Examination Council announced today its approval of
a policy statement on the analysis of the geographic distribution
of lending for CRA. The Council is recommending to the Federal
Reserve Board, Federal Deposit Insurance Corporation, Office of
the Comptroller of the Currency, and Office of Thrift Supervision
that they adopt the attached policy statement.

This Statement of Policy addresses the agencies' views
concerning the need for institutions to analyze the geographic
distribution of their lending patterns as a part of their CRA
planning process, to indicate what the agencies expect of the
institutions they supervise, and to give guidance on how
financial institutions can meet these expectations.

A copy of the Council-approved policy statement is
attached. For further information, contact Debra Clements,
FFIEC, Consumer Compliance Analyst, at (202) 357-0186.

(revised)

Board of Governors of the Federal Reserve System, Federal Deposit Insurance Corporation, National Credit Union Administration
Office of the Comptroller of the Currency, Office of Thrift Supervision

Federal Financial Institutions Examination Council

Community Reinvestment Act

Policy Statement on Analyses of Geographic

Distribution of Lending

The Community Reinvestment Act (CRA) contains a Congressional finding that regulated financial institutions are "required by law to demonstrate that their deposit facilities serve the convenience and needs of the communities in which they are chartered." It also directs the agencies to assess the institution's ".... record of meeting the credit needs of its entire community, including low- and moderate-income neighborhoods." The regulations that implement the CRA state that two of the twelve factors that will be considered by the agencies in assessing the performance of the institutions they supervise are (1) the extent of participation by the institution's board of directors in formulating the institution's policies and reviewing its performance with respect to the purposes of the CRA (Assessment Factor C) and (2) the geographic distribution of the institutions credit extensions, credit applications, and credit denials (Assessment Factor E).

The purpose of this policy statement is to articulate the agencies' views concerning the need for institutions to analyze the geographic distribution of their lending patterns as part of

- 2 -

their CRA planning process, to indicate what the agencies expect of the institutions they supervise, and to give guidance on how financial institutions can meet these expectations.

NEED FOR AN EFFECTIVE CRA MANAGEMENT PROCESS

The Statement of the Federal Financial Supervisory Agencies Regarding the Community Reinvestment Act (54 F.R. 13742, April 5, 1989), states the agencies' belief that an effective CRA program includes a sound process for managing the institution's responsibilities under the law, including the involvement of the board of directors and senior management in setting policy and reviewing results. This position was further reflected in the revised CRA examination rating system issued by the agencies (55 F.R. 18163, May 1, 1990) to implement the Financial Institutions Reform, Recovery, and Enforcement Act of 1989 (FIRREA).

The agencies believe that an effective CRA management process involves (a) developing a plan for addressing the institution's CRA responsibilities, (b) implementing the plan, and (c) reviewing the results and making any necessary revisions to the plan. As part of the review element of this process, an

- 3 -

annual or more frequent analysis of the disposition of loan
applications should be made to ensure that potential borrowers
are treated in a fair and nondiscriminatory manner and that all
segments of the delineated community are appropriately served.
As reflected in the interagency rating system, this analysis
should be used by the board of directors and senior management in
their CRA planning, implementation and monitoring processes.

Analyzing the geographic distribution of credit
applications, credit extensions and credit denials is an integral
part of effective CRA management. Therefore, the agencies
consider the analysis essential to the CRA management process.
The agencies expect that the institution will appropriately
document this analysis and make the documentation readily
available to their examiners.

A comprehensive and accurate analysis performed by the
institution can provide valuable information in several
respects. It can help ensure that policy and program goals and
objectives are achieved and indicate whether any adjustments are
necessary. It can assure that the institution receives
appropriate recognition for its activities from the public and
the examiners. It can help an institution recognize and avoid
the problems that may result from having unexplained geographic
skewing of its lending distribution. And, finally, these
analyses may provide the institution with knowledge of its

— 4 —

market, and its own position in that market, that it may not otherwise have.

TYPES OF GEOGRAPHIC DISTRIBUTION ANALYSIS SYSTEMS

The key to geographic distribution analysis is the demonstration of lending activities in response to identified credit needs within the institution's delineated community. The first element of such a system would entail collecting sufficient data to make a reliable analysis and sorting it in a geographic format that will be useful in reviewing the institution's lending efforts. The second element of such a system would involve overlaying information about the demographics (e.g. income levels, percent of minority population, age of housing stock, number of owner-occupied housing units, etc.) of the local community. The analysis would result from the merger of these data in a way that the institution could draw a conclusion about how well it is serving its entire community, including the low- and moderate-income areas and what changes it should make, if any.

The type and sophistication of the analysis will vary depending on such factors as the size of the institution, the number and types of products it offers, and the size and makeup of the community it serves. Small institutions in rural settings, for example, would not have the need for as

- 5 -

sophisticated a system for developing data to do this analysis as
would a large institution in a large city. Also, there are
various degrees of institutional need and community size and
composition between those two extremes. It is not the agencies'
intent to prescribe a system of data gathering and analysis that
is appropriate for every institution in every setting. Rather,
the intent is to provide guidance regarding the types of systems
various institutions might consider when they attempt to put such
a program in place.

HMDA Data. For mortgage-related lending, one available
source of data for most institutions in large metropolitan areas
that are designated by the United States Bureau of the Census as
Metropolitan Statistical Areas (MSA's), is the data generated
under the Home Mortgage Disclosure Act (HMDA). This is data on
home mortgage lending and home improvement lending that is
reported to the institution's federal supervisory agency,
aggregated and made public by the Federal Financial Institutions
Examination Council. The agencies believe that an analysis by
each covered institution of its own HMDA data is a necessary
element of an analysis of that institution's geographic lending
patterns.

HMDA data has several important aspects. First, it is
collected and reported by the institution itself. Second, when
aggregated, it is linked to important demographic data for the

- 6 -

areas involved. Therefore, the data should be seen as reliable by the institution that carefully collects and reports it, and it can be used without change to reach some conclusions about the demographic impact of the geographic lending patterns of the institution's housing related loans.

Other Lending. Most institutions list other types of lending on their CRA statement as part of their lending plan for meeting their responsibilities under CRA. Therefore, it will be necessary to have data at least about the major product lines offered, and to apply the demographics to that lending data in making the analysis. What follows are intended as examples of the types of systems the agencies believe would be appropriate. However, they are not intended to be exclusive or to preclude institutions from designing different systems that fit their needs more adequately.

Many institutions, especially the larger ones, are likely to find that it is desirable to use some sort of computer application to keep track of the data necessary to make this analysis. For example, it may be useful to identify activity by location, based on codes entered into the lending databases. Alternatively, some institutions may find it sufficient to use self-developed or purchased software that facilitates an analysis through spreadsheet applications, or that correlates lending records with such things as census tract information and that

- 7 -

develop reports using maps, tabular displays, or other
representations of the community's demographics.

Other lenders, especially smaller institutions in small
towns or rural areas, may find a significantly lesser effort to
be sufficient to analyze their lending record. For example, the
institution's lending record may be adequately demonstrated by
using a paper-based reporting of lending volume by local branches
or by individual lending officers. Alternatively, the data about
lending location may be gleaned from plotting the actual location
of the loans on a map and then correlating the resulting array
with the demographics for the areas involved. All such systems,
other than the HMDA system, may involve the collection of all
relevant lending data or a sample that is representative of the
overall lending patterns for the type of loan being reviewed.

Demographic data. Demographic data resources may be found
in various locations, including county or city planning offices,
regional planning authorities, and economic research studies from
area colleges and universities. Personal knowledge of the
institution's directors, officers, and employees regarding the
community's demographic makeup should be incorporated,
particularly in smaller communities. Information obtained from
the institution's own community outreach and marketing efforts
can be usefully correlated with raw data on geographic lending
patterns to reach conclusions about the impact of the
institution's lending patterns and practices.

- 8 -

THE ANALYSIS

The important elements in this policy statement are (1) that a documented analysis of the institution's geographic lending patterns should be done and (2) that the analysis should be reviewed and considered by the board of directors and appropriate levels of management in setting and evaluating the institution's CRA program and its lending policies. To do that, it is recognized that some data collection will be necessary and that it will be necessary to correlate that data with the relevant demographic data relating to the institution's community. The agencies believe this process will render important insights for the institutions, as well as their communities. They also believe that this effort should be an ongoing part of the management of the institution.

If an institution needs guidance regarding the specific method it can or should use for analyzing the geographic distribution of its lending activity, it may contact its supervisory agency.

\#   \#   \#

Appendix 5

CRA Evaluation Format

<u>(EVALUATION FORMAT)</u>

<u>PUBLIC DISCLOSURE</u>

(Date of Evaluation)

COMMUNITY REINVESTMENT ACT PERFORMANCE EVALUATION

(Name of Depository Institution)
(Institution's Identification Number)

(Address)

(Name of Supervisory Agency)

(Address)

NOTE: This evaluation is not, nor should it be
          construed as, an assessment of the financial
          condition of this institution. The rating
          assigned to this institution does not represent
          an analysis, conclusion or opinion of the
          federal financial supervisory agency concerning
          the safety and soundness of this financial
          institution.

GENERAL INFORMATION

This document is an evaluation of the Community Reinvestment Act (CRA) performance of (Name of depository institution) prepared by (Name of agency), the institution's supervisory agency.

The evaluation represents the agency's current assessment and rating of the institution's CRA performance based on an examination conducted as of (the date on the cover). It does not reflect any CRA-related activities that may have been initiated or discontinued by the institution after the completion of the examination.

The purpose of the Community Reinvestment Act of 1977 (12 U.S.C. 2901), as amended, is to encourage each financial institution to help meet the credit needs of the communities in which it operates. The Act requires that in connection with its examination of a financial institution, each federal financial supervisory agency shall (1) assess the institution's record of helping to meet the credit needs of its entire community, including low- and moderate-income neighborhoods, consistent with safe and sound operations of the institution, and (2) take that record of performance into account when deciding whether to approve an application of the institution for a deposit facility.

The Financial Institutions Reform, Recovery and Enforcement Act of 1989, Pub. L. No. 101-73, amended the CRA to require the Agencies to make public certain portions of their CRA performance assessments of financial institutions.

Basis for the Rating

The assessment of the institution's record takes into account its financial capacity and size, legal impediments and local economic conditions and demographics, including the competitive environment in which it operates. Assessing the CRA performance is a process that does not rely on absolute standards. Institutions are not required to adopt specific activities, nor to offer specific types or amounts of credit. Each institution has considerable flexibility in determining how it can best help to meet the credit needs of its entire community. In that light, evaluations are based on a review of 12 assessment factors, which are grouped together under 5 performance categories, as detailed in the following section of this evaluation.

<u>ASSIGNMENT OF RATING</u>

Identification of Ratings

In connection with the assessment of each insured depository institution's CRA performance, a rating is assigned from the following groups:

Outstanding record of meeting community credit needs.

An institution in this group has an outstanding record of, and is a leader in, ascertaining and helping to meet the credit needs of its entire delineated community, including low- and moderate-income neighborhoods, in a manner consistent with its resources and capabilities.

Satisfactory record of meeting community credit needs.

An institution in this group has a satisfactory record of ascertaining and helping to meet the credit needs of its entire delineated community, including low- and moderate-income neighborhoods, in a manner consistent with its resources and capabilities.

Needs to improve record of meeting community credit needs.

An institution in this group needs to improve its overall record of ascertaining and helping to meet the credit needs of its entire delineated community, including low- and moderate-income neighborhoods, in a manner consistent with its resources and capabilities.

Substantial noncompliance in meeting community credit needs.

An institution in this group has a substantially deficient record of ascertaining and helping to meet the credit needs of its entire delineated community, including low- and moderate-income neighborhoods, in a manner consistent with its resources and capabilities.

DISCUSSION OF INSTITUTION'S PERFORMANCE

Institution's Rating:

This institution is rated [Insert Applicable Rating] based on the findings presented below.

I. ASCERTAINMENT OF COMMUNITY CREDIT NEEDS

Assessment Factor A - Activities conducted by the institution to ascertain the credit needs of its community, including the extent of the institution's efforts to communicate with members of its community regarding the credit services being provided by the institution.

(Conclusion/Support):

Assessment Factor C - The extent of participation by the institution's board of directors in formulating the institution's policies and reviewing its performance with respect to the purposes of the Community Reinvestment Act.

(Conclusion/Support):

II. MARKETING AND TYPES OF CREDIT OFFERED AND EXTENDED

Assessment Factor B - The extent of the institution's marketing and special credit-related programs to make members of the community aware of the credit services offered by the institution.

(Conclusion/Support):

Assessment Factor I - The institution's origination of residential mortgage loans, housing rehabilitation loans, home improvement loans, and small business or small farm loans within its community, or the purchase of such loans originated in its community.

(Conclusion/Support):

Assessment Factor J - The institution's participation in governmentally-insured, guaranteed or subsidized loan programs for housing, small businesses, or small farms.

(Conclusion/Support):

III. GEOGRAPHIC DISTRIBUTION AND RECORD OF OPENING AND CLOSING OFFICES

Reasonableness of Delineated Community

(Conclusion/Support):

Assessment Factor E - The geographic distribution of the institution's credit extensions, credit applications, and credit denials.

(Conclusion/Support):

Assessment Factor G - The institution's record of opening and closing offices and providing services at offices.

(Conclusion/Support):

IV. DISCRIMINATION AND OTHER ILLEGAL CREDIT PRACTICES

Assessment Factor D - Any practices intended to discourage applications for types of credit set forth in the institution's CRA Statement(s).

(Conclusion/Support):

Assessment Factor F - Evidence of prohibited discriminatory or other illegal credit practices.

(Conclusion/Support):

V.   COMMUNITY DEVELOPMENT

Assessment Factor H - The institution's participation, including investments, in local community development and redevelopment projects or programs.

(Conclusion/Support):

Assessment Factor K - The institution's ability to meet various community credit needs based on its financial condition and size, legal impediments, local economic conditions and other factors.

(Conclusion/Support):

Assessment Factor L - Any other factors that, in the regulatory authority's judgment, reasonably bear upon the extent to which an institution is helping to meet the credit needs of its entire community.

(Conclusion/Support):

APPENDIX 6

CRA PROFILES

COMMUNITY REINVESTMENT ACT PROFILES

Outstanding	Satisfactory	Needs to Improve	Substantial Noncompliance
An institution in this group has an outstanding record of ascertaining and helping to meet the credit needs of its entire local community, including low- and moderate-income neighborhoods, in a manner consistent with its resources and capabilities. CRA is a demonstrated and important component of the institution's planning process and is explicitly reflected in its formal policies, procedures, and training programs. The management of the CRA process is thorough and includes comprehensive and readily available documentation of the institution's CRA-related activities. The board of directors and senior management are highly involved in planning for, implementing, and monitoring the institution's CRA-related performance. The institution has played a leadership role in promoting economic revitalization and growth and/or has engaged in other activities to help meet community credit needs. The institution is highly involved with a broad spectrum of community organizations and	An institution in this group has a satisfactory record of ascertaining and helping to meet the credit needs of its entire local community, including low- and moderate-income neighborhoods, in a manner consistent with its resources and capabilities. CRA is routinely considered in the institution's planning process. The CRA program, including goals, objectives and methodology for self-assessment, is articulated and generally understood by all levels of the institution, but may not be explicitly reflected in its formal policies, procedures, and training programs. Employee training for CRA is adequate. The management of the CRA process is satisfactory and includes adequate documentation of the institution's CRA-related activities. The board of directors and senior management have regular involvement in the institution's CRA planning, implementation and monitoring process. The institution has a satisfactory level of involvement with most community organizations and the public sector. The institution determines its	An institution in this group needs to improve its overall record of ascertaining and helping to meet the credit needs of its entire local community, including low- and moderate-income neighborhoods, in a manner consistent with its resources and capabilities. The institution's program for meeting responsibilities under CRA is inadequate; specific, identifiable weaknesses are apparent. The board of directors and senior management provide only limited support to the CRA training of personnel. The institution does not adequately document or monitor its CRA-related activities. The board of directors and senior management have limited involvement in the institution's CRA planning, implementation and monitoring process, if such process exists. The institution engages in limited affirmative outreach to the community, passively determines credit needs and addresses them primarily with existing standard loan products. The institution has limited, if any, involvement with local community organiza-	An institution in this group has a substantially deficient record of ascertaining and helping to meet the credit needs of its entire local community, including low- and moderate-income neighborhoods, in a manner consistent with its resources and capabilities. CRA responsibilities are rarely, if ever, considered within the institution's planning process or its policies, procedures, or training programs. The institution does not have a viable program for meeting responsibilities under CRA. The institution does not actively monitor its CRA activities. Little or no documentation exists to demonstrate an adequate level of performance. The board of directors and senior management have little, if any, involvement in the institution's CRA planning, implementation and monitoring process. The institution has no meaningful interaction with community organization and the public sector. The institution has not actively promoted community economic revitalization or growth, and it has shown very limited interest in

COMMUNITY REINVESTMENT ACT PROFILES   PAGE 2

Outstanding	Satisfactory	Needs to Improve	Substantial Noncompliance
the public sector. The institution employs affirmative outreach efforts to determine community credit needs and addresses them through innovative product development. The institution's marketing aggressively promotes credit services including, when appropriate, special programs which are responsive to the needs of the community and, as a result, the institution has significantly benefit the extended loans which significantly benefit its local community. The CRA statement correctly lists all of the institution's credit products available throughout its local community. The institution's delineated community meets the purpose of the CRA and does not exclude low- and moderate-income neighborhoods. The geographic distribution of the institution's credit extensions, applications, and denials reflect a reasonable penetration of all segments of its local community. Internal monitoring procedures are well documented. The institution is in substantial compliance with all provisions	community credit needs and normally addresses them through appropriate loan product development. The institution has played a supportive role in promoting and participating in economic revitalization and growth and/or has demonstrated a willingness to explore other activities which help to meet community credit needs. The institution has marketed credit services which address identified community credit needs and has extended loans which benefit its local community. The CRA statement correctly lists the majority of the institution's credit products available throughout its local community. The institution's delineated community meets the purpose of the CRA and does not exclude low- and moderate-income neighborhoods. The geographic distribution of the institution's credit extensions, applications, and denials demonstrates a reasonable penetration of all segments of its local community. The institution is in compliance with the substantive provisions of antidiscrimination laws and regulations,	tions and the public sector. The institution has played only a limited role in developing projects to foster economic revitalization and growth, but management may express a willingness to consider participation in other activities which help meet community credit needs if they are presented to the institution. The institution has limited marketing of credit services responsive to community credit needs, and advertisements are not generally reflective of identified community credit needs. The CRA statement may not accurately reflect certain credit products that the institution makes available throughout its local community. The institution's delineated community is unreasonable and may exclude some low- and moderate-income neighborhoods. The geographic distribution of the institution's credit extensions, applications, and denials demonstrates an unjustified, disproportionate lending pattern, adversely impacting low- and moderate-income neighborhoods within its local community. The institution is not in	pursuing other activities to address community credit needs. The institution is not generally aware of existing credit needs and may not have appropriate loan products to address them. The institution does not advertise credit services based upon identified community needs. The CRA statement is materially inaccurate with respect to the types of credit the institution is willing to make available throughout its local community. The institution's delineated community is unreasonable and excludes low- and moderate-income neighborhoods. The institution's restrictive credit policies contribute to unjustified, disproportionate lending patterns, adversely impacting low- and moderate-income neighborhoods within its local community. The institution is in substantial noncompliance with antidiscrimination laws and regulations, including fair lending and fair housing laws. The institution is of significant supervisory concern in CRA matters and requires the strongest supervisory encouragement to be responsive to

COMMUNITY REINVESTMENT ACT PROFILES			PAGE 3
Outstanding	Satisfactory	Needs to Improve	Substantial Noncompliance
of the antidiscrimination laws and regulations, including fair lending and fair housing laws. The institution has demonstrated the ability to monitor and assess its own performance, and it presents no supervisory concern in CRA matters.	including fair lending and fair housing laws. The institution does not present a supervisory concern in CRA matters. It may, however, benefit from additional encouragement to ascertain and and help meet community credit needs, initiate community contacts, or pursue special programs on an ongoing and more aggressive basis.	compliance with the substantive provisions of anitdiscrimination laws and regulations, including fair lending and fair housing laws. The institution is of supervisory concern in CRA matters and requires strong encouragement to improve the level of performance.	community credit needs.

I. ASCERTAINMENT OF COMMUNITY CREDIT NEEDS

Assessment Factor A	Outstanding	Satisfactory	Needs to Improve	Substantial Noncompliance
Activities conducted by the institution to ascertain the credit needs of its community, including the extent of its efforts to communicate with members of its community regarding the credit services being provided by the institution.	The institution has an outstanding record of determining the credit needs of its local community, including low- and moderate-income neighborhoods. This may take the form of: • ongoing, meaningful contacts with a full range of individuals and groups representing civic, religious, neighborhood, minority and small business organizations, and commercial and residential real estate development; • ongoing contact with officials and leaders from city, county, state and federal governments and active participation in public programs; and, • established, productive relationships such as those with private, non-profit developers or financial intermediaries resulting in public/private partnership activities. The institution regularly collects and analyzes local demographic data in relation to its lending activities. The board of directors and senior management maintain a proactive attitude and a high degree of responsiveness in addressing community credit needs through product development, including loans for residential mortgages, housing rehabilitation,	The institution has a satisfactory record of determining credit needs of its local community, including low- and moderate-income neighborhoods. This may take the form of: • regular contacts with a large range of individuals and groups representing civic, religious, neighborhood, minority and small business organizations, and commercial and residential real estate development; • regular contact with officials and leaders from city, county, state, and federal governments and some participation in public programs; and, • regular contact with private, non-profit developers or financial intermediaries that may be used for public/private partnership opportunities. The institution periodically reviews published, local demographic data in relation to its lending activities. The board of directors and senior management satisfactorily respond to local input regarding community credit needs through product development, including loans for residential mortgages, housing rehabilitation, home improvement, small businesses, small farms and rural	The institution needs to improve its contacts within the community to determine the credit needs of its local community, including low- and moderate-income neighborhoods. This is represented by: • limited contact with individuals and groups representing civic, religious, neighborhood, minority and small business organizations, and commercial and residential real estate development; • limited contact with officials and leaders from city, county, state, and federal governments and marginal effort to participate in public programs; and, • a lack of productive contact with private, non-profit developers or financial intermediaries that may be used for public/private partnership opportunities. The institution occasionally considers or analyzes published demographic data in relation to its lending activities. The board of directors and senior management show limited response to outside input regarding community credit needs through product development, including loans for residential mortgages, housing rehabilitation, home improvement, small business,	The institution does not conduct, or has little involvement in, activities that determine credit needs of its local community, including low- and moderate-income neighborhoods. This is represented by few, if any contacts with: • representatives of civic, religious, neighborhood, minority and small business organizations, and commercial and residential real estate development; • private, non-profit developers or financial intermediaries that may be used for public/private partnership opportunities; and, • officials and leaders from city, county, state and federal governments, and the institution makes little or no effort to participate in public programs. The institution is unaware of, or ignores, the existence of demographic data and does not use it to analyze its lending activities. The board of directors and senior management rarely (or, do not) respond to community credit needs through product development, including loans for residential mortgages, housing rehabilitation, home improvement, small businesses, small farms, and rural development. Lending services are rarely

I. ASCERTAINMENT OF COMMUNITY CREDIT NEEDS

Assessment Factor A	Outstanding	Satisfactory	Needs to Improve	Substantial Noncompliance
	home improvement, small businesses, small farms, and rural development. Senior management performs systematic and regular reviews of lending services. The institution offers products well-suited to identified needs, which may include products that make use of government-insured and publicly-sponsored programs. The board of directors and senior management demonstrate willingness to explore and offer conventional products with special features and more flexible lending criteria to make credit more widely available, throughout the institution's local community, within the bounds of safe and sound lending practices.	development. Senior management performs informal reviews of lending services. The institution offers products reasonably suited to identified needs, which may include products that make use of government-insured and publicly-sponsored programs. The institution offers a variety of conventional products, and may explore and offer conventional products with special features and more flexible lending criteria to make credit more widely available, throughout its local community, within the bounds of safe and sound lending practices.	small farms, and rural development. Senior management infrequently reviews its CRA-related activities or its lending services in response to changing credit needs. Credit products may not be structured or sufficiently varied to address the identified credit needs of certain segments of the institution's local community, especially in low- and moderate-income neighborhoods. The institution is not a significant participant in government-insured and/or publicly-sponsored programs. Limited efforts have been made to offer a variety of conventional products or explore special features and more flexible lending criteria to make sound credit more widely available throughout the institution's local community.	(or, are not) reviewed in response to changing credit needs. Customer input and/or information on credit needs is rarely (or, is not) taken into account in product development, especially from customers in low- and moderate-income areas. There is nominal or no participation in government-insured and/or publicly-sponsored programs. There is little or no effort made to offer a variety of conventional products or explore special features and more flexible lending criteria to make sound credit more widely available throughout the institution's local community.

I. ASCERTAINMENT OF COMMUNITY CREDIT NEEDS

Assessment Factor C	Outstanding	Satisfactory	Needs to Improve	Substantial Noncompliance
The extent of participation by the institution's board of directors in formulating policies and reviewing the institution's performance with respect to the purposes of the Community Reinvestment Act.	CRA is a demonstrated and important component of the board of director's planning process. A formal, written CRA program exists with goals, objectives and methodology for self-assessment. The board of directors and senior management: • Are an integral part of the CRA process and activities. • Exercise active policy oversight and conduct regular reviews of CRA activities and performance. • Ensure that an annual, or more frequent, analysis of the disposition of loan applications is made to ensure that potential borrowers are treated in a fair and nondiscriminatory manner. • Are personally involved in activities designed to develop, improve and enhance the local community. • Consistently support prudent but innovative underwriting criteria that help address community credit needs and that may not fall within the criteria of the institution's more conventional loan products. • Provide active support to the CRA training of personnel. • Have expanded their CRA	CRA is routinely considered in the board of directors' planning process. The institution's CRA program, including goals, objectives and methodology for self-assessment, is articulated and generally understood by all levels of the institution, but may not be explicitly reflected in its formal policies, procedures and training programs. The board of directors and senior management: • Are generally involved in the CRA process and activities. • Exercise policy oversight and conduct occasional reviews of CRA activities and performance. • Ensure that at least an annual analysis of the disposition of loan applications is made to ensure that potential borrowers are treated in a fair and nondiscriminatory manner. • Have some involvement in activities designed to develop, improve and enhance the local community. • Consider prudent but innovative underwriting criteria that help address community credit needs and that may not fall within the criteria of the institution's more conventional loan products. • Provide adequate support	CRA is sometimes considered in the board of director's planning process. The institution's CRA program is inadequate and may lack goals, objectives and methodology for self-assessment. The board of directors and senior management: • Have limited involvement in the CRA process and activities. • May exercise some policy oversight but conduct infrequent reviews of CRA acitivities and performance. • Do not ensure that any more than a limited analysis of the disposition of loan applications is made to ensure that potential borrowers are treated in a fair and nondiscriminatory manner. • Have limited involvement in activities designed to develop, improve and enhance the local community. • May be reluctant to consider prudent but innovative underwriting criteria that help address community credit needs and that may not fall within the criteria of the institution's more conventional loan products. • Provide only limited support to the CRA training of personnel.	CRA is rarely (or, is not) considered in the board of director's planning process. The institution does not have an articulated and implemented program for dealing with its responsibilities under CRA. The board of directors and senior management: • Have little, if any, involvement in the CRA process and activities. • Exercise little, if any, policy oversight with respect to CRA and rarely (or, do not) conduct reviews of CRA activities and performance. • Rarely (or does not) ensure that an analysis of the disposition of loan applications is made to ensure that potential borrowers are treated in a fair and nondiscriminatory manner. • Have little, if any, involvement in activities designed to develop, improve and enhance the local community. • Are reluctant to consider prudent but innovative underwriting criteria that help address community credit needs and that may not fall within the criteria of the institution's more conventional loan products. • Provide little, if any, support to the CRA training of personnel.

I. ASCERTAINMENT OF COMMUNITY CREDIT NEEDS

Assessment Factor C	Outstanding	Satisfactory	Needs to Improve	Substantial Noncompliance
	Statement describing the institutions's CRA policies and programs, discussing the results of their self-assessment, and summarizing documentation of the institution's performance. • Effectively ensure that CRA technical regulatory requirements are consistently met.	to the CRA training of personnel. • Generally ensure that CRA technical regulatory requirements are consistently met. The institution's CRA Statement satisfactorily meets the regulatory requirements. The board of directors and senior management have expanded the statement to describe the institution's CRA policies, programs and results; however, the material in the expanded statement might not be fully descriptive of the institution's performance.	• May be lax in ensuring that CRA technical regulatory requirements are met.	• Rarely (or, do not) ensure that CRA technical regulatory requirements are met.

II. MARKETING AND TYPES OF CREDIT OFFERED AND EXTENDED

Assessment Factor B	Outstanding	Satisfactory	Needs to Improve	Substantial Noncompliance
The extent of the institution's marketing and special credit-related programs to make members of the community aware of the credit services it offers.	The institution has implemented sound marketing and advertising programs that are approved, reviewed and monitored by senior management and the board of directors. The programs inform all segments of the institution's local community of general financial products and services offered, including those that have been developed to address identified community credit needs. Marketing strategies ensure that products and services are responsive to identified community needs. Advertisements are designed to stimulate awareness of credit services throughout the institution's entire local community, including low- and moderate-income neighborhoods. This includes use of special media aimed at particular segments of the community. Complete, readily available marketing and advertising records are maintained and internally reviewed for compliance with applicable laws and regulations. Personnel routinely provide assistance to individuals and groups in understanding and applying for credit.	The institution has implemented adequate marketing and advertising programs that function outside the formal oversight of senior management and the board of directors. The programs are designed to inform all segments of the institution's local community of general financial products and services offered and any products that may have been developed to address identified community credit needs. Although advertisements, including those for credit products, are carried in widely circulated local media, additional advertising in media directed toward low- and moderate-income neighborhoods may be needed in order for the advertising program to be effective throughout the institution's local community. The institution maintains adequate records of its advertising, and these are occasionally reviewed for effectiveness in all segments of its local community. The institution may have established, but limited, policies and procedures to review proposed marketing campaigns for compliance with applicable laws and regulations. Personnel generally provide assistance to individuals and groups in understanding and applying for credit.	The institution's marketing and advertising programs have limited oversight by senior management and the board of directors, and may require revision or expansion to inform all segments of the institution's local community of general financial products and services offered. Marketing strategies are primarily designed to promote an image of the institution as a provider of general financial products and services or as a provider of only deposit services. Although advertisements are primarily carried in local media, the institution does not advertise in media specifically directed to low- and moderate-income neighborhoods within its local community. The institution maintains limited documentation of its advertising. The advertising is infrequently reviewed for compliance with applicable laws and regulations. Marketing campaigns are infrequently reviewed for their effectiveness in informing all segments of the institution's local community. Personnel make limited effort to assist individuals and groups in understanding and applying for credit.	The institution's marketing and advertising programs, if existent, are inadequate as they do not address credit products directed to all segments of the institution's local community, including low- and moderate-income neighborhoods. The institution does not maintain sufficient documentation of its advertising. The advertising is rarely (or, is not) reviewed for compliance with applicable laws and regulations. There is little, if any, effort to assist individuals and groups in understanding and applying for credit.

II. MARKETING AND TYPES OF CREDIT OFFERED AND EXTENDED

Assessment Factor I	Outstanding	Satisfactory	Needs to Improve	Substantial Noncompliance
The institution's origination of residential mortgage loans, housing rehabilitation loans, home improvement loans, and small business and small farm loans within its community; or the purchase of such loans originated in its community.	The institution has undertaken significant efforts to affirmatively address a substantial portion of the identified community credit needs through the origination and purchase of loans, including those for residential mortgages, housing rehabilitation, home improvement, small businesses, small farms, and rural development. Lending levels reflect exceptional reponsiveness to the most pressing community credit needs. A substantial majority of loans are within the delineated community. Loan volume, in relation to the institution's resources and the community's credit needs, exceeds expectations. The CRA Statement correctly lists all of the institution's credit products available throughout its local community.	The institution has undertaken efforts to address a significant portion of the identified community credit needs through the origination and purchase of loans, including those for residential mortgages, housing rehabilitation, home improvement, small businesses, small farms, and rural development. Lending levels reflect a general responsiveness to the most pressing community credit needs. A significant volume of loans are within the institution's delineated community. Loan volume is adequate in relation to the institution's resources and its community's credit needs. The CRA Statement correctly lists the majority of the institution's credit products available throughout its local community.	The institution is marginally involved in addressing identified community credit needs through origination and purchase of loans, including those for residential mortgages, housing rehabilitation, home improvement, small businesses, small farms, and rural development. Lending levels reflect marginal responsiveness to the most pressing community credit needs. A significant volume of loans may be outside the institution's delineated community, and/or loan volume may be low in relation to the institution's resources and its community's credit needs. The CRA Statement may not accurately list certain credit products that the institution makes available throughout its local community and/or may list some credit products that the institution does not make available.	The institution is minimally involved in addressing identified community credit needs through origination and purchase of loans, including those for residential mortgages, housing rehabilitation, home improvement, small businesses, small farms, and rural development. Lending levels reflect little, if any, responsiveness to the most pressing community credit needs. A substantial majority of loans are outside the institution's delineated community, and/or loan volume is excessively low in relation to the institution's resources and its community's credit needs. The CRA Statement is materially inaccurate with respect to the types of credit the institution is willing to make available throughout its local community.

II. MARKETING AND TYPES OF CREDIT OFFERED AND EXTENDED

Assessment Factor J	Outstanding	Satisfactory	Needs to Improve	Substantial Noncompliance
The institution's participation in governmentally-insured, guaranteed, or subsidized loan programs for housing, small businesses or small farms.	When an identified community credit need exists, the institution takes a leadership role in meeting that need and affirmatively participates in governmentally-insured, guaranteed, or subsidized loan programs for housing, small businesses, small farms, and rural development.	When an identified community credit need exists, the institution generally takes some steps to help meet that need and frequently participates in governmentally-insured, guaranteed, or subsidized loan programs for housing, small businesses, small farms, and rural development.	When an identified community credit need exists, the institution sometimes becomes involved in helping to meet that need and infrequently participates in governmentally-insured, guaranteed, or subsidized loan programs for housing, small businesses, small farms, and rural development.	When an identified community credit need exists, the institution rarely (or, never) becomes involved in helping to meet that need or in participating in governmentally-insured, guaranteed, or subsidized loan programs for housing, small businesses, small farms, and rural development.

III. GEOGRAPHIC DISTRIBUTION AND RECORD OF OPENING AND CLOSING OFFICES

Assessment Factor	Outstanding	Satisfactory	Needs to Improve	Substantial Noncompliance
Reasonableness of Delineated Community	The institution's delineated community meets the purpose of the CRA and does not exclude low- and moderate-income neighborhoods.	The institution's delineated community meets the purpose of the CRA and does not exclude low- and moderate-income neighborhoods.	The institution's delineated community is unreasonable and may exclude some low- and moderate-income neighborhoods. The institution's guidelines for defining its community need revision.	The institution's delineated community is unreasonable and excludes low- and moderate-income neighborhoods. The institution's guidelines for defining its community need substantial revision.

III. GEOGRAPHIC DISTRIBUTION AND RECORD OF OPENING AND CLOSING OFFICES

Assessment Factor E	Outstanding	Satisfactory	Needs to Improve	Substantial Noncompliance
The geographic distribution of the institution's credit extensions, credit applications, and credit denials.	The institution has a documented analysis demonstrating that the geographic distribution of its credit extensions, applications, and denials reflect a reasonable penetration of all segments of its local community, including low- and moderate-income neighborhoods. The institution has formulated procedures to identify the geographic distribution of its loan products. This information is documented and used by the board of directors and senior management in the institution's establishment of loan policies, products and services, and marketing plans.	The geographic distribution of the institution's credit extensions, applications, and denials demonstrates a reasonable penetration of all segments of its local community, including low- and moderate-income neighborhoods. The geographic distribution of the institution's loan products may be used by the board of directors and senior management in the establishment of loan policies, products and services, and marketing plans.	The geographic distribution of the institution's credit extensions, applications, and denials demonstrates an unjustified, disproportionate pattern with respect to the activity inside its delineated community as compared to the activity outside the delineated community and/or with respect to the distribution of loans, applications and denials within the various segments of its community. The board of directors and senior management may be unaware of the geographic distribution of the institution's loan products or accord inadequate or no review of lending policies and practices with regard to how they affect lending patterns within their local community. Senior management has not taken adequate corrective action on previously identified unreasonable lending patterns.	The geographic distribution of the institution's credit extensions, applications, and denials does, in fact, indicate unreasonable lending patterns inside and outside its delineated community, particularly in low- and moderate-income neighborhoods. The board of directors and senior management disregard the geographic distribution of the institution's loan products and have taken limited or no corrective action on previously identified unreasonable lending patterns. Loan policies and procedures contain restrictions which have or can be expected to have a significant adverse impact on loan availability in low- and moderate-income neighborhoods within the institution's local community.

III. GEOGRAPHIC DISTRIBUTION AND RECORD OF OPENING AND CLOSING OFFICES

Assessment Factor G	Outstanding	Satisfactory	Needs to Improve	Substantial Noncompliance
The institution's record of opening and closing offices and providing services at offices.	Offices are readily accessible to all segments of the institution's local community. Business hours and services are tailored toward the convenience and needs of the community and are reviewed for their effectiveness on an ongoing basis. Prior to closing offices, the institution assesses the potential adverse impact of an office closing on its local community. This assessment includes the institution's taking into consideration information and ideas obtained from consultations with members of the community to minimize the adverse impact of an office closing. The institution's record of closing offices has not had an adverse impact on its local community.	Offices are reasonably accessible to all segments of the institution's local community. Periodic review of services and business hours assures accommodation of all segments of the institution's local community. The institution makes an adequate assessment of the potential adverse impact of an office closing on its local community. This assessment includes contacts with members of the community for their views on the impact and ways to minimize it. The institution's record of opening and closing offices has not adversely affected the level of services available in low- and moderate-income neighborhoods within its local community.	Accessibility to the institution's offices is difficult for certain segments of its local community. Business hours may be inconvenient relative to the needs of the institution's local community, particularly low- and moderate-income neighborhoods, and they are infrequently reviewed for effectiveness. The institution's assessment of the potential adverse impact of an office closing will have on its local community and of methods needed to minimize that impact is inadequate and needs revision or expansion. The institution's record of opening and closing offices indicates adverse impact upon certain segments of its local community, particularly low- and moderate-income neighborhoods, although the result may be unintentional.	There is limited accessibility to the institution's offices for certain segments of its local community, particularly low- and moderate-income neighborhoods. Business hours are inconsistent with the needs of the institution's local community, and they are rarely, if ever, reviewed for effectiveness. The institution rarely, if ever, makes an assessment of the potential impact of its office opening and closing practices on its local community. The institution's record of opening and closing offices suggests a continuing pattern of adverse impact upon certain segments of its local community, particularly low- and moderate-income neighborhoods.

IV. DISCRIMINATION AND OTHER ILLEGAL CREDIT PRACTICES

Assessment Factor D	Outstanding	Satisfactory	Needs to Improve	Substantial Noncompliance
Any practices intended to discourage applications for types of credit set forth in the institution's CRA Statement(s).	The institution affirmatively solicits credit applications from all segments of its local community, with a strong focus on low- and moderate-income neighborhoods. The board of directors and senior management have developed complete written policies, procedures, and training programs to assure the institution does not illegally discourage or prescreen applicants. The institution regularly assesses the adequacy of implemented, nondiscriminatory policies, procedures and training programs through internal reviews and management reporting mechanisms.	The institution generally solicits credit applications from all segments of its local community, including low- and moderate-income neighborhoods. The board of directors and senior management have developed adequate policies, procedures and training programs supporting nondiscrimination in lending and credit activities. Minor revisions or expansions may be required. The institution periodically assesses the adequacy of implemented, nondiscriminatory policies, procedures, and training reviews and management reporting mechanisms.	Although the institution accepts credit applications from all segments of its local community, available data suggests the possibility of isolated, illegal discouraging or prescreening of applicants. The institution's policies, procedures and training programs are inadequate and require significant revision or expansion to support nondiscrimination in lending and credit activities. The review and/or reporting mechanisms developed by the board of directors and senior management need improvement to fully assure that the institution does not illegally discourage or prescreen applicants.	Available data indicates that the institution rarely, if ever, considers credit applications from all segments of its local community. The volume of applications from low- and moderate-income neighborhoods is very low or nonexistent. The institution's policies, procedures and programs are either nonexistent or in need of substantial revision to properly support nondiscrimination in lending and credit activities. The review and/or reporting mechanisms developed by the board of directors and senior management and designed to assess implemented policies, procedures and training programs to support nondiscrimination in lending and credit activities are inadequate and require substantial revision. Or, the institution has not developed any review or reporting mechanisms to assure that the institution does not illegally discourage or prescreen applicants.

IV. DISCRIMINATION AND OTHER ILLEGAL CREDIT PRACTICES

Assessment Factor F	Outstanding	Satisfactory	Needs to Improve	Substantial Noncompliance
Evidence of prohibited discriminatory or other illegal credit practices.	The institution is in substantial compliance with all provisions of the antidiscrimination laws and regulations, including: the Equal Credit Opportunity Act, the Fair Housing Act, the Home Mortgage Disclosure Act, and any agency regulations pertaining to nondiscriminatory treatment of credit applicants.	The institution is in compliance with the substantive provisions of antidiscrimination laws and regulations, including: the Equal Credit Opportunity Act, the Fair Housing Act, the Home Mortgage Disclosure Act, and any agency regulations pertaining to nondiscriminatory treatment of credit applicants. Any violations disclosed are nonsubstantive in nature, and corrections are promptly made by senior management.	The institution is not in compliance with the substantive provisions of antidiscrimination laws and regulations, including: the Equal Credit Opportunity Act, the Fair Housing Act, the Home Mortgage Disclosure Act, and any agency regulations pertaining to nondiscriminatory treatment of credit applicants. Substantive violations are not ed on an isolated basis. Violations may be repeated from previous examinations.	The institution is in substantial noncompliance with antidiscrimination laws and regulations, including: the Equal Credit Opportunity Act, the Fair Housing Act, the Home Mortgage Disclosure Act, and any agency regulations pertaining to nondiscriminatory treatment of credit applicants. The institution has demonstrated a pattern or practice of prohibited discrimination, or has committed a large number of substantive violations of the antidiscrimination laws and regulations. Violations may be repeated from previous examinations.

V. COMMUNITY DEVELOPMENT

Assessment Factor H	Outstanding	Satisfactory	Needs to Improve	Substantial Noncompliance
The institution's participation, including investments, in local community development and redevelopment projects or programs.	The institution has maintained, through ongoing efforts, a high level of participation in development and redevelopment programs within its local community, often in a leadership role.	The institution is generally aware of any community development and redevelopment programs within its community, and periodically participates in such programs.	The institution has limited awareness of any community development and redevelopment programs within its local community and rarely seeks them out or participates in them.	The institution is unaware of, or not interested in, the existence and nature of community development programs within its local community. The institution has made little or no effort to participate in these programs.

V. COMMUNITY DEVELOPMENT

Assessment Factor K	Outstanding	Satisfactory	Needs to Improve	Substantial Noncompliance
The institution's ability to meet various community credit needs based on its financial condition and size, and legal impediments, local economic conditions and other factors.	The institution has played a leadership role in developing and/or implementing specific projects promoting economic revitalization and growth, consistent with its size, financial capacity, location, and current local economic conditions. Its participation in these projects may have taken, for example, the form of investment, direct loans or loans through intermediaries, financial services, and technical assistance. The institution has established good working relationships with government and private sector representatives to identify opportunities for the institution's involvement in addressing community development needs.	The institution generally supports the development or implementation of specific projects promoting economic revitalization and growth, consistent with its size, financial capacity, location, and current local conditions. Its participation in these projects may have taken, for example, the form of investment, direct loans or loans through intermediaries, financial services, and technical assistance. The institution has informed government and private sector representatives of its interest in participating in community development projects, and is already involved in some aspects of planning or implementation.	The institution has played only a limited role in developing projects to foster economic revitalization and growth, and has taken limited action to learn or support the specific features of existing programs. The institution has rarely contacted government and private sector representatives to discuss community development needs and opportunities.	The institution has played a very small, if any, role in developing or implementing specific projects promoting economic revitalization and growth. The institution has made little, if any, effort to contact government or private sector representatives to learn about community development needs or the features of existing programs.

V. COMMUNITY DEVELOPMENT

Assessment Factor L	Outstanding	Satisfactory	Needs to Improve	Substantial Noncompliance
Other factors that, in the regulatory authority's judgment, reasonably bear upon the extent to which an institution is helping to meet the credit needs of its entire community.	The institution has engaged in other meaningful activities, not covered under other performance categories, which contribute to the institution's efforts to help meet community credit needs.	The institution has demonstrated a willingness to explore other activities contributing to its efforts to help meet community credit needs which are not covered in other performance categories.	The institution expresses a willingness to consider participation in other activities designed to meet community credit needs only when specific proposals or requests are brought to its attention.	Senior management has shown little, if any, interest in pursuing other activities, not covered under other performance categories, which would enhance the institution's effectiveness in helping address community credit needs.

APPENDIX 7

SUMMARY OF CRA RATING SYSTEM

Reproduced with permission of the Individual Banking Regulatory Compliance Division of Chase Manhattan Bank, N.A.

CRA Rating System

PERFORMANCE CATEGORIES AND ASSESSMENT FACTORS	Outstanding	✔	Satisfactory	✔	Needs to Improve	✔	Substantial Noncompliance	✔
I. Ascertainment of Community Credit Needs (A) Activities to ascertain credit needs and efforts to communicate with the community								
■ contact with individuals and groups	Ongoing, meaningful		Regular contact		Limited contact		Few if any	
■ contact with government officials and community leaders	Ongoing		Regular contact		Limited contact		Few if any	
■ participation in public programs	Active		Some effort		Marginal effort		Nominal or none	
■ relationships with private nonprofit developers and financial intermediaries resulting in public-private partnerships	Established and productive		Regular contact		Lack of productive contact		Few if any	
■ collection and analysis of local demographic data regarding lending activities	Regularly collected and analyzed		Periodically reviewed		Occasionally considered or analyzed		Unaware or ignorant of	
■ responsiveness of board of directors and senior management in addressing community credit needs through product development and lending	Proactive attitude and highly responsive		Satisfactory		Limited		Rare or never	
■ senior management review of lending services	Systematic and regular		Informal		Infrequent		Rare or never	
■ credit products structured or varied to meet identified needs; may include government-insured and publicly sponsored programs	Well-suited products, including those that make use of government-insured or publicly sponsored programs		Reasonably suited products, including those that make use of government-insured and publicly sponsored programs		May not meet needs; insignificant participation in government-insured and publicly sponsored programs		Rare or none; nominal or no participation in government-insured and publicly sponsored programs	
■ board of directors and senior management efforts to explore and offer conventional products with special features and more flexible lending criteria within safe and sound practices	Demonstrated willingness		May explore and offer		Limited effort		Little or no effort	
(C) Board of directors participation in formulating policies and reviewing institution's CRA performance								
■ extent of participation and review	Integral part of CRA process and activities		Generally involved		Limited involvement		Rare or no involvement	

continued

-1-

CRA Rating System (continued)

PERFORMANCE CATEGORIES AND ASSESSMENT FACTORS	Outstanding	✓	Satisfactory	✓	Needs to Improve	✓	Substantial Noncompliance	✓
■ CRA program with goals, objectives, and methodology for self-assessment	Formal, written program		Articulated and generally understood, but possibly not explicitly reflected in formal program		Inadequate program		No program	
■ policy oversight of CRA activities	Active oversight		Oversight exercised		Some oversight		Little or no oversight	
■ review of CRA activities and performance	Regular review		Occasional review		Infrequent review		Rare or no review	
■ analysis of disposition of loan applications to check fairness and nondiscrimination compliance	Annual or more frequent analysis		At least annual analysis		Only limited analysis		Rare or no analysis	
■ activities designed to develop, improve, and enhance local community	Personally involved		Some involvement		Limited involvement		Little, if any, involvement	
■ prudent but innovative underwriting criteria to address community credit needs	Consistent support		Consideration given		May be reluctant to consider		Reluctant to consider	
■ CRA training of personnel	Active support		Adequate support		Limited support		Little, if any, support	
■ Expanded CRA Statement adoption	Yes; includes self-assessment and documentation of performance		Yes, but might not be fully descriptive of institution's performance		No		No	
■ CRA technical regulatory requirements being met	Effective efforts to ensure compliance		Generally ensures		Lax		Rarely or never	
II. Marketing and Types of Credit Extended (B) Extent of marketing and special credit-related programs								
■ marketing and advertising programs	Sound programs, approved, reviewed, and monitored by senior management and board		Adequate, but exist outside formal oversight of senior management and board		Limited oversight by senior management and board		If exist, are inadequate	
■ programs inform all segments of the community of products and services offered	Yes		Designed to inform		May require revision or expansion		No	
■ advertisements of credit services throughout the community	Designed to stimulate awareness		Ads carried in widely circulated local media		Ads designed only to promote institution's image as provider of products and services		No	

continued

-2-

CRA Rating System *(continued)*

PERFORMANCE CATEGORIES AND ASSESSMENT FACTORS	Outstanding	Satisfactory	Needs to Improve	Substantial Noncompliance
■ use of special advertisement media aimed at particular segments of community	Yes	Additional targeted advertising may be needed	No	No
■ maintenance of advertising and marketing records	Complete, readily available	Adequate	Limited	Insufficient
■ review of advertising and marketing programs to ensure compliance with applicable laws and regulations	Routinely reviewed	Occasionally reviewed	Infrequently reviewed	Rarely or never reviewed
■ personnel involvement to assist individuals and groups applying for credit	Routinely provide assistance	Generally provide assistance	Limited effort	Little, if any, effort
(I) Origination or purchase of loans within community				
■ meeting identified community credit needs through origination and purchase of loans	Affirmatively addresses a substantial portion of identified needs	Addresses a significant portion of needs	Marginal	Minimal
■ lending levels in response to community credit needs	Exceptional responsiveness to most pressing needs	General responsiveness	Marginal responsiveness	Little, if any, responsiveness
■ number of loans within delineated community	Substantial majority	Significant volume	Significant volume may be outside delineated community	Substantial majority outside delineated community
■ loan volume relative to institution's resources and community's needs	Exceeds expectations	Adequate	Low	Excessively low
■ CRA Statement lists credit products available from the institution	Correctly listed	Majority correctly listed	Not accurately listed	Statement is materially inaccurate
(J) Participation in governmentally insured, guaranteed, or subsidized loan programs				
■ approach to meeting identified community credit needs	Assumes leadership role	Generally takes some steps	Sometimes becomes involved	Rarely or never involved
■ level of participation	Affirmatively participates	Frequently participates	Infrequently participates	Rarely or never participates

continued

CRA Rating System *(continued)*

PERFORMANCE CATEGORIES AND ASSESSMENT FACTORS	Outstanding	✓	Satisfactory	✓	Needs to Improve	✓	Substantial Noncompliance	✓
III. Geographic distribution and record of opening and closing offices								
(*) Reasonableness of delineated community	Meets CRA purpose and does not exclude low- and moderate-income areas		Meets CRA purpose and does not exclude low- and moderate-income areas		Delineation unreasonable and may exclude some low- and moderate-income areas; delineation guidelines need revision		Delineation unreasonable and excludes low- and moderate-income areas; delineation guidelines need substantial revision	
*not included as one of the 12 assessment factors, but considered under this category.								
(E) Geographic distribution of credit extensions, applications, and denials								
■ geographic distribution within delineated community	Documented analysis reflects reasonable penetration of all segments of community		Reasonable penetration of all segments of community		Unjustified, disproportionate pattern within delineated community compared with outside community, or regarding distribution within community		Unreasonable lending pattern inside and outside delineated community	
■ procedures formulated to identify geographic distribution	Yes		N/A		N/A		N/A	
■ geographic data documented and used by board and senior management to establish policies, products and services, and marketing plans	Yes		May be documented and used		N/A		N/A	
■ awareness of board and senior management of geographic distribution	N/A		N/A		May be unaware		Disregards	
■ review by board and senior management of lending policies and practices and effect on geographic distribution	N/A		N/A		Inadequate or no review		N/A	
■ corrective action on previously identified unreasonable lending patterns	N/A		N/A		Inadequate or no action		Limited or no action	
■ loan policies and procedures impact on local community	N/A		N/A		N/A		Contain restrictions that adversely affect loan availability	

continued

-4-

CRA Rating System *(continued)*

PERFORMANCE CATEGORIES AND ASSESSMENT FACTORS	Outstanding	Satisfactory	Needs to Improve	Substantial Noncompliance
(G) Record of opening and closing offices and providing services				
▪ accessibility of offices to all segments of the community	Readily accessible	Reasonably accessible	Difficult to access	Limited access
▪ accommodation through business hours and services	Tailored to convenience and needs; ongoing review	Reviewed periodically to assure accommodation	May be inconvenient and infrequently reviewed	Inconsistent and rarely if ever reviewed
▪ assessment of potential adverse impact of office closings	Detailed assessment prior to closing, including consultation with community members	Adequate, including contacts with community members	Inadequate; needs revision or expansion	Rare or none
▪ record of opening and closing offices as it affects local community, particularly low- and moderate-income areas	No adverse impact	Level of service available in low- and moderate-income areas not adversely affected	Adverse impact; may be unintentional	Continuing pattern of adverse impact
IV. Discrimination and Other Illegal Credit Practices **(D) Practices to discourage applications for types of credit set forth in CRA Statement**				
▪ solicitation of credit applications from all segments of community	Affirmatively solicits; strong focus on low- and moderate-income areas	Generally solicits from all segments of community	Possibility of isolated, illegal discouraging or prescreening	Rarely, if ever, considers credit applications from all segments of community; volume of applications from low- or moderate-income areas low or nonexistent
▪ board of directors and senior management development of policies, procedures, and training programs to prevent illegal discouragement and prescreening of applicants	Effectively assures absence of illegal discouragement or prescreening of applicants	Adequate; minor revision or expansion may be required	Inadequate; requires significant revision or expansion	Nonexistent or needs substantial revision
▪ adequacy of review and reporting mechanisms to assure nondiscriminatory policies, procedures, and training programs	Regularly assessed	Periodically assessed	Improvement needed	Inadequate and requires substantial revision; or no mechanisms exist

continued

CRA Rating System (continued)

PERFORMANCE CATEGORIES AND ASSESSMENT FACTORS	Outstanding	Satisfactory	Needs to Improve	Substantial Noncompliance
(F) Evidence of prohibited discriminatory or other illegal credit practices				
■ compliance with antidiscrimination laws and regulations	In substantial compliance	In compliance with substantive provisions	Not in compliance with substantive provisions	In substantial noncompliance
■ violations and corrective action	N/A	Nonsubstantive; promptly corrected	Substantive violations on isolated basis; violations may be repeated from previous exams	Demonstrates pattern or practice of prohibited discrimination or committed large number of substantive violations; violations may be repeated from previous exams
V. Community Development				
(H) Participation, including investments, in local development and redevelopment projects and programs				
■ awareness of programs	Thoroughly aware	Generally aware	Limited awareness	Unaware of or ignores programs
■ level or frequency of participation in programs	High level of participation, often in leadership role	Periodic participation	Rarely seeks out or participates	Little or no effort made to participate
(K) Ability to meet community credit needs consistent with institution's characteristics				
■ role in development of projects to foster economic revitalization and growth	Leadership role	Generally supports projects	Limited role	Small, if any, role
■ level of contact with government and private sector representatives to identify community development needs and opportunities	Has established good working relationships	Informed others of interest and involved in some aspects of planning or implementation	Rare	Little or none
(L) Participation in other activities not covered under other performance categories that bear on extent to which institution meets community credit needs	Engages in other meaningful activities	Demonstrates willingness to explore	Demonstrates willingness to consider only when approached	Exhibits little or no interest

Appendix 8

Glossary of CRA Acronyms

ARM Adjustable Rate Mortgage

ATM Automated Teller Machine

BNA Block Numbering Area

B&T Bank and Trust

CAMEL Bank regulatory safety and soundness rating measuring Capital Adequacy, Asset Quality, Management, Earnings and Liquidity

C&D Cease and Desist Order

CMSA Consolidated Metropolitan Statistical Area

CDC Community Development Corporation

CRA Community Reinvestment Act of 1977

CSS Community Support Statement

DSR Data Submission Report

ECOA Equal Credit Opportunity Act

FA Federal Association

FDIC Federal Deposit Insurance Corporation

FDICIA FDIC Improvement Act of 1991

FED Federal Reserve System and Federal Reserve Board

FFIEC Federal Financial Institutions Examination Council

FHA Federal Housing Administration

FHFB Federal Housing Finance Board

FHLB Federal Home Loan Bank

FHLBB Federal Home Loan Bank Board

FHLMC Federal Home Loan Mortgage Corporation

FIRREA Financial Institutions Reform, Recovery and Enforcement Act of 1989

FmHA Farmers Home Administration (also FmHome)

FNB First National Bank

FNMA Federal National Mortgage Association

FOIA Freedom of Information Act

FRB Federal Reserve Bank

FSB Federal Savings Bank

FS&LA Federal Savings and Loan Association

GAO General Accounting Office

GNMA Government National Mortgage Association

HFA Housing Finance Authority

HMDA Home Mortgage Disclosure Act

HUD U.S. Department of Housing and Urban Development

LAR Loan Application Register

M $000

MM $000,000

MACRO Thrift regulatory safety and soundness rating measuring **M**anagement, **A**sset Quality, **C**apital Adequacy, **R**isk Management and **O**perating Results

MSA Metropolitan Statistical Area

MSB Mutual Savings Bank

NA National Association

OCC Office of the Comptroller of the Currency

OTS Office of Thrift Supervision

PMI Private Mortgage Insurance

PMSA Primary Metropolitan Statistical Area

RTC Resolution Trust Corporation

S&LA Savings and Loan Association

SB Savings Bank

SBA Small Business Administration

SSB State Savings Bank

VA Veterans Administration

INDEX

About the Publisher

PROBUS PUBLISHING COMPANY

Probus Publishing Company fills the informational needs of today's business professional by publishing authoritative, quality books on timely and relevant topics, including:

- Investing
- Futures/Options Trading
- Banking
- Finance
- Marketing and Sales
- Manufacturing and Project Management
- Personal Finance, Real Estate, Insurance and Estate Planning
- Entrepreneurship
- Management

Probus books are available at quantity discounts when purchased for business, educational or sales promotional use. For more information, please call the Director, Corporate/Institutional Sales at 1-800-PROBUS-1, or write:

Director, Corporate/Institutional Sales
Probus Publishing Company
1925 N. Clybourn Avenue
Chicago, Illinois 60614
FAX (312) 868-6250